**Architectural
Drawing
and
Design**

Architectural Drawing and Design

George C. Beakley, P.E.
College of Engineering and Applied Sciences
Arizona State University

Donald D. Autore, P.E.
College of Engineering and Applied Sciences
Arizona State University

Terry L. Patterson, A.I.A.
School of Architecture
University of Oklahoma

With contributions by

David G. Scheatzle, A.I.A., P.E.
College of Architecture
Arizona State University

John R. Rummell, A.I.A.
College of Architecture
Arizona State University

Macmillan Publishing Company
New York
Collier Macmillan Publishers
London

Copyright © 1984, George C. Beakley.

Printed in the United States of America.

All rights reserved. No part of this book may be reproduced or transmitted in any form or by any means, electronic or mechanical, including photocopying, recording, or any information storage and retrieval system, without permission in writing from the Publisher.

Macmillan Publishing Company
866 Third Avenue, New York, New York 10022

Collier Macmillan Canada, Inc.

Library of Congress Cataloging in Publication Data

Beakley, George C.
  Architectural drawing and design.

  Includes index.
  1. Architectural drawing. 2. Architectural design.
I. Autore, Donald D.   II. Patterson, Terry L.   III. Title.
NA2700.B39   1984   720'.28'4   83-9407
ISBN 0-02-307440-X

Printing: 2345678   Year: 56789012

ISBN 0-02-307440-X

Preface

This book is an introduction to the field of architectural drawing and design. It has been written for individual or class use for students having a wide range of skill levels. Normally, students studying this material will have completed a course in mechanical drawing, but such previous training is not required. Instructions in the fundamentals of architectural drawing are presented in the beginning of the text. However, this material may be omitted for more experienced users.

The text takes a somewhat unique approach to architectural drawing and design in that it is both *more theoretical* and *more practical* than other books written at this level. It is more theoretical because the "why" is explained for procedures and practices that are standard and traditional but may be taken for granted by some authors. It is more practical because in the text an *actual* architectural project is followed from start to finish, including photos of representative stages in construction. Stages of the building project are separated from each other in the text by chapters covering the theory that will be applied later.

All architects and architectural drafters need to become proficient in freehand drawing and sketching. This subject is given special attention in Chapter 2. This chapter is an adaptation of the authors' earlier work, *Freehand Drawing and Visualization* (Bobbs-Merrill Educational Publishing). Again, the authors gratefully acknowledge the contributions of Todd T. Smith and William E. Sadler in the preparation of this material. The instructional material may be studied in sequence with the other text material and prior to considering the design aspects of architectural drawing, or competency in this important skill may be developed progressively throughout the course.

The authors have provided instructional material for both the beginner and the more experienced student. Design material not usually included in elementary texts is provided in the chapters that emphasize the engineering aspects of home building and light construction. Also, the appendixes include comprehensive material on architectural planning and on the selection of building components. This approach has been made possible because of the unusual blends of architectural and engineering backgrounds of the authors, who are themselves registered professionals in their respective fields.

A special effort has been made to present the text material in a clear and concise manner. In addition, it was believed to be especially important that the text illustrations be instructionally clear and effective. They also have been prepared to represent an excellent quality of professional work to show the student how finished work should be prepared. A number of practical exercises for the reader are provided at appropriate locations throughout the text.

The authors have used a step-by-step instructional technique where practical. The theory discussed is illustrated with sequential two-color drawings. In each step the linework being drawn is shown in color. This work reverts to black in the next step, while the new linework being added is once again presented in color. This procedure enables the student to follow each step in the sequence. Conventional discussions of theory and application are accompanied by a large number of related drawings and/or photographs. However, in addition, the authors have incorporated summary comments of theory *to accompany each drawing and photograph*. This feature helps the student to better understand the theory and also provides a convenient method of review.

The authors are especially appreciative of the work of Yin K. Pang, AIA, for his preparation of most of the architectural figure drawings in the text. He was ably assisted by Terrance Y. V. Pang. The authors are also appreciative of the many industries and professionals who have provided pertinent illustrative materials for the text. Individual recognition of these permissions is recorded in the Acknowledgments section, pages xi–xiv. Also, the manuscript reviews and advice received from practicing architects and instructors throughout the country has been especially helpful and is gratefully acknowledged.

George C. Beakley
Donald D. Autore
Terry L. Patterson

Contents

I Drawing Fundamentals

1 History and Development of Architectural Drawing *1*

    1.1 Primitive Structures   *1*
    1.2 Early Architectural Drawing   *1*
    1.3 Types of Architectural Drawing   *4*
    1.4 Opportunities in Architectural Drawing   *8*

2 Freehand Drawing *11*

    2.1 Drawing As a Language   *11*
    2.2 Sketches As Symbols   *12*
    2.3 The Marker and the Drawing Surface   *14*
    2.4 Avoid Drafting Tools in Sketching   *14*
    2.5 Holding the Marker   *16*
    2.6 Preparation for Sketching   *16*
    2.7 Beginning the Sketch   *17*
    2.8 Overlapping Shapes   *18*
    2.9 Relative Size   *19*
    2.10 Aerial Positioning   *20*
    2.11 Atmospheric Effects   *21*
    2.12 Introduction to Perspective   *21*
    2.13 Locating Vanishing Points   *23*
    2.14 Construction of a Simple Perspective Sketch   *24*
    2.15 Sketching Objects in Perspective   *26*
    2.16 Eye Level and Proportion Relationships   *30*
    2.17 Perspective Complexities   *31*
    2.18 Circles in Perspective   *34*
    2.19 Cylinders in Perspective   *36*
    2.20 Inclined Planes   *37*
    2.21 Value and Value Contrast   *37*
    2.22 Light and Shade   *40*
    2.23 Shadows in Perspective Cast on a Horizontal Surface   *42*
    2.24 Space Illusion Using Value Contrast   *43*

3 Drawing Tools and Supplies *45*

    3.1 Pencils, Leads, and Pens   *45*
    3.2 Line Drawing   *48*
    3.3 Curve Drawing   *51*
    3.4 Measuring Tools   *55*
    3.5 Miscellaneous Tools   *59*
    3.6 Drafting Papers and Films   *60*

4 Architectural Drafting Fundamentals *62*

    4.1 Drafting Concepts   *62*
    4.2 Linework   *62*
    4.3 Geometric Constructions   *65*
    4.4 Orthographic Drawing   *67*
    4.5 Sections   *71*
    4.6 Floor Plans   *74*
    4.7 Pictorial Drawings   *75*
    4.8 Axonometric Drawings   *77*
    4.9 Oblique Drawings   *79*
    4.10 Perspectives   *82*
    4.11 Lettering   *95*
    4.12 Dimensioning   *99*
    4.13 Cleanliness in Drawing   *100*

5 Time Saving Methods *102*

    5.1 New Drawing Techniques   *102*
    5.2 Photoreproduction   *102*
    5.3 Pin Registration   *103*
    5.4 Typewritten Notations   *104*
    5.5 Xerography As a Drafting Technique   *105*
    5.6 Transfer Lettering and Symbols   *105*
    5.7 Photocompositors   *106*
    5.8 Template Lettering   *106*
    5.9 Rubber Stamps   *106*
    5.10 Electronic Lettering Machines   *107*
    5.11 Computer Drafting   *107*

II Architectural Design

6 Aesthetic Considerations in Design   111

    6.1 Historic Influences   *111*
    6.2 Roofs   *115*
    6.3 Design Principles   *120*

7 Functional Considerations in Design   123

    7.1 Functional Requirements   *123*
    7.2 Functional Requirements for a Residence   *128*

8 Energy Conservation in Design   148

    8.1 Energy and Environment   *148*
    8.2 Active Energy Systems   *148*
    8.3 Passive Energy Systems   *151*
    8.4 Direct Gain Heating   *152*
    8.5 Indirect Gain Heating   *153*
    8.6 Isolated Gain Heating   *154*
    8.7 Energy Conservation Through the Use of Shading   *155*
    8.8 An Energy Design Case Study   *163*

9 Budget and Legal Considerations in Design   170

    9.1 Budget Limitations   *170*
    9.2 Codes and Regulations   *171*

10 The Design Process   179

    10.1 The Concept   *179*
    10.2 The Program   *179*
    10.3 Bubble Diagrams   *181*
    10.4 Schematic Drawings   *183*

11 Design Presentation   185

    11.1 Presentation Plans   *185*
    11.2 Presentation Elevations and Sections   *190*
    11.3 Renderings   *199*

12 Model Building   209

    12.1 Types and Materials   *209*
    12.2 Construction Preparations   *211*
    12.3 Constructing the Model   *212*

13 A Design Case Study   219

    13.1 Selecting the Architect   *219*
    13.2 Selecting the Lot   *219*
    13.3 Family Preferences   *220*
    13.4 Minimum Standards   *220*
    13.5 The Design Studies   *220*

III Building Systems

14 Light Construction Methods   227

    14.1 Structural Systems   *227*
    14.2 Foundations   *227*
    14.3 Floors   *233*
    14.4 Walls   *237*
    14.5 Roofs   *253*
    14.6 Prefabricated Construction   *260*

15 Sizing Structural Members   264

    15.1 Basic Structural Principles   *264*
    15.2 Bending Stresses   *265*
    15.3 Deflection   *266*
    15.4 Wood Joist Selection   *268*
    15.5 Wood Beam Selection   *269*
    15.6 Wood Decking Selection   *270*
    15.7 Wood Truss Selection   *270*
    15.8 Steel Joist Selection   *271*
    15.9 Open Web Steel Joist Selection   *271*
    15.10 Steel Decking Selection   *272*

16 Design of Residential Climate Control Systems   273

    16.1 Comfort Conditions   *273*
    16.2 Heat Transfer   *274*
    16.3 Resistance (R) Values   *275*
    16.4 Coefficient of Transmission (U) Values   *277*
    16.5 Heat Losses   *277*
    16.6 Transmission Losses   *278*
    16.7 Heat Loss at Slab Perimeter   *280*
    16.8 Air Infiltration Losses   *281*
    16.9 Heat Loss Calculations   *281*
    16.10 Types of Heating Systems   *285*
    16.11 Warm Air Systems   *285*
    16.12 Types of Warm Air Furnaces   *286*
    16.13 Types of Air Distribution   *288*
    16.14 Warm Air Controls   *289*

16.15 Hot Water Systems   *289*
16.16 The Boiler   *290*
16.17 Hot Water Piping Systems   *291*
16.18 Sizing Baseboard Convectors   *293*
16.19 Hot Water Radiant Heating   *295*
16.20 Heat Pumps   *295*
16.21 Electric Heating Systems   *296*
16.22 Cooling Systems   *296*
16.23 Evaporative Cooling   *296*
16.24 Heat Gain   *297*
16.25 Using the Cooling Load Form   *299*
16.26 The Compression Refrigeration Cycle   *302*
16.27 Typical Air Conditioning Equipment   *303*
16.28 Sizing the Air Conditioning System   *304*
16.29 Forced Air Distribution   *305*
16.30 Air Duct Construction and Sizing   *306*
16.31 Planning and Designing the Entire System   *307*

17 Plumbing Systems   *311*

17.1 Plumbing   *311*
17.2 Water Supply   *311*
17.3 Supply Pipes and Sizing   *311*
17.4 Water and Waste Disposal   *312*
17.5 Disposal Pipe Sizing   *314*

18 Electrical Systems   *320*

18.1 Basic Electrical Terminology   *320*
18.2 Electric-Hydraulic Analogy   *320*
18.3 Electrical Power   *321*
18.4 Series and Parallel Circuits   *321*
18.5 Wire Sizes   *321*
18.6 Electrical Generation and Distribution   *322*
18.7 Service Entrance   *322*
18.8 Electrical Service   *324*
18.9 Safety   *325*
18.10 Lighting Fixtures   *326*
18.11 Electrical Layout   *329*
18.12 Low Voltage Switching   *330*
18.13 Electrical Plans   *330*

IV Construction Documentation

19 Construction Documents   *335*

19.1 Architectural Specifications   *335*
19.2 Working Drawings   *337*
19.3 Organization of Working Drawings   *337*
19.4 Standards and Symbols   *338*
19.5 Title Blocks   *340*

20 Developing Plans   *341*

20.1 Site Plans   *344*
20.2 Foundation Plans   *344*
20.3 Floor Plans   *344*
20.4 Roof Plans   *347*
20.5 Schedules   *348*

21 Developing Elevations and Building Sections   *350*

21.1 Elevations   *350*
21.2 Cross Sections   *351*

22 Developing Details   *354*

22.1 Detail Drawings   *354*
22.2 Wall Sections   *354*
22.3 Door and Window Details   *354*
22.4 Miscellaneous Details   *357*
22.5 Detail Drawing Sequence   *357*
22.6 Clarity in Communications   *360*
22.7 The Drawing Check   *360*

23 Developing Stair and Fireplace Details   *365*

23.1 Stair Details   *365*
23.2 Nonresidential Stairs   *369*
23.3 Fireplaces   *373*

24 Engineering Drawings   *385*

24.1 Types of Engineering Drawings   *385*
24.2 Structural Working Drawings   *385*
24.3 Mechanical Working Drawings   *385*
24.4 Electrical Working Drawings   *393*
24.5 Plumbing Working Drawings   *399*

25 A Working Drawing Case Study   *403*

V Computers in Architectural Drawing and Design

26 Computer Equipment *425*

    26.1 Introduction *425*
    26.2 The Workstation *425*
    26.3 The Computing Equipment *429*
    26.4 The Documentation Equipment *431*
    26.5 Equipment Selection *433*

27 Computer Applications *434*

    27.1 Computer Software *434*
    27.2 Design Calculations *434*
    27.3 Word Processing *434*
    27.4 Computer-Aided Drafting *435*
    27.5 Computer-Aided Design *437*
    27.6 Conclusions *441*

VI Appendixes

A. Architectural and Construction Abbreviations *445*
B. Glossary of Architectural and Construction Terms *451*
C. Program Development Case Study *465*
D. Doors and Windows *483*
E. Structural Tables *501*
F. Fasteners and Fastening Systems *527*

Index *531*

Acknowledgments

Fig. 1–5	Monastery Library, St. Gallen © Julius Hoffman, Stuttgart, Germany 4	
Fig. 1–6	Leonardo da Vinci ca 1500. Studies for a central structure © Julius Hoffman, Stuttgart, Germany 5	
Fig. 1–7	Paolo Soleri 5	
Fig. 1–8	Law Faculty, Paris © Julius Hoffman, Stuttgart, Germany 5	
Fig. 1–9	The Office of Max O. Urbahn 6	
Fig. 1–10	Auguste Hubert, 1780 (photo: Tosi) 7	
Fig. 1–11	Gruen Associates 7	
Fig. 1–12	Baptistry for St. Paul's Cathedral, London © Julius Hoffman, Stuttgart, Germany 7	
Fig. 1–13	National Forest Products Association 8	
Fig. 1–14	*The Practical Builder*, 1789, Plate LXXXVIII 9	
Fig. 2–1	North Texas State University 11	
Fig. 2–2	Robert Hershberger, AIA 12	
Fig. 2–3 thru Fig. 2–100	*Freehand Drawing and Visualization*, George C. Beakley and Donald D. Autore, Bobbs Merrill, 1982 12–44	
Fig. 3–5	Berol USA 46	
Fig. 3–8A	J. S. Staedtler, Inc. 46	
Fig. 3–8B	KOH-I-NOOR Rapidograph, Inc. 46	
Fig. 3–9	J. S. Staedtler, Inc. 48	
Fig. 3–13	Keuffel & Esser Co. 49	
Fig. 3–23	Berol USA 53	
Fig. 3–24	J. S. Staedtler, Inc. 54	
Fig. 3–25	J. S. Staedtler, Inc. 54	
Fig. 3–28	Keuffel & Esser Co. 56	
Fig. 3–32	Keuffel & Esser Co. 57	
Fig. 3–34	J. S. Staedtler, Inc. 57	
Fig. 3–37	J. S. Staedtler, Inc. 58	
Fig. 3–43	Teledyne Rotolite 61	
Fig. 4–47	Wausau Homes, Inc. 80	
Fig. 4–72	Crossfield Products Corporation 94	
Fig. 4–73	Crossfield Products Corporation 94	
Fig. 4–82	Terry L. Patterson, AIA 97	
Fig. 5–2 thru Fig. 5–5	Bishop Graphics, Inc. 103–105	
Fig. 5–6	IBM Corporation 105	
Fig. 5–7	Keuffel & Esser Co. 105	
Fig. 5–8	Stanpat Products, Inc. 106	
Fig. 5–9	Kroy, Inc. 106	
Fig. 5–10	Keuffel & Esser Co. 107	
Fig. 5–11	KOH-I-NOOR Rapidograph, Inc. 107	
Fig. 5–12	Alpha Merics Corporation 107	
Fig. 5–13	Radio Shack, a division of Tandy Corporation 108	
Fig. 6–1	Red Cedar Shingle and Handsplit Shake Bureau 111	
Fig. 6–2	Terry L. Patterson, AIA 111	
Fig. 6–3	Maine Publicity Bureau 111	
Fig. 6–4	Scholz Homes, Inc. 112	
Fig. 6–5	Colorado Historical Society 112	
Fig. 6–6	Georgia Pacific Corporation 112	
Fig. 6–7	Maine Publicity Bureau 112	
Fig. 6–8	Dept. of Commerce, State of Michigan 113	
Fig. 6–9	Aladdin Readi-Cut Homes 113	
Fig. 6–10	Wisconsin Division of Tourism 113	
Fig. 6–11	Aladdin Readi-Cut Homes 113	
Fig. 6–12	Terry L. Patterson, AIA 113	
Fig. 6–13	Colorado Historical Society 114	
Fig. 6–14	Terry L. Patterson, AIA 114	
Fig. 6–15	Florida Division of Tourism 114	
Fig. 6–16	Wisconsin Division of Tourism 114	
Fig. 6–17	Aladdin Readi-Cut Homes 114	
Fig. 6–18	Aladdin Readi-Cut Homes 115	
Fig. 6–19	The Frank Lloyd Wright Memorial Foundation 115	
Fig. 6–20	The Frank Lloyd Wright Memorial Foundation 115	
Fig. 6–22	Georgia Pacific Corporation 116	
Fig. 6–23	California Redwood Association 116	
Fig. 6–24	Red Cedar Shingle and Handsplit Shake Bureau 116	
Fig. 6–25	Terry L. Patterson, AIA 117	
Fig. 6–26 thru Fig. 6–28	Red Cedar Shingle and Handsplit Shake Bureau 117	
Fig. 6–29	Terry L. Patterson, AIA 117	

Fig. 6–30	Aladdin Readi-Cut Homes *117*
Fig. 6–31	Brick Institute of America *117*
Fig. 6–32	Terry L. Patterson, AIA *117*
Fig. 6–33	Elwin G. Smith Division, Cyclops Corp. *118*
Fig. 6–34	Red Cedar Shingle and Handsplit Shake Bureau *118*
Fig. 6–35	American Plywood Association *118*
Fig. 6–36	American Plywood Association *119*
Fig. 6–37	Red Cedar Shingle and Handsplit Shake Bureau *119*
Fig. 6–38	A.E.P., SPAN *119*
Fig. 6–39	Red Cedar Shingle and Handsplit Shake Bureau *119*
Fig. 6–40	Terry L. Patterson, AIA *119*
Fig. 6–41	Red Cedar Shingle and Handsplit Shake Bureau *119*
Fig. 6–42	Red Cedar Shingle and Handsplit Shake Bureau *120*
Fig. 6–43	Margaret Ann Smith *120*
Fig. 6–44	The Frank Lloyd Wright Memorial Foundation *121*
Fig. 6–45	The Frank Lloyd Wright Memorial Foundation *121*
Fig. 6–46	American Plywood Association *121*
Fig. 6–47	The Frank Lloyd Wright Memorial Foundation *121*
Fig. 6–48	College of Architecture, Slide Library, Arizona State University *121*
Fig. 6–49	John C. Haggard *122*
Fig. 7–15	Deck House, Inc. *129*
Fig. 7–16 thru Fig. 7–20 John R. Rummell, AIA *130–134*	
Fig. 7–22 thru Fig. 7–24 Deck House, Inc. *136–137*	
Fig. 7–25	Quaker Maid *137*
Fig. 7–26	American Woodmark Corporation *137*
Fig. 7–28	Deck House, Inc. *138*
Fig. 7–29	Weyerhauser Co. *138*
Fig. 7–30	Georgia Pacific Corporation *138*
Fig. 7–31	Acorn Structures, Inc. *139*
Fig. 7–33 thru Fig. 7–35 American Woodmark Corporation *141*	
Fig. 7–36	Quaker Maid *142*
Fig. 7–37	Quaker Maid *142*
Fig. 7–38	Dwyer Products Company *142*
Fig. 7–40	Deck House, Inc. *143*
Fig. 7–42	Weyerhouse Co. *144*
Fig. 7–43 thru Fig. 7–48 Quaker Maid *145*	
Fig. 8–2	U.S. Dept. of Commerce National Weather Service *149*
Fig. 8–7	Terry L. Patterson, AIA *151*
Fig. 8–8	Edmond M. Stryker *151*
Fig. 8–9	Terry L. Patterson, AIA *151*
Fig. 8–10	Owen Corning Fiberglass *151*
Fig. 8–13	*Solar Design Workbook,* U.S. Dept. of Energy *153*
Fig. 8–14	Owen Corning Fiberglass *153*
Fig. 8–15 thru Fig. 8–17 *Solar Design Workbook,* U.S. Dept. of Energy *154–155*	
Fig. 8–18	Terry L. Patterson, AIA *155*
Fig. 8–19	*Solar Design Workbook,* U.S. Dept. of Energy *156*
Fig. 8–22	Libbey-Owens-Ford Company *157*
Table 8–1 thru Table 8–4 ASHRAE *158–161*	
Fig. 8–28	John Wiley & Sons, Inc. *164–165*
Fig. 8–29 thru Fig. 8–35 Deck House, Inc. *166–169*	
Fig. 9–1	The City of Pittsburg, Kansas *174*
Fig. 10–1	J. Adams & Associates, Inc. *180*
Fig. 10–5	Terry L. Patterson, AIA *183*
Fig. 10–6	Terry L. Patterson, AIA *184*
Fig. 11–23	Architectural Media Ltd. *191*
Fig. 11–24	Georgia Pacific Corp. *192*
Fig. 11–25	Architectural Media Ltd. *192*
Fig. 11–43	Architectural Media Ltd. *197*
Fig. 11–44	Vogt-Buelow & Associates, Inc. *197*
Fig. 11–45	Deck House, Inc. *198*
Fig. 11–46	Georgia Pacific Corporation *198*
Fig. 11–48	Architectural Media Ltd. *198*
Fig. 11–52	Terry L. Patterson, AIA *200*
Fig. 11–53	Georgia Pacific Corporation *201*
Fig. 11–54	Georgia Pacific Corporation *201*
Fig. 11–59	Architectural Media, Ltd. *203*
Fig. 11–60	J. Adams & Associates, Inc. *204*
Fig. 11–61	Vogt-Buelow & Associates, Inc. *204*
Fig. 11–62	Day and Ertman, Architects *205*
Fig. 11–63	Vogt-Buelow & Associates, Inc. *205*
Fig. 11–64	Day and Ertman, Architects *206*
Fig. 11–65	Georgia Pacific Corporation *206*
Fig. 11–66	Day and Ertman, Architects Acorn Structures, Inc. *207*
Fig. 11–67	Georgia Pacific Corporation *207*
Fig. 11–68	Follansbee Steel Corporation *208*
Fig. 12–1	Terry L. Patterson, AIA *209*
Fig. 12–2	Terry L. Patterson, AIA *209*
Fig. 12–3	Brian L. Freese *209*
Fig. 12–4 thru Fig. 12–7 Terry L. Patterson, AIA *210*	
Fig. 12–8	Owen Corning Fiberglass *211*
Fig. 12–9	Owen Corning Fiberglass *211*
Fig. 12–10	Day & Ertman, Architects *211*
Fig. 13–1	John R. Rummell, AIA *221*
Fig. 13–2	John R. Rummell, AIA *223*
Fig. 14–1	Colorado Historical Society *227*
Fig. 14–2	Colorado Historical Society *228*

Fig. 14–3	Red Cedar Shingle and Handsplit Shake Bureau	229
Fig. 14–6	U.S. Dept. of Commerce National Weather Service	230
Fig. 14–28	American Plywood Association	236
Fig. 14–30	INRYCO, Inc.	236
Fig. 14–32	U.S. Dept. of Agriculture	237
Fig. 14–38	National Concrete Masonry Association	240
Fig. 14–41	John R. Rummell, AIA	241
Fig. 14–42	John R. Rummell, AIA	241
Fig. 14–46	INRYCO, Inc.	243
Fig. 14–48 thru Fig. 14–51	Deck House, Inc.	243–245
Fig. 14–52	California Redwood Association	246
Fig. 14–53	American Plywood Association	246
Fig. 14–56	California Redwood Association	248
Fig. 14–57	California Redwood Association	248
Fig. 14–58	Georgia Pacific Corporation	249
Fig. 14–59	California Redwood Association	249
Fig. 14–60	California Redwood Association	249
Fig. 14–62	Reynolds Metals Company	250
Fig. 14–63 thru Fig. 14–66	Gypsum Association	251
Fig. 14–67	Georgia Pacific Corporation	252
Fig. 14–68 thru Fig. 14–70	California Redwood Association	252–253
Fig. 14–74	American Plywood Association	254
Fig. 14–75 thru Fig. 14–78	Alpine Engineered Products, Inc.	254–256
Fig. 14–79	Scholz Homes, Inc.	257
Fig. 14–80	Red Cedar Shingle and Handsplit Shake Bureau	257
Fig. 14–81	Terry L. Patterson, AIA	257
Fig. 14–82	Trus Joist Corporation	258
Fig. 14–83	Trus Joist Corporation	258
Fig. 14–84	National Forest Products Association	259
Fig. 14–85	Wausau Homes, Inc.	259
Fig. 14–87 thru Fig. 14–89	Deck House, Inc.	261
Fig. 14–90	Scholz Homes, Inc.	262
Fig. 14–91	Wausau Homes, Inc.	262
Fig. 14–92	Scholz Homes, Inc.	262
Fig. 14–93	Scholz Homes, Inc.	263
Table 16–1	*ASHRAE Handbook of Fundamentals,* 1981	276
Table 16–2	*ASHRAE Handbook of Fundamentals,* 1981	278
Fig. 16–8	*ASHRAE Handbook of Fundamentals,* 1981	279
Fig. 16–9	*ASHRAE Handbook of Fundamentals,* 1981	280
Table 16–3	*ASHRAE Handbook of Fundamentals,* 1981	279
Table 16–4	*ASHRAE Handbook of Fundamentals,* 1981	281
Table 16–5	*ASHRAE Handbook of Fundamentals,* 1981	281
Table 16–8	Lennox Industries, Inc.	286
Fig. 16–13 thru Fig. 16–16	Lennox Industries, Inc.	287–288
Fig. 16–21	A.O. Smith Corporation	290
Table 16–9	A.O. Smith Corporation	291
Fig. 16–33	Carrier Corporation	296
Fig. 16–38	Lennox Industries, Inc.	304
Fig. 16–39	Lennox Industries, Inc.	304
Fig. 16–40	Carrier Corporation	305
Fig. 18–6	Arizona Public Service Company	323
Fig. 18–14	General Electric Company	326
Fig. 19–1	Frankfurt-Short-Emery-McKinley, Inc.	335
Fig. 21–5	James Risinger	352
Fig. 23–1	Maine Publicity Bureau	365
Fig. 23–2	Virginia State Travel Service	365
Fig. 23–3	Deck House, Inc.	366
Fig. 23–10	U.S. Dept. of Agriculture	368
Fig. 23–11	U.S. Dept. of Agriculture	368
Fig. 23–13	PICO Stairs	370
Fig. 23–14	PICO Stairs	371
Fig. 23–15	American Stair Corporation, Inc.	372
Fig. 23–16	Zephyr Metal Craft	373
Fig. 23–17	Heatilator, Inc.	373
Fig. 23–18	Terry L. Patterson, AIA	374
Fig. 23–19	Heatilator, Inc.	374
Fig. 23–20	California Redwood Association	374
Fig. 23–21	California Redwood Association	375
Fig. 23–22	Weyerhauser Co.	375
Fig. 23–23	Heatilator, Inc.	375
Fig. 23–24	Wausau Homes, Inc.	375
Fig. 23–26 thru Fig. 23–29	U.S. Dept. of Agriculture	376–378
Fig. 23–30	Heatilator, Inc.	378
Fig. 23–31	Heatilator, Inc.	378
Fig. 23–32	Superior Fireplace Company	379
Fig. 23–33 thru Fig. 23–38	Heatilator, Inc.	379–380
Fig. 23–39 thru Fig. 23–41	Superior Fireplace Company	381–382
Fig. 23–42	Heatilator, Inc.	383
Fig. 23–43	Superior Fireplace Company	383
Fig. 23–44	Superior Fireplace Company	383
Fig. 23–45	California Redwood Association	384
Fig. 23–46	Superior Fireplace Company	384
Fig. 24–1, 24–2, 24–4 thru 24–8, 24–13 thru 24–15, 24–17 thru 24–19, 24–21, 24–22, 24–26	U.S. Army Corps of Engineers/Yandell & Hiller, Inc./Wukasch & Associates	385–401

Fig. 25–1 thru Fig. 25–7   John R. Rummell, AIA   *404–417*

Fig. 26–1	Honeywell Information Systems, Inc. *425*
Fig. 26–2	Intergraph Corporation *426*
Fig. 26–3	Bausch & Lomb *426*
Fig. 26–4	Computervision Corporation *426*
Fig. 26–5	Bausch & Lomb *427*
Fig. 26–6	Computervision Corporation *427*
Fig. 26–7	Bausch & Lomb *428*
Fig. 26–8	Evans & Southerland Computer Corporation *428*
Fig. 26–9	IBM Corporation *428*
Fig. 26–10	Apple Computer, Inc. *429*
Fig. 26–11	IBM Corporation *429*
Fig. 26–12	Honeywell Information Systems, Inc. *430*
Fig. 26–13	Aristographics Corporation *431*
Fig. 26–14	Hewlett-Packard Company *431*
Fig. 26–15	Computervision Corporation *432*
Fig. 26–16	Computervision Corporation *432*
Fig. 26–17	Bausch & Lomb *432*

Fig. 27–1	Computervision Corporation *435*
Fig. 27–2	Computervision Corporation *436–437*
Fig. 27–3	Intergraph Corporation *437*
Fig. 27–4 thru Fig. 27–8	Computervision Corporation *438–440*
Fig. 27–9	Bausch & Lomb *441*

Appendix C	J. Adams & Associates, Inc. *472–482*
Appendix D	Caradco Corporation *483–500*
Table E–3 thru E–10	Southern Forest Products Association *501–508*
Table E–11	American Institute of Timber Construction *509–511*
Table E–12	Western Wood Products Association *512*
Table E–13	Western Wood Products Association *513*
Table E–14	Alpine Engineered Products *514–515*
Table E–15	United States Gypsum *516*
Table E–16	United States Gypsum *517*
Table E–17	Steel Joist Institute *518–524*
Table E–18	Steel Joist Institute *525*

**Architectural
Drawing
and
Design**

I

Drawing Fundamentals

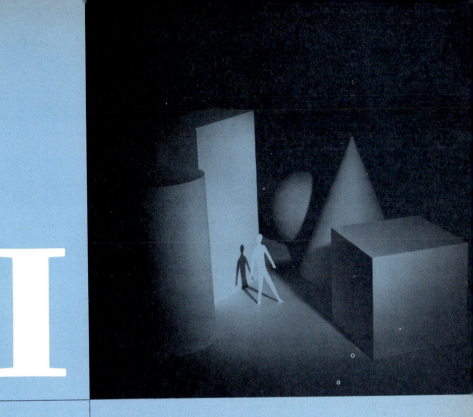

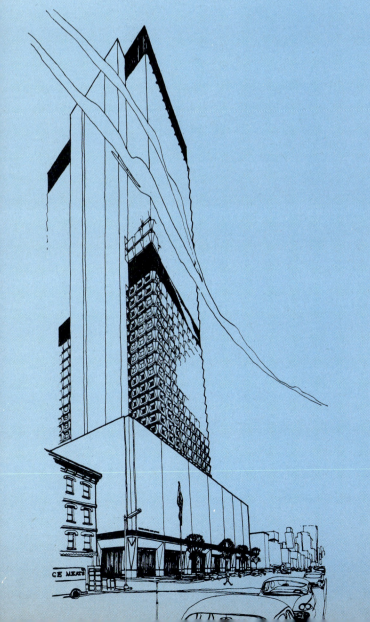

1 History and Development of Architectural Drawing

1.1 Primitive Structures

From his appearance on earth to the end of his cave-dwelling days, man had very little need for architectural drawing. Although man-made shelters of skins and bones of animals coexisted with cave homes for thousands of years, architectural drawings were not required for their construction. When man for the most part abandoned cave dwelling, cavelike shelters appeared [1–1]. They were simple in design and their construction matched the technology of that day. Drawings were not necessary. Although ancient graphic impressions have been found, the informal arrangements of the earliest communities suggest that formal drawings were not used in their construction [1–2].

1.2 Early Architectural Drawing

The appearance of formal shapes with remarkably accurate dimensions, however, suggests there was a need for architectural drawing [1–3]. It is difficult to imagine achieving such precision work with the limited construction technology available without some form of pictorial planning and documentation [1–4].

Some shelters have been built without formal drawings.

Figure 1–1

Catal Huhuk, a Neolithic town in Anatolia . . . arrangement appears informal.

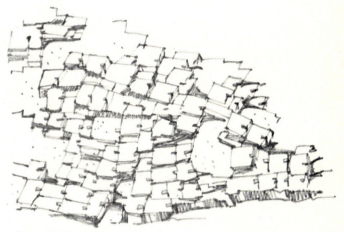

Figure 1–2

The ancient architects and builders were as limited in their tools of documentation as they were in their tools of construction. The Egyptians wrote on river reeds split and sewn together. Ink was made from soot. The delicacy of their recording medium has left us with no samples of architectural drawings from ancient times. We are hardly better off in our documentation of more recent architectural drawing history since fragile parch-

Egyptian pyramids built over 4500 years ago . . . almost perfectly square in plan.

Figure 1–3

A magnificent Greek temple . . . designed by architects Ictinus and Callicrates. Drawings would have been helpful in achieving the precise proportional relationships between the parts of this building.

Figure 1–4 *The Parthenon (432 B.C.).*

ment and paper was the primary recording media used. Also, the economics of storing drawings with no apparent value and the absence of reproduction capabilities have left us with few examples of historic architectural drawing. One of the oldest samples in existence was drawn in the ninth century and is a copy of an earlier drawing that was destroyed [1–5].

With more complex buildings being built, it became necessary to develop more elaborate drawing methods. In the last few hundred years architectural drawing has evolved into several general types. These range from concept sketches to intricate details drawn to scale.

1.3 Types of Architectural Drawing

Design sketches are rough drawings that are used as "idea sketches," made to explore concepts that will be refined at a later date. They are drawn approximately to scale, and are characterized by free-flowing lines drawn with a soft marking device. They may appear crude to the casual observer, but a closer study of sketches drawn by talented designers will usually reveal a theme and sensitivity containing the elements of good design. It is the purpose of these drawings to establish such elements. Design sketches have changed very little from the earliest known examples [1–6] to those of today's architects [1–7].

Usually, clients are not trained in grasping concepts

Drawn on five pieces of vellum sewn together . . . original lines in red ink . . . lettering in black ink.

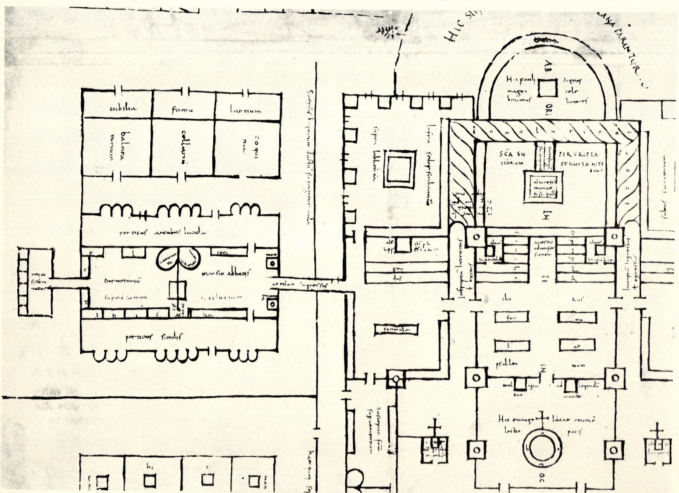

Figure 1–5 *Idea for a Carolingian imperial abbey, ca. A.D. 820.*

Drawing Fundamentals

Leonardo da Vinci (1452–1519) used freehand sketches to picture his ideas.

Paolo Soleri (1919–   ) continues to use rough design sketches to develop his ideas, as do all designers.

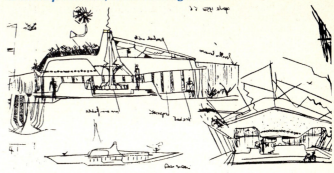

Figure 1–7

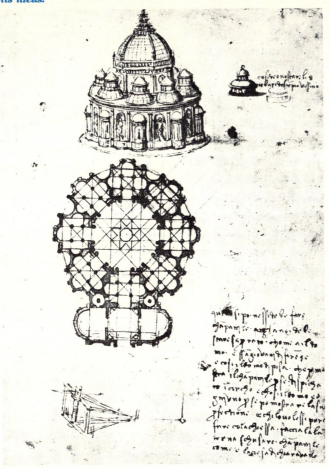

Figure 1–6

from rough sketches. Therefore, a more picturelike drawing, known as a *presentation drawing*, is required to explain a proposed building to the prospective owner. Such a drawing may also be required for the banker or loan company who will be asked to lend money to build the project and for other persons or committees that must first understand, then approve or disapprove of the proposal.

Presentation drawings are usually necessary for commercial work and custom homes, while homes built on a speculative basis (with no owner committed) usually do not require this preparation. Often, modern design presentation drawings are characterized by realistic features, such as shades, shadows, people, trees, plantings, and automobiles. The techniques for making these drawings have changed over the years as drawing technology has advanced and attitudes have changed concerning what parts of the building or setting are most important. Early drawings were usually done in black or colored ink [1–8] on nonreproducible paper. Modern presenta-

An early ink drawing on paper.

Figure 1–8 A law faculty building in Paris by Jacques-Germain Soufflot.

History and Development of Architectural Drawing

Modern presentation drawings may be in full color . . . or in pencil or ink on tracing vellum as in this example by Richard Bergmann.

Figure 1-9

tion drawings are often done with pencil or ink on tracing paper so that copies can easily be made [1-9]. However, many contemporary renderings are also done on nonreproducible stock since color photography has simplified the copying of drawings.

Another type of design drawing is the *competition drawing*. Since competitions often result in prizes or commissions for the winners and are usually associated with large projects, the drawings are often grand in nature and of very high quality [1-10]. The goal of the competitors has not changed over the years, but drawing styles have changed. For example, in the last century the front view was the most common drawing used for design presentation and competition drawings. In this century perspective views have become popular, and more recently axonometric views are often seen [1-11].

Once the design has been accepted, drawings must be prepared to guide the builders of the project. These are called *working drawings*. They are precisely drawn and include plan views, elevations, and details, all with dimensions and notes. A more complete discussion of these drawings appears in Part IV, Construction Documents. The working drawing has changed a great deal over the years. At one time a working drawing included only a plan view and one elevation drawn to scale with general dimensions. Many drawings were not needed since the first architects were themselves master builders.

As styles were repeated year after year, proportions and details became standardized. In later periods, books of standardized details were published. One or two drawings, a standard detail book, and the knowledge and skill of the craftsmen were enough to guide in the construction of magnificent buildings [1-12]. As technology advanced, buildings became more complicated. Many crafts' work had to fit harmoniously with that of other trades, mechanical equipment had to be included, and legal considerations became important. The one-sheet working drawing grew into a legal document of hundreds of sheets of drawings for larger jobs and at least several sheets for the smallest of projects.

Working drawings, which are instructions for constructing a building, require "rules" for their own development. These basic rules, discussed in later chapters, describe the techniques of architectural drawing that are now used throughout the world. A common drafting "language" has evolved which enables architects, contractors, engineers, and technicians to communicate with one another and, in turn, with the workmen assembling the final product. Drafting offices vary in some specific drawing procedures, but once you understand the concepts of architectural drafting, adaptation to different interpretations of the "rules" is easily accomplished.

The art and skills of engineering graphics and particularly the rules of multiview projection apply to the profession of architecture just as they do to the machine designer, electronics drafter, or the aerospace designer. The major differences in presentation technique used for the various specialties is brought about by the relative

Competition drawings are often grand and of very high quality.

Figure 1-10 *Elevation of Castello d'Acqua, Auguste Hubert Parma Competition, 1780.*

size of the projects. Because most structures drawn by architectural drafters are huge in comparison to machine or electronic parts, certain variations in the drafting rules become necessary. Figure [1–13] shows how architectural drawings are related to the various parts of a building. In order to preserve the elevation in [1–13], a true floor plan has not been shown. A true architectural floor plan is drawn by making a horizontal cut through the building several feet above the floor. This technique is explained in Chapter 4.

Another type of architectural drawing is one that is completed after the construction of a building. It is called an *as-built drawing* if it contains dimensions and other technical data. It may be for use in further technical

Modern competition drawings usually use pictorial views.

Sir Christopher Wren drawing . . . pen on paper.

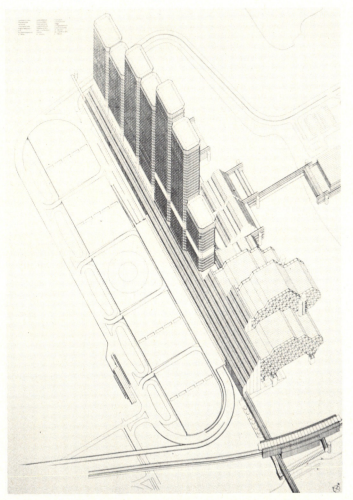

Figure 1-11 *U.N. city competition, Vienna. Drawn by Doug Meyer for Gruen Associates, Architects.*

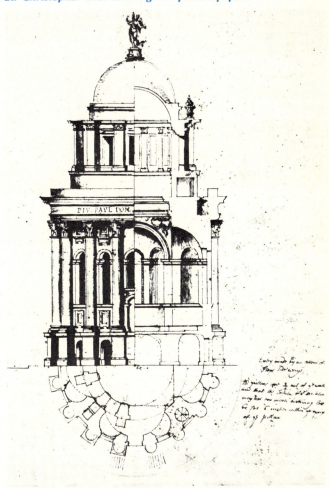

Figure 1-12 *Chapter house or baptistry for St. Paul's Cathedral, London ca. 1675.*

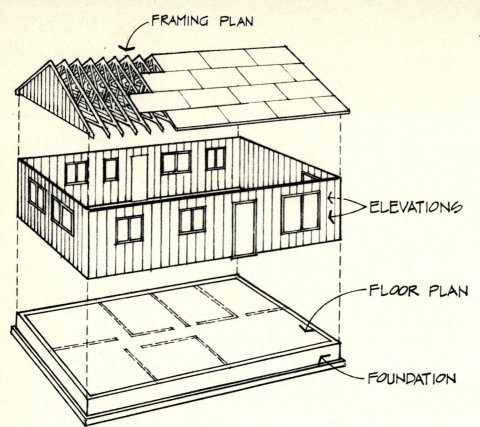

Separate architectural drawings are made for each part of a building.

Figure 1–13

work, for maintenance of the building, or it may be used for publication. Before photography became an integral part of the printing industry, drawings had to be specially prepared for publication. The drawings were usually of very high quality. They were produced through a process called *engraving* and contained great detail and fine linework [1–14].

Modern published works sometimes contain photographic reproductions of the drawings done in the course of a project. At times, simplified plans and sections may be specially drawn for magazine publication. This is an expensive undertaking, however, because the publication does not usually produce direct income for the drafting office.

1.4 Opportunities in Architectural Drawing

Architectural drawing is the means of graphic communication used within the professions and businesses that are concerned with the design and construction of buildings. The building profession falls generally into two categories, *residential* and *nonresidential*. Nonresidential includes commercial, institutional, industrial, recreational, and other types of buildings that are not houses. This group is sometimes referred to simply as *commercial*. Small commercial buildings built with residential methods are called *light construction*. Residential work includes both multi-family (apartments, condominums, town-houses) and single family buildings.

Although state laws vary, typically it is a legal requirement that new nonresidential and multifamily buildings be designed by registered architects. Employees of a registered architect need not be licensed, however. Usually it is not required to have an architectural registration seal (license) to design and detail single family and duplex residences. To become a licensed architect one typically earns a degree in architecture from an accredited university, serves an apprenticeship under a registered architect, and then passes a lengthy examination. The architect is a major source but not the only generator of architectural drawings. Architects work closely with and often coordinate the efforts of many consultants who perform design and drawing work. Engineers, interior designers, landscape architects, acoustical consultants, and hospital specialists are some of the professionals who are associated with architects and who also employ architectural drafters.

The contractors and subcontractors involved in the construction industry may communicate to the architect their intentions regarding construction and installation of certain components with *shop drawings*. These are detailed drawings that show limited variations to the

An engraved drawing published in The Practical Builder, 1789.

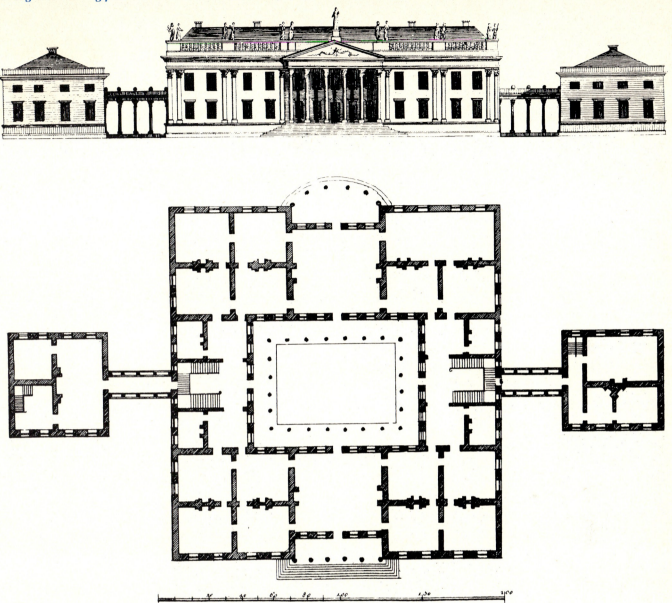

Figure 1-14

original architectural drawings. An employee of the contractor must be skilled in architectural drafting to prepare this type of drawing, even if he or she does not do it full time. The contractor's foremen may need to interpret detail drawings for the craftsmen with pictorial sketching. Sometimes the contractor is required to record what was actually constructed in the form of as-built drawings, as previously described.

For construction that does not require an architectural seal, a contractor or other firm may do the design and prepare presentation and working drawings. There are many home production firms that design and detail custom homes or produce drawings for a series of typical house configurations. These companies then may build the houses themselves or employ an associated contractor to build them. Due to the repetition of details in standardized house configurations, working drawings for these types of homes will be more brief than those prepared for custom-designed homes.

Companies that manufacture materials and components for construction must communicate how their products will look and how they should be installed. Drawings used to convey this information may resemble part of a working drawing or may be more like a pictorial drawing. In either case, typical architectural drawing skills are required of the drafter who prepares them.

Generally, residential construction is more simple and standardized than commercial work, although there are exceptions. Homes designed by E. Fay Jones, an award-winning Arkansas architect, include unique detailing.

These complex features required many drawings to describe their configurations to the contractor.

In summary, we have seen that the growth in sophistication of architectural drawing is related to the increase in complexity of building technology. Several types of architectural drawing have been examined, and we have seen that architectural design and drawing skills are needed in architectural and related offices. Since building is a visual industry, participants at many levels must be skilled in communicating graphically. A basic application of graphic communication is the freehand sketch that the designer may show to a client, a professional may show to an associate, or a foreman may show to a crew to explain construction that is difficult to describe with words. The next chapter is designed to help you develop the basic graphic communication skill of sketching.

EXERCISES

1-1. Why have drawings become necessary in the design and construction of buildings?

1-2. Why are ancient architectural drawings not available to us for study today?

1-3. Name five types of architectural drawings and describe how they are used.

1-4. Why is an architectural license usually required to conduct the design and detailing of "commercial" buildings but usually not required for houses?

1-5. How does one become a registered architect?

1-6. How may an architectural drafter who is not a registered architect participate in the building industry?

1-7. Who are Ictenus, Callicrates, Leonardo da Vinci, Paolo Soleri, and E. Fay Jones? What has been their contribution to the world of architecture? Use the library to expand your discussion of these people.

2 Freehand Drawing

Truly the key to my artistic creation is my pictorial work begun in 1918 and pursued regularly each day.
Le Corbusier, Architect, 1948

2.1 Drawing As a Language

Drawing is a form of language that uses lines and symbols to convey meaning. Written language, spoken language, and body language are other forms of idea communication [2–1]. Each has its own application.

Freehand drawings are frequently called *sketches*. In many respects the sketch is a superior representational system as compared with other types of language. Freehand drawings are commonly used by architects in the conceptual stage of design [2–2A and 2–2B]. For example, it might be difficult to describe in words your idea for an entry to a house. On the other hand, a quick sketch could easily describe the entry in its proportions and relationship to surrounding features [2–3]. A sketch has the additional quality of being easy to learn and understand.

It is a rare designer who can totally envision the complete development of a building in his or her mind. Sketches are particularly useful in idea development. A basic concept may be added to other ideas, changed, or expanded to become a new, more potent idea. Since the mind works more quickly than the hand, ways of improving and modifying the sketch can be fed to the eye–hand system even as the first marks are being drawn on paper.

Freehand sketching is an important means of communicating with oneself [2–4]. However, sketching is most often used as a means of communicating complicated ideas from one person to another [2–5]. Sketching is a natural method of recording a mental image for further study, for clarification or modification, or for idea transmission to others. Keep a sketchbook and record your ideas for later reference.

Since sketching is a *symbolic* representation of reality, it is not completely perfect. For example, the dimension of depth is missing because the image is drawn on a flat piece of paper. Natural color and the awareness of true size and true relationships between objects are also lost. To some degree these characteristics can be restored to the paper surface by means of various forms of illusion. These illusions and how to use them are the bases of this study of sketching.

The meaning of certain body language actions is unmistakenly clear to even the most average of audiences.

Figure 2–1

Sketches record ideas . . .

Figure 2–2A Freehand sketch by Le Corbusier, an architect and artist, of his Chapel at Ronchamp, France.

. . . and help bring them to reality.

Figure 2–2B Chapel at Ronchamp, France, 1950–1953. Le Corbusier.

In the following material we will discuss general guidelines for freehand sketching, explore methods of increasing your ability to visualize a three-dimensional object as an image, and develop the means to translate this image onto a two-dimensional piece of paper. You may also become more visually aware of how one idea reproduced in sketch form can lead to or generate other creative thoughts.

2.2 Sketches As Symbols

A symbol is a sign by which we know or infer something. Sketches are symbols. An examination of children's sketches provides us with a better understanding of this fact [2–6]. The sketch in [2–7] more completely describes a specific house and captures some of its character. Note that while this sketch does not have the depth, size, and color of the original house, these basic elements are restored somewhat through illusion. Sketches most often employ the illusions of depth, shape, and proportion. The loss of color does not generally hinder our acceptance of a sketch as being representational.

You will learn a number of procedures and techniques that will improve the quality of your sketches, but the most important of all factors is *attitude*. And the most important ingredient in attitude is *confidence*. Draw confidently, not timidly! Remember that the objective in making a sketch is to produce a "representation" of reality—not a copy. You want the sketch to be accurate, but do not be concerned with the fine detail [2–8]. *Do not be afraid to make a mistake!* Allow your arm to move freely and with rhythm. Use a large piece of paper and draw boldly.

A sketch is more effective than words . . . proportions and relationships are easily shown.

Figure 2–3

12 **Drawing Fundamentals**

Sketches are used to communicate with ourselves . . .

. . . and also with others.

Figure 2–4

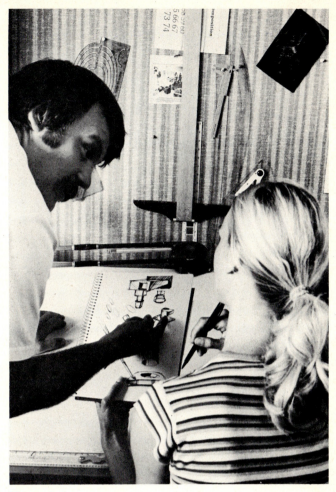

Figure 2–5

Figure 2–6

A child can represent "house" with a few simple lines.

This sketch captures more of the true character of the house.

Figure 2–7

A sketch should be accurate . . . but do not be concerned with fine detail.

Figure 2–8

2.3 The Marker and the Drawing Surface

Sketches can be made using various types of markers and drawing surfaces. For the beginner it is advisable to use a combination that encourages freedom of movement and discourages self-criticism. This approach is employed by many experienced designers in the early stages of concept development. Use simple, bold strokes with a broad-tipped marker to help establish the central character of a building without cluttering your mind with fine line refinements [2–2A].

First try a broad-point felt-tip pen, preferably one using black ink [2–9]. Use a large piece of inexpensive paper such as newsprint for a drawing surface. As confidence is gained, other tools, such as soft charcoal, fine-point felt-tip pens, and soft lead pencils, may be used. Other surfaces, such as tracing paper, textured cardboard, or fine-grain paper, may be chosen later.

2.4 Avoid Drafting Tools in Sketching

The common drawing instruments, guides, scales, triangles, templates, and so on, *should not* be used in freehand sketching [2–10]. Their use should be reserved for technical and presentation drawing. With practice you should be able to sketch freehand the many straight lines—parallel, perpendicular, and converging—that are often seen in architectural drawings [2–11].

The use of an eraser should also be avoided. This is one reason that a felt-tip ink pen is recommended—to avoid the temptation to make adjustments with the aid of an eraser. Correct errors in a freehand sketch by drawing over the original lines. If the error is too serious for this remedy, discard the paper and begin again [2–12]. Don't hesitate to discard an undesirable sketch. If you have been approaching sketching with vigor and speed, as you should, you will have invested only a very little time in the sketch.

Marking tools for sketching . . .

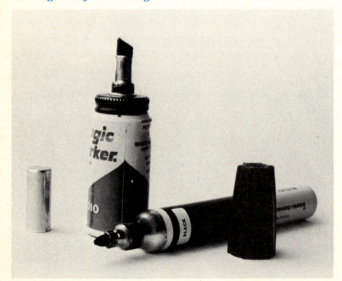

Figure 2–9

Don't use drafting instruments.

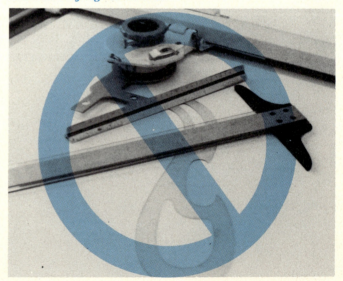

Figure 2–10

14 Drawing Fundamentals

Buildings, even with their many straight lines, can be sketched freehand.

Figure 2-11

No sketch should become "too precious."

Figure 2-12

"Cradle" marker in the hand.

Figure 2–13

EXERCISES

2–1. Who is Le Corbusier? What has been his contribution to the world of art and architecture? Use your library to expand your discussion.

2–2. How is freehand sketching useful to the architectural drafter?

2–3. What are some of the practices you may employ to develop confidence in your sketching?

2–4. What are some advantages of using broad-tipped marking tools in your sketchwork?

2–5. Why should you avoid using drafting tools in your sketchwork?

2.5 Holding the Marker

The way in which you hold the marker determines the accuracy and "looseness" of the final result. Unlike writing, where the fingers are important in guiding the writing instrument, sketching involves the free use of the hand and arm. The marker is held by the hand so that one end rests in the palm [2–13]. The thumb and forefinger are used loosely to steady the marker as shown. Rotate your hand into a sketching position and make a few random marks on a large piece of paper [2–14]. At first the hand position will be awkward, and the feeling will not be natural. With practice you will feel comfortable in this new position.

Rotate hand into sketching position.

Figure 2–14

Most people are tempted to return to the writing position. Don't let this happen to you! Draw with your arm, not your fingers. Imagine that your wrist and hand are bound together in a cast and that you cannot move them separately. This encourages full arm movement and emphasizes a boldness of stroke.

Where possible it is advisable to stand rather than sit at the drawing table. This position helps keep you energetic and your arm free to move. If sitting is required, don't get lazy and allow your hand or elbow to rest on the table.

2.6 Preparation for Sketching

Just as an athlete "warms up" prior to a race, the sketcher should complete some drawing exercises prior to sketching. The exercises described here should be completed in a *minimum* amount of time. Make the strokes as rapidly as your muscles will allow. Do not be concerned with accuracy. It will improve with practice. Use a separate large piece of newsprint (18 × 24 inches approximately) for each of the following exercises.

EXERCISES

2–6. With the paper horizontal in front of you, stroke a series of lines from left to right (using the full width of the paper), and then right to left [2–15]. The lines should be straight and horizontal. It is usual for them to be slightly arched at first, and for one end of the lines to sag. Keep practicing until the sheet of paper has been filled on both sides. Strive to make the lines rapidly and accurately. (Time limit of 30 seconds)

2–7. Using another piece of paper, stroke lines vertically—first from top to bottom, and then from bottom to top [2–16]. Ideally the lines will be straight and vertical. Don't be discouraged if at first the lines tend to be shaky and to fan out at the edges of the paper. Don't slow down in an attempt to increase accuracy! (Time limit of 30 seconds)

2–8. On a piece of newsprint lay down a series of circular coil strokes horizontally across the paper [2–17]. On another piece of paper lay down a series of different-sized ellipses. Experiment with differences in stroke "weight." Make some strokes with a light pressure, some with a

Figure 2–15

Drawing Fundamentals

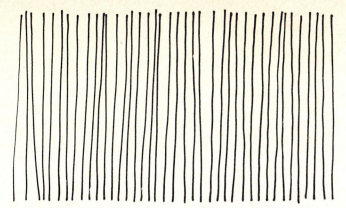

Figure 2–16

Contour exercises develop eye–hand coordination.

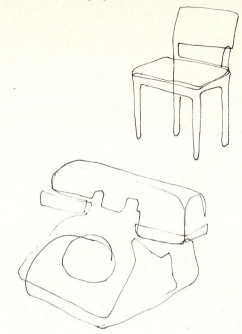

Figure 2–18

heavy pressure. Notice the differences in line qualities that result. Now make a series of lines that have a variation in line weight. (Time limit of 2 minutes)

2–9. Contour exercises develop confidence and understanding. Select a common object in the room, such as a chair or a telephone. With the object located in front of you, place your marker on a piece of paper. After this initial contact between the marker and paper *do not* look at the paper again. Look only at the object. Convince yourself that you are touching it. Then slowly follow the lines of the object with your eyes and make corresponding moves with your arm, marking the paper. *Do not look at the paper!* Continue to draw until you believe that you have captured the lines of the object. Now look at your image [2–18]. (Time limit of 1 minute)

The contour exercise points out a very important fundamental of drawing. A good visual familiarity with the subject is essential. Consequently, *more time should be spent in looking at the subject than at the surface of the paper.*

2.7 Beginning the Sketch

Proficiency in sketching will improve with practice. The important thing is to begin and not to be overly concerned with the apparent quality of the first sketches. Whenever you get a chance, practice making simple sketches of common objects—a book, a cup, a wastebasket, a box, a drawer, and so on [2–19]. Sketch each object as your mind first perceives it. Omit decorative surface designs and minor details such as screws and other fasteners. No attempt should be made to portray

Sketch coils and ellipses . . . try varying line weights.

Figure 2–17

Practice sketching simple common objects.

Figure 2–19

Freehand Drawing

Construction lines act as an initial framework.

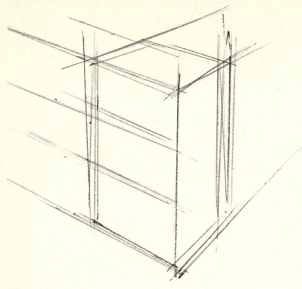

Figure 2–20

The finished sketch retains construction lines.

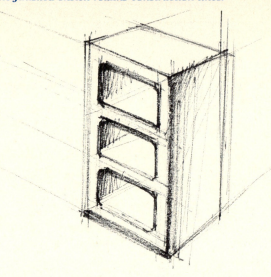

Figure 2–22

surface texture or color. Only the overall shape should concern you at this stage.

Many beginners believe that every line drawn in a sketch will be a part of the finished work. This is not so. Some lines may be drawn lightly. In this way they may serve as the initial framework for the final heavier lines, just as an outline is used in writing a story. These lightweight lines are called *construction lines* [2–20]. They help identify errors while laying out the sketch. Generally these errors are the result of initial inaccuracies in judgment. They can be corrected by simply drawing more heavily over the original line work [2–21]. Avoid using an eraser. The construction lines are retained on the finished sketch [2–22].

Some new information added . . . some errors corrected.

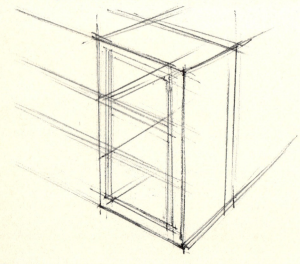

Figure 2–21

EXERCISE

2–10. Make sketches of five common objects using light construction lines to form a framework for each. Select large objects of simple shape such as (1) a cardboard box on a table, (2) a beverage vending machine, (3) a garage, or (4) an air conditioning unit. Concern yourself with basic proportions. Avoid details. Don't become attached to your sketches and be prepared to discard them. (Time limit of 5 minutes for each object)

In drawing an object as though it were real, you are creating a two-dimensional illusion of three-dimensional space. There are several conditions that will assist you in adding the quality of realism to two-dimensional sketches. Several of these are discussed in the following paragraphs.

2.8 Overlapping Shapes

The quality of *depth* in a sketch is important in creating the illusion of three-dimensional space. Overlapping shapes are often used for this purpose. When an object or part of an object is hidden behind another object, it is interpreted by your mind as being located farther away than the shielding object [2–23]. However, it is not always evident just how far away the object is located. You might not know, for example, whether a few inches or several feet separate the shapes.

EXERCISE

2–11. Sketch a circle, a square, and a diamond. All three should be of approximately equal size. Using the principle of overlapping shapes, sketch the circle in front of the

Overlapping shapes create the illusion of depth . . . but how far apart are they?

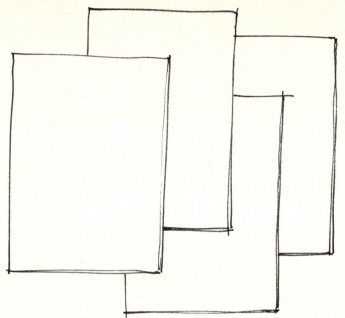

Figure 2–23

The mind stores information concerning relative sizes . . . the sign appears larger than the plane, so it is assumed to be closer.

Figure 2–25

square with the diamond in back of the square. Repeat this exercise twice, changing the order of the shapes each time. Remember to use arm movement—not your fingers. Make the sketches quickly, and keep them "free and loose." No drafting tools such as compasses or straightedges should be used. (Total time limit—5 minutes)

2.9 Relative Size

If you see two objects that you know to be identical, and one appears to be larger than the other, it is natural

If the sizes are identical . . . then the larger one must be closer.

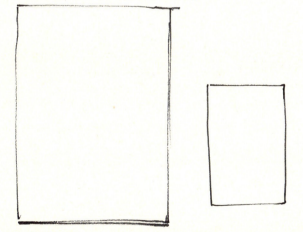

Figure 2–24

to assume that the one appearing larger is closer [2–24]. This illustrates the conditions of relative size. You are not always aware of your brain's work since it functions automatically and frequently beyond the level of consciousness. Your mind stores a large amount of information concerning the relative size of objects and is particularly adept in making instantaneous judgments about the size of the objects that your eye sees. For example, if you see a traffic sign and an airplane at the same time, and the sign appears to be larger, you ordinarily will assume that it is closer to you [2–25]. The cumulative effect of overlapping shapes and relative size increases the illusion of depth [2–26].

EXERCISE

2–12. Use a circle, square, and diamond as in Exercise 2–11. Place the circle in front of the square but diminish the size of the square. Place the square in front of the diamond, but diminish the size of the diamond. Repeat the sketches of Exercise 2–11, but in each case diminish the size of each overlapped shape. (Total time limit—5 minutes)

Freehand Drawing

Combining overlapping shapes and relative sizes . . . increases the illusion of depth.

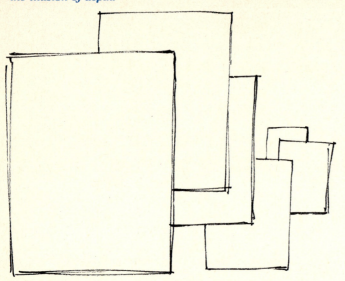

Figure 2–26

2.10 Aerial Positioning

Another condition affecting the illusion of depth is aerial positioning. This condition is based on the fact that human beings are constructed with their eyes located about 1.6 meters above the ground. This gives the human being an advantage over most animals by providing an increased ability to see over objects and into the distance. Closer objects therefore appear lower in your field of vision and objects farther away appear higher [2–27]. Look across the room. The chairs that are close appear lower in your field of vision and those farther away appear higher [2–28].

The cumulative effect of overlapping shapes, relative

Aerial positioning . . . closer objects appear lower in the field of vision.

Figure 2–27

The chairs that are close appear lower . . . farther ones appear higher.

Figure 2–28

size, and aerial positioning further increases the illusion of depth [2–29]. You can make good use of these conditions to supply realism to your sketches.

EXERCISE

2–13. Sketch a circle, square, and diamond. Position them with the square in front of the diamond and the diamond in front of the circle. Obtain depth illusion using the conditions of overlapping shapes, relative size, and aerial positioning. Repeat the exercise using other shape sequences.

Combining overlapping shapes, relative size, and aerial positioning . . . further increases the illusion of depth.

Figure 2–29

20

Drawing Fundamentals

More distant objects appear less distinct.

Which depth illusion techniques are used here?

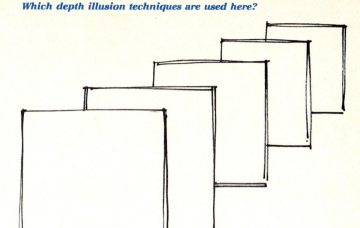

Figure 2–30

Figure 2–32

as a uniform, fine texture with suggestions of darks and lights. As the fairway recedes, continues on to the next hill, and approaches the horizon, the individual grass blades are no longer identifiable and only shades of green-gray appear. Taking these atmospheric effects into account will help to add depth quality to your sketches [2–31]. It is most effective, however, when combined with the other conditions of overlapping shapes, relative size, and aerial positioning [2–32].

2.11 Atmospheric Effects

The feeling of space and depth is also influenced by the clarity of the atmosphere. This includes the effects that air, smoke, fog, and haze have on the appearance of objects. As an object recedes into the distance, detail becomes less defined and more obscure [2–30]. This principle provides you with yet another means of adding depth illusion to your sketches.

If the light level remains constant, distant surfaces appear as middle-tone grays. Careful visualization of grass on a golf course will help us to understand this principle. In the near foreground, you can see individual blades of grass with contrasting dark shadows and brightly lit surfaces. Some 30 feet away, the grass surface appears

EXERCISE

2–14. Make a sketch of a diamond, circle, and square. Arrange them so that the diamond is in front and the square is farthest away. Achieve the illusion of depth using the condition of atmospheric effects. Repeat the exercise using other sequences of the shapes.

2.12 Introduction to Perspective

Perspective is probably the most effective method used to add the illusion of depth to a sketch. This procedure follows fundamental principles of vision because the lines you draw on paper appear to your eye as they

Atmospheric effects . . . the closest object appears sharpest and clearest.

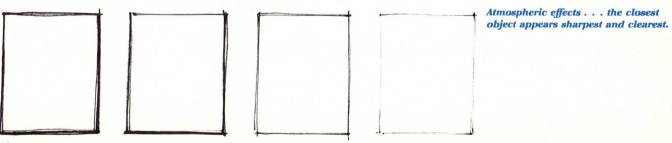

Figure 2–31

Freehand Drawing

21

The sense of reality evidenced in the photograph . . .

. . . can be achieved in perspective sketching.

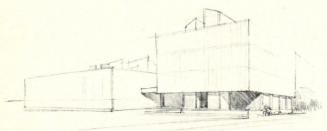

Figure 2–33

do in life situations [2–33]. An in-depth technical discussion of perspective drawing is beyond the scope of this material. However, it will be helpful to describe some basic principles of perspective that will assist you in adding realism to your sketches.

Many forms in our society are basically rectangular. This permits most perspective sketches to be drawn using a few basic principles. It is only when inclined planes, intersecting planes, circles, and other variations are added that perspectives are complex to draw.

In perspective an object appears to grow smaller in a determinable way as it recedes into the distance [2–34]. This effect may be referred to as *foreshortening*. The top and the bottom edges of any vertical surface, when represented by lines, disappear toward each other. If extended to the extreme, they will eventually meet. The location of the point where these lines meet is critical. It is called the *vanishing point* [2–35]. This is the point where the surface bounded by these lines vanishes.

For the moment you may assume that vanishing points are always located on the *horizon line* [2–36]. The horizon is an imaginary line that represents the apparent meeting point of the earth and sky. Mountains and valleys are ignored and the earth is assumed to be flat. If you stand on a beach and look out to sea, you will see a true horizon line [2–37]. The horizon line is always assumed to be straight and horizontal. It accompanies you wherever you go—whether you sit, stand, or climb stairs. The horizon line's position in relation to what you are viewing can be determined by imagining that the line is located straight ahead from your eyes and that it cuts horizontally across the scene that you are viewing.

EXERCISE

2–15. Cut out several newspaper or magazine pictures. Locate the horizon line and vanishing points in each and draw

An object appears to grow smaller as it recedes into the distance.

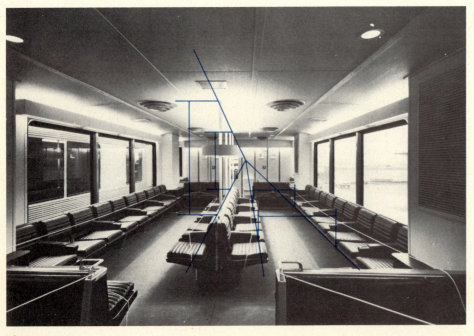

Figure 2–34

Drawing Fundamentals

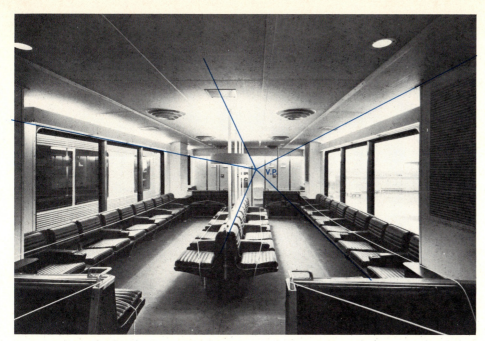

The vanishing point is the distant point where horizontal lines appear to meet.

Figure 2–35

them on the picture. Draw lines on the edges of major elements that converge toward the vanishing points.

2.13 Locating Vanishing Points

The first step in locating a vanishing point is to imagine that the parallel horizontal top and bottom-edge lines of an object extend toward the horizon line until they appear to merge into a single point [2–38]. This technique requires practice. It is frequently helpful to close one eye and hold a marker in a horizontal position in front of your eye so that the marker appears to rest on the top and then on the bottom of the closest vertical line of the object [2–39]. This makes it easier to judge the angles of the top and bottom lines as they lead to vanishing points on the left and on the right.

In some cases the size or location of an object may make it particularly difficult to locate the vanishing points. If it is not possible to extend directly an edge line of the object to locate a vanishing point, you can sight along an imaginary line running parallel to it

Vanishing points are located on the horizon.

Figure 2–36

Freehand Drawing

A true horizon line is seen when looking out to sea.

Figure 2–37

Extensions of the horizontal edge lines meet on the horizon at the vanishing point.

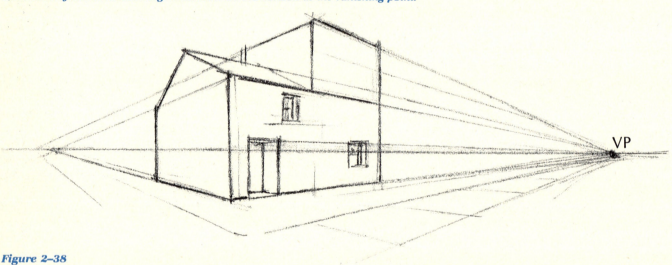

Figure 2–38

A marker held horizontally helps estimate angles.

Figure 2–39

[2–40]. Your imaginary sight line will intersect the horizon line at the same vanishing point as the object lines that are parallel to it. All parallel lines disappear to the same vanishing point.

2.14 Construction of a Simple Perspective Sketch

The horizon line is the foundation of the sketch [2–41]. Always draw it first (assuming it is located on the paper). In some instances it may be well above or below the object. The next construction line drawn should be one representing the closest vertical edge of the object

If extensions of edge lines are difficult to see . . . sight along lines parallel to them to locate vanishing points.

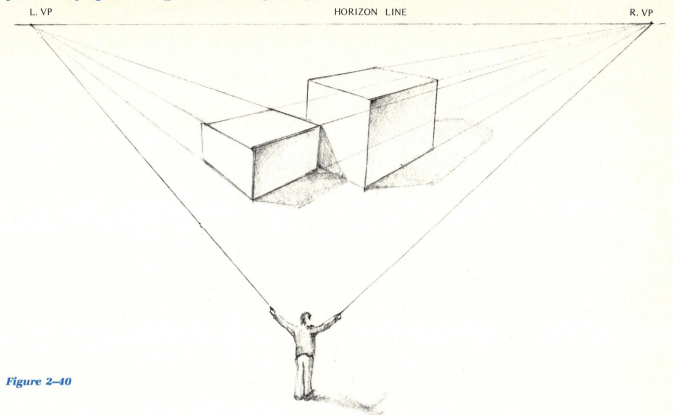

Figure 2–40

The horizon line is the foundation of the sketch . . . draw it first.

HORIZON LINE

Figure 2–41

[2–42]. Establish the height of the object by marking points on the vertical line to designate the top and bottom of the object [2–43]. If the horizon line passes through the object, proportion the height of the object above and below the horizon as it appears to your eye.

Estimate the angular relationships of the top and bottom edges of the object to the horizon line. Using these angles, extend light angular construction lines to the right and left from the top and bottom of the front edge of the object to the horizon line [2–44]. The vanishing points will be established where these pairs of receding lines meet at the horizon. Finally, make a judgment about the comparative width and depth dimensions of the object and represent them with vertical construction lines drawn to the left and right of the front edge line [2–45]. Figure [2–46] shows the sequence of steps used in sketching a more complicated object in perspective.

Draw the closest vertical edge . . .

. . . and establish the height.

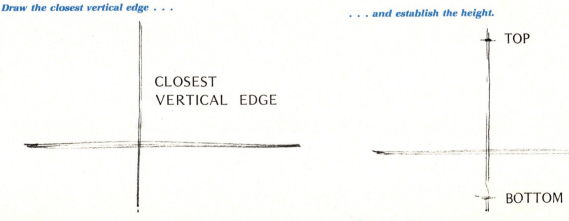

Figure 2–42

Figure 2–43

Freehand Drawing

25

Estimate the angles with the horizontal and draw lines that meet at the vanishing points.

Steps in sketching a more complex object.

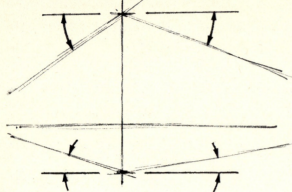

Figure 2–44

Establish the width and depth by drawing vertical lines.

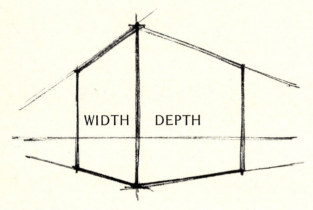

Figure 2–45

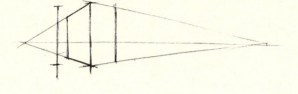

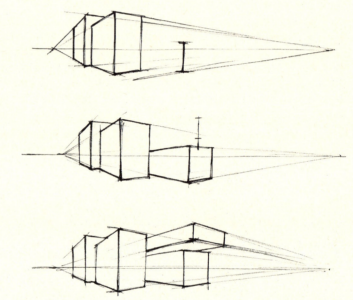

2.15 Sketching Objects in Perspective

Figure 2–46

If you look directly ahead, the view recorded in your mind takes the form of a picture. It is framed by the limits of your vision. When making a perspective sketch, you are actually transferring the visual image or "picture" of the object from your mind to paper.

To assist you in picturing an object, assume that a transparent pane of glass has been placed on edge and extends upward in front of your face with its flat surface perpendicular to your line of sight. This forms a *picture plane* through which you can see. (This is sometimes

The viewer sees an image of the object projected onto the picture plane.

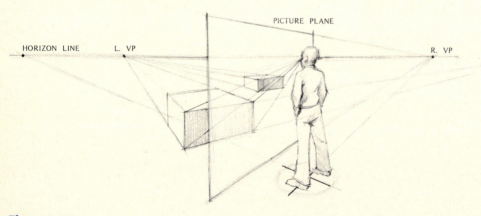

Figure 2–47

Drawing Fundamentals

referred to as a *viewing plane*.) The images of all objects visible to you are projected onto it [2–47]. If a camera were to be positioned where your eyes are located, the resulting photograph would record the same view that has been projected onto the picture plane.

Since drawing paper isn't as transparent as glass, it can't be positioned between your eyes and the object to receive the image directly. Instead, the paper must be placed to one side and the image transferred to it by a mental process rather than by a tracing operation [2–48].

Parallel and perpendicular lines and surfaces are very evident in most objects that we see in our daily lives. Buildings are generally designed with most of their surfaces perpendicular to each other. Streets and sidewalks are commonly laid out in rectangular patterns [2–49]. For this reason there usually are at least two sets of parallel lines to consider in sketching—those concerned with the width of the object and those concerned with the depth. In perspective sketching the parallel width lines vanish to one side of the object and the parallel depth lines vanish to the other side [2–50]. This condition is called *two-point perspective*.

The sketcher must transfer the image on the picture plane to the drawing paper.

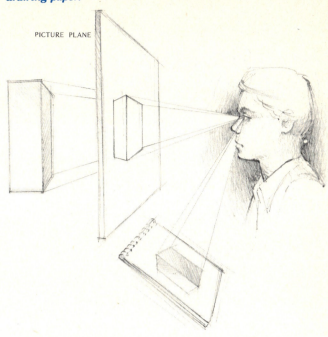

Figure 2–48

Figure 2–49

Rectangular patterns are frequently seen in our everyday activities.

Freehand Drawing

27

In two-point perspective . . . the horizontal lines vanish to the left and to the right.

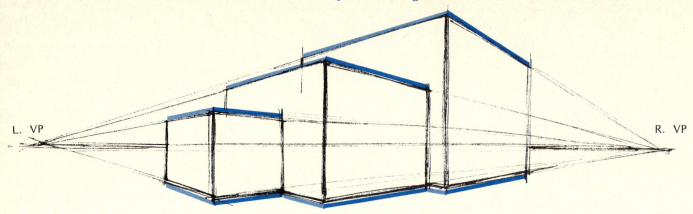

Figure 2–50

As you walk around a building, your viewing direction relative to the building changes as you move from left to right [2–51]. This movement causes a continual change in the location of the width and depth vanishing points. As you approach the closest vertical edge of the building (the left corner of the front surface), the extensions of the horizontal top and bottom edges of the left side of the building converge more quickly. This forces the left vanishing point to move closer to the building. At the same time, the extensions of the top and bottom horizontal edges of the front surface of the building converge more gradually. This causes their vanishing point to move farther to the right. As you move closer to the center of the front of the building, the horizontal lines of the front surface converge less and less and their vanishing point moves off to infinity to the right [2–52]. At the same time, your view of the left side of the building is vanishing and its horizontal lines are converging rapidly to a point behind the building.

On arriving at the exact center of the front of the building, you will be looking directly at (perpendicular to) the front surface [2–53]. The top and bottom lines of the front surface will be parallel and the horizontal lines of the left side will have converged to a point centered behind the building. If you were to sketch the object from this viewing direction, you would produce what is known as *one-point perspective*. This is because the horizontal lines of both the left-side and right-side parallel surfaces converge to the same vanishing point.

As you walk to the right you will see part of the right side of the building [2–54]. Note that the horizontal lines of this surface converge very rapidly at first as their vanishing point moves out from behind the building. At the same time, the horizontal lines of the front surface are converging very slowly to a distant left vanishing point. As you continue walking to the right you will see that the vanishing point for the right side moves more to the right and the vanishing point for the front surface moves from the far left to a position closer to the building.

The left vanishing point is moving closer to the building . . . the right farther away.

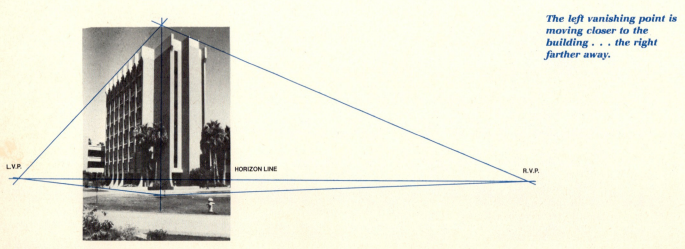

Figure 2–51

Drawing Fundamentals

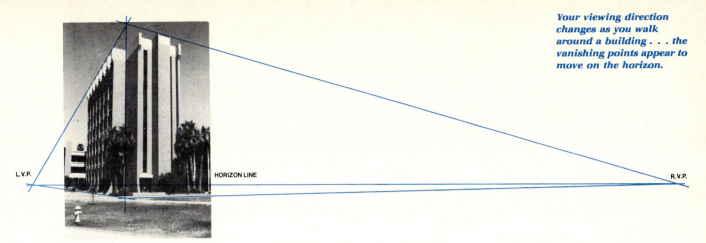

Your viewing direction changes as you walk around a building ... the vanishing points appear to move on the horizon.

Figure 2-52

When you are looking directly at the front of the building ... the vanishing points for the left and right sides are centered behind the building.

Figure 2-53

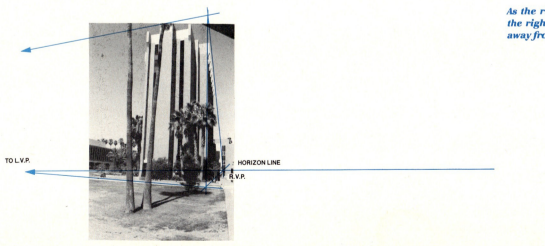

As the right side comes into view, the right vanishing point moves away from the building to the right.

Figure 2-54

29

EXERCISE

2–16. Using a box or some other rectangular solid as a subject, make a series of five sketches. Begin the first sketch by establishing the horizon line. Add the closest vertical line of the object. Then locate the left and right vanishing points. Finally, establish the width and depth of the object. For the second and each following sketch rotate the object approximately 70° around a vertical axis. (Time limit of 5 minutes maximum for each sketch)

2.16 Eye Level and Proportion Relationships

The appearance of an object drawn in perspective is always influenced by the height of the sketcher. If the base of the object that you are sketching is on the same ground level as you are, the height of your eyes determines the distance between the base of the object and the horizon line. When standing, your eyes are about 1.6 meters above the ground. On your sketch the distance from the base of the object to the horizon line must, therefore, represent 1.6 meters [2–55]. If you are kneeling down, your eyes will be about 1 meter above the ground. In this case the location of the horizon line above the base of the object on your sketch will represent 1 meter.

The actual dimension that you select for this distance in your sketch may be any length. This selection is critical, however, because all other dimensions of the object will be established in proportion to it.

The first dimension on your sketch that the distance from the base of the object to the horizon line will influence is the height of the object. If your eyes are 1 meter above the ground as you look at a building, the total building height of 6 meters must be drawn six times as large as the distance from the base to the horizon [2–56]. The portion of the height between the horizon and the top of the building represents 5 meters. In sketching, the distance from the base of the object to the horizon line is usually visualized as one unit and *eye judgment* is used to decide how many of these units appear above the horizon line.

Eye judgments of distances and proportions are very important in sketching. One aid to accomplishing this is to sight over a marker held in line with the object. To estimate a vertical distance, hold your marker vertically at arm's length with your arm straight and elbow locked [2–57]. Sight past the marker with one eye closed and position the marker in line with the distance you wish to measure. Slide your thumb along the marker to adjust its length, matching the apparent distance on the object. This unit measurement can then be easily compared with other dimensions of the object to establish its basic proportions. Measurements in other directions can be estimated by aligning your marker in those

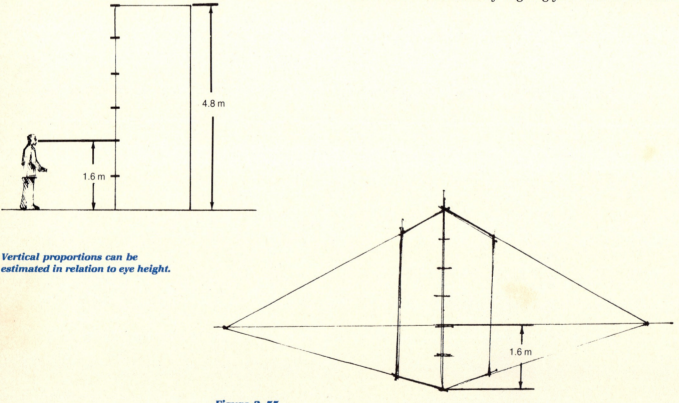

Vertical proportions can be estimated in relation to eye height.

Figure 2–55

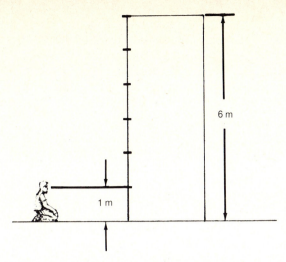

Lowering eye height decreases the proportion of the building below the horizon.

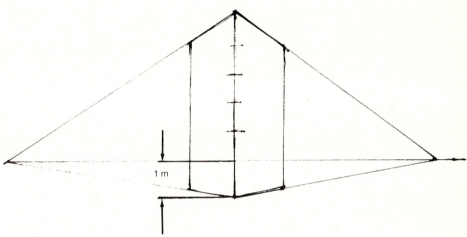

Figure 2-56

Sight over a marker to estimate distances and proportions . . . hold your arm straight with elbow locked.

Figure 2-57

directions [2-58]. Although this procedure is a useful tool to help train your eye, don't become overly dependent on it. Make distance and proportion judgments directly with your eye as much as possible. This will greatly speed up your sketching.

2.17 Perspective Complexities

Occasionally, a building is constructed, a street located, or a box set down so that it is not aligned in an orderly rectangular pattern with other nearby objects. This presents a new problem for the sketcher who is trying to portray accurately each object in the sketch. What must be realized is that while the group of objects has a common horizon line, each object has its own separate set of vanishing points on this horizon line [2-59].

Occasionally, you will need to sketch an object from a high viewpoint [2-60]. This is often referred to as a "bird's eye view." It may be difficult or even impossible to include the horizon line in the sketch [2-61]. In this event, the lines representing the horizontal edges of the

Freehand Drawing

Distances can be estimated in any direction.

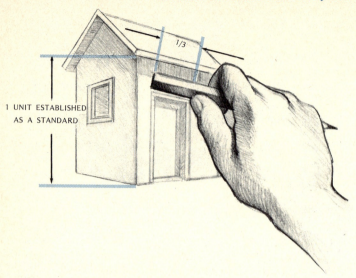

Figure 2–58

Each object has its own set of vanishing points on the horizon line.

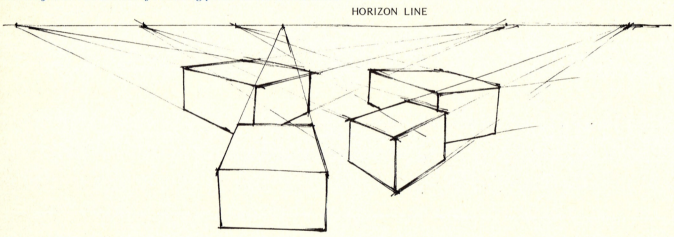

Figure 2–59

If you look down on an object . . .

. . . the horizon line may not appear on the drawing of the object.

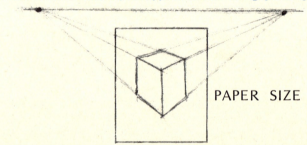

Figure 2–61

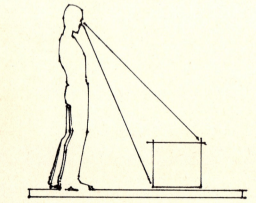

Figure 2–60

32

Which line does not vanish to the same point?

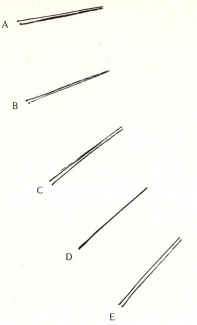

... with the lines extended, it is obviously "C."

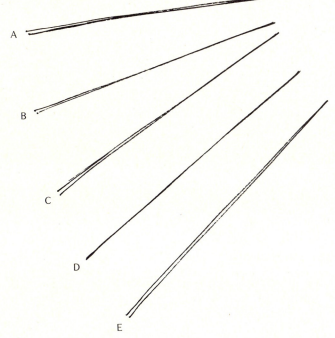

Figure 2–62

object must be extended to meet at vanishing points located some distance off the paper. Only a small portion of these construction lines will be used to frame the object, but the longer these lines can be extended on the paper, the better. People's eyes are more adept at identifying directional trends of long lines [2–62]. It may be helpful to identify vanishing points that exist off the paper by marking them on the table with a thumb tack

Vanishing points remain constant when you move from a distant to a closer view.

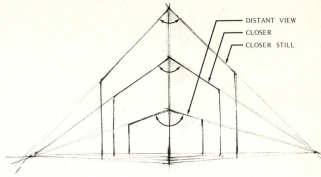

Figure 2–63

or a chalk mark. If you do this, be careful not to move your paper while making the sketch.

EXERCISE

2–17. Use the same or a similar object to that used in Exercise 2–16. Place the object on a table high enough so that the horizon line intersects the object. Sketch it in this location. Then move the object to a lower table or shelf and sketch that view of the object. Finally, sketch the object as it appears when placed on the floor. (None of these sketches should take longer than 5 minutes.)

Another problem occurs in perspective sketching as the sketcher moves from a distant to a closer view of the same object. Examination of a rectangular building at three different distances demonstrates that the horizon line and the vanishing points remain constant for the three views [2–63]. The problem arises in that the closer the viewer is to the object, the longer the edges appear. Also, the nearest vertical edge of the object appears to lengthen at a rate greater than the distant vertical edges. This causes the angle on the top corner to become more acute. A similar situation occurs when sketching objects of varying sizes. The best way to determine the various angles is to observe how they occur on real objects. As you become more skilled in sketching objects that exist only in your mind, you will be able to imply the size or nearness of an object by merely manipulating these angles.

EXERCISES

2–18. Find a small rectangular object. Place it on your desk as far away from your eye as possible. Position it high enough so that the horizon line intersects the object. Make a quick sketch on paper large enough to include both vanishing points. Next, move the object as close as possible to you and sketch it on top of your previous sketch. Use the same vanishing points. It may help you to close one eye when sketching close objects. Compare

Freehand Drawing

the angles of the lines that converge to the vanishing points on the two sketches.

2–19. Go outdoors. Quickly sketch several (at least five) large buildings. Avoid details such as windows, doors, and decorations. Pay attention to overall perspective and proportion. Repeat the exercise on another day. Compare your best sketches each day. (Time limit of 10 minutes for each sketch)

2.18 Circles in Perspective

Sooner or later those who sketch objects in perspective need to draw a circle in perspective [2–64 and 2–65]. Fortunately, circles are not difficult to sketch if a few simple fundamentals are kept in mind.

In some ways a circle and a square are closely related. A circle can always be placed within a square so that it touches the midpoint of each side of the square and shares the square's center [2–66]. This basic relationship is preserved when the square and circle are viewed in perspective [2–67]. The circle now appears as an ellipse but is still tangent to the midpoints of the sides of the distorted square and shares its center. If a line runs through the center of the circle and is perpendicular to its surface, the line becomes an "axle" [2–68]. This axle has the same relationship to the circle as a true axle would have to a wheel [2–69].

A line drawn at 90° to the axle so that it runs across the ellipse at its widest point is known as its *major axis* [2–70]. The major axis crosses the axle close to, but not

When drawing a perspective sketch of a circular building such as this one, several ellipses must be drawn.

Figure 2–64

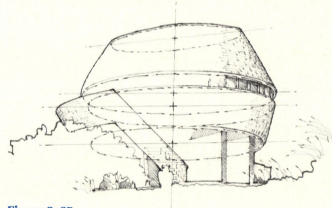

Figure 2–65

A line perpendicular to the ellipse at its center is the "axle."

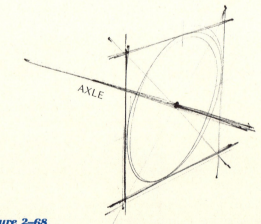

A circle drawn inside a square shares its center and is tangent at the midpoints of the sides.

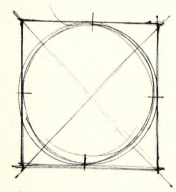

Figure 2–66

When the square is drawn in perspective, the circle becomes an ellipse.

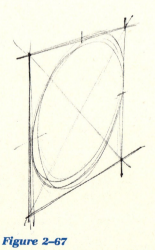

Figure 2–67

Figure 2–68

Drawing Fundamentals

The perpendicular shaft at the center of this satellite is like the axle of a wheel.

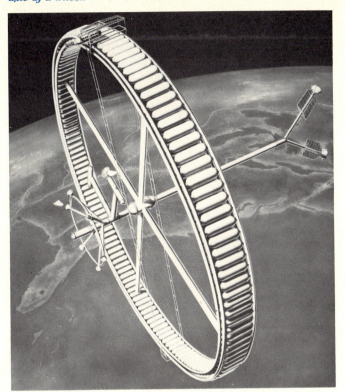

Figure 2–69

exactly at, the center of the circle in the perspective view. The shortest distance across the ellipse is known as its *minor axis*. The minor axis is also located at a right angle (90°) to the major axis and appears to lie over the axle. The relationship of these parts of the ellipse allows us to sketch them easily.

To sketch an ellipse, draw a line that is approximately 90° to the long direction that you expect the ellipse to take [2–71]. This will represent the axle. Next, draw a

The major axis is the widest dimension of the ellipse . . . the minor axis is perpendicular and in line with the axle.

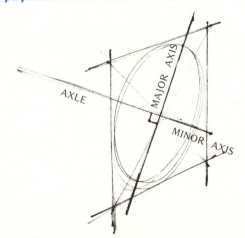

Figure 2–70

To sketch an ellipse . . . draw a line to represent the axle.

Figure 2–71

Draw major axis at a right angle . . . mark width and length proportions.

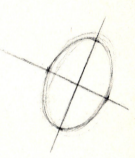

Figure 2–72

Sketch the ellipse through the marks on the axes.

Figure 2–73

line at right angles to it, close to where you expect the center of the circle to be [2–72]. This will be the major axis. The direction of the minor axis was established automatically when the axle was drawn. The proportions of width and length of the ellipse are now defined by making small marks on opposite ends of the major and minor axes. These marks will serve as references as you sketch the actual lines of the ellipse [2–73].

The only successful way to sketch an ellipse is to let your arm do it for you—easily, naturally, and rapidly. Try it! Set up some construction lines as previously discussed, then loosen up and let your arm muscles work by themselves [2–74]. This will require some practice. As you sketch your ellipses, imagine that the marker is trying to get around the ellipse as fast as possible. Make a few imaginary passes with the point of the marker just above the paper. Let the point drop to the paper surface and make a few more passes. To save time, avoid turning the paper.

EXERCISE

2–20. First, practice sketching several ellipses of varying sizes and in various positions. Allow your arm to move easily, naturally, and rapidly. Next, sketch an axle that recedes into the distance to meet a horizon line. Mark six intervals along the axle. At each interval sketch an ellipse that would describe a wheel attached to the axle [2–75].

Freehand Drawing

Let your arm move freely and rapidly as you sketch.

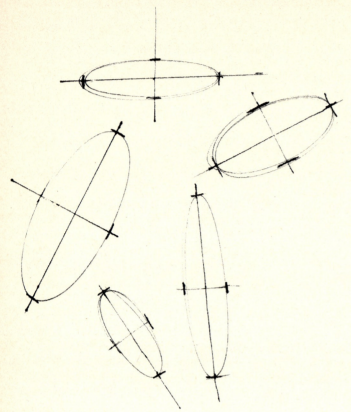

Figure 2-74

2.19 Cylinders in Perspective

When sketches are used to define the shape of objects, circles are frequently seen as the ends of cylinders. A cylinder may be hollow as in the case of a round tube, or it may be a solid shape. In the most common case of a cylinder, such as a beverage can, the circular end surfaces are perpendicular to the longitudinal centerline

Sketch a set of wheels on an axle that recedes into the distance.

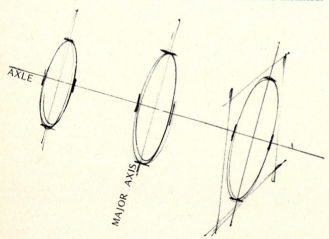

Figure 2-75

Sketch the edge lines of the cylinder.

Figure 2-76

The axis lies midway between the edge lines and forms the axle.

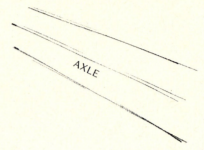

Figure 2-77

Establish cylinder length and sketch the major axes perpendicular to the axle.

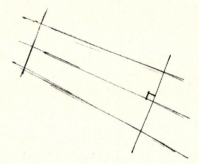

Figure 2-78

Mark minor axis proportions.

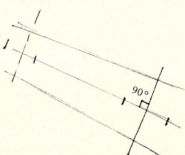

Figure 2-79

Sketch end ellipses.

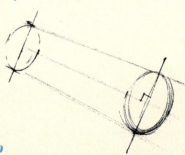

Figure 2-80

Vertical cylinders with horizontal ends . . . the major axes of the ellipses are horizontal . . . the minor axes are vertical.

Figure 2–81

2.20 Inclined Planes

Up to this time you have dealt with vanishing points that always lie on the horizon line. This is true for objects that are composed of vertical and horizontal surfaces. What happens in perspective when part of an object or a surface is positioned at an angle to the other elements of your sketch? Examples of this situation occur commonly—pitched roofs, cars parked on a hill, and so on.

Consider [2–82]. A common cardboard box rests on a flat surface with its two vanishing points located on the horizon line. The top flap farthest from you has been opened out flat. As this flap is lifted away from a horizontal position (parallel to the ground) into an angled position, the vanishing point to the right rises with it. The more erect the flap is, the *higher* the vanishing point is *above* the horizon line. These new vanishing points are directly *above* the original one. Note that the left vanishing point of the flap lines remains stationary because these lines are still horizontal lines.

In [2–83] the flap closest to you is raised from an open horizontal position. The right vanishing point will drop down *below* the original vanishing point. Again, the vanishing point to the left remains stationary.

Examine the sketch of a simple "houselike" structure [2–84]. The front surface of the roof angles upward toward the rear. Its right vanishing point has moved up with it. The rear surface angles downward. This causes its right vanishing point to move down.

Figure [2–85] shows what can happen when several angled surfaces appear on the same object. No two surfaces are angled in the same direction. Their vanishing points all move up or down from either the left vanishing point or the right vanishing point depending on which direction the surface is pointing as it moves away from you. When seen from the front, a surface either rises or falls. This determines whether its vanishing point will also rise or fall.

EXERCISE

2–22. Find roofs and other inclined planes on buildings in your community. Sketch the outlines and major features of these buildings. Select both steep and low sloped planes. Try to find a building that has several inclined planes in a variety of positions. Sketch the building.

or *axis* of the cylinder. This axis, therefore, is the same as the "axle" of the end circles.

To sketch a solid cylinder lying on its side, establish as the first step the direction of the longitudinal edge lines as they converge toward a vanishing point on the horizon [2–76]. You can then sketch a centerline representing the axis of the cylinder and the axle for the end circles. Place it midway between the edge lines [2–77]. Mark on the axis the end points defining the length of the cylinder. Now you can sketch the long major axes of the end ellipses passing through the end points and perpendicular to the axis [2–78]. The minor axes coincide with the axle. Points are marked to establish their lengths relative to those of the major axes that are terminated by the cylinder's edge lines [2–79]. The proportions can be estimated by eye or by holding up a marker and sighting past it as described earlier. You are now ready to sketch the end ellipses tangent to the edge lines and passing through the major and minor axes points [2–80]. Darken in only the visible portion of the ellipse representing the far end of the cylinder.

Vertical cylinders have a vertical axis that also forms the axle for the end ellipses. If sketched in two-point perspective, the edge lines will be parallel, vertical lines. The major axes of the ellipses will be horizontal since they must be perpendicular to the vertical axle [2–81]. The minor ellipse axes are aligned with the axle.

EXERCISE

2–21. Find several circular and cylindrical building features in your community. Find both horizontal and vertical orientations. Sketch simple outlines of the buildings and then circular components. At an equal distance from each building, prepare three sketches as viewed from three different angles.

2.21 Value and Value Contrast

There are several ways to imply space, depth, form, texture, and volume in sketching. Among these are the use of overlapping shapes, relative size, aerial positioning, atmospheric effects, and perspective. Another very effective illusion technique is the use of value. First, the term

Freehand Drawing

37

As the far flap rises, its right vanishing point rises . . . the left does not change.

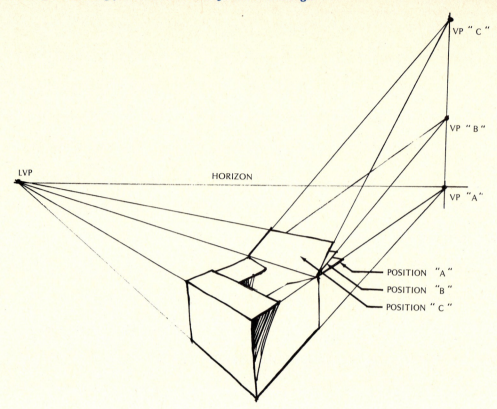

Figure 2–82

As the near flap rises, its right vanishing point drops . . . the left does not change.

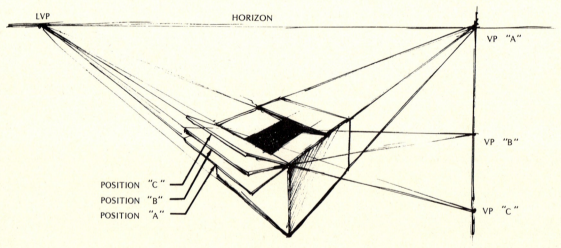

Figure 2–83

As the roof angles up, its vanishing point rises . . . as it angles down, the point drops.

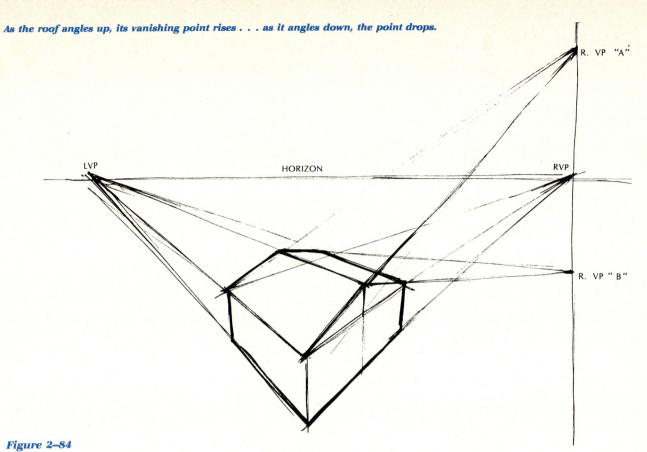

Figure 2–84

Vanishing points rise or fall as surfaces angle up or down from the viewer.

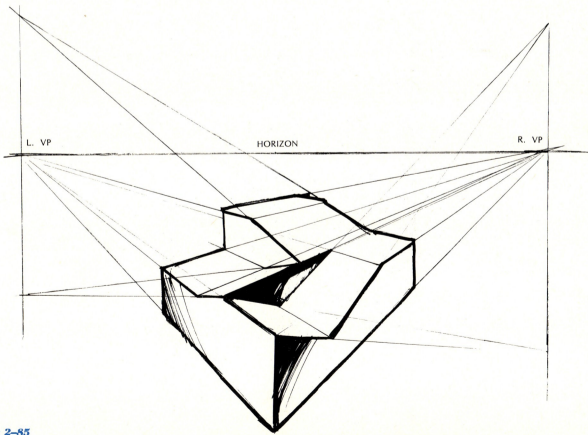

Figure 2–85

39

Low value contrast . . . heavy values adjacent.

Figure 2–86

Low value contrast . . . light values adjacent.

Figure 2–87

High value contrast . . . light and heavy values adjacent.

Figure 2–88

A value scale . . . the value contrast between each of the pairs of shaded blocks is equal.

Figure 2–89

value must be understood. Value refers to how light or dark each surface of an object appears to a viewer. Surface colors have a relative lightness or darkness in relation to each other. Yellow, for example, appears much lighter than black, yet darker ("heavier" value) than white. On the other hand, the same tint of yellow may appear to be heavier or lighter under changing lighting conditions.

Value contrast refers to the relation of two color areas to each other. When two color areas similar in value are placed together, low value contrast is produced [2–86 and 2–87]. A distinctly light color placed next to a very dark (heavy value) color produces high value contrast [2–88].

EXERCISE

2–23. Make a 10-unit "value scale" study using a soft lead pencil or charcoal. First, lay out a rectangle 25 centimeters (cm) long and 3 centimeters wide. Subdivide this rectangle into 10 smaller rectangles using very light lines. Each rectangle should measure approximately 2.5 × 3 cm. Leave the white of the paper in the top rectangle. Now make the bottom rectangle as dark as possible. Progressively darken each area in between by the same amount so that the value contrast between adjacent areas remains equal all along the scale [2–89]. Some people prefer to darken the rectangles separately, cut them out, correct where necessary, then paste them all together to make a total pattern. There is one caution: inserting visible lines to separate the areas will destroy the effectiveness of this exercise.

2.22 Light and Shade

In addition to representing color variations, value contrast is used to portray conditions of *light* and *shade*. These conditions are a part of life and daily experience. Looking at [2–90], you can readily appreciate how adding value contrast to portray light and shade conditions improves the perception of the shapes as solid forms [2–91].

In [2–92] you can see three basic value areas on a cylinder: (1) a lighted surface, (2) a shadow "core," and (3) a reflected light area. The lighted surface is always the lightest value tone, whereas the shadow core is always the darkest. The reflected light area lies somewhere in between. The shadow core is the area on an object where the lighted surface stops and the shaded area begins. It exists on both sides of the object. The shadow

When value contrast is absent . . . only line and perspective are available to show depth and form.

Value contrast may portray light and shade to clarify forms.

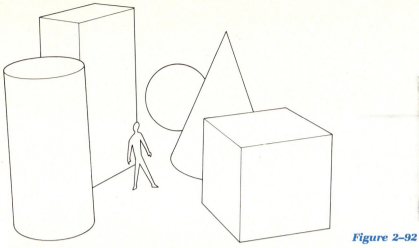

Figure 2–90

Figure 2–92

Value contrast used to portray light and shade helps clarify form and depth.

Figure 2–91

41

The shadow cast on an adjacent surface starts at the shadow core.

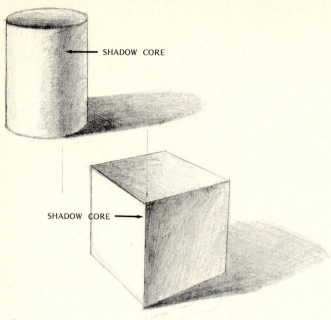

Figure 2-93

A cast shadow drawn correctly adds to the illusion of reality.

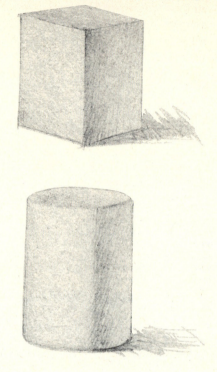

Figure 2-95

core is also the starting point for any *shadow* that is *cast* by the object onto an adjacent surface [2-93].

EXERCISE

2-24. Obtain several objects such as a small 20 × 20 × 50 cm cardboard box, a beverage can, a paper cone, and a ball. Paint them flat white. Shine a light on each object as shown in [2-94]. Now sketch each object. To shade the darker areas with their full values, use charcoal as your marker. Use care to keep areas of contrast separate. Avoid smudging and an overall gray appearance. With experience you may switch to a soft pencil.

Components of good lighting.

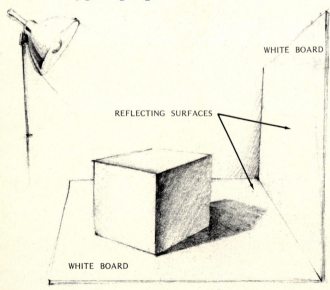

Figure 2-94

2.23 Shadows in Perspective Cast on a Horizontal Surface

The sketching of shadows cast by objects needs understanding in regard to perspective. A cast shadow drawn correctly adds immeasurably to the illusion of reality in a sketch and is well worth the effort required

42 Drawing Fundamentals

[2–95]. An incorrectly drawn shadow, on the other hand, can do much to destroy the third dimension illusion that you are trying to establish. Remember that the objective of your sketch is to transfer your ideas to others by creating a sense of reality for them.

The cast shadow is formed because the object blocks direct light. If the light source is overhead, the light will pass over the object and create shadow edge lines on the far side of the object. The shadow lines produced by vertical edges of this object converge toward the horizon in the direction of the light [2–96]. The shadow line produced by a horizontal edge vanishes to the same vanishing point as the edge line of the object that produced it.

Light source overhead . . . the shadow lines produced by vertical edges converge toward the horizon in the direction of the light . . . the shadow line produced by a horizontal edge vanishes to the same point as the edge itself.

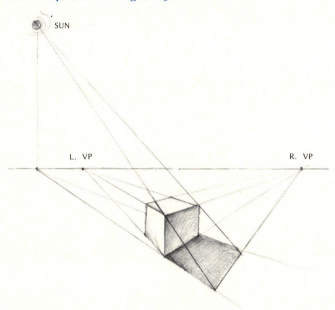

Figure 2–96

EXERCISE

2–25. Find a small building with a few major features protruding from the surface. A canopy, sign, or balcony is appropriate. Sketch the building from the same viewpoint in the morning, midday, and in the afternoon. Each time sketch the shadows cast on the building by its protruding features and also the building's shadow cast on the ground. Does one of the shadow positions make your sketch look more three dimensional than the others? Which one? Why?

2.24 Space Illusion Using Value Contrast

One of the most positive uses of value contrast is the creation of the illusion of depth, even of vast spaces. In nature your eye depends heavily on value contrast to identify depth. The more value contrast that is evident, the greater the illusion of space [2–97]. In sketching, value contrast is especially important in separating objects from other objects and their background. To achieve a visual perception of depth, it doesn't matter whether the closest or farthest object is darker or lighter [2–98 and 2–99].

The effects of atmospheric perspective can be used to provide the illusion of deep space. Here the use of high value contrast will make the objects appear closer to the viewer. Low value contrast will push surfaces into the distance. Figure [2–100] illustrates this effect with a lightly shaded object nearby and a much darker object farther away. Beyond the second object several other objects appear to be positioned farther and farther away. As they recede into the distance they grow closer together in value, approaching a middle-tone value (that is, midway between white and black).

It may be difficult for you to measure value. Try squinting your eyes when looking at an object. This temporarily blurs details and surface texture that tend to obscure the true values of the object and its surroundings. Squinting helps you see contrasts and patterns of values.

Space illusion is heightened by greater value contrast.

Figure 2–97

Freehand Drawing

43

Space illusion depends on value contrast . . .

. . . not on the order of light and dark objects.

Figure 2–98

Figure 2–99

Value contrast decreasing with distance provides the illusion of deep space.

Figure 2–100

EXERCISES

2–26. Select four simple objects of differing surface color. Sketch each object using a value of gray to represent the color.

2–27. Arrange the objects in Exercise 2–26 in a pleasing group. Sketch the group controlling your perception of depth through the use of value contrast. Introduce background value and begin to use value changes instead of lines to define edges.

Drawing Fundamentals

3 Drawing Tools and Supplies

Technical drawings may be drawn formally with instruments, or they may be sketched freehand using only a pencil or some other marking tool. Freehand sketches are often used in developing design concepts and in planning formal drawings. Instrument drawings are normally required when it is necessary to provide accurate and detailed descriptions for construction. When making instrument drawings, specialized tools are used to draw the different types of lines required to describe an object.

3.1 Pencils, Leads, and Pens

Most technical architectural drawings are done in pencil. The *lead holder,* also called a *mechanical pencil,* has generally replaced the wooden pencil as it is more convenient to use [3–1]. It consists of a hollow metal or plastic shaft in which pencil leads of various degrees of hardness are inserted. A "springlike" device causes the grips near the tip to hold the lead in place. Usually,

Lead holders are used by many architectural drafters . . .

Figure 3–1

Revolving lead pointers may be used to sharpen the lead.

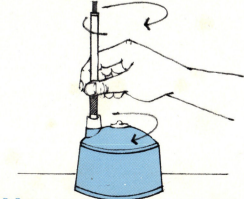

Figure 3–2

A fine point can also be obtained using a pointer having sharp metal blades.

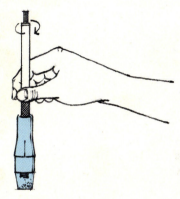

Figure 3–3

about ⅜ inch is exposed for drawing. The point can be easily sharpened with a revolving *lead pointer* [3–2]. It will produce a tapered point. This type of pointer has a sandpaper strip inside that can be changed when it becomes worn. Another type of lead pointer has one or more sharp metal blades, also replaceable, that shave the lead to a fine tapered point [3–3].

Traditional wood-encased drafting pencils are still available. They are sharpened by cutting away the excess wood with a sharp knife or with a special pencil sharpener that removes the wood only. This exposes the lead for pointing with a pointer, a fine steel file, or a sandpaper pad. Keeping wooden pencils sharp is both time consuming and troublesome, so they are seldom used today.

For a minimum of point breakage, damage to drawing paper, and variation in line thickness, you should not draw with the sharpest point that the lead pointer will produce [3–4]. An easy way to achieve an appropriate

The lead pointer can produce a point too sharp for drawing . . .

. . . a slightly rounded tip will produce more uniform line thickness.

Figure 3–4

Ultra-thin lead holders do not require sharpening.

Figure 3–5

drawing point is to first sharpen the lead to the maximum. Then, tap the tip lightly on scratch paper. The fine tip will break off. Draw one or two freehand circles on the scratch paper. The resulting point should be about the right sharpness.

Lead holders are also marketed that use ultrathin (0.3 mm, 0.5 mm, 0.7 mm, or 0.9 mm) leads that do not require sharpening [3–5]. Since these leads are thinner than those for the standard-size lead holder, you may require some practice with them to develop the right pressure for the desired line weight without breaking the lead. The advantages of ultrathin lead holders are more consistent line weights and increased drafting speed due to the omission of sharpening.

Drawing techniques with the various types of pencils are similar. When drawing, the lead should be pulled (not pushed) across the paper [3–6]. To achieve this, tilt the lead holder in the direction of the hand movement when drawing a line. To reduce the frequency of sharp-

Correct . . . pencil is pulled across the paper . . . tilt the pencil in direction of movement.

Incorrect . . . pencil should not be pushed across the paper.

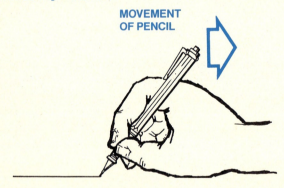

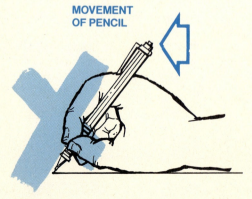

Figure 3–6

A right handed person should slowly rotate the pencil clockwise to maintain uniform line weight.

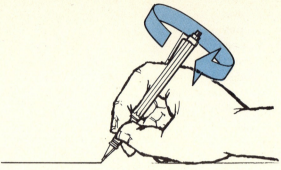

Figure 3–7

ening standard size leads, slowly rotate the pencil as you draw a line [3–7]. This has the effect of sharpening the lead with the drawing paper. The lead rotation helps to keep the line thickness uniform since it would

Technical pens . . . used alone or in compasses to draw lines. Keep capped between uses to prevent clogging. Clean frequently.

Figure 3–8

Drawing Fundamentals

broaden if the lead became dull. This sharpening effect is not enough to avoid using the lead pointer periodically, however. Although the ultrathin leads do not require sharpening, rotation of the pencil is still recommended to ensure uniformity.

A disadvantage of pencil line work is that it can be easily smudged. *A good rule to follow is to use the softest weight of lead that will allow a clean sheet*. Each drafter has a different "touch"—no universal rule can be followed to specify the correct lead for each person to use.

Drawing paper or film with more "bite" or "tooth" (the roughened surface upon which the drawing is made) does not require as soft a lead as does a smooth, hard finish board or paper. Degrees of lead hardness range from 9H (extremely hard) to 6B (extremely soft). Leads commonly used by architectural drafters vary from the relatively hard 4H to the softer HB. Each person must experiment with lead hardness until the most suitable is found. The paper on which you work and the touch of your hand will affect the results. Only experience will determine which lead is best for you.

The following is a list of leads and their suggested uses. The list refers to the use of graphite lead on vellum drawing paper. If graphite lead is used on plastic drafting film, you will find that harder leads will be appropriate to achieve the same line weight because of the more abrasive nature of the plastic film's surface. Plastic leads are manufactured especially for use on plastic film. Their use is discussed in Section 3.6, where the film is described.

5H through 9H: very hard lead, not popular for architectural drafting.
4H: hard and dense lead used for layout work, difficult to erase and will dent or groove soft drawing paper; very difficult to draw darkly enough to produce a good print.
2H: medium hard lead, sometimes used for layout work; adequate for finished work if you have a "heavy" hand; medium difficult to erase and can groove the paper if pressed too hard into the surface.
F or H: medium to medium soft lead, most commonly used for general work; excellent for lettering; maintains a good point even under relatively heavy pressure; can smudge easily if you are not careful.
HB: soft lead, good for bold linework; can yield good work for the person with a light touch; easy to erase, but also smudges easily, prints very well; requires that good control be exercised to obtain fine linework; ultrathin good for both lines and lettering.
B through 6B: very soft lead, good for sketching and rendering; specific degree of softness appropriate will vary with the user; smudges very easily; difficult to erase cleanly due to ease of smudging; fine linework not practical due to rapid dulling of pencil point.

Regardless of the weight of lead used, it is best to purchase a good-quality lead. The cheaper-quality lead breaks easily, is difficult to sharpen to a fine point, and may produce inconsistent quality linework due to manufacturing irregularities. Use good-quality materials and practice with the leads that you find perform the best for you.

Ink may be used for drawing border lines or as framing to set off different types of work on the same sheet. It is usually used for overlay drafting using pin-bar registration systems. Ink is also used extensively in architectural renderings or delineations of finished structures that are drawn in perspective. Several brands of *technical pens* are available that make drawing with ink fairly easy [3–8].

The advantages of ink are that once dry it doesn't smear, and it results in a strong readable image in both original work and reproductions. The disadvantages are that it is very easy to smear while wet, and once dry it is difficult to erase on vellum. Ink may be easily erased from plastic drafting film using a slightly moistened soft rubber or special plastic eraser. Care must always be taken not to damage the drawing surface when doing any erasing, especially if an electric eraser is used.

A variety of line thicknesses may be drawn by using different-size pens [3–9]. Standard pen points are made of stainless steel, but harder carbide and jeweled points are also available to resist the abrasive action of drafting film. Pens must be cleaned regularly and kept capped when not in use to prevent clogging. It is also important always to use fresh ink.

A common cause of smearing wet ink is allowing a drawing tool to touch a freshly drawn line. Moving the tool will then smear the ink. To avoid this, use special inking triangles with recessed edges [3–10] or raise your standard triangle above the drawing surface by attaching spacers to the bottom side [3–11]. Technical pens work best when held exactly vertical. You should experiment with how much you can tilt your pen so as to not interfere with the flow of ink.

EXERCISES

3–1. Describe the advantages of a lead holder over a wooden pencil.
3–2. What are the advantages of an ultrathin lead holder over the standard size? What are the disadvantages?
3–3. What techniques are used to draw a uniform line?
3–4. What pencil lead weights are recommended for most general architectural drafting?
3–5. What are the disadvantages of using hard leads?
3–6. What are the disadvantages of using soft leads?
3–7. What are the advantages and disadvantages of drafting with ink?
3–8. How can ink smears be prevented?
3–9. What can be done to keep ink flowing freely in a technical pen?

Drawing Tools and Supplies

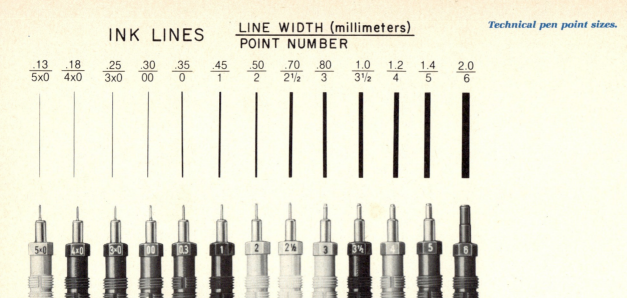

Figure 3–9

3.2 Line Drawing

A smooth drawing surface of appropriate hardness is necessary to produce high-quality linework. This is best achieved by using a drawing board with a special vinyl drafting surface. A drawing board without such a cushioned surface is too hard to be used directly under the drawing paper. Drawing on a "bare" board may result in nonuniform linework and damage to both the drawing paper and the board surface. The "self-healing" surface of vinyl board covering also resists the repeated punctures of compass points. An inexpensive substitute for the vinyl covering, such as illustration board, may be used but will not last long. Even an inexpensive board, such as a piece of plywood, will serve well when covered with vinyl if a true edge is not required to guide a T-square.

Some drafting offices use desk-height drawing boards. In this case an office chair is used instead of a stool. This system allows great ease of movement between layout tables, files, and bookshelves as one's feet are on the floor while seated and can readily move a wheeled chair. Many offices still prefer higher drafting tables with a drafting stool. These have the advantage of allowing drafting while standing and being at a convenient height for other people to examine the drawings while standing at the table.

Horizontal lines are drawn with a *T-square*, a *parallel rule*, or a *drafting machine* [3–12]. When using a T-square for drawing horizontal lines and guiding other instruments, a smooth square edge is necessary on the board. The square edge is not important on boards equipped with a parallel rule or a drafting machine. Drafting machines not only replace the T-square, but also the triangle, and to some extent the scale, since the blades can be turned at any angle and scales are frequently printed on their edges. Drafting machines are not used as often in architectural offices as they are in machine drafting offices. Parallel rules are frequently preferred in architecture work.

If you do not have a drafting machine, *triangles* are necessary for vertical and angled lines [3–13]. Standard

Special inking triangles are shaped so the edge never touches the ink line.

Spacers may be attached to the bottom of standard triangles and templates to avoid contact with the wet ink.

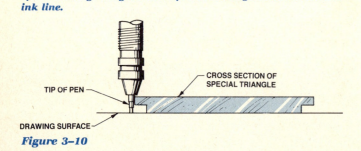

Figure 3–10

Figure 3–11

48   **Drawing Fundamentals**

Horizontal lines are drawn with a T-square, a drafting machine, or a parallel rule . . . the drafting machine can also be used for vertical and angled lines.

Vertical and inclined lines are drawn with triangles.

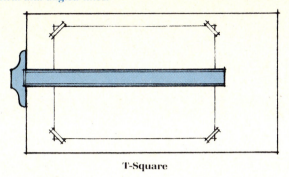
T-Square

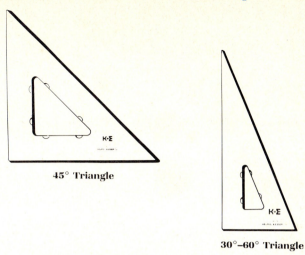
45° Triangle

30°–60° Triangle

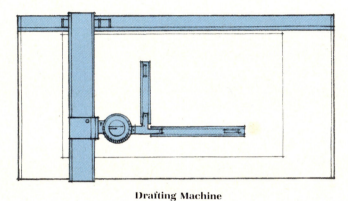
Drafting Machine

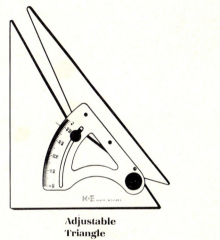
Adjustable Triangle

Figure 3–13

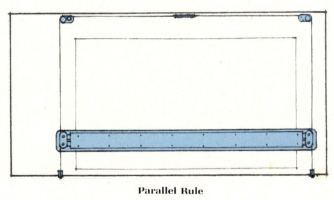
Parallel Rule

Figure 3–12

45° and 30°–60° triangles may be used alone or in combination to draw lines in 15° increments from 15 to 90°. Other angles may be quickly obtained by using an adjustable triangle. Some adjustable triangles having graduations that designate slope and pitch as well as degrees are especially valuable to the architectural drafter. One side of the adjustable triangle changes position by loosening a knob. This knob is also a convenient device with which to lift the triangle. This is important in helping to keep the drawing clean.

Right-handed drafters normally draw vertical lines by guiding their pencil on the left side of the triangle [3–14]. The triangle is held in place with the left hand,

Right handed drafters draw on the left side of the triangle.

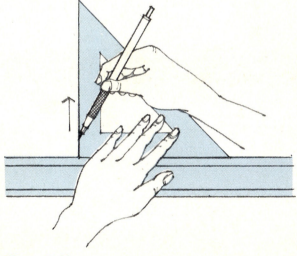

Figure 3–14

Drawing Tools and Supplies

49

The paper is aligned and the corners are taped to the board.

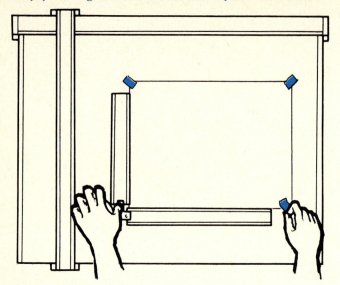

Horizontal lines are drawn directly.

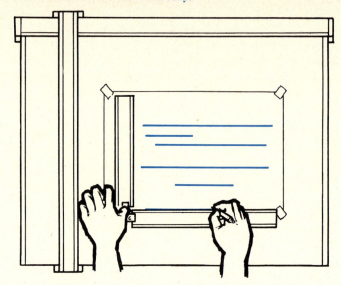

Vertical lines are drawn with a triangle placed on a T-square or parallel rule . . .

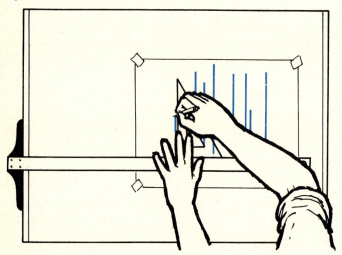

. . . or drawn directly with a drafting machine.

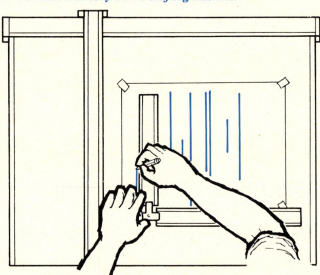

Angled lines are also drawn with a triangle . . .

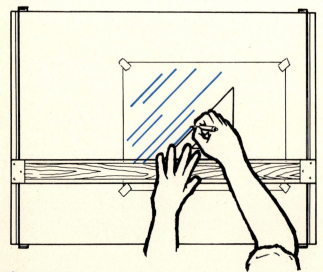

. . . or directly with a drafting machine.

Figure 3–15

and the line is drawn by moving the pencil up on the sheet. As the line is drawn, the pencil is slowly rotated to prevent forming a flat spot on the point that would change the thickness of the line. Left-handed drafters draw vertical lines on the right side of the triangle. This method causes the pencil point to help press the triangle to the sheet instead of lift it. It also makes the line more visible as you draw it and consequently gives you more control over it. A summary of basic line drawing procedures is shown in [3–15].

EXERCISES

3–10. What are the three instruments that can be used for drawing horizontal lines? What are their advantages and disadvantages?

3–11. How many different angles can be drawn with a 30°–60° and a 45° triangle—separately and in combination?

3.3 Curve Drawing

Circles are drawn with either a *compass* [3–16] or a *circle template* [3–17]. The circle template is preferred due to the relative ease with which you can draw a uniform line of the same weight as the straight lines on your drawing. The template has, however, a limited number of circle sizes available. Compasses are available in a variety of sizes, including "beam" compasses for very large radii.

With either a circle template or a compass, it is important to draw a line of uniform thickness. Since the lead is fixed in a compass, you cannot rotate it as you turn the compass. As the lead continues to mark on the paper it develops a flat spot, and the thickness of the line increases. It is not convenient to stop with a partially completed circle to sharpen the lead. Sharpening the lead changes the radius that has been set on the compass and requires that it be reset. It is difficult to match the exact diameter of the partially completed circle and also to match the thickness of the line already drawn. Therefore, it is better to complete each circle without stopping to sharpen the lead.

To help reduce the rate of dulling, a wedge point is used instead of a conical point on the compass lead [3–18]. The wedge point is achieved by rubbing the lead back and forth on sandpaper or scratch paper. The flat

Circles may be drawn quickly with a template.

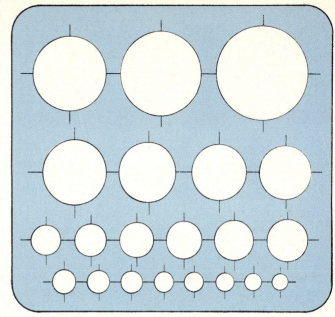

Figure 3–17

A compass can draw a variety of circle sizes.

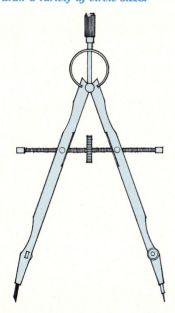

Figure 3–16

A wedge point is used for the compass lead.

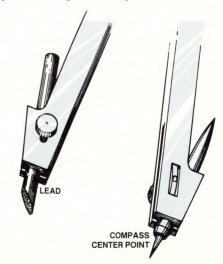

Figure 3–18

Drawing Tools and Supplies

51

face of the wedge is positioned so that it faces away from the center of the circle. Since the position of the lead remains constant with respect to the drawn line, the fine edge of the wedge produces a fine line. This type of point also has a greater mass of graphite behind it than does a conical point, and it does not dull as quickly.

To draw a circle with a compass, first locate its center. Place the center point of the compass on the center and (if you are right-handed) rotate the compass clockwise. Tilt the compass slightly in the direction of rotation so as to "pull" the lead across the paper rather than "push" it [3–19]. Note that the compass center point is designed with a flat ledge back of the point to provide a bearing surface on the paper as the compass is rotated [3–18]. This ledge keeps the point from digging deeper into the paper as the compass is turned, thus making a larger hole and slightly altering the radius setting. Since many compasses are supplied with a center point that has a plain conical dividers point on the other end, be sure to use the correct end for drawing circles.

A large circle probably will require stopping and repositioning your fingers on the compass. Be sure that when you stop and start, and also when you meet the beginning of the circle, the line weight does not change. Gradually apply increasing pressure as you start to draw a circle and gradually reduce the pressure as you stop. This will help blend the lines at the beginning and end of the circle. Since circles are more awkward to draw than straight lines, the line weight tends to be lighter. You may have to trace over your circle a second time to make its weight match that of adjacent straight lines. When going over a circle, be sure that you draw exactly

Tilt the compass slightly in direction of rotation.

Figure 3–19

Carefully align template center line marks with the circle's center lines.

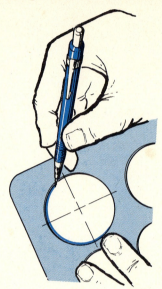

Figure 3–20

on top of the previously drawn line. If you are not precise, a "fuzzy" or double circle may result. Using a slightly softer lead in the compass also helps maintain uniform line weight.

There are several things to keep in mind when drawing a circle with a template. Be sure to align the center line marks on the template exactly on the center lines of the desired circle [3–20]. When purchasing a template be sure that the center line marks are printed accurately on the holes in the template. If you are right-handed, draw the circle in a clockwise direction and slowly rotate the pencil to maintain uniform line weight. Keep the angle of the pencil to the template constant [3–21]. If this angle changes, the shape drawn will not be a true circle. The safest method is to hold the pencil exactly perpendicular to the paper.

In selecting the proper hole size to use on a circle template, it is always wise to draw a sample circle first on a piece of scrap paper and measure it. The printed sizes on templates cannot always be relied upon. The manufacturer makes each hole slightly larger than the stated size to allow for lead thickness. The amount of this "pencil allowance" often varies, however, from hole to hole in the same template, from manufacturer to manufacturer, and even between different style templates from the same manufacturer. There is also considerable difference in the way each drafter holds a pencil, the way that the lead is pointed, and whether it is standard or ultrathin lead. The difference in point sizes when using technical pens also influences the size of a circle drawn with a template.

Templates are also available with which to draw ellipses. Since ellipses not only vary in size but also in angle, several *ellipse templates* will be required if you

52 Drawing Fundamentals

Correct... angle of pencil with template held constant... circle is true.

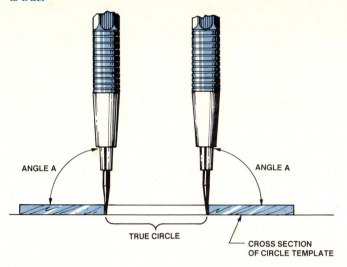

Incorrect... angle of pencil varies producing a distorted circle.

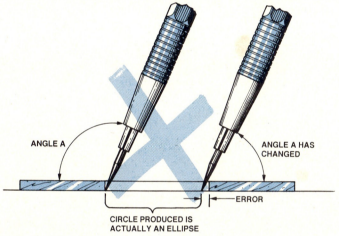

Figure 3–21

Drawing ellipses... lay out the rhombus that results from drawing a square tangent to the circle that the ellipse represents...

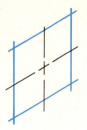

... use the rhombus as a guide in selecting an ellipse template opening that is tangent to the four sides at their midpoints.

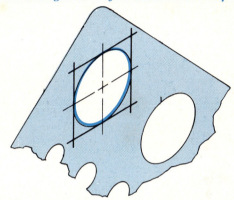

Figure 3–22

expect to draw a variety of ellipses. An ellipse is the result of looking at a circle in a tipped position. Its size is related to the size of the circle, and its angle is the angle of the circle with the viewer's line of sight. To help select the right ellipse template and to position it correctly, first draw a rhombus with its center on the center of the desired ellipse [3–22]. The dimensions and shape of this rhombus are obtained from a view where it would be seen as a square tangent to the original circle.

Templates are available for drawing various symbols.

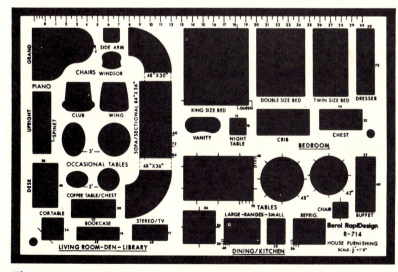

Figure 3–23

Drawing Tools and Supplies

53

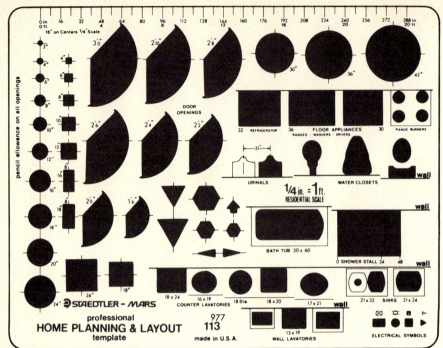

Fixture shapes are time consuming to draw without a template.

Figure 3–24

Select an ellipse template opening that is tangent to the rhombus at the midpoints of its sides. The same techniques as described for drawing a circle with a template are used to draw the ellipse. When positioning an ellipse template, it is also helpful to know the correct orientation of the minor axis of the ellipse. This procedure was introduced in Section 2.18, Circles in Perspective.

Many other common shapes are needed on drawings. Squares, hexagons, triangles, and rectangles are often used for certain symbols. Nongeometric shapes such as the outline of plumbing fixtures are necessary for floor plans. Templates are available for drawing various symbols [3–23] and standard fixtures [3–24]. Fixture templates are made in different scales. You must select one with the same scale as your drawing.

Irregular or *"French" curves* are used for drawing lines that have varying curvature [3–25]. They are available in many sizes and shapes. Drawing an irregularly curved line becomes more difficult as the number of times the instrument must be repositioned increases. The line must be kept uniform in thickness and darkness. The joints of short segments that make up a long line must be blended so that their individual lengths are not apparent in the final line. The technique described for starting and stopping a circular line may be used to achieve a smooth line.

Generally, a minimum of three points are used to draw a curved segment of a line [3–26]. To guide you in posi-

Irregular curves are located by plotting points . . . the curve is lightly sketched . . . then darkened in with an irregular curve.

Irregular "French" curves are used to draw lines of varying curvature.

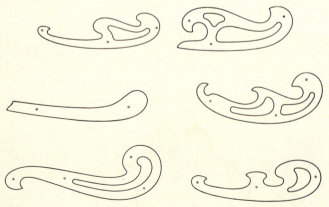

Figure 3–25

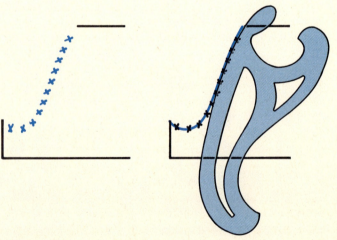

Figure 3–26

Drawing Fundamentals

tioning the instrument, first plot reference points along the desired curve. Lightly sketch a curve through the points and then darken it in by positioning your irregular curve along the sketched curve. If you wish to draw the same curve elsewhere, make temporary pencil "tic" marks on the plastic of the irregular curve to identify the exact portion that was used to draw the first line. The marks will rub off easily when you are done with them. If you wish to make a curve in the mirror image of the original line, turn the irregular curve over. The tic marks will be visible through the clear plastic.

EXERCISES

3-12. Draw a circle of ¼ inch diameter with a template and with a compass. Which produces the better linework?

3-13. Draw a circle of 2 inch diameter with a template and with a compass. Which produces the better linework?

3-14. Draw circles, all of 3'–6" diameter, measured with the following scales.
  (a) ⅛" = 1'–0"
  (b) ¼" = 1'–0"
  (c) ½" = 1'–0"
  (d) 1" = 1'–0"
  (e) 1" = 20'
  (f) 1" = 40'

3-15. Trace this series of points onto drawing paper and connect them with a smooth curved line.

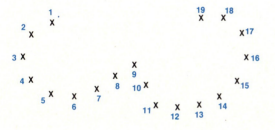

3.4 Measuring Tools

Various types of measuring tools are available to assist in making accurate drawings. Since architectural linework usually represents objects that are much larger than the drawing paper, a proportional measuring system must be used. The amount of size reduction is called the *scale* of the drawing and is normally stated on the drawing. When a drawing is made "to scale," this means that all distances on it are related to the real object by some chosen scale ratio. In a "large-scale" drawing, the amount of size reduction is relatively small as compared to a "small-scale" drawing, where considerable size reduction has been made.

The term *scale* also refers to the physical device used by the drafter to quickly and accurately reduce linear distances to their correct scale lengths. Scales commonly

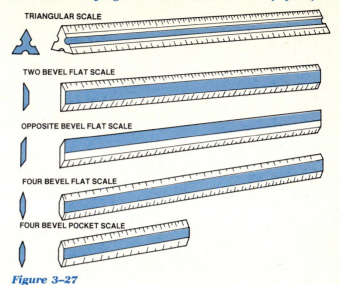

Architectural drafting scales are available in a variety of shapes.

Figure 3-27

used in architectural drafting are made in different shapes and lengths [3-27]. Triangular scales are very popular because more scales can be printed on them. The triangular shape also makes them convenient to pick up and use. Flat scales have beveled edges so that the graduations can be printed close to the edge. The bevel also provides a convenient lifting edge. Flat scales may be either two-bevel or four-bevel depending on the number of scales required. A good-quality scale must have sharply defined graduations close to the edge for accurate measurements. To preserve this accuracy, you must *never* use the edge as a pencil guide when drawing a line.

Drafting scales are identified by the types of scales marked on them. In architectural drafting, *architect's scales* and *engineer's scales* are most commonly used. Architect's scales are graduated in feet and inches and also fractions of an inch in some cases. The numerical values on engineer's scales are decimally divided. In architectural work these values usually represent feet, but they could also represent larger units such as miles.

Most of the scales on an architect's scale are based on some measured interval in inches representing 1 foot [3-28]. The markings on five of the six faces of the usual triangular architect's scale are ³⁄₃₂, ³⁄₁₆, ⅛, ¼, ⅜, ¾, ½, 1, 1½, and 3. These numbers indicate the length in inches that represents 1 foot. The sixth face on the scale is marked 16. This is a "full-size" scale where a 1-inch interval (with 16 divisions) represents 1 inch.

In order to accommodate the maximum number of scales on an architect's scale, there are usually two scales printed on each face. For example, one face has ⅛ marked

A triangular architect's scale

Figure 3–28

Representative ⅛" = 1'–0" scale readings . . . this scale reads from left to right . . . the 1-foot end unit is divided into 2-inch increments.

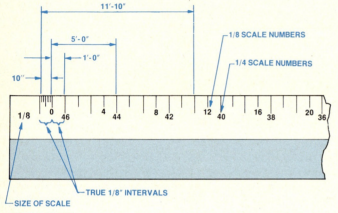

Figure 3–29

on one end and ¼ on the other [3–29 and 3–30]. These are the ⅛" = 1'–0" and the ¼" = 1'–0" scales. With this arrangement only the extreme end intervals are subdivided into finer increments. A scale of this type is called an *open divided* scale. The ⅛-inch interval on the left end of the ⅛ scale is divided into six increments. Since this is a ⅛" = 1'–0" scale, each of the six increments represents 2 inches. At the opposite ¼ end of the ⅛ scale there is a ¼-inch interval divided into 12 parts, each

representing 1 inch. Only marks representing whole numbers of feet appear in the middle portion of an architect's scale between the subdivided ends. You must be very careful in reading the dual set of numbers in the middle to be sure that you are reading in the correct direction. The ⅛ scale reads from left to right—the ¼ scale reads from right to left.

When laying out or measuring a specific distance with an architect's scale, you must use both the divided end unit and the whole-number marks. In [3–29] a distance of 11'–10" on the ⅛" = 1'–0" scale is read from the fifth small mark to the left of the zero to the eleventh whole-number mark to the right of the zero. The 46, 44, 42, and 40 represent numbers of feet read from the right end ¼" = 1'–0" scale. Figure [3–30] shows a distance of 7'–4" read on the ¼" = 1'–0" scale from the fourth small mark to the right of the zero to the long mark between the whole numbers 6 and 8 to the left of the zero.

On larger architectural scales such as the 1" = 1'–0" scale shown in [3–31], the end unit is divided into inches and fractions of an inch. There are long marks at 3, 6, and 9 inches, medium length marks at 1-inch intervals, and shorter marks at each ¼ inch. A 2'–9¼" distance is read from the first short mark to the left of 9 in the end unit to the whole number 2 to the right of zero. The 20 and 18 represent whole numbers of feet read from the right end ½" = 1'–0" scale.

The ¼" = 1'–0" scale on the right end of the ⅛ scale reads from right to left . . . the 1-foot end unit is divided into 1-inch increments.

This 1" = 1'–0" scale reads from left to right . . . the 1-foot end unit is divided into ¼-inch increments . . . the right end is a ½" = 1'–0" scale.

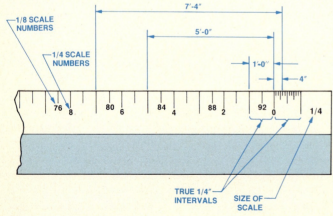

Figure 3–30

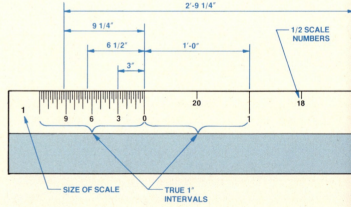

Figure 3–31

Drawing Fundamentals

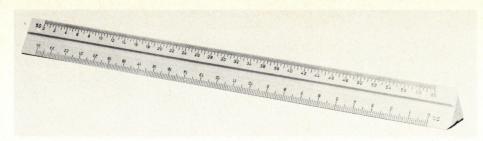

A triangular engineer's scale.

Figure 3-32

When printing a dimension measured in feet and inches on a drawing, you must place a small dash between the numbers to separate the two types of units. Place a foot mark after the first number and inch marks after the second. For a whole number of feet and no inches, a zero is shown after the dash, as in 6′–0″. If there is only a fraction and no whole number of inches, a zero precedes the fraction—for example, 1′–0¼″.

When making drawings covering large areas, such as site plans, you will find it convenient to use engineer's scales because dimensional information provided by land surveys is usually expressed in feet and decimal portions of a foot rather than in feet and inches. Engineer's scales read from left to right and have subdivisions printed throughout their entire length [3–32]. This type of scale is said to be *fully divided*. The usual triangular engineer's scale has six faces marked 10, 20, 30, 40, 50, and 60. These numbers refer to the fact that a true 1-inch distance on a particular scale has that number of subdivisions. For example, the 20 scale shown in [3–33] has 20 marks between 0 and the number 2. The subdivision marks are arranged in groups of 10 as shown by the whole numbers on this scale.

An engineer's scale is very versatile because 1 inch can be used to represent any decimally divided quantity by merely shifting the decimal point. In [3–33] a 20 scale is shown being used to read dimensions at a scale of 1″ = 20′. This is accomplished by considering the 1-inch distance at which the number 2 appears to be 20 feet. The 20 individual marks between 0 and 2 will then each represent 1 foot. Decimal portions of a foot must be approximated by eye between each mark. A 28.0-foot distance is read at eight marks to the right of the 2 mark.

If a 20 scale is used to lay out a drawing at a scale of 1″ = 200′, the true 1-inch distance at which the number 2 appears will represent 200 feet. At eight marks past 2, the distance read will be 280.0′. A 20 scale can also be used to lay out longer distances at a scale of 1″ = 20 miles or 1″ = 200 miles by considering the number 2 to be 20 miles or 200 miles.

In the coming years, the construction industry will gradually change to the metric system of measurement. As this occurs you will find it necessary to become familiar with scales that read in millimeters, meters, and kilometers. The arrangement of metric scales and the scale ratios for architectural drawings are not fully standardized yet, but they are relatively easy to use because of their decimal subdivisions.

An important measuring tool associated with scales is an instrument called a *divider* [3–34]. Distances can

Dividers are often used to transfer dimensions between drawings and scales.

Representative 1″ = 20′ scale readings on an engineer's 20 scale . . . each of the 20 divisions in 1 inch represent 1 foot . . . the numbers are 10's of feet.

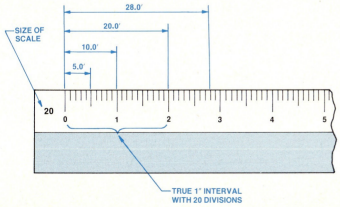

Figure 3-33

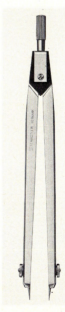

Figure 3-34

Drawing Tools and Supplies

57

Dividers are also used to transfer distances from one location to another on a drawing.

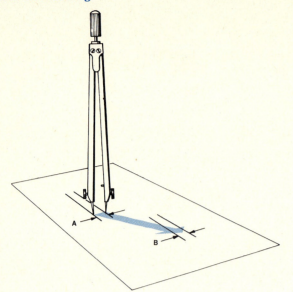

Figure 3–35

be laid out or measured by carefully aligning a scale directly on a drawing or by transferring them between the drawing and a scale with a divider. The divider shown in [3–34] is called a "friction" type because the setting is held by friction. If there is too much friction, the legs of the divider will act "springy" and may cause inaccurate measurements. Be sure that the desired distance that you have set does not change when you release your fingers from the instrument. Smaller dividers having adjusting wheels are easier to use for accurately laying out a series of equal intervals.

In addition to transferring dimensions to or from scales, dividers may be used to transfer distances from one location to another on a drawing [3–35]. The transferred dimensions can be marked by pricking tiny holes in the paper with the divider's points or by using a pencil to mark the limits. Measurements may also be enlarged a multiple number of times by setting the dividers to the original measurement and then "walking" the instrument [3–36]. To double the measurement, the dividers are rotated 180°. To triple the distance, they are rotated another 180° and so on.

A *protractor* is used to measure the angle between lines on a drawing [3–37]. Simple angle measurements between slanted lines and horizontal lines are easily read with an adjustable triangle or with a drafting machine. However, if the angle to be measured is between two slanted lines, reading the angle directly on a protractor is more convenient and less subject to error. The same is true in laying out a specific angle between slanted lines.

Most protractors have angular graduations on the perimeter reading both clockwise and counterclockwise. Always be careful to read the correct set of numbers. When measuring an angle between short lines, lightly extend the lines with a sharp, hard pencil to permit accurate alignment with the base line and graduation lines on the protractor.

The measurement at A has been transferred to B and tripled without using a scale.

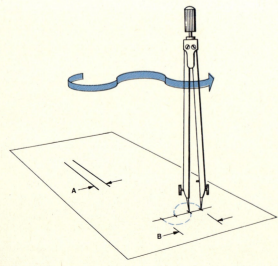

Figure 3–36

Protractors . . . used to measure or lay out angles.

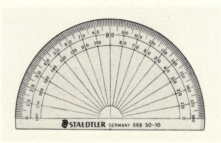

180° Protractor

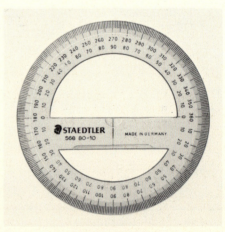

360° Protractor

Figure 3–37

Drawing Fundamentals

EXERCISES

3-16. How long is the line below when measured on the following scales?
- (a) $\frac{1}{8}'' = 1'-0''$
- (b) $\frac{1}{4}'' = 1'-0''$
- (c) $\frac{1}{2}'' = 1'-0''$
- (d) $1'' = 1'-0''$
- (e) $1\frac{1}{2}'' = 1'-0''$
- (f) $3'' = 1'-0''$
- (g) $1'' = 20'$
- (h) $1'' = 40'$

3-17. How long are the lines below when measured on the scales indicated?
- (a) $1'' = 10'$
- (b) $1'' = 60'$
- (c) $1'' = 1'-0''$
- (d) $3'' = 1'-0''$

3-18. Triple the length of the line below on a separate sheet of paper without tracing it or using a scale.

3-19. Measure the angles below with an adjustable triangle and with a protractor. Compare convenience, accuracy, and chances for error with each tool.

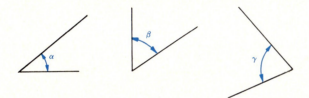

3.5 Miscellaneous Tools

Guidelines for lettering are drawn with a *lettering guide* [3-38]. The height for various size letters is set by rotating the circular disk. The pencil point is inserted into a hole in the disk to move the instrument on a straightedge across the paper from left to right as the line is drawn

A popular type of lettering guide used to draw guidelines for lettering.

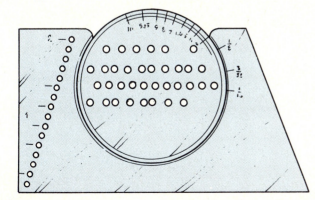

Figure 3-38

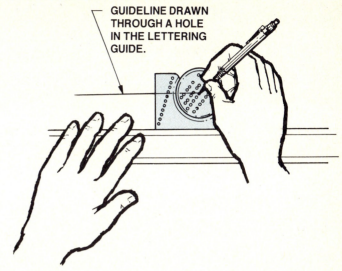

The lettering guide is pulled along a straightedge by the pencil point . . . the next line is drawn by placing the pencil in a second hole and pulling in the reverse direction.

GUIDELINE DRAWN THROUGH A HOLE IN THE LETTERING GUIDE.

Figure 3-39

[3-39]. The next line is drawn by inserting the pencil in an adjacent hole and sliding the guide from right to left. Other types of lettering guides working on the same principle are also available.

A soft pink rubber or white plastic *eraser* is recommended for removing lines from your drawing. They tend to leave less discoloration on the sheet than other types of erasers. Electric erasers remove lines better and faster than ordinary erasers [3-40]. They are, however, expensive. Plug-in and rechargeable cordless types are available.

An *erasing shield* is necessary to limit the area of an erasure and to help keep the drawing clean [3-41]. Positioning a hole in the shield over an unwanted line or letter prevents the eraser from removing adjacent linework or letters. An erasing shield can also be used to clean an eraser. Moving the eraser across the short dimension of the slots scrapes the graphite from its surface so that it won't be transferred back to the drawing.

A *drafting brush* is used to help keep the drawing

Electric erasers are useful in removing unwanted lines.

Figure 3-40

Drawing Tools and Supplies

Erasing shields permit erasing specific items quickly.

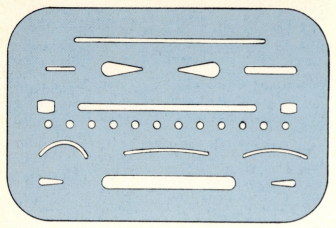

Figure 3–41

clean by brushing eraser crumblings and powdered graphite from the sheet [3–42]. After drawing several lines, brush them along their axes to remove the excess graphite. Brushing across a line has a greater tendency to smear the graphite.

3.6 Drafting Papers and Films

Most architectural drawings are made on semitransparent paper, known as *vellum*, or on polyester *drafting film* (commonly known by the DuPont trade name Mylar). The drafting film is very tough and dimensionally stable. It is resistant to tearing and does not significantly shrink or expand with changes in humidity as will traditional drawing paper. It will withstand repeated erasures with little wear and ink can be easily erased from it. It is also more expensive than vellum. If vellum is used, be certain it is fresh. It sometimes deteriorates with age and eventually acquires a yellowish tinge that will affect the reproducibility of the work drawn on it.

The pencil "lead" manufactured for use on drafting film is a plastic-based substance whose waxlike composition is resistant to smudging. It can be erased best with a special plastic eraser or with an ordinary soft rubber eraser. It is also possible to draw on the surface of drafting film with ordinary graphite drafting pencils, but the lines will smudge easily. When using an electric erasing

A drafting brush helps keep the drawing clean.

Figure 3–42

machine, you must be careful not to press too hard to avoid removing the roughened surface from the polyester film.

The standard sizes of architectural drafting sheets are 18 × 24 inches, 24 × 36 inches, 30 × 42 inches, and 34 × 44 inches. Purchasing roll stock is more economical than buying precut sheets. However, time must be spent drawing the border and title block. Before using roll stock, it should be cut into one of the standard sizes to reduce reproduction costs and to simplify storage. Metric standard-size sheets are also commercially available.

Sketching paper is a particularly important item for the architectural drafter. It is used for idea sketches, preliminary drawing, rough graphics, and as a protective covering for work already completed. A thin, buff-colored paper is often used for this purpose. It is not transparent enough to use for making reproductions with high contrast. Sketching paper is most economically bought in long rolls. Since sketching paper is conveniently used in widths of 6, 12, or 18 inches, the original roll can be cut to a desired width with an electric saw. Drawings on sketching paper are ordinarily discarded after the final architectural drawings have been completed and approved.

When drawings on vellum or drafting film are completed, they must be reproduced for use by others. The *prints* are used for bidding and for construction while the original drawings remain in the drafting office for safekeeping. Prints are also made at various times during the drawing process for use in checking the work. The most widely used method for making prints of architectural drawings is the *diazo* process [3–43]. This process requires that the original drawing be made on some material through which light can pass.

In the diazo printing process, the original drawing is placed face up on light-sensitive print paper [3–44]. The face of the print paper has a pale yellow, light-sensitive coating. The two sheets are sent through the rollers of a printing machine while in contact with each other. The linework on the drawing shields the yellow coating on the print paper that is directly underneath from exposure to a brilliant light in the machine. All unshielded print paper is exposed to the light and the yellow coating is bleached away. When the print paper and the drawing come out of the machine, the drawing is unchanged while the print paper has turned white except for the unexposed pale yellow lines in the exact format as the linework on the drawing. The drawing is removed and the print paper is returned to another section of the machine that develops the print using ammonia or some other chemical. This turns the yellow lines into permanent blue or some other color.

The linework on the print may be blue, black, or brown depending on the type of print paper used. The background is white. The most widely used color is blue,

A typical diazo type printing machine for making copies of original drawings.

In the diazo printing process, the original drawing and the light sensitive print paper travel past a strong light . . . the original is removed, and the print paper continues on through a developer.

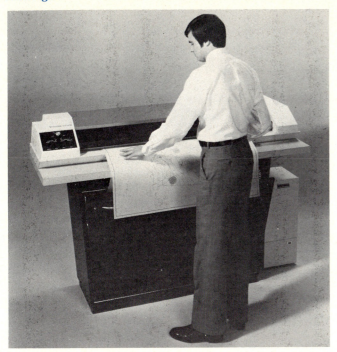

Figure 3–43

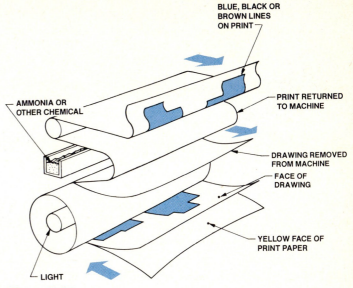

Figure 3–44

and the prints are called *blueline prints*. These are not to be confused with "blueprints," which have white lines on a blue background. Blueprints are more expensive and are no longer in common use. Their advantage is that they remain readable longer than bluelines because they fade less and show dirt less. An advantage of blueline prints, besides price, is that they have a white background on which notes can be made.

Some types of print paper can be used as a drawing medium. *Sepia* print paper produces brown lines on a light tan background. Its unique feature is that a sepia print is reproducible similar to a drawing made on vellum. For example, a floor plan may be drawn on vellum and four sepias printed. Each of these sepias could then become an "original" on which framing, mechanical, electrical, and plumbing plans are completed. Using this method the floor plan need not be redrawn four times. The printed lines on a sepia are semipermanent. They won't smear but can be removed with a chemical that is "painted" on the line with a small brush. Erasable sepia paper is also available. Reproducible second originals can also be printed on plastic film if more durability is desired. When using any type of light-sensitive print paper, be sure to keep it covered in its original wrapping for protection from exposure until you are ready to use it. It should also be stored away from any fumes from the developing chemicals.

Blue-, black-, or brownline prints are sometimes used as the base for presentation drawings. Plans, elevations, and perspectives may be printed, and then color added to the print using colored pencils or felt-tip markers. Print paper is also available with a light plastic coating on the face. The appearance is the same as a regular print except that color applied with a felt-tip marker is softer and does not "bleed" or spread beyond the guidelines. A professional appearing result is obtainable and at a lower cost than by using some of the more permanent color techniques.

EXERCISES

3–20. Compare the advantages and disadvantages of vellum and plastic drafting film.

3–21. Describe how a print is made from an original drawing.

3–22. Describe the various types of prints that are available and their uses.

Drawing Tools and Supplies

4 Architectural Drafting Fundamentals

4.1 Drafting Concepts

Many drafting procedures such as the construction of basic geometric shapes and the principles of multiview drawing are typical of both architectural and machine drafting. Certain rules, however, in lettering, dimensioning, and other specialized areas are unique to architectural drafting. The differences between machine and architectural drafting are not unlike the differences in machines and buildings. Machines often require great precision in their manufacture and assembly. The materials used in machines also lend themselves to close tolerances in manufacture. Machines must obey the strict laws of physics to achieve success as functional tools. On the other hand, buildings must achieve a balance between the mechanics of nature and the emotional impact of their artistic features. Building materials vary greatly in their properties and are often crude and incompatible. The process of "manufacturing" a building is often performed under primitive conditions and with tools dating back to ancient times.

The designer of a building by definition must be a person who has original ideas, and one who has unique thoughts about how to proceed with the task at hand. Consequently, architectural drafting has a system of rules that in some respects varies from office to office. It is a system of rules that mixes artistic influences with functional ones.

Knowledge of the capabilities and limitations of construction practices is as integral a part of architectural drafting as awareness of manufacturing processes is of machine drafting [4–1]. This sensitivity is a drafting fundamental that will mature with study and practical experience.

Two goals of the architectural drafter are to be as precise as construction practices will allow and to be as clear as possible. Although this may mean breaking strict drafting rules upon occasion, without these rules as a base, graphic communication would be highly inefficient and confusing at best.

4.2 Linework

The architectural drafter must communicate ideas clearly and precisely. In addition to procedures already described in the use of drafting tools, there are "tricks of the trade" that will help you to produce clear linework. To be precise, a line must be uniform in thickness and darkness [4–2]. It must be dense and have smooth

Understanding the limitation of precision in construction results in a door that will look more precise when built than one that looks more precise on a drawing.

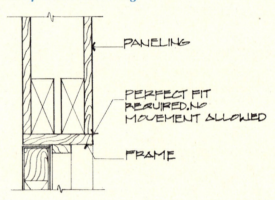

UNREALISTIC – PRECISE DETAIL

It is doubtful that the edge of the paneling and door frame will be true and plumb. The slightest movement at a later date would open the joint or disalign the materials.

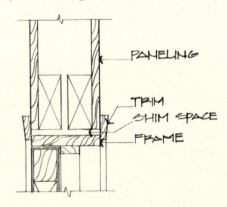

REALISTIC – IMPRECISE DETAIL

Tolerance is allowed (shim space) to slide the door frame into place after the wall is built. The edge of the paneling and door frame need not be perfect since the trim covers both and the shim space.

Figure 4–1 Door head detail.

Incorrect... lines below are not clear and precise.

Probable causes:
A, B, C. Pencil rotated incorrectly.
D. Pencil too dull.
E. Drawing or paper too rough.
F. Pencil lifted too soon.
G. Retracing a line inaccurately drawn.

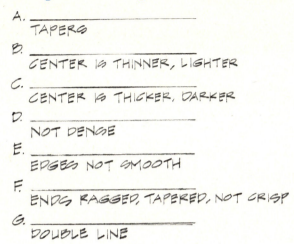

Figure 4-2

Slight retracing at the start of a line helps produce a clean, blunt line end.

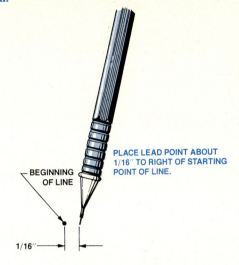

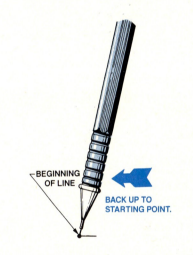

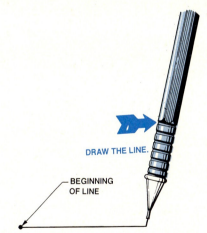

Figure 4-4

edges. It must meet other lines cleanly. The ends of a line must end crisply. The ends must be blunt, without extraneous marks [4-3].

It is difficult to achieve dark blunt ends to lines since you can't be sure of the exact condition of the pencil lead when you start or finish a line. A desirable habit that will give you more control over the ends of lines is to touch the pencil to the paper a little beyond where you want to start the line and "back up" to the starting point. By the time the lead reaches the starting point, irregular edges on the lead will have rounded off. Once you reach the starting point, reverse direction and draw the line [4-4]. Any irregularity in the beginning of the line will be covered as the lead retraces its path. This also prevents lightness from occurring at the beginning of the line.

Line ends must be blunt... no extraneous marks.

Figure 4-3 An enlargement of the ends of lines. (The thickness of these short lines is magnified many times.)

Use the same technique in reverse at the end of the line. Draw to the end of the line and as you start to lift the pencil, back up, or retrace a fraction of an inch [4-5]. With practice this will help you achieve crisp dark

Architectural Drafting Fundamentals

Slight retracing at the end of a line is also helpful.

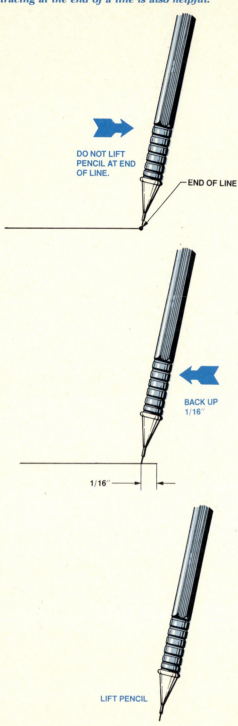

Figure 4–5

Lines may cross at corners in architectural drafting.

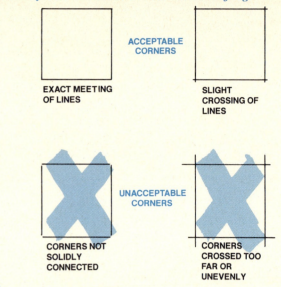

Figure 4–6

ends to your lines without your noticing that you are actually retracing them.

Architectural drafters have more flexibility in drawing the meeting of lines at corners than in other types of drafting. The intent is to make corners appear solidly connected. While attempting to gain speed in drawing, the tendency is to lift the pencil too quickly at a corner and not achieve a solid connection. To compensate for this tendency, in architectural drafting you may cross the lines [4–6]. This way you can get both speed and a solid corner. The crossing must be limited to about 1/16 inch and must be uniform.

There is a great range of line weights (darkness and thickness) available for the many types of lines needed in an architectural drawing. In practice, however, you may find that two weights—*dark thick* and *dark thin*—will serve most purposes [4–7]. Of course, you will use very light thin lines for construction (temporary) lines and lettering guidelines, but these are not part of the final graphic communication vocabulary. The desirability of darkness of lines is stressed since it is a common error among beginning drafters to draw too lightly. Remember that original pencil drawings are not used themselves, but rather they are printed. Some darkness of lines is lost in the printing process. To see approximately how strongly your lines will appear on a print, turn your paper over and hold it up to the light to examine the line work as seen through the paper. In ink drawing, there is no variation in darkness. As a practical matter, as you draw thin lines, you will naturally apply less pressure to the pencil. The thin pencil lines will tend to be a little lighter than the dark ones without your intending them to be so.

The desire to achieve a great variety of weights varies with the taste of the drafter . . . two are generally sufficient.

DARK THICK LINE

DARK THIN LINE

Figure 4–7

64   Drawing Fundamentals

Types of lines . . . a standard "alphabet" of lines is used to describe an object on a drawing.

TYPE	WEIGHT	LINES
OBJECT (VISIBLE)	THICK	———————
HIDDEN	THIN	– – – – – – –
CENTER	THIN	— – — – — – —
PHANTOM	THIN	— — – – — — – –
EXTENSION & DIMENSION	THIN	←————→
LEADER	THIN	↘
SECTION	THIN	/////
CUTTING PLANE	THICK	↑– – – –↑
SHORT BREAK	THICK	∼∼∼∼∼
LONG BREAK	THIN	—–∧–—–∧–—

Figure 4–8

The choice of line weight is related to the function of the line [4–8]. *Object lines* describe the contour of the object. They are drawn dark and thick. The function of a line may also cause it to be interrupted by short blank spaces. For example, *hidden lines* describing features hidden from view, are indicated by a special type of line that is not only dashed but also thin. *Center lines* indicating the center of an object are thin with long segments interrupted by a short dash. *Dimension lines*, *extension lines*, *leaders*, and *material symbol lines* representing the cut material in a section view are all thin lines. *Cutting-plane lines* showing the position of a cutting plane are thick and may be broken in a variety of ways so as not to be confused with object lines. Lines cutting off a portion of an object, called *break lines*, are thin with a periodic zigzag. The use of many of these line types will be examined further in later chapters.

EXERCISES

4–1. Draw two vertical lines, two horizontal lines, and two 45° lines, all 4 inches long. Draw a 2-inch-diameter circle. Exchange your drawing with another drafter. Identify such irregularities as nonuniform line thickness, ragged ends, and lines that are too light.

4–2. Draw three squares with sides of 1, 2½, and 3¾ inches. Exchange your drawing with another drafter. Identify corners that do not solidly connect, have lines with ragged ends, and lines that cross too far.

4–3. Draw four sets of alternating thick and thin dark lines 4 inches long. Exchange your drawing with another drafter. Identify pairs of adjacent lines that do not have enough contrast in their thicknesses. Identify irregularities as described in Exercise 4–1.

4.3 Geometric Constructions

In drawing any geometric shape it is essential to know how to quickly and accurately draw fundamental line relationships. Knowledge of the construction of a few basic geometric shapes is also helpful in drawing more complicated subjects.

Slanted parallel lines may be drawn by setting the desired angle on the head of a drafting machine or on an adjustable triangle and simply moving to the location of each line. Should a drafting machine or an adjustable triangle not be available, a pair of standard triangles will also do the job [4–9]. Two triangles are positioned longside to longside with another side of the top triangle aligned with the first slanted line. The bottom triangle is held in position while the top triangle slides to the location of the second slanted line. The required parallel line can now be drawn. Perpendicular slanted lines may be drawn in a similar way [4–10]. When the top triangle

Parallel slanted lines can be drawn by sliding triangles on one another.

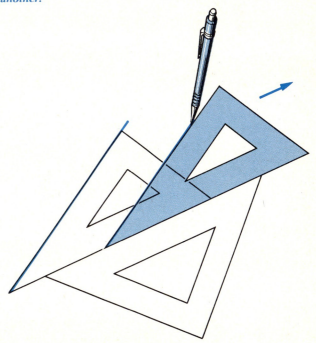

Figure 4–9

Architectural Drafting Fundamentals

Perpendicular slanted lines can be drawn by sliding triangles on one another.

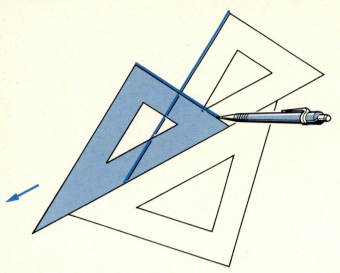

Figure 4–10

Bisecting a line with a compass.

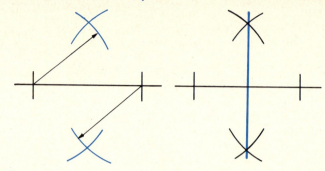

Figure 4–12

is moved to its new position, the side at 90° to the one used to draw the parallel line is used to draw the perpendicular line.

Perpendicular lines may also be constructed with a compass [4–11]. Select the point on a line at which a second line will be drawn perpendicular. Set the compass at a convenient radius (the larger it is, the more accurate the construction will be). Center the compass on the selected point and swing arcs to mark equal distances on both ends of the line. Using the same or a larger radius, set the compass on each mark in turn and draw overlapping arcs directly above the selected point. Connect the "x" created by the crossing arcs to the selected point. The connecting line will be perpendicular to the first line at this point.

A line may be divided into equal halves using a compass [4–12]. Set the compass at a convenient radius and swing arcs on both sides of the line with the compass set on each of the ends of the line in turn. Connect the two "xs" resulting from the overlapping of the arcs. The connecting line will bisect the original line and be perpendicular to it.

When drawing a line tangent to a circle at a certain angle, first locate the point of tangency with a radial line drawn from the center of the circle to the circumference at a 90° angle to the desired angle [4–13]. Then draw a line perpendicular to the radial line at the tangent point. The perpendicular line will be tangent to the circle. An adjustable triangle is very useful for this procedure.

A square may be constructed by drawing four tangents to a circle with a 45° triangle [4–14]. A hexagon may be constructed by drawing six tangent lines to a circle with a 30°–60° triangle. An octagon may be constructed by drawing eight tangent lines to a circle with a 45° triangle. These geometric shapes can be drawn faster by using triangles and will usually be more accurate than if their angles were measured with a protractor.

A hexagon may also be constructed using a compass by drawing a circle and dividing its circumference into six equal parts [4–15]. Each part is equal to the radius of the circle. A compass is used to place the marks without changing its setting from the radius used to draw the circle. There is room for six marks. If you place the compass on the last mark, you should find that the last arc should exactly meet the starting point. Connecting the marks with straight lines will result in a hexagon.

An approximate ellipse may be drawn using a compass [4–16]. First draw the rhombus that represents a square drawn tangent to the circle from which the ellipse is derived. Now draw a line perpendicular to each side of the rhombus at its midpoint. The intersections of these lines will be the centers for compass arcs that can be drawn tangent to the four sides of the rhombus. The four arcs when joined will form an approximate ellipse.

To divide a line into any number of equal parts, first draw a light line perpendicular to the line at each end

Perpendicular lines can be constructed with a compass.

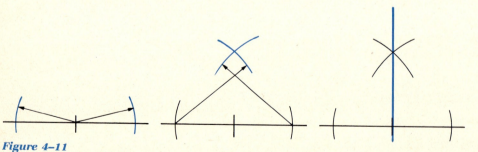

Figure 4–11

Drawing Fundamentals

Drawing a line tangent to a circle or an arc . . . the line is perpendicular to a radial line drawn to the point of tangency.

A hexagon may be drawn using a compass . . . draw a circle and mark six arcs equal to the radius of the circle.

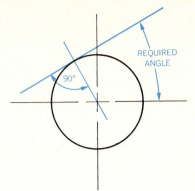

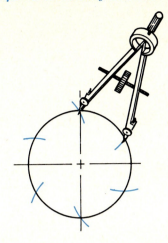

Figure 4–13

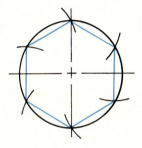

point [4–17]. Select any scale having the desired number of equal divisions that will fit between the two perpendicular lines. Slant the scale so that the zero is on one perpendicular line and the number identifying the correct number of divisions rests on the other. Mark the paper at each division on the scale. Drop lines from these marks parallel to the perpendicular end lines. These lines will divide the original line into the desired number of equal parts.

Figure 4–15

EXERCISES

4–4. Draw a 2-inch-long line at an angle of 25° to the horizontal. Using only two triangles, draw three 2-inch-long lines parallel to the first line and spaced one inch apart.

4–5. Draw a 2-inch-long line perpendicular to each of the lines of Exercise 4–4. Use only the two triangles. Space the lines one inch apart.

4–6. Draw a 4-inch-long horizontal line. Bisect it with a compass.

4–7. Draw a 4¼-inch-diameter circle. Draw a line tangent to it at an angle of 68° to the horizontal.

4–8. Using a 2-inch-diameter circle, first construct a hexagon using a 30°–60° triangle and then using only a compass.

4–9. Draw a 4-inch-long line at an angle of 20° to the horizontal. Divide it into nine equal parts using the method shown in [4–17].

To draw an approximate ellipse . . . draw a rhombus representing a square tangent to the circle from which the ellipse is derived . . . draw perpendiculars from the midpoints of the sides to locate centers for compass arcs.

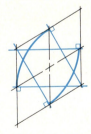

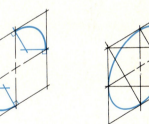
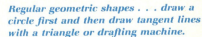

Figure 4–16

Regular geometric shapes . . . draw a circle first and then draw tangent lines with a triangle or drafting machine.

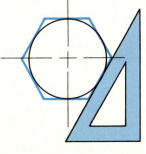

Figure 4–14

Architectural Drafting Fundamentals

Dividing a line into any number of equal parts . . . drop parallel lines from a slanted scale having the desired divisions.

Orthographic projection . . . the drawing is the picture a viewer sees on a transparent viewing plane placed perpendicular to the line of sight.

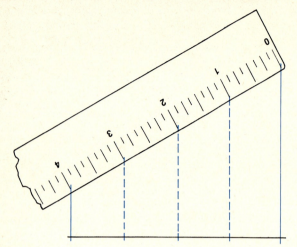

Figure 4–17

Figure 4–18

4.4 Orthographic Drawing

The terms "plans" and "elevations" may already be familiar to you. They are architectural drawings made using the *orthographic projection system*. In this system the drawing on paper is the picture that the viewer sees on the surface of a transparent viewing plane that is placed perpendicular to the line of sight between the viewer's eyes and the object [4–18]. By placing the object in different positions relative to the viewing plane, a variety of views may be recorded [4–19]. Since buildings are relatively large, a coordinated arrangement as shown

By placing the object in different positions relative to the viewing plane, a variety of views may be recorded.

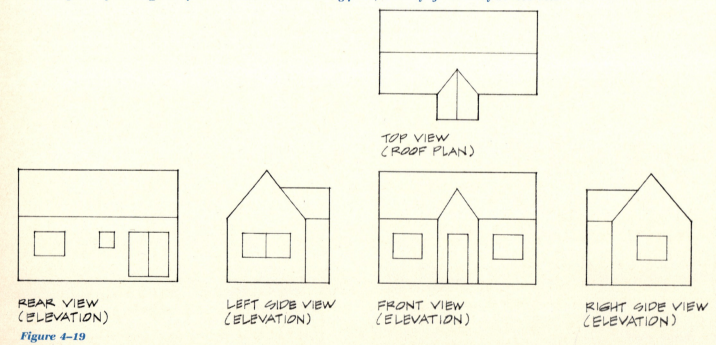

Figure 4–19

68

Drawing Fundamentals

Elevations of interior walls may also be needed.

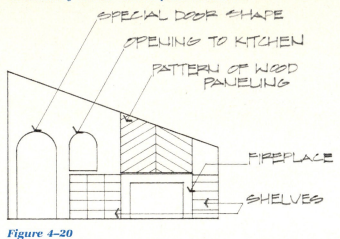

Figure 4–20

is rarely possible due to limited space on the drawing sheet.

The term *elevation* is usually used in architectural drafting to refer to views of the various vertical surfaces of a building. The front, right and left, and rear views seen in [4–19] are all elevations. The word itself refers to altitude (technically, height above sea level). It is in these views that the "altitude" of the components on the sides of a building are shown. The "altitude" of some components are dimensioned in the elevations, usually with reference to the first floor rather than sea level. Thus the term "elevation" (drawing showing altitude) has become a common term.

An elevation drawing expresses the true horizontal and vertical relationships between the parts exposed on only the vertical surfaces of a building that are parallel to the viewing plane. If a building has slanted surfaces, the elevation drawing shows an image that is somewhat different from that which the eye actually sees. When viewing a building, the eye sees a distortion of the corresponding horizontal and vertical relationships due to its perception of depth. Since an elevation does not show depth, examining only one elevation may not give the viewer a true idea of the building configuration. Therefore, elevations are usually drawn for all sides of a building. In drawing plans for less complex buildings repetitive or very simple elevations are sometimes omitted.

The precise way to identify an elevation is by compass direction. Commercial buildings may have more than one major entry or important facade. For this reason the terms "front," "side," and "rear" may not be meaningful. The titles "north elevation," "east elevation," and so on, leave less possibility for misunderstanding concerning the side of the building to which the drafter is referring. The north elevation is the north side of the building. In other words, it is the side that faces north. Designations such as "side view," "front," "right elevation," or "left side" are sometimes used on residential drawings or drawings of very small commercial structures. They are considered to be less professional expressions.

Elevations may also be drawn of interior vertical surfaces [4–20]. These are called *interior elevations*. The principles for drawing exterior elevations apply to interior elevations as well. Elevations may be needed to explain the appearance of the components of an interior wall. The walls of kitchens and bathrooms, fireplace walls, and other walls with permanently installed items such as bookshelves and openings may be described with interior elevations. Elevations are often drawn of cabinets, counters, and other special features to be built by the contractor. All elevations must have their scale indicated.

Elevations are particularly useful for construction purposes. They are drawn to scale and all vertical and most horizontal lines are true length lines. The true relationship between features appearing on any vertical plane that is parallel to the viewing plane is shown [4–21]. This is important to the builder.

Elevations show the true relationship between features on a vertical plane.

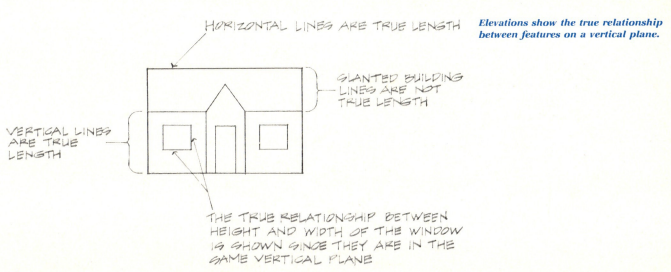

Figure 4–21

Architectural Drafting Fundamentals

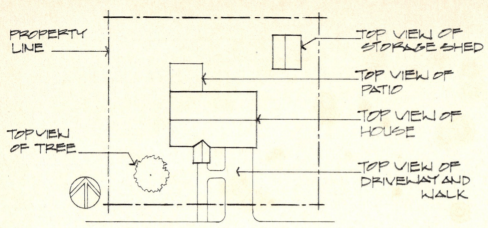

The site plan shows the outline of structures on the building site.

Figure 4–22

With experience, the drafter should develop the sensitivity to visualize the actual three-dimensional image of a building by examining the elevations. This sensitivity is very important during design since you will need to draw a variety of proposed elevations and examine them to see if the visual goals of the design concept are being achieved. Since the owner of the proposed building may not be skilled in such visualization, perspective drawings are often used in addition to the elevations to describe the design.

EXERCISE

4–10. Draw an elevation of a wall in the room where you are drafting. Use a scale of ⅛" = 1'–0". Use a tape measure to get exact dimensions. Simplify detail that is too small to draw. Draw the same elevation at a scale of ¼" = 1'–0". Include as much detail as possible. Compare the two drawings. Does the smaller drawing adequately describe the wall? Is a larger scale than ¼" = 1'–0" needed to add useful detail?

The top view of a building may also be drawn with the orthographic system. The resulting drawing is the *roof plan* [4–19]. If the surface of the ground around the building and extending to the property lines is shown, the drawing becomes a *site plan* (sometimes referred to as the *plot plan*). The site plan may also be drawn by showing the outline of structures on the building site rather than the roof plans [4–22]. The site plan shows the position of the building with respect to the property lines and other features, such as paving, lawn, trees, planting, water, and so on. Parking areas are shown, if they exist, as well as surrounding streets (with names). The scale at which the site plan is drawn is always shown.

To orient the viewer to the environment and to other drawings, the north direction must be indicated on plan drawings. To accomplish this, an arrow is drawn on the plan pointing north [4–23]. The word "north" may be omitted as a standard practice. Whenever possible orient all plans so that north is up on the sheet. This standard practice provides a uniformity that aids in comprehension of the drawings. A north arrow symbol is not included with elevations.

EXERCISE

4–11. Draw a site plan for the building in which you are drafting. Extend the plan to a distance of about 100 feet on all four sides of the building. Step off approximate measurements for all features on the site and for the outline of the building. Use a scale of 1" = 20' for the drawing. Exchange drawings with another drafter. Compare the drawing to the actual site to see if anything was omitted.

A few of the large variety of north arrows appropriate for use on plans.

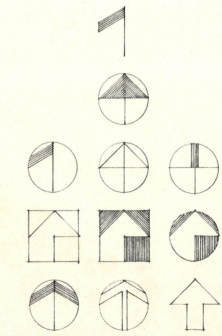

Figure 4–23

Drawing Fundamentals

A section view shows information behind the outer surface... an imaginary plane "cuts" through the building... the segment on one side of the "cutting plane" is removed.

4.5 Sections

In the previous discussion, drawings were described that showed the outer surfaces of a building. Information behind the surfaces may be shown with a drawing called a *section* [4–24]. An imaginary plane called a *cutting plane* is passed through the building or building component. Removal of all building parts between the viewer and the imaginary plane exposes previously hidden components. The section is viewed with sight lines perpendicular to the cutting plane. Identifying letters are used to link the section view with the cutting plane that produced it.

Sections through buildings are drawn at small scales such as $\frac{1}{16}''$, $\frac{1}{8}''$, or $\frac{1}{4}'' = 1'-0''$. Sections through large components such as walls are drawn at larger scales such as $\frac{3}{4}''$ or $1'' = 1'-0''$ [4–25]. Sections through small components of buildings such as connections are usually drawn at even larger scales, such as $1\frac{1}{2}''$ or $3'' = 1'-0''$.

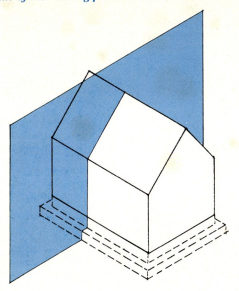

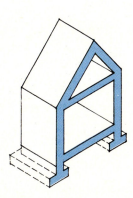

Figure 4–24A

In the orthographic views the location of the cut is shown with a cutting plane line... arrows indicate the direction of viewing.

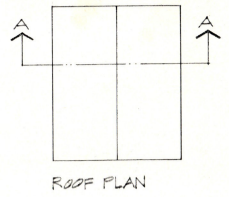

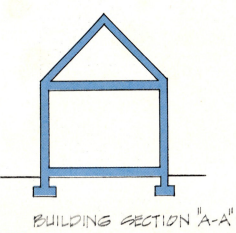

Figure 4–24B

Architectural Drafting Fundamentals

71

Section views may cut through only a portion of a building.

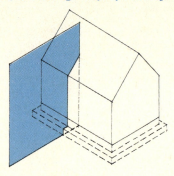

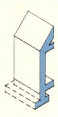

Figure 4–25A

The section view must be drawn at a large enough scale to show internal parts clearly.

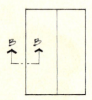

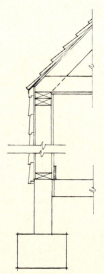

Figure 4–25B Wall Section B-B (Simplified).

The purpose of such a section is to show "detailed" information, thus requiring a larger scale. Such sections are called *details* [4–26]. A section of a component is only useful if drawn at a large enough scale to show the internal parts clearly. The scale at which any section or detail is drawn must be indicated. North arrows are not shown with sections.

Sections are often not "pure" sections in that part of the component beyond the cut line may be seen. These segments that have not been touched by the cutting plane are seen in elevation [4–27]. That is to say, they are projected forward to the cutting plane as any object is projected to the viewing plane in an orthographic projection. The parts of the assembly seen in elevation are drawn with lighter lines than the segment seen in section. They aid the viewer in understanding the section since they give the section a context and add realism to the drawing.

Section views differ in orientation on an architectural drawing as compared to a machine drawing. In architectural drawing the section view is always oriented so that horizontal components are drawn horizontal [4–28A]. In machine drawing the section view retains its direct projected orientation [4–28B].

Only the parts touched by the cutting plane are seen in section . . . parts beyond the plane are seen in elevation.

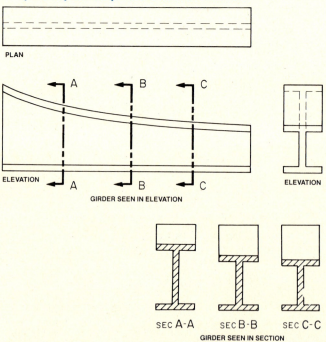

Figure 4–27

72   Drawing Fundamentals

Details are section views cut through a small segment of a building.

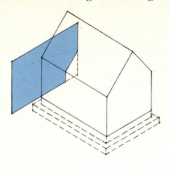

A detail is often an enlarged segment of another section.

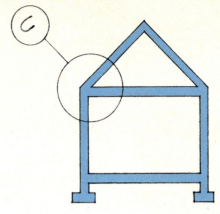

Figure 4–26A

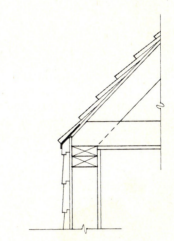

Figure 4–26B Detail C.

In architectural drawing, section views are orientated so horizontal components are seen horizontal . . .

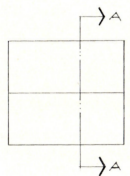

ROOF PLAN

In machine drawing, section views retain their direct projected orientation.

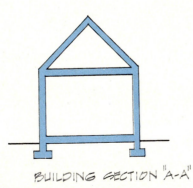

BUILDING SECTION "A-A"

Figure 4–28A

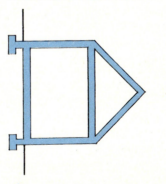 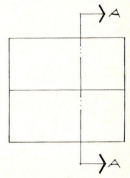

Figure 4–28B

Architectural Drafting Fundamentals

73

EXERCISE

4–12. Draw a building section of the example shown in [4–29]. Draw the section at the location shown by the cutting plane. The exterior door is 3'-0" wide. Use your dividers and the door width to find the other dimensions. Draw the section at a scale of ½" = 1'-0".

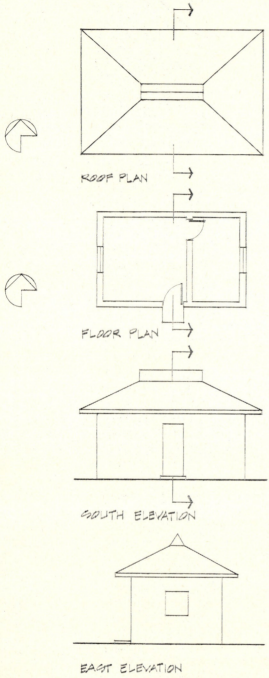

Figure 4–29

4.6 Floor Plans

A floor plan is a horizontal section of a building [4–30]. The cutting plane is passed through the building parallel to the floor at a distance of 3 to 4 feet above the floor. This is not a fixed distance because the plane cuts selectively. It must be high enough to pass through windows and must pass over all built-in furniture and appliances. Since a cutting plane in only one position cannot do this, it is allowed to be raised and lowered in various parts of the building as needed to clearly show the appropriate information. The floor plans should be oriented with north in the same direction on the sheet as that used for the site plan.

Typically, the floor plan indicates partition locations, positions of built-in cabinetry and plumbing fixtures, door swings, and the position of windows [4–31]. The wall thicknesses are drawn to scale. The windows and doors may be a single or a double line depending on the scale of the drawing. Windows are drawn closed, but doors are drawn open. A line is drawn showing the path of the edge of the door when it swings. Drawings made by architectural firms usually show doors open at 90°. Drawings made by drafting services may show doors open at 45°. The 90° position is considered the more professional convention.

Thus far, the discussion of floor plans, as with elevations and sections, has been general in nature. The information given is typical of both presentation and working drawings. Detailed information unique to each type of drawing is discussed in the design presentation and working drawing chapters.

EXERCISE

4–13. Draw a floor plan of the room in which you are drafting. Use a tape measure to find exact dimensions. Include furniture and cabinets if they exist. Use a scale of ¼" = 1'-0".

A floor plan is a horizontal section of a building . . . the cutting plane is parallel to the floor at a short distance above it . . . the upper part of the building is removed.

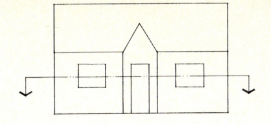

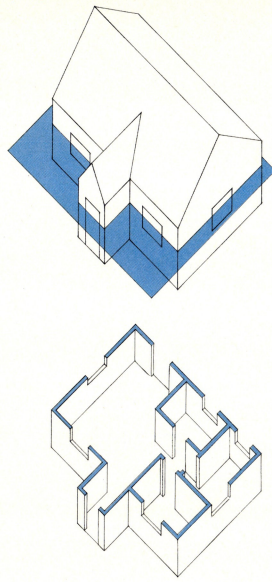

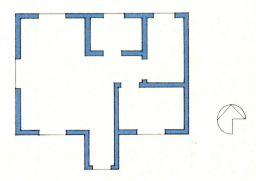

FLOOR PLAN (SIMPLIFIED)

Figure 4–30B

Figure 4–30A

4.7 Pictorial Drawings

To aid both the professional and the nonprofessional in visualizing a proposed building, *pictorial drawings* are used. These drawings "picture" an object as we normally see it with all three dimensions of space appearing at the same time. In order to do this, a certain amount of distortion is necessarily involved, and true-shaped surfaces are seldom seen. The most realistic pictorial drawing is a *perspective drawing* because it most nearly duplicates the way our eyes actually see an object in space. Any parallel lines on the object appear to converge in the distance rather than remaining parallel, and the features of the object that are farther away appear smaller. To duplicate this convergence in a drawing involves complicated, time-consuming procedures.

Most of the difficulties encountered in pespective drawing can be avoided by using one of several simpler approximate pictorial drawing systems. In all of these systems, parallel lines are drawn parallel and the features

Architectural Drafting Fundamentals

The method of drawing doors and windows on a floor plan varies with the type, the scale, and the preference of the drafter . . . wall thicknesses are drawn to scale.

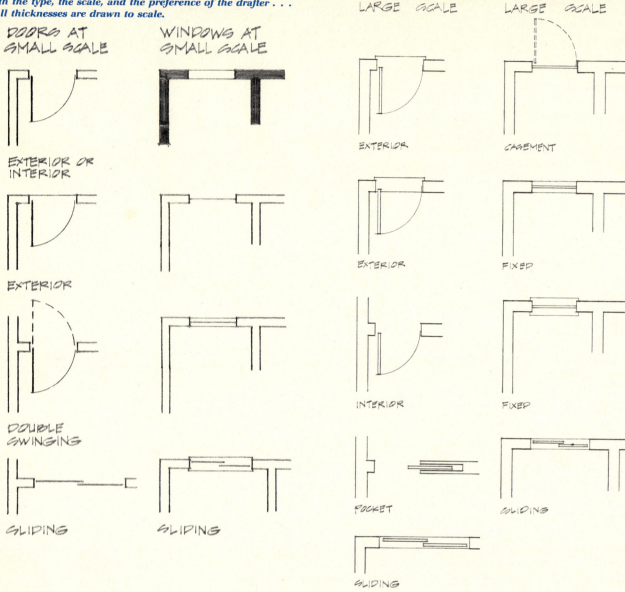

Figure 4–31A

Figure 4–31B

retain their size as they recede in the distance. Since parallelism is retained, these drawings are sometimes referred to as *paraline drawings*.

There are two types of parallel line pictorial drawings—*axonometric* and *oblique*. Both types are easier to draw than perspective because of the parallelism and because distances parallel to the width, height, and depth axes can be measured directly with a scale. Although relatively easy to produce, these drawings tend to create a distorted appearance in long objects. Since our eyes expect parallel lines to converge as they move away from us, an unnatural illusion of diverging is produced when receding lines are drawn parallel.

Although very little of a true perspective drawing is measured directly, it has the advantage of resembling a photograph, something familiar to any client. Perspectives may be interior or exterior. They may be drawn at eye level, thus appearing as they would to a person standing on the ground, or drawn as an aerial view, appearing as a view seen by a person in an airplane or on a hill looking down at the building. Interior perspectives are usually reserved for buildings with large interior spaces such as shopping centers or auditoriums. They are usually drawn as one-point perspectives. Exterior perspectives are usually drawn as two-point perspectives.

4.8 Axonometric Drawings

In *axonometric drawing* the object is positioned at an angle to the viewing plane [4–32]. The lines of sight are parallel and perpendicular to the viewing plane. The three axonometric systems—*isometric, dimetric,* and *trimetric*—differ in the degree to which the three principal faces of the object are visible. This is done by increasing or decreasing the angle between each face and the viewing plane. As the angle with the viewing plane increases, the dimensions of the face appear smaller. In drawing the view, this shortening is produced by using appropriate reducing scales on the width, height, and depth axes.

In *isometric* the three principal faces of an object are equally visible because they are positioned at the same angle with the viewing plane [4–33]. This causes the width and depth axes to appear at 30° angles with the horizontal on an isometric drawing. The same 0.82 reducing scale is required on all three axes because the dimensions are equally distorted. In practice, to save time, a reducing scale is not used. The dimensions along all three isometric axes are transferred directly at full size from the multiview drawing. This makes the isometric system the easiest of the axonometric systems to use.

In *dimetric* two principal faces of the object are equally visible, with the third face given greater or less visibility by varying its angle to the viewing plane [4–34]. For example, to obtain a better view of the top surface than in an isometric drawing, the object can be tilted up more. The width and depth scales remain equal, but the height scale is reduced. The angles selected for the axes dictate the reducing scale required for each axis. Scales are the same for two of the three axes.

Dimetric is more versatile than isometric since there are a variety of positions in which the object can be viewed, thus allowing a choice of the feature that will be emphasized [4–35 and 4–36]. Dimetric is more time consuming to draw, however, due to the different reductions that must be made to the building dimensions.

In *trimetric* each principal face of the object is at a different angle with the viewing plane [4–37]. This gives greater flexibility in positioning the three faces but is more time consuming to draw since a different scale must be used on each axis. Dimetric is more widely used than trimetric because it provides adequate views while requiring only two scales.

The various types of axonometric drawings may be constructed by following the same general construction procedures [4–38 to 4–43].

Axonometric drawing . . . lines of sight are parallel and perpendicular to the viewing plane . . . the object is at an angle with the viewing plane.

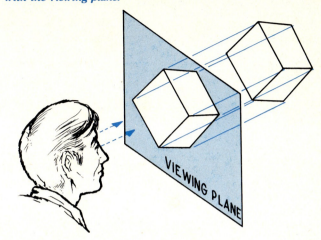

Figure 4–32

Isometric . . . the three faces are at the same angle with the viewing plane . . . the .82 reducing scale is usually drawn full size.

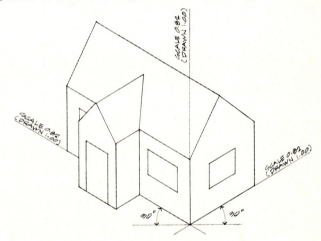

Figure 4–33

Dimetric . . . two faces are at the same angle with the viewing plane . . . the angle of the third face can be varied to increase or decrease its visibility.

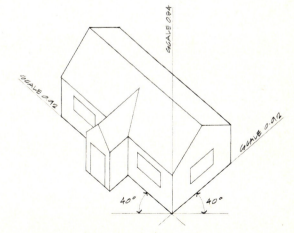

Figure 4–34

Architectural Drafting Fundamentals

In dimetric if the angle of tilt is less than in isometric, the top surface will be less visible . . . width and depth scales remain equal, but the height scale is increased.

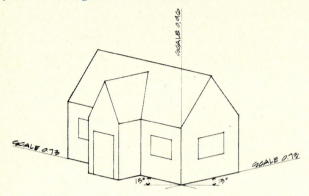

Figure 4–35

In dimetric a better view of the front surface can be obtained by rotating the object so that the front is at a smaller angle with the viewing plane . . . the depth scale varies with the degree of rotation while the width and height scales remain equal.

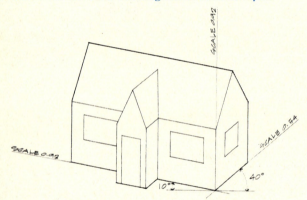

Figure 4–36

Trimetric . . . each face of the object is at a different angle with the viewing plane . . . different scales must be used on each axis.

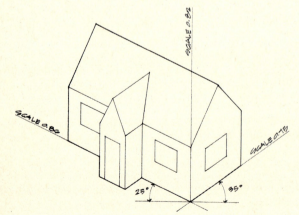

Figure 4–37

To lay out an axonometric drawing . . . set up the axis system desired with the required angles and scales.

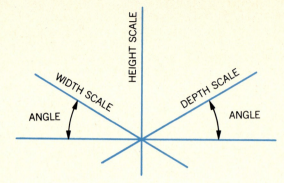

Figure 4–38

Imagine the object enclosed in a rectangular box that just touches its outermost points and surfaces.

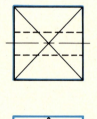
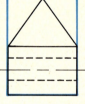
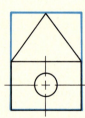

Figure 4–39

Lay out the width, height, and depth of the enclosing box along the axonometric axes . . . be sure to use the correct scale for each axis.

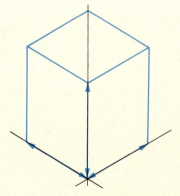

Figure 4–40

Drawing Fundamentals

On the outline of the enclosing box draw in the surfaces of the object that are in contact with the outside faces . . . omit hidden lines.

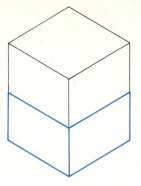

Figure 4–41

Next, draw in the surfaces of the object that fall inside the box . . . locate the beginning and ending points of angled lines with measurements parallel to the width, height, and depth axes.

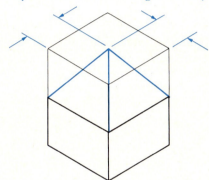

Figure 4–42

The circular opening on the right side of the object is drawn by laying out an enclosing square on the surface . . . the resulting rhombus serves as a guide for selection of an ellipse template opening that is tangent to the four sides.

A circle appearing on a surface is represented in axonometric by an ellipse, the minor axis of which is parallel to the direction of a line perpendicular to the surface (the width axis in this example) . . . a 35° ellipse template is used for circles on the principal faces of an object drawn in isometric.

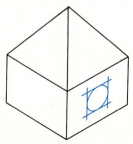

Figure 4–43

4.9 Oblique Drawings

The word oblique in *oblique drawing* describes the relationship between the viewer's lines of sight and the viewing plane [4–44]. The lines of sight are parallel but at any angle other than 90° with the viewing plane. The other criterion for an oblique drawing is that one face of the object must be positioned parallel to the viewing

Oblique drawing . . . the lines of sight are parallel but at an angle with the viewing plane . . . one face of the object is parallel to the viewing plane.

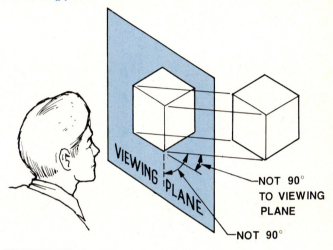

Figure 4–44

plane. Architectural drawings can be made in the oblique system [4–45]. In the case of an elevation oblique, the one face that is parallel to the viewing plane and is in true proportion can be traced from a building elevation. In a plan oblique the true face can be traced from a floor plan. The receding lines on an elevation oblique and the vertical lines on a plan oblique are often drawn shorter than true size to reduce distortion.

The true face of an elevation oblique can be traced from an elevation . . . the true face of a plan oblique is traced from a floor plan.

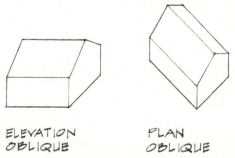

Figure 4–45

Architectural Drafting Fundamentals

There are three types of elevation oblique drawings. They are identified by the amount of reduction in the receding lines. In *cavalier oblique* the receding lines are drawn true length [4–46]. In *cabinet oblique* the receding lines are drawn half true length. The receding axis is cutomarily drawn at 45° in both types. The third option is to draw the receding lines at some scale between the cavalier and cabinet. This option may be referred to simply as *oblique*. The receding axis can be drawn at any angle less than 90°, but angles between 30° and 60° are common. Cavalier and cabinet obliques are the easiest to draw due to the simplicity of measuring the receding lines. They, however, show the most distortion. The proportions of the object will help you decide which is the appropriate choice. Sketch several simplified versions of your subject freehand and choose the option that appears the least distorted and is easiest to draw.

A plan oblique drawing is useful when you wish to emphasize a horizontal surface such as a roof or a floor [4–47]. It has an advantage over the similar-appearing isometric drawing in that the roof or floor plan on which it is based need not be reconstructed to make the walls meet at a 120° angle. The walls in a plan oblique meet at 90° just as in the multiview drawing of the floor plan. The floor plan is usually rotated 45° from the horizontal as the base for this construction. This gives a more three-dimensional appearance to the finished drawing [4–48].

Elevation oblique drawings . . . on the true shape face a circle appears as a circle . . . on other faces a circle appears as an ellipse.

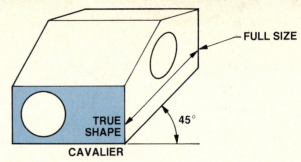

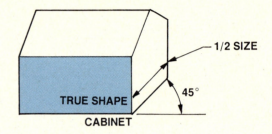

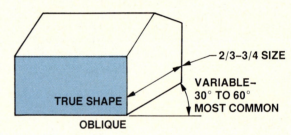

Figure 4–46

Plan oblique drawings . . . the true shape plan is rotated 45° with the horizontal . . .

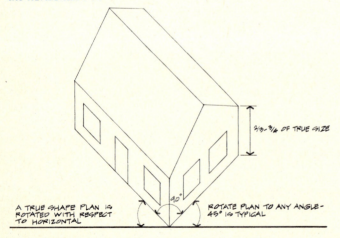

Walls may be extended up from a standard scaled floor plan . . . a circle in the plan view is true shape.

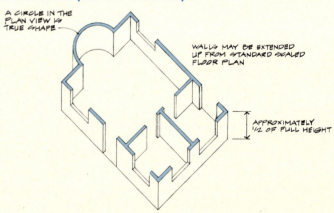

Figure 4–47

Drawing Fundamentals

The various types of elevation oblique drawings may be constructed by following the same general construction procedures [4–49 to 4–53].

Plan oblique of a two story duplex with the roof removed from one unit to show second floor plan.

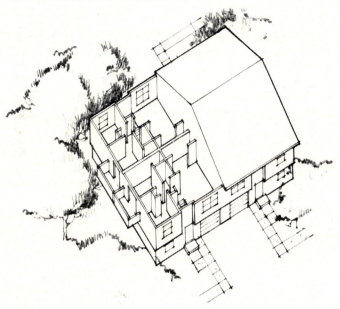

Figure 4–48

To lay out an oblique drawing . . . orient the object so that the face needing emphasis is in the "front" viewing position and can be drawn undistorted.

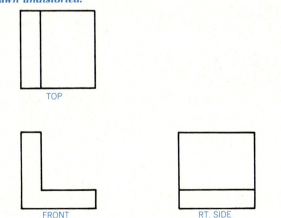

Figure 4–49

The depth axis is usually drawn at 45° with the horizontal . . . for convenience, depth measurements may be made to the same scale as that used for width and height . . . lines parallel to the depth axis remain parallel.

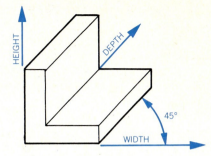

Figure 4–50

To create a more realistic appearance, depth measurements may be made to a reduced scale . . . the angle of the depth axis may also be changed and its scale changed accordingly.

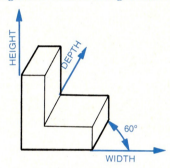

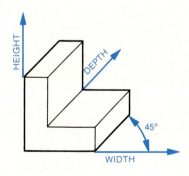

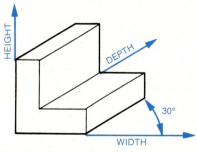

Figure 4–51

Architectural Drafting Fundamentals

For objects that are basically rectangular, an enclosing box can be used to help in the layout . . . orient the object so that circles and irregular contours appear on the undistorted front face.

Note that the square box in this example appears to have greater depth than width . . . to reduce this distortion the receding lines could be drawn to less than true size.

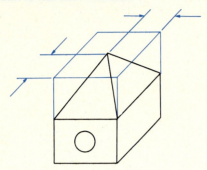

Figure 4–52

For cylindrical objects, a longitudinal center line is laid out first . . . depth measurements are marked off on this axis to locate the centers of the circular faces.

Notice that the planes containing the circles are positioned parallel to the viewing plane . . . being able to draw the circles true shape greatly simplifies the construction of this drawing . . . to position the object any other way would unnecessarily complicate the work and increase distortion considerably.

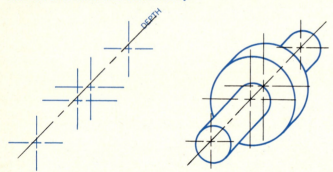

Figure 4–53

EXERCISES

4–14. Draw an isometric of the building in Exercise 4–12. Use a scale of ½" = 1'–0".

4–15. Draw a dimetric of the building in Exercise 4–12. Use a scale of ½" = 1'–0". Orient the building 40° to the base line.

4–16. Draw an elevation oblique of the building in Exercise 4–12. Use a scale of ½" = 1'–0". Draw all three variations (cavalier, cabinet, and oblique). Which appears least distorted?

4–17. Draw a plan oblique of the building in Exercise 4–12. Use a scale of ½" = 1'–0". Which of the drawings from Exercises 4–14 to 4–17 seems most realistic? Which was easiest to draw?

4–18. Draw a floor plan oblique of the building in Exercise 4–12 (roof removed). Use a scale of ½" = 1'–0".

4.10 Perspectives

In *perspective* drawing more realistic pictorial views are produced. Although quite similar to the views produced in axonometric drawing, perspective drawing produces views that more closely duplicate how the human eye sees an object in space. Since the lines of sight are not perpendicular to the viewing plane, parallel lines on the object must be drawn so as to converge at an imaginary point in the distance [4–54]. Width, height, and depth measurements must be made progressively smaller as they vanish into the distance. These variations from axonometric require additional time to draw accurately. This makes perspective drawing more suitable for artistic presentations.

You may wish to review the introduction to perspective drawing in Chapter 2. It will give you a general overview of the subject before starting the following step-by-step explanation. There are three perspective systems available—*one-point*, *two-point*, and *three-point*. They differ in the direction in which the object is viewed and the degree of realism produced.

Perspective . . . lines of sight are not parallel to each other or perpendicular to the viewing plane . . . they converge in the distance.

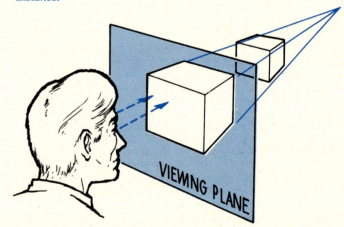

Figure 4–54

In *one-point perspective*, object lines that are parallel to the depth axis converge to a single vanishing point on the horizon [4–55]. This is similar to the apparent vanishing of receding lines of real buildings on the line where the real sky seems to meet the real earth or ocean. One-point is the easiest perspective to draw as the features in any plane parallel to the viewing plane are in true shape. The object is positioned so that one set of parallel planes is parallel to the viewing plane (also called the picture plane).

One point perspective . . . object lines parallel to the depth axis converge to a single vanishing point on the horizon . . . position the object so one set of planes is parallel to the viewing plane.

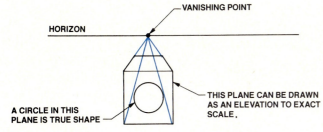

Figure 4–55

It is especially convenient to set the plane having the most information (wall of a room, face of a building, and so on) in such a position that it can be drawn as an elevation with a standard scale [4–56]. Projections that come forward and recesses that go behind the selected exact scale plane cannot be drawn at the same scale. They are still in true shape but unless their slight

An elevation of a plane having the most information is first drawn to scale . . .

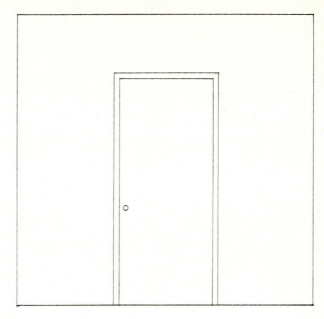

Projecting and recessed features are then drawn at larger and smaller scales.

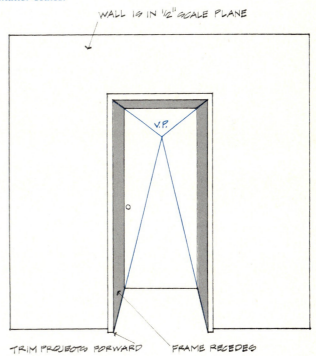

Figure 4–56

Architectural Drafting Fundamentals

projection is drawn, some of the three-dimensional effect will be lost. This principle becomes more important as the size of the perspective drawing increases.

One-point perspective is popular for describing interior spaces [4–57]. A courtyard or plaza may be outside, but still have the nature of an interior space in that features are surrounded by "wall-like" construction.

In one-point perspective a line from the viewer to the vanishing point will be perpendicular to the viewing plane [4–58]. The vanishing point, then, represents the position of the eyes of the viewer projected to the viewing plane. There are nine general positions in which the one-point perspective may be drawn. These are based on the position of the viewer with respect to the actual object drawn. The three horizontal choices are: the viewer may be to the (1) left, (2) right, or (3) exactly on the center of the object. The vertical choices are: the viewer may be (1) above (*bird's-eye* or *aerial perspective*), (2) below (*worm's-eye perspective*), or (3) exactly at eye level. An infinite number of exact positions are possible within these general categories.

The vanishing point represents the position of the viewer . . . the object may be drawn in several basic positions relative to the viewer.

One point perspective is popular for interior spaces . . . including courtyards and plazas.

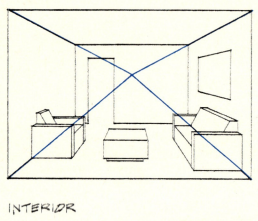

INTERIOR

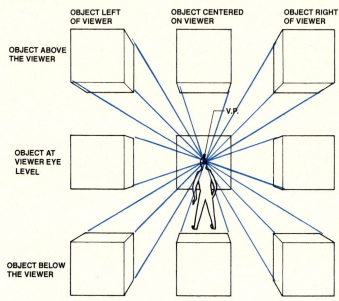

Figure 4–58

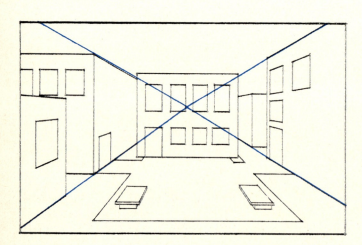

PLAZA OR COURTYARD
Figure 4–57

There are several ways to lay out a perspective drawing. The easiest of these is the use of a perspective grid. A one-point perspective grid consists of a network of lines parallel to the picture plane and a series of receding lines converging toward a vanishing point. A sheet of tracing paper is placed over the grid. The grid lines corresponding to the major lines of the building are located and traced.

Even if you use a grid you should understand the principles of constructing a perspective drawing. This is necessary to understand the grid and will equip you to draw a perspective when the appropriate grid is not available. A simplified method for constructing a one-point eye-level perspective will be discussed here. Once you have mastered it, you may want to learn variations and refinements.

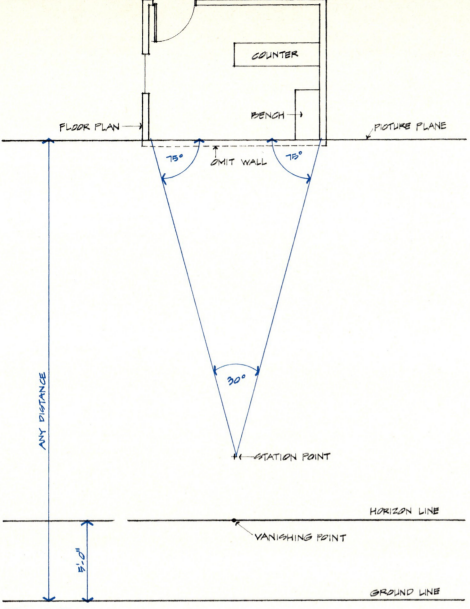

Setting up a one point perspective drawing . . . start by laying out the floor plan . . . locate the station point and the vanishing point.

Figure 4-59

A one-point perspective may be constructed using the following procedures:

1. Set up the drawing [4–59].

Lay out the floor plan of the space for which you will draw the perspective. Use the largest scale that will allow the drawing to fit on the sheet and still provide room for the perspective elevation view that will be projected from it. Draw a line representing the edge of the *picture plane* along the wall separating the viewer from the space. Locate the desired position of the viewer. This is called the *station point*. In [4–59] the viewer has been centered on the picture plane. The distance of the viewer from the picture plane has been selected to give an average 30° angle of vision.

At some convenient distance in front of the picture plane draw a *ground line* parallel to the picture plane. This will be the bottom line of the perspective elevation view that we will draw. Draw a *horizon line* parallel to the ground line and at a scaled 5'–0" distance above it. Five feet represents an approximate distance from the ground to the level of the viewer's eyes. Locate the *vanishing point* on the horizon line directly below the station point.

Architectural Drafting Fundamentals 85

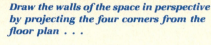
Draw the walls of the space in perspective by projecting the four corners from the floor plan . . .

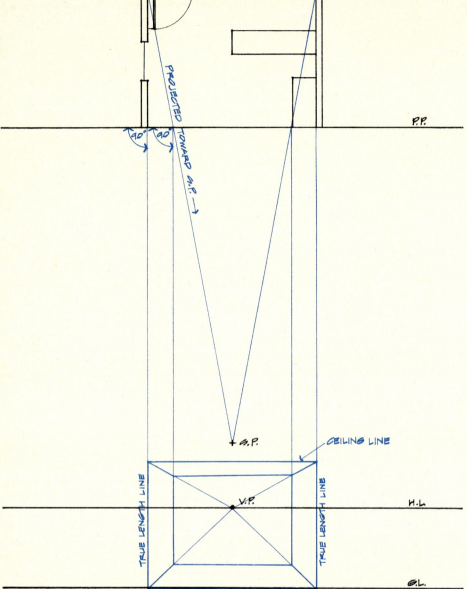

Figure 4–60

2. Draw the walls of the space in perspective [4–60].

Project the front corners of the room that touch the picture plane to the ground line. Between these two projections draw a ceiling line parallel to the ground line at a distance above it equal to the ceiling height of the room. Use the same scale as you used for the floor plan to measure this distance. You now have a rectangle representing the cross section of the room at the picture plane. The vertical edges of this rectangle are true length lines. Connect the four corners of this rectangle to the vanishing point.

To establish the back wall of the room in the perspective view, draw lines on the floor plan from the back corners to the station point. Project the points where those lines cross the picture plane to intersect the four receding lines drawn from the front corners of the room to the vanishing point. Connect these four intersections. This small rectangle represents the back wall of the room.

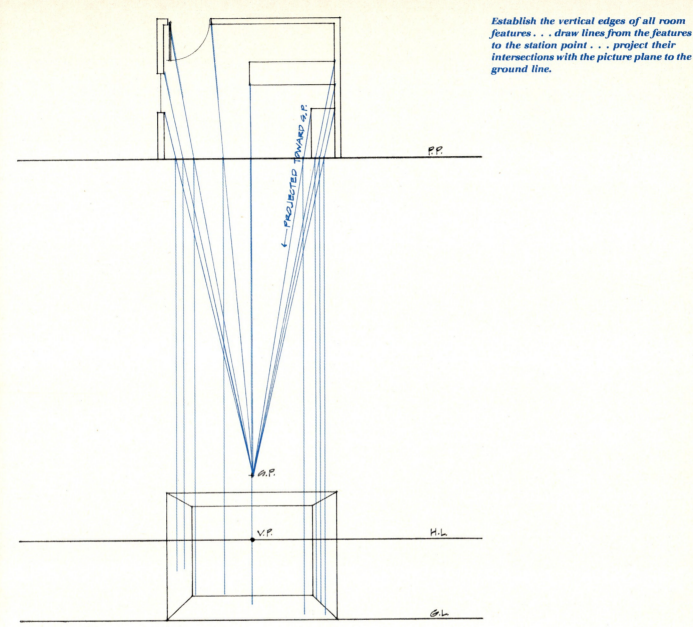

Establish the vertical edges of all room features . . . draw lines from the features to the station point . . . project their intersections with the picture plane to the ground line.

Figure 4–61

3. Establish the vertical edges of all features in the room [4–61].

Draw lines on the floor plan from the various features to the station point. Project the intersections of these lines with the picture plane to the ground line.

Architectural Drafting Fundamentals

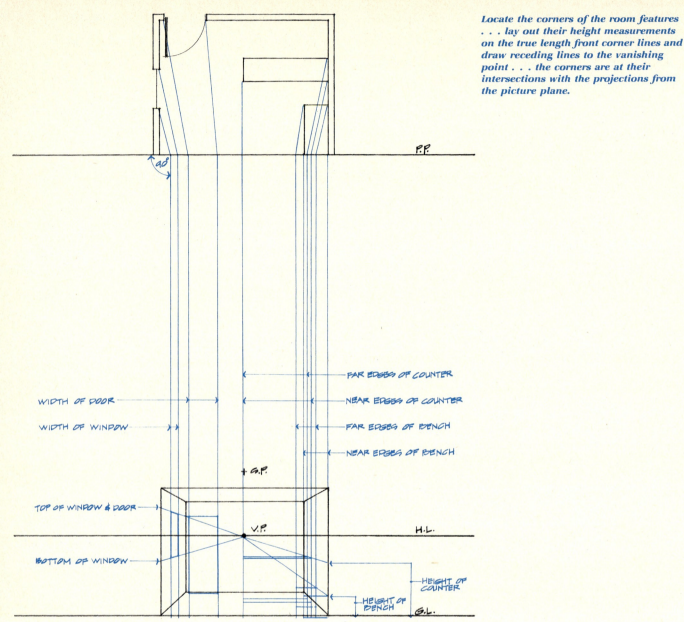

Locate the corners of the room features . . . lay out their height measurements on the true length front corner lines and draw receding lines to the vanishing point . . . the corners are at their intersections with the projections from the picture plane.

Figure 4–62

4. Locate the corners of the room features in the perspective view [4–62].

   Measure the height of the room features on the true length lines (the vertical edges of the large rectangle in the perspective). Draw receding lines from these heights to the vanishing point. The crossings of the receding lines and the vertical projections from the picture plane are the corners of the room features.

5. Complete the outline of each feature in the room [4–63].

   Draw horizontal, vertical, and receding lines connecting the corners of each feature.

Complete the perspective view by connecting the corners of the room features with horizontal, vertical, or receding lines.

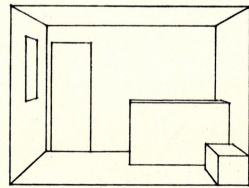

Figure 4–63

88 Drawing Fundamentals

This completes the basic construction of a simple one-point perspective of the interior of a room. Further refinements would include adding details, such as door and window recesses [4–56] and trim. You may wish to trace the perspective construction for the final version rather than erase all the construction lines.

EXERCISE

4–19. Draw an eye-level one-point perspective of the main room in the building in Exercise 4–12. Set the wall with the exterior door parallel to the picture plane. Place a 3′-0″ cube on the floor in the center of the room. Select a scale for the plan that will result in a perspective that will fill an 8½- × 11-inch sheet of paper. This may require experimentation.

Two-point perspective is the most common perspective used in architectural drafting. It is more difficult to draw than one-point perspective since there is no plane seen in true shape. As the name implies, two vanishing points are used [4–64]. The viewer may be positioned in a variety of positions in order to emphasize various planes of the object [4–65]. In the bird's-eye view, the roof of a building would be seen. In the worm's-eye view the underside of roof overhangs, balconies, and other horizontal planes would be emphasized. The eye-level perspective, however, is a good choice because it is the position in which most people see a building. Positioning the viewer halfway between the left and right edges of the object is also desirable, as this location helps keep distortion to a minimum. The viewer may move a short distance to the left or right to increase the emphasis on walls on these respective sides, but distortion may occur if the viewer moves too far off center.

As with a one-point perspective, a perspective grid may be used to construct a two-point perspective. A simplified method for constructing a two-point, eye-level perspective of a simple building will be discussed here [4–66]. Several other procedures may be used. Further study will make it possible for you to include more complex detail in your perspective drawings.

Draw a two point perspective of this building . . .

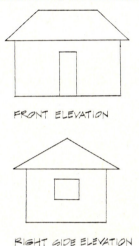

Figure 4–66

Two point perspective . . . object lines parallel to the width and depth axes converge to two vanishing points on the horizon.

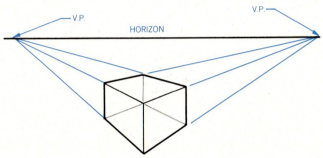

Figure 4–64

In two point perspective the viewer may stand to the left or right of the center of an object but must always see two sides . . . the viewer's eyes and the vanishing points are on the horizon line.

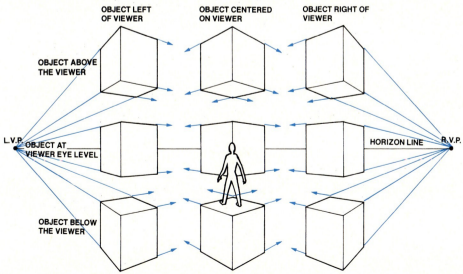

Figure 4–65

Architectural Drafting Fundamentals

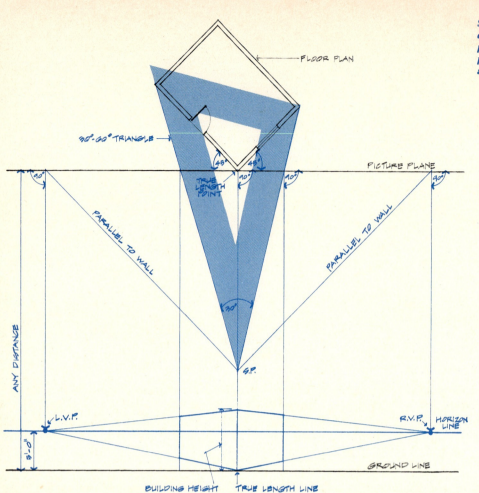

Setting up a two point perspective drawing... start by laying out a floor plan at a 45° angle with the picture plane... establish the station point and the vanishing points.

Figure 4-67

A two-point perspective may be constructed using the following procedures:

1. Set up the drawing [4–67].

Lay out the exterior walls of the building in a floor plan drawn to a convenient scale. Use this scale for all future measurements. Tilt the plan 45° to a *picture plane line* drawn through the corner nearest the viewer.

The intersection of this corner and the picture plane is the true length point. Draw an elevation view of this line by projecting down to a *ground line* drawn at a convenient location near the bottom of the sheet. This is the *true length line.* It is the only line in the perspective on which you can measure true lengths with a scale. Place your 30°–60° triangle on the floor plan with the 30° angle pointing down the sheet and on the true length line. Slide the triangle down the true length line until its two sides touch the far left and far right corners of the floor plan. Keep the 30° angle on the true length line. Make a dot at the tip of the 30° angle on the true length line. This is the *station point*.

Draw a *horizon line* 5'–0" above the ground line. Extend lines from the station point to the picture plane parallel to the left and right sides of the floor plan. Project their intersections with the picture plane down to the horizon line. These two points on the horizon line are the *vanishing points.* Draw lines from the left and right corners of the floor plan to the station point. Project their intersections with the picture plane down to the ground line.

On the true length line, measure the building height. From the top and bottom of the height measurement draw lines to both vanishing points. Mark the four points where these receding lines cross the vertical projections of the far corners of the building from the picture plane. Darken the vertical lines between the marks. Darken the receding lines from the marks to the true length line. Darken the true length line between the receding lines. You now have a perspective of the rectangular volume representing the building without a window, door, or roof.

Locate the door and the window in the perspective view . . .

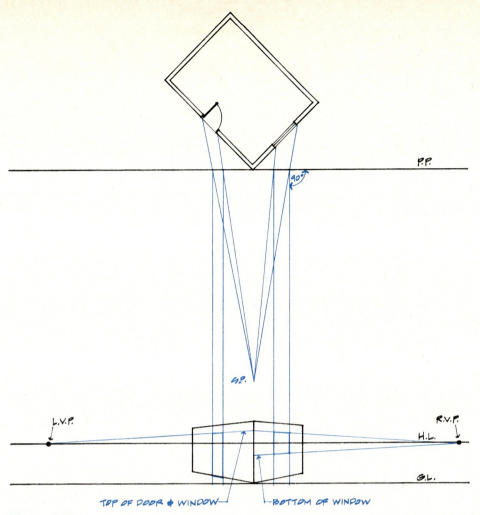

Figure 4–68

2. Locate the door and the window in the perspective view [4–68].

   Draw lines from the edges of the door and the window to the station point. Project their intersections with the picture plane down to the ground line. Measure the height of the window and the door on the true length line. Draw receding lines from these heights to both vanishing points. Darken the segments of these lines between the two vertical door projections and the two vertical window projections previously drawn. You have drawn the top of the door and window.

   Measure the height from the ground line to the bottom of the window on the true length line. Draw a receding line from this height to the right vanishing point. Darken the segment on this line where it crosses the two vertical window projections. Darken the vertical lines between the end points of this segment and the segment at the top of the window. You now have the entire window outlined. Darken two vertical lines from the top of the door to the bottom edge of the building. This completes the drawing of the door.

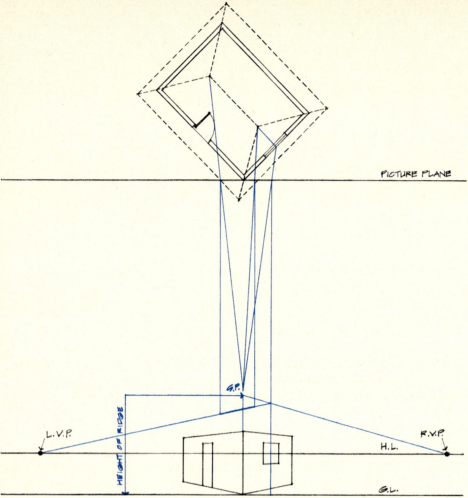

Figure 4–69

3. Draw the ridge of the roof [4–69].

Using dashed lines draw the configuration of the roof on the floor plan. Extend the ridge line to the face of the right side wall with a construction line. Draw a line from this intersection point to the station point. Project its intersection with the picture plane down to the ground line. Measure the height of the ridge on the true length line. Draw a receding line from this height to the right vanishing point. Mark the point where this line crosses the vertical projection just drawn from the picture plane. From this mark draw a line to the left vanishing point. This line is the line on which the ridge lies.

Draw lines from the ends of the ridge line in the plan view to the station point. Project their intersections with the picture plane down to the ridge construction line in the perspective view. Darken the ridge construction line between these two vertical lines. You now have the ridge drawn in perspective.

Finish drawing the roof.

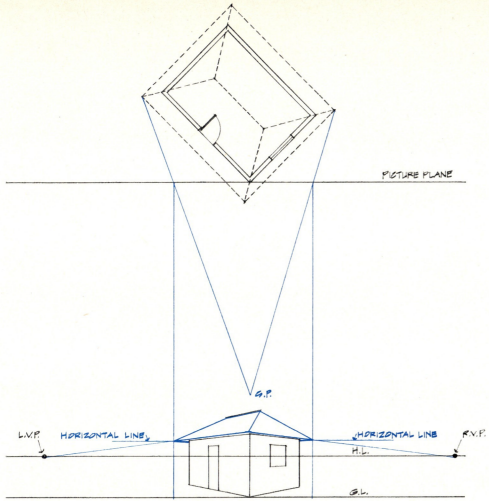

Figure 4–70

4. Finish drawing the roof [4–70].

Draw lines to the station point from the left and right corners of the roof in the plan. Project their intersections with the picture plane down to the ground line. From the far left and right, upper corners of the building walls in the perspective, draw horizontal lines to the vertical projections just drawn from the picture plane. The left and right corners of the roof are at these intersections. (Note: This works only when the overhang is equal on all sides and the building is tilted at 45° in plan.)

Draw lines from both vanishing points to the left and right corners of the roof. Extend these lines to the true length line to identify the front edges of the roof. The third visible roof corner is located where these extended lines cross. From this corner and the far right corner, draw lines to the right end of the roof ridge. From the far left corner, draw a line to the left end of the roof edge.

This completes the basic construction of a two-point perspective of a simple building. You may wish to trace the perspective construction for the final version rather than erase all construction lines.

EXERCISE

4–20. Draw an eye-level two-point perspective of the building in Exercise 4–12. Select a view that shows the south and east sides. Select a scale for the plan that will result in a perspective that will fill an 8½- × 11-inch sheet of paper. This may require experimentation.

Architectural Drafting Fundamentals

Three point perspective . . . object lines parallel to width, depth, and height axes converge to three vanishing points.

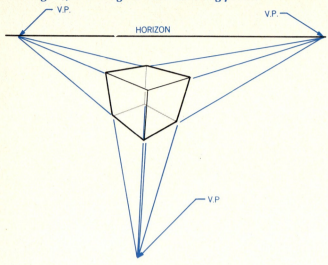

Figure 4–71

Three-point perspective is rarely used. It is complicated to draw since there are no parallel lines in it and a third vanishing point is used [4–71]. The advantage of three-point perspective is that for very tall buildings, the illusion of height is magnified. Two-point perspectives ignore the fact that as one observes a tall building its walls seem to converge to a point in the sky if you are looking up at it. If you are looking down from an airplane, the walls seem to converge to a point in the ground [4–72]. For any but the tallest buildings [4–73], the third vanishing point may be ignored and two-point perspective drawing is sufficient. The procedure for drawing a three-point perspective will not be examined in this text.

Looking down on a tall building . . . the walls seem to converge to a point in the ground.

Figure 4–72 *World Trade Center, New York City.*

Three point perspective is appropriate only for drawing very tall structures.

Figure 4–73 *The world's tallest building—Sears Tower in Chicago.*

Drawing Fundamentals

4.11 Lettering

Architectural lettering differs somewhat from that employed by other drafters. There is a "correct" way to form letters [4–74 and 4–75], but individual lettering style in architectural drawing is flexible. The prime requisite is readability. Lower-case lettering is seldom used.

Figure [4–76] shows a recommended style of architectural lettering. It is simple, without peculiar or attention-attracting features. Resist the temptation to use a lettering style that is clever or artistic. This only draws attention to the lettering and makes it harder to read. Individualistic styles are hard for other drafters to match. When several people work on the same drawing, which is very common, several widely differing lettering styles make the sheet look less professional. Note that the letters are vertical. All the connections of the lines in the letters are closed. The letters are all about the same size. Uniformity is important for readability.

Some drafting offices use inclined lettering [4–77]. This practice is more common with engineers than with architects. In fact, few architects use inclined lettering. However, inclined lettering is easier to do than vertical lettering; it is also a little faster. Many who use vertical lettering believe that it looks neater than the inclined style. A variation of the standard proportioned letter is the wide-letter style [4–78]. Some believe the wide letter is more attractive than the standard-width letter. The extra space requirement is a drawback when lettering in places of restricted size.

Variations that are sometimes used but not recommended are shown in [4–79]. Using a triangular shape for the "A" is artistic but hard to read. Shortening the middle bar of the "E" and "F" is a machine drafting style. Architectural "Es" and "Fs" generally have horizontal bars of equal length. Many people can't resist putting serifs on "Is" and "Js." They worry that without the short horizontal trim lines (serifs) on the ends of the strokes, these letters have an appearance that is weaker than other letters. Using serifs, however, is a completely different style of lettering. Adding serifs to standard lettering requires extra time and seldom improves legibility.

Do not mix lettering styles, just as you would not mix Roman numerals with Arabic numbers. Note that the lower leg of the "K" should meet the vertical leg at the same point that the upper leg meets it. It does not con-

These letters illustrate traditional stroke patterns in lettering. Some letter configurations shown, such as the E, F, K, and R, are not popular with architectural drafters. Refer to [4–76] for preferred architectural style.

Figure 4–74 Vertical Lettering.

Figure 4–75 Inclined Lettering.

Architectural Drafting Fundamentals

A recommended style of architectural lettering . . .

ABCDEFGHIJKLMNOPQ
RSTUVWXYZ 12345
67890

FLOOR CEILING ROOF

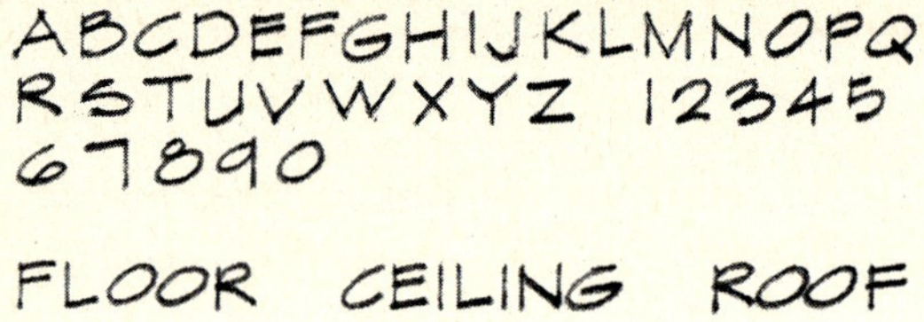

. . . some variations are used but are not as readable.

EFGGKKMMRRS
W 13

Figure 4–76

Some drafting offices use inclined lettering.

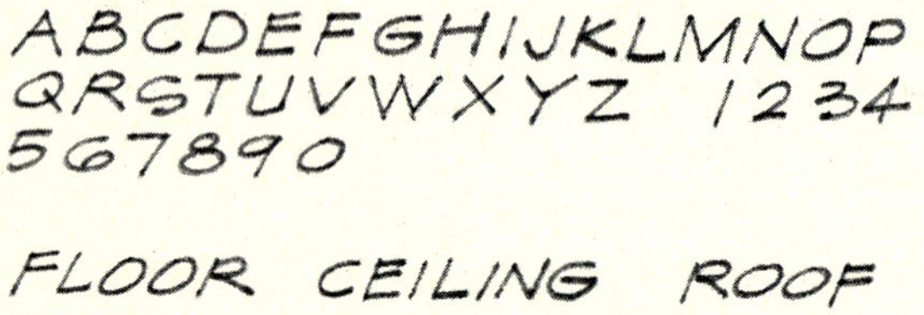

ABCDEFGHIJKLMNOP
QRSTUVWXYZ 1234
567890

FLOOR CEILING ROOF

Figure 4–77

A wide-letter style requires extra space.

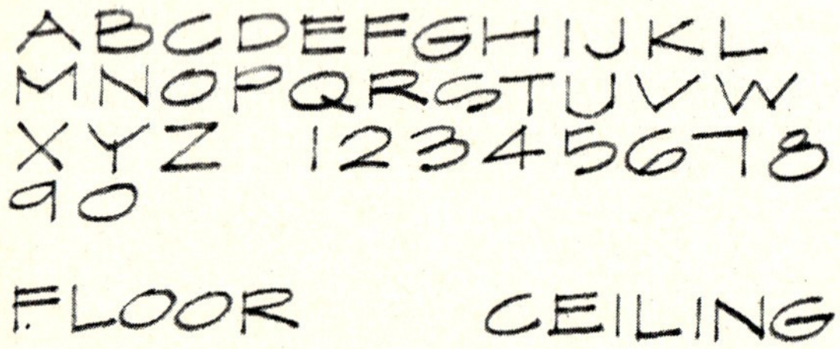

ABCDEFGHIJKL
MNOPQRSTUVW
XYZ 12345678
90

FLOOR   CEILING

Figure 4–78

Letter shapes that are not recommended . . .

AGIJKMNSWY
14

Figure 4–79

nect to the upper leg at its midpoint as shown in [4–79]. Technically the middle of the "M" should touch the lower guideline. It should not stop at the midpoint of the letter. However, many drafters ignore this recommendation and still produce excellent lettering. The sides of the "M" are vertical, not sloped.

The curved leg of the "R" is another artistic touch. Do not use it. Make the slanted leg of the "R" straight and connect it to the vertical leg at the point where the curved line connects. The artistic "W" shown in [4–79] is hard to read. The "W" in which the middle part does not touch the upper guideline is treated like the "M." Technically, the middle part should extend to the same height as the legs. The "Y" shown appears to be slanted, but the upper part is not. Avoid this style for "Ys." The number "1" should not have serifs except in special situations where it is necessary to distinguish it from the letter "I." Close the top of the "4."

Architectural fractions are also different from machine drafting fractions [4–80]. Note that the numerator is not directly above the denominator. The numerator and denominator are nearly as large as the whole number. The fraction extends slightly above and below the guidelines. The idea is to show the fraction as large as possible without interfering with the lettering on the lines above and below it. Since architectural lettering is often placed in a cramped space, the lines are very close together, leaving no space for a fraction that is very tall.

Architectural fractions are only slightly higher than whole numbers.

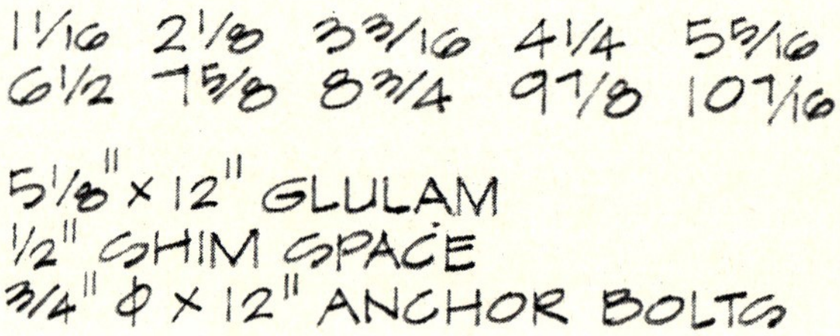

1 1/16 2 1/8 3 3/16 4 1/4 5 5/16
6 1/2 7 5/8 8 3/4 9 7/8 10 7/16

5 1/8" × 12" GLULAM
1/2" SHIM SPACE
3/4" ⌀ × 12" ANCHOR BOLTS

Figure 4–80

Uniform letter height is maintained by always using light guidelines. These can be easily and quickly drawn with a lettering guide [3–38 and 3–39]. A popular size for architectural note lettering is 3/32 inch. This is a little smaller than machine drafting lettering, which is typically 1/8 inch. On most working drawings the goal is to get a lot of lettering in a small space. Dimensions are also 3/32 inch high. Main titles are 3/16 inch, while subtitles and room names are 1/8 inch. All note lettering should be the same size. Plan ahead when lettering. Do not get yourself into a situation where you reduce the size

Drawing Fundamentals

of the note lettering in order to fit it into a tight space. The lettering should be very dark. It should be as dark as the object lines on the drawing.

Letters are not spaced an equal distance apart. The *area* between each letter should be about equal [4–81]. This is not always possible as the area between an "L" and "A" can't be reduced to that between an "N" and an "E"... but this is the goal. The distance between words is about equal to the width of a letter. These distances should be estimated rather than measured.

It is difficult for most beginning drafters to achieve "professional-looking" lettering. Good-quality lettering comes from lettering every day on the job. It is distinguished by a character that portrays confidence. This does not mean that the letters are perfectly shaped. They are formed boldly as if the drafter had no doubts about his or her ability. There is no sign of shakiness that often occurs when a letter is formed slowly as if to avoid a mistake.

To achieve this professional touch takes much practice. Begin by practicing lettering with fairly quick dark strokes. When you can achieve uniformity, you are on your way to good lettering. One method used by many architectural drafters to improve speed and uniformity is to use a triangle as a guide in making vertical letter strokes. The triangle is quickly slid along on the T-square or parallel rule with the left hand while lettering with the right.

The lines forming a letter should be drawn using the same principles as drafted linework (Section 4.2). The end of each line in a letter should be dark and blunt. The same habits used to achieve this in linework will achieve it in lettering. Start each line of a letter a little beyond its actual starting point. Move the pencil point back to the starting point and begin the letter. As you lift the pencil at the end of the stroke, move it back on the line. This will help prevent ragged ends on each letter and keep them dark. Some drafters like to exaggerate this habit to the point of almost creating tiny serifs with the darkened ends of the letter lines [4–82].

Letter spacing... maintain equal area between letters... areas 1, 2 and 3 are approximately equal... distances 4, 5 and 6 are not equal.

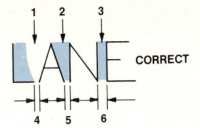

Poor letter spacing... areas 1, 2 and 3 are not equal... distances 4, 5 and 6 are equal.

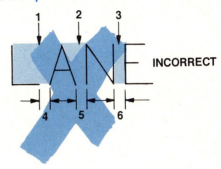

Figure 4–81

A variety of examples of lettering is shown in [4–83]. They are not perfect or even recommended in every case. They do demonstrate a variety that is typical among different architectural drafters.

EXERCISES

4-21. What is the most important characteristic necessary for all lettering, regardless of style?

4-22. What are some of the characteristics of the lettering in [4–76] that make it look professional?

4-23. Select a paragraph related to design or construction from a newspaper or magazine.
(a) Copy it using the style of [4–76].
(b) Copy it using the style of [4–77].
(c) Copy it using the style of [4–78].
Which style is best suited to you? Why?

4-24. Select the lettering style that is the most legible from [4–83]. Why is this style better than the others?

4-25. Select the lettering style that is the most difficult to read from [4–83]. Why is this style less legible than the others?

4-26. What advantage does style C from [4–83] have over style B?

4-27. What characteristic does style G from [4–83] have that makes it difficult to read?

4-28. Identify the distinguishing characteristic of each style of lettering in [4–83]. Decide whether the characteristic makes the lettering harder or easier to read.

Exaggerate dark ends of letters.

ABCDEFGHIJKLM
NOPQRSTUVWXYZ
1234567890

Figure 4–82

A variety of lettering styles are found among architectural drafters . . . some good and some bad.

A. REMOVE TWO EXISTING INCANDESCENT FIXTURES AND INSTALL 2'X4' RECESSED FLUORESCENT FIXTURE.

B. 3'-6" CERAMIC TILE WAINSCOT ON CONCRETE BLOCK AT TOILET AND KITCHEN.

C. COLUMNS SHALL BE PRIMED AND GIVEN 3 COATS OF FLAT EXTERIOR ENAMEL. WALLS SHALL BE PRIMED AND SHALL RECEIVE 2 COATS OF FLAT EXTERIOR ENAMEL.

D. 6-12" DEEP SHELVES SHALL BE INSTALLED ON ADJUSTABLE METAL SIDE TRACKS ON WEST WALL. SOUTH WALL SHALL RECEIVE 2 SHELVES.

E. ALL BIDDERS SHALL VISIT THE JOB SITE TO DETERMINE THE ACTUAL WORKING CONDITIONS. ALL FACTORS AFFECTING THE BID SHALL BE CONSIDERED.

F. PROVIDE DUCT THROUGH THE ROOF. SEAL ALL JOINTS AIR TIGHT WITH DUCT TAPE. INSULATION SHALL FIT TIGHT TO DUCT.

G. CONTRACTOR SHALL VERIFY ALL EXISTING BUILDING DIMENSIONS AND NOTIFY THE ARCHITECT OF ANY DISCREPANCIES WITH THE DRAWINGS.

H. FOOTING SIZES ARE BASED ON SOIL BEARING CAPACITY OF 5000 LBS./SQ.FT. ALL FOOTINGS SHALL BE FORMED WITH WOOD OR METAL PANELS.

I. Flexible neoprene expansion member with 15 lb. felt strip shall be secured with aluminum screws @ 12" o.c.

Figure 4–83

Architectural dimensions are usually stated in feet and inches... such as 2'-3"... or 35'-11".

Architectural arrowhead practices...

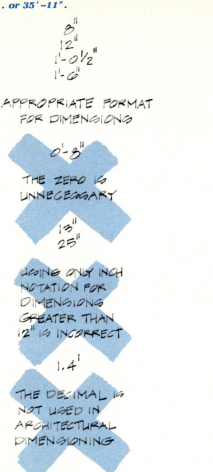

Figure 4–84

Figure 4–86

Architectural dimensions are placed above the dimension line.

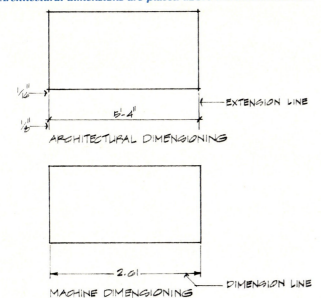

Figure 4–85

4.12 Dimensioning

Architectural dimensions are usually stated in feet and inches rather than in decimal-inches or in millimeters [4–84]. As in machine drafting, the extent of a dimension is usually shown with a *dimension line* [4–85]. Architects usually prefer to place their dimension numbers above the dimension lines rather than breaking the lines, as is common in machine drawing. Architectural drafters may use arrowheads, slash ("tic") marks, or solid dots to indicate the end of a dimension [4–86]. The choice may be dictated by office policy. The dimension line stops at an *extension line*. The extension line starts ¹⁄₁₆ inch away from the object and extends ⅛ inch past the dimension line. Extension and dimension lines are the same thickness and darkness.

One important rule for dimensioning of architectural work is that the dimension numbers should always be readable from the bottom or right-hand edge of the paper. Correct and incorrect examples of architectural di-

Architectural Drafting Fundamentals

Correct and incorrect dimensioning practices.

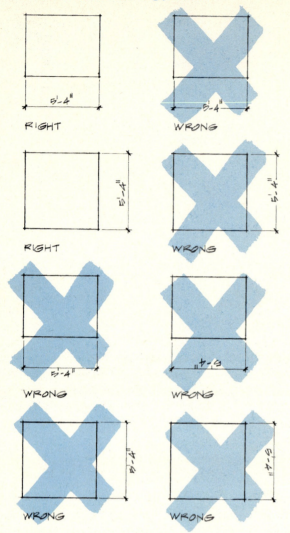

Figure 4–87

Work from the top of the drawing downward to reduce smearing.

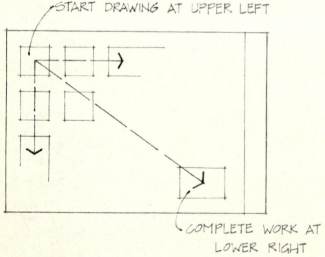

Figure 4–88

mensioning are shown in [4–87]. More specific dimensioning practices will be discussed in the working drawing chapters.

4.13 Cleanliness in Drawing

Because you will usually draw with a pencil, there is always the problem of keeping the work clean and neat. Drawings that are sharp and clear will provide better prints for the worker in the field. Smudged work produces smudged prints. These can be difficult to read. After use in the field where they are subjected to wrinkling, rolling, and folding, and to a dusty environment, prints can become almost impossible to read in a short time. Sunlight also tends to fade blueline prints.

Graphite from your pencil can smear the most carefully executed drawings if certain drafting procedures are not followed. First, keep all lines very light—only faint outlines—until the drawing is finished and all changes are made. Then darken the final lines as desired. Lettering is usually done last because the softer leads used for lettering smudge more readily than the harder leads used for linework

Second, it is good practice always to begin work at the upper left corner of the sheet of drafting paper and to finish at the lower right corner of the sheet [4–88]. Left-handed drafters may want to begin at the upper right corner of the paper. In any case the work should start at the top of the paper and progress toward the bottom.

These techniques will assure that instruments, hands, arms, and elbows are not smearing the linework as it is drawn. They will also help avoid smudging the pencil lines with perspiration and oils from your skin. Washing your hands frequently will further guard against smudging, especially when the softer leads are used. If your hands perspire profusely, you should keep talcum powder and a piece of cloth or paper towel handy for frequent hand wiping.

Drafting tools are a source of "dirt." They pick up graphite from the linework and lettering and deposit it back on the sheet. To reduce soiling by instruments, wash them frequently and do not slide them on the drafting surface. Pick triangles, scales, templates and parallel rules up when moving them. Pressure on the head of a T-square will lift the blade up off the sheet so that it may be moved without touching the drawing. This may seem awkward at first, but once it becomes a habit, you won't notice that you are doing it.

Another good idea is to cover all completed work with an inexpensive piece of semitransparent paper secured with drafting tape [4–89]. In this way completed portions of the drawing are protected and only that portion of the work is exposed on which you are actively working.

Cover completed portions of the drawing to avoid smudging.

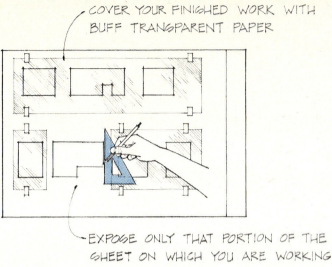

Figure 4–89

Fixative may be sprayed over the completed drawing to keep it clean.

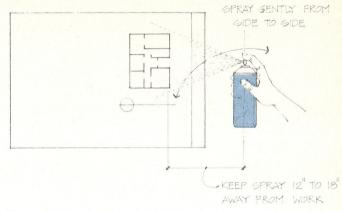

Figure 4–91

Some drafters like to use a preparation made of soft eraser crumblings to clear smudges from their work [4–90]. This product can be obtained in a small bag and sprinkled onto the paper while you work, much like salt on a hamburger. You can brush it away as the work progresses so it won't become dirty and in turn cause additional smudging. Poor linework will result unless you brush it away from the portion of the drawing on which the work is being done. Excess use will also reduce the darkness of the finished linework.

Soft eraser crumblings can be sprinkled on top of the drawing to minimize smearing linework.

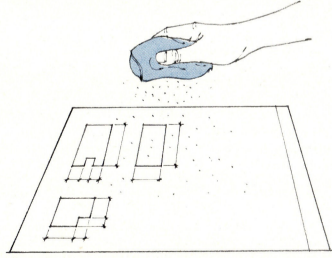

Figure 4–90

Many drafters prefer to use plastic drafting film and plastic-based leads instead of the more traditional paper and leads. Although it is possible to draw on drafting film with ordinary graphite drafting pencils, they wear down and become dull very quickly on the abrasive surface. The inevitable smearing of graphite will be worse than on paper. Plastic is impermeable and will not readily absorb the material in the graphite leads. Smearing becomes a real problem. This can be greatly reduced by using the special plastic-based leads.

Finally, if you want to keep the finished drawing clean, it can be sprayed with a fixative [4–91]. Fixative is an invisible plastic spray and comes in a matte or gloss finish. Matte is generally preferred. A caution is appropriate here. *Do not* spray the drawing until you are certain that it is completed, has been checked, and is unlikely to require any changes. The fine, impermeable, misty coating placed on the work is also nearly impossible to remove without damaging the paper. Also, the fixative must be applied with care. Spray the drawing lightly with a side-to-side motion, holding the spray can 12 to 18 inches from the drawing. Several light coatings are preferable to a single, thick coat. Too heavy a spray is likely to run and cause streaking of the drawing.

Applying fixative is a delicate process and one should practice on several old tracings to develop the technique of "fixing" before attempting it on work that will be retained and printed. Practice this technique and remember to make certain that the work is truly finished before spraying.

EXERCISES

4–29. List several procedures that will help keep your drawing clean.

4–30. What is a disadvantage of using powdered eraser?

4–31. What safeguards should you observe when using fixative?

5 Timesaving Methods

5.1 New Drawing Techniques

Ink, a common medium of drafting offices of the past, was time consuming to use and lines were not easily changed. Reproduction of drawings was done by hand copying. Although the tools and supplies were both awkward and time consuming to use, labor was cheap and working drawings were kept simple and few in number. The increase in the complexity of buildings, the increase in the number of drawings required, and the increase in the cost of labor have all caused modern drafting offices to seek methods to reduce drafting costs. This does not mean that the drafter's work is being eliminated. Rather, the complexity of today's structures has led architects to adopt new ways of picturing the manner in which a building is to be constructed without employing often tedious and time consuming hand-drawn linework and lettering. The drafter who is familiar with these more modern techniques and is skilled in their use will be in great demand. Some of these timesaving methods are described in the following sections.

5.2 Photoreproduction

Many advanced techniques do not include "drafting" at all. That is, hand-held pencils are not always needed to produce drawings. This is particularly true where the drafter's work consists of producing detail drawings that have been used many times before or when repetitive use of plans or elevations would normally call for tedious redrawing.

Often a substantial part of a drawing can be completed by fastening photoreproductions of details from other drawings, standard details, specifications from manufacturers' catalogs, or repetitive plans and elevations on a prepared drawing form. This procedure, diagrammed in [5–1], is known as paste-up or "scissors" drafting. When completed, new photoreproductions of the complete sheet are made on drafting vellum or film. Then you can fill in or add details or do other work as required.

Floor plans and site plans must be used several times in the same set of construction drawings, each with different detailed information (architectural, mechanical, electrical, and so on). Rather than drawing the basic plan several times, some offices prepare the various sets of detailed information on transparent overlay sheets that do not have the floor plan or site plan on them. Each overlay sheet is placed on top of a master sheet containing the basic plan. Information is drawn on the overlay sheet in the appropriate location relating to the plan. Later each overlay sheet is photographically combined with the basic plan sheet on one reproducible page. Matching crossed-line targets ("bulls-eyes") are drawn

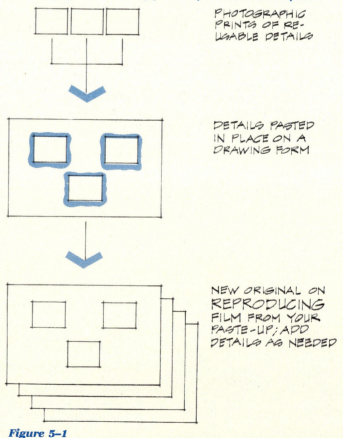

Time may often be saved by photo-reproduction techniques.

PHOTOGRAPHIC PRINTS OF REUSABLE DETAILS

DETAILS PASTED IN PLACE ON A DRAWING FORM

NEW ORIGINAL ON REPRODUCING FILM FROM YOUR PASTE-UP; ADD DETAILS AS NEEDED

Figure 5–1

in the corners of each sheet so that the two sheets may be separated and rematched at any time. These matching symbols are used during the photographic process to superimpose the detailed information exactly in the correct position on the plan.

When the plan drawing is subordinate to the detailed information placed on it (such as in the engineering sheets), the plan may be photographically printed lighter than the detailed information. This is called a *screened plan*. It will appear gray or light blue in a printed set of drawings, while the superimposed information will show up as black or dark blue.

5.3 Pin Registration

Where a number of drawing sheets or overlays need to be accurately aligned, the *pin registration* system is recommended. Precise alignment from one drawing sheet to another is termed *registration*. The demand for precise registration of drawings has created the need to develop a system that will assure a high degree of registration accuracy.

Many industrial firms have developed their own system of pin registration. There are also several commercially available pin registration systems. These systems are all based on drafting media that has been punched with accurately spaced holes, causing the various sheets of drawings to be registered when mounted on alignment pins. Generally, the holes are punched along the upper edge of the drafting media [5–2]. The alignment pins are less likely to be an obstruction if they are located

Drawings can be hung by the alignment pins for photography.

Figure 5–3

at the top edge of the drawing. Drawings that require photographing may be hung during the process using the pins and holes [5–3]. This also requires that the pins and holes be located near the top edge.

On large drawings an additional pin and hole are placed at the center of the bottom edge [5–4]. This is called a tail pin and hole. The drafting media may change size due to the effects of temperature and/or humidity.

Registration holes are punched along the upper edge of the drafting media.

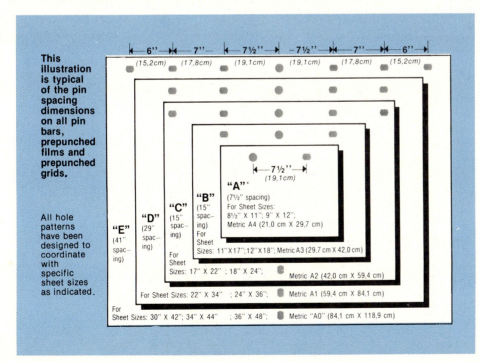

Figure 5–2

Timesaving Methods

103

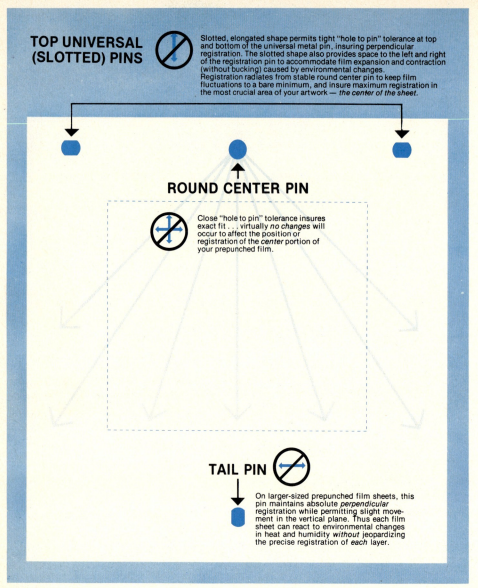

Figure 5-4

To avoid buckling or wrinkling, registration holes are punched elongated, except for the center hole that is round.

There are several types and sizes of prepunched polyester drafting films commercially available: clear film, matte one-side or two-side, and clear inking film. The prepunched drafting film is also available in various thicknesses. Many industrial firms have their own precision punch which is capable of punching all required holes simultaneously. Some industrial firms place one extra hole on the right or left side of the center hole to prevent (through error) the film from being placed upside down.

If prepunched drafting film is not used, holes may be punched oversize with a hand punch at the pin locations. The drafting film is then placed onto the pins, and self-adhesive adapter pads with accurately punched holes are placed on each pin and adhered to the film [5-5].

Alignment pins are avilable in two shapes—round and elongated. They are also available in several styles: pins mounted on a bar with a predetermined spacing that is mounted on the drafting surface, pins mounted on a base plate that may be taped to the drafting surface, or individual pins with no base plate that may be adhered to the drafting surface with a double-stick pad.

5.2 Typewritten Notations

Another timesaving technique eliminates much of the hand lettering formerly required in architectural drawing. This requires the use of a special typewriter that accepts the larger sheets often used in the drafter's work.

Oversize holes may be hand-punched at the pin locations . . . the film is placed on the pins and adhesive adapter pads are pressed into place.

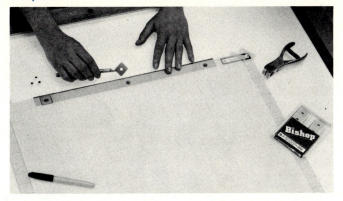

Figure 5-5

A popular and versatile machine of this type is the IBM Selectric II with a correcting tape feature [5–6]. This machine accepts a 15-inch-wide sheet of drawing paper and can print in a number of type styles. Typing errors can literally be "lifted off" the paper by a special correcting ribbon mounted in front of the typing element. Other manufacturers offer wider carriage machines that will accept even the largest of tracing sheets. For those cases where the drawing is too large to fit in a typewriter, the note can be typed on special transparent, self-adhesive paper and applied to the drawing.

5.5 Xerography As a Drafting Technique

Electrostatic reproduction through the use of the xerography process is gaining popularity in many architectural firms. Original work can be reproduced on an adhesive-backed, decal-like material called *appliques*. After printing, the protective backing is peeled from the special paper and the applique is pressed firmly onto the drawing sheet in the desired location. If this process is used, it is important to employ heat-resistant transfer paper to prevent the press-on material from peeling off in the printing process. Specially prepared, heat-resistant, adhesive-backed film for this work is known by trade names such as Mactac, Stikybac, Dulseal, and Zip-a-tone.

The advantage of using xerographic reproduction is that multiple copies of details, title blocks, and schedules can be reproduced on machines that are generally available in most architects' offices. Disadvantages lie in the difficulty in correcting or changing work after it has been applied. Also, the laminated materials often print with a "ghost," or darker background than does work that is drawn or typed directly onto a sheet of drawing vellum.

5.6 Transfer Lettering and Symbols

A great variety of press-on and rub-on lettering and drafting symbols are available [5–7]. These are manufactured under trade names such as Prestype, Letra-set, Chart Pak, and Zip-a-tone. An enormous variety of print styles are available in almost any size. Also, shading, crosshatching, and halftone patterns can be obtained. Use of these trans-

Transfer lettering . . . used in special situations where large letters and special letter forms are needed. Individual letters are pressed or rubbed onto the drawing surface.

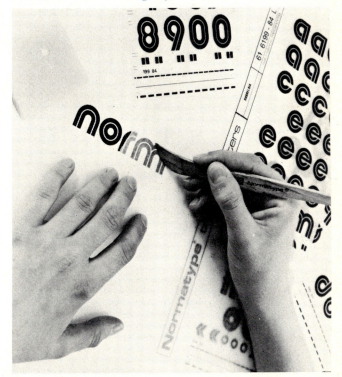

Figure 5-7

An IBM Selectric II typewriter can be used for typing notes.

Figure 5-6

Timesaving Methods

fer techniques will greatly reduce your work. Further, these transfers can be easily removed if a change is desired. They can be made more permanent when sprayed with a fixative.

In addition to lettering and symbols, the transfer system offers representations of trees, shrubbery, human figures, artwork, and trademarks. If a sufficient quantity is warranted, the manufacturers of the transfer material will print almost any symbol, lettering, shading pattern, or drawing desired. One problem with these graphic aids is that they print much darker than adjacent pencil work and consequently stand out strongly. This is not a problem, however, when working with ink.

5.7 Photocompositors

Photocompositors print lettering on clear, adhesive, positive or negative film strips [5–8]. The strips are simply pressed onto the tracing at the desired positions. Opaque tape can also be obtained, but it is suitable only for photo-reproduction work. Diazo-type reproductions must be made on a transparent medium since prints are made by projecting light through them onto light-sensitive paper and then developing the light-sensitive paper into the final print. Manufacturers of photocompositors claim considerable savings in time and expense over transfer type or hand-operated template-type devices such as Leroy or Wrico lettering guides. Their initial cost is high, however, and presently they are limited in type styles and sizes. The Kroy lettering machine prints type on adhesive-backed clear tape [5–9]. This is especially useful for use on architectural drawings.

Press the adhesive-backed lettering into position at the desired location.

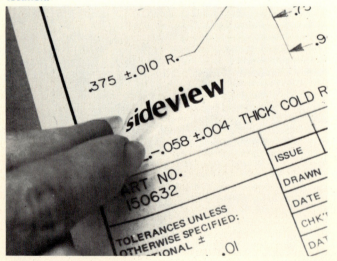
Figure 5–8

A Kroy lettering machine prints type on adhesive backed tape.

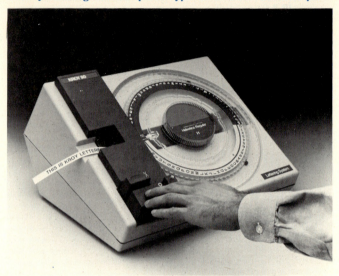

Figure 5–9

5.8 Template Lettering

Uniform lettering of various sizes and styles can be done in ink using technical pens and various types of templates. Ink lettering is used on a drawing where greater clarity and reproducibility is required than is possible with pencil lettering. This is especially important if the drawing will be reduced in size when it is duplicated.

One type of lettering template is marketed under trade names such as Leroy and Rapidograph. This template uses a penholder (called a *scriber*) that follows grooves in a plastic guide strip [5–10]. The scriber can be adjusted to produce vertical or inclined lettering with the same guide. In the Wrico and similar template lettering systems, a plastic stencil is used instead of a guide strip [5–11]. The technical pen is directly guided by the letter outline holes in the template.

All of these devices yield consistent and uniform letters but require considerable practice for best results. They are employed primarily in lettering title blocks or in major title lettering on drawings. Templates are available in a wide variety of letter styles and sizes.

5.9 Rubber Stamps

In listing timesaving drafting devices, we should not forget the use of the "old-fashioned" rubber stamp. Stamps are relatively inexpensive to make, but are limited in their utility. Once the message is set, it cannot be changed. For this reason, they are used more often on prints to indicate dates of issue, to identify work, or to print the professional seals of the architect and engineer. Rubber stamps are also useful to represent landscaping,

One type of lettering template . . . a pen-holding scriber follows grooves in a guide strip.

Figure 5–10

such as bushes and trees. Unless a special rubber stamp ink is used, the stamped image on drawing vellum may produce an inferior reproduction. Special stamp pad ink, such as Carter's Microporous Plastic Ink, yields good results. Two problems in using rubber stamps are alignment and removal. It is difficult to place the stamp in a precise location because of its bulky back and handle. Also, removal of the impression is almost impossible once the ink has permeated the paper. For this reason

A technical pen is guided directly by the holes in this type of lettering template.

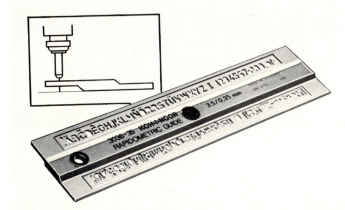

Figure 5–11

you must be sure that the desired stamped imprint is correct before application. Another problem is that stamp pad ink will smear until it is completely dry. With some inks drying may take several minutes.

5.10 Electronic Lettering Machines

Several types of electronically driven lettering machines are available that mount directly on the drafting board. Figure [5–12] shows an electronic lettering machine manufactured by Alpha Merics Corp. Some electronic lettering and symbol-generating instruments have a plotter with a motorized pen and keyboard that can be attached to a drafting machine. A large variety of preprogrammed standard or custom letter and symbol template modules can be inserted in a separate microprocessor-based controller and activated by the plotter keyboard to print directly on a drawing.

5.11 Computer Drafting

Computers not only can be used for calculation, but they also can be programmed to draw. They may be used during the design phase to develop floor plans that best meet the criteria programmed into the computer. Optimum room relationships requiring the least circulation are typical solutions of which the computer is capable.

Dimensional data may also be entered in a computer to produce perspective constructions from any viewing angle. The viewer may "walk around" the building or through it by watching the changing perspective views on a display screen. Prints may be produced of any of the perspective outlines seen on the screen. A finished

The motorized pen of the lettering and symbol generating instrument prints directly on a drawing.

Figure 5–12

Timesaving Methods

107

Computers can be programmed to draw as well as to calculate.

Figure 5–13

rendering can then be done by hand on an overlay using the computer-produced perspective construction as a guide.

Technical drawings may also be done by a computer [5–13]. Precise details and dimensioning may be produced that are appropriate for a set of construction documents. Computers with this capability are expensive, so they tend to be used by only the largest offices. Since computers do only what they are told, someone knowledgable in architecture must determine what information is entered into the machine and must know how to efficiently use the data that the computer produces. Part V of this text further explores the use of computers in architecture.

EXERCISE

5–1. List advantages and disadvantages for the following time-saving techniques. Through group discussion develop suggestions in addition to those listed in the text.
   (a) Photoreproduction.
   (b) Pin registration.
   (c) Typewritten notations.
   (d) Xerography.
   (e) Transfer lettering and symbols.
   (f) Photocompositors.
   (g) Template lettering.
   (h) Rubber stamps.
   (i) Electronic lettering machines.
   (j) Computers.

II

Architectural Design

6 Aesthetic Considerations in Design

Characteristics that make a building attractive are sometimes the most difficult to discuss due to their abstract nature. The appearance of a home falls into one of the following categories: similar to styles of the past, similar to current styles, and a third group which includes styles similar to neither the past nor present. If styles from the third group become popular and are copied, this category could be called styles of the future.

6.1 Historic Influences

Some homeowners wish to attempt to capture the spirit of past societies by copying their spirit through the copying of the forms of their homes and other buildings. This is not a new trend. Early settlers of America brought with them images of their European homes and built new homes reflecting these forms. These early styles in America have become the inspiration for many current home styles.

The *Saltbox* form [6-1], found in early colonial America, is still built today [6-2]. A very popular style is simply called *Colonial* [6-3]. The same window and door arrangement is readily apparent in modern versions of this same style [6-4]. The Pearce–McAllister House in

Contemporary version of the historic Saltbox style.

Figure 6–2

Denver, Colorado, is a *Colonial Revival (Dutch)* home [6-5]. The main feature of this style is the gambrel roof, which is repeated in a contemporary interpretation of this historic style [6-6]. The *Federal* style popular in the late 1700s and early 1800s, which is identified by its two-story configuration with a relatively smooth facade and low hip roof [6-7], is not as widely copied as the colonial styles.

A Colonial style home built in Standish, Maine.

This New England Saltbox-style farm home was the birthplace of John Howard Payne, and inspired his writing of the immortal "Home Sweet Home."

Figure 6–1

Figure 6–3 Marrett House.

Modern version of the popular Colonial style.

Figure 6–4

The two slopes of the gambrel roof identify this contemporary home as a Dutch Colonial style.

Figure 6–6

In the early to middle 1800s, Greek temples were the inspiration for a style called *Greek Revival* [6–8]. Although the historic examples are imposing, scaled-down versions of this style are available to today's homeowner [6–9]. Many variations of both historic and contemporary versions of popular styles exist. Greek Revivial homes may have the columns either on the gable end of the house as in previous illustrations or on the eave side [6–10 and 6–11]. Note also that in this second set of examples, a porch is supported at the second-floor level by the columns.

In the mid-1800s, homes patterned after the *Gothic* style began to appear in America. The Gothic style was popular in Europe, especially for cathedrals, during the 1200s through the 1500s [6–12]. This style is easily recognized by the pointed arches at windows. The style may be seen in a few historic examples in America [6–13], but it is not widely copied today. In the late 1800s two heavily detailed styles for homes became popular: first, the *Victorian* [6–14], followed by the *Queen Anne* [6–15]. Neither style lends itself to the economy-minded homeowner today. If these styles are copied today, it will be only for the more elaborate and expensive homes.

A style that did not have a popular "revival" period

A Colonial Revival (Dutch) example.

Figure 6–5 The Pearce-McAllister House, Denver, Colorado.

Federal style.

Figure 6–7 Ruggles House, Columbia Falls, Maine.

Architectural Design

Greek Revival style.

Figure 6–8 Harold Brooks Home, Marshall, Michigan.

A modern home building company's version of a Greek Revival home.

Figure 6–9

Historic example of the Greek Revival-style architecture.

Figure 6–10 The Wade House at Wade House State Park in Wisconsin.

A Greek Revival-style home being built today.

Figure 6–11

A Gothic cathedral in Cambridge, England.

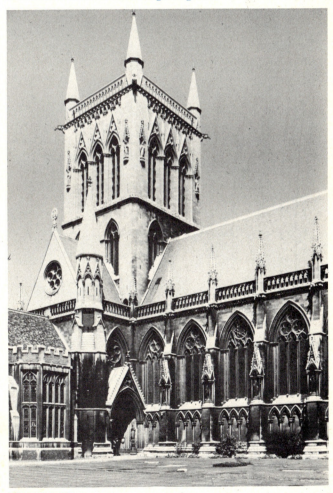

Figure 6–12

113

Gothic Revival-style house in Colorado.

Figure 6–13

A Queen Anne-style home in Key West, Florida.

Figure 6–15

Half-timber construction common in medieval Europe.

but has continued to be built over the years is patterned after European medieval half-timber construction [6–16]. In the original building, the timber elements held up the buildings while in today's examples they are non-structural decoration [6–17]. This style is often referred to as *Tudor*.

A relatively new style, and one which has its roots in America, is the *ranch* style [6–18]. The long, low, rambling, ranch style house reflects the nature of the great plains in the central United States and the relatively cheap land available in that area during the developing stages of this country. Low-cost land meant that it was economical to build "out" instead of "up" as people were forced to do in the more crowded East. Frank Lloyd Wright is given credit for laying the groundwork for the

Figure 6–16

Contemporary home with decorative elements resembling half-timber construction—often referred to as Tudor.

A Victorian-style home in Nevada, Missouri.

Figure 6–14

Figure 6–17

Architectural Design

A rectangular ranch style home.

Figure 6–18

ranch style house in his prairie houses, such as the Robie House [6–19 and 6–20].

Due to economic limitations and a shortage of craftsmen, the original character of a historic style is difficult to achieve in new construction. A compromise is often the result. The success of the appearance is left to the judgment of the individual viewer. Usually, for the untrained observer, the grander the scale, the more successful the design is adjudged to be. Designs with limited

An architectural rendering of the Robie House.

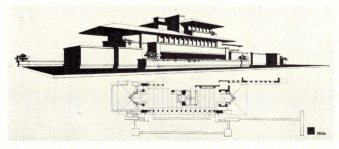

Figure 6–19

The Robie House, Chicago, 1909, designed by Frank Lloyd Wright . . . the style known as the "Prairie School" was created by Wright, used in several of his homes, and was copied by other architects . . . it is the forerunner of today's ranch style.

Figure 6–20 *A photograph of the Robie House.*

budgets, size, and sites often blend into the nondescript nature typical of many housing areas and are not noticed or appreciated.

Often a family wishes to live in a house that does not pretend to be of another era. They simply want a home with a character typical of a current style. Many styles are popular today. In some cases they vary with the part of the country in which they are located. Two-story styles are popular in highly populated areas with high land costs. As suggested earlier, the one-story or ranch style house is common in less populated areas with lower land costs. Both of these types and many others are mixed in all areas, as you can see by examining the styles of homes in the town in which you live.

6.2 Roofs

The character of a small building may be dominated by its roof [6–21]. Selection of a roof shape requires consideration of appearance, utility, and economic factors. A relatively inexpensive roof is the *flat* roof [6–22]. This configuration utilizes the least material and compared to other styles it goes into place quickly. The absence of attic space has two disadvantages. First is the loss of storage space, and the second is the lack of ventilation. Heat from the sun is more easily transferred to the interior of the house if there is no ventilated space to act as a buffer (such as an attic). The *shed* roof [6–23 and 6–24] is a popular contemporary roof. It uses slightly more material than the flat roof and gives the option of an attic or an exposed sloped ceiling in the space below. The acute angle between the wall and the upper part of the roof has a crisp, dynamic appearance.

The *gable*, probably the most common roof type, is least interesting when it has a relatively flat slope [6–25 and 6–26]. It may be constructed with either trusses or rafters and usually has an attic. In some contemporary applications, the attic is omitted to achieve a "cathedral" ceiling [6–27]. Its flexibility and widespread acceptance make it a popular choice for traditional and contemporary homes.

The *gambrel* roof provides the most headroom for attic bedroom space [6–28]. It also provides a small attic above the second-floor rooms that can be ventilated. The gambrel roof reduces the apparent scale of the house because (from the eave side) the home appears to be a one-story building. Since this roof has such a strong traditional identity, it is not common in contemporary styles. An exception is the church shown in [6–29].

The *hip* roof is popular for both contemporary and traditional applications [6–30 and 6–31]. Less siding material is used than for the gable, but the roof construction is slightly more complicated. Rafters are common in this type of roof. Trusses are possible, as well, but a greater variety of sizes and shapes are required than for the

The character of a small building may be dominated by its roof shape.

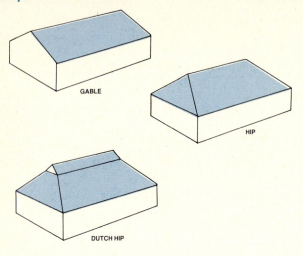

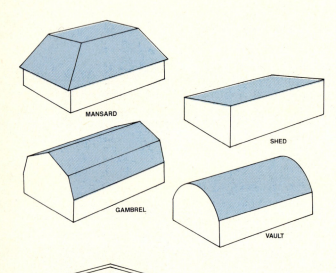

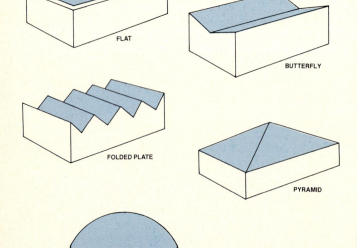

Figure 6–21

The horizontal nature of this roof is emphasized by the flat overhanging elements.

Figure 6–22

Shed roofs on a condominium project in Salt Lake City.

Figure 6–23

A shed roof can be used in combination with variations for increased interest.

Figure 6–24

116

A gable roof is more dynamic if the steepness of the slope is increased above the minimum for drainage.

Figure 6–25

A gable roof on a contemporary log house.

Figure 6–26

The A-frame shaped building is simply a steep gable roof carried down to the ground or close to it.

Figure 6–27

A gambrel-roofed home with a gable-roofed garage.

Figure 6–28

Carrying this otherwise traditional gambrel roof to the ground gives this church a contemporary appearance. The clerestory windows are another contemporary feature.

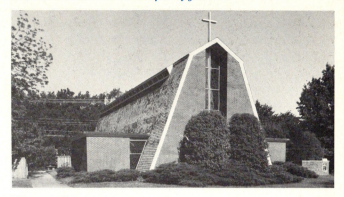

Figure 6–29

A hip roof on a traditional home.

Figure 6–30

A contemporary variation on a hip-roof. A vault with glass at its ends has replaced the ridge.

Figure 6–31

A mansard roof on a residence near Buras, Louisiana.

Figure 6–32

gable roof. Hip roofs typically have attics. Vents are easily installed at the eaves but are more difficult to locate at the ridge. A continuous ridge vent is possible, but it is noticeable and some may object to the interruption of the roof with this feature. A gable-like vent is possible if the *Dutch hip* variation is used [6–21].

The *mansard* roof [6–32] has an advantage similar to the gambrel roof in that it provides a great amount of space on the upper level for living space while giving the appearance of a one-story building. It has been popular for apartment buildings because it tends to lower the apparent height of the building while not reducing the rental space. Sometimes more than one floor is covered by a mansard roof [6–33]. Since the roof can be easily added to any flat-roofed building, it is now extensively used for small commercial structures. The widespread use of this roof has reduced its novelty, as is the case with any widely used feature. It has the additional disadvantage of requiring two types of maintenance because it has both built-up and shingle (or sheet metal) roofing.

Pyramid-shaped roofs are a variation on the hip roof. They are not common and therefore have the advantage of being unique [6–34 and 6–35]. Due to their special nature you can expect to pay a little more for their construction. Trusses are not likely choices due to the absence of an opportunity for repetition of the same shape and size. With the uniqueness of the shape, you probably would want to expose the framing from below, thus eliminating an attic.

Given a few basic shapes to work with, designers continue to search for variations to provide interest and excitement. The gable roof is the basis for a number of variations called *folded plate* roofs [6–36 to 6–38]. These variations tend to be applied to nonresidential buildings due to their scale. The economics of a residence may not allow such unique shapes nor do many homeowners wish to attract the attention that these roofs may receive in a residential neighborhood.

Vaults are not a common roof for residences but are

Several pyramid roofs with eaves extended so that each plane is a square rather than the more common triangle.

Figure 6–34

occasionally used [6–39]. They are more common in larger applications, such as apartments, condominiums, or commercial buildings [6–40]. They are more costly to build than roofs with straight lines and more difficult to waterproof. They do have the advantage of being interesting. The purely rounded *dome* is not a common residential roof in the United States, although it is found in religious buildings. The *geodesic dome*, however, has gained in popularity in the last few years [6–41]. This dome is made up of flat triangles. It has the advantage of enclosing a lot of space with a minimum of material. This is also important in reducing utility bills for heating and cooling. Two disadvantages are that some of the

Curved surfaces give this pyramid roof a unique character.

Variation on a mansard roof . . . three floors are covered by the roof, as evidenced by the windows.

Figure 6–33

Figure 6–35

Economy was achieved in this application of a folded plate roof on a school due to the repetition possible in the long building.

Figure 6–36

A hyperbolic paraboloid shaped roof adds interest and expense.

Figure 6–37

If the ridge lines of this folded plate roof were level, it would be a simple gable roof.

Figure 6–38

interior space has limited use due to reduced head room, and it is difficult to make this shape watertight.

It is a challenge for the designer to use traditional roofs in new and interesting ways. Upon occasion, however, existing forms may not meet the unique desire of the homeowner. Designers welcome the challenge of creating new shapes that are both interesting and functional [6–42].

Radial vaults on a country estate in Illinois.

Figure 6–39

The Kimball Museum in Fort Worth, Texas, designed by Louis Kahn has a series of vault-shaped roofs, although structurally they are not actually vaults.

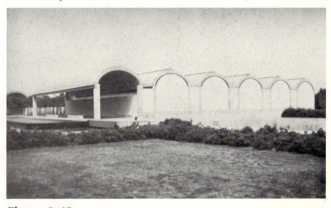

Figure 6–40

A geodesic-dome residence in Pennsylvania.

Figure 6–41

Aesthetic Considerations in Design

A unique vaulted dome having great height for a relatively small usable floor area.

Figure 6-42

South side view of the Herb Greene House. Although constructed in 1961, this house, designed by Herb Greene, Norman, Oklahoma, still appears somewhat futuristic . . . because it resembles no traditional style.

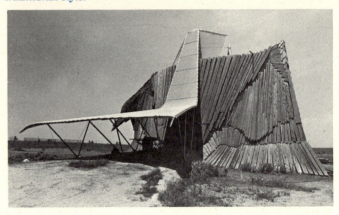

Figure 6-43A

North side view of the Herb Greene House.

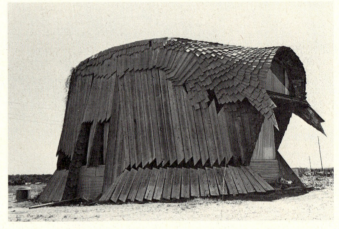

Figure 6-43B

6.3 Design Principles

Some families will want to live in a home whose appearance reflects only their own life-style and personality. In this case the architect will disregard historical and current stylistic influences. He or she will attempt to create a character reminiscent only of that of the owners [6-43A and 6-43B]. Since an individual's interpretation of what he perceives is affected by his own character, one can expect to find traces of the architect's personality in the buildings he designs. The home is, after all, a perception of the client's needs and desires. When the architect's personality is strongly reflected in his designs, you will find common traits in many of his buildings [6-20]. This is the first step in the emergence of a new style. Naturally, another necessary ingredient for such an evolvement is that the common traits be pleasing to the eye.

Regardless of historical, current, or personal design influences, an architect usually attempts to adhere to certain ageless design standards. Among these are unity, rhythm, balance, and proportion. These and others are usually included in many types of design, such as in furniture, graphics, household products, and many other man-made items. The study of these traits could consume several hundred pages. We will limit our discussion to a few comments on each.

A building that exhibits *unity* is one that repeats a theme. The theme may include shapes, materials, or more abstract concepts. A simple example would be the repetitive use of a circular shape in the floor plan, windows, and ornament [6-44 and 6-45].

Rhythm is a type of repetition also. If sizes and shapes reoccur in a consistent pattern, the building is said to have rhythm [6-46]. Repetition is not always successful in architecture or in music. Rhythm must be interesting and cleverly achieved. Sometimes subtlety enhances a rhythm. The use of the word "rhythm" is not accidental, in that architecture is often compared to music.

The characteristic of *balance* is easy to grasp. If a stack of blocks is unbalanced, it will collapse. If a building is not balanced in its appearance, the apparent tendency to collapse is unnerving and consciously or subconsciously renders the building unpleasant to view. Balance that is achieved by merely positioning equal shapes on each side of a center is not necessarily successful. Again,

An architectural rendering of the Guggenheim Museum.

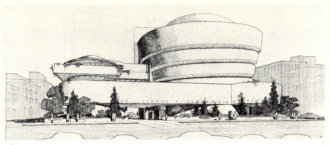

Figure 6–44

The Guggenheim Museum, 1943, New York, designed by Frank Lloyd Wright . . . note use of the circle to unify a building design . . . even the control joints in the sidewalk are circular.

Figure 6–45 *A photograph of the Guggenheim Museum.*

Note the periodic appearance of the various shapes. This facade exhibits the characteristic of rhythm.

Figure 6–46

A residence designed by Frank Lloyd Wright . . . an example of both visual and physical balance . . . horizontal light shapes are balanced against vertical, slightly darker shapes.

Figure 6–47 *An architectural rendering of Fallingwater House.*

Figure 6–48 *A photograph of Fallingwater House, 1937, Bear Run, Pennsylvania.*

subtlety and cleverness are important to achieve interest. Shapes of different size may achieve balance by their differing proximity to the center or by their differing visual impact due to their varied tones [6–47 and 6–48].

Proportion is the most difficult trait to define. Briefly, it is the comparison of a shape's length to its width.

We could determine the most pleasing proportions of a rectangle by taking a vote from a group of observers, but to prove that one proportion is more pleasing than another is more difficult. Some designers achieve pleasing proportions by deriving them from nature. The theory is that those shapes and sizes that occur in nature, including the human figure, must be acceptable to our senses since they are such a permanent part of ourselves and our environment [6–49]. Pleasing proportions are sometimes achieved by trial and error. The success of the selection of the pleasing proportions from those that are not will depend on the designer's sensitivity.

Le Corbusier developed a system of proportions based on the human figure called Le Modulor. Centre Le Corbusier, an exhibition hall in Zurich, Switzerland, was designed according to the system of proportions by Le Corbusier.

Figure 6–49

EXERCISES

6–1. Locate the following historical styles in your town:
- (a) Saltbox.
- (b) Colonial.
- (c) Dutch Colonial.
- (d) Federal.
- (e) Greek Revival.
- (f) Victorian.
- (g) Tudor.
- (h) Ranch.

List the identifying characteristics of each.

6–2. Locate a home in your town that seems to be of no identifiable style. List the similarities and differences with the historic styles in Exercise 6–1. Do you like this design? Why or why not?

6–3. Identify homes or buildings in your city that exhibit the characteristics of unity, rhythm, balance, and proportion. Draw a diagram of the building showing each trait. How would you improve each trait in the buildings that you have selected?

7 Functional Considerations in Design

7.1 Functional Requirements

Several functional principles are common to design regardless of the building type. Efficient circulation of people, for example, is almost always a goal. "Efficient" may be defined slightly differently in some cases. Usually it means that spaces are planned so that the minimum possible distance is traveled by the users of the building. In a store it means that customers move in a pattern that encourages them to buy the most goods. Generally, however, walking between work stations or rooms in a home is considered wasted time and also tiresome.

Every square foot of *hallway* beyond the absolute minimum adds unnecessary cost to the construction, monthly utility bills, and maintenance. Consequently, hallways and traffic paths through rooms should be kept to a minimum. The least useful hall is one with merely an opening at each end. A more useful hall is one with many additional doors and functions along the sides [7–1]. An ideal use of a hall in a home is to have it double as a room, such as a *laundry*. For example, if a washer and dryer are enclosed with a folding door on one side of a hall, the hall becomes a laundry room when the door is opened [7–2]. A *linen closet* opposite the laundry alcove is handy to the washer and dryer and further increases the usefulness of the hall.

Hallway space requirements can be reduced by the

In this office suite only about 3 feet of hallway wall is not used.

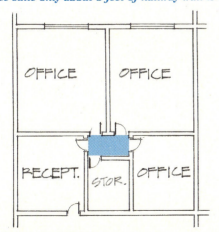

Figure 7–1

A hall can be designed to double as a room.

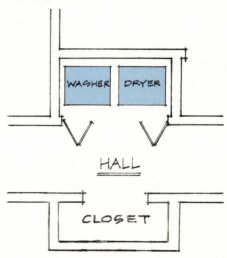

Figure 7–2

way adjoining rooms are oriented. When placing a room at the end of a hall, orienting the short dimension of the room perpendicular to the hall will reduce the length of the hall [7–3]. If the hall passes by a room, the length of the hall can be reduced by orienting the long dimension of the room perpendicular to the hall. When possible, plan the traffic pattern through a room so that it is perpendicular to the long dimension of the room [7–4]. In this way less of the room will be lost to traffic space.

Even if a hall cannot have double use, it may be useful as a visual extension to a room. If the requirements for privacy will allow it, remove one wall of a hall so that the adjacent room seems larger [7–5]. This may be possible more frequently in a home.

In a commercial building, a glass wall may be used between a room and a hall to give both the room and the hall a feeling of being larger. The apparent length of an office hallway may be reduced by orienting fluorescent light fixtures across the width of the hall [7–6]. If oriented lengthwise, the hall will appear longer.

Halls may serve as buffers between noisy and quiet spaces. By positioning a noisy room across a hall rather than adjacent to a quiet room, sound transmission to the quiet room will be reduced [7–7]. A short straight

123

Hallway size can be reduced by the way that adjoining rooms are oriented.

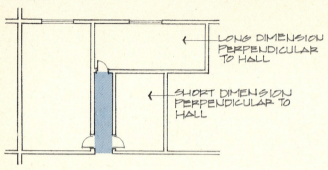

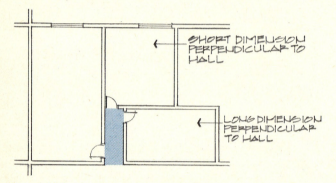

Figure 7–3

Incorporating a hall into a room increases apparent room size.

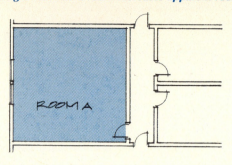

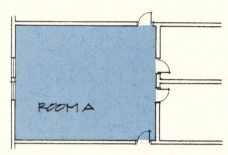

Figure 7–5

Plan efficient traffic patterns through a room.

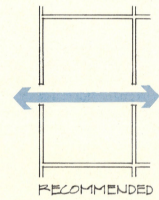

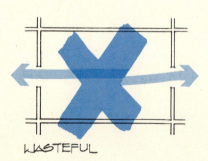

Figure 7–4

Light fixtures can be oriented to visually reduce the length of the hall . . .

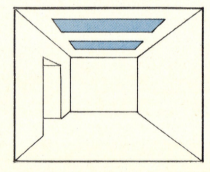

. . . or to accent the length of the hall.

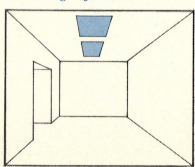

Figure 7–6

In this layout, noise must travel through two walls and an air space to get to quiet spaces.

Simple hall patterns are more efficient.

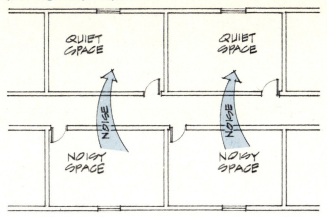

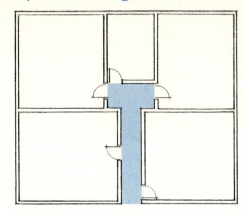

In this layout, noise travels through walls to adjacent quiet spaces.

Irregular hall shapes are inconvenient.

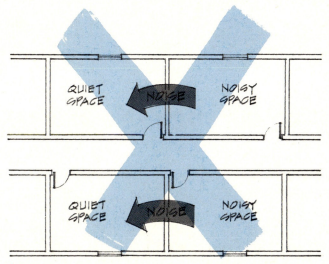

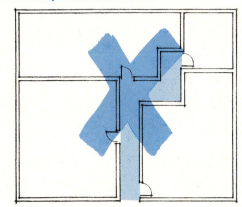

Figure 7–7

Figure 7–8

Even in the simplest of houses, there should be a distinction between private and public areas.

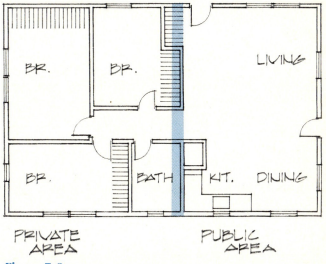

Figure 7–9

hall will keep the number of turns a person must negotiate to a minimum. If a hall must turn, keep the configuration simple [7–8]. Irregularly shaped halls are inconvenient to use. They may also be a sign of inefficiently planned rooms and unnecessarily complicated construction.

Another goal typical of both commercial and residential design is to separate private and public activities. In residential planning the distinction between the two is subtle since a home is a private building [7–9]. Living and dining areas are often used to receive visitors. The bedrooms, however, are not as public. This affects the placement of rooms so that non-residents of the home aren't forced to pass through the private area in the course of their visit. It may be desirable to provide a toilet for guests separate from the bathrooms serving

Functional Considerations in Design

the bedrooms. Both private and public areas may be in use at the same time, making their separation an important practical matter.

In businesses where there are areas for employees only, the separation between public and private use is easily accomplished. Walls and locked doors are clear barriers. In situations where limited public access to private areas is allowed, the design must provide for control of the access but not make it difficult. A receptionist can provide such control if the rooms are arranged properly [7–10]. The presence of a receptionist or secretary should be an implied physical barrier so that it is apparent that permission is required to pass.

The need for acoustical privacy may be met in a home with the same plan that provides physical privacy for the bedrooms. If the bedrooms are grouped together and separated from public areas, noise is less likely to be bothersome to those sleeping while activity continues elsewhere in the house. Acoustical privacy in commercial buildings is not usually solved by the private/public separation. The need for solving noise problems in nonresidential buildings ranges from little to very important. Some businesses do not generate noise, or at least the noise level in all spaces is about equal. Offices with few typewriters and no machines may simply need privacy for conversation [7–11]. Several business machines in use will require at least a separate closed room. The location of doors is also an important consideration in controlling noise [7–12].

Light manufacturing may need to be located at one end of a building while the office functions take place at the other. Heavy manufacturing may require a building separate from the offices.

An increasing part of a building's cost are the service components. If you can achieve other design goals while increasing the efficiency of the heating, air conditioning, electrical, and plumbing systems, it is obvious that you should do so. Since plumbing involves only certain rooms, the position of these rooms is important to reduce the cost of the plumbing system. Kitchens (or kitchenettes), toilets, and water heaters are common in many buildings. It is standard practice to try to bring these items together to reduce the cost of piping and the labor to install it [7–13]. Features such as drinking fountains, janitor's closets, and other commercial plumbing needs

Receptionist has control of access to all offices.

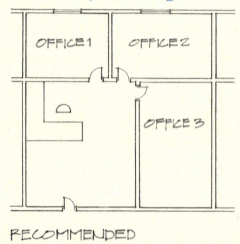

Receptionist has only limited control of access to offices 1 and 2 and almost no control of access to office 3.

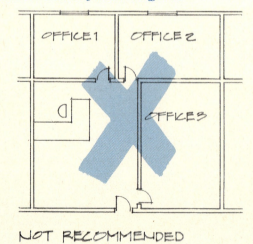

Figure 7–10

Running the partition all the way to the ceiling structure helps reduce sound transmission from room to room.

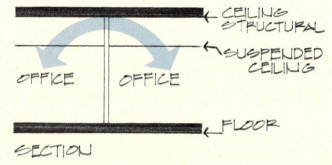

Sound can easily pass over a partition that stops at a suspended ceiling.

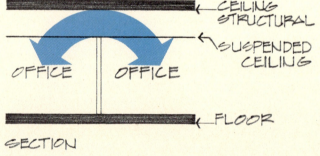

Figure 7–11

Staggering doors and increasing the space between them increases acoustical privacy.

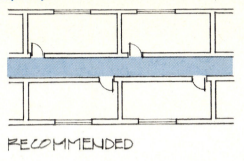

Alignment of doors across a hall reduces acoustical privacy.

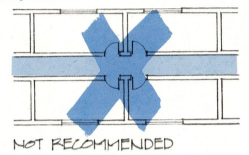

Figure 7–12

The rooms requiring plumbing are grouped together in this house plan to save plumbing costs.

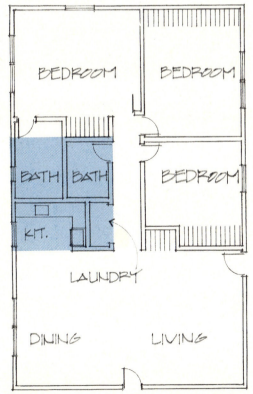

Figure 7–13

are, of course, included in this grouping when they are present. In multistory buildings, the stacking of rooms having plumbing is a standard procedure. The savings in a single small house may not be great, but that small savings multiplied by a hundred units in a subdivision or in an apartment building becomes significant.

In the discussion of general requirements thus far, we have seen that the solution to several goals has been the grouping together of functions that have something in common. These groupings are called *zones*. The process of identifying zones and planning a building in zones is an important technique in achieving efficiency of function in both residential and nonresidential design. Exploring in detail the appropriate zones and the relationships that exist between their functions for the great variety of commercial building types is beyond our scope here. However, we will study in detail the functional needs of a residence. The same approach to analyzing and arranging spaces may be applied to nonresidential design.

EXERCISES

7–1. Name several ways in which efficiency may be achieved in the planning of a building.

7–2. List the building types where achieving the minimum amount of circulation is not an appropriate goal.

7–3. Suggest functions that may be combined with a hallway to give it a "multipurpose" nature. List your own ideas in addition to those discussed in the text.

7–4. Study the room in which you are working to see if it could be redesigned to reduce circulation space. Draw a floor plan of the room showing furniture and proposed new locations for doors.

7–5. Look above a suspending ceiling in the building where you are working. Note which partitions extend to the structure above and which do not. Decide if it would be appropriate to extend some partitions all the way up to reduce noise transmission between rooms. It will be necessary to conduct noise experiments on opposite sides of such partitions and to ask the occupants of the rooms if they need more acoustical privacy.

7–6. Study the locations of doors and rooms in the building where you are working. Make a list of suggested rearrangement of room functions and doors if acoustical privacy needs improvement.

7–7. Study the hall pattern in your building. Do you think it could be simpler and more efficient? How?

7–8. Identify major zones in your building. Determine if similar functions are grouped together. How would you improve the arrangement of the existing functions into zones so that efficiency of circulation is improved?

7–9. Examine an office in your building that has a secretary or receptionist. Is there adequate control of access to adjacent private areas? How would you improve it?

7–10. Study the location of plumbing in your home. Can you suggest how the plumbing could have been grouped more tightly in the original design?

Functional Considerations in Design

7.2 Functional Requirements for a Residence

For average-size homes, there is little flexibility in planning the site. The lot may have access from one street or two, if located on a corner. Usually there is not enough land to do anything but run a straight driveway from the street to the front of the house, where the garage door must be located. Side-yard setback requirements may force the house to be located within a few feet of the center of the lot. Tradition or zoning ordinances may cause the house to be located the same distance (setback) from the street as neighboring homes. If enough land is available, some variations are possible [7–14]. Given a relatively fixed position for the "front" of the house, planning the interior for privacy and with respect to environmental influences can be more of a challenge.

The main entry to a home—the "front" door—is usually visible from the street so as to not confuse visitors. The family may use a secondary entry more often than the front door. An *entry foyer* is desirable at the front

The most common lot arrangement . . . the driveway goes directly from the street to the front of the house.

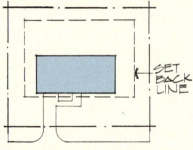

Figure 7–14A

If the lot is wide, the garage entrance may be on the end of the house.

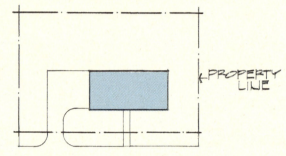

Figure 7–14B

A garage entrance in the rear of the house requires many turns.

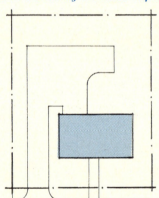

Figure 7–14C

A curved drive can eliminate having to back into the street.

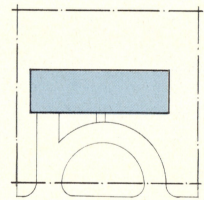

Figure 7–14D

A corner lot is more flexible. The garage entrance can face the side street.

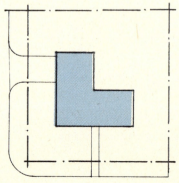

Figure 7–14E

The garage may be positioned in front of the house.

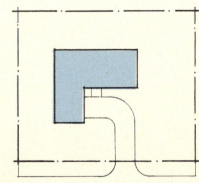

Figure 7–14F

door [7-15]. If space allows, the foyer may be an alcove located adjacent to the living room with a closet and a durable floor covering to accommodate wet shoes. Separation of the foyer increases the elegance of the living room and helps divert blasts of cold air from sweeping directly across the room. Even without a separate foyer, a closet near the front door is necessary. A depth of 2 feet and a width of 3 feet are minimum dimensions for the closet.

The *living room* is typically located in a position that makes it accessible to guests without their having to pass through or by more private parts of the house. Having the living room adjacent to the entry foyer accomplishes this. Although the living room is commonly located on the street side of the house [7-16, 7-19 and 7-20], other locations are popular [7-17 and 7-18]. A position on the back side of the house has the advantage of having a more quiet and private view. Observation of the childrens' play area may also be desirable for some families. Both positions are possible with a long room that runs across the floor plan from front to rear. The living room may be located on the second floor if adequate control of the front door is provided.

A few general design guidelines will help provide a living room that is efficient and flexible enough to allow a variety of furniture arrangements. Circulation through one end of a space will leave the majority of the area free for watching TV, conversation, and other activities [7-21A and 7-22]. At least 60 inches should be provided between facing seating and also between seating and a TV. Allow an open 24-inch space for circulation between furniture and an open 36 inches for main traffic ways. The living room typically accommodates the furniture shown in Table 7-1. Bookshelves may be desirable. If the home has a family room or study, the television and desk may not be needed in the living room. Always draw living room furniture to scale on the presentation plan to be sure that adequate wall space is provided

This one-story house has a large entry foyer with a half bath and closet.

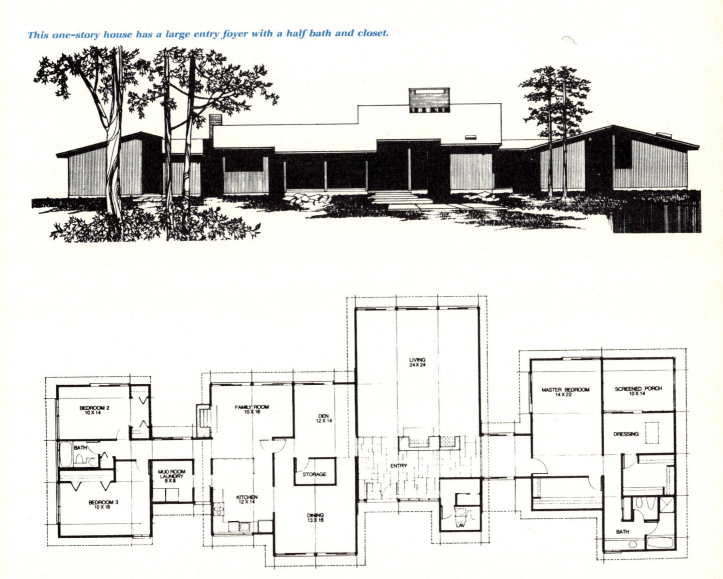

Figure 7-15

Functional Considerations in Design

The living room is commonly on the street side of the house.

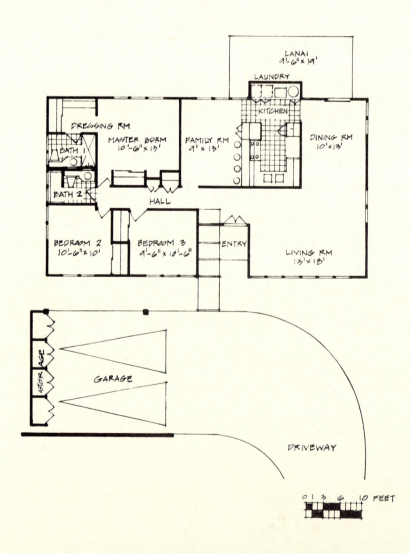

Figure 7–16

Some families prefer to have the living room overlook the backyard . . . the dining room may be a part of the living room.

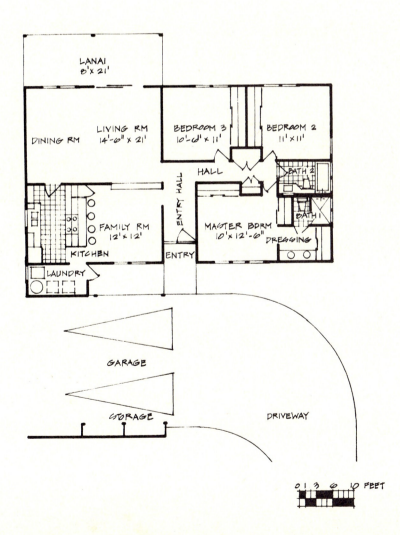

Figure 7–17

Another arrangement with the living room on the back side of the house . . . the dining room is adjacent.

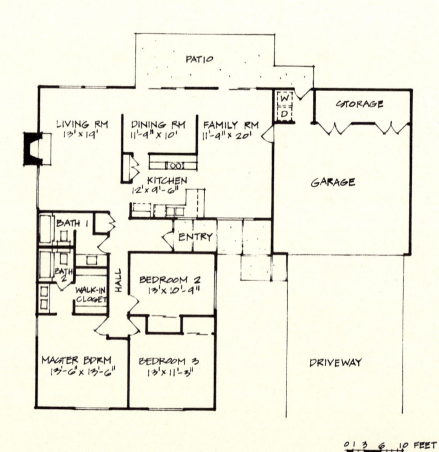

Figure 7-18

A family room should be adjacent to the kitchen.

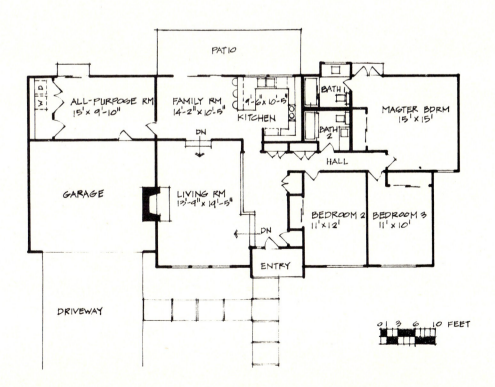

Figure 7–19

The dining room and kitchen must be adjacent.

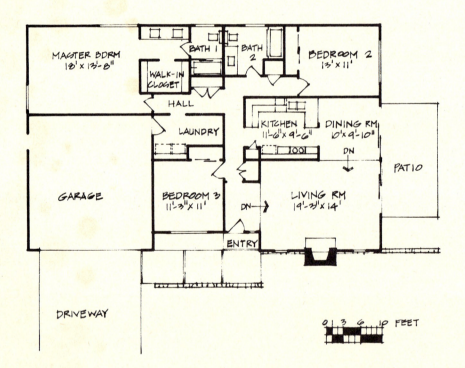

Figure 7–20

Through circulation and activities are separated.

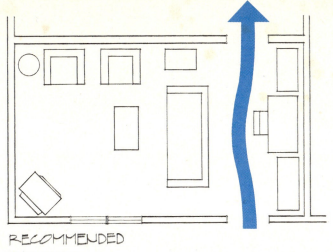

RECOMMENDED

Figure 7-21A

Circulation through the center of a room interrupts activities.

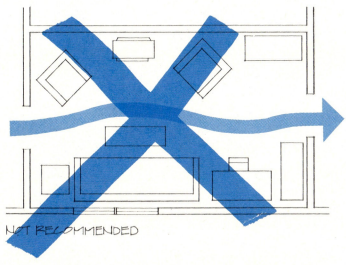

NOT RECOMMENDED

Figure 7-21B

for its placement. Although placing furniture in front of windows is a common practice, this makes opening the windows difficult. Remember that heat and air conditioning registers must not be blocked with furniture. Several living room layouts are shown in [7-23 to 7-26].

Table 7-1. Furniture for a Living Room

1	couch, 3'-0" × 6'-10"
2	easy chairs, 2'-6" × 3'-0" (3 for four or more bedroom homes)
1	desk, 1'-8" × 3'-6"
1	desk chair, 1'-6" × 1'-6"
1	television set, 1'-4" × 2'-8"
1	coffee table, 1'-6" × 2'-6"
2	end tables, 1'-6" × 2'-0"

SOURCE: Adapted from HUD Minimum Property Standards, 1973 ed.

For many years *family rooms* have been popular as second living rooms or dens. Design guidelines similar to those for living rooms apply. Family rooms tend to be less formal than living rooms since eating, TV watching, and recreation usually occur here. This frees the living room for quieter activities. The family room is adjacent to the kitchen [7-16 to 7-19]. This room might face the backyard while the living room faces the street [7-16 and 7-19]. Certainly, the reverse may be true if the family life-style so dictates [7-17].

The *dining room* often is located next to the living room since guests may be invited to dinner [7-18]. The dining area is also often included in the living room without a wall separating the two [7-17]. Whether combined with the living room or separate, the furniture shown in Table 7-2 should be accommodated in the dining room.

Table 7-2. Furniture for a Dining Room

Number of Bedrooms in the House	Number of Occupants	Size of Table
2	4	2'-6" × 3'-2"
3	6	3'-4" × 4'-0" or 4'-0" round
4 or more	8	3'-4" × 6'-0" or 4'-0" × 4'-0"

Dining chairs: 1'-4" × 1'-4"
China cabinet or buffet: 1'-6" × 5'-0" ±

SOURCE: Adapted from HUD Minimum Property Standards, 1973 ed.

The activities in a dining room have less variety than those in a living room. Eating is, of course, the main function. If there are other activities such as recreation, they will still most likely center around the dining table. Use of and access to the dining table then dictates the minimum dimensions of this room. Figure [7-27] suggests minimum clearances for the dining table. Several dining room layouts are shown in [7-28 to 7-30].

Since the kitchen serves the dining room, it is necessary to have these rooms adjacent [7-16 to 7-18 and 7-20]. There are many demands on the kitchen. If a family room is planned, the kitchen is usually nearby to serve lunch, dinner, or snacks while the family watches TV [7-16 to 7-19]. Groceries are usually brought into the kitchen from the garage or driveway where the car is parked [7-17]. This requires the kitchen be near one or both of these areas.

Much of the work done during the day occurs in the kitchen, especially if a laundry is combined with it [7-16 and 7-17]. The kitchen then becomes the control center for daily activities. Supervising childrens' play from the kitchen is often necessary. Therefore, it should be adjacent to indoor and outdoor play areas [7-19]. It

Functional Considerations in Design

In this split-level house circulation through the dining room is across the short dimension at one end.

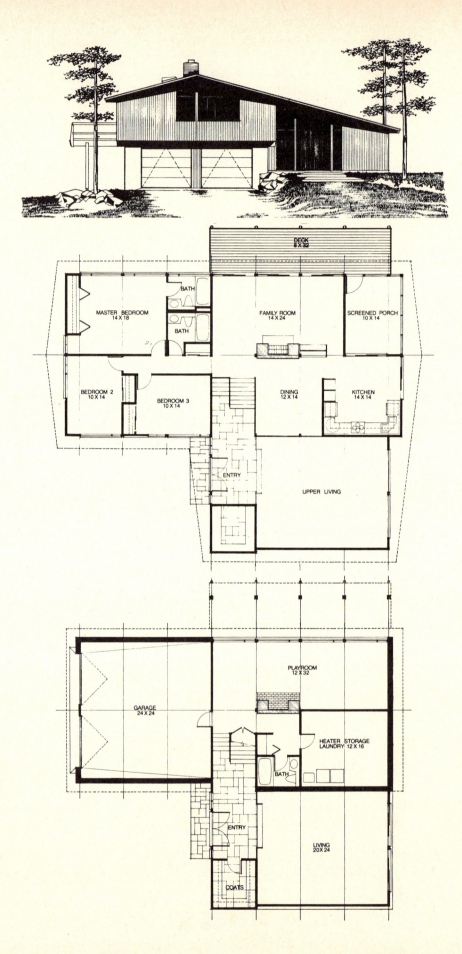

Figure 7-22

This dining space is open to adjacent areas of the home. Lack of privacy is offset by the appearance of a larger dining area due to the visual extension of the room.

Figure 7-23

An "outdoor" oriented living room. One entire wall is glass.

Figure 7-24

A traditional living room with an internal focus rather than an orientation to the outdoors.

Figure 7-25

A living space with the dining area adjacent.

Figure 7-26

Traffic across the short dimension of the room is preferred. Extra circulation is shown here to illustrate clearances.

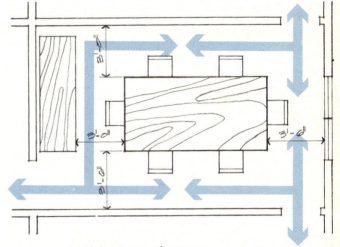

Figure 7-27 Dining Room Clearances.

is convenient to have visual control of the entry to the home so one can see who is coming to the front door. It must, of course, be close to any eating area, such as a breakfast nook or an outdoor eating space [7-19]. Some people prefer a sunlit kitchen in the morning, especially if a breakfast nook or breakfast bar is provided. This could be accomplished by having an east-facing window in this area. In an informal approach, the kitchen may be entirely open to the dining and living rooms [7-31].

The kitchen should be planned for minimum circulation. A guideline for controlling circulation is to keep the distance between the stove, sink, and refrigerator to a minimum of 12 and a maximum of 17 feet. The triangular path between these main work stations is

Functional Considerations in Design

Glass on two sides of the dining area give this space an outdoor orientation. The table is lighted in the evening with a globe pendant above.

Figure 7–28

This informal dining space is adjacent to an open kitchen. A light hangs close to the table from the high ceiling on a long pendant.

Figure 7–29

The view from this dining space is through a very special round window. Such a feature must be carefully coordinated with the exterior appearance of the home.

Figure 7–30

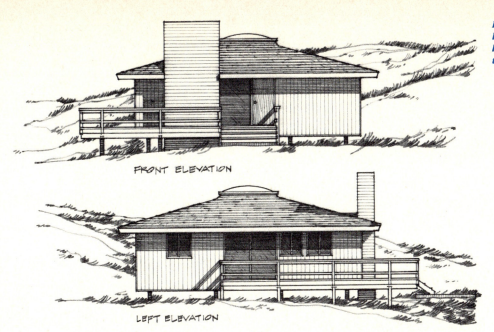

In this one-story square plan, the kitchen is at the geometric center of the house. It has no walls separating it from the dining and living room.

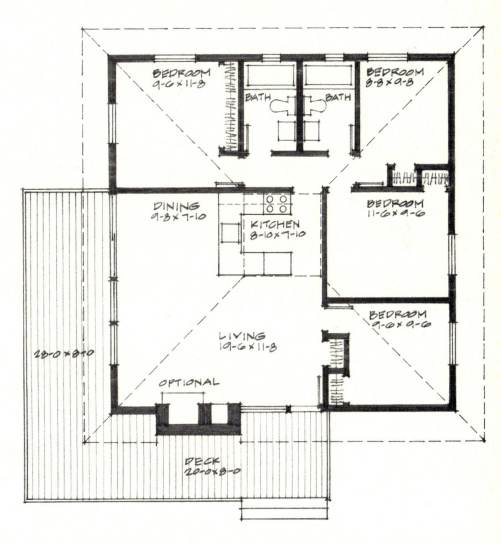

FLOOR PLAN

Figure 7–31

sometimes called the "work triangle" [7-32]. Do not locate the kitchen stove under a window. Also, avoid positioning a stove at the end of a counter. The lack of counter on the one side of the stove is an inconvenience and is also dangerous should a pot handle be bumped by a passerby.

Recommended kitchen storage space is shown in Table 7-3. Minimum countertop and appliance sizes are shown in Table 7-4. Several kitchen layouts are shown in [7-33 to 7-37]. Kitchen cabinets have certain dimensions that are standard, that is, height of counter and depth of cabinets. In most homes, the cabinets are prefabricated rather than custom-built. You may obtain available sizes from a cabinet manufacturer and select the units needed for your kitchen design. Prefabricated sink, refrigerator, stove, and cabinet units are available in metal for kitchenettes for offices and other nonresidential use [7-38].

Bedrooms have already been identified as belonging in a quiet and private zone of the house. Grouping them so that "public" and other daily traffic is not directed through this zone is standard procedure [7-17 to 7-19]. Persons who like to wake up in a sunlit room may want their bedroom on the east to receive the morning sun. A position away from the street side will result in a quieter room. In two-story homes the bedrooms are typically on the upper level for added privacy. Certainly, variations to this practice may be appropriate [7-39 and 7-40]. Bedrooms typically accommodate the furniture shown in Table 7-5.

All bedrooms should be designed so that there is an option of at least two walls against which to position

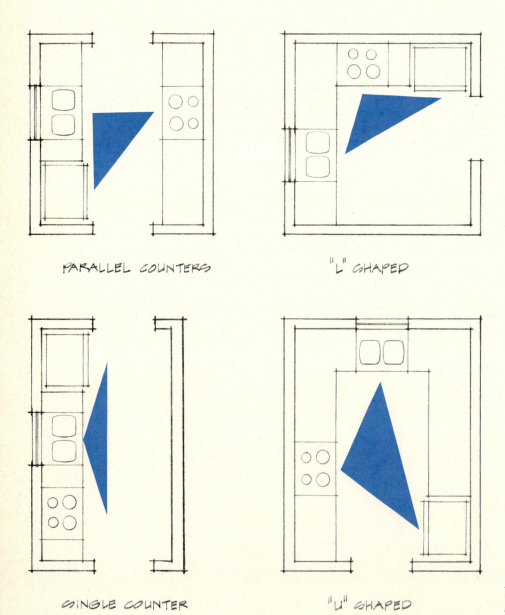

Figure 7-32

Four basic kitchen layouts showing work triangles. Larger kitchens may have more counter space and a table.

Table 7-3. Kitchen Storage Area (minimum ft^2)

Storage Location	Number of Bedrooms				
	0	1	2	3	4
Shelf area	24	30	38	44	50
Drawer area	4	6	8	10	12

SOURCE: HUD Minimum Property Standards, 1973 ed., April 1977 revision.

Table 7-4. Kitchen Counter Tops and Fixtures: Minimum Frontages (lineal in.)

Work Center	Number of Bedrooms				
	0	1	2	3	4
Sink	18	24	24	32	32
Counter top, each side	15	18	21	24	30
Range or cook-top space	21	21	24	30	30
Counter top, one side	15	18	21	24	30
Refrigerator space	30	30	36	36	36
Counter top, one side	15	15	15	15	18
Mixing counter top	21	30	36	36	42

SOURCE: HUD Minimum Property Standards, 1973 ed., April 1977 revision.

Table 7-5. Furniture for a Bedroom

Master Bedroom	Bedroom for Two	Bedroom for One
2 twin beds, 3'-3" × 6'-10" (this assures that any size double bed will fit)	1 double bed, 4'-6" × 6'-10"	1 twin bed, 3'-3" × 6'-10"
1 dresser, 1'-6" × 4'-4"	1 dresser, 1'-6" × 3'-6"	1 dresser, 1'-6" × 3'-6"
1 chair, 1'-6" × 1'-6"	1 chair, 1'-6" × 1'-6"	1 chair, 1'-6" × 1'-6"
2 night tables, 1'-0" × 1'-0"	2 night tables, 1'-0" × 1'-0"	1 night table, 1'-0" × 1'-0"

SOURCE: Adapted from HUD Minimum Property Standards, 1973 ed.

An L-shaped kitchen . . . the space above the upper cabinets provides shelf space for open storage.

Figure 7-34

This kitchen has parallel counters . . . space above the upper cabinets conceals indirect lighting.

Figure 7-33

A U-shaped kitchen with an island stove top . . . note built-in desk at the left and the "pass-through" opening in the wall.

Figure 7-35

An L-shaped kitchen with a sink island . . . note the lower eating counter that is a part of the island.

Figure 7–36

Natural light is brought into this kitchen with a large skylight . . . extensive use of plants is feasible with such lighting conditions.

Figure 7–37

Prefabricated sink, refrigerator, stove, and cabinet units are especially popular for offices and other nonresidential use.

Figure 7–38

With a site sloping to the rear, the more private floor may be on the lower level.

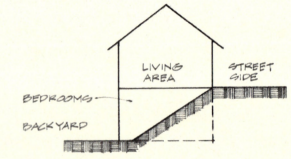

Figure 7–39

the bed [7–41]. This gives the family a chance to move the furniture periodically for variety. There should be space beside a double bed for a night table on each side or on one side for a single bed. Bedrooms for two people should have a closet space at least 2 feet deep and 5 feet wide. A bedroom for one person needs a closet 2 feet deep and at least 3 feet wide. All bedrooms need access to a bathroom without having to pass through

Architectural Design

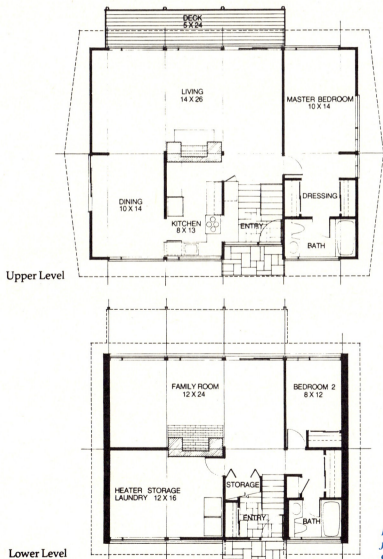

Upper Level

Lower Level

Entry into this home is halfway between the two floors . . . the living room and master bedroom are on the upper level, while the family room and a bedroom are on the lower level.

Figure 7–40

The bed may be placed in two locations ... a better design.

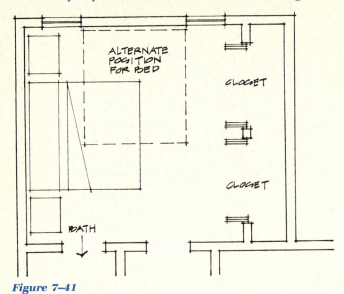

Figure 7–41

The bed may be placed in only one location ... not recommended.

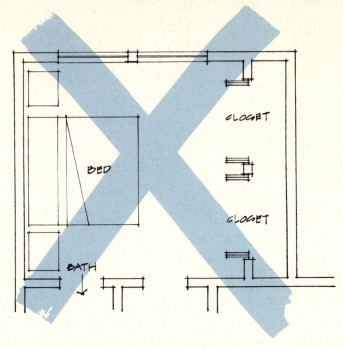

another room (except a hall). Do not plan the circulation so that one must pass through a bedroom to reach another room or so that the only path to the bedroom is through a bathroom. Several bedroom layouts are shown in [7–42 to 7–44].

If a choice is possible, some people like to have the morning sun in their *bathroom*. This of course requires the room to be on an east exterior wall and have a window. A skylight may be desirable for a bathroom with no exterior walls. If a home has only one bathroom, it is naturally associated with the bedrooms. It must be accessible from all bedrooms without having to pass through another bedroom. Positioning the bathroom next to a hall accomplishes this and makes it reasonably available for guests.

Having two bathrooms is popular in today's home. One may serve secondary bedrooms and guests from a hall while the other serves only the master bedroom [7–16 to 7–20]. The typical arrangement is to have these two bathrooms "back to back" so that the plumbing will be more economical. The wall between the bathrooms is thicker than other partitions because of the plumbing in the walls.

In larger homes a half bath may be provided for guests, leaving the two full baths for private use. A half bath has only a sink and a toilet and no bathtub. It would normally be located in the more public zone, such as near the dining room for washing hands before dinner. If the half bath is close to a backyard entrance, a small shower booth might be desirable, especially if a swimming pool is planned.

Provide a bathtub as well as a sink and a toilet in at least one bathroom. It is a good idea to make the bathtub a combination tub and shower. Typical bathtubs are 5 feet long and 2½ feet wide. The second bathroom may have a shower instead of a bathtub, if desired. One mistake often made by beginning designers is to make a shower stall too small. The minimum length of any side of a shower stall is 30 inches. Thirty-six inches is more comfortable.

Some typical bathroom layouts are shown in [7–45]. More spacious bathrooms are shown in [7–46 to 7–48].

A traditional bedroom in a contemporary "log" home ... this bedroom is large enough to provide seating for reading and dressing.

Figure 7–42

A study-oriented bedroom . . . bookshelves and a desk match the headboard/storage.

Figure 7–43

A storage-oriented bedroom . . . the dresser wraps around the room to become a headboard . . . lighting is provided above the counter top.

Figure 7–44

Typical bathroom layouts with interior dimensions.

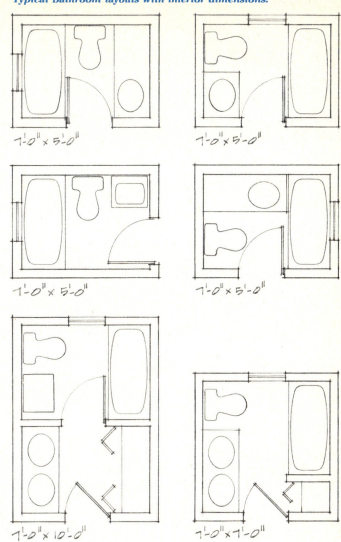

Figure 7–45

This all-ceramic tile bathroom has a large "bay window"-type shower . . . ample storage is provided for linens and toilet articles.

Figure 7–46

A *linen closet* should be provided near the bathrooms. This closet should have at least 10 square feet of shelf space for a two-bedroom house and 15 square feet for three or more bedrooms.

Provision should be made somewhere on the main floor of the house for a washing machine and a dryer. This may be desirable even in homes with basements to avoid carrying laundry up and down basement stairs. Although a typical washer and dryer will fit into a 3-foot by 5-foot space, it is sensible to allow extra room for counter space if the plan permits. The laundry alcove [7–2] or *laundry room* may be near the kitchen [7–16] for doing laundry while working in the kitchen or near the bedrooms [7–20] to reduce the distance that clothes must be carried.

Functional Considerations in Design

A dormer window brings light onto the oversize bathtub in this spacious bathroom . . . with the high humidity typical of bathrooms, plants are a natural and pleasing accessory.

This bathroom includes storage above the tub unit . . . a separate shower stall is adjacent . . . seating is provided at the vanity.

Figure 7–47

Figure 7–48

If no basement is provided, space must be planned for the furnace and water heater. The water heater will typically fit into a 2-foot by 2-foot closet, while a small furnace will fit into a 3-foot by 4-foot closet. The water heater should be located near the bathrooms. However, a central location for the furnace is usually most appropriate.

A two-car *garage* or a *carport* is almost always desirable in contemporary homes. The minimum size is 22'–0" × 22'–0" but additional space is desirable for storage and work space [7–16 to 7–18]. An additional 4 feet of length or width is recommended to accommodate a work counter and circulation space at the back or on one side. Direct access to the kitchen is recommended for carrying in groceries. If the site allows, placement of the garage on the north side of the house will allow it to act as a buffer against cold north winds in the winter. For southern regions, locating the garage or carport on the west side of the house will help insulate it from the hot summer sun.

With increased family needs and budget, a variety of miscellaneous rooms may be added to the basic group presented here. A sewing room, study, greenhouse, dressing room, utility room, basement, and recreation room are a few of the options. Extra storage is always in demand. These additional spaces vary in size and location according to their function. Minimum sizes for various areas have been discussed, but these should not limit you if the budget allows more space. Regardless of the size of any room, however, efficiency of circulation and functional layout of the space should be basic goals. A summary of minimum room sizes is shown in Table 7–6.

EXERCISES

7–11. Expand the list of important features for home design by adding subcategories to those already shown and adding any new major categories that you can think of.

Table 7–6. Minimum Room Sizes[a]

Name of Space	Minimum Area (ft^2)				Least Dimension
	LU with 1 BR	LU with 2 BR's	LU with 3 BR's	LU with 4 BR's	
LR	160	160	170	180	11'–0"
DR	80	80	95	110	8'–0"
BR (primary)	120	120	120	120	9'–4"
BR (secondary)	NA	80	80	80	8'–0"
Total area, BR's	120	200	280	380	—

[a] LU, living unit (home); BR, bedroom; LR, living room; DR, dining room; NA, not applicable.
SOURCE: HUD Minimum Property Standards, 1973 ed., May 1979 revision.

7-12. Make a list of the rooms and their sizes that your family would require in a new home. Identify any relationships between rooms that you believe are important.

7-13. Sketch the floor plan of your home. Identify activity zones and draw a line around them. How would you change the zone layout to meet your personal preferences? How do your zones differ from those of other members of the class?

Figures [7-16 to 7-20] are abbreviated floor plans and renderings of five separate homes. Complete the following exercises for these homes.

7-14. Which house has the greatest number of square feet of living space?

7-15. Which house has the least number of square feet of hallway?

7-16. In which house do you think the laundry is most conveniently located? Why?

7-17. Which kitchen do you like the best? Why?

7-18. Which house would you prefer to live in? Why?

7-19. Sketch the two elevations not seen in [7-20].

7-20. On sketch tracing paper revise the house plan in [7-20] to include a fourth bedroom and bring all bedrooms closer together in a more private zone.

8 Energy Conservation in Design

Now in houses with a south aspect, the sun's rays penetrate into the porticos in winter, but in the summer, the path of the sun is right over our heads and above the roof, so that there is shade. If then this is the best arrangement, we should build the south side loftier to get the winter sun and the north side lower to keep out the winter winds. To put it shortly, the house in which the owner can find a pleasant retreat at all seasons and can store his belongings safely is presumably at once the pleasantest and the most beautiful.
Socrates, in Xenophon's *Memorabilia*

8.1 Energy and Environment

In the 2500 years since Socrates gave us this architectural design advice, attention to the environment has found expression in many cultures—from the Persians to the Pueblos. Now we are experiencing a renaissance of these basic concepts which enable shelters to cooperate with nature rather than impose upon and dominate their environment.

Since the oil embargo in 1973 the United States has become more aware of our fragile national energy balance. We do not now produce enough fossil fuels in a usable form (oil, coal, natural gas) to supply our present and anticipated energy needs. It is impractical, for instance, with our present technology to operate an automobile on coal. This means that each of us must do what we can to conserve our own energy resources and reduce our dependence on foreign sources to supply our energy needs.

The auto is not the only wasteful consumer of our limited supply of fossil fuel. The homes that we live in, most of which were constructed in times of plentiful supplies of oil and gas, are also wasteful of energy resources. You can make a significant contribution to our national welfare through careful consideration of energy conservation.

Much of the energy waste from our homes results from a past indifference to the critical nature of our energy problems. Many homes are not properly insulated or ventilated. Others are not properly oriented to utilize available natural energy such as that from the sun or wind. Also, in the past homes have not made full use of available solar energy devices. These are all areas where the architectural designer can become involved and contribute to the enhancement of our standard of living and conservation of energy supplies.

Before examination of the more sophisticated considerations of the environment, let us look at some traditional guidelines. Bedrooms are often placed on the south side of the house where they receive more sunshine and are naturally warmer than other rooms. The reflected light that enters windows on the north side of a house is excellent for artwork, sewing, and other tasks that require good light without glare. Since the sun rises in the east, some like to have certain rooms positioned to receive the early morning sun. The bathroom, breakfast room, and even the bedroom for people who like a bright cheerful room in which to awake, can be located on the east to receive the first sunlight. Avoiding a western exposure for a picture window in the living room will reduce the load on the air conditioner in the summer and preserve drapes, carpeting, and furniture.

Seasonal breezes will usually come from the same direction in a given location. A home can be arranged with windows to force the breeze through the house, thus reducing the need for air conditioning [8–1]. However, windows need not be facing the breeze to ventilate a room. Large ventilated attics were once popular, and they still have the same cooling effect on a house today that they had years ago. Let us now examine more involved solutions to climate control. Recently, a revival of interest in controlling the sun's energy has been stimulated by architects and engineers.

8.2 Active Energy Systems

The sun is an unlimited source of energy [8–2]. Using solar energy from the sun to heat and cool homes has become an important architectural consideration. The use of this resource can be divided into two classifications—active and passive energy-producing and energy-conserving systems. *Active solar energy systems* utilize mechanical devices to recover, store, and deliver thermal energy. Some common solar energy collectors are the open flat collectors, the closed flat collector, and the closed circular parabolic collector.

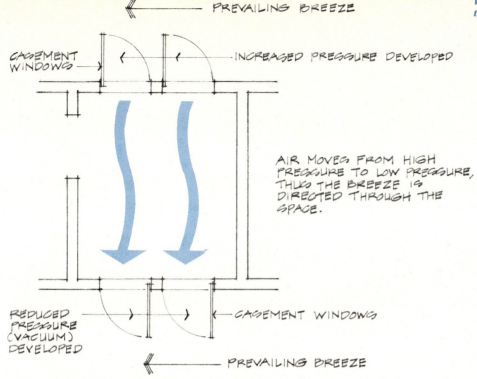

Windows can be arranged to force a breeze through a house.

Figure 8–1

Average exposure to the sun in the United States.

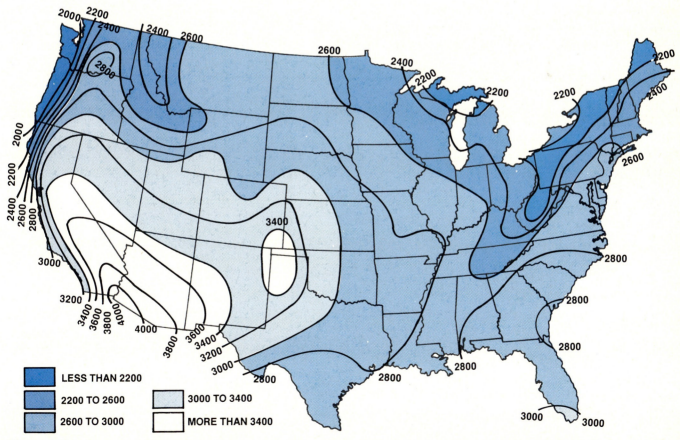

Figure 8–2

An open type flat solar energy collector.

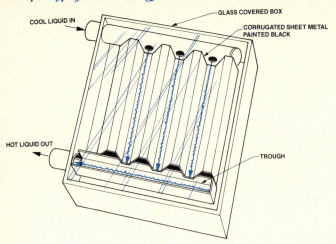

Figure 8–3

The *open flat collector* [8–3] is a reasonably simple mechanism. It can be built with relatively unsophisticated tools and components. Many have been built on the job and by the homeowner. Water or some other liquid is pumped to a position above a sloped corrugated sheet metal panel that is painted black. The liquid flows over the surface of the sheet metal that has become hot from exposure to the sunshine. The liquid gains heat from the metal and leaves the unit hotter than when it entered. It is then used to heat air or water for use in the building. The entire panel is covered with glass to keep out dust and leaves and to help concentrate the heat. Disadvantages of this system include evaporation of the liquid and the possibility of freezing of the liquid in the winter. If water is used to transport the heat energy in the open system, it is usually not routed back into the plumbing system for direct use in the home.

In the *closed flat collector* [8–4], water may be circulated and reused in the building. However, water is not the most efficient liquid to use. Generally antifreeze-type solutions are more popular. The liquid enters the collector in a tube at the top and flows back and forth downward through the tube. The zigzag shape of the tube increases the amount of metal that can be heated by the sun and consequently increases the amount of heat available to enter the liquid.

Flat collectors are usually fixed in a position that faces south. The exact position and angle (about 60° with the horizontal) varies with the geographic location of the building. Slightly different orientations are more efficient in different parts of the country.

Parabolic collectors [8–5 and 8–6] have the ability to concentrate intense solar energy on a line or a point. Relatively high temperatures can be achieved with these fairly simple systems. They may be stationary or they can be designed to "track" the sun. That is, they can move their orientation as the sun moves so as to always be in the most efficient position. Increased cost and more maintenance problems are the penalties for the higher efficiency of the parabolic systems.

The appearance of parabolic collectors is unmistakably technological. Unless a building is designed in a technological style, such systems may be identified by the viewer as an element that is aesthetically foreign in comparison with other building parts. Flat collectors are more easily blended with traditional and contemporary styles [8–7]. They are still noticeable but are rapidly becoming an accepted visual feature.

A careful study of available mechanical equipment must be made prior to selection of an active system. Active solar water heaters, for example, are available that can economically supply residential winter and summer hot water for most areas of the country. Other active solar energy systems and applications are available, but careful economic and engineering analyses should precede their use in the design of a structure. Consultation with a professional engineer familiar with solar systems is advised before attempting to select any active system. The engineer must size the system, select and design controls, and specify installation of freeze protection.

A closed type flat solar energy collector.

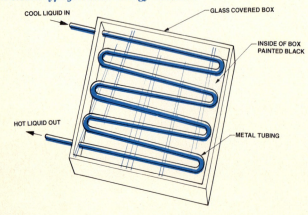

Figure 8–4

A linear parabolic solar energy collector . . . the sun's energy is concentrated by reflection on a tube containing moving liquid.

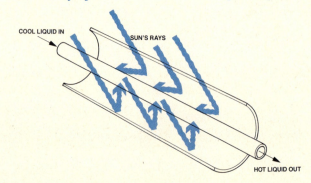

Figure 8–5

A circular parabolic solar energy collector . . . the sun's energy is concentrated on a point in a tube through which liquid passes.

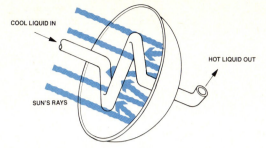

Figure 8–6

8.3 Passive Energy Systems

A *passive energy control system* is defined as one in which heat flows through or away from a building by natural means, enabling the system to operate without external power. Some climates are more suitable for passive systems than others; however, the designer must be very careful in applying design concepts to a particular climate. In some cases too much heat may be worse than not enough. Successful passive design requires skill and knowledge about the site's year-round climate. Such systems are relatively easy to design and apply. In many cases, however, they present difficulties that limit the production of exact results. In general, passive systems fall into four categories: (1) *insulation,* (2) *building orientation,* (3) *shading,* and (4) *infiltration control.* Each has some effect on the principal factors involved in heat loss or gain.

In the category of insulation, a primitive but still workable solution for stabilizing temperatures in a building is to surround it with earth [8–8 to 8–10]. Earth does not have high insulative value per unit thickness, but it is inexpensive. Therefore, large quantities at relatively

An active solar energy system . . . flat solar collectors are part of the roof of this contemporary home.

Figure 8–7

An earth-insulated dwelling used by pioneers wintering in Kansas.

Figure 8–8

An earth-sheltered building . . . the earth rises about halfway up the exterior wall.

Figure 8–9

This energy conserving design will require only about 35% of the energy needed for a traditional design.

Figure 8–10 A model of the Washington/Jefferson Elementary School, Walla Walla, Washington, an earth sheltered building.

Energy Conservation in Design

151

low cost may be used to increase the total insulative value. In [8–8], only the entry to this pioneer "dugout" is visible (or exposed to the elements). It is located in southeast Kansas, where it once served as the winter home of a family moving west. The 10-foot by 10-foot room with a 6-foot high ceiling has stone walls and a roof of logs covered with stone and earth.

Five or six feet down into the earth, the temperature is nearly constant (about 55°F). However, there is some variation in both depth and temperature in different parts of the country. A building recessed in the earth benefits from the earth's temperature in both summer and winter, since the earth is warmer than typical winter air and cooler than typical summer air. The effect is much like that of a cave, which is relatively warm in winter and cool in summer. You can get an idea of these temperature advantages by going into a basement when air conditioning is not being used in a home. The air in the basement will feel cooler than in the rooms of the floor above. Moisture problems must be solved in earth-sheltered rooms just as they must be with any basement. Leaks and condensation cause greater obstacles to the usability of an earth-sheltered office or living room than they would in the case of a basement, however, because of the types of activities taking place.

In the northern hemisphere a house should be oriented to take advantage of the low rays of the winter sun while excluding the high rays of the summer sun [8–11]. This arrangement will assist in warming the house during cold winter months. This means that where possible most of the windows should be located on the southern exposure to admit the heat-giving winter light rays. The entry of hot southern rays is reduced during the summer because the sun is at a higher angle during the hottest, middle part of the day. An overhang will also help reduce entry of the hot summer rays.

In addition, it is usually best to orient the longer sides of the house to the north and south. This will place the relatively narrow ends of the structure on the east and west ends of the building [8–12]. This orientation will assure maximum exposure to the warm rays of the southern sun to gain wintertime supplemental heat. It also reduces the impact of the hot rays of the western

Orient the house to maximize southern exposure for natural winter heating.

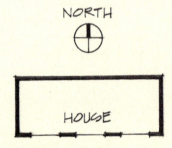

Figure 8–11

Orient the narrow ends of the house east and west for minimum wall exposure to the hot western sun in the summer.

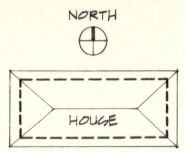

Figure 8–12

sun in the summer by confining them to minimal wall areas.

Consideration of orientation alone, however, is not sufficient. It must be combined with other passive systems to make it most effective. To cut down on unwanted summer heat gain, shading devices can be employed to exclude the summer rays. Shading is discussed later in Section 8.7, after taking a closer look at some aspects of heat gain.

EXERCISES

8–1. List several ways in which the rooms of a house may be oriented in consideration of the environment.

8–2. What is the difference between active and passive energy-conserving systems? Give an example of each.

8–3. What are the advantages and disadvantages of flat solar collectors compared to parabolic collectors?

8–4. Why are the surfaces of the flat solar collector painted black?

8–5. What are the advantages and problems of earth-sheltered buildings?

8–6. What is the best orientation in this hemisphere for a rectangular house?

Heat gain in passive solar energy systems falls into several general categories—direct gain, indirect gain, and isolated gain. Each of these three basic passive solar heat gain concepts have different relationships between the sun, the storage mass, and the living space.

8.4 Direct Gain Heating

In the *direct gain passive system* (sun to living space to storage mass), solar radiation passes through the living space before it strikes a surface, is converted to heat, and then stored in the thermal mass for longer-term heating [8–13 and 8–14].

The storage mass can be some building structure, such as concrete, brick, or stone. Or it could be, for example, containers of water. To avoid overheating in the summer,

Direct gain heating . . . solar energy enters the south-facing glass and is stored in the concrete floor and masonry walls in the winter.

An example of direct gain heating.

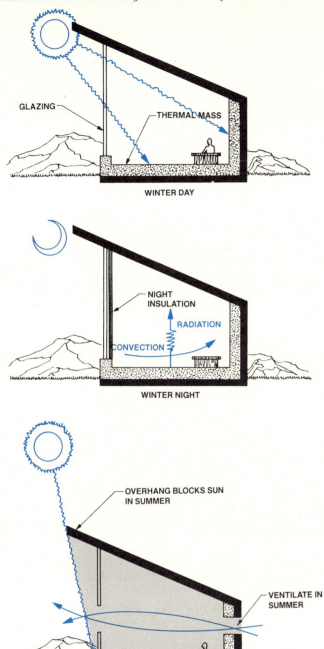

Figure 8–13

Figure 8–14 *Transit operations and maintenance facility, Chapel Hill, North Carolina.*

8.5 Indirect Gain Heating

In an *indirect gain passive system* (sun to storage mass to living space), a thermal mass collects and stores heat directly from the sun and then transfers the heat to the living space. The storage mass intercedes between the sun and the living space. The storage wall and the storage roof are two types of thermal masses used.

In the *storage wall* system, the thermal mass is placed directly behind the glazing [8–15]. After some time delay, depending on the material and thickness used, heat is transmitted through the wall by conduction. The heat is then distributed in the room by radiation and convection. By adding vents high and low in the wall, heat can also be supplied immediately to the space by convection.

In the storage wall system, the delivery of heat to the space is much more controllable than in a direct gain system. Delivery can be immediate through convection vents to satisfy the daytime loads or be delayed through conduction and reradiation from the wall's inside surface to meet nighttime loads. Glare, ultraviolet deterioration, and nighttime privacy are not problems with this system; but visual access to the outside is lost. To minimize overheating during the summer months, a storage wall must be shaded and vented to the outdoors.

The *storage roof* system is also referred to as a *roof pond*. The design concept is the same as for the storage wall except that the intercepting thermal mass is located in the roof of the building [8–16]. The thermal mass is usually water that is enclosed in plastic bags. Movable insulation is required to control heat gains and losses.

A storage roof is able to provide both heating and cooling. In the winter, the insulation is removed from above the roof during the day to absorb the sun's heat. The insulation covers the roof at night to prevent heat

exposed glass should be shaded by some means, for example, a roof overhang. To reduce winter heat losses, some type of movable insulation is recommended. Large glass areas can present special problems. Daytime glare, nighttime loss of privacy, and the degrading effects of ultraviolet light on fabrics, furniture, and artwork are special problems to consider in installing a direct gain system.

Energy Conservation in Design

Indirect gain heating with a storage wall . . . solar energy is stored first in a wall and then transmitted inside the house.

Indirect gain heating and cooling with a storage roof . . . energy is stored in the roof and then transmitted inside or outside.

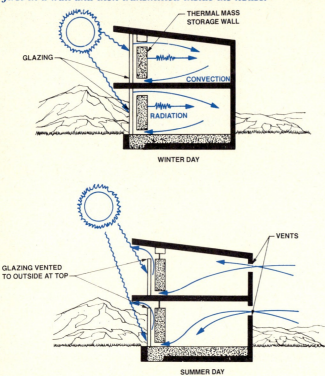

Figure 8–15

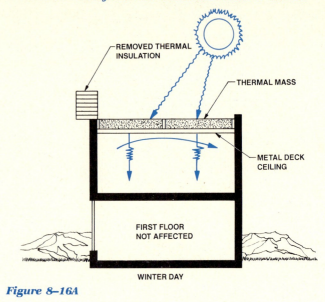

Figure 8–16A

Figure 8–16B

loss. The stored heat is then radiated into the house. In the summer, the insulation covers the roof during the day. Heat from inside the house is absorbed into the roof. At night the insulation is removed, allowing the stored heat to radiate to the cool night air.

The storage roof system has some advantages over a storage wall in that the thermal mass is evenly distributed over the floor area, thereby providing more evenly distributed heating and cooling. Also, wall openings can be located to take advantage of additional heat gains and desirable views. Some other problems exist, however. These concern the weight of the system on the structure and the mechanics of controlling the movement of the insulation in the morning and evening.

8.6 Isolated Gain Heating

The *isolated gain passive system* (sun to collector space to storage mass to living space) incorporates a collector storage component separate from the primary living spaces. Solar radiation is collected in an area separate from the building for transfer to a storage mass or for distribution to the living spaces. The attached sunspace and the thermosiphon are two types of isolated gain systems.

The *attached sunspace* is really a direct gain heating space with a south-sloping aperture [8–17 and 8–18]. It tempers the south wall of the primary living space. In the winter, the temperature in the sunspace floats over a fairly large range. In the summer, overheating is partially controlled by venting. Plants are often grown in the sunspace in the same manner as in a greenhouse. If this is done, thermal storage must be included in the sunspace to keep the temperatures from dropping below freezing.

An attached sunspace provides a relatively inexpensive additional living space that is usable much of the year. In most areas of the country, food can be grown all the year long. Thermal control, primarily by shading and natural ventilation, is critical to reduce overheating in the summer. Often, the hot air from the top of the space will be drawn by a fan through ducts to a rockbed

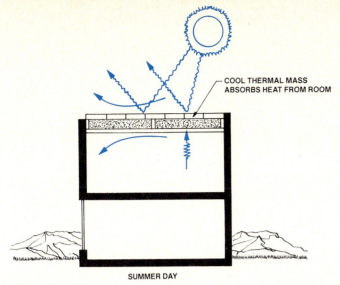

Figure 8–16C

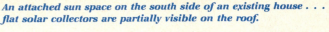

An attached sun space on the south side of an existing house . . . flat solar collectors are partially visible on the roof.

Figure 8–18

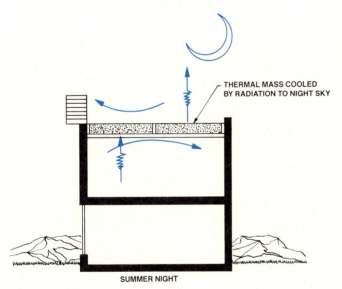

Figure 8–16D

Isolated gain heating using an attached sunspace . . . solar energy heats a collector space first and is then stored or distributed.

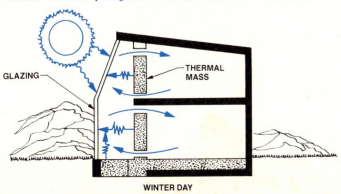

Figure 8–17

storage and back to the sunspace. This will improve the system's efficiency and reduce overheating.

In the *thermosiphon isolated gain system*, the natural convection of a fluid—either a liquid or air—is induced by using a flat plate collector [8–19]. To successfully collect and store energy, the design of the system can vary only slightly.

To allow the heated fluid to rise up into storage, the storage container must be located either at the same height or above the top of the collector. The driving force of the system is the difference in density between the fluid in the collector (hotter and lighter) and the fluid in storage (warm and slightly heavier). The velocity of flow is a function of this difference in density.

The storage can be thermally isolated or connected to the living space. Dampers or valves can be used to control the flow. In an air system, heat may be supplied directly to the space or to storage. In a water system, a method of preventing freezing must be provided.

EXERCISES

8–7. Name three categories of passive solar heating systems and very briefly outline their basic operating principles.

8–8. What are the advantages and disadvantages of direct gain heating systems as compared to indirect gain heating?

8–9. How can a "greenhouse" contribute to the energy efficiency of a house?

8.7 Energy Conservation through the Use of Shading

The control of sunlight is a very important consideration in energy conservation. The sun's rays can be controlled by shading to either heat or to prevent the heating of

Energy Conservation in Design

155

Isolated gain heating using a thermosiphon ... the sun heats a fluid passing over a flat plate collector and causes it to rise into a heat collector.

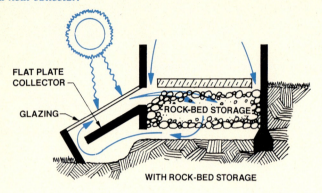

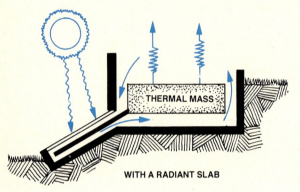

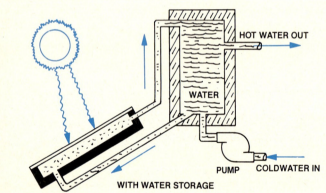

Figure 8–19

Knowledge of the sun's altitude angle is essential to effective shading.

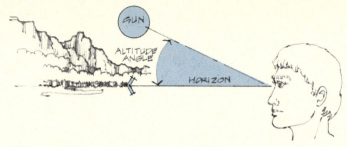

Figure 8–20

temperate zone of the United States. In the temperate zone, sunshine is desired during the late fall and winter. Usually, the shading device is designed to admit sun between September 21 and March 21. It is designed to omit sun between 9 A.M. and 3 P.M. (when the sun is most intense) between March 21 and September 21. For other than south-oriented glass, and for other climate zones, the student is encouraged to do further research on shading devices.

The following definitions are important in understanding shading devices:

Solar altitude: the angle between the rays of the sun and a horizontal plane [8–20].
Solar azimuth: the angle of the sun from true south [8–21].
Angle of incidence: the angle between the sun's rays and a normal (90°) to the window.
Normal to the window: a line perpendicular (90°) to the plane of the window.
Profile angle: the angle between a normal to the window and the component of the sun's rays that acts in a plane perpendicular to the window plane.

Solar azimuth is the angle of the sun from true south.

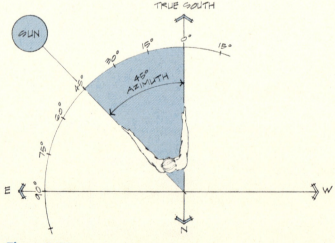

Figure 8–21

certain areas. To do this effectively, you should know the variations in sun angles that will occur during the year [8–20].

The design of shading devices must be based on the specific geographic location and climate in question. Sunlight can strike all four sides of a structure, but for most cases you will only need to be concerned with the south, east, and west orientations. Glass with a south exposure is the simplest to deal with, since you can use a horizontal overhang. However, southeast, southwest, east, and west orientations are difficult to shade when the sun is low in the sky.

In this section we will examine the simplest case of south-facing glass using a horizontal overhang in the

156

Architectural Design

Overhang: a roof extension or other horizontal device above a window to intercept the rays of the sun (or to provide protection from the elements, or for aesthetic reasons).

Figure [8–22] will help visualize some of the above definitions. Angle *HIJ* is the true solar altitude angle. *H* and *A* are two points on the edge of an overhang. Line *CB* is a normal to the window, and line *AB* represents the direction of the component of the sun's rays that acts in a plane perpendicular to the window plane. *ABC* is the profile angle. The profile angle must be determined in order to compute the position and dimensions of a shading device.

Tables 8–1 to 8–4 give solar data, including altitude, azimuth, and profile angles for the various times of day on the twenty-first day of each month at different latitudes (24°, 32°, 40°, and 48° north latitude). The general compass directions marked at the tops and bottoms of the profile and incidence angle columns indicate the direction in which the vertical surface of a building faces. Note that, for example, the angles for a north by northeast (NNE) facing are the same as for a north by northwest (NNW) facing. You should also note as you read across the table that for a particular solar A.M. time, there is a comparable P.M. time. For example, the angles for 7 A.M. on December 21 at 24° north latitude (Table 8–1) are the same as those for 5 P.M. on the same day. Afternoon times are read along the right-hand column with respective orientations along the bottom of the chart.

Let us consider a typical case. Assume that a building is located at 40° north latitude. Using the appropriate sun angle (Table 8–3) for this latitude, evaluate the effect of the sun and suggest shading devices that may be employed to compensate for it. Note that a house facing due south at latitude 40° will have a profile angle of

The profile angle is the angle between a normal to the window and the component of the sun's rays that acts in a plane perpendicular to the window plane.

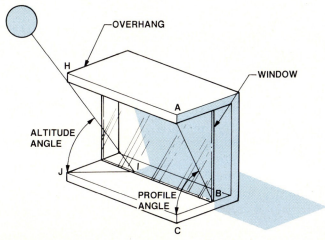

Figure 8–22

Maximum and minimum profile angles on December 21 at 40° north latitude . . . the sun provides useful warmth.

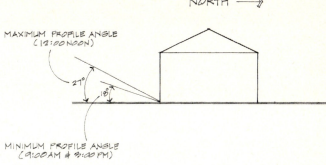

Figure 8–23

27° at 12 noon on December 21. It will have a profile angle of 18° at either 9 A.M. or 3 P.M. In this example the date of December 21 was chosen because that is the day in winter that the sun assumes its lowest position in the sky. The effect of this information can be seen in diagrammatic form on an elevation of a house [8–23]. This will help assess the amount of useful solar energy that can be reasonably expected between 9 A.M. and 3 P.M. in midwinter.

During the winter it is important to determine the height of useful window area that will allow the maximum desired natural heating effect from the sun. For example, let us choose a typical 8-foot-high south-facing wall with a 4-foot overhang and predict the maximum effective window height [8–24]. Don't forget to include the overhang in the silhouette drawing. By drawing the maximum and minimum profile angles through the edge of the overhang, the extent to which the sun's rays will enter the house can be readily seen. The maximum effective window height can be measured where the 18° line intersects the wall.

Winter heating is not the only consideration you will

Maximum effective window height on December 21 at 40° north latitude.

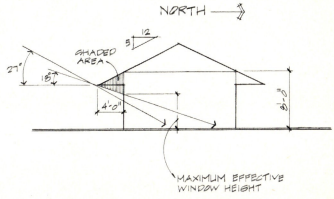

Figure 8–24

Energy Conservation in Design

157

Table 8–1. Solar Position and Related Angles for 24° North Latitude for the 21st Day of Each Month

Date	Solar Time A.M.	Solar Position Alt.	Az.	N	NNE	NE	ENE	E	ESE	SE	SSE	S	SSW	SW	WSW	Solar Time P.M.
Dec.	7	3	63			10	5	4	3	3	4	7	33			5
	8	15	55			56	26	18	15	15	18	25	52			4
	9	26	46			88	50	34	52							3
		34	34				74	51	39	35	35	39	51	74		2
	11	40	18					70	53	44	40	42	48	62	85	1
	12	43	0					90	67	52	45	43	45	52	67	12
Jan. and Nov.	7	5	66			13	7	5	5	5	7	11	69			5
	8	17	58			53	27	20	17	17	20	30	62			4
	9	28	49			83	50	35	29	28	31	39	59			3
	10	37	36				73	52	42	38	38	43	56	79		2
	11	44	20					71	55	47	44	45	52	66	87	1
	12	46	0					90	70	56	48	46	48	56	70	12
Feb. and Oct.	7	9	74		55	18	11	9	9	10	14	30				5
	8	22	66			48	30	24	22	23	29	45	87			4
	9	34	57			73	50	39	34	35	39	51	75			3
	10	45	44				70	55	47	45	46	54	68	88		2
	11	52	25				88	72	60	54	52	55	62	75		1
	12	55	0					90	75	64	57	55	57	64	75	12
Mar. and Sept.	7	14	84		41	21	16	14	14	17	27	66				5
	8	27	77		73	44	32	28	27	31	41	66				4
	9	40	68		90	65	50	42	40	43	50	66				3
	10	52	55			82	68	58	53	53	57	66	80			2
	11	62	33				84	74	66	62	62	66	73	84		1
	12	66	0					90	80	73	68	66	68	73	80	12
Apr. and Aug.	6	5	101	24	9	6	5	5	6	8	22					6
	7	18	95	76	36	23	19	18	20	27	47					5
	8	32	89		60	42	34	32	34	41	57	88				4
	9	46	82		76	60	50	46	47	52	64	82				3
	10	59	72		87	75	65	60	59	62	69	79				2
	11	71	52			88	81	75	72	71	73	78	85			1
	12	78	0					90	85	81	79	78	79	81	85	12
May and July	6	8	108	24	12	9	8	8	11	17	63					6
	7	21	103	59	34	24	21	22	26	36	67					5
	8	35	98	78	53	41	35	35	39	49	71					4
	9	48	94	87	69	56	50	48	51	59	74					3
	10	62	88		80	70	64	62	63	69	77	89				2
	11	76	77		88	82	78	76	76	78	81	87				1
	12	86	0					90	88	87	86	86	86	87	88	12
June	6	9	112	24	13	10	9	10	13	22	85					6
	7	22	107	55	33	25	22	23	28	41	76					5
	8	36	103	73	51	40	36	36	41	53	76					4
	9	49	99	82	66	55	50	49	53	63	78					3
	10	63	95	87	77	68	64	63	65	72	81					2
	11	76	91	90	84	80	77	76	77	80	85					1
	12	89	0					90	90	90	89	89	89	90	90	12
	A.M.			N	NNW	NW	WNW	W	WSW	SW	SSW	S	SSE	SE	ESE	P.M.

Table 8–2. Solar Position and Related Angles for 32° North Latitude for the 21st Day of Each Month

Date	Solar Time A.M.	Solar Position Alt.	Az.	N	NNE	NE	ENE	E	ESE	SE	SSE	S	SSW	SW	WSW	Solar Time P.M.
Dec.	8	10	54			50	19	13	11	10	12	17	37			4
	9	20	44				45	28	22	20	21	26	42	86		3
	10	28	31				74	45	33	28	28	31	41	65		2
	11	33	16					66	46	36	33	34	40	53	81	1
	12	35	0					90	61	44	37	35	37	44	61	12
Jan. and Nov.	7	1	65			4	2	2	1	2	2	3	32			5
	8	13	56			48	22	15	13	13	15	22	49			4
	9	22	46			88	46	30	24	22	24	31	48			3
	10	31	33				73	47	36	31	31	35	46	71		2
	11	36	18					68	49	39	36	37	44	58	83	1
	12	38	0					90	64	48	40	38	40	48	64	12
Feb. and Oct.	7	7	73		52	14	9	7	7	8	10	22				5
	8	18	64			46	27	20	19	19	24	37	79			4
	9	29	53			76	48	35	30	30	33	43	66			3
	10	38	39				70	52	42	39	40	46	59	82		2
	11	45	21					70	55	47	45	47	54	68	89	1
	12	47	0					90	70	57	49	47	49	57	70	12
Mar. and Sept.	7	13	82		42	21	15	13	13	16	24	58				5
	8	25	73		78	45	31	26	25	28	36	58				4
	9	37	62			69	50	40	37	38	44	58	83			3
	10	47	47			88	69	56	49	47	50	58	72			2
	11	55	27				87	72	62	56	55	58	65	78		1
	12	58	0					90	77	66	60	58	60	66	77	12
Apr. and Aug.	6	6	100	32	11	7	6	6	7	11	26					6
	7	19	92	84	39	25	20	19	20	27	44					5
	8	31	84		65	44	35	32	33	38	52	80				4
	9	44	74		83	63	51	45	44	48	57	74				3
	10	56	60			80	67	59	56	57	62	71	85			2
	11	65	37				83	74	68	66	66	70	77	87		1
	12	70	0					90	82	75	71	70	71	75	82	12
May and July	6	10	107	32	16	12	10	11	13	22	63					6
	7	23	100	67	38	27	23	23	27	36	63					5
	8	35	93	86	59	44	37	35	38	47	65					4
	9	48	85		75	60	52	48	49	55	67	85				3
	10	61	73		87	75	66	62	61	64	70	81				2
	11	72	52			88	81	76	73	72	74	79	85			1
	12	78	0					90	85	81	79	78	79	81	85	12
June	5	1	118	1	1	1	1	1	1	2						7
	6	12	110	32	18	13	12	13	16	27	79					6
	7	24	103	63	38	28	25	25	29	41	71					5
	8	37	97	81	57	44	38	37	41	50	70					4
	9	50	89		72	59	52	50	52	59	72	90				3
	10	62	80		84	73	66	63	63	67	74	85				2
	11	74	61			86	80	76	74	75	78	82	88			1
	12	81	0					90	87	84	82	81	82	84	87	12
	A.M.			N	NNW	NW	WNW	W	WSW	SW	SSW	S	SSE	SE	ESE	P.M.

Table 8-3. Solar Position and Related Angles for 40° North Latitude for the 21st Day of Each Month

Date	Solar Time A.M.	Solar Position Alt.	Az.	N	NNE	NE	ENE	E	ESE	SE	SSE	S	SSW	SW	WSW	Solar Time P.M.
Dec.	8	5	53			35	11	7	6	6	6	9	21			4
	9	14	42				37	20	15	14	15	18	30	78		3
	10	21	29				72	38	26	21	21	23	31	54		2
	11	25	15					61	37	28	25	26	31	43	75	1
	12	27	0					90	53	35	28	27	28	35	53	12
Jan. and	8	8	55			38	15	10	8	8	10	14	34			4
Nov.	9	17	44				40	24	18	17	18	23	37	87		3
	10	24	31				72	41	29	24	24	27	36	61		2
	11	28	16					63	41	32	29	29	35	48	78	1
	12	30	0					90	56	39	32	30	32	39	56	12
Feb. and	7	4	72		43	9	6	4	4	5	7	14				5
Oct.	8	15	62			43	23	17	15	15	19	29	69			4
	9	24	50			80	45	31	25	24	27	35	56			3
	10	32	35				70	47	36	32	33	38	50	75		2
	11	37	19					67	49	40	37	39	45	60	85	1
	12	39	0					90	65	49	41	39	41	49	65	12
Mar. and	7	11	80		43	13	13	12	12	14	21	50				5
Sept.	8	23	70		85	45	29	24	23	25	31	50				4
	9	33	57			72	48	37	33	33	38	50	75			3
	10	42	42				69	53	45	42	43	50	64	87		2
	11	48	23				90	71	57	50	48	50	57	71		1
	12	50	0					90	72	59	52	50	52	59	72	12
Apr. and	6	7	99	40	14	9	8	8	9	12	29					6
Aug.	7	19	89		42	26	20	19	20	26	41	88				5
	8	30	79		71	46	35	31	31	35	47	72				4
	9	41	67			67	51	44	41	43	51	66	90			3
	10	51	51			85	69	58	52	51	55	63	77			2
	11	59	29				86	73	64	60	59	62	69	81		1
	12	62	0					90	78	69	63	62	63	69	78	12
May and	5	2	115	5	3	2	2	2	3	6						7
July	6	13	106	40	20	15	13	13	16	25	62					6
	7	24	97	75	42	30	25	24	27	36	58					5
	8	35	87		65	47	38	35	37	44	59	86				4
	9	47	76		82	64	53	48	47	51	61	77				3
	10	57	61			80	68	61	58	58	63	73	86			2
	11	66	37				84	75	69	66	67	71	77	87		1
	12	70	0					90	82	76	71	70	71	76	82	12
June	5	4	117	9	6	4	4	5	7	14						7
	6	15	108	40	22	16	15	16	19	31	75					6
	7	26	100	71	42	31	27	26	30	40	66					5
	8	37	91	89	63	47	39	37	40	48	64					4
	9	49	80		79	63	54	49	50	54	65	82				3
	10	60	66			78	68	62	60	61	67	77	89			2
	11	69	42				83	76	71	69	70	74	81	89		1
	12	73	0					90	84	78	75	73	75	78	84	12
	A.M.			N	NNW	NW	WNW	W	WSW	SW	SSW	S	SSE	SE	ESE	P.M.

Table 8–4. Solar Position and Related Angles for 48° North Latitude for the 21st Day of Each Month

Date	Solar Time A.M.	Solar Position Alt.	Solar Position Az.	N	NNE	NE	ENE	E	ESE	SE	SSE	S	SSW	SW	WSW	Solar Time P.M.
Dec.	8	1	53			5	1	1	1	1	1	1	2			4
	9	8	41				24	12	9	8	8	10	17	63		3
	10	14	28				68	27	17	14	14	15	21	40		2
	11	17	14					51	27	20	17	18	21	31	66	1
	12	19	20					90	41	25	20	19	20	25	41	12
Jan. and	8	3	55		20	6	4	4	4	4	6	15				4
Nov.	9	11	43			29	16	12	11	12	15	25	78			3
	10	17	29			68	32	21	17	17	19	26	48			2
	11	21	15				55	32	24	21	21	25	37	71		1
	12	22	0				90	47	30	24	22	24	30	47		12
Feb. and	7	2	72	23	4	2	2	2	2	3	6					5
Oct.	8	11	60		37	18	13	11	11	14	21	56				4
	9	19	47		83	39	25	20	19	21	27	45				3
	10	25	33			69	41	30	26	26	30	40	66			2
	11	30	17				63	42	33	30	31	36	51	81		1
	12	31	0				90	58	41	33	31	33	41	58		12
Mar. and	7	10	79	42	18	12	10	10	12	18	42					5
Sept.	8	20	67		44	27	21	20	21	26	42	88				4
	9	28	53		75	46	34	29	28	32	42	66				3
	10	35	38			70	49	39	36	36	42	55	80			2
	11	40	20				68	52	43	40	42	49	63	87		1
	12	42	0				90	67	52	44	42	44	52	67		12
Apr. and	6	9	98	48	17	11	9	9	10	14	31					6
Aug.	7	19	87	46	27	20	19	20	24	38	80					5
	8	29	75	77	47	34	29	29	32	42	64					4
	9	38	61		70	51	42	38	39	45	58	82				3
	10	46	45			70	56	48	46	48	55	69	90			2
	11	51	24			89	72	60	53	52	54	61	74			1
	12	54	0				90	74	62	56	54	56	62	74		12
May and	5	5	114	13	7	6	5	6	8	15						7
July	6	15	104	48	24	17	15	15	18	27	60					6
	7	25	93	83	47	32	26	25	27	34	54					5
	8	35	82		71	49	39	35	35	41	53	78				4
	9	44	68		89	68	54	46	44	47	54	69				3
	10	53	51			85	70	60	54	53	57	65	78			2
	11	59	29				86	74	65	61	60	63	70	81		1
	12	62	0				90	78	69	64	62	64	69	78		12
June	5	8	117	17	10	8	8	9	12	24						7
	6	17	106	48	26	19	17	18	22	33	70					6
	7	27	96	79	47	33	28	27	30	39	61					5
	8	37	85		69	50	41	37	38	44	58	83				4
	9	47	72		86	67	55	48	47	50	58	74				3
	10	56	55			83	70	61	56	56	60	69	81			2
	11	63	31				86	75	67	63	63	66	73	83		1
	12	65	0				90	80	72	67	65	67	72	80		12
	A.M.			N	NNW	NW	WNW	W	WSW	SW	SSW	S	SSE	SE	ESE	P.M.

want to take into account. During the warmer months it will be necessary to block the sun's rays. If we want to start admitting sunlight through the windows on September 21 and to stop its entrance on March 21, the overhang and the window sill height must be designed to do this. It so happens that the sun is in the same position in the sky on these two dates. These dates are known as the *equinoxes*. From Table 8–3 we see that the profile angle at 40° north latitude for a south-facing wall at 9 A.M. and 3 P.M. is 50° on those dates.

Either the length of the overhang or the height of the windowsill must be adjusted so that the sun just touches the bottom of the glass at 9 A.M. and 3 P.M. on the equinoxes. As an example, if the overhang is kept at 4 feet, what window sill height will just block the sun at the equinoxes? By graphical solution in [8–25], after plotting the 50° profile angle, we see that the bottom of the window sill must be at 1'—6" above floor height.

During the hot summer months in addition to blocking the sun's rays from passing through the windows, the entire wall should be shielded from the rays. To do this we should check the sun angle tables for June 21. This is the day when the sun reaches its highest point in the sky. For a south-facing wall at 40° north latitude, the profile angle is 73° at 12 noon and 82° at 9 A.M. and 3 P.M. (Table 8–3). The 4-foot overhang used in the design for the equinoxes completely shades the wall when the sun is higher during the summer months [8–26].

By combining the information from both summer and winter sun angle consideration, you can intelligently plan window heights and overhangs to provide maximum use of the sun in winter while providing shading to exclude the hot rays of the summer sun. In [8–27] we can see that the dimensions determined in the preceding examples will provide adequate protection against summer sun intrusion while allowing winter sun warmth to enter the window area.

While sun angle tables can help predict direct sun infiltration at various locations, dates, and times of day, they do not show the effect of glare. Exclusion of glare is an important factor in sun control. Glare effects and methods of control are shown in [8–28]. These diagrams also show a number of sun control devices that may be employed to control direct sun intrusion. Using these devices (in addition to varying the overhang), you have considerable flexibility in controlling the solar effects on a home.

One of the most common and successful methods of solar control is to use the natural shade provided by trees and shrubbery. The diagrams [8–28] show how simply a tree can be used to control solar intrusion. By proper selection and planting, trees can be extremely good solar control devices, as well as making the landscape more attractive. It is common to consider the use of *deciduous* trees (those that lose their leaves in winter) for this use. During the summer they can provide effective shading, and in winter, without leaves, the sun can filter into the home through the bare branches.

Maximum and minimum profile angles on June 21 at 40° north latitude . . . an overhang is needed to shade the wall.

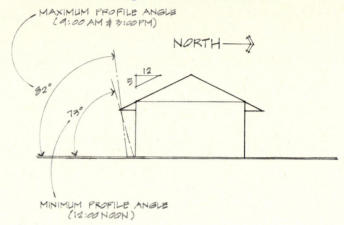

Figure 8–26

Windowsill height required to block the sun's rays at the equinoxes.

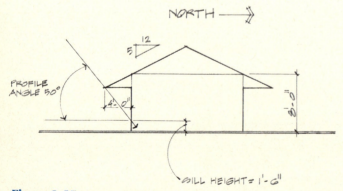

Figure 8–25

Planning for maximum winter, equinox, and summer sun produces an effective all-year design.

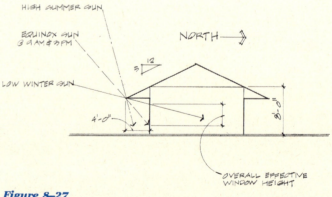

Figure 8–27

EXERCISES

8–10. Assume that you are at 48° north latitude. Determine the sun angle at 1 P.M. on July 21. What would the sun angle be on October 21?

8–11. If a house facing directly south at 24° north latitude has a 2-foot overhang, how far below the overhang will the wall be shaded at 3 P.M. on April 21?

8–12. Assume that the house in [7–16] has a flowerbed on the south wall that is located on the ground and extends outward 1 foot from the wall of the house. On June 21 at 2 P.M., does the sunlight strike the bed? If not, how far from the outer edge of the bed is the direct sunlight?

8–13. A flat-roofed house faces directly south. The bottom of the overhang is 8 feet above the ground. The top of a 5-foot high window is 7 feet above the ground. At 12 noon on June 21 at 40° north latitude, how far must the overhang project to completely shade the window?

8.8 An Energy Design Case Study

Solving isolated problems in energy conservation is only half the problem that must be faced by the building designer. You must be able to assemble the various principles and components into a whole so that the result is a building that meets functional and aesthetic as well as energy needs. The following is a case study of a housing system based on such a synthesis [8–29].

The most important feature in this system is the conservatory sunspace [8–30]. While this room is an attractive environment for living, it also functions as the house's primary heating system. The solar collector consists of sloped and vertical windows oriented to the south to receive maximum winter heat and sunlight. Two-story walls of brick thermal mass in the conservatory and a remote rockbed under the kitchen floor absorb heat during the day and release it slowly at night, providing free solar heat long after sunset. The amount of mass has been carefully sized with the help of computer analysis to keep temperatures from dropping too low on winter nights. No "backup" heating is required for the conservatory. To keep the conservatory from overheating, a control sensor near the roof peak monitors the temperature of the space and determines whether to send excess heat to the rockbed for storage in winter or to exhaust it outdoors in summer.

Prime living spaces are arranged along the south side of the design to take best advantage of direct warmth, daylight, and view through properly oriented windows. An added benefit is that the key living areas are coordinated with the conservatory. Sliding glass doors in shared walls expand visual space and allow easy access— both on the ground level and from overlook balconies upstairs. These doors can be opened to allow the warmth, soothing humidity, and the flower fragrance to flow freely from the conservatory into adjacent spaces.

Secondary areas—entry, baths, laundry, stairs, and hallways—are designed along the north wall, where severe winter winds and virtually no solar gain mandate few windows in the exterior wall. Since less time is spent in these areas, lower temperatures and reduced natural light pose no inconvenience. The garage is also located on the north to serve as an added thermal buffer. The low, continuous profile of the garage roof aerodynamically deflects air currents up and over the house to give wind protection as well.

The room layout offers spatial zoning. The segregation of living areas not only assures privacy for adults and children, but also offers the option of closing off areas during extreme periods of heat and cold. If no children or guests are home, some of the bedrooms can be isolated from the conditioned space for all or part of the winter.

A family room in the plan offers supplemental space for recreation, home office, or guest accommodations. In addition to zoning benefits, this provides pleasing variation in architectural space and feeling. It is a cozy niche that complements the more open areas and serves as a natural retreat for intimate conversations and quiet moods.

Consideration has been given to a wide range of environmental factors—the seasonal sun angles, prevailing winds, soil temperatures, and natural convection patterns. The most important factor is the seasonal path of the sun [8–31]. In summer it travels high in the sky, but in winter it is low along the southern horizon. This simple phenomenon, all but forgotten in the era of cheap energy, is the key to passive solar heating. Accordingly, our energy-efficient house design offers broad expanses of south-facing windows to collect the winter sunlight without overheating in summer.

When short-wave radiation in the form of sunlight passes through clear glass, it is transformed to long-wave radiation, or heat, as soon as it touches a solid object. This occurs when sunlight strikes the brick wall or tile floor of the conservatory. Since glass will not readily transmit long-wave radiation, the heat "manufactured" in the conservatory stays in the conservatory, and is available for immediate circulation or storage. Strategically placed sliding glass doors in the conservatory can be opened to allow warm air to flow freely into living spaces and bedrooms.

Because the conservatory will generate more heat than the house requires during the day, thermal mass has been incorporated into the design [8–32]. Masonry's conductivity gives it the ability to absorb heat, and its density allows it to hold a substantial amount of heat for later release. Some heat is absorbed directly into the tile floor and brick wall of the conservatory to prevent daytime temperature extremes within this space. The rest of the heat, rising naturally to the peak of the two-story conservatory, is channeled to a remote rockbed under the kitchen, family, or living room. At night, stored heat

Figure 8-28 Sun control.

DIAGRAM		A EXCLUDES DIRECT SUN RAYS	B RE-RADIATES HEAT	C CONTROLS SKY GLARE	D CONTROLS GROUND GLARE & HEAT	E EFFECTIVE ORIENTATION	F RESTRICTS VIEW	G HINDERS FREE AIR MOVEMENT	H CONTROLS WINTER RAYS	I MAINTENANCE (NOT CLEANING)
1. OVERHANG	Length of overhang calculated to eliminate summer sun.	Seasonal	No	No	No	South	No	Yes	Yes	Minimum unless otherwise noted
2. VERTICAL SCREEN (WITH OVERHANG)	Length of louver calculated to eliminate summer sun. Length of louver for sky glare dependent on amount of control desired on exterior conditions and occupants normal eye level.	Optional: Completely or seasonal.	Minimal	Yes	Some—amount varies with design.	Any direction. depends on design.	Yes— If opaque blade in louver. No— if tinted glass blade.	Slight	Depends on design	High for louver.
3. VERTICAL SCREEN (WITHOUT OVERHANG)	Length of louver or glass panel calculated to eliminate summer sun. Length of louver for sky glare dependent on amount of control desired on exterior conditions and occupants normal eye level.	Optional: Completely or seasonal.	Minimal	Yes	Some—amount varies with design.	Any direction. depends on design.	Yes— If opaque blade in louver. No— if tinted glass blade.	No— if louvers. Yes— if glass panel unless vent slats are provided.	Depends on design	Low for glazing
4. ADJUSTABLE EXTERIOR HORIZONTAL LOUVERS	Louvers can be adjusted to control direct rays of sun.	Optional	Minimal	No	Yes	Any direction. South is least restrictive to view.	Yes	No	Depends on design	Varies—depending on scale and materials used.
5A. OVERHANG VERTICALLY LOUVERED	Length of overhang calculated to eliminate summer sun.	Seasonal	No	Yes	No	South	No	No	Yes	Varies—depends on material used.
5B. OVERHANG ANGLE LOUVERED	Length of overhang and pitch of louvers calculated to eliminate summer sun and permit winter rays full penetration.	Seasonal	No	No	No	No	No	No	Yes—with louvers as shown, can permit maximum winter sun if desired.	Varies—depends on material used.
6. EXTERIOR VERTICAL LOUVERED	If fixed louvers can be set so as to eliminate low angle sun rays for predetermined orientation. If operable, maximum control any orientation but with various amount of view interference.	Optional: Completely or seasonal depending on orientation or other factors.	Minimal	Some	Some	East or west, south with adequate overhang.	Yes	No	Depends on design	Moderate
		As desired.	Minimal	Can be good see J	Some	Any	Yes	No	Yes	High
7. SPEC. GLAZING (GLASS, PLASTIC, COATED GLASS)	Heat absorbing glazing controls solar heat gain. Heat absorbing and low transmission glazing controls heat gain and sky glare. Sandwich of glass and fixed louvers can control direct sun rays and sky glare and admits greater amounts of useful daylight.	No—reduces—depending on glazing material.	Can be substantial unless double glazing used.	Yes—ideal if darker sheets used in upper portion of window.	Yes	Any	No	See K	Yes—more than others	Low
		Seasonal	Low to minimal.	Yes	Same	Any	Yes	See K	Less than 7A	Low

164

J EFFECT ON INTERIOR LIGHTING	K CAUTIONS	L VARIATIONS
Harsh without ideal exterior conditions, or with no glare control in glass or interior control devices.	Tends to trap warm air. High sash if open may let heat into building.	Overhang with light & heat transmission glass. Overhang with open framing with removable material (fabric, fiber glass). Trellis with plant material—permits entry of winter sun. Fixed awning—similar characteristics, except maintenance is high. Operable awning—also similar, plus lower sun angle control (west), restricts view when down.
Good	Check clearance for operating sash and window cleaning.	Addition of vertical member may be used to cut off low angle oblique rays. Adjustable vertical blinds or awnings afford good control for low sun, or glare from beach or water, without permanent restriction of view. Maintenance is high.
Good	Check clearance for operating sash and window cleaning.	Addition of vertical member may be used to cut off low angle oblique rays. Adjustable vertical blinds or awnings afford good control for low sun, or glare from beach or water, without permanent restriction of view. Maintenance is high.
Good—could be used for darkening device.		Exterior operating shutters have similar characteristics, and can be opened when not required but with loss of sky glare control.
Diffused reflected light from louvers improves quality of daylighting by reducing contrast between interior ceiling and bright sky.		Egg crate overhang instead of louvers to control oblique sun rays. Adjustable louvered awnings (questionable in cold climates) require high maintenance.
Diffused reflected light from louvers improves quality of daylighting by reducing contrast between interior ceiling and bright sky.		Egg crate overhang instead of louvers to control oblique sun rays. Adjustable louvered awnings (questionable in cold climates) require high maintenance.
Varies depending on position in room.	Check clearance for operating sash and window cleaning.	Narrow windows with adequate side reveals or projecting blades have similar sun and glare control.
Good—if a limited view is acceptable.		When used with adequate overhang on south will eliminate all sun in summer months.
Good (see C) w/high levels of artificial light, interior visual comfort is improved as reduces contrast between work surfaces and window area. Good—combine w/7A for ideal sky glare control w/a restricting eye level view.	Open sash may defeat sun & glare control, but is appropriate for a/c buildings. Replacement delay is probable. Open sash may defeat sun & glare control, but is appropriate for a/c buildings.	Allow only storm sash to be tinted to eliminate problem noted under B. Louvered screen placed in front of glazing would control sun but restricts view, maintenance factor if movable, and sky glare control is lost.

GENERAL NOTES

Uncontrolled glare, generated by the sun's rays, can become uncomfortable in winter; in summer, this glare plus solar heat can be intolerable. Glare can be effectively controlled by either interior or exterior devices, but solar heat gain is best controlled by interception outside the building. Tinted glass and/or interior devices such as shades, horizontal blinds, vertical blinds, as well as various screening methods may be used to control sky glare and glare from the direct rays of the sun. However, they do little to reduce interior air temperature because the sun rays have been allowed to enter the room. Do not use any form of translucent glass where sun will fall directly on it because this will produce glare similar to the dirty windshield of a car. Objectionable glare (i.e., a brightness ratio in excess of 10:1 between peripheral vision and the immediate area of vision) can occur at any orientation, including north, through indirect sources, by reflection from various surfaces. For example, light from a slightly overcast sky or from patches of white clouds can be 30 to 300 times greater than the light reflected from a well-lighted work surface. Provisions for shielding these secondary sources are particularly important to good vision when occupants of a space must remain in relatively fixed positions.

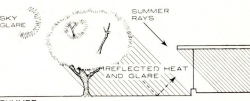

SUMMER
SUN AND GLARE AND HEAT CONTROLLED; I.E. EXCLUDED

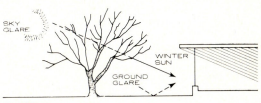

WINTER
SUN ACCEPTED—GLARE CAN BE A PROBLEM (SNOW IN PARTICULAR). CLOSELY SPACED LIMBS CAN CONTROL SKY GLARE.

SOUTH EXPOSURE

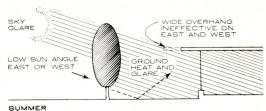

SUMMER
SUN GLARE AND HEAT CONTROLLED

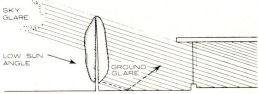

WINTER
LOW SUN ANGLE NOW ACCEPTED; GLARE CONTROLLED BY DENSE BRANCH STRUCTURE; HEAT CAN BE REASONABLY CONTROLLED AS DESIRED BY INSIDE DEVICES (SHADES, BLINDS, OR DRAPES).

EAST AND WEST EXPOSURE

APPLICATIONS IN CONJUNCTION WITH PLANTING

EXAMPLES OF HOW BASIC CONTROL DEVICES CAN BE USED IN CONJUNCTION WITH NATURAL FEATURES TO ACHIEVE GOOD SEASONAL RESULTS

NOTE
For more positive sky glare control in winter and summer, coniferous trees should be used.

An energy-conserving house . . . the rooms are grouped around a conservatory sunspace.

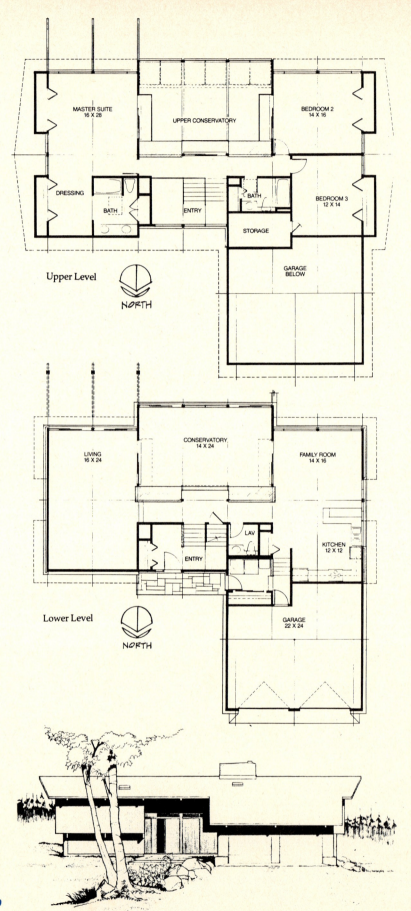

Figure 8–29

An energy-conserving house . . . the most important feature is the conservatory sun space.

- GARAGE AT NORTHWEST CORNER SERVES AS INSULATION BUFFER WHILE DEFLECTING HARSH WINTER WINDS
- ROLLING SUNSCREEN PROTECTS SOLARIUM FROM SUMMER HEAT
- CHIMNEY VENT EXHAUSTS HOT AIR DIRECTLY OUTDOORS IN SUMMER
- UNDERGROUND COOLPIPE EXTENDS FROM HOUSE TO SHADED, SCREENED OUTLET TO INTRODUCE FRESH, COOL AIR IN SUMMER
- SLOPED GLASS PERPENDICULAR TO THE WINTER SUN'S ANGLE OF INCIDENCE TRANSMITS MAXIMUM WINTER SOLAR GAIN
- CANTILEVERED CLOSET PODS INSULATE BEDROOMS. RECESSED EAST AND WEST WINDOWS ARE PROTECTED FROM WINTER WIND AND SUMMER HEAT
- LARGE EXPANSES OF GLASS FACE SOUTH FOR PASSIVE SOLAR GAIN
- OVERHANGS PROTECT SOUTH-FACING GLASS FROM HOT SUMMER SUN
- EARTH BERM MINIMIZES TEMPERATURE DIFFERENTIAL BETWEEN INDOORS AND OUT
- "PERGOLA" SUPPORTS DECIDUOUS VINES WHICH PROVIDE ADDITIONAL SUMMER SHADE
- STRATEGICALLY LOCATED SLIDING DOORS AND OPENING SASH FACILITATE NATURAL VENTILATION

Figure 8–30

within the rockbed gradually radiates through the floor to the living area long after the sun has set. The warm radiant floor is a benefit. Due to the higher mean temperatures produced, the rooms so heated will "feel" warmer than a conventionally heated space would at the same air temperature.

In summer, warm air from the solarium will be automatically vented outdoors [8–33]. Cooler replacement air is brought in through an underground cool pipe that extends from the house to a planted, shaded outlet. Excess humidity from the air condenses on the walls of the pipe as the air cools. This moisture drains away from the house, and cool, dry, fresh air filters into the house. There is also a security benefit in these automatic temperature control systems. The house ventilates itself, so it is not necessary to leave windows open.

The seasonal sun path is the most important factor in the efficient use of solar energy.

The conservatory collects more heat than it needs during the day . . . excess heat is absorbed by masonry during the day and released at night.

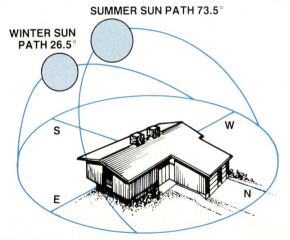

Figure 8–31

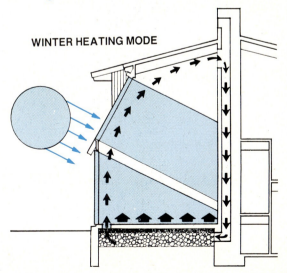

Figure 8–32

Energy Conservation in Design

Sunlight is reflected away from the conservatory due to the high sun angle and the exterior screen . . . warm air within the solarium is automatically exhausted outdoors, with fresh, cooler air drawn inside through an underground cool pipe.

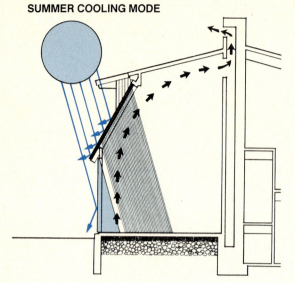

Figure 8–33

A simple control system maximizes the solar efficiency of the house with little involvement on the part of the homeowner [8–34]. Once the desired temperature setting is chosen on the control panel, temperature sensors in the conservatory and the rockbed automatically activate the heat storage mode in winter and the exhaust mode in summer. Aside from the control panel itself, the solar system is completely hidden from view, inside and out.

The solar features incorporated into the house's design contributes a large proportion of the energy requirements for both heating and cooling. However, this represents only part of their overall energy efficiency. The rest is attributed to conservation. Whether a house is heated by the sun or by a conventional furnace, it cannot be energy efficient unless it can hold heat. A leaky house cannot retain heat any better than a leaky bucket can hold water. Care must be taken to assure an efficient thermal envelope in the house. Preengineered building components and precise construction on the site assure a tight building envelope, while careful attention to caulking and weather stripping minimize air infiltration. These important techniques conserve the free heat that is collected by the conservatory and stored by the thermal mass.

Another fundamental feature inherent in this house design is earth sheltering. Since the soil temperature is moderate all year, less heat is required to keep the living spaces comfortable. Accordingly, the lower level of this design is tucked into the ground on three sides. Careful site planning maintains architectural openness and the solar benefit of the southern elevation.

The earth-sheltered walls are also among the most heavily insulated walls in the house, with rigid foam insulation both inside and outside of the foundation walls. The concrete or block wall components would otherwise readily conduct heat from the warm rooms to the earth. Walls that are not earth-sheltered incorporate full thickness fiberglass insulation and a polyethylene vapor barrier, while the roof features a thermal barrier of rigid foam.

Windows are designed for energy efficiency as well as for aesthetics. Solid mahogany frames are double-glazed, with mahogany-framed storm windows providing added protection at the opening sash. The post-and-beam building system of this house enables closet units in the bedrooms to cantilever from the outside walls. The closets therefore do double duty as storage and thermal buffers. In addition, the extended side walls of the closets shield the east and west windows from winter wind and summer sun.

The closet "pods" are but one of the shading techniques that prevent summer overheating. The cantilevered overhangs at the floor of the upper level and at the roof provide shade for the windows and prevent unwanted heat gain from the high summer sun [8–35]. This feature is greater than seven times more effective than shading done inside the glass using conventional drapes and blinds. The overhangs are sized so that windows receive the full benefit of winter sunlight. The sloped windows of the conservatory are shaded by a roll-down exterior screen, blocking up to 84% of the heat without sacrificing natural daylight or the sweeping view of sky and natural landscape.

Extended beams on the south side of the living room serve as a trellis for wisteria vines or grape arbors, with

The desired temperature is set on a control panel . . . temperature sensors in the conservatory and the rockbed automatically activate the heat storage and exhaust systems.

Figure 8–34

Architectural Design

Overhangs at the floor of the upper level and at the roof shade the window.

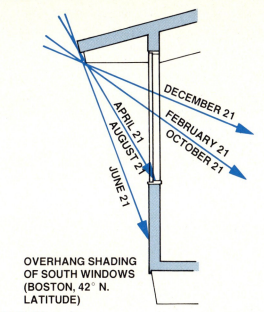

Figure 8–35

deciduous foliage providing summer shade without impeding the welcome winter sun. Proper shading—intercepting sunlight before it is transmitted through the glass—can save up to one ton of air conditioning installation and operation cost per hundred square feet of glass. Effective shading techniques, in conjunction with the automatic exhaust of warm air and introduction of cool fresh air via the cool pipe, make the house as comfortable in summer as it is in winter.

EXERCISES

8–14. What is the main energy-conserving feature of the case study house? How does it work?

8–15. What rooms are assigned to the south side of the house? Which rooms have a north orientation? Why was this arrangement provided?

8–16. How is shading used in this house to conserve energy?

8–17. Has the kitchen been efficiently located in the house? Why or why not? What improvements would you recommend in the arrangement of the work area or the access to the kitchen?

9 Budget and Legal Considerations in Design

9.1 Budget Limitations

It is the designer's responsibility to inform the client of the estimated cost of a building program. If the available budget is too low, the designer should work with the client to revise the program. A common misconception of some clients is that the designer can always create the building that the client wants at a cost that he or she wants to pay. Since clients do not deal with construction costs daily, they usually underestimate the cost of what they want in a building. Although it is the building contractor that ultimately establishes the cost of the building, the designer should be able to predict the cost closely enough to be able to warn the client if the program is too extensive.

Some ways in which the designer may bring a program within budget limitations are to combine room functions and thereby reduce the number of rooms, to omit certain spaces until some future time, to reduce the size of rooms, and to omit special features. Cost data based on recently constructed buildings are published and can be used in estimating the cost of a new home or other building. You may get a rough idea of what a building will cost by comparing its size, quality, and location to cost statistics for buildings with similar characteristics. Table 9-1 gives average costs for the various systems within one type of building for each square foot of floor area. You must decide whether the various systems shall be constructed with inexpensive, average, or expensive materials and methods. Practical experience is necessary to relate your concept for the construction to these broad cost categories.

Cost reference publications typically include conversion factors to adjust the standard figures to your area. A slightly more detailed estimate may be made if you refer to a table listing general materials within each system (Table 9-2). This table gives the low, mid-range, and high costs for the material types shown. By showing the range of costs associated with each type of material that might be used for a particular system, such as exte-

Table 9-1. Average Building Systems Costs: Building Type—Branch Banks[a]

Building System	Low Average Cost	Low Average Percent of Total	Average Cost	Average Percent of Total	High Average Cost	High Average Percent of Total
Foundations	6.82	11.9	10.59	13.2	11.65	12.1
Floors on grade	2.41	4.2	2.64	3.3	2.79	2.9
Superstructure	6.65	11.6	9.38	11.7	13.00	13.5
Roofing	1.54	2.7	1.68	2.1	1.73	1.8
Exterior walls	6.70	11.7	9.22	11.5	12.42	12.9
Paritions	4.18	7.3	5.62	7.0	7.51	7.8
Wall finishes	1.32	2.3	2.89	3.6	3.76	3.9
Floor finishes	1.61	2.8	1.61	2.0	3.18	3.3
Ceiling finishes	1.32	2.3	2.25	2.8	2.70	2.8
Conveying system	0.0	0.0	0.0	0.0	0.0	0.0
Specialties	1.09	1.9	1.12	1.4	1.83	1.9
Fixed equipment	7.14	12.5	15.02	18.7	16.95	17.6
HVAC	8.19	14.3	9.22	11.5	9.25	9.6
Plumbing	3.21	5.6	3.45	4.3	3.47	3.6
Electricial	5.09	8.9	5.55	6.9	6.07	6.3
Gross building cost	$57.27	100	$80.24	100	$96.31	100

[a] Costs are in dollars per square foot of floor area (2500–3500 SF).

SOURCE: 1983 Dodge Construction Systems Costs, McGraw-Hill Information Systems Co., 1221 Avenue of the Americas, New York, NY 10020.

rior walls, the user can quickly conceptualize the cost implications of various selections. All units are expressed in costs per square foot of wall area. The sophistication of detailing and construction methods must be considered and will be a factor in selecting the low, medium, or high typical costs for the materials you have selected. The next logical refinement is to examine costs based on specific materials within each subsystem (Table 9-3).

For detailed estimates complete cost data concerning materials, labor, overhead, profit, crew size, crew output, and other information is helpful. Such data are published and updated each year (Tables 9-4 and 9-5).

The best way to keep costs under control is to work closely with a reliable contractor. Since he is a realistic authority on the current price of materials and labor, getting his opinion on costs early in the planning process is recommended. A contractor may also suggest ways to save money through changes in design details.

EXERCISES

9-1. A branch bank is to be designed and built using average cost materials and methods. The bank contains 5000 square feet. What is your estimate of the approximate total cost of the building? Use Table 9-1.

9-2. How does the average cost of masonry compare to that of framing with various types of siding? Use Table 9-2. What are some advantages of masonry over siding? Do the advantages of the more expensive material seem justified by the higher cost?

9-3. A rectangular wood frame building 20'-0" × 30'-0" has an 8-foot high exterior wall covered with clapboard siding. Assuming that you want to use very high quality materials, what is an approximate cost for this wall? Use Table 9-3. The square-foot costs listed are per square foot of wall area.

9.2 Codes and Regulations

Buildings must be safe. Some areas of concern are protection from collapse, fire, electrical shock, asphyxiation, and unsanitary conditions. State and local governments typically endeavor to protect the public from unsafe building practices by creating laws requiring compliance with minimum safety standards by persons in the building industry. This often means adoption of a broadly accepted book of rules concerning design and construction called a *building code*. Although every city or other governmental body has the authority to prepare their own building code, many have chosen to adopt one of several that have been written by groups interested in building safety.

The broadly accepted codes are the *Basic Building Code* (commonly called the *BOCA Code*). *The National Building Code*, the *Standard Building Code*, the *Uniform Building Code*, and the *One and Two Family Dwelling Code*. Several of these codes have associated volumes covering mechanical and plumbing work. Although there are several choices for building codes, only one major code is customarily used for electrical construction. This is the *National Electrical Code*.

The designer and builder are obliged to follow the rules of the code adopted by the community in which the building is to be constructed. An example of a typical code requirement concerning the fire resistance of construction is illustrated in Table 9-6. Practical experience is helpful in understanding the terms used since drafters deal with many of them on a daily basis. For example, one-hour fire-resistant construction refers to the length of time that a wall will maintain certain properties during a fire. Materials and wall construction appropriate for this rating may be looked up elsewhere in the code or in other handbooks.

Table 9-2. Average Material Costs[a]

Exterior Walls	Low	Medium	High
Wood siding	2.62	2.94	4.04
Galvanized iron siding	2.39	2.95	3.50
Aluminum sidings (nonresidential)	2.75	3.10	3.67
6 to 12 in. CMU	3.25	3.58	4.71
Stuccos on sheathing/lath/insulation	3.62	3.94	4.90
Galbestos	3.88	4.20	6.13
Aggregate finished plywood	4.04	4.84	5.21
4 to 12 in. adobe brick	5.43	6.55	8.60
8 to 12 in. CMU split faced	3.96	4.87	6.07
Porcelain enamel panel	5.11	6.47	9.50
4 to 10 in. poured concrete	7.09	7.98	8.64
Curtain walls, metal and glass	14.49	16.20	28.39
10 in. brick cavity (with and without insulation)	6.85	8.03	10.65
8 to 12 in. face and common	9.50	10.98	12.23
Precast concrete panel	10.23	11.45	12.99
6 to 12 in. glass block	10.90	11.86	12.22
Stone and CMU backup	13.85	14.65	16.77

[a] Costs are in dollars per square foot of wall area.
SOURCE: 1983 Dodge Construction Systems Costs, McGraw-Hill Information Systems Co., 1221 Avenue of the Americas, New York, NY 10020.

Table 9-3. Exterior Walls: Wood[a]

Cedar siding			
Cedar ⅝ in. T-11	0.76	0.84	1.60
15-lb felt	0.09	0.12	0.21
Sheathing	0.33	0.37	0.70
Insulation	0.24	0.22	0.46
Paint, three coats	0.34	0.20	0.54
Total per square foot	1.76	1.75	3.51
Basic stud framing (Add as appropriate)			
2" × 4" wood studs 16 in. O.C.	0.48	0.48	0.96
Total per square foot	0.48	0.48	0.96

[a] Costs are in dollars per square foot of wall area.
SOURCE: 1983 Dodge Construction Systems Costs, McGraw-Hill Information Systems Co., 1221 Avenue of the Americas, New York, NY 10020.

Table 9-4. Formwork Costs

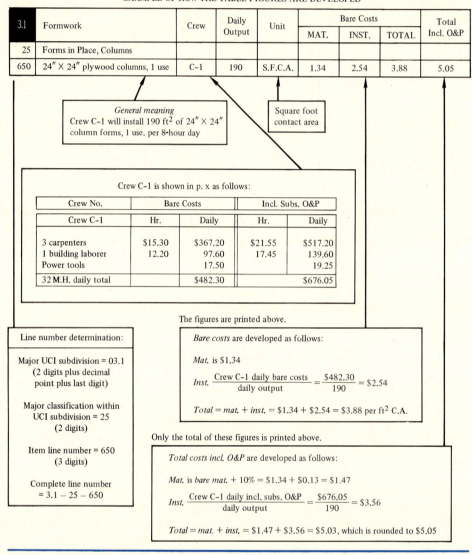

SOURCE: 1983 Means Residential/Light Commercial Cost Data, Robert Snow, Means Company, Inc. 100 Construction Plaza, Kingston, MA 02364.

Another way to provide protection from fire is to provide a means of escape. If the exits are too far away, an occupant may not be able to leave the building safely during a fire. Table 9-7 shows how a code limits the distance between exits to avoid this problem.

Structural soundness is controlled by specifying either the forces that must be resisted or the strength of building materials, by specifying minimum sizes allowed for structural components (Table 9-8), or by specifying methods of construction (Table 9-9).

Local governments may wish to control physical and functional characteristics of the community by enacting a *zoning ordinance*. Such a law typically designates the function allowed for buildings constructed in different zones of the city. A *zoning map* [9-1] is used to designate zones in which certain types of buildings, such as only

Table 9–5. Rough Carpentry Costs[a]

		Crew	Man-Hours	Unit	Bare Costs				Total Incl. O&P
					Mat.	Labor	Equip.	Total	
33	**Partitions,** metal studs with runners, Partitions 10' high								
002	Load bearing, 24 in. O.C., 20 ga. galv., 2½ in. wide	F-2	.016	S.F.	.34	.19	.01	.54	.68
004	3⅝ in. wide		.016		.38	.20	.01	.59	.74
006	4 in. wide		.017		.38	.21	.01	.60	.76
008	6 in. wide		.018		.47	.22	.01	.70	.88
010	18 ga. 2½ in. wide		.016		.41	.19	.01	.61	.77
012	3⅝ in. wide		.017		.45	.20	.01	.66	.83
014	4 in. wide		.018		.46	.21	.01	.68	.86
016	6 in. wide		.019		.60	.22	.02	.84	1.03
018	16 ga, 2½ in. wide		.016		.47	.20	.01	.68	.84
020	3⅝ in. wide		.017		.54	.21	.01	.76	.94
022	4 in. wide		.018		.56	.22	.01	.79	.97
024	6 in. wide		.019		.71	.23	.02	.96	1.15
026	8 in. wide		.020		.80	.23	.02	1.05	1.27
030	Nonload bearing, 24 in. O.C., 25 ga. galv., 1⅝ in. wide		.016		.14	.19	.01	.34	.46
032	2½ in. wide		.016		.14	.19	.01	.34	.46
034	3⅝ in. wide		.016		.18	.20	.01	.39	.52
036	4 in. wide		.017		.20	.21	.01	.42	.56
038	6 in. wide		.018		.24	.21	.01	.46	.61
040	20 ga., 2½ in. wide		.016		.23	.19	.01	.43	.56
042	3⅝ in. wide		.016		.29	.20	.01	.50	.64
044	4 in. wide		.017		.31	.21	.01	.53	.68
046	6 in. wide		.018		.39	.21	.01	.61	.78
048									
101	Wood stud with single bottom plate and double top plate,								
102	no waste, std. & better lumber								
104	2" × 4" studs, 8 ft. high, studs 16" O.C.	F-2	.160	L.F.	2.59	1.87	.13	4.59	5.95
106	24 in. O.C.		.128		1.98	1.50	.10	3.58	4.64
108	10 ft. high, studs 16 in. OC.		.160		3.08	1.87	.13	5.08	6.45
110	24 in. O.C.		.128		2.31	1.50	.10	3.91	5
112	12 ft. high, studs 16 in. O.C.		.200		3.74	2.34	.16	6.24	7.95
114	24 in. O.C.		.160		2.75	1.87	.13	4.75	6.10
116	2" × 6" studs, 8 ft. high, studs 16" O.C.		.177		4.01	2.08	.14	6.23	7.85
118	24 in. O.C.		.139		2.75	1.63	.11	4.49	5.70
120	10 ft. high, studs 16 in. O.C.		.177		4.73	2.08	.14	6.95	8.65
122	24 in. O.C.		.139		3.52	1.63	.11	5.26	6.55
124	12 ft. high, studs 16 in. O.C.		.228		5.45	2.67	.18	8.30	10.40
126	24 in. O.C.		.177		4.02	2.08	.14	6.24	7.85
128	For horizontal blocking, 2" × 4", add		.026		.21	.31	.02	.54	.74
130	2" × 6", add		.026		.34	.31	.02	.67	.89
134	For openings, add	F-2	.064	L.F.		.75	.05	.80	1.23L
138	For headers, add			B.F.	.38				.42M

[a] Costs are in dollars per unit.
SOURCE: 1983 Means Residential/Light Commercial Cost Data, Robert Snow Means Company, Inc. 100 Construction Plaza, Kingston, MA 02364.

residential buildings or only industrial buildings, may be constructed.

By zoning, the community can control noise levels, type and amount of traffic, odors, smoke, and other characteristics that affect the desirability of various areas. Zoning ordinances or similar laws by other names may also control physical features of buildings and exterior space. The minimum distance a building may be positioned from the property line and the maximum height of a building are commonly controlled dimensions. Paving may be controlled by specifying the minimum distance between driveways, minimum driveway angle to the street, maximum driveway width at the curbs, maximum and minimum driveway widths, minimum driveway return radius, number of parking places required, screening and landscaping of paving, setback requirement for paving, and minimum dimensions within a parking lot [9–2].

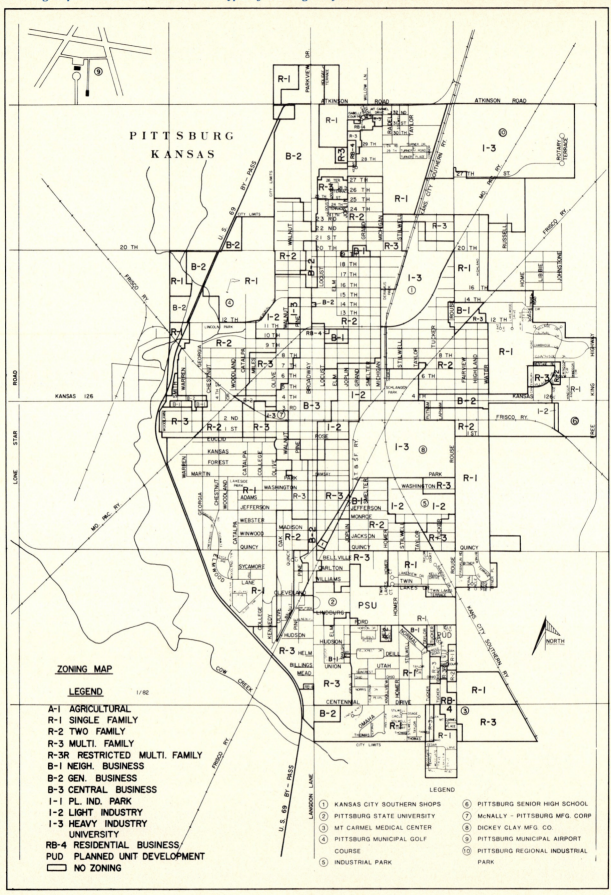

A zoning map shows areas in which certain types of buildings may be constructed.

Figure 9-1

Table 9-6. Excerpt from the Standard Building Code

702.3 – WALL AND PARTITIONS REQUIREMENTS BY OCCUPANCY

All walls and partitions shall provide not less than the degree of fire resistance required in Table 700, except as may be specified elsewhere in this code.

GROUP B: BUSINESS BUILDINGS–Partitions along exit access corridors shall be of one (1) hour fire resistant construction. Regardless of Type of Construction, non-fire rated partitions may be constructed within rooms or spaces not exceeding three thousand (3,000) square feet in area. Such rooms or space shall be enclosed with permanent partitions having not less than one (1) hour fire-resistive construction. (See Section 403 for mixed occupancy and separation requirements, Section 403.2 for tenant separation and Section 704.3 for ceiling and interior wall finish requirements.)

GROUP R: RESIDENTIAL–Except in one and two family dwellings, all partitions along exit access corridors or partitions that separate apartments, dormitory rooms, or hotel rooms from other occupancies, shall be of not less than one (1) hour fire resistive construction. Non fire rated partitions may be permitted within individual dwelling units.

SOURCE: Southern Building Code Congress International, 900 Montclair Road, Birmingham, AL 35213.

Table 9-7. Excerpt from the Standard Building Code

SECTION 1103 – ARRANGEMENT AND NUMBER OF EXITS

1103.1 – ARRANGEMENTS

(a) Exits shall be so located that the distance from the most remote point in the floor area, room or space served by them to the nearest exit, measured along the line of travel, shall be not more than specified in Table 1103. Where floor areas are sub-divided into small spaces or rooms, and the egress travel in the room or space does not exceed fifty (50) feet, the distance of travel to an exit shall be measured from the corridor entrance to such rooms or spaces. See Section 1103.1(d) for factory-industrial buildings.

TABLE 1103 – MAXIMUM DISTANCE OF TRAVEL OF AN EXIT IN FEET

Occupancy	Unsprinklered	Sprinklered
Group A–Assembly	150	200
Group B–Business	150	200
Group E–Educational	150	200
Group H–Hazardous	NP	75
Group F–Factory-Industrial	150	200
Group I–Institutional	NP	200
Group M–Mercantile	150	200
Group R–Residential	150	200
Group S–Storage	150	200
Open Parking Structures	200	200

(b) Where more than one (1) exit is required, at least two (2) shall be located as remote from each other as practicable and shall be so arranged and constructed to provide direct access in separate directions from any point in the area served and to minimize the possibility that both may be blocked by any one fire or other emergency condition.

SOURCE: Southern Building Code Congress International, 900 Montclair Road, Birmingham, AL 35213.

Table 9–8. Excerpt from the Standard Building Code

1404.2–THICKNESS OF BEARING WALLS

The minimum thickness of masonry bearing walls shall be at least twelve (12) inches in thickness for the uppermost thirty-five (35) feet of their height and shall be increased four (4) inches in thickness for each successive thirty-five (35) feet or fraction thereof measured downward from the top of the wall.

SOURCE: Southern Building Code Congress International, 900 Montclair Road, Birmingham, AL 35213.

Table 9–9. Excerpt from the Standard Building Code

SECTION 1706 – VERTICAL FRAMING

1706.1–EXTERIOR WALL FRAMING

(a) Stud Size and Spacing

Studs in one-and-two story buildings shall be not less than two (2) by four (4) inches with the wide face perpendicular to wall. In three-story buildings, studs in first story shall be not less than three (3) by four (4) inches or two (2) by six (6) inches.

(b) Studs shall be spaced not more than the following:

Stud Size	Supporting Roof and Ceiling Only	Supporting 1 Floor Roof and Ceiling	Supporting 2 Floors Roof and Ceiling
2 x 4	24"	16"	—
3 x 4	24"	24"	16"
2 x 5	24"	24"	—
2 x 6	24"	24"	16"

SOURCE: Southern Building Code Congress International, 900 Montclair Road, Birmingham, AL 35213.

Table 9–10. Minimum Requirements of Ventilation and Natural Light[a]

Location	Natural Light (Glazed Area as Percent of Floor Area)	Natural Ventilation (Percent of Floor Area)		Mechanical Ventilation (Air Changes/Hour)
Living rooms	10	5		—
Dining rooms	10	5		—
Bedrooms	10	5		—
Heater rooms	—	—		—
Kitchens	—	5	or	15
Baths	—	5	or	8
Laundry	—	—		[a]
Other habitable rooms	10	5		—
Basement	1	1		—
Attics and structural spaces	—	1/150		—
Basement-less spaces	—	1/150		—

[a] A detailed set of requirements is listed in another section of the Minimum Property Standards.

SOURCE: HUD Minimum Property Standards, 1973 ed.

Parking lot dimensions are often controlled by ordinances.

> (Official Publications)
> **VILLAGE OF EDEN PRAIRIE**
> **HENNEPIN COUNTY, MINNESOTA**
> **ORDINANCE NO. 141**
> **AN ORDINANCE AMENDING**
> **ORDINANCE NO. 135**
>
> The Council of the Village of Eden Prairie does hereby ordain as follows:
>
> Section 1. Section 12 of Ordinance No. 135 is hereby amended by deleting Subdivision 12.1, 12.2, 12.3 and substituting therefor the following:
>
> Subdivision 12.1 Purposes
>
> | Description of Dimensions | Parking Angle | | | | | | | | | |
> |---|---|---|---|---|---|---|---|---|---|---|
> | | 0 Deg. | 20 Deg. | 30 Deg. | 40 Deg. | 45 Deg. | 50 Deg. | 60 Deg. | 70 Deg. | 80 Deg. | 90 Deg. |
> | Parking space width perpendicular to angle | 9' | 9' | 9' | 9' | 9' | 9' | 9' | 9' | 9' | 9' |
> | Parking space dimension perpendicular to aisle | 9' | 14'6" | 16'10" | 18'6" | 19'5" | 20' | 20'8" | 20'9" | 20'2" | 19' |
> | Parking space dimension parallel to aisle | 23' | 24'8" | 17' | 13'2" | 12' | 11'1" | 9'10" | 9' | 9' | 9' |
> | Aisle width | 12' | 11' | 11' | 12' | 13'6" | 12'6" | 18'6" | 19'6" | 24' | 25' |

Figure 9–2

Energy codes set standards for thermal efficiency of various building elements.

2. EXPOSED WALLS: The overall thermal transmittance value, U_o, for the combined gross area of walls consisting of opaque wall, window, and door areas, and foundation walls above grade, enclosing an interior heated space shall not exceed 0.17 Btu/hr/ft²/°F for one- and two-family dwellings, and 0.22 Btu/hr/ft²/°F for all other buildings. Equation 6006–1 shall be used to determine acceptable combinations of construction materials and to calculate U_o of the exposed walls.

Equation 6006–1

$$U = \frac{U_o A_o + U_g A_g + U_d A_d}{A}$$

where
- U = average or combined transmittance of the gross wall or ceiling area
- A = external exposed (above-grade) gross area (wall or ceiling) of the building that faces heated spaces
- U_o = thermal transmittance of all elements of the opaque area (wall or ceiling)
- A_o = opaque wall area
- U_g = thermal transmittance of the glazing area (window or skylight)
- A_g = glazing area
- U_d = thermal transmittance of the door or similar opening, considered as an assembly, including the frame
- A_d = door or similar opening area

SOURCE: Design and Evaluation Criteria for Energy Conservation in New Buildings, Additions and Remodeled Elements of Buildings, Jan. 30, 1976.
State of Minnesota, Department of Administration
Building Code Division
St. Paul, Minnesota

Figure 9–3

With the continued emphasis on conservation of energy, codes affecting the energy efficiency of buildings are appearing. An *energy code* may designate temperatures for which you must design, thermal transmittance values for walls [9–3] and roofs, tightness of construction, control of condensation, HVAC (heating, ventilating, and air conditioning) systems, lighting levels and hardware, and other components and practices affecting the annual consumption of energy by a building.

Budget and Legal Considerations in Design

Standards may be specified by agencies that will be asked to guarantee or provide loans for construction projects. For example, all projects, that are sponsored by the U.S. Department of Housing and Urban Development must follow the HUD Minimum Property Standards. These standards are very specific. They control such design items as minimum room sizes (Table 7–6), minimum kitchen counter-top space (Table 7–4), kitchen storage (Table 7–3), and minimum ventilation and natural light in a home (Table 9–10).

Institutional buildings, such as nursing homes and hospitals, have additional guidelines that must be met due to their critical and specialized nature. One cannot memorize all the legal requirements affecting a design. The designer must know generally what requirements exist, where they are explained, how to interpret the explanations, and must have access to the publications that detail the requirements. The many legal requirements are complicated and sometimes confusing, but they can also be used as a design aid. Dimensions, quality of materials, and sometimes configurations of detailing are specified, thereby relieving the designer of the necessity of developing an individual set of minimum standards.

EXERCISES

9–4. What is the purpose of a building code?

9–5. How do building codes become required standards in different communities?

9–6. What is the building code required in your community?

9–7. Select an example of a building code requirement not already listed in this text and explain it to a group. (You can perhaps find a copy of a code in your library or at your city building department.)

9–8. Obtain a city zoning map. How does it differ from [9–1]?

9–9. How does a zoning ordinance differ from a building code?

9–10. Select an example of a zoning ordinance requirement not already listed in this text and explain it to a group. (You may find a copy of a zoning ordinance in your library or at your city zoning department.)

9–11. Examine a zoning map at your library or city zoning department. Identify the zone in which you live. Draw a sketch of this zone showing the streets and their names at its boundaries. Identify the zones that border "your" zone. List the types of buildings that may be built in all the zones on your sketch.

9–12. The following data applies to a particular single family home:

Area of opaque outside wall = 6400 ft².
Amount of glazed area (glass) = 144 ft².
Total area of all doors = 42 ft².

Thermal transmittance of opaque outside wall = 0.125.
Thermal transmittance of glass = 0.58.
Thermal transmittance of doors = 0.51.

Does the exterior wall of this home meet the requirements of the energy code shown in [9–3]?

10 The Design Process

10.1 The Concept

Familiarity with the regional climate, topography of the site, surrounding man-made and natural features, and the purpose of the proposed building help in establishing a *concept* for the building design. The concept summarizes the designer's attitude concerning the nature of the building, that is, what its character should be, or what general impression it should have on those who use it or see it. Certainly, designers seek to create an attractive building, but such adjectives as dynamic, delightful, powerful, delicate, dignified, serene, unique, traditional, and others may describe more specific visual goals. A visual theme or "order" will help unify the appearance and contribute to achieving the goals of the concept. Frank Lloyd Wright designed many houses that had a horizontal visual theme [6–20]. This concept was related to the regional topography (the flatness) of the midwestern prairie. Religious buildings often have a vertical theme. Although this is sometimes a recognition of tradition, the vertical theme developed as designers followed a concept relating churches to "the heavens."

Electing to design a building in an established style is based on the designer's attitude of what the building "should be," and is therefore one type of concept. You should be able to justify your concept by reasoning based on characteristics of the project, such as those mentioned in the beginning of this discussion. There are many more themes of visual order than just "vertical" or "horizontal." Each project is an opportunity to create a fresh concept with an original theme or system of visual order. The designer who develops a unique or controversial visual order that is not immediately recognized can expect criticism before praise. To pursue untested design goals is one of the challenges of creativity [1–7 and 6–20].

10.2 The Program

Given all the considerations the architect must include in a design, one may think the design process is a near impossible task. It is not easy, but methods have been developed to help keep the process orderly and successful. One indispensible design tool is the *program*. The program is a list of functional requirements of a proposed building.

Developing a program for a commercial building is a more involved process than for a home. Naturally, the depth of research, the complexity of assimilating the data, and the thoroughness of the resulting program increase in proportion to the size of the building. Certain types of buildings require more complex programs than other structures of similar size due to the nature of their function. A hospital, for example, is far more complicated than an office building of the same size.

Examination of existing operations and interviews with people who will use the building is necessary to understand what spaces are required and what relationship the spaces will have to each other. You must learn what furniture and equipment are necessary. You must also learn what special characteristics are required for certain spaces, such as quietness, privacy, easy access by the public, visibility, security, and so on. The client may not know all the plan requirements of his or her business. It may be your job to analyze the various known needs and to discover the relationships and requirements that are not apparent. You must document your findings so that both you and your client understand the functional design goals.

Figure [10–1] is a page from an architect's program for a small commercial building. Areas (rooms) are given numbers as well as names. Areas that closely relate to each other have the same first number. The present space requirements in square feet are listed together with predicted future space requirements. You may need to include future space needs in the building or provide for easy expansion to accommodate those needs later. A column is provided to list area numbers that should be adjacent to the space in question. Fixtures and equipment are listed for each area. The last column is for miscellaneous remarks pertaining to the needs of each area. A step-by-step development of a complete program for a small commercial building is illustrated in Appendix C, at the end of this book.

The specific needs of a home owner often make "stock

One page from a five-page program for a small commercial building.

SPACE PROGRAM FOR: Rural Electric Association   PROJECT NO. A75-12   DATE Apr 19 '83   PAGE 3 OF 5

Description of Area-Subareas	Area No.	Space Requirements Present	Space Requirements Future	Adjacent Area Nos.	Fixture & Equipment (PRESENT)	Remarks (PRESENT)
Accounts Receivable Clerk	2.3	145	195	3.2	billing machine 3'x6', 6 card files, receipt file, Check writer, typewriter, 1 file cabinet	Present area is at capacity
Bookkeeper	2.4	110	110	3.6		Privacy, auditors need larger space
Work/Conference Area	2.5	140	280			Private but multi-purpose
Work Order Clerk	2.6	80	160		Desk, chair, old billing machine, 2 file cabinets	
Vault	2.7	115	115	2.4		Adequate for future needs
Staff Lounge	2.8	150	200	2.0, 3.0	small refrigerator, table, chairs, coffee maker	
Staff Toilets	2.9	120	120			
ADMINISTRATIVE SERVICES	3.0	1135	1255			
Operational Superintendent	3.1	160	160	4.2	Catalog storage desk, chair, work top, conference table, 4 file cabinets	Overall map of system accessible by Engineer, Assistant Operations Superintendent
General Manager	3.2	220	220	1.0, 2.0, 3.0, 4.0	3-2 drawer file bookcase, 10'L credenza, table, work, 30x60 desk, WC & lav.	Intercom
Toilet	3.3	35	35			Access from General Manager Office
Board Room	3.4	500	500		14 people/table	Very comfortable, adjacent to toilet

NOTES:

james j adams
architecture / planning   s main st   nevada mo 64772   417·667·3568

Figure 10-1

plans" unacceptable. To design a home for the unique needs of a family you should develop a program much like that described for commercial clients. Development of a residential program is simpler than for a commercial building because you are dealing with fewer people and the general concept of the function of a home should already be familiar to you.

To design a home for the use of a certain family, you must know what makes that family different from any other. Knowing the members' ages, hobbies, and habits will help you understand their life-style. You must meet with the family several times and ask many questions that will help determine space requirements and desired relationships between spaces. Do they need rooms for recreation, sewing, or study? Do they want a family room in addition to a living room? Do they prefer single or multilevel living? Will each child have his or her own room? Does the family prefer an open, informal type of home or a more rigidly separated and formal plan? A socially oriented family may entertain frequently and require large open living and dining spaces. A bar and kitchen arrangement that facilitates serving to large groups may be needed. They may like to eat outdoors when weather permits. If so, this requires a patio or deck that is easily accessible from the kitchen.

The combinations of preferences by the owners are limitless and cannot all be suggested here. You may wish to use a form similar to the example in [10–1] or adopt

A bubble diagram may be started by using a series of squares to represent the various area requirements.

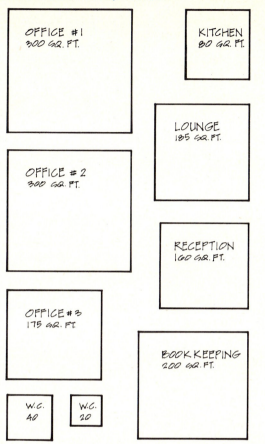

Figure 10–2

some other format. Some type of formal list of spaces required and information about their relationships should be prepared so that the client can comment on it and you can refer to it throughout the design process. In Chapter 13 a design case study illustrates the process of researching a typical family's needs for a new home.

10.3 Bubble Diagrams

The complexity of most design programs will require the designer to "think graphically." Ideas need to be sketched and studied in order to progress toward a solution. Trying to solve all the requirements of design and construction in each idea sketch is not an efficient approach. A hierarchy of design goals should be established and studied in turn. Identifying major zones and their relationships to each other and to the site is a logical beginning. So as to not be delayed by including refinements too early in the process, rough outlines called

Using the area requirement squares, circular bubble diagrams are drawn to represent the relationships and circulation patterns.

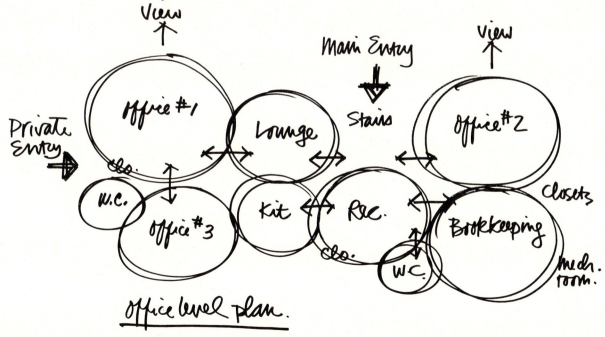

Figure 10–3

The Design Process

181

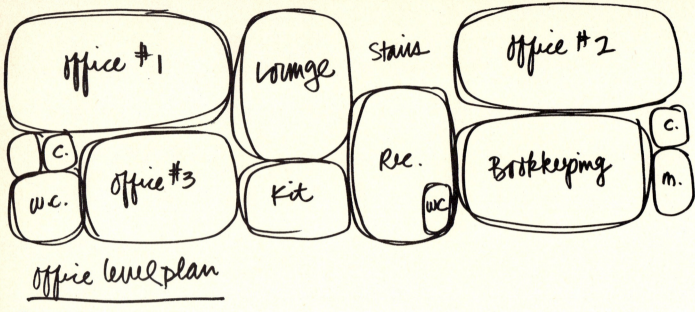

The finalized circular bubbles are transformed into rectangular areas approximating the anticipated proportions of the rooms.

Figure 10–4

bubble diagrams are used to establish basic space relationships. Circular shapes (called *bubbles* or *balloons*) contain the approximate area required for each room. The bubbles are arranged and rearranged until the desired relationship between spaces is achieved.

To get started on the bubble diagrams, the following procedure may be used. On scratch paper draw a square representing each room [10–2]. The side of each square may be determined by computing the square root of each room area desired. For example, a 300-square-foot area would be represented by a square that is about 17 feet square. The squares are drawn to a small scale such as the scale of the site plan. The bubble diagrams that will be drawn from the squares may then be drawn on an overlay of the site plan, thus encouraging a strong relationship of building to site.

The bubble diagram is now drawn to approximate scale by tracing freehand circles equivalent to each square [10–3]. Since the final room shapes will probably not be exactly square, the circles may be squeezed into ovals or other shapes as needed. Using rounded shapes instead of rectangular ones is a flexible technique that increases speed and reduces the tendency to be delayed by shapes that won't fit where you want them to. Knowing that the circles are only approximations encourages overlapping and discourages refinement at this stage.

The circular bubble diagrams are prepared on sketch tracing paper. When one sketch does not yield the desired room relationship, an overlay is drawn on another sheet of sketch paper. This allows you to trace the acceptable parts of the previous sketch and change other parts. With this method you can establish relationships and circulation patterns without having to solve the demands of logical construction and structural considerations. You should study room relationships in plan, but relationships between volumes should be studied in elevation. While the room arrangement is still in the diagram stage, the elevations will be simple outlines. Neither should be finalized without cross-checking it with the other to see if design goals are being achieved in each.

Once a bubble diagram is established, it is transformed into a sketch that maintains the desired room relationships and begins to exhibit structural patterns that will allow economical construction detailings. This is done by making an overlay of the bubble diagram in which you trace the room bubbles, transforming them into rough rectangular shapes [10–4]. The corners of the rectangles are still rounded at this stage. The rectangular shapes approximate the final proportions of the rooms but are still unsettled enough to be squeezed and pushed, as necessary, to begin solving the problems of construction.

With additional refinement the rectangular bubble diagram will become a *schematic plan* [10–5]. Refinement of the corresponding rough elevation diagrams will lead to a *schematic elevation*. The drawings may be freehand or instrument drawn. Walls are drawn in single line and a minimum of detail is shown.

Schematic plan and elevation drawings are made from the finalized bubble diagrams.

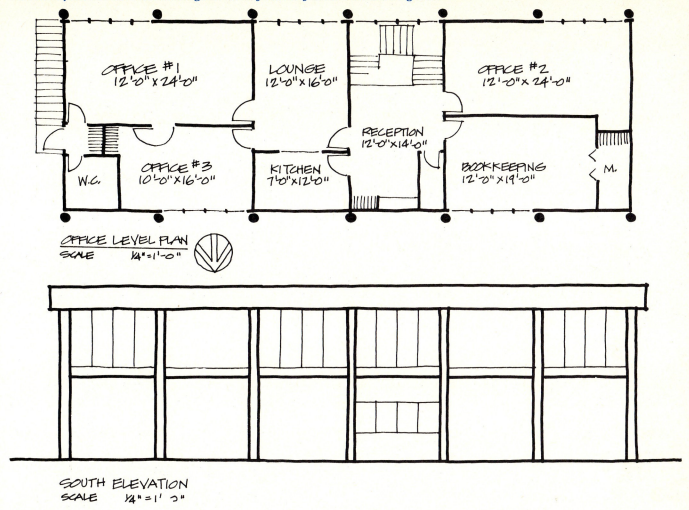

Figure 10–5

10.4 Schematic Drawings

During the preparation of the schematic drawings that are developed from the bubble diagrams the appearance of the building must be considered. If you wait until the plan is finalized to do this, it may be too late to make significant changes in the outside appearance of the building. Placement and size of windows, roof configuration and slope, and shapes that protrude from or recede from the external surfaces are some of the features that have an effect on the character of the home. These are closely related to the floor plan and should be planned together. Views of the sides of a building that are not perfected but show basic relationships and proportions of the parts appear in the schematic elevations [10–5].

The schematic drawings (including a site plan) are usually the first sketches shown to an owner. They are meant to show the intent of the designer for all aspects of the project, including function, structure, and appearance. More complete drawings are not prepared at this stage since if major changes are to occur, this is the point at which they should be requested by the owner. The designers do not want to invest a great deal of drawing time prior to acceptance of their concept by the client. Major changes at this point may require other meetings with the client prior to the preparation of design *presentation drawings* [10–6]. These drawings are very complete and are drawn to look as realistic as possible. The design presentation is discussed in Chapter 11.

Make presentation drawings as realistic as possible using the schematic drawings as a reference.

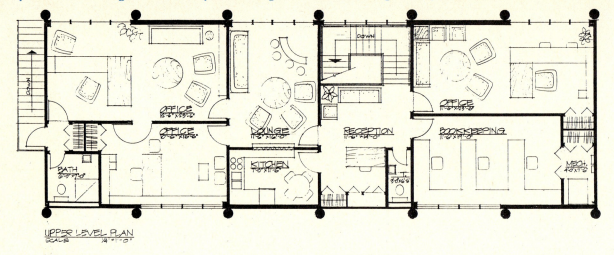

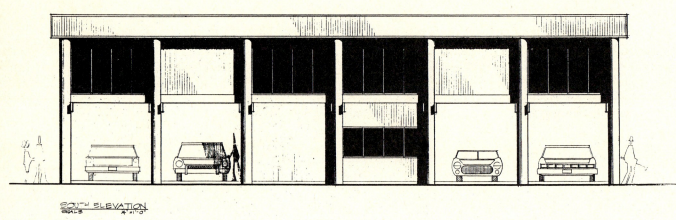

Figure 10–6

EXERCISES

10–1. Study Frank Lloyd Wright's "Fallingwater House" at Bear Run, Pennsylvania [6–46]. (Visit your library to find other views of this house.) What system of visual order is apparent? In a group discussion arrive at a conclusion as to the concept for this house.

10–2. Make a list of ways in which visual order may be achieved in a building.

10–3. Outline your concept for a home for yourself in a mountainous region. Do the same for a site in a desertlike area. How do the concepts differ? How are they alike? Why? What additional information is needed to complete the ideas?

10–4. What is the purpose of a design program? List the items that should be included in a program.

10–5. Visit a fire station in your community. Find out how the station works by talking with the fire chief and firemen. Write a program for a similar fire station, including changes that the firemen recommend.

10–6. Prepare a formal program for a home for yourself. Identify the spaces that are closely related to each other. List furniture for all rooms.

10–7. Prepare a brief program for a gas station. (Frank Lloyd Wright designed a gas station in Minnesota.) Prepare bubble diagrams for the design of the station. Include exterior spaces in the diagramming process.

10–8. Using the program from Exercise 10–6, prepare bubble diagrams for the house. Refine the diagrams to the point where the intended proportions in the plan and elevations are apparent.

10–9. Refine the diagrams from Exercise 10–8 into schematic sketches. Be sure that design goals are achieved in both plan and elevations.

11 Design Presentation

The owner of a building being designed must understand what the new building will look like and how it will function. He or she is rarely trained in understanding the rough sketches and technical drawings prepared by architects and drafters. Design presentation techniques have been developed to help the client visualize the project while still in the drawing stage. The first technique that we will examine is rendering, and the second is model building.

Rendering is preparing a drawing to look as much like a photograph as possible. Thus with only two dimensions, the drafter creates an illusion of three dimensions that the layperson can more readily understand. This is done with plans, sections, elevations, and pictorial drawings by using textures, shades and shadows, and other aids to give the illusion of depth and to make relative scale apparent.

11.1 Presentation Plans

The key to making a drawing "read" (be easily understood) is to make all its elements easily recognizable. To be able to distinguish one element from another, it must have contrast with the adjacent elements. Since a floor plan is a drawing showing the location of walls, the walls must read strongly. This is often accomplished by darkening them to a solid black [11-1]. This method is relatively easy and fast. Walls shaded with lines are not as strong and are time consuming to draw [11-2 and 11-3]. A double-line wall with no shading can be understood better if the surrounding elements are darker. Some architectural offices prefer to leave the walls unshaded so that the floor plan can be converted into a construction drawing. This means that other rendering techniques must be omitted also. Windows are shown with a single line representing the glass, double lines representing the sill and stool, or all three lines can be shown if the scale of the drawing is large enough [4-3].

To illustrate that the size and shape of each room is appropriate, furniture may be drawn on the presentation floor plan [11-4]. A large-scale plan will allow more detail to be shown than on a small-scale plan. The furniture

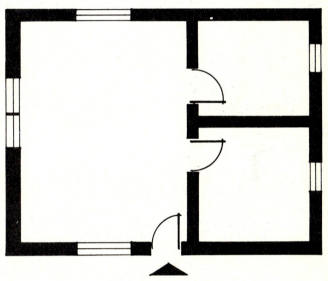

Solid black walls are the easiest to draw and will read the strongest.

Figure 11-1

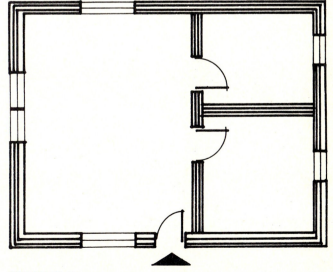

Lined walls are not often seen.

Figure 11-2

Short freehand lines across guidelines give an artistic feeling but are time consuming to draw.

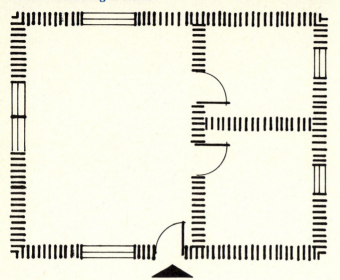

Figure 11–3

is drawn lighter than the walls. Rectilinear furniture is easy to draw. It is usually used regardless of what the actual furniture will look like. Furniture fabric is shown with dots, denser around the edges than in the center. The edges of fabric covered furniture are shown rough.

Furniture "in plan" . . .

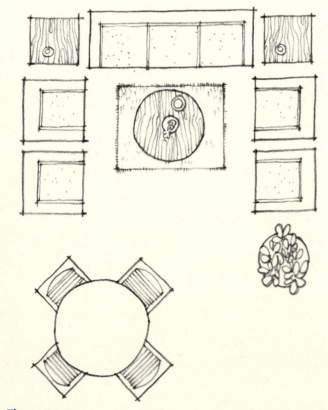

Figure 11–4

Loose carpeting . . .

Figure 11–5

Tables may be rectangular or circular. In addition to providing a feeling of scale realism, showing the owner a suggested layout for furniture assures both the client and the architect that the furniture will fit into the room. Even when furniture is omitted, built-in items such as kitchen counters, sinks, toilets, and bathtubs should be shown. A stove and refrigerator should always be included in the kitchen.

Floor textures, like furniture, add richness to the plan. Carpeting can be represented with dots [11–5]. If the carpeting is a loose rug, the edge can be fringed. The edges of wall-to-wall carpeting are not fringed. In both cases, the dot intensity fades out toward the center. Care should be taken to see that the dots do not stop abruptly and form an apparent pattern.

Kitchen and bathroom tile may be shown as a grid pattern of joints [11–6]. Sometimes hallways have such a grid pattern even if there is no tile in the hall. This is done as a graphic procedure to identify circulation space. Stone at an entry foyer will have a symbol representing the shape of the stones [11–7].

Communication aids such as room names and room sizes are included [7–9 and 7–13]. A north arrow [4–23] is required. The scale of the drawing should be indicated. Entry arrows can be placed on the drawing as an aid in quickly locating the main entrances to a build-

Floor tile . . .

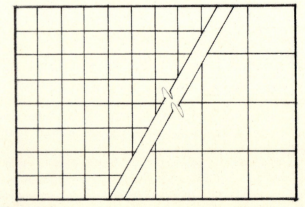

Figure 11–6

186   Architectural Design

Flagstone . . .

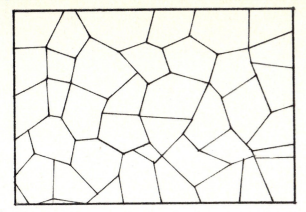

Figure 11-7

Grass, neat but time consuming.

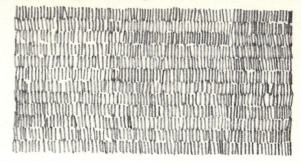

Figure 11-9

Grass, a compromise for speed.

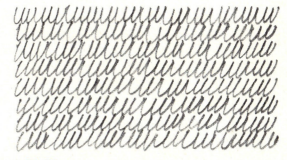

Figure 11-10

Concrete, gravel, or sand . . .

Figure 11-11

Brick or stone paving . . .

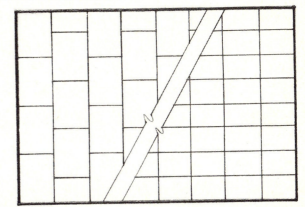

ing [11-8]. They are usually drawn as a simple darkened broad triangle.

With the exception of the building itself, certain techniques for rendering a floor plan and a site plan differ only in scale. If the building is large enough, and the site plan small enough, both plans may be shown as one drawing. If this is not possible, some site features near the building may be shown on the floor plan.

To distinguish between types of surfaces and give an illusion of reality, symbols representing textures may be drawn on the site plan. Some common textures represented are grass, concrete, brick and stone, paving, water, wood, and roofing. Several workable and relatively easy-to-do techniques are available for representing these textures.

Grass is a time-consuming symbol to draw [11-9]. Light guidelines 3/16 inch or less apart are drawn across lawn areas. Blades of grass are drawn between the guidelines. To save time, the pencil strokes may be a series of connected U shapes [11-10]. The strokes must be kept close together to avoid the appearance of waves in water. Another method to save time is to let the grass fade out in the central part of the grassy area. Composing the faded area requires an experienced hand. Filling the entire area with grass is recommended for beginners.

Concrete, gravel, or sand have a similar appearance [11-11]. Dots are used to resemble tiny shadows on the surface caused by the pitted concrete surface or irregularities in a gravel or sand surface.

The symbols for masonry paving used for patios, walls, and streets is easy to draw [11-12]. The joint pattern is shown to scale. The same technique is used for wood decks [11-13]. Showing the joints between the boards

Entry arrows quickly locate entrances.

Figure 11-8

Figure 11-12

Design Presentation

187

Wood deck . . .

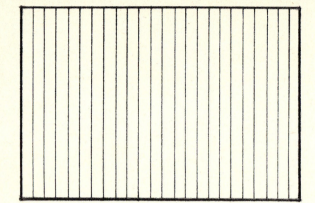

Figure 11–13

Standing seam metal roof . . .

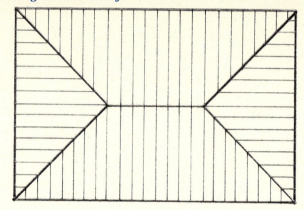

Figure 11–15

results in a tone and gives the deck contrast with the surrounding grass or adjacent inside floor area. Any roofing materials having joints may also be shown with lines [11–14 and 11–15].

Water can be shown with lines at the edges representing ripples caused by the water moving against the edge of a pool. The lines may also be representative of contour lines showing the relative depths of a large body of water such as a lake [11–16]. An island is shown in the center of this illustration. The edge line representation is a fast technique, but it leaves the water as a light area. If a dark tone is desired for the water, the area may be covered with closely spaced straight lines [11–17].

Trees in a plan view may be drawn with or without leaves [11–18]. Plan view tree symbols may also be used to represent bushes and planting. A plant symbol is just a smaller version of a tree symbol. Large-scale plants will show individual leaves, while plants drawn at a small scale will show an outline of leaf mass.

Automobiles are very useful in site plans and plot plans. Seen from the top, they are simple to draw [11–19]. You need not trace them. Draw a rectangle the size of an average car and draw a smaller rectangle on top of it. Keep the drawing reasonably simple. Fill about

Water . . . light tone.

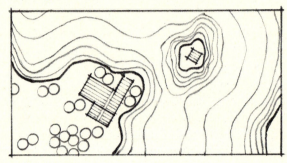

Figure 11–16

20 to 25% of the parking spaces shown in the site plan with car symbols of this type. This gives the drawing a nice texture and sense of detail.

The illusion of three-dimensional space on a drawing is enhanced by using shadows. A shadow is a darkened area on an object caused by the blocking of sunshine by another object. Shadows may be used to establish distance between objects or parts of an object. In a site plan the feeling of height is created when high objects cast shadows on lower ones.

The size and position of a shadow area are related to the sun's position in the sky. Shadows are short around noon in the summer when the sun is high. They

Shingle hip roof . . .

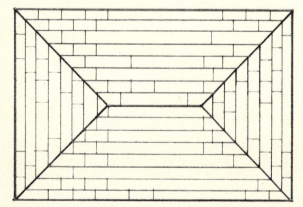

Figure 11–14

Water . . . dark tone.

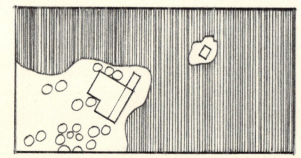

Figure 11–17

188

Architectural Design

Trees and plants . . .

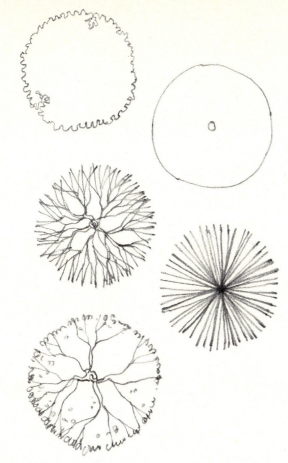

Figure 11–18

are long in the late afternoon and in the winter when the sun is low in the sky. The exact position of the sun can be determined for any time of day and year in any part of the world from solar angle charts (see Tables 8–1 to 8–4). Precise positioning of shadows is not necessary or even recommended for presentation drawing purposes.

In presentation drawing it is convenient to assume that the sun's rays are approaching the building at an angle of 45° regardless of the time of year. A ray of the

Automobiles . . .

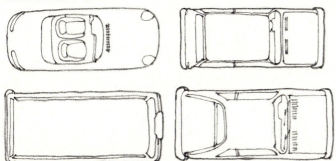

Figure 11–19

The sun's rays are assumed to be at a 45° angle . . . the length of the shadow on the ground equals the height of the object.

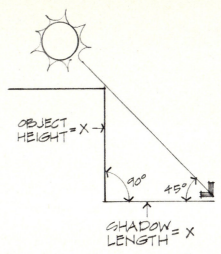

Figure 11–20

sun touching the top of a flagpole, building, or any object will cast on the ground a shadow of a length equal to the height of the object [11–20]. This may be easier to visualize if you compare it to a 45° right triangle. The object is represented as the height of the triangle. The sun's ray is the hypotenuse. The shadow is equal to the height of the object. The top of a 1-foot tall box would cast a shadow on the ground 1 foot long.

Another convenient assumption in drawing shadows is that the sun's rays pass the object at an angle that causes the edge of the shadow to make an angle of 45° with the building. This is not critical, but it matches a standard triangle and can be very convenient in drawing shadows on a perspective, as we shall see later in this chapter.

Some architectural drafters like to match the perpendicular distance that the shadow extends on the ground to the height of the building [11–21]. The sun in this case is at an angle of 35°16′ to the ground and causes a slightly longer shadow. This is a perfectly satisfactory way of measuring shadows. At this altitude angle any portion of the shadow that is cast on the elevations of a building will appear at a 45° angle. This has advantages when sizing shadows in elevation.

Having the sun in exactly the same position in all views is not necessary. Drawing all angled shadow lines at 45° is an accepted procedure, however, due to its convenience.

All shadows that fall on relatively smooth surfaces such as brick, wood, or concrete should be drawn with closely spaced parallel lines [11–21]. Avoid the temptation of shading with the broad side of the pencil or with scratchy strokes in random directions. This results in a messy shadow. If the shadow density is not perfectly even, by using parallel strokes the irregularities will at least be relatively uniform. Parallel shadow lines are not

Design Presentation

Another shadow measurement approximation . . . the shadow on the ground extends for a perpendicular distance equal to the object's height.

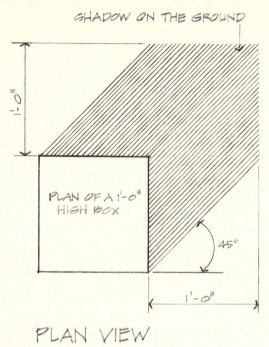

Figure 11–21

A shadow cast on grass is shown by darkening the grass symbol.

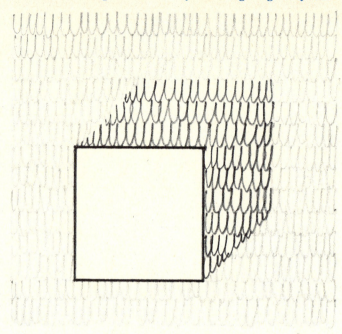

Figure 11–22

used on grass. In the shadowed area, draw the grass symbol darker than for the area that is in the sunshine [11–22]. This looks more realistic than using straight lines superimposed on top of the grass symbol.

Rendering site plans [11–23 and 11–24] and floor plans [11–25] increases readability, richness, and warmth of the presentation. In addition to using standard symbols, a drafter can apply his or her own technique to give the drawing depth and realism.

EXERCISES

11–1. What is meant by rendering? How can it be applied to a plan drawing?

11–2. What is the purpose of a design presentation?

11–3. Sketch the furniture in your living room in plan view.

11–4. Find a paved area in your neighborhood using masonry (brick or stone). Sketch a symbol to represent it in plan view.

11–5. Draw three 4-inch squares. Fill them with guidelines $\frac{1}{8}$, $\frac{3}{16}$, and $\frac{1}{4}$ inch apart, respectively; fill each one with the grass symbol.

11–6. Find a house in your neighborhood with wood, vinyl, or metal siding. Sketch an elevation of the house showing symbols for all the materials, including glass.

11–7. Draw two plan views of a 20 × 30 foot swimming pool at a scale of $\frac{1}{4}'' = 1'-0''$. Put a 6-foot strip of 12-inch square tile on all four sides. Place a rubber raft in the pool and locate a ladder at each side of the deep end. Show the water with two different symbols. Which do you prefer? Why?

11–8. Draw 10 light circles with a 1-inch diameter. Draw two samples each of five different plan symbols for trees. Which one do you prefer? Why?

11–9. Examine four different types of cars in your community. Sketch simple plan views of each at a scale of $\frac{1}{4}'' = 1'-0''$.

11–10. Find two small boxes such as ones in which a stapler or a pencil sharpener might be sold. Tape or glue them together in any arrangement and fix them to a flat cardboard base. Now draw them in plan view and draw the shadow that they would cast using the 45° system. Transfer the shadow lines to the cardboard base. Move the assembly into the sunshine. Can you tilt and turn the assembly until the actual shadow matches your drawn shadow lines?

11–11. Copy the floor plan of [7–13] at a scale of $\frac{1}{4}'' = 1'-0''$. Determine the scale of the illustration by assuming that the hall is 3 feet wide. Render the floor plan. Show furniture in all rooms and place grass around the house for a distance of 20 feet. Show a car in the driveway.

11.2 Presentation Elevations and Sections

Many plan rendering techniques apply to presentation elevations as well. The preferred types of line weights are illustrated in [11–26]. Typical materials seen in elevation are masonry, wood, shingles, and glass.

A rendered site plan showing apartment buildings with hip roofs.

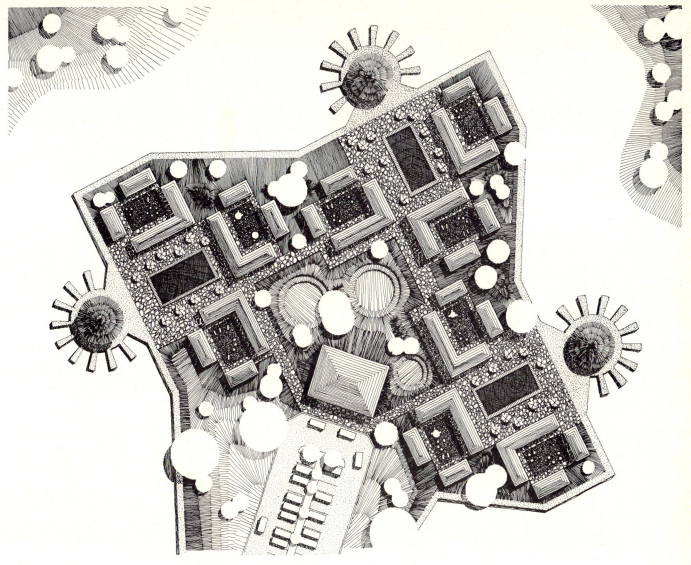

Figure 11–23

The method of representing brick is often more time consuming than it should be. The simplified method seen in [11–27] shows only the horizontal joints. Examine any brick wall at different times during the day. Notice that the shadows on the horizontal joints are usually more prominent than the vertical ones. The sun casts a shadow almost continuously in the horizontal joints since it is above them at all times except at sunrise and sunset. A shadow is cast in the vertical joints only when the sun is to one side of the joint. Architects generally use only horizontal lines as the brick symbol because of this and also because the method is much faster. Brick should be drawn to scale on large-scale drawings. On small-scale drawings, the size of the brick may be exaggerated as needed for a readable drawing. In both cases,

lines for concrete block are drawn farther apart than for brick. Typically, one concrete block is equal in height to three bricks.

The stone symbol is easy to draw but often is drawn incorrectly by beginners [11–28]. The illustration shows very tight joints between the stones; in fact, nearly all the stones touch. Do not draw wide joints. Measure your joints after you have drawn a few. If their scale dimension is larger than an inch, draw them smaller. Stone can be set with wide joints, but it usually isn't. The narrow joint looks more professional on a drawing. Time may be saved by letting the stones fade out in the center. This requires an artistic touch to keep the stones from stopping in an apparent pattern. A few stones can be drawn "floating" in the blank area to help achieve a

Design Presentation

A site plan showing clustered single family housing rendered with a wash (nonlinear) technique.

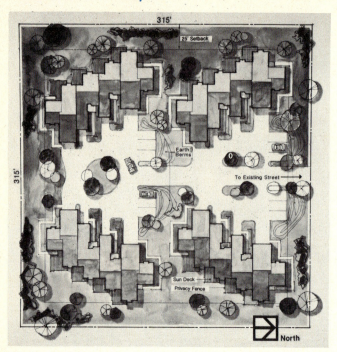

Figure 11–24
A rendered floor plan showing surrounding site features.

natural appearance. Although stones can be round, the more rectangular they look in your drawing, the neater the drawing will look.

All types of shingles are best drawn as wood shakes [11–29]. Shakes vary in thickness because they are hand split. This produces an irregular shadow line. The shadow line adds a rich texture to the drawing and is used for asphalt shingles too. It is achieved with a wedge-pointed pencil drawn back and forth for short distances and tipped up and down as the hand moves across the sheet. A number of vertical joints can be added to help distinguish this symbol from the brick symbol. The central area can be left free of joint lines to save time and to control the overall tone of this area in relation to other areas.

Wood siding (or vinyl and metal that imitate wood) should be shown without wood grain [11–30]. The joints between boards is enough to give the feeling of the material. For interior elevations, some drafters like to exaggerate the grain of wood wall panels [11–31]. The grain is also exaggerated on table tops in plan view. Care should be taken to see that adding the grain does not reduce the readability by making the drawing too "busy."

On a pencil drawing the grain lines can be smudged

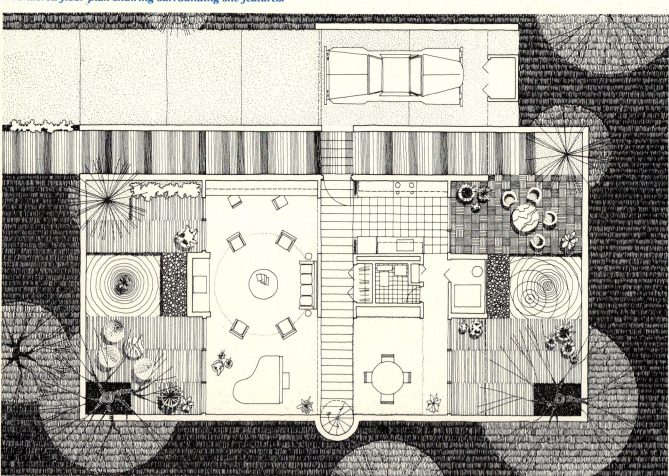

Figure 11–25

Line weights for presentation elevations.

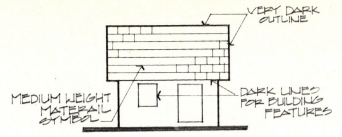

Figure 11-26

Brick or concrete block . . .

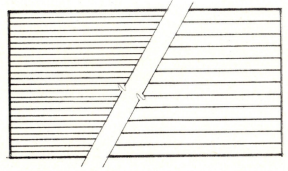

Figure 11-27

Stone . . .

Figure 11-28

Shingles . . .

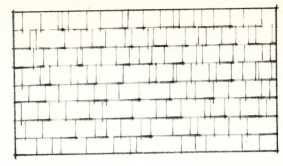

Figure 11-29

Wood siding . . . horizontal and board and batten.

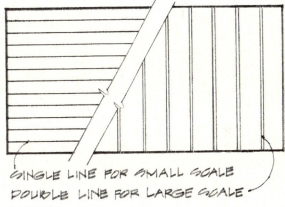

Figure 11-30

Interior wood paneling . . .

Figure 11-31

with the thumb to give the wood a darker tone. The smudge need not be even since light spots look like light being reflected on the surface. The grain lines should be reasonably straight and angular. Curved lines do not look crisp. Commercial transfer sheets are available for a wide variety of textures. Their use can simplify texture representation as well as save considerable time. The texture is transferred to the drawing with a burnishing tool.

A greatly misunderstood symbol is that of glass. The beginner usually draws a few slash lines across the glass to represent reflections. One of the secrets of graphic representation is to draw a feature to resemble the original object. This seems self-evident, but often it is not done. There are no slash lines on the surface of real glass. Look at a window from the outside that has no curtains or blinds. The glass appears solid black. An easy and successful way to represent windows is to draw the glass solid black [11-32]. Since it is difficult to achieve solid blackness, blacken the glass with vertical pencil strokes. If light streaks show, they will at least be uniform.

Elevations, being orthographic projections, do not naturally indicate depth. Shadows are helpful in creating the illusion of depth. The same approach to shadows discussed for plans may be used in elevations. Assume

Design Presentation

Glass is best shown solid black.

Figure 11–32

Shadows cast by vertical elements.

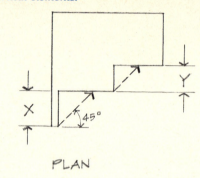

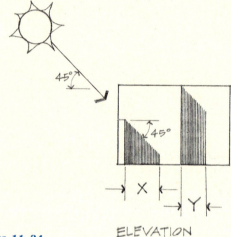

Figure 11–34

that the sun rays are at an angle of 45° in each elevation. Overhanging features such as roofs, canopies, balconies—even window sills—will cast a shadow on the face of the building with a vertical height equal to the width of the overhang [11–33].

Shadows of walls and other vertical elements may be sized in a similar way. The length of the projection of a wall forward of a perpendicular surface will be equal to the size of the shadow it casts on the elevation [11–34]. The projecting wall and the width of shadow in the plan view form two legs of a 45° triangle. The sun's rays become the hypotenuse. If the rays pass over the top of the projecting element, the top of the shadow in elevation will be sloped at 45°.

In drawing elevations you should position the sun to cause objects in the foreground to cast shadows on parts farther back [11–35]. Positioning the sun so that few or no shadows are cast is a waste of one of the

Shadows drawn on vertical surfaces . . . the shadow height equals the width of the overhang.

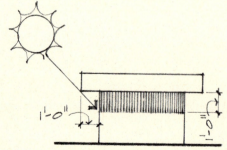

Figure 11–33

Recommended sun position to produce a shadow in the elevation view . . . this gives the illusion of depth.

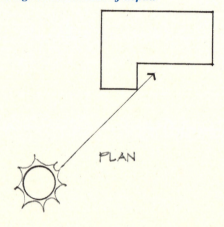

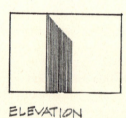

Figure 11–35

194 Architectural Design

techniques available to you to create the feeling of depth [11–36].

In the northern hemisphere, little sunlight shines on the north face of a building. For the most part the north elevation is in shade. To draw a completely shaded north elevation, although technically correct, is of little graphic value. If you show shadows that will never exist, an unrealistic idea will be presented. This may draw complaints from the client. One solution is to place a very light tone on the north elevation to acknowledge reality but not obscure information. Avoid showing the sun as shining from the north at an angle of 45° on other elevations since this is not a realistic condition. Except for these "north sun" limitations, it is recommended that the sun be positioned differently in each elevation to yield the best three-dimensional effect for the building.

Presentation elevations are not complete without giving a feeling of "scale." In this sense we are not talking about the proportional scale at which the view has been drawn. Scale also means visual comparison of size to the human figure. In other words, how will the building size compare to a person and to objects that are familiar to people? Including people in the views is an obvious way to make this comparison [11–37]. Other items, such as cars, trees, plantings, and furniture, help the viewer understand the scale and add realism to the presentation.

Drawing people may seem difficult, but it is probably the easiest scale aid to include. You are not expected to be expert in drawing human figures. Many books are published that include figures of all sizes that can be traced. Also, you can maintain a less expensive file of traceable people by collecting pictures from newspapers, magazines, and mail-order catalogs. School yearbooks are an excellent source for figures in all sizes and positions.

When tracing a figure keep the drawing simple. Facial details and shading are usually omitted. An outline is adequate to give the desired impression. Use people of the correct size. To select people for elevations, measure the figures with the same scale at which the elevation is drawn.

Sun position not recommended . . . no shadow is produced in the elevation view.

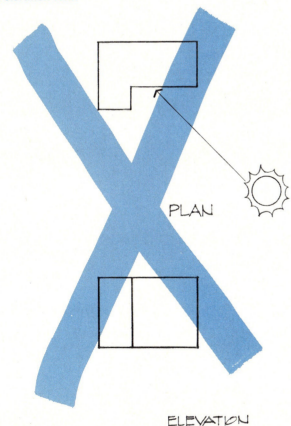

Figure 11–36

Including people and familiar objects in an elevation adds realism and permits size comparisons . . . use only simple outlines of the correct scale.

Figure 11–37

Design Presentation

195

Draw only true elevations of cars . . . use simple outlines and maintain correct scale.

Figure 11–38

Automobile shapes may also be traced from publications printed for this purpose or from newspapers and magazine ads. True elevations of cars are not common in newspapers and magazines. Usually, cars are photographed at an angle, making them appear in perspective. Trace only true elevations [11–38]. Also, be sure the car is "in scale" with your drawing. Use the same rule of detail as was used for drawing people. Represent the cars as simple outlines. Omit shading even if the drawing has shades and shadows elsewhere. We do not want to call attention to these accessory details by making them too noticeable.

Trees are helpful in adding realism and richness to elevations. Since photographs of trees are hard to trace, it is advisable to trace drawings from a publication that shows trees graphically. Nearby trees have more detail. The individual leaves can be seen. Midground trees show leaf shapes, but they are very close together. Several circular pencil strokes can be run together to give the impression of many, many leaves [11–39]. Distant trees show no leaves [11–40]. Simple outlines are adequate to portray all the leaves in one large shape. You may be more comfortable in drawing all trees without leaves (winter trees) [11–41]. They are less realistic but more easily drawn.

Do not show a north arrow on an elevation. Its use is only appropriate on plan views. The scale of the drawing should be included somewhere near the title. A thick black line is often drawn under the building [11–42].

Individual leaves are shown on nearby trees.

Figure 11–39

Use simple outline shapes for distant trees.

Figure 11–40

Trees without leaves may be easier to draw . . . but are less realistic.

Figure 11–41

This represents the ground and gives the appearance that the building is resting on a solid base.

Elevations are usually drawn for all sides of the building unless some of the views would be repetitive. The heavily rendered elevations in [11–43 to 11–46] bring together many techniques we have discussed. Note that the sky has been left blank in three of the elevations. This is a safe and acceptable approach. Clouds are difficult to draw and require great artistic skill and experience.

A thick black line drawn under the building gives the appearance of resting on solid ground.

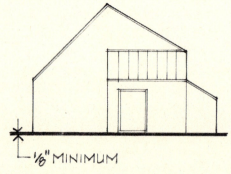

Figure 11–42

Individual leaves are shown on nearby trees.

Figure 11-43

A *building section* is sometimes included in the presentation if the floor or ceiling levels change [11-47]. The floor, ceiling, roof, and walls are usually drawn solid black so as to avoid showing detail that is not important at this time. The title may be general such as "Typical Building Section" or may be identified by letters such as "Section A-A." The actual position of the section cut would be indicated on the floor plan and identified with the same letters. Room names may be included and as always, the scale should be shown. Some drafters prefer to omit detail seen in elevation from the building section. Others like to show very complete interior elevations within the presentation section [11-48].

Presentation sections may be rendered with trees, cars, and people as in elevations. Note that the section in [11-48] leaves the walls and roof blank and relies on the heavy rendering surrounding these items to make them "read."

Line rendering technique with windows solid black . . . roof shingles shown . . . trees shown with leaves . . . blank sky.

Figure 11-44

Design Presentation

197

Line rendering with press-on toned film for windows . . . shingled roof left blank . . . background trees without leaves . . . blank sky.

Figure 11–45

Wash rendering (transparent paint) with partial wash tone on windows . . . shingles suggested on roof . . trees shown with suggested leaves . . . hint of clouds in sky.

Figure 11–46

A building section may be included if floor or ceiling levels change.

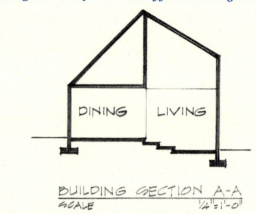

Figure 11–47

A fully-rendered presentation section.

Figure 11–48

198

EXERCISES

11–12. Sketch a line elevation of your home at a scale of ¼″ = 1′–0″. Use three different line weights to establish a hierarchy of line weights.

11–13. Show symbols for all materials on the elevation in Exercise 11–12, including glass.

11–14. Draw a second version of the elevation in Exercise 11–12 and change the materials (siding becomes brick, brick becomes stone, and so on.) Can you arrive at a selection of materials that you prefer over the actual materials? Compare sketches to make your decision as a designer would.

11–15. Select the elevation you prefer from [7–19] and draw shadows on it using the 45° method. Include the small shadows around window trim, and so on.

11–16. Trace some people from a magazine or newspaper onto the front elevation of [7–19]. Select two adults and a child.

11–17. Draw one simple car in the front elevation of [7–16]. Put it to one side of the house.

11–18. Draw the front elevation of [6–28] at a scale of ¼″ = 1′–0″. Render the elevation. Show all the features that a rendering usually shows.

11–19. Add trees to the elevation in [6–28]. Draw a large tree behind the building and rising above the roof. Add a low row of trees in the distance to the left and right of the building.

11.3 Renderings

Not all design presentations will contain all of the features that have been discussed in this chapter. A perspective or other type of pictorial drawing having most of the items discussed is called a *rendering*. Elevations and plans with these features are called *rendered elevations and plans*. When you are drawing them it is called "to render" or "to delineate." A rendering is also called a *delineation*. One who prepares renderings professionally is called a *delineator*. Renderings containing some of these aids may be seen in other sections of this book. Figure [1–9], for example, does not include shadows but has cars. Figure [2–7] has shadows but no cars or people. The symbols described for rendering plans and elevations are drawn in a similar manner in perspectives except for the fact that horizontal lines should converge toward the vanishing points.

Furniture must be included in interior perspectives. Furniture that is basically rectangular is easier to draw in perspective than curved types [11–49 and 11–50]. With so many drawing aids available for tracing, you do not need to construct perspective furniture graphically, however. Furniture that is parallel to the walls have the same vanishing points as the wall lines. When tracing furniture, be sure that the vanishing points are on the horizon line of the perspective. If they aren't, the furniture will look like it has been tipped up or down. Furniture size may be judged by constructing a few guidelines in the perspective at appropriate heights for tables and chairs.

Interior and exterior planting is easily sized since there is a wide range of sizes appropriate for a building. They may be traced or drawn freehand. Large plants may show complete leaf shapes [11–51], while smaller plants and plants in the distance may show an outline or silhouette of the leaf mass.

Furniture must be included in interior perspectives.

Figure 11–49

Design Presentation

199

Curved furniture is more difficult to draw in perspective.

Large plants may show complete leaf shapes.

Figure 11–51

Figure 11–50

One-point is the most popular perspective system for drawing an interior [11–52]. It is relatively easy to construct, and it is realistic. Two-point perspective may be used for interior views with equal success, but it is more time consuming to construct [11–53].

The representation of a relatively flat surface in perspective requires increased detailing to give the illusion of depth. When showing cabinets, a fireplace, or book-

A one-point interior perspective using a linear technique. Since the outside is lighter than the interior of the room, exterior glass is rendered clear . . . the glass in the oven is shown dark. The absence of lines on the edges on many items gives a less harsh and more three-dimensional effect.

Figure 11–52

200   Architectural Design

A two-point interior perspective using a wash technique . . . note that no lines are parallel to the bottom of the page as they are in a one-point perspective.

Figure 11–53

shelves, you are dependent on relatively small increments of depth and scale features (plants, furniture) to achieve a three-dimensional effect [11–54].

Trees seen in elevation views and in perspective views are the same in appearance. The elevation trees seen in [11–39 to 11–41] are perfectly acceptable for perspectives. Additional depth can be added to a perspective view by drawing a tree in a location near the viewer. The tree, in this case, would be higher than the viewer's head and be too large to draw in its entirety. Drawing a large branch and detailed leaves in one corner of the perspective gives the feeling that you are viewing from under a tree in the foreground [11–55]. The building, being partially framed by this tree, appears to recede into the middle ground.

Drawings of people may be used to give a feeling of foreground and background as well as give a sense of scale. Having a "sense of scale" means understanding how the building relates to a human being. Drawing people in the perspective is a direct way of establishing this relationship.

Selecting people for perspectives is relatively easy. If you have an eye level perspective, all figures are the correct size. Simply position them with their eyes on the horizon line. Small figures will appear to be in the background and large figures will seem to be close to the viewer. You must be careful, however, to position

A portion of a very close tree placed in the corner of the drawing adds depth.

A one-point perspective of a fire-place with bookshelves . . . the extension of furniture into the foreground supplements the detailing of the trim and shelf depth in distinguishing this drawing from an elevation.

Figure 11–54

Figure 11–55

Design Presentation

the figures in logical places. After setting the figure's eyes on the horizon line, be sure that the feet are not in a flowerbed or a pool of water. Shorter people such as children will have their eyes below the horizon line. Use the adults in the drawing as a guide for placing children.

The same people outlines that are used in elevations [11–37] are used in perspectives. A perspective requires a greater variety of sizes, however, in comparison to an elevation where all people are drawn at the same scale.

Automobiles are often drawn in a rendering to provide a sense of scale and realism. Selecting the size of a car is done by comparing it to other items in the drawing. The top of a car is slightly below the shoulder of an average-height person [11–38]. Small cars appear to be in the background, so do not draw them in front of an object that is obviously in the foreground. The reverse is true for large cars. Location is important but easily solved. Don't position a car in a place that is peculiar, such as on the grass or on a sidewalk.

Since cars are basically box-like shapes, they have vanishing points just like a building. Be sure that the vanishing points of the car are on the horizon line of the building. Also, be sure that you are tracing a car whose photograph was taken from the same eye level as the perspective was drawn [11–56]. Do not heavily render cars with shadows and textures. They are supplementary to the building and should not compete with it for attention.

Although a perspective will seem three-dimensional because of its construction, shadows are important to further strengthen the photographic effect. There are ways to construct shadows directly on a perspective. It is easier for beginners, however, to simply draw the shadows on the elevations and plans and then transfer them to the perspective during the course of constructing

When tracing car outlines . . . be sure to select a photo taken from the same eye level as the perspective.

Figure 11–56

If the object is at 45° with the picture plane, a shadow cast at 45° will have horizontal lines.

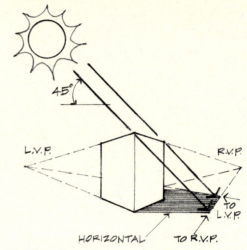

Figure 11–57

the perspective. If the principal faces of the object have been positioned at an angle of 45° with the picture plane, a shadow cast at 45° will appear parallel to the bottom of the sheet in the perspective view [11–57]. Since few lines are horizontal in a perspective, it reduces the complexity of its construction if half the shadow edges are parallel to the bottom of the drawing.

Shade is a darkened area on an object caused by the blocking of the sun's rays by the object itself [11–58]. That is to say, it occurs on the side of the object opposite to the one in the sunshine. Shade is relatively easy to draw. It is shown on the sides of objects on which the sun does not shine. Use the same line symbolism as used for shadows. Shade shows only in a perspective view, unless angled walls are seen in an elevation.

Figure [11–59] is a one-point exterior perspective. It includes all the aids that we have discussed plus some lines in the sky to represent clouds. Figure [11–60], a two-point perspective, uses a heavy linear technique to represent clouds. Care must be taken so that such a tech-

Shade is the dark area on the side opposite the sun . . . the same line symbol is used as for shadows.

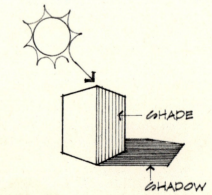

Figure 11–58

A one-point exterior perspective rendering.

Figure 11–59

nique does not draw attention away from the building. Note that in this rendering, the automobiles are left unrendered (except for glass) and the people are either light or dark to contrast with the shade behind them. The paving in the foreground has a linear shading that is a relatively smooth texture to distinguish it from grass.

Figure [11–61] utilizes a tone for the sky that is darkest at the building and fades quickly to white as it progresses up the sheet. This technique is fairly easy to master as long as you are able to produce a reasonably even tone. It has the advantage of helping the building stand out without the more difficult task of drawing clouds. Sky tones tend to give the feeling of stormy weather. This method may become monotonous if you use it in all your renderings.

One way to avoid a blank looking sky or an artificial one is to fill the sky with foreground trees [11–62]. The white sky gives contrast to the trees which in turn helps to give an impression of depth. Note that the grass darkens as it approaches the townhouses in the distance to give increased contrast to the lined siding. The roofs are left blank to achieve contrast with the siding tone and the trees behind.

A blank sky combined with blank foreground paving gives prominence to a darker building but leaves a relatively washed out appearance to the rendering as a whole [11–63]. This rendering contains vanishing sign lettering that requires fairly tedious and time-consuming precision. When faced with signs, you must resist the temptation to rush through the construction of the letters. Inaccurate letters in a rendering are noticeable even to the untrained eye. Precision and patience are necessary to make vanishing letters accurate. You may wish to avoid this problem by arranging your perspective so that signs appear parallel to the picture plane as in a one-point perspective. In this position all letters appear

Design Presentation

203

A two-point rendering of an addition to a small historic building . . . an attempt has been made to border all light areas with dark areas and vice-versa, to increase contrast and therefore increase the three-dimensional effect.

Figure 11–60

This two-point perspective is nearly a one-point due to the great distance away of the left vanishing point. The light building is framed by a sky and grass tone is done in pencil. The dark glass of the greenhouse is faded to a light tone as the glass curves to a slanted position . . . this gives the feeling that it is reflecting the sky.

Figure 11–61

An unusual combination of a one-point (foreground building at the right) and a two-point perspective (buildings in the background). Since units in a multifamily project may not be perpendicular to each other, such a mix of perspectives is appropriate.

Figure 11–62

Technically, this is a two-point perspective, but the left vanishing point is so far away that the left vanishing lines are almost horizontal. Care has been taken to see that the sign lettering becomes appropriately smaller as it approaches the right vanishing point.

Figure 11–63

A one-point perspective with the vanishing point at the far left of the picture. Note that the tree and post shadows are incomplete . . . fading out shadows frees the delineator from the time-consuming process of reproducing complete shadows. Complete shadows may confuse the drawing and, if drawn inaccurately, may detract from the rendering . . . this is an artistic decision and requires artistic skill to select appropriate places to use this technique.

Figure 11–64

in their true proportion to each other. Press-on letters might even be found that are the appropriate size.

One-point exterior perspectives need not be constructed with the vanishing point near the center of the rendering [11–64]. A feeling of the more complex two-point perspective can be achieved by positioning the single vanishing point far to one side of the picture. The illusion created is that of a second vanishing point at a great distance to the other side of the drawing. One-point perspectives are especially appropriate for courtyards or entryways where structures surround a central space [11–65].

Water in perspective can be tricky since the appearance of water is different when it is motionless than when it is moving. You may find the most success if you draw still water almost as if it were a mirror. You should examine a still pond or lake on a sunny day to see just how objects are reflected. Typically, they are simply drawn upside down in the water area. To account for the fact that reflected images are not as bright as actual images, the reflections may be drawn light or the water may have a tone applied to it. Do not apply a tone to water with horizontal lines. Vertical lines give a better illusion of depth. With practice you may be

A typical one-point perspective of an entry court . . . the vanishing point is in the center of the drawing.

Figure 11–65

206 Architectural Design

A one-point perspective in pencil. Note that the trees change darkness to contrast with their backgrounds . . . this can be justified by the variety of shades and shadows encountered in a wooded area. The water reflects this variety of tones and thus seems reflective and transparent at the same time

Figure 11–66

able to achieve lively and rich-looking water by rendering a variety of reflections and tones in water areas [11–66].

Up to this point most of the renderings have been *linear* in nature (tones achieved with lines). Increased realism may be achieved with *continuous-tone* renderings (ink or paint washes applied with a brush). *Painted* renderings require a high level of skill, but may be more highly appreciated by the general public due to their picturelike quality [11–67].

Figure 11–67

A two-point perspective rendered with a transparent-type paint . . . the continuous tones are harder to achieve than lined tones but are more reminiscent of reality if done well.

Design Presentation

An aerial one-point perspective . . . time was saved in this heavily rendered drawing by utilizing a border to save drawing everything all the way to the horizon.

Figure 11–68 *Rehabilitation Center, Buffalo State Hospital, Buffalo, N.Y.*

You should not try water color or other paint techniques until you have mastered perspective construction and the basic principles of contrast in rendering. These are best studied in pencil, which is easier to control and to achieve reasonable results.

The renderings studied thus far have all been drawn at eye level. This is the appropriate level for most perspective drawings since it represents the angle at which buildings are viewed by most people. Aerial perspective (a view from higher than eye level) may be appropriate for projects with several buildings [11–68] or with buildings that are very long compared to their height (such as shopping centers).

Be sure that an aerial view is absolutely necessary before you decide to draw one. They require more drawing than the eye-level view due to the great amount of land that shows. Unless you cut the perspective off at the top with a border, or let it fade out, you will need to draw trees and buildings all the way to the horizon.

In all presentation drawings you must decide how much detail is needed to explain your design and then balance that with how much time is available to prepare the drawings. A client may feel that a very thorough presentation is too expensive, and you may too.

An economical approach to presentation drawing is to prepare a drawing that may be converted into a construction drawing at a later date. When doing this you must not include any items that are inappropriate for construction drawings, such as blackened walls, furniture, textures, shadows, and scale realism aids. In effect you would be presenting a construction drawing without details. This saves redrawing the views of the building, but it is not an impressive presentation.

EXERCISES

11–20. Sketch the furniture in your living room in perspective.

11–21. Sketch a plant while looking at a real one or at a magazine picture.

11–22. Draw a wide street vanishing to a single point on a horizon line located 5′–0″ above a ground line. Using magazine and newspaper illustrations, trace 20 different-size adult people on the street. Place their eyes above, on, or below the horizon line depending on whether they are tall, medium, or short people. Add five children of different sizes. Use the adult figures to estimate the appropriate placement of the children.

11–23. Find an automobile that you can view from three levels (near an outside stairway, for example). Sketch a line drawing of the car from eye level, a few feet above normal eye level, and 10 to 15 feet above eye level. Compare the drawings to see how the view of the car roof increases as the eye level rises.

11–24. Copy the perspective of the house in [6–20B]. Enlarge it to fill an 8½- x 11-inch sheet of paper. Use grids to transfer the linework. Render the drawing. Show people on the sidewalk and an automobile on the street that runs parallel to the sidewalk (just out of the picture on the right side).

12 Model Building

12.1 Types and Materials

The second type of design presentation is the architectural model. Models are generally of two types: those built for study and those built for display. *Study models* have a wide range of sophistication. Since their prime purpose is to assist in studying the three-dimensional aspects of a design, it may be only necessary that they be built to an accurate scale without refined craftsmanship. The materials used for a study model can consist of almost any material that can be easily formed to a selected scale. Chipboard, matboard, flat foam plastic sheets, and, quite often, corrugated cardboard cartons from a grocery store can be used for this purpose.

Chipboard is a homogeneous, relatively inexpensive material [12–1 and 12–2]. Models done in chipboard are typically tan or gray without attempt made to indicate true material color or texture. Windows may be cutouts or omitted.

Matboard is not homogeneous [12–3]. It has a colored surface paper with white (usually) backing material. Consequently, flush joints show the inner color in contrast

A chipboard study model of an apartment building. Windows are recessed and represented in a dark color . . . balconies are constructed . . . existing adjacent buildings are of contrasting color chipboard but show no detail.

Figure 12–2

A chipboard study model of a residence. No detail is included . . . glass areas are left open . . . a model of this type is useful for studying relationships of forms prior to finalizing the design.

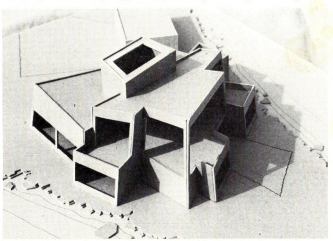

Figure 12–1

A matboard model used to study the relationships of a proposed building to surrounding buildings . . . windows and doors of the existing buildings are drawn on the surface of the matboard.

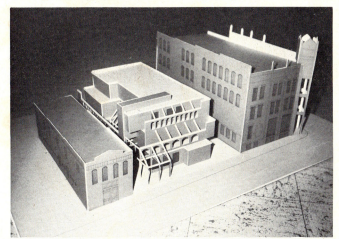

Figure 12–3

A polystyrene foam model used to study the relationships between buildings in a downtown area . . . no windows or other details are shown.

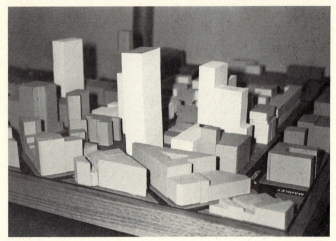

Figure 12–4

A chipboard model of six blocks on the Lower East Side of New York City. The proposed renovation is built with gray board . . . existing buildings that will remain unchanged are made with tan.

Figure 12–6

to the colored surface. This is not a problem in study models and may actually add crispness to the model. The colored surface may be useful to suggest the color of the building material. Windows may be drawn on the walls or cut out.

Polystyrene plastic foam may be used for models done at small scale where gluing individual walls together would be too time consuming [12–4]. Discarded plastic foam packing material or insulation scraps may be large enough for some models. Large blocks may be purchased if necessary. Polystyrene may be smoothly and accurately cut with a hot wire that is mounted in a device to hold it straight and heat it with an electrical current [12–5]. Simple solid shapes are formed quickly by moving the polystyrene against the wire. This method may also be used to make models of small buildings at large scale.

Chipboard may be used for small-scale models if you have the time to cut the many small pieces and fit them together [12–6]. The small-scale chipboard model can be more refined than the polystyrene since parapets and overhangs are easily constructed.

A very small scale model covering several square miles may be done in chipboard and wood [12–7]. Do not attempt to represent sloping ground by a smooth surface. Cut chipboard pieces to conform to the contours of the site plan and stack them. If the chipboard is $\frac{1}{16}$ inch thick and the model is made at a scale of $\frac{1}{32}'' = 1'-0''$, every layer of board represents a 2-foot vertical drop.

This is not an accurate representation of what happens at each contour on a site plan since the ground usually

A hot-wire cutter for polystyrene. The polystyrene is pressed against a taut resistance wire that has been heated with electric current . . . this melts the plastic, producing a relatively straight "cut" surface.

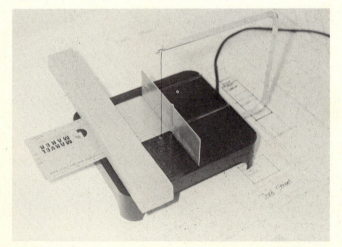

Figure 12–5

Chipboard can be layered horizontally to show contours of the land . . . the thickness of the chipboard must be exactly equal to the contour interval to present a realistic view of the steepness of the topography. At such a small scale, buildings can be represented by small lengths cut from balsa wood sticks.

Figure 12–7

A presentation model of the Farr Credit Banks Building, Spokane, Washington . . . cars and trees give a sense of scale to the building.

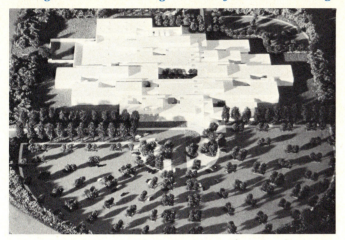

Figure 12–8

A presentation model of the Department of Justice, Sacramento, California . . . models can show the landscape design as well as the building configuration.

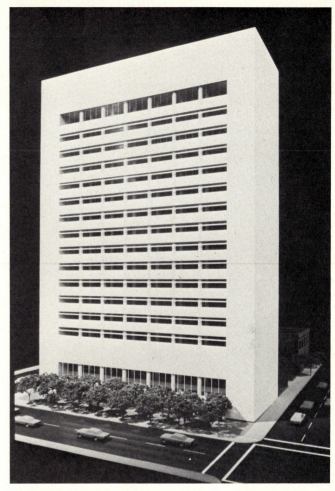

Figure 12–9

has a continuous slope between contours with no sudden drops. However, it is a representation that gives an impression of the overall configuration of the land and is easily understood by professionals. It is an aid to realism if the scaled distance represented by each board is small. Complicated contour models may be cut from a polyurethane plastic foam block by a computer-controlled machine. The contour intervals may be indicated by vertical drops or by a smooth slope. Such models would typically be made by companies specializing in this type of work.

Display models [12–8 to 12–10] require more accuracy in the use and cutting of materials. Most are constructed of cardboard or wood. A mat knife, modelmaker's knife, or even a single-edged razor blade can be used to cut the cardboard to the shapes desired. Always use a steel straightedge for a cutting guide. *Never* attempt to use a T-square, triangles, or scales for this purpose because a slight miscut will ruin a wood or plastic drawing edge. Power saws are used to cut wood elements. Materials are shown realistically with color and texture. Plantings can be represented with certain weeds that you may find in your community. Materials may also be purchased to represent trees and shrubbery.

12.2 Construction Preparations

The following paragraphs describe the step-by-step process of making a model relatively fast. It involves using scale drawings as patterns for the model as well as for the representation of windows, doors, patterns, and textures. Typically prints from presentation drawings are used since this type of model may be useful in explaining the proposed building to a client. This example, however, uses working drawing prints instead of presentation

A presentation model for condominiums in Hanover, New Hampshire. The buildings are made of mahogony . . . the wood grain suggests brick joints and the deep red color is similar to the color of the brick.

Figure 12–10

prints. This is not the usual approach because by the time the working drawings are done, study models have little use. The procedure that is used here is for purposes of clarification and instruction.

Frequently, it is desirable to construct a model at a different scale than originally drawn in the plans. As an example, a ¼" = 1'-0" scale model of a house may be too bulky to transport. A model of this size also requires considerably more detail than one built to a smaller scale. This is particularly true if you also wish to model the building site by showing landscaping, trees, topographic contours, and perhaps, even miniature people and cars. Fortunately, it is possible to either reduce or enlarge the original drawing to prepare a pattern for the model. This is made possible by reducing or enlarging your original drawings using a xerographic copying machine or a copy camera.

Let us build a model of the home design developed in Chapter 13. We will use the working drawings produced in Chapter 25 as a pattern. A more typical approach would be to use the presentation drawings as a pattern. The techniques shown are the same in either case. The original drawings were made at a scale of ¼" = 1'-0". We should reduce them to a more workable size so that the site plan can be included. For this purpose we will need a 50% reduction print of the floor plan and elevations. The original site plan was already drawn at ⅛" = 1'-0", so a direct diazo print of it is adequate to serve as a model base and pattern. The reduced floor plan and elevations are shown in [12-11] and [12-12], and the site plan is shown in [12-13].

Simple materials and tools, such as cardboard and a sharp knife, can be used for model building. You will also want to include spray adhesive or rubber cement, white glue, an architect's scale, pins (to hold the model while the glue is drying), and bits of sponge, shrubbery, and lichen to represent landscape planting. All of these materials can be obtained from a handicraft or art supply store. Model railroad shops sell scale models of cars, trees, and people that you may want to use to complete your model. An assortment of tools and materials that are commonly used to build models is shown in [12-14].

12.3 Constructing the Model

In our sample model, ¹⁄₁₆-inch-thick corkboard is used as a surface material to represent the ground. This material is available at art supply stores, hobby shops, and some hardware stores, where it is sold by the roll. Particleboard can be obtained from a building materials supply store and used as a base for the model. The site plan print is trimmed to the size of the lot and used as a pattern to cut the particleboard and the corkboard to size. These two materials are then cemented together with spray adhesive.

The trimmed site plan print is lightly sprayed with adhesive for temporary attachment to a piece of matboard obtained at an art supply store. In our example, a cream color has been chosen for the matboard since it will be used to represent the concrete surfaces on the model. The matboard is trimmed to match the site plan. The mounted site plan is now lightly sprayed with adhesive and temporarily mounted on the surface of the corkboard [12-15].

Using a sharp utility knife, carefully make a cut around the outlines of those areas of the print that are to be represented as concrete on the finished model. The cut should be made deep enough to pass through the print, the matboard, and the corkboard. By peeling off the concrete portion of the print, the cream-colored matboard will be exposed [12-16].

The remainder of the site plan print (along with the matboard on which it is mounted) is now peeled off, exposing the underlying corkboard surface that represents the ground. The "concrete" matboard along with the corkboard under it is lifted off the particleboard. The corkboard is removed from the underside of the matboard, and lines are drawn on the colored matboard surface at the appropriate scale intervals to represent joints in the concrete. The house's floor area is cut out from a floor plan print and spray-cemented to the "concrete" matboard in its proper location. The matboard is then sprayed with adhesive and returned to its opening in the corkboard [12-17].

The reduced-scale elevation print is lightly sprayed with adhesive and temporarily attached to a sheet of matboard of the desired color and texture to represent the exterior wall surfaces [12-18]. Cuts are then carefully made around the outlines of the walls. After removing the mounted wall panels from the matboard, cuts passing only through the print are made around the outlines of the windows and doors. After peeling the print off of the window areas, the exposed matboard is darkened in with black ink. Some model makers prefer to make the window area cuts a little deeper so that the top layer of the matboard can also be peeled off. This gives the window a feeling of depth.

The remaining wall print is now peeled off of the matboard except for the doors which are left cemented in place. Vertical lines are drawn on the matboard to suggest the texture of the finished wall paneling. Figure [12-19] shows the front wall of the house completed in the manner just described along with two other walls that still need cutting out and finishing. Note that a heavy dark outline has been drawn on the front wall to represent the garage door.

When the four walls are finished, they can be glued to the floor plan in their proper location using white glue [12-20 to 12-23]. Pins are used to hold the walls in place while the glue dries. The walls should also be glued to one another at the inside corners to provide stability. In addition it may be advisable to place a small

The floor plan is reduced to the scale of the site plan.

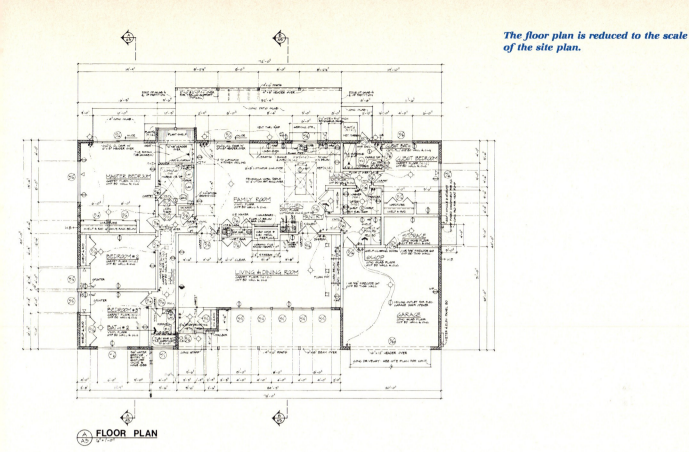

Figure 12–11

The elevations are also reduced to the scale of the site plan.

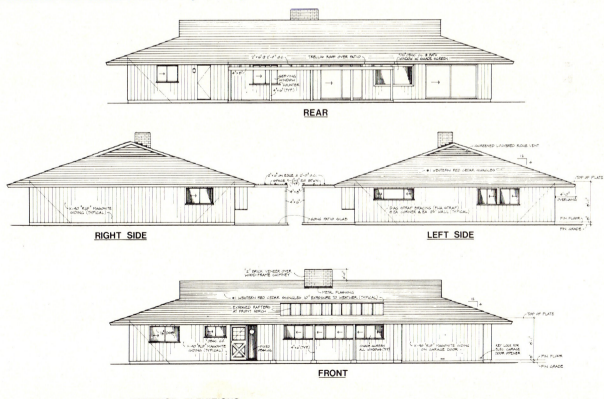

Figure 12–12

The site plan is used at its original drawn size.

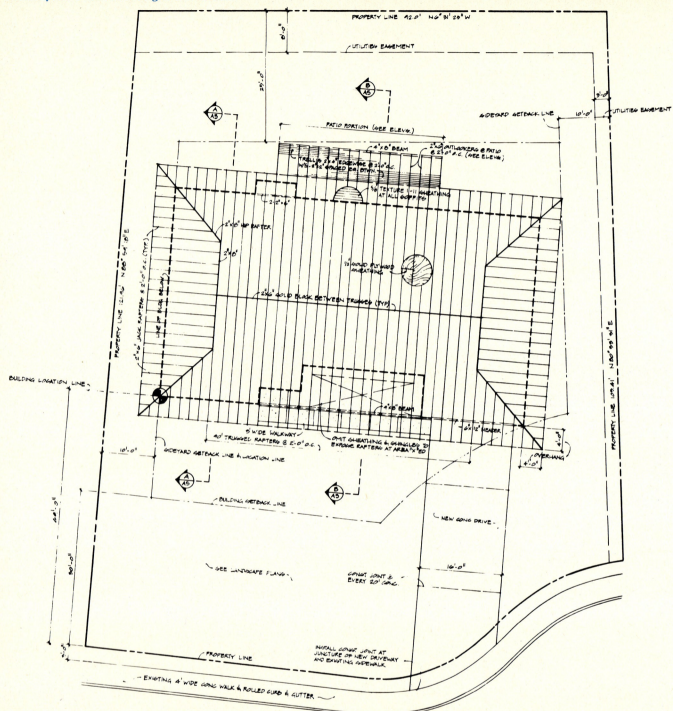

Figure 12–13

piece of balsa wood (about ¼ inch × ¼ inch) in each inside corner to provide a gluing base and to furnish extra rigidity to the walls.

After completing the walls, the roof panels are cut from brown matboard. Ink lines are drawn on the surface to represent a wood-shingled roof. The panels are then mounted on a roof support frame and glued together [12–24]. Attic vents on the gable ends of the roof are cut from the elevation print and glued in place. The chimney is cut from brick-printed paper and glued over a matboard box. It is then fitted to the roof and glued. The roof can now be placed loosely on top of the walls.

Figures [12–25 to 12–28] show the completed model's appearance from the four sides. The exposed rafters at

An assortment of tools and materials used to build and finish the model . . . including spray adhesive, materials, and straightedge.

Figure 12–14

Spray-cement a trimmed site plan print to cream-colored matboard . . . mount on corkboard that has been cemented to a particleboard base.

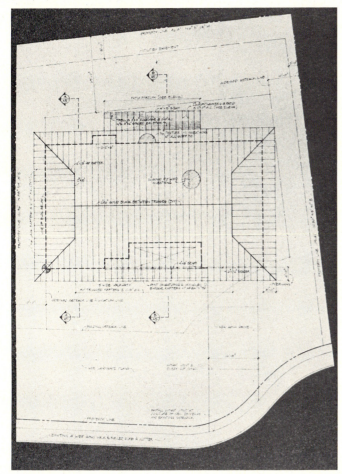

Figure 12–15

Peel off the concrete portion of the site plan print . . . the exposed cream-colored matboard will represent these concrete areas.

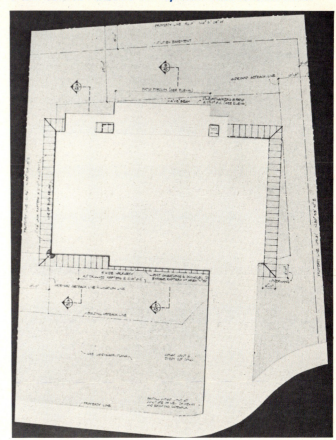

Figure 12–16

Peel off the remaining site plan print and underlying matboard exposing the cork (ground) . . . remove the corkboard from under the "concrete" matboard . . . cut out the floor plan and cement in place on the "concrete" matboard.

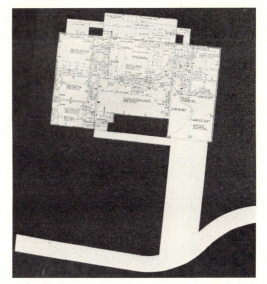

Figure 12–17

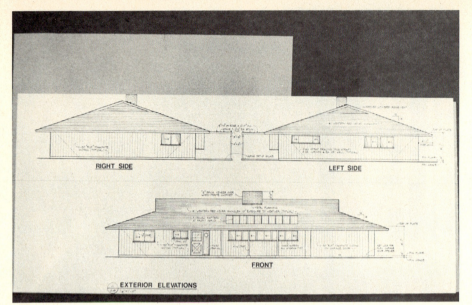

Spraymount the elevation print onto matboard wall surface material.

Figure 12–18

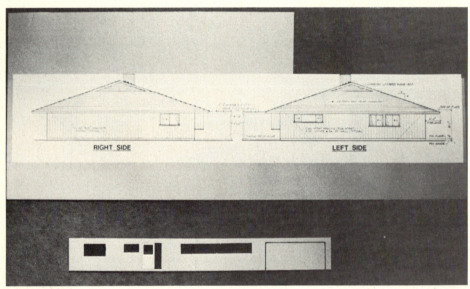

Door and window outlines and glass areas are inked in . . . walls are cut out from the mat board and the paper print is peeled off . . . vertical lines are drawn on the mat board to suggest exterior paneling.

Figure 12–19

Glue the finished walls onto the floor plan . . . first the left side . . .

Then the front wall . . .

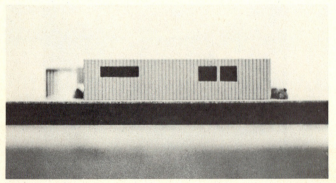

Figure 12–20

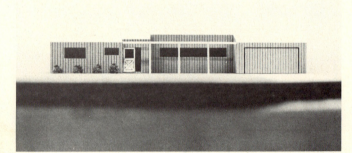

Figure 12–21

The right side . . .

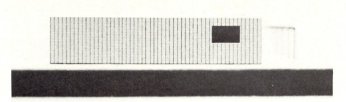

Figure 12–22

. . . and finally the rear wall.

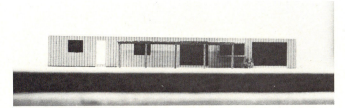

Figure 12–23

Roof panels are cut from brown matboard and lined to indicate shingles . . . the panels are glued together on a roof frame, shown in the underside view of the roof.

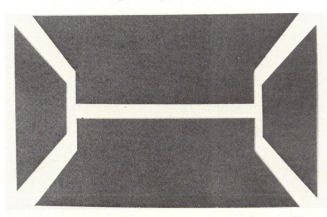

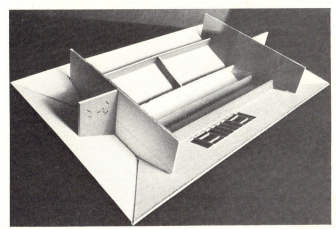

Figure 12–24

The completed model showing the right side . . .

Figure 12–25

The front . . .

Figure 12–26

the front are cut from balsa wood and glued in place. The palm trees are made from paper fronds glued to the surface of a drinking straw. Other trees can be made from sprigs of bushes and shrubs. Carefully trim them and spray with a plastic fixative material. Sumac, parsley, and bits of juniper and other shrubs can be used along with small pieces of sponge and lichen to represent plants and shrubs. These are best prepainted with a quick-drying acrylic spray or lacquer prior to gluing onto the model.

Coarse grades of sandpaper can be used to represent a graveled surface. Dark-colored, heavy-textured emery paper is a good representation of an asphalt surface. Brown paper nipped at the edges and cut into strips can serve as miniature roof shingles. Spanish tiles can be made from drinking straws slit in half lengthwise and sprayed a terra-cotta red color. Brick patterns can be inked onto cardboard.

A bit of skill can turn small pebbles into decorative rock textures. Very coarse sand particles sprinkled on a wet glue surface and allowed to dry will help create a rock garden. Blue paper or mat board can serve to imitate water. Flocking material available from a handicraft store can be sprinkled on a wet glue surface to simulate grass. Fine sand on a glued surface can be used for desert landscaping. Using your imagination, you can discover a wealth of other materials that can be used to represent desired textures for your models.

You must be careful to keep textures in scale with the model. For example, be sure that a texture representing grass does not look like grass a foot or more high! If sandpaper is used to represent a gravel-covered roof, its scaled texture should not look like rocks several inches

The left side . . .

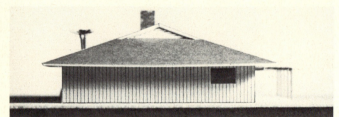

Figure 12–27

and the rear.

Figure 12–28

An overhead view of the finished model.

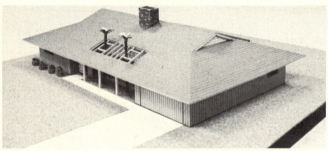

Figure 12–29

The removable roof permits viewing the floor plan.

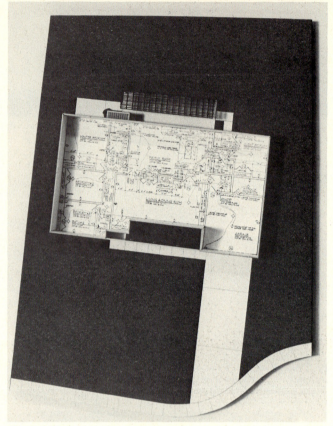

Figure 12–30

in diameter. If textures are out of scale, the model will look "clumsy." Also, avoid the use of shiny surfaces. Water and glass have a more representative appearance if they are represented by nonreflective materials.

Figure [12–29] shows the completed model as if viewed from an airplane. The removable roof permits us to see the floor plan layout of the house [12–30].

EXERCISES

12–1. What are the two types of architectural models? How are they different? How are they alike?

12–2. What are the advantages of a chipboard model over a polystyrene model? What are the advantages of polystyrene over chipboard?

12–3. What are the advantages of a matboard model over chipboard? Disadvantages?

12–4. Why is it useful to show existing buildings that are adjacent to the proposed new building in a model? How should they be shown?

12–5. Chipboard for a certain model is $1/16$ inch thick. What is the contour interval using this board on a $1/8'' = 1'-0''$ scale model? Try making a sample contoured area with this material.

12–6. Of what must you be careful when applying textures to a model?

12–7. Why shouldn't a T-square be used as a guide for cutting chipboard or matboard for a model? What should be used?

12–8. Build a study model of the house in [7–18]. Do not include windows, doors, patterns, or textures. Use a scale of $1/4'' = 1'-0''$. Use grocery carton cardboard.

12–9. Build a study model of the building in [14–3]. (The pilings are $12'-0''$ on center). Use a light-colored board for the building and dark-colored board for the windows. Find a round tube that scales about 18 inches in diameter for the piling (try a straw). Use a scale of $1/8'' = 1'-0''$.

13 A Design Case Study

A real situation is used here to show how an architect and a drafter worked together to produce the plan of an *actual* home designed and constructed for a specific family. In this way you can see how information gathered about a family's needs gradually evolves into the formation of a home in which the family can be comfortable. Authentic notes, sketches, and drawings pertaining to the actual project have been reproduced here. This includes some of the questions that were asked to establish the family's needs, the architect's rough sketches, and finally (as presented in Chapter 25) the drafter's working drawings. The building of a model of the home has been described in Chapter 12. Actual photographs of the home under construction are included in Chapter 25 so that you can relate the progress of the step-by-step construction process with the drawings.

First, we should introduce ourselves to the homeowners, Mr. and Mrs. Browne. Henry Browne and his wife, Dorothy, have two children—a boy, John (age 16), and a girl, Mary (age 12). Although their home was erected in the southwestern portion of the United States, its development, design, and construction are so typical that it could just as well have been erected in many other places.

13.1 Selecting the Architect

A family may find help in designing and constructing a new home in several ways. One way is to select a home from one of the numerous house plan booklets available and then to contract with a home builder to construct it. Minor alterations may be made to the plans by the contractor if the owners desire. If major alterations to the "stock plans" are required, a family may wish to have a "design-build" contracting firm draw new plans and build the home.

If the family wishes to have a home designed especially to meet their living needs and to have professional help in working with the contractor who will build the house, they may decide to employ an architect. Although 90% of the homes that are built are not custom designed by an architect, this was the preferred procedure for the Browne family.

An architect may be selected in several ways. If you see a home that you like, you may decide to use its architect for your own home. You may obtain recommendations from friends that have worked with architects. The family in our example was acquainted with an architect prior to deciding to build a new home. Henry Smith, the architect, lived in the same city as Browne and they had become acquainted through mutual friends. Mr. Browne selected Smith as his architect shortly before deciding to buy the land on which to build a family home.

13.2 Selecting the Lot

The Brownes had learned that a new subdivision was opening in a neighborhood that they had long admired. It was within walking distance of the high school attended by John and only a block from Mary's intermediate (junior high) school. Browne is an electronics engineer. He has been working for the same firm for more than 10 years. A recent promotion, the desire to move into a larger home closer to the company for which he works, and the need for a place for Mrs. Browne's widowed mother prompted them to think about securing a newer, custom-designed home.

The Brownes started by looking at vacant lots in the subdivision where they thought they might like to live. They found several that appealed to them. Finally, after selecting about four likely prospects, Smith, the architect, was contacted to assist them in making the final decision. Smith and the Brownes spent several weekends looking at available property. One lot in particular seemed to satisfy their needs above all others. Finally, with the architect along, they approached the real estate agent who had listed the property for sale.

The price was a bit higher than they wanted to pay. With Smith's assistance they were able to obtain favorable purchase terms from the seller. Smith then helped them select a financial institution that would agree to finance the purchase of a lot and the design and construction of the home. Browne made a substantial security deposit on the lot, and an agreement was drawn up for Smith's architectural services.

13.3 Family Preferences

Several long question-and-answer sessions followed. Smith probed into the Browne's design preferences and discussed the life-style that would dictate the home they would soon enjoy as their own. Smith talked individually to each member of the family. He learned that they liked to entertain frequently, particularly during the warm spring and summer months when maximum use could be made of outdoor activities.

Being a closely-knit family, but with a need for individual privacy, the architect determined that a three-bedroom, two-bath house would amply serve their basic needs. In addition, Mrs. Browne's widowed mother, who wanted to be close to the family, would be able to move into the house with them if a guest bedroom and bath were added. It was made clear, however, that on occasion she enjoyed her quiet and privacy away from the active life of the Brownes and their children. For this reason it would be desirable to separate her area in some way. Henry Browne liked to "putter around" in his workshop on weekends. Dorothy Browne loved to cook, and she wanted the latest in kitchen equipment. She also requested that there be a family room–kitchen relationship that would allow easy access to the outdoors for summer entertainment. John and Mary, the children, were good students and needed a private place to study and complete their homework assignments.

Mr. and Mrs. Browne had long admired the Southwest ranch style architecture. Such homes generally have wide overhangs and rough-hewn shingle roofs. Also, they wanted a spacious master bedroom adjoined by a large private bath. They further specified that they would prefer that their bedroom have primarily an eastern exposure since they both enjoyed the cool, early daylight hours of the morning. Mr. Browne requested that their master bedroom be placed as far away from the street as possible since he was a light sleeper and was easily awakened by street traffic noises.

Finally, all agreed that their new home should take advantage of all the available energy-conserving measures. Since they lived in the hot, dry southwest, the installation of air conditioning was considered a necessity. Chilly winters also required that a central heating system be used. This, the family agreed, should be supplemented by a heat-circulating fireplace that all the family could enjoy.

13.4 Minimum Standards

The neighborhood residential restrictions required construction of a minimum of 2200 square feet of "liveable area," exclusive of garages and patios. The family owns two cars, one (a compact model) that Mr. Browne drives to work, and the second (a station wagon) that his wife uses for her numerous activites with church and social groups and for family shopping.

The building ordinances for the neighborhood established a minimum side-yard setback of 10 feet on each side of the house and 30 feet on the front or street side. All of the family wanted to include a swimming pool in their future plans. Therefore, it was decided that space should be allowed for a swimming pool at a later date.

13.5 The Design Studies

With all the data clearly in mind, architect Smith began his design studies. At first, he made some "thumbnail" sketches of design ideas that indicated relationships of activities. The first likely solution to the Browne's requirements emerged as a bubble diagram [13–1]. In a casual and rough manner, this diagram indicates a basic configuration for the plan of the home. Made with a felt-tip pen, it shows in a very tentative manner how the architect felt their needs for privacy, circulation, and orientation might be satisfied.

After several more conferences, architect Smith developed a tentative floor plan and elevation sketches of the home. The Brownes immediately liked the proposed solution. Mrs. Browne asked if she could have a storage cabinet in the dining area to display her chinaware collection. Browne requested the addition of a beverage bar that would be accessible from both the living room and family room to serve adult needs for entertainment. It would also provide a place where teenagers could store soft drinks that are always in demand on warm summer days.

Mrs. Browne wanted space for a large chest-type freezer. She also wanted a laundry room that was separate from the other activity areas of the home. Finally, the Brownes asked the architect for another consideration. They wanted a large "Roman-type" tub–shower combination where Mr. Browne could relax and bathe after a busy day at the electronics plant. Smith agreed that all of these requests seemed reasonable, and he proceeded to refine the bubble diagram and finally developed a rough draft floor plan [13–2] and elevations for the Browne's approval.

A perspective rendering of the finished house was drawn so that the Brownes could visualize their future home [13–3]. Smith presented his completed design to the Brownes for approval. To save time, Smith presented somewhat simplified schematic drawings to the Brownes as his final design presentation. Abbreviated procedures such as this may be utilized on small projects or on those in which the relationship between parties is informal. Typically, at the end of the design development phase on large projects, a full design presentation is prepared. The Brownes approved the design and Smith was ready for the next phase. The continuation of his work is described in Chapter 25, where the actual working drawings are displayed.

A bubble diagram is drawn to show the physical relationships of the various functions of the home.

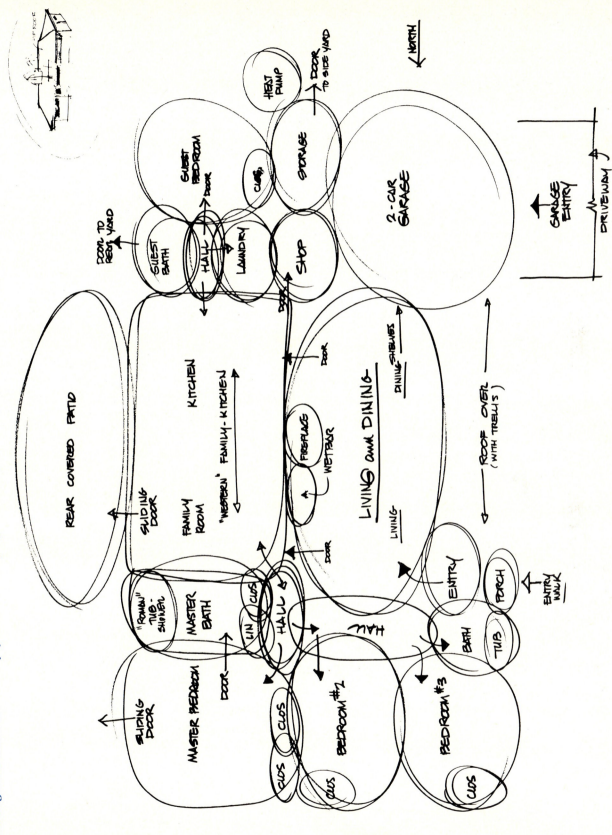

Figure 13–1

A perspective rendering helps to show how the house would appear after construction.

Figure 13-3

EXERCISES

13-1. The city has hired you as a consultant for the building of some housing units for the elderly. They wish to select a designer for the project. Assuming that you are ineligible to be selected as the designer, what advice would you give the city officials as to how to proceed with this decision?

13-2. What life-style characteristics and special needs do the Browne family have that required special consideration in the design of their home?

13-3. How did local zoning ordinances affect the design of the Browne home?

13-4. What adjustments were necessary so that the initial bubble diagrams would satisfy the needs of the Brownes? Why do you think these items weren't covered by the initially suggested layout?

13-5. Why do you think that fully developed presentation drawings were not necessary for the Browne project?

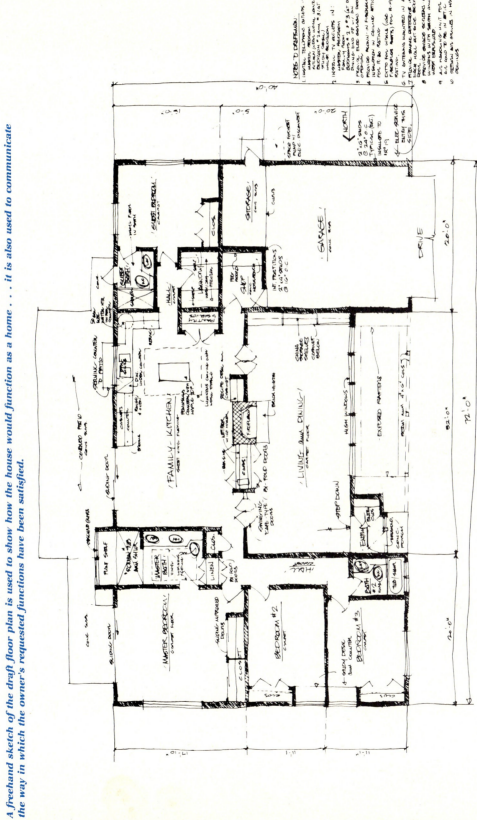

A freehand sketch of the draft floor plan is used to show how the house would function as a home . . . it is also used to communicate the way in which the owner's requested functions have been satisfied.

Figure 13–2

III

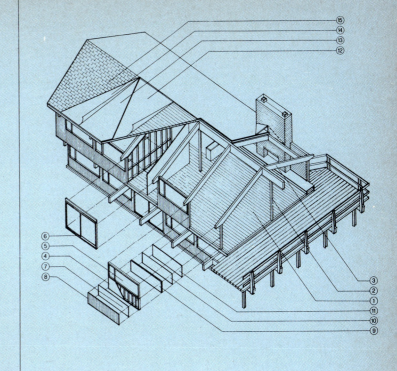

Building Systems

14 Light Construction Methods

As the population of the United States expanded west, people sometimes moved faster than tools and materials of the current building technology. Consequently, buildings in newly settled areas were often constructed with fairly primitive techniques while at the same time sophisticated structures were going up in the East where the building industry had long been established. Sod houses [14–1] were common in the Plains states, where trees were scarce. The weathering of the walls, especially due to rain, was one reason this construction method was only a temporary solution.

The log cabin [14–2], although crude, provided reasonable insulation if the joints between logs could be sealed adequately. It is doubtful that the charm associated with contemporary log homes was much appreciated when the early prototypes were first built and used. These early construction systems addressed many problems that modern construction must solve. The protection of occupants from wind, rain, and cold is a timeless economic and aesthetic challenge in design and construction.

14.1 Structural Systems

During the design development phase you should be considering the various types of structural systems that might be used for your building. The system chosen will undoubtedly affect the layout and appearance of the building. The selection of a particular structural system should be finalized just prior to beginning the construction documents.

Most architectural structural systems employ four basic materials: wood, concrete, masonry, and steel. They are often used in combination with one another. Glass, plastics, ceramic tile, and other materials are not usually considered to be "structural." The basic parts of the structural system are the foundation, floors, walls, and roof.

14.2 Foundations

The function of the *foundation* is to prevent the building from moving in any direction. A foundation should prevent settling, heaving (upward movement), or lateral shifting. The weight of a building tends to push it downward through the earth. Wind tends to move a building laterally or lift it during severe storms. Earthquakes also typically cause lateral movement. Freezing and thawing of ground moisture and the expansion and contraction of soil that is sensitive to moisture changes may move a structure vertically. Also, shifts of the earth may move the building in any direction.

Figure 14–1

A sod house in Colorado . . . this type of house uses a construction system similar to masonry in both configuration and material . . . the raw soil, however, is no match for clay units (brick) burned at high temperatures.

A log cabin in Colorado . . . typically houses of this type were built with simple rectangular plans . . . every corner meant laboriously cutting every log to fit with the adjacent member. Even today, increasing the number of corners in a building increases the cost.

Figure 14–2

The shape and material of the foundation are dictated by soil conditions, economics, and occasionally aesthetic considerations [14–3]. The foundation types available are continuous spread footings, pad footings, piling, and piers. The *continuous spread footing* spreads the weight of a building over a broad enough area so that the soil is not penetrated by the foundation, allowing it to move downward [14–4]. If some areas of the soil are softer than others, the foundation should still span over these areas without sinking.

Forces tending to move the building upward are common. Every winter, in all but very warm climates, the moisture in the ground freezes. In the northern states the moisture freezes to depths of as much as 5 feet. This distance, called the *frost depth*, becomes less as we move south. It is reduced to a few inches in states that have only very brief freezing spells and to zero in areas that never have temperatures below freezing. As the moisture in the earth freezes, it expands. The expanding earth is strong enough to lift entire buildings. This lifting and lowering (upon melting of the frozen moisture) of buildings or their parts causes cracking of walls and floors because the movement is rarely evenly distributed.

To avoid this type of movement, you must prevent freezing moisture from occurring under the foundation of any building. Since it is impossible to eliminate all of the moisture from the earth, the solution is to place the footings below the *frost line* (the lowest point below ground level that freezes) [14–5]. If the moisture under the foundation cannot freeze, it cannot lift the building. Based on climate history, approximate frost depths are established for various parts of the country. To allow for a rare winter that exceeds historical data, it is necessary to place the bottom of the foundation at least 12 inches below the known frost depth. The frost depth in your area may be determined by contacting the city building department or examining a weather bureau map [14–6].

The foundation must resist sidewise pressure when it serves as a basement wall. Resistance to sliding of the foundation wall off the footing can be provided by the floor slab, by locating a "key" between the wall and footing, and by reinforcing that interconnects the footing to the wall [14–7]. Reinforcing rods placed between the footing and the wall also help prevent the wall from tipping over.

The thickness of the foundation wall should be designed to resist the forces already mentioned. Residential foundations are usually a minimum of 12 inches thick if they are concrete block, or 10 inches if they are concrete. Local ordinances sometimes control this mini-

This lakefront home is an example of design that takes its cue from an unusual site . . . the site is a rock slide with 40° slope to the water's edge. The home is a three-story structure suspended 60 feet above the water on cedar posts anchored to footings in the slide.

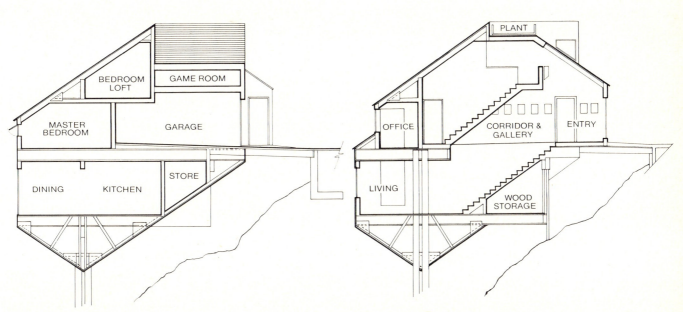

Figure 14–3

A continuous spread footing . . . the weight of the building is spread over a broad area.

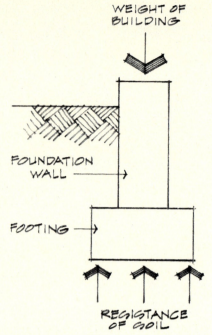

Figure 14–4

The bottom of the footing is placed below the frost line.

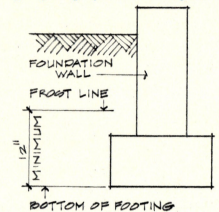

Figure 14–5

Frost penetration map . . . average depth of frost penetration in inches.

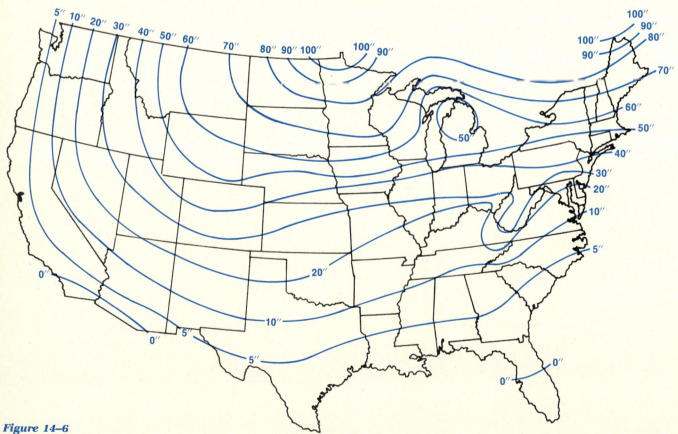

Figure 14–6

The floor slab, the key, and reinforcing provide resistance to sliding off the foundation.

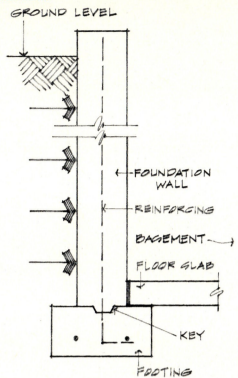

Figure 14–7

Typical foundation and footing proportions.

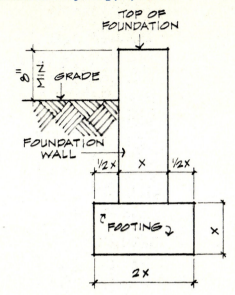

Figure 14–8

A stepped footing may be used on a sloping site.

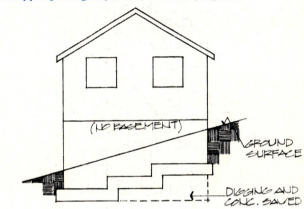

Figure 14–9

Rule of thumb dimensions for a residential pad footing.

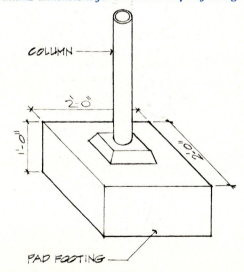

Figure 14–10

mum. A "rule of thumb" for the size of a footing is that it should be at least twice as wide as the foundation wall and equal to it in thickness [14–8]. Actual size should be determined by calculations accounting for the strength of the soil and the weight of the building. The foundation wall should extend at least 8 inches above the *grade* (ground level) when supporting wood construction. This is to keep any wood on top of the foundation from rotting due to moisture that results from light flooding or melting snow.

Concrete block is commonly used for foundations in residential and light commercial construction. Poured concrete is common for commercial work and is used in residences if the contractor finds it economically competitive with block. With concrete block, concrete is used for the footing. It must rest on soil that has not been disturbed by digging. Disturbed soil tends to settle unless compacted extensively. Dependable compacting is a very expensive process.

On a sloping site, the footing on the high side of a building may be much deeper than necessary if there is no basement. For this reason the foundation wall and footing may be stepped up [14–9] if it appears that the savings in digging and concrete exceeds the extra cost in labor required to form the special configuration.

Any support columns used in a building typically require a *pad footing* [14–10]. Since a column or post trans-

Light Construction Methods

231

fers a concentrated load to the soil, the final size of the pad must be calculated based on the load applied and the strength of the soil. Although "rule of thumb" dimensions allow a 2'-0" × 2'-0" pad for residences [14–10], commercial pad footings may be several feet across.

Wood foundation walls and footings have appeared recently. Special procedures must be taken with wood foundations to prevent deterioration due to fire and decay. Concrete and masonry are naturally immune to both of these hazards.

Piling is used when the soil near the surface of the site is not structurally sound. In areas near the ocean or other water, the ground may be too weak to support the weight of a building. In areas where expansive soil changes volume with changes in moisture, piling may be desirable to bypass this layer of earth to reach more stable material. Piling consists of polelike structural members [14–11] driven through the earth until they reach sound material, such as bedrock, or until the friction of the soil is great enough to prevent further penetration [14–12].

Due to economy and workability, wood piling is usually the choice for residential and light construction. Steel and concrete piling is used for heavier construction. A grid pattern of piling will result in a network of sound supports that can be spanned by beams to support the building weight over the undesirable soil [14–13 to 14–15].

Wood, steel, and round concrete piers are essentially short piling. They are appropriate when great depth is not needed to achieve sound support. If a spread concrete footing (pad) is used, masonry may be added to the list of pier materials. A pier may extend to bedrock, or if the soil will support a spread footing, it need only extend to a point 12 inches below the frost line [14–16 to 14–18]. Steel piers are not as common as wood, concrete, and masonry in light construction.

Typical piling . . .

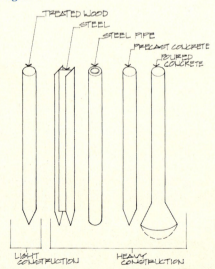

Figure 14–11

A pile can be supported by friction . . .

. . . or a pile can extend to stable material.

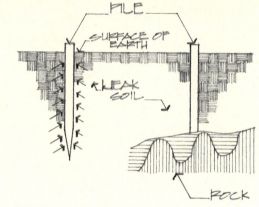

Figure 14–12

Beams span a piling grid to provide a sound support over soft soil.

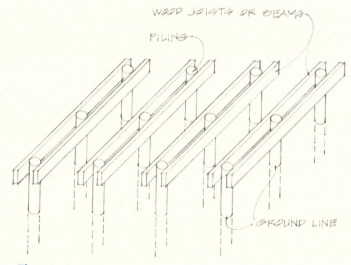

Figure 14–13

Spanning beams may be concrete.

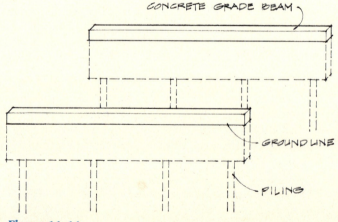

Figure 14–14

The piling may be spanned by a concrete slab with built-in beams.

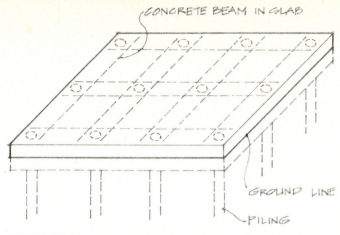

Figure 14–15

A pier may extend to bedrock . . .

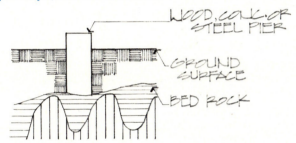

Figure 14–16

. . . or to 12 inches below frost line for spread footings.

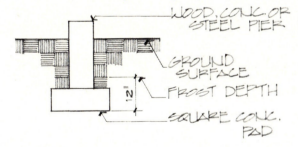

Figure 14–17

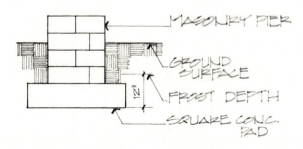

Figure 14–18

14.3 Floors

A concrete slab is typical for floors on or below grade in all types of construction [14–19]. It is the logical choice because of its economy and resistance to the deteriorating agents in soil. Basement slabs and slabs on grade are typically 4 inches thick. They are usually placed on a sheet of plastic six thousandths of an inch thick (6-mil polyethylene) to prevent moisture from the earth from rising through the slab. The plastic (called a *vapor barrier*) rests on 4 inches of *aggregate* such as crushed stone or sand. This provides a level base at an appropriate elevation on which to pour the concrete. The slab should be independent of the foundation for some soil conditions or tied to the foundation for others.

A common misconception is that a slab provides a firm span from foundation wall to foundation wall. A 4-inch thick concrete slab can span only a few feet without support. It cannot span the distance that typically occurs between foundation walls. The slab simply rests on a base supported entirely by the earth below it. Generally, the slab and wall are independent of each other for unstable soil conditions and are connected for stable soil conditions.

If the earth is not stable, the slab should be free to move as the soil moves [14–20 and 14–21]. If the foundation prevents the slab from moving with the soil, the slab may crack, enabling the parts to move independently of the wall. Concrete floor slabs above grade are rarely found in residential construction.

In [14–22] a steel structure provides the support for a corrugated steel deck. The corrugations provide strength for the relatively thin decking but are obviously not appropriate as a base for carpet or other flooring

A concrete slab is typical for floors on or below grade.

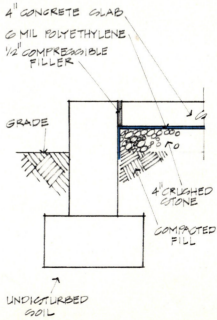

Figure 14–19

Correct relationships of slabs to foundation walls based on soil conditions.

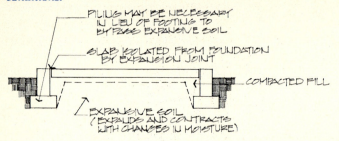

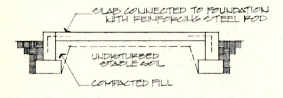

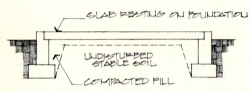

Figure 14-20

A corrugated steel deck may be supported on a steel structure.

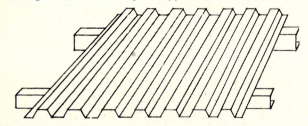

Figure 14-22

Lightweight concrete fill provides a smooth hard surface over the steel deck.

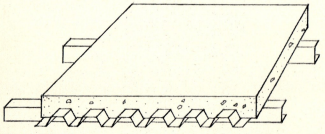

Figure 14-23

Incorrect relationships between slabs and foundation walls based on soil conditions

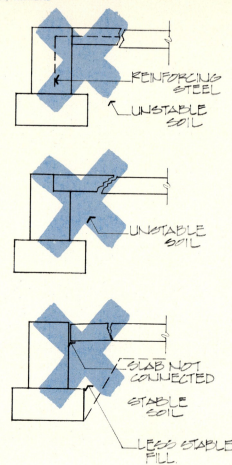

Figure 14-21

finishes. A relatively lightweight concrete is poured over the steel deck to provide a smooth, hard surface [14-23]. In a heavier-duty system, reinforcing steel may be used with structural concrete to create a structural slab over a corrugated steel deck.

Purely concrete floor systems are not used in light construction. Flat slab without steel decking, one-way ribbed slab, and two-way ribbed slab are used in heavier commercial construction such as multistory work [14-24 to 14-26].

Wood floor support beaming is used only in very light commercial and residential work. In commercial buildings the use of wood framing is very limited because of the fire hazard. Ceilings and floors above grade are supported by members called *joists*. Wood joists are usually 2 × 6's, 2 × 8's, 2 × 10's, or 2 × 12's. These identification numbers give their approximate or *nominal* sizes in inches. The actual sizes are less (Table 14-1). Joists are set on the 2-inch edge with the longer dimension being vertical. They are usually spaced at a distance of 16 inches from the center of one to the center of the adjacent one. The longer the distance the joist must span, the greater must be its vertical size dimension. The selection of joist sizes is described in Chapter 15.

A flat slab has enough strength to span between beams . . . all members are reinforced concrete.

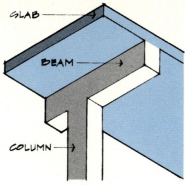

Figure 14–24

A one-way ribbed slab . . . all members are reinforced concrete . . . the slab has only enough strength to span between ribs.

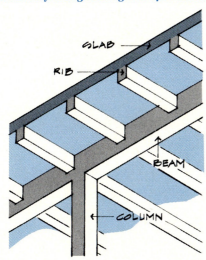

Figure 14–25

A two-way ribbed slab . . . called a "waffle" slab because of its appearance . . . all members are reinforced concrete.

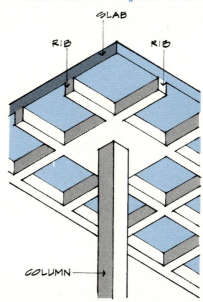

Figure 14–26

Table 14–1. Lumber Sizes

Thickness (in.)		Width (in.)	
Nominal	Actual Dry	Nominal	Actual Dry
2	1½	2	1½
2½	2	3	2½
3	2½	4	3½
3½	3	5	4½
4	3½	6	5½
		8	7¼
		10	9¼
		12	11¼

If the first floor of a house is wood, the joists will rest on a *sill plate* that is attached to the foundation wall [14–27]. The sill plate is a 2 × 4, 2 × 6, or 4 × 4. It is anchored to the foundation wall with ½-inch diameter anchor bolts spaced at a maximum of 6 feet apart ([B–1], Appendix B). The bolts are set into the concrete foundation while the concrete is still soft. In a block wall, an opening in the block is filled with mortar and the bolt is set in it. Anchors may also be shot into hard concrete with a powder-activated tool much as a gun would shoot a bullet.

It is the function of the sill to prevent the house from moving with respect to the foundation. Because the sill must be strong enough to resist failure during wind storms, some communities require sill plates larger than 2 × 4.

The sill can be set back from the outer face of the foundation wall a distance equal to the thickness of the *wall sheathing,* or it can be set flush with it. Wall sheathing is usually ½-inch thick. A member of the same size as the joists is placed on the sill flush with the sill's outer edge. This member, called a *header,* is set on its 2-inch edge in the same way as the joists [14–27]. The

Floor joists rest on a sill plate anchored to the foundation.

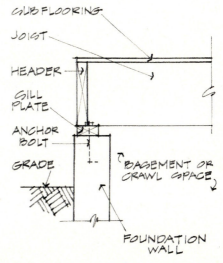

figure 14–27

header is nailed to the joists and the sill plate. The joists are also nailed to the sill plate.

Subflooring, which is most commonly plywood, is nailed to the top of the joists [14–28]. The subflooring can be a total of ½ to ¾ inch thick, in a single or double layer, depending on what type of finished flooring will be used. Weak floor finishing materials, such as tile or carpeting, require thicker subflooring than stronger finishes, such as hardwood flooring.

A ½- or ⅝-inch plywood subfloor may be covered with an *underlayment* of ¼-inch hardboard or ⅜-inch particleboard. The joints between the sheets of underlayment are arranged so they do not coincide with those of the plywood. The underlayment provides a smooth surface with a minimum of movement at the joints. The soundness of the joints between sheets of one-layer subfloors can be improved by using tongue-and-groove plywood.

Subflooring is nailed to the top of the joists.

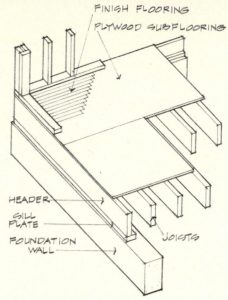

Figure 14–28

A C-shaped steel joist . . . light gauge steel framing is popular for light commercial construction.

Figure 14–29

Steel joists supporting a lightweight concrete floor poured on a corrugated steel deck.

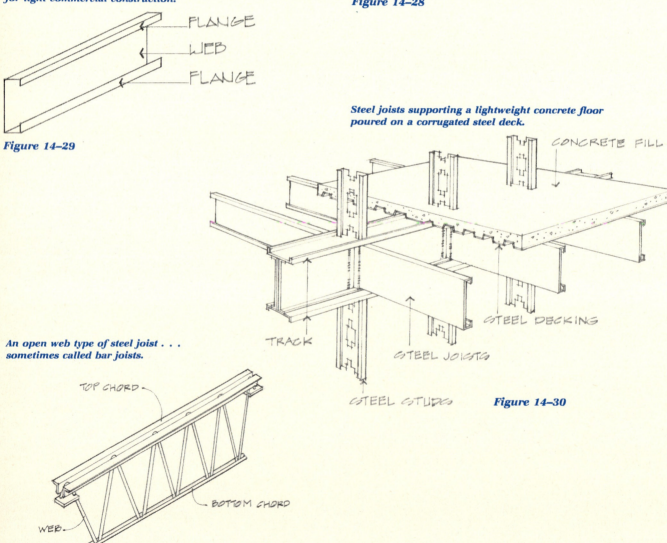

An open web type of steel joist . . . sometimes called bar joists.

Figure 14–30

Figure 14–31

236   Building Systems

Light-gauge steel framing is popular for light commercial construction since it does not burn [14–29]. *C-shaped* steel joists resemble the profile of typical wood framing members and fit together in a similar way [14–30].

Steel joists may also be the *open web* type [14–31]. These are sometimes called *bar joists* because the web is a continuous round bar bent in a zigzag shape. Open web joists are stronger than C-shaped joists and can therefore span longer distances. They may span between light-gauge steel-framed walls, masonry or concrete bearing walls, steel beams, or open web girders. Open web joists are rarely used in residential construction since their span capability is not needed. C-shaped steel joists are sometimes used in residential work, although this is not common.

14.4 Walls

Residential walls are limited to a few types, whereas commercial construction utilizes numerous shapes and materials. Walls may be *load-bearing* or *non-load-bearing*. Load-bearing walls carry the weight of the floors and roof. This includes everything resting on the floors and roof.

Walls for both residential and light commercial construction can be built with concrete, masonry, steel studs, or wood studs. Both concrete and masonry are common for basement walls [14–32]. Masonry bearing wall construction is often used in commercial construction. This type of construction offers a variety of configurations. Typically, they consist of two vertical layers

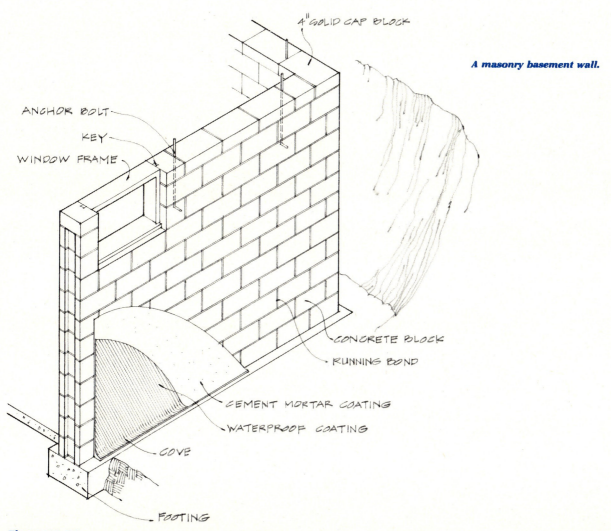

A masonry basement wall.

Figure 14–32

(*wythes*). The exterior wythe may be stone, brick, or concrete block. The interior wythe may be brick, concrete block, or clay tile. The wythes may touch or be separated by an air space (*a cavity wall*) [14–33].

Insulation may be placed between the wythes [14–34] or on the room face of the interior wythe [14–35]. In recent years systems have been developed in which the insulation is placed on the outside of the wall. As in the case of placing insulation on the room face of the wall, the masonry is hidden from view. The masonry wythes are tied together with metal ties [14–36] or continuous steel reinforcing [14–37].

Wood joists may tie into a masonry bearing wall by spacing the units of the interior wythe around each joist.

Basic nomenclature for masonry walls.

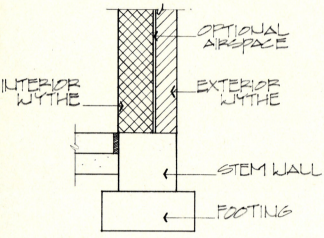

Figure 14–33

Insulation may be placed between wythes in a masonry wall.

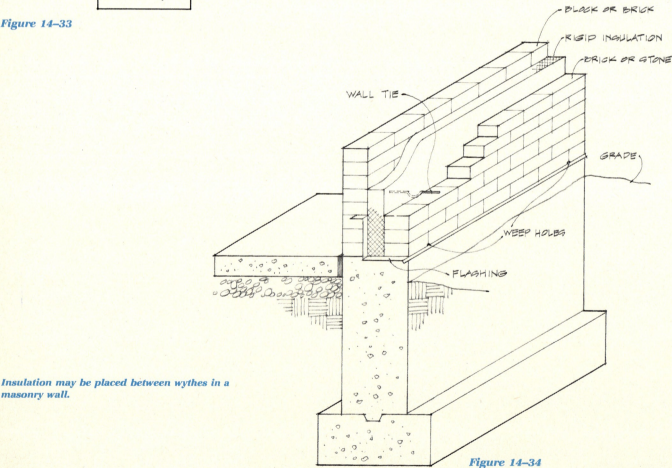

Figure 14–34

238

Building Systems

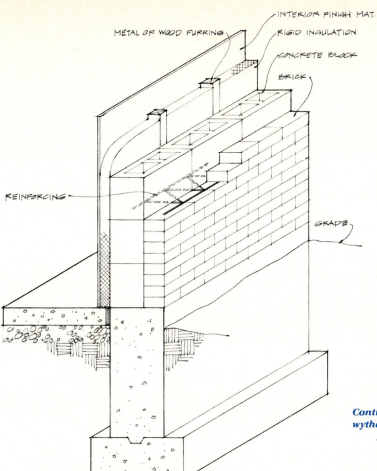

Insulation may be placed on the room face of the interior wythe.

Figure 14-35

Continuous reinforcing may be used to tie together the masonry wythes.

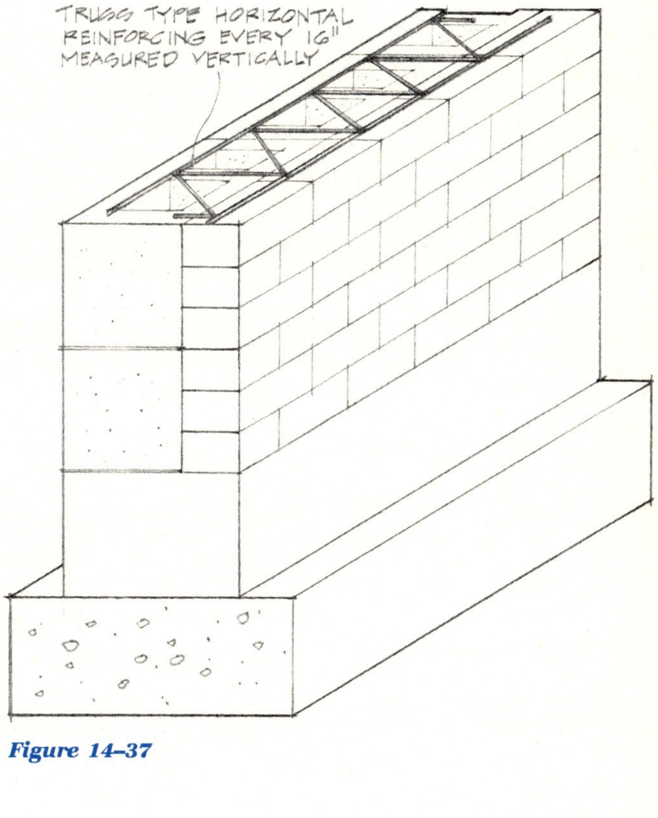

Figure 14-37

The masonry wythes are tied together with metal ties.

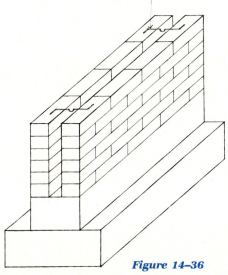

Figure 14-36

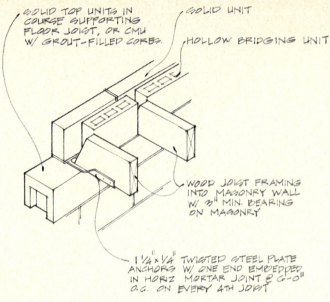

Wood joists supported on a masonry wall are tied to the wall with metal straps.

Figure 14–38

To support steel open web joists on a masonry wall . . . omit one large block to provide bearing for the joist . . . fill the void with smaller stock sizes of brick or block.

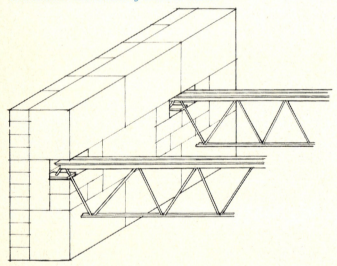

Figure 14–39

Open web joists are tied to the masonry wall by embedding steel anchors between masonry units.

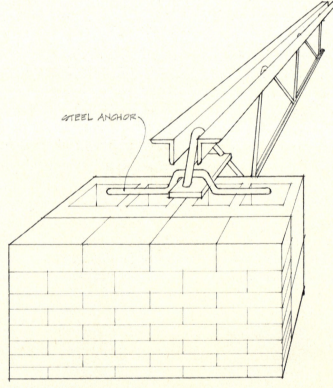

Figure 14–40

Balloon framing uses studs that are two stories high.

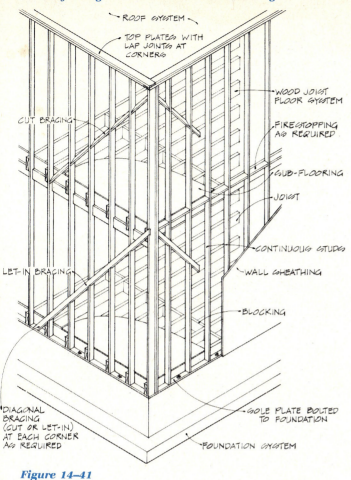

Figure 14–41

The joists must be tied into the wall with metal straps [14–38]. Steel open web joists may rest in a masonry bearing wall by omitting regular units at each joist and filling the hole with stock size smaller units [14–39]. The joists are held in the wall by steel anchors [14–40].

Residential walls are almost exclusively load-bearing. Wood frame construction is most common, but masonry exterior walls and steel stud frame walls are also used. The wood frame usually consists of 2 × 4 *studs* standing on end spaced at a distance of 16 inches from center to center [14–41 and 14–42]. With the increased interest in energy conservation, 2 × 6 studs at 24 inches on center have made their appearance in home construction. The deeper stud allows the installation of thicker insulation.

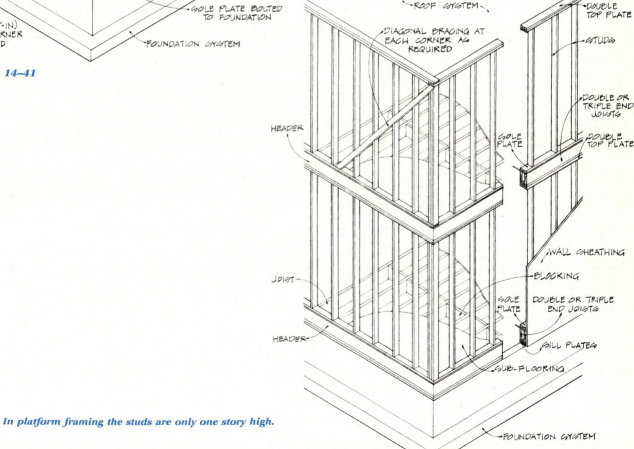

In platform framing the studs are only one story high.

Figure 14–42

Light Construction Methods

241

Balloon framing used to be common in two-story homes. Today, platform (Western) framing is more common. *Balloon framing* gets its name from its lightweight "shell-like" nature [14–41]. It incorporates studs that are two stories high. They run continuously from the foundation to the roof. *Platform framing* utilizes studs that are one story high [14–42]. The second floor is built as a platform on top of the first-floor studs. Advantages of platform framing include the increased availability and lower cost of the shorter studs and the ease of handling. Balloon framing has less vertical shrinkage.

In platform framing, the studs may be assembled on the floor and tilted up into place. The bottom (*sole plate*) and *top plate* may be nailed to the ends of the studs while in the horizontal position. The wall is tilted up, *plumbed* (set exactly vertical), and braced. The sole plate is nailed to the joists through the subfloor. With either balloon or platform framing, the sole plate is bolted directly to the foundation in place of the sill plate if an on-grade concrete floor is used. A second top plate is used to tie sections of wall together in a straight line or at intersections. Doors and windows have double studs at the *jambs* (sides) and double *headers* across the top [14–43]. Windows also have double members at the *sill* (bottom).

In platform framing the attachment of the second floor to the walls resembles the connection of the first floor to the foundation wall [14–44]. The floor construction configuration attached to the top plate is the same as the configuration attached to the sill plate on the foundation. At the top of the second-floor studs, a double top plate is used in the same way as on the top of the first-floor studs.

Lightweight steel framing is similar in configuration to wood framing [14–45]. Steel studs are usually spaced 24 inches on center. Thin-gauge steel studs, such as for nonbearing partitions, may be fastened together by screws, whereas heavier members are welded together. A steel-stud bearing wall may support C-shaped joists or open web steel joists [14–46].

Non-load-bearing walls are found not only within load-bearing systems but also in structural system called *post-and-beam construction* [14–47]. In this type of construction, the roof and floor loads are carried by beams that are supported by columns. The walls carry no weight other than their own and thus are non-load-bearing.

Typical framing at a window.

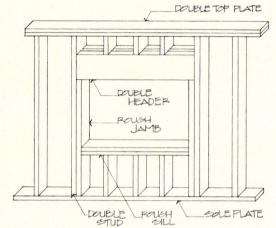

Figure 14–43

Attaching a second floor in platform framing.

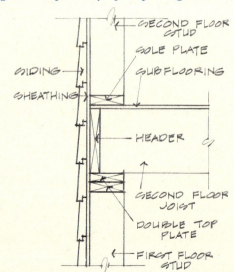

Figure 14–44

Lightweight steel framing is similar to wood framing.

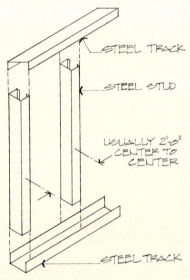

Figure 14–45

Load bearing steel studs supporting open web joist floor or roof framing.

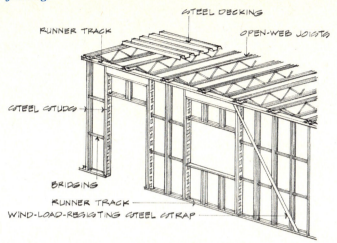

Figure 14–46

A post-and-beam system under construction . . . curtain walls will be installed next.

Figure 14–48

Post-and-beam construction . . . does not depend on walls to carry the weight of the building and occupants . . . curtain walls are installed after the posts and beams are in place.

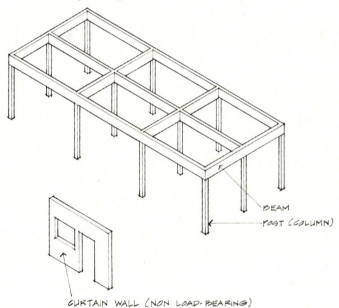

Figure 14–47

Exterior non-load-bearing walls are called *curtain walls* [14–47 and 48]. They may be made of any material that is weather-tight and can resist the force of the wind. Brick, glass, and thin metal panels mounted on metal studs are common materials for curtain walls.

A post-and-beam system may be integrated with other construction systems. In [14–49] interlocking laminated decking (1) is nailed to the framework of posts (2) and beams (3) to form the floor and roof system. Exterior walls are next installed between the perimeter posts. These are combinations of various-sized solid panels consisting of 2 × 4's and plywood sheathing (4), glass panels (5), or sliding glass doors (6). Once these panels are in place, asphalt paper (7) and exterior siding (8) are applied. Wall insulation (9), a polyethylene vapor barrier (10), and an interior surface of gypsum board (11) complete the exterior walls. The exterior surface of the roof decking is covered with asphalt felt (12), a layer of rigid insulation (13), a second layer of asphalt felt (14), and asphalt roof shingles (15).

Post-and-beam systems are relatively easy to recognize because the posts usually are not hidden in the curtain wall nor are the beams covered with a ceiling material [14–50 and 14–51]. The posts and beams are often used as important visual features. Beams may be provided in pairs (one on either side of a post), or posts may be doubled or even quadrupled to achieve a feeling of a certain scale and character. Beams may vary in their shape, especially if laminated wood is used [14–52]. Selecting beam sizes is discussed in Chapter 15.

The outside of the studs that make up a curtain wall or a frame bearing wall are usually covered with *sheathing* before a final surface material is attached [14–53]. Sheathing may be plywood or some other sheet material that is not as strong as plywood but has a higher insulating value.

The installation of ½-inch-thick plywood sheathing provides bracing to keep the wood frame square [14–54] and is a good support for the final surface material. If insulative sheathing is used, codes usually require either plywood or diagonal bracing at the building corners for rigidity [14–41 and 14–42].

Light Construction Methods

A post-and-beam system may be integrated with other construction systems.

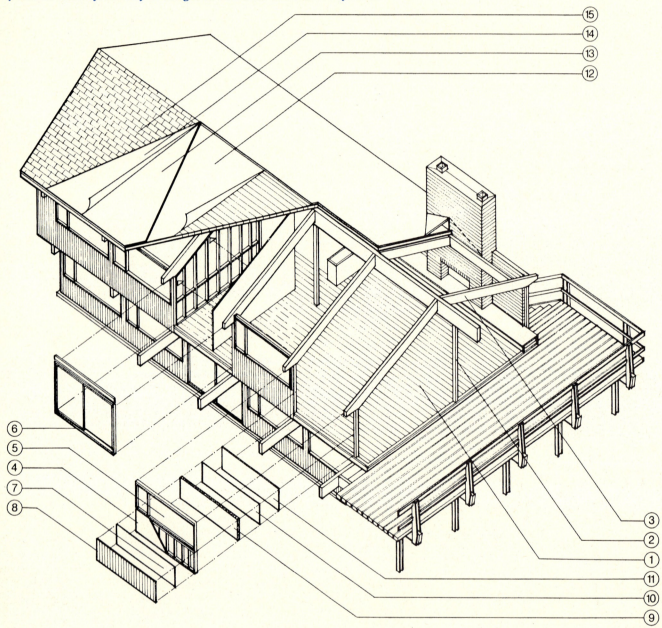

Figure 14–49

Exposed beams span posts between windows in this home.

Figure 14-50

The post-and-beam frame of this house is easily seen because the curtain walls on the near side are glass.

Figure 14-51

Curved laminated wood beams create a unique ceiling shape.

Figure 14-52

The wall framing is covered with sheathing before applying the surface material.

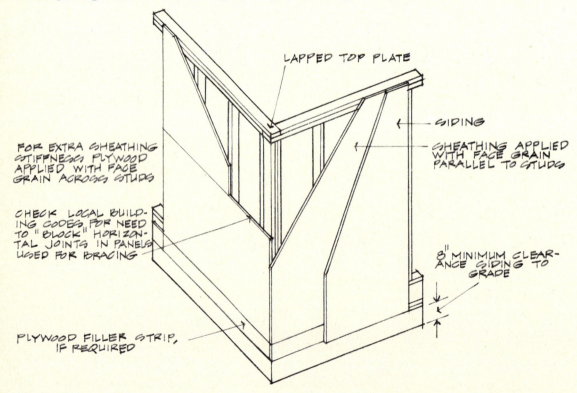

Figure 14-53

Plywood sheathing braces the frame to keep it square.

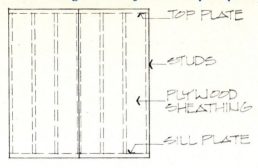

Nails joining the studs and plates are not strong enough to keep the wood frame square.

Figure 14–54

A variety of surface materials are available to cover the sheathing. Brick homes, in most cases, are actually built with wood framing covered with a single layer of brick [14–55]. This is called *brick veneer.* The brick does not carry any load other than its own weight. It merely provides an attractive appearance, resistance to exterior fire, and a low maintenance surface.

Other surfaces, such as board or sheet siding, may be applied to the framing [14–44 and 14–53]. Horizontal or vertical lines of various intensities may be achieved with bevel siding [14–56], grooved siding [14–57], board-and-batten siding [14–58], or other types of siding. Siding may also be applied in a diagonal pattern [14–59] or may achieve a special character if the grain patterns and colors are not uniform. Sections of several siding types are shown in [14–60].

Brick veneer may be used to cover the sheathing.

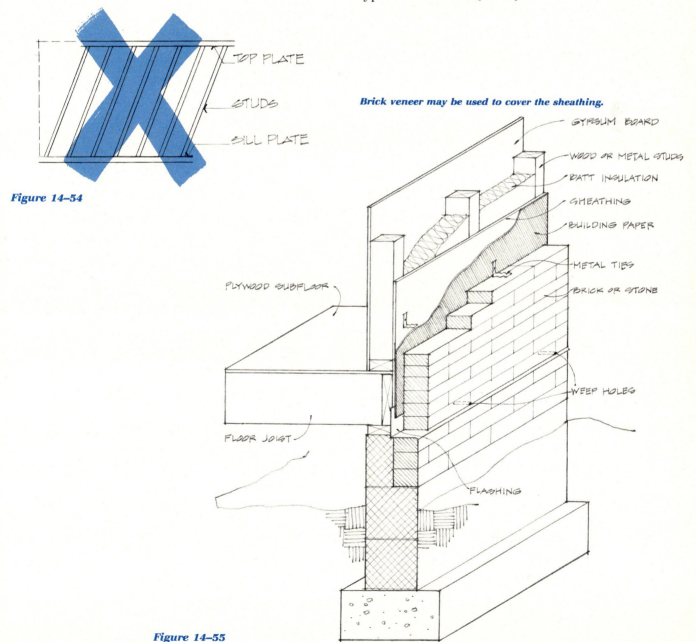

Figure 14–55

Light Construction Methods

247

Bevel siding . . .

Figure 14–56

Vertical-groove redwood siding . . .

Figure 14–57

248

Board-and-batten redwood siding . . .

Figure 14–58

Siding applied in a diagonal pattern . . .

Figure 14–59

The intensity of appearance of shadow lines in siding varies with the shape and size of the joints.

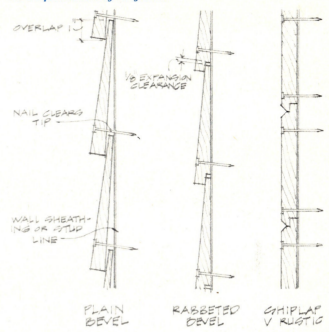

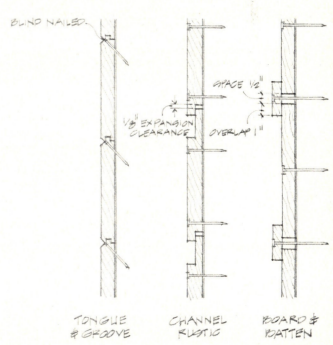

Figure 14–60

249

Metal commercial siding usually has vertical grooves and joints.

Deep groove commercial aluminum siding applied in a horizontal position shows large horizontal shadow lines.

Figure 14–61

Figure 14–62

Steel, aluminum, and vinyl sidings are available that resemble wood siding patterns. They usually have horizontal lines when used in residential construction. Metal commercial sidings usually have vertical grooves and joints [14–61]. They come in large sheets or in long interlocking strips. In [14–62] deep-groove commercial aluminum siding has been applied in a horizontal position in a residential application to achieve a unique effect.

The interior surfaces of framed walls are often covered with gypsum board since it is economical and can have a variety of finishes [14–63]. A smooth painted finish is the most common, but textured paint, wallpaper, and vinyl wall coverings are also popular. A rough plaster appearance may be achieved by applying an inexpensive spackling compound with a texture to the gypsum board. True plaster, once a very common interior finish, is now found only in the more expensive homes. The extra expense is due to the fact that some form of lathe must be installed first, and then the plaster must be applied by a skilled workman.

For sound vertical corners, gypsum board should have framing behind both edges [14–64]. The joint between the wall and ceiling requires continuous or periodic backing of the ceiling gypsum board. When the joint is parallel to the ceiling framing, a joist is required directly above the edge of the ceiling board [14–65]. When the joint is perpendicular to the ceiling framing, continuous support above the joint is not required. The periodic support of the ceiling board by the joists at their normal spacing is adequate [14–66].

Gypsum board is a popular, economical interior surface for framed walls.

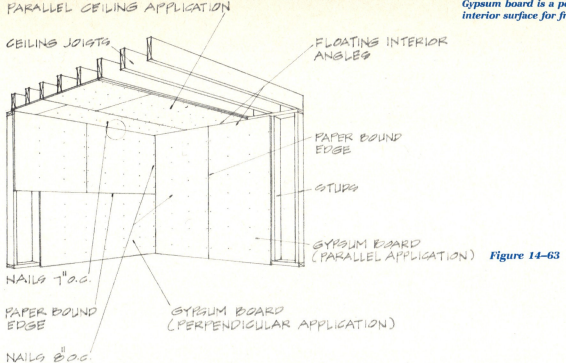

Figure 14–63

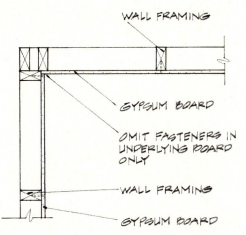

Figure 14–64

A horizontal section showing a gypsum board joint in a vertical corner.

A vertical section showing a gypsum board ceiling-to-wall joint parallel to the ceiling framing.

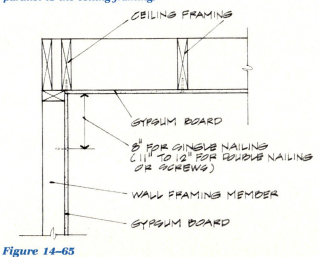

Figure 14–65

A vertical section showing a gypsum board ceiling-to-wall joint perpendicular to the ceiling framing.

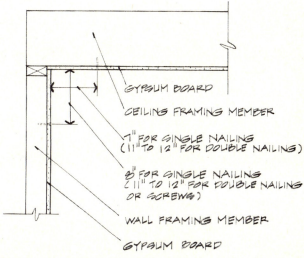

Figure 14–66

Gypsum board spans between framing just as a beam spans between columns. Thin gypsum board (as compared to thick board) is more likely to sag or be broken by impact if it spans between widely spaced framing. The maximum spacing of framing for various thicknesses of gypsum board is shown in Table 14–2.

Gypsum board can be applied to both straight and curved walls. The thinner sheets can curve to smaller radii. The minimum bending radii for various thicknesses of gypsum board are shown in Table 14–3.

Paneling of various compositions, thicknesses, and sizes is available in wood textures, patterns, and colors. Sheet paneling with grooves [14–67] may be applied directly to the studs giving the appearance of more expensive board paneling [14–68]. Single boards may be applied horizontally [14–69], diagonally [14–70], or in any position that is desired.

Sheet paneling with grooves gives the appearance of more expensive board paneling.

Figure 14–67

Table 14–2. Maximum Framing Spacing for Gypsum Board

Single-Ply Gypsum Board (Thickness)		Application to Framing	Maximum O.C. Spacing of Framing	
in.	mm		in.	mm
Ceilings				
3/8	9.5	Perpendicular[a]	16	406
1/2	12.7	Perpendicular	16	406
1/2	12.7	Parallel[a]	16	406
5/8	15.9	Parallel	16	406
1/2	12.7	Perpendicular[a]	24	610
5/8	15.9	Perpendicular	24	610
Sidewalls				
3/8	9.5	Perpendicular or parallel	16	406
1/2	12.7	Perpendicular or parallel	24	610
5/8	15.9	Perpendicular or parallel	24	610

[a] If ceiling to receive a water-base spray texture finish, gypsum board should be applied perpendicular to framing and board thickness increased from 3/8 in. (9.5 mm) to 1/2 m. (12.7 mm) for 16 in. (406 mm) O.C. framing and from 1/2 in. (12.7 mm) to 5/8 in. (15.9 mm) for 24 in. (610 mm) O.C.

Board paneling applied vertically.

Table 14–3. Bending Radii for Gypsum Board

Gypsum Board Thickness		Bent Lengthwise		Bent Widthwise	
in.	mm	ft	meters	ft	meters
1/4	6.4	5	1.5	15	4.6
3/8	9.5	7.5	2.3	25	7.7
1/2	12.7	10[a]	3.0	—	—

[a] Bending two 1/4-in. (6.4-mm) pieces successively permits radii shown for 1/4 in. (6.4 mm).

Figure 14–68

Boards may also be applied horizontally...

Figure 14–69

...or applied diagonally.

Figure 14–70

14.5 Roofs

In frame construction, the connection of the wall to the roof is the same for one- and two-story buildings [14–71 to 14–73]. The structural member of the sloped roof of a house is called a *rafter*. Rafters are usually 2 × 6's but could be larger or smaller depending on the span. Rafters are placed either 24 or 16 inches on center. Roofs carry less load than floors, so a wider spacing is feasible.

The rafters meet at the peak of the roof at a *ridge board* that runs perpendicular to the rafters and is sandwiched between them. The ridge board is 1 inch thick and is the next standard depth larger than the depth of the rafters. For example, 2 × 6 rafters would connect to a 1 × 8 ridge board. However, 2 × 8's are often used since they are more commonly available at the project site.

Residential roofs are usually sloped. Commercial roofs are usually flat. The commercial floor systems previously discussed are also used for roof construction. Instead

One-story-wood frame roof construction.

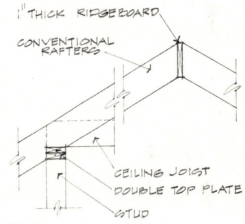

Figure 14–71

One-and-a-half-story wood-frame roof construction.

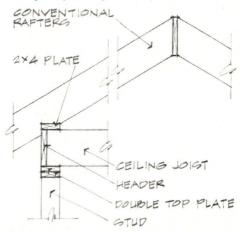

Figure 14–72

Light Construction Methods

Wood-frame roof construction using trusses.

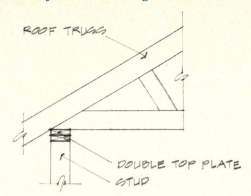

Figure 14–73

Sheathing is fastened to the rafters... followed by building paper and shingles.

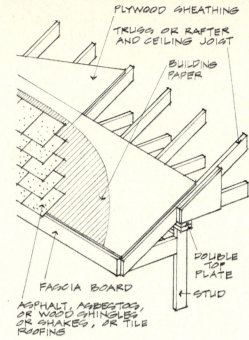

Figure 14–74

of finished floor material, alternating layers of roofing felt and bituminous cement are applied to make the roof watertight. This is known as *built-up roofing* ([B–11], Appendix B). Insulation is usually placed between the structural deck and the built-up roofing but can also be placed under the deck or on top of the roofing.

Sheathing to support the shingles is fastened to the top of the rafters [14–74]. The sheathing is usually

A common truss with bearing details shown.

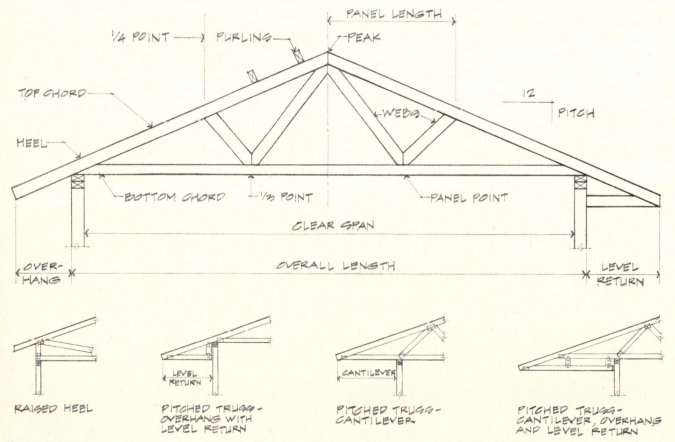

Figure 14–75

254 Building Systems

½-inch plywood but could be ¾-inch thick boards. A heavy water-resistant paper called *building paper* is nailed to the top of the sheathing as an underlayment for the shingles. It reduces air infiltration through the roof and helps protect the sheathing from any moisture that may get under the shingles. The finished roofing on a sloped residential roof is usually asphalt or wood shingles. Other materials, such as metal and clay products, are also used. In southern climates, 1 × 6's spaced up to 10 inches on center may be used as sheathing for wood shingles and shakes.

When rafters are used, joists are required to support the ceiling below [14–71 and 14–72]. Ceiling joists are similar to floor joists except that they carry less weight and are often smaller. When ceiling joists, rafters, and intermediate bracing members are nailed together prior to installation, this assembly is called a *truss* [14–75 to 14–78]. The combined system is so strong that the sizes of the individual members may be reduced below the required sizes of the same components used separately.

Typical residential trusses are made of 2 × 4's with the members being fastened together with gusset plates ([B–19], Appendix B). These trusses may be factory manufactured or made on the job just prior to erection. They are light enough in weight to be handled by two people or by a small hoist [14–79].

Since trusses eliminate the cutting and assembly of the roof and ceiling structure on the site, the site erection time for the roof is faster than rafter and joist construction. Due to their depth and efficiency, trusses span from exterior wall to exterior wall, thus eliminating the need for interior bearing partitions [14–80]. This gives flexibility in laying out the floor plan. The space between the chords and webs is available for locating ductwork. The large number of web members in a typical truss makes use of the attic space difficult for the homeowner. Trusses cost more than the individual pieces of lumber for traditional roofs, but they save on labor costs. They are generally considered to be economical and are common in new construction [14–81].

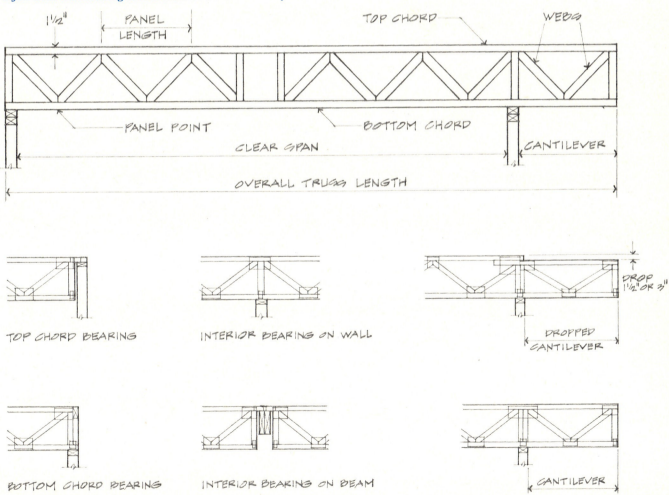

Figure 14–76

Light Construction Methods

Another type of flat truss with bearing details shown.

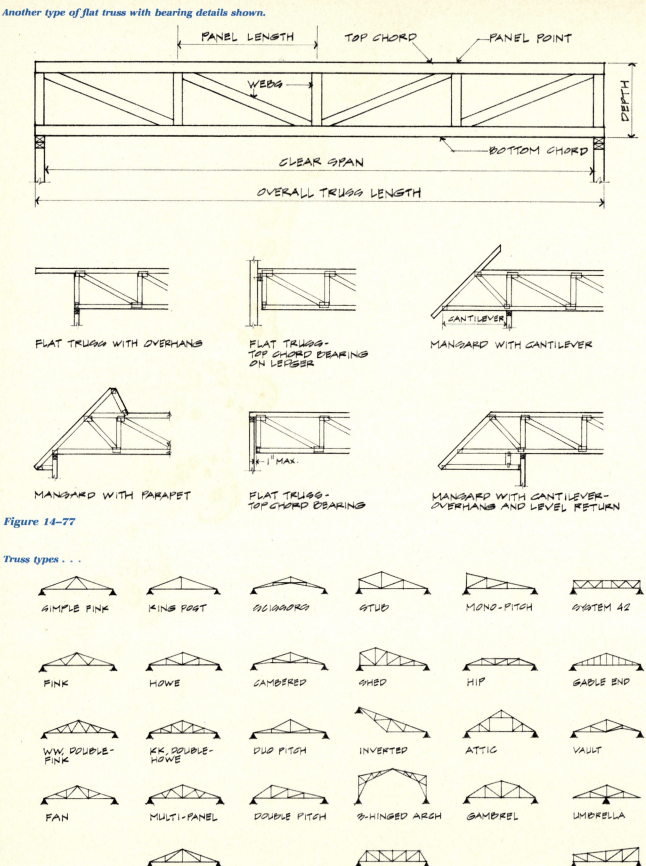

Figure 14-77

Truss types . . .

Figure 14-78

Lightweight residential trusses can be lifted onto a roof with a small crane and moved into final position by hand.

Figure 14–79

Trusses span long distances eliminating intermediate supports.

Figure 14–80

Roof trusses in home construction.

Figure 14–81

257

A truss made with wood chords and steel tubing webs spans long distances with relatively light total weight.

Figure 14–82

Wood and tubing trusses are available in curved shapes.

Figure 14–83

Trusses are also used for floor construction in both residential and nonresidential construction. Flat trusses made from 2 × 4's positioned with the 4-inch dimension horizontal utilize very short lengths of 2 × 4's for web members [14–76]. The ability to utilize short lengths of lumber to help span long distances is an economical arrangement.

The combination of steel tubing web members with wood chords results in a truss that will span long distances with a relatively light total weight [14–82]. These units may be obtained in curved shapes for very long spans [14–83]. The wood chord provides a surface that allows nails to be driven into it. This is a convenience not available in all-steel trusses or joists.

You have now seen the basic parts of standard home construction and a sampling of variations of these systems used in light commercial construction. It may be helpful at this point to review the residential components as a whole. Figure [14–84] shows how the individual details relate to each other in a house. Figure [14–85] shows a summary of some of the important nonstructural subsystems involved in home construction. These are as follows:

A. Entry: overhang protects users and the opening itself from rain.
B. Plumbing: should be within the insulated space and not too distant from the water heater.
C. Insulation under the floor: appropriate for ventilated crawl spaces.
D. Insulation inside the foundation wall: appropriate for concrete slab floors and crawl spaces without insulation in the floor.
E. Interior wall materials and finishes.
F. Ridge vent for the attic.
G. Ceiling insulation.
H. Heat distribution system.
I. Wall insulation.
J. Insulated windows.
K. Insulation at joint between window and wall.

In the following chapters, you will see how the structural elements and the various subsystems are drawn and specified and how they relate to each other in a set of construction drawings.

EXERCISES

14–1. List 12 basic structural parts of a residence or light commercial building.
14–2. What elements prevents the building from sinking into the ground?
14–3. What are the directions of the forces that must be resisted by the foundation wall?
14–4. What is the frost depth in your locale? Is it the same throughout your state?
14–5. If a foundation wall is 14 inches thick, what should be the minimum size of the footing? (Use the "rule of thumb.")
14–6. What is the correct name for the concrete slab commonly called a "waffle" slab?
14–7. What are the two types of steel joists?
14–8. What is the purpose of the vapor barrier under an interior concrete slab?
14–9. What is the purpose of a sill on a foundation wall?

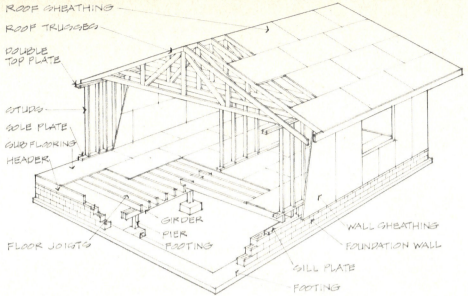

Structural elements in a home.

Figure 14–84

Some of the important nonstructural subsystems in a home.

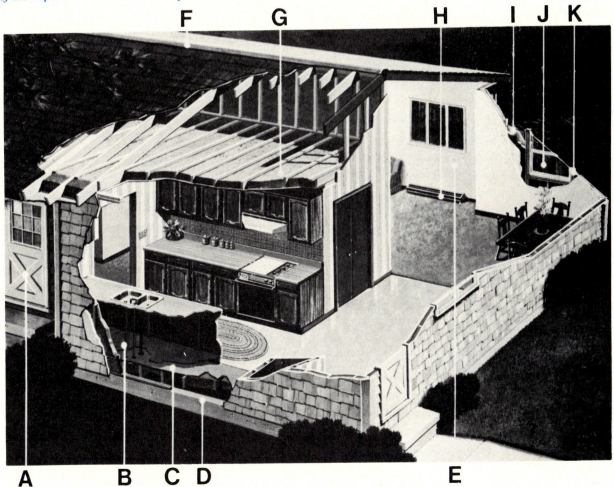

Figure 14–85

259

14–10. What is the actual size of a 2 × 4? A 2 × 12?

14–11. What is the typical spacing of 2 × 4 studs in residential construction?

14–12. What is the main difference between balloon and platform framing?

14–13. What element supports the ceiling and roof structure of a brick veneer house?

14–14. What is the 2 × 4 member called that is at the base of a stud wall?

14–15. What are the two types of framing used in residential roof construction?

14–16. What are four functions of wall sheathing?

14.6 Prefabricated Construction

A prefabricated item is one that is made at a location other than where it is used. In the strict sense, lumber and nails are "prefabricated," as are almost all construction materials with the possible exception of poured-in-place concrete and foamed-in-place insulation. The use of manufactured building materials is not, however, considered prefabrication. The assembly of lumber into trusses at a factory is a prefabrication that is in very common use today. Their use, however, does not automatically cause a building to be identified as prefabricated. Prefabricated buildings employ major factory-produced components such as walls, bathrooms, kitchens, habitable rooms, or groups of rooms.

After World War II, housing was in short supply. Factory-made housing was quickly produced to solve the shortage. Due to the urgency of the problem, quality was not maintained, and "prefab" housing developed a reputation as being "shoddy" construction. Because of this image it was many years before people began taking prefabricated housing seriously. Since the 1960s, however, the prefabricated housing industry has done much to overcome old prejudices against it.

Although prefabrication is sometimes considered to be economical, this is not always true. Factory labor is typically less costly than field labor, but other considerations often offset this saving. The equipment necessary to produce the components must be included in the cost of the component produced. This means that a very large number of sales is necessary on which to apportion the equipment cost. As small pieces are assembled into large components, delivery of the product becomes a cost factor. Economic limits on the distance large units may be transported also reduces potential sales.

An obvious way to reduce costs is to reduce waste in building materials. Lumber is manufactured in length multiples of 2 feet, and much sheet material is 4 feet × 8 feet or 4 feet × a length that is divisible by 2 feet [14–86]. Waste can be reduced by planning a building with dimensions that are compatible with these material sizes.

Certain other advantages in prefabricated building have become more clear. On-site project planning time is decreased. It is also generally possible to reduce the total time necessary to produce a finished building. This can have economic advantages, such as fewer months during which an owner must pay for two buildings (the old one *and* the new one under construction) and a shorter time over which interest for the construction loan must be paid. Housing shortages and shortages of building space in general may also be solved relatively quickly with prefabrication techniques.

Working conditions in a factory are consistently better than outdoors on a building site. With constant temperatures and the absence of rain and snow indoors, it is possible to improve quality control. Disadvantages include possible damage to finished components during handling. Also, there is increased difficulty in joining large components, as compared to joining traditional materials on site.

The *precut home* is a compromise between using only prefabricated trusses and the other extreme of prefabricated building modules containing several rooms built in a factory. Relatively small components, such as stairs, wall sections, prehung doors, studs, joists, and trusses, are factory-built [14–87 to 14–89]. Handling is reasonably easy with these small units. All of the pieces for a home may be delivered in one or two truckloads. The components are then assembled on the site like pieces of a large puzzle [14–90]. Each piece is numbered and drawings provide the instructions for fitting them together. Utility cores may be installed traditionally, or they may also be prefabricated [14–91].

There are a variety of precut systems available. Some may install much of the finished surfaces in the factory, while others apply the finishes on the site. With the mixture of factory-built and site-built features, it is often difficult to identify precut houses by their finished appearance. Choices of such units range from simple vacation houses [11–66] to large homes of varied complexities [14–93].

Buildings made of large modules are slightly easier to identify by appearance. The limiting factor in module size is the maximum size that is allowed to be moved on a highway. Such modules tend to be the size and shape of the typical mobile home because these units are usually built using the largest possible dimensions.

Variety is achieved in the appearance of modular buildings by arranging the modules in different ways and by adding a variety of accessories with different shapes [14–92]. Some systems may have "pull-out" modules that fit into the main unit. Once the main

The use of standard sizes of building materials will reduce cost.

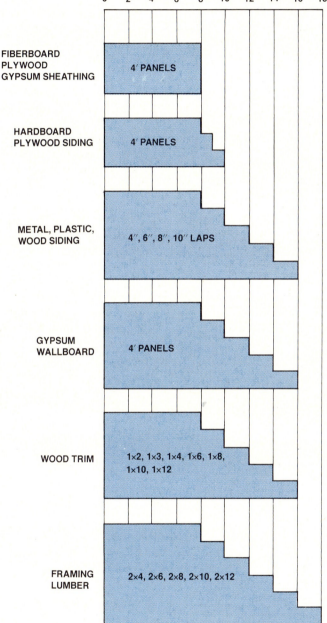

Figure 14–86

The cutting and assembly of framing members for a precut home is done in a factory.

Figure 14–87

Cutting and assembling stairs in a factory reduces both time and cost.

Figure 14–88

Cutting and assembling prehung doors simplifies the construction process.

Figure 14–89

Premade wall panels are assembled on the site.

Figure 14–90

A factory-made utility core (kitchen back to back with bathroom) is installed on a subfloor system at the site. The rest of the building will be assembled around this unit.

Figure 14–91

Modules containing one or more rooms are assembled on the site . . . the modules may be completely finished on the inside and even contain appliances and furniture.

Figure 14–92

module is in place, the submodules are pulled out of its sides, like drawers. Modular units are often entirely finished on the inside, sometimes including appliances and furniture. Since the modules are all or partially enclosed during shipment and installation, the interior finishes are protected from weather and handling. This degree of finishing is difficult to achieve in systems assembled from prefabricated panels.

EXERCISES

14–17. List several advantages of prefabricated building methods over traditional methods.

14–18. List several problems that must be solved with prefabricated building methods that are not problems with traditional methods.

14–19. List the maximum dimensions of a building module that is allowed to be transported on the highways in your state. (Contact the State Highway Patrol.)

A two-story precut home.

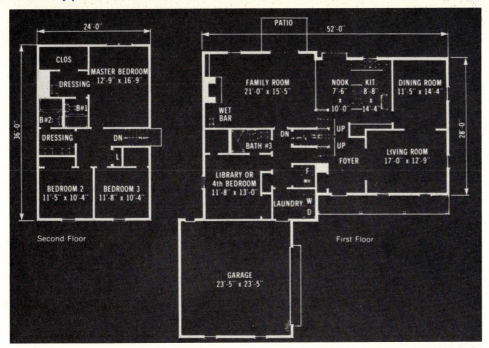

Figure 14-93

15 Sizing Structural Members

15.1 Basic Structural Principles

Since the soundness of a building structure affects the life and safety of its occupants, it must be designed by competent personnel. The seriousness of this aspect of architecture and building construction has never been more clearly summarized than in Hammurabi's building code of Babylon in 1800 B.C. In effect, it stated that if a building collapsed and killed the owner, the architect/builder would be put to death.

Although light construction is often relatively simple to build, the structural members of the building must be designed by people with professional training and experience. Design firms may have such people on their staff, or an engineering firm may be employed to make the calculations. The architectural designer must often prepare drawings that show the location of structural components before the engineer has calculated their minimum sizes. It is helpful, therefore, if you can estimate member sizes for generalized design and drawing purposes. This is important because if you can draw structural components reasonably close to their final sizes, the architectural details will not have to be revised after the engineer selects the actual members.

The ability to make some basic calculations and a knowledge of how to use structural tables are especially helpful to the drafter for structural size estimating purposes. The information in this chapter will help you make such size estimates.

Girders, beams, and joists must meet three basic conditions, among others, to be acceptable. They must not fail by part of the member sliding past the adjacent part (*shear failure*) [15–1]. They must not fail by breaking of the member when bent (*bending failure*) [15–2]. They must not bend so much as to damage surrounding components (*deflection failure*) [15–3]. A structural deflection may crack ceiling materials (especially plaster) cause doors and windows to stick, or result in "springyness" of a floor as one walks across it.

In light construction, shear failures are very rare. Because of the relatively light loads and long spans involved, a beam or joist will fail in bending or have too great a deflection before its shear strength is exceeded. Usually it is the deflection criterion that governs the design. We will not, therefore, examine beam sizing for shear.

Structural members must not fail in shear . . .

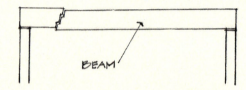

Figure 15–1

. . . or fail in bending.

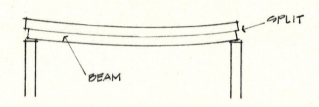

Figure 15–2

. . . or fail by excessive deflection.

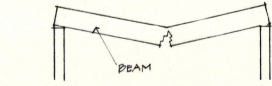

Figure 15–3

15.2 Bending Stresses

The property of a structural member that indicates its bending strength is its *section modulus* represented by the letter *s*. Section modulus is easily computed for any member with a rectangular cross section if the dimensions are known. Computing *s* for steel beams and joists is more difficult since their profiles are not usually rectangular. The section modulus and other properties for standard steel members are available from tables published by the American Institute of Steel Construction. They may also be found in structural engineering texts and handbooks. The equation for the section modulus (*s*) of a structural member with a rectangular cross section is as follows:

$$s = \frac{bh^2}{6}$$

where b = base of the section [15–4]
h = height of the section

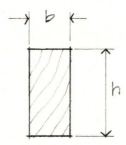

Figure 15–4

Example 15–1

The section modulus of a 4 × 12 timber [15–5] is found as follows:

$$s = \frac{3.5 \text{ in.} \times 11.25 \text{ in.} \times 11.25 \text{ in.}}{6}$$
$$= 73.8 \text{ in}^3$$

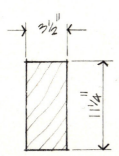

Figure 15–5

EXERCISE

15–1. Determine which member has the greater resistance to bending forces, a 2 × 12 or a 4 × 6. (Hint: Compute the section modulus of each and see what result is larger. Use actual dimensions from Table 14–1.)

The section modulus (*s*) required for structural members to resist failure by bending may be computed by the equation

$$s = \frac{M}{F_b}$$

where M = maximum bending moment caused by the load
F_b = bending stress allowable in the structural material

The allowable bending stress (F_b) for various materials may be found in structural texts and handbooks (see Table E–3, Appendix E) for properties of Southern Pine lumber).

The maximum moment (*M*) caused by the load is based on the total load and the length of span of the member. If either increases, so does the maximum moment. The maximum moment (*M*) on a uniformly loaded beam or joist (such as a typical floor joist) may be computed by the equation

$$M = \frac{Wl}{8}$$

where M = maximum moment, lb-ft
W = total load on the beam, lb
l = length of span, ft.

The total load (*W*) on the beam or joist may be computed by multiplying the area of the floor (or roof) times the design load on the floor (or roof) divided by the number of beams or joists:

$$W = \frac{\text{area} \times \text{design load}}{\text{number of members}}$$

The design load is the live load plus the dead load. *Live load* consists of loads that are not permanent. Snow, wind, occupants, and furniture are examples of live loads. *Dead load* is permanent. The weight of the construction materials resting on the member and the weight of the structural member itself are dead loads.

The live load is selected from handbooks listing typical loads for specific building uses or from code books and ordinances. Since structural design affects the safety of building occupants, it is often controlled by law. Representative live loads are listed in Tables E–1 and E–2. You may estimate the typical dead load of a wood-framed floor or roof to be 10 pounds per square foot (lb/ft² or psf). The following example illustrates how to compute the size required for a wood floor joist. When making any sizing calculations using equations, always be sure that the units used for any value are compatible with the equation and with each other.

Example 15–2

Given: A floor 15 ft × 40 ft has No. 2 Southern Pine floor joists (for nonsleeping areas) spaced 16 in. on center [15–6].

Required: Compute the size of the floor joists.

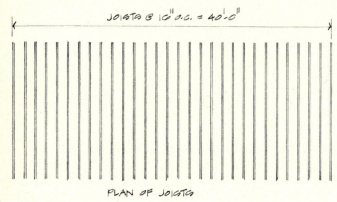

Figure 15–6

Step 1 Find the total design load on the floor.

dead load = 10 lb/ft² (estimated)
live load = 40 lb/ft² (Table E–1)
10 lb/ft² + 40 lb/ft² = 50 lb/ft²

Step 2 Find the number of joists. (Assume that the joists span the short distance.)

number of joists = 40 ft ÷ 16 in./joist
or
40 ft ÷ 1.33 ft/joist
$N = 30$ joists

Step 3 Find the total load on one joist.

$$W = \frac{\text{area} \times \text{design load}}{\text{number of members}}$$

$$= \frac{(15 \text{ ft} \times 40 \text{ ft}) \times 50 \text{ lb/ft}^2}{30 \text{ joists}}$$

= 1000 lb/joist

Step 4 Compute the maximum moment on each joist.

$$M = \frac{Wl}{8}$$

$$= \frac{1000 \text{ lb} \times 15 \text{ ft}}{8}$$

= 1875 lb-ft
or
= 22,500 lb-in. (convert feet to inches)

Step 5 Compute the section modulus required. The value of F_b is found in Table E–3. Use the column marked $1.15 F_b$ because at least three joists are being used. We will assume that a 5-inch or deeper joist will be required.

$$s = \frac{M}{F_b}$$

$$= \frac{22,500 \text{ lb-in.}}{1400 \text{ lb/in}^2}$$

= 16.07 in³

Step 6 Compute the size of the joist.

$$s = \frac{bh^2}{6}$$

Solve for h.

$$h = \sqrt{\frac{6s}{b}}$$

$$= \sqrt{\frac{6 \times 16.07 \text{ in}^3}{1.5 \text{ in.}}} \quad \text{(Wood joists are typically 1.5 in. thick, so } b = 1.5 \text{ in.)}$$

= 8.02 in.

The actual size required is 1.5 inches × 8.02 inches.

Use 2 × 10's to satisfy the resistance to failure by bending requirement. Note that we are still not sure that the 2 × 10's are satisfactory because we don't know yet whether this size will satisfy the deflection requirements.

EXERCISE

15–2. A floor 12 ft × 30 ft has No. 2 KD* Southern Pine floor joists spaced 16 in. on center. Compute the size of the floor joists.

15.3 Deflection

Deflection is the distance that a structural member sags in the center when compared to the position of its supported ends [15–3]. *Allowable deflection* usually falls into three categories. If the member has a plaster or gypsum board ceiling fastened directly to it, its deflection in feet is usually limited to a distance equal to the length (L)

* KD is explained in Appendix Table E–3.

in feet divided by 360. An 18-foot long joist in this case could sag 0.6 inch without problems. This value is obtained by dividing the 18 feet by 360 and converting the result to inches. An allowable deflection of $L/240$ may be used when the structural member does not have a plaster or gypsum board ceiling fastened directly to it, or when the appearance of the ceiling is not as important. The $L/240$ ratio permits a larger deflection, thus giving a less uniform appearance than would the $L/360$ deflection ratio. A deflection ratio of $L/180$ permits an even greater allowable sag, but is still sometimes used.

EXERCISE

15–3. Determine the allowable deflection for a rafter that spans 12 feet. Assume the allowable deflection is $L/240$.

The *actual deflection* of a structural member when a uniform load is applied may be determined by the equation

$$\Delta = \frac{5Wl^3}{384EI}$$

where Δ = symbol for deflection, in.
W = design load, lb
l = length of span, in.
E = modulus of elasticity of the structural material, lb/in.²
I = moment of inertia of the structural member, in.⁴

The modulus of elasticity (E) of a material is an indication of its stiffness (ability to resist deflection). It may be found in structural handbooks in tables that also show other properties for materials. The value of E for Southern Pine may be found in Table E-3.

The moment of inertia (I) is a measure of the stiffness provided by the cross-sectional shape of a structural member in resisting deflection. It may be found in structural tables for standard wood and steel shapes. The value of I for a rectangular cross section may be computed with the equation

$$I = \frac{bh^3}{12}$$

where b = base of the section, in.
h = height of the section, in.

Example 15–3
The moment of inertia for a 4 × 12 timber is found as follows:

$$I = \frac{3.5 \text{ in.} \times 11.25 \text{ in.} \times 11.25 \text{ in.} \times 11.25 \text{ in.}}{12}$$

$$= 415.3 \text{ in.}^4$$

EXERCISE

15–4. Determine which member has the greater resistance to deflection, a 2 × 12 or a 4 × 6. (Hint: Compute the moment of inertia of each and see which result is larger. Use actual dimensions as shown in Table 14–1.)

The following example illustrates how to check the actual deflection of a given structural member.

Example 15–4
Given: The 2 × 10 floor joist system described in Example 15–2.
Required: Determine if the actual deflection is within the allowable limit of $L/360$.

Step 1 Compute the moment of inertia.

$$I = \frac{bh^3}{12}$$

$$= \frac{1.5 \text{ in.} \times 9.25 \text{ in.} \times 9.25 \text{ in.} \times 9.25 \text{ in.}}{12}$$

$$= 98.9 \text{ in.}^4$$

Step 2 Find the total load on one joist. Often, only the live load is used to compute deflection. This is because the materials that may be damaged by sagging joists are applied after the joists have already deflected due to their own weight (dead load). Once the materials are installed, only the additional deflection due to live load will tend to crack them. If the dead load is very large, it may be included in the deflection computation. Here, we will compute W (design load) based on live load only.

$$W = \frac{\text{area} \times \text{live load}}{\text{number of members}}$$

$$= \frac{(15 \text{ ft} \times 40 \text{ ft}) \times 40 \text{ lb/ft}^2}{30 \text{ joists}}$$

$$= 800 \text{ lb/joist}$$

$$\Delta = \frac{5Wl^3}{384EI}$$

$$= \frac{5 \times 800 \text{ lb} \times 180 \text{ in.} \times 180 \text{ in.} \times 180 \text{ in.}}{384 \times 1{,}600{,}000 \text{ lb/in.}^2 \times 98.9 \text{ in.}^4}$$

$$= 0.38 \text{ in. actual deflection due to live load.}$$

Step 3 Compare the actual deflection to the allowable deflection.

$$\text{allowable } \Delta = \frac{L}{360}$$
$$= \frac{180 \text{ in.}}{360}$$
$$= 0.5 \text{ in.}$$

The actual deflection (0.38 in.) is less than the allowable deflection (0.5 in.). Therefore the 2 × 10 joists are satisfactory to resist deflection.

Since we have designed the joists adequately to resist bending forces and have shown that the joists have satisfactory stiffness to resist deflection, we can conclude that 2 × 10 floor joists are satisfactory for this floor system.

EXERCISE

15–5. Check the actual deflection for the joists you selected in Exercise 15–2 against the allowable limit of $L/360$ to see if the joists you selected for bending strength are also stiff enough to resist excessive deflection.

When sizing structural members, if you select a beam for bending strength and discover that it is not satisfactory in deflection, select the next larger size and try the deflection computation again. Continue to select larger sizes until you find a satisfactory structural member. If no standard sizes are appropriate, you may have to combine members, build a special member, shorten the span, or change materials.

15.4 Wood Joist Selection

When dealing with standard materials, shapes, and loads, the span capabilities of structural members may be computed and arranged in tabular form. This has been done for most standard structural members and the information can be found in handbooks published by agencies representing the various segments of the structural products industry. Appendix E contains some sample tables. The remainder of this chapter will be devoted to learning how to use these tables. It is easy to see after having done a few simple calculations that much time can be saved during the design and working drawing phases if structural sizes are estimated from tables.

Structural tables differ slightly in their format, and you must be able to understand the abbreviations and the footnotes. You must also understand how to convert the known information about the loading on a structural member into a form that is compatible with the available table.

Tables E-4 to E-10 show allowable spans for wood joists and rafters. These tables do not apply to all joists and rafters, however. To use a table, you must match the loading conditions, construction application, and allowable deflection to the table. Loading conditions are noted in pounds per square foot (psf) of live load and dead load. This is the weight that the member must carry. Construction application relates to the function of the member within the construction system. There are separate tables for floor joists, ceiling joists, and rafters. These divisions are further subdivided according to what types of floors, ceilings, and roofs are involved.

Once you have selected the appropriate table for your construction application, additional information is required to use it. To select a member size for a given span, you must know how far apart the members are spaced. In modern construction we have already noted that floor joists are usually spaced 16 inches on center, while ceiling joists and rafters may be at 16 or 24 inches on center. The on-center spacings are listed vertically in the tables beside each member size in the Appendix E tables.

The last item required is the type and quality of wood used. Tables E-4 to E-10 are for Southern Pine only. If, for example, you are using Douglas Fir on your project, you cannot use these tables. Across the top, the tables show various grades of Southern Pine. The strongest grades are in the first column on the left. The grades get progressively weaker as you move to the right side of the tables. Selection of the appropriate grade depends on economics and availability. On an actual project you would have to balance the increased cost of the better lumber against their longer span capability. If the lumberyards in the project locale are limited in the grades that they have in stock, you will have to take this into consideration. For lumber that will be exposed to view, appearance becomes an important consideration. The cheaper grades are not attractive.

If you were selecting joist sizes for typical residential floors, you would use Table E-4 or E-5. Assuming that the standard joist spacing of 16 inches on center is used and that the lumber available is No. 3 Grade Southern Pine, you could select a joist for spans from 6′-5″ to 16′-0″. A span of 12′-0″, for example, would require a 2 × 10. The 2 × 10 can span farther than 12′-0″ (it can span 13′-1″), but a 2 × 8 can only span 10′-3″. The 2 × 10 is the smallest standard-size member that can span the required 12 feet.

Example 15–5

Given: the conditions specified in Examples 15–2 and 15–4.
Required: Select a floor joist from a span table.

Step 1 Find the appropriate table in Appendix E. We will use Table E-5. Read the description at the top of the table to see that it matches the requirements of the problem. Note that this table is based on a 40-psf live load and that it limits live load deflection to $L/360$.

Step 2 Find the column that is designated for the type of wood used (No. 2).

Step 3 Examine each row specified for a 16-inch joist spacing. Note the span listed in the appropriate column in each row as follows:

Member Size	Span for No. 2
2 × 5	8′–0″
2 × 6	9′–9″
2 × 8	12′–10″
2 × 10	16′–5″
2 × 12	19′–11″

The designated span of 15′–0″ is not listed. You must select a standard size that will span *at least* 15′–0″. A 2 × 8 will span only 12′–10″. A 2 × 10 will span 16′–5″. Use 2 × 10 joists.

Note that this table selection matches the joist size selected by calculations in Examples 15–2 and 15–4. The table includes checks of both bending strength and deflection.

EXERCISES

15–6. Select a joist from the span tables in Appendix E to meet the requirements of Exercises 15–2 and 15–5. Compare your table selected member to the one you selected by computation. They should be the same size.

15–7. An attic floor is to be designed for a 30-psf live load and a 10-psf dead load. Deflection is limited to $L/360$. No. 3 Dense KD Southern Pine joists are spaced at 16 in. on center. What size joists are required if they span 12′–6″?

15–8. The first floor of a house is to be designed for a 40-psf live load and a 10-psf lead load. Deflection is limited to $L/360$. No. 1 Dense KD Southern Pine joists are spaced at 16 in. on center. What size joists are required if they span 20′–0″?

15–9. Ceiling joists that support a gypsum board ceiling are spaced at 24 in. on center. Use of the attic is not planned. They carry a 10-psf live load and a 5-psf dead load and are limited to a deflection of $L/240$. What size Select Structural Southern Pine joists are required if they span 18′–0″?

15–10. Ceiling joists that support a gypsum board ceiling and limited attic storage are to be designed to carry a 20-psf live load and a 10-psf dead load. They are limited to a deflection of $L/240$. What size Select Structural KD Southern Pine joists are required if they are spaced 16 in. on center and span 16′–0″?

15–11. Rafters in a roof that slopes 2 in 12 are exposed to view from below. They carry a 20-psf live load and a 10-psf dead load. They are spaced at 24 in. on center and are limited to a deflection of $L/240$. What size No. 2 Dense KD Southern Pine members are required if they span 21′–0″?

15–12. Rafters in a 4 in 12 sloped roof carry no finished ceiling. They carry a 20-psf live load and a 15-psf dead load. The deflection is limited to $L/180$. What size Dense Select Structural KD Southern Pine joists are required if they are spaced 16 in. on center and span 25′–0″?

15.5 Wood Beam Selection

Beams may be sized in a way similar to the process used for joists. Allowable bending stresses and moduli of elasticity tend to be higher in laminated beams than in beams consisting of one piece of wood [15–7]. This is because characteristics that may reduce the strength of the beam can be cut out of the individual laminations. Knots may be positioned in areas requiring less strength (the stresses in a beam are not distributed uniformly) and split wood may be eliminated entirely. Also, laminated beams need not be made entirely of the same kind of wood. Stronger wood may be positioned where it is needed the most. Table E-11 lists laminated wood beams sizes for various spacing and spans.

Allowable bending stresses tend to be higher for laminated beams than for one-piece beams.

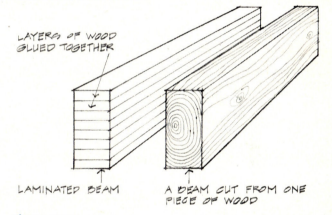

Figure 15–7

Example 15–6

Given: Laminated wood beams span 12 feet, are spaced 8 feet on center, and carry a 30-psf total load on a roof.

Required: Select a laminated beam for the given conditions.

Step 1 Examine Table E-11. Find the 12-foot span row in the farthest-left column, SPAN-FT.

Step 2 The adjacent column, SPACING-FT, lists spacings of 6, 8, 10, and 12 feet. Select the row of beam sizes for 8-ft spacing.

Step 3 Move to the right until you find a beam size listed in a column with a heading of 30 psf. In this case, it is the first column that has a beam size listed. This shows the estimated beam size to be a 3⅛ × 6 in. beam. Note that laminated beam sizes do not match the typical 2 in. increments between sizes of one-piece beams.

EXERCISE

15–13. A floor system has a total load of 50 psf. Laminated wood beams will be used to span 16 feet. The beams will be spaced 8 feet on center. Select a beam size for the given conditions.

15.6 Wood Decking Selection

Since beams are typically spaced farther apart than 2 feet, plywood subfloor is not strong enough to span between them. Thick wood *decking* is used because of its strength, and in most cases its appearance. The decking is often left exposed to view in ceiling applications. The decking is designed using the same principles as are used for beams and joists. Decking may also be selected from tables such as Tables E-12 and E-13.

Example 15–7

Given: The laminated roof beam system described in Example 15–6.
Required: Determine the size of Douglas Fir–Larch Select wood decking to span between the beams.

Step 1 Examine Tables E-12 and E-13. Note that several loading conditions are available. The second chart in each table meets the requirements of this example. These charts are entitled Roof Decking: 10-psf Dead Load/20-psf Live Load. This total load of 30 psf meets our requirement.
Step 2 The charts are divided into columns with the wood types listed at the top. Douglas Fir–Larch is in the first column.
Step 3 Note that each wood type column is divided into two sections—"Select" and "Common." We will use the "Select" half of the column.
Step 4 We have now narrowed the selection to two choices. The chart is divided into two rows—"Simple" and "Controlled Random." The term "Simple" refers to decking of a length equal to the spacing of the beams. "Controlled Random" refers to decking of random lengths in a system where there are at least four beams. Assuming a simple span condition, we see that 2-in. decking will span 8′–9″ and 3-in. decking will span 14′–7″. Since our required span is only 8′–0″, the 2-in. decking should be satisfactory.

EXERCISE

15–14. Western Hemlock Common decking is to be installed on the floor system described in Exercise 15–13. Assuming a simple span condition, select a decking thickness to meet the given conditions.

15.7 Wood Truss Selection

Trusses are more complicated to design than beams. Truss span tables, however, are similar to beam and joist span tables and just as easy to use. Table E-14 lists allowable spans for several types of wood roof trusses.

Example 15–8

Given: A shingle roof is designed with a 4 in 12 pitch. The walls of the building are 45 feet apart. The live load is 20 psf. Trusses spaced 24 in. on center will be used to support the roof.
Required: Select a Common type truss to meet the given requirements.

Step 1 Examine Table E-14. The table is divided into four groups of truss types. We are interested in the first group of Common trusses. Note that the table is based on a 24-in. truss spacing (see the footnote at the bottom of the table).
Step 2 The table is divided into several rows relating to different roof pitches. The 4 in 12 pitch is the fifth row from the top.
Step 3 The table is also divided into four main columns relating to the types of loading listed at the top. Each column relates to several types of loading that result in the same requirement for truss strength. Note that our loading (20 psf live load) is listed in the last column.
Step 4 Each loading column is divided into three columns relating to the size of individual members within the truss. Our truss must span 45 feet. Three different trusses will accomplish this according to the table. A 2 × 6 top and bottom chord truss will span 63 feet. A 2 × 6 top and 2 × 4 bottom chord truss will span 51 feet. A 2 × 4 top and bottom chord truss will span 42 feet. Select the truss with the smallest members (least cost) that will span the distance. The appropriate choice is the 2 × 6 top and 2 × 4 bottom chord truss in the center of the three columns. This truss will span 51 feet, which is more than the required 45 feet. The next smaller truss will not span 45 feet.

EXERCISE

15–15. Flat trusses 24 in. on center must span 44 ft. carrying a 30-psf snow load and roofing weighing about the same as shingles. (Shingles are not used on flat roofs.) Select a truss of the least depth to meet these requirements.

Example 15–9

Given: A floor system must span 25 ft. with trusses spaced 24 in. on center. The live load is 40 psf and the dead load may be assumed to be 15 psf.
Required: Select a wood floor truss of the least depth to meet the given requirements.

Step 1 Examine Table E-15. Two overall loading conditions are available. We want the column labeled "55 psf" (40-psf dead load plus 15-psf live load).

Step 2 Note that trusses made of wood of different strengths are available in each size. The truss with the least depth that will span 25 ft. is 18 in. deep. A No. 1 Dense Kiln Dried Southern Pine truss will span 26′–6″. A Select Structural Douglas Fir 19% truss will span 25′–4″. (The value 19% means that the wood has been air dried to a 19% moisture content.) The final choice between these two trusses will be made based on which wood is available in your area. Should both be available, price probably will be the deciding factor in your selection.

EXERCISE

15–16. A 22-foot span floor system will carry a 40-psf live load and a 15-psf dead load. Select a truss having the least depth that will meet the given requirements at a spacing of 24 in. on center.

15.8 Steel Joist Selection

Metal framing members typically do not have simple rectangular cross sections. Physical properties are, consequently, difficult to compute. Fortunately, it is not necessary to make such computations since tables are available that list section moduli and moments of inertia for the various products available. As in wood construction, tables exist that contain spans versus loading conditions for metal structural members. Table E-16 lists allowable spans for solid web steel (C-type) joists.

Example 15–10

Given: A floor system must span 14 ft. with C-type steel joists spaced 24 in. on center. The floor must carry a 40-psf live load and a 10-psf dead load.
Required: Select a joist having the least depth that meets the given requirements.

Step 1 Examine Table E-16. The left column contains joist styles (sizes) as follows: The first numbers represent the depth of the joist (115 represents 11.5 in., 60 represents 6.0 in.). The letters describe the member (SJ is a member that may be used as a *stud* or *joist*). The last numbers represent the thickness of the steel (20 represents 2.03 mm, 13 represents 1.25 mm). Note that there are three columns representing different loading conditions. We will use the middle of these three columns since it covers our loading requirements.

Step 2 The loading columns are divided into two subcolumns, titled "1-span" and "2-span." 1-span refers to joists that are supported only at each end [15–8]. 2-span refers to joists that are supported at each end and also in the center. Assume a 1-span condition for this example.

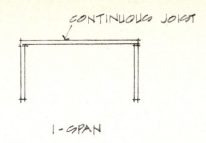
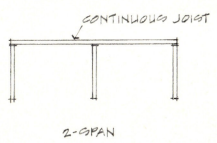

Figure 15–8

Step 3 There are three rows for each joist designation, relating to different spacings. This example calls for a 24-in. spacing. Follow the 1-span column down until you find the least depth joist in a 24-in. row that will span 14 ft. or greater. Select a 725SJ20 joist.

EXERCISE

15–17. A floor system must span 18 ft. with C-type steel joists spaced 24 in. on center. The floor must carry a 50-psf live load and a 10-psf dead load. Assume a 2-span condition. Select a joist having the least depth to meet the given conditions.

15.9 Open Web Steel Joist Selection

Open web steel joist tables are often arranged differently from the tables we have examined thus far. Many open web joists can be used for both floor and roof as long as the load and deflection requirements are met. Table E-17 lists safe loads for open web steel joists.

Example 15–11

Given: Open web steel joists will be used to span 20 ft. at a spacing of 48 in. on center in a floor system. The live load is 60 psf and the dead load is 12.5 psf.
Required: Select a joist that meets the given conditions.

Step 1 Examine Table E-17. Note that joist designation (sizes) are listed as headings of columns across the top of the table. The spans are listed in a column at the

Sizing Structural Members

left of the table. The table itself contains total loads in black and live loads in color. The loads above the colored lines are governed by shear stresses. This division in the table may be ignored for our purposes. To use this table you must locate a load in the table that is equal to or greater than the allowable load per linear foot that can be carried by the joist. The given loads stated in pounds per square feet must be converted to pounds per linear foot.

Step 2 Determine the load per linear foot on each joist. See [15–9] for a plan diagram of several joists. Each linear foot of joist must support a strip of floor 4'–0" wide and 1'–0" long for the length of the joist. The amount of live load on this strip is

60 lb/ft² × 4 ft² = 240 lb/linear foot

The amount of dead load on this strip is

12.5 lb/ft² × 4 ft² = 50 lb/linear foot

The total load on this strip is

240 lbs + 50 lbs = 290 lb/linear foot

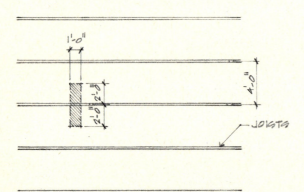

Figure 15–9

Step 3 Select a joist that will carry 290 lb/linear foot total load and 240 lb/linear foot live load in the 20-foot span row. A 12H6 will carry 390 lb of total load and 246 lb of live load. A 14H4 will carry 350 lb of total load and 245 lb of live load. The 12H6 is 12 in. in depth and weighs 8.2 lb/ft. The 14H4 is 14 in. in depth and weighs 6.5 lb/ft. Unless the greater depth is a problem, the lighter member is often less expensive (less steel) and is selected. Lighter members are deeper, which may force a building to be taller per floor and therefore more expensive to build. Experience will help determine the more economical choice in a real situation.

EXERCISE

15–18. Open web steel joists are used to span 24 ft. at 60 in. on center in a floor system. The live load is 60 psf. The dead load is 15 psf. Select a joist having the least depth that meets the given conditions. Now select a joist having the least weight that meets the given conditions.

15.10 Steel Decking Selection

Steel deck is typically used to span between open web steel joists. Deck size may be selected from a table (see Table E-18). Many deck profiles are available with different strengths.

Example 15–12
Given: The floor system of Example 15–11.
Required: Select the appropriate size steel deck.

Step 1 Examine Table E-18. Note that three deck profiles are available in this table as are three span conditions. Assume a simple span condition and Narrow Rib Deck Type NR.
Step 2 The columns in the table represent spans. The 4'–0" span required in our case is the far left column.
Step 3 Select the decking that can carry at least 72.5 psf of total load. Note that NR 22 decking can carry 73 psf. The other two choices for a simple span condition can support greater loads because they are thicker and therefore heavier. This would result in unnecessary expense. Use NR 22 steel decking.

EXERCISE

15–19. Using the same conditions as in Exercise 15–18, select a steel decking for these requirements. Use Narrow Rib Type NR Deck in a 2-span condition.

16 Design of Residential Climate Control Systems

Most of us are not fortunate enough to live in a climate that produces ideal year-round comfort conditions. Much of the year the weather conditions are either too cold, too hot, too wet, too dry, or too dusty for our bodies to be comfortable. In order to create an environment where we can function efficiently, it has been discovered that certain climate variables must be controlled. This can be accomplished best by constructing an *envelope* (a controlled space). Within this envelope we can vary an array of climate variables. These variables include: temperature, humidity, air motion, and air cleanliness. Complete climate control or "year-around air conditioning" would include heating and cooling, humidification and/or dehumidification, ventilation (fresh air), and filtering, all provided within an acceptable noise level.

Most residential installations do not provide a measure of all these variables. Perhaps the most basic and necessary item is heating. Nowhere in the United States can it be completely avoided. However, in certain geographic locations, mechanical equipment for heating may be kept to a minimum or even eliminated by employing passive solar heating techniques (see Chapter 8). Mechanical cooling is optional except in certain southern states.

This chapter discusses the considerations to be made in the selection of a residential size heating or cooling system. It enables you to become familiar with the major components of a typical system, to compute the size of the equipment needed, and to know where system components can be located.

16.1 Comfort Conditions

Thermal comfort results from a desirable combination of temperature, humidity, air movement, and air cleanliness. We may feel comfortable under varying combinations of these variables. As an example, high relative humidity (which of itself tends to make one uncomfortable) may be counteracted by a relatively lower temperature and more rapid air movement. The other extreme, a frequently occurring low relative humidity, is found in many homes in wintertime. As far as comfort is concerned, this condition can be compensated for by increasing the room temperature and air movement.

Studies on comfort have been carried out since about 1900. The American Society of Heating, Refrigerating, and Air Conditioning Engineers (ASHRAE) has sponsored much of this research. In 1975, ASHRAE published energy conservation guidelines that call for the following indoor design conditions: winter—72°F and 30% relative humidity maximum; summer—78°F.* Figure [16–1] shows a range of temperatures and relative humidites in which most people will feel comfortable. It must be noted that this figure assumes that the person is not in direct sunlight, nor exposed to air movement of more than 50 feet per minute.

Air motion is desirable, within certain limits, in an occupied room. It improves the general feeling of comfort by unifying the thermal conditions in the space and by clearing out stuffy spots. As air gently passes the occupants, it carries away accumulated warm air and humid-

The comfort zone . . . based on temperature and relative humidity.

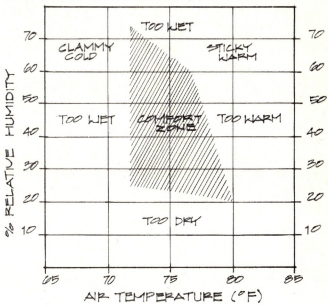

Figure 16–1

* For normal residential design, relative humidity in summer is not specified by ASHRAE.

273

Heat is transferred by conduction from one end of an iron bar to the other.

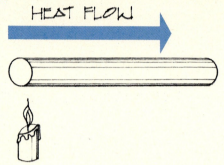

Figure 16–2

Heat is transferred by radiation by energy waves flowing through space.

Figure 16–4

ity given off by the body. This results in a feeling of freshness. Air velocity within the occupied zone (from the floor to 6 feet in height) should not exceed 50 feet per minute.

To maintain comfortable temperature levels within a building envelope, it may be necessary to add or subtract heat. During the winter, heat is lost. It flows from inside the building to the outside and must be replenished by some means. In the summer, heat will most probably be flowing into the building envelope. Thus, to maintain comfort, heat must be added to or removed from the occupied space. In either case, the designer must understand how to compute the rate of heat being transferred in order to size the heating and/or cooling systems.

16.2 Heat Transfer

Heat energy always migrates in the direction of decreasing temperature. This transfer of energy can be by three different methods: conduction, convection, and radiation.

Conduction: Heat transfer occurs when materials at different temperatures are in contact. The molecules at a higher temperature are moving more rapidly; they collide with slower (lower temperature) molecules, thus transferring some of their energy. As an example of conduction, imagine the heating of an iron bar at one end [16–2]. The temperature of the bar will gradually increase from left to right until the right end becomes too hot to hold. Likewise, when you touch a cold glass window, heat is rapidly conducted away from your skin and you have a cold sensation. In general, the denser the material, the better it will conduct heat. For example, metal will conduct heat better than wood.

Convection: Thermal energy can be moved through a fluid (air can be considered to be a fluid) not only by conduction as discussed above, but also by the movement of the fluid from one region to another. A warm surface will heat the air in contact with it [16–3]. The warmed air becomes less dense and rises, allowing more dense cool air to take its place.

Radiation: Heat energy flows from a warm surface to a cold surface through space in the same way that light travels from one place to another. This radiation does not heat air as it travels through a space. However, when the radiation warms a cooler object, the object in turn will warm the surrounding air by conduction. In [16–4] the person's side that faces the fire is warmed

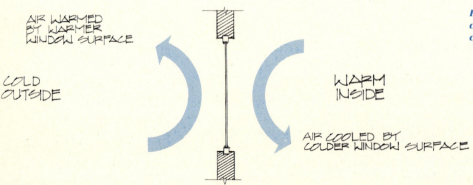

Heat is transferred by convection as air currents are formed by heating or cooling.

Figure 16–3

by radiation, while his back remains cold. The air is not being heated by radiation. Similarly, when you sit next to a window on a cold day, you are radiating body heat to the cold glass and to the colder objects beyond. The glass and the objects are radiating much less heat to your body. There is a net loss in radiant heat energy and therefore you feel a cold sensation.

Heat is transmitted through the building shell by the three methods of heat transfer: conduction, convection, and radiation. All materials will offer some resistance to heat flow. Those that are specifically used to stop heat flow are called *insulators*. They help keep the heat on the inside in the winter and outside in the summer. Without these insulation materials the heating or cooling equipment must work harder to overcome the heat loss or heat gain.

16.3 Resistance (R) Values

Certain construction materials have been tested and given a rating (R value) that indicates relatively how much *resistance* they offer to heat flow. The higher the R value the better the insulating value of the material. Figure [16–5] gives an indication of the relative values of common materials. Manufacturers mark R values on insulation materials. An extensive listing of R values can be found in the *ASHRAE Handbook of Fundamentals*. A partial list of these values is shown in Table 16–1.

Let us consider how these resistance (R) values are utilized. Consider the cross section of a typical frame wall [16–6]. Note that even the air film on the surface of a material offers some resistance to heat flow. Also, the dead air space between the studs offers about as much resistance as any of the other items.

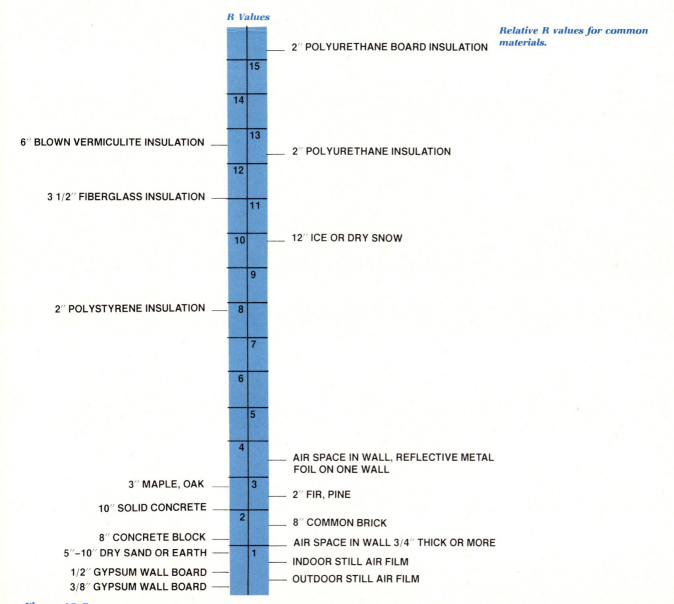

Relative R values for common materials.

Figure 16–5

Design of Residential Climate Control Systems

275

Table 16–1. Resistance (R) Values of Air Films, Air Spaces, and Common Construction Materials (°F-ft²-hr/Btu)[a]

Surface (nonreflective) resistances for still air	
Horizontal (heat flow up)	0.61
Horizontal (heat flow down)	0.92
Vertical	0.68
Surface (nonreflective) resistances for moving air (any surface)	
Winter, 15-mph wind	0.17
Summer, 7½-mph wind	0.25
Air spaces	
Horizontal (heat flow up)	0.9
Horizontal (heat flow down)	0.94
Vertical (heat flow horizontal)	1.0
Building and insulating materials	
Building board gypsum or plaster board, ½ in.	0.45
Plywood (Douglas Fir)	1.25 per inch
Fiber board sheathing, ½ in.	1.32
Particle board, medium density	1.06 per inch
Vapor seal, plastic film	Negligible
Floor materials	
Carpet with rubber pad	1.23
Terrazzo, 1 in.	0.08
Tile, asphalt	0.05
Wood, hardwood	0.68
Insulating materials	
Blanket and batt mineral fiber, fibrous form processed from rock, slag or glass	
Approximately 2–2.75 in.	7
Approximately 3–3.5 in.	11
Approximately 3.5–6.5 in.	19
Approximately 6–7 in.	22
Approximately 8.5 in.	30
Board and slabs	
Glass fiber, organic bonded	4 per inch
Polyurethane (board)	6.25 per inch
Expanded polystyrene, extruded smooth skin surface	5.26 per inch
Expanded polystyrene, molded beads	3.57 per inch
Mineral fiberboard, wet-molded acoustical tile	2.38 per inch
Wood, shredded (cemented in preformed slabs)	1.67 per inch
Loose fill	
Perlite, expanded	2.70 per inch
Mineral fiber	
Approximately 3.75–5 in.	11
Approximately 6.5–8.75 in.	19
Approximately 7.5–10 in.	22
Approximately 10.25–13.75 in.	30
Foamed fill: polyurethane	6
Masonry materials	
Cement mortar	0.20 per inch
Lightweight aggregate	
80 lb/ft³	0.40 per inch
40 lb/ft³	0.86 per inch
Sand and gravel concrete (140 lb/ft³)	0.08 per inch
Stucco (116 lb/ft³)	0.20 per inch
Masonry units	
Brick, common	0.20 per inch
Concrete block	
8 in.	1.11
12 in.	1.28
Plastering materials	
Cement plaster, sand aggregate	0.20 per inch
Gypsum plaster, lightweight aggregate, ⅝ in.	0.39 per inch
Roofing	
Asphalt shingles	0.44
Built-up roofing, ⅜ in.	0.33
Wood shingles	0.94
Siding materials	
Wood	
Drop, 1 × 8 in.	0.79
Bevel, 0.5 × 8 in. lapped	0.81
Plywood, ⅜ in.	0.59
Woods	
Hardwoods	0.91 per inch
Softwoods	1.25 per inch

[a] Values are approximate. For more exact and complete information, see *ASHRAE Handbook of Fundamentals*.

To make the wall in [16–6] more energy efficient, the air space could be filled with a variety of insulation materials that have high R values. A flexible batt insulation is commonly used. It can be bought in roll form and in various widths that accommodate common stud and joist spacings. For instance, the 14½-inch width fits be-

The thermal resistance of a wall is the sum of the individual component resistances.

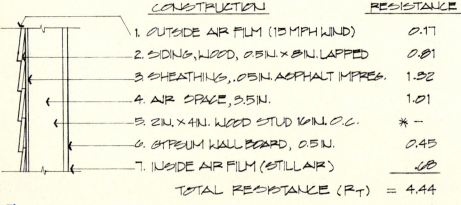

CONSTRUCTION	RESISTANCE
1. OUTSIDE AIR FILM (15 MPH WIND)	0.17
2. SIDING, WOOD, 0.5 IN. × 8 IN. LAPPED	0.81
3. SHEATHING, .05 IN. ASPHALT IMPREG.	1.32
4. AIR SPACE, 3.5 IN.	1.01
5. 2 IN. × 4 IN. WOOD STUD 16 IN. O.C.	*—
6. GYPSUM WALLBOARD, 0.5 IN.	0.45
7. INSIDE AIR FILM (STILL AIR)	.68
TOTAL RESISTANCE (R_T) =	4.44

Figure 16–6

* Although the studs contribute slightly to the total R of the wall, we will assume zero R value for this computation.

tween studs spaced 16 inches on center. Table 16–1 shows the R values for commonly available thicknesses.

By using 3½-inch mineral fiber batts in the air space of the wall section shown in [16–6], we could recompute the total resistance of the wall to be 14.43 (4.44 previous total − 1.01 air + 11 batt). Remember that if you want to stop heat flow, the *higher* the R value, the better.

16.4 Coefficient of Transmission (U) Values

The *coefficient of transmission* (U value) represents the heat flow through 1 square foot of construction material in 1 hour if there is a temperature difference of 1 degree Fahrenheit from inside to outside. This is a very important concept for the designer. The U value must be known in order to compute the heat loss through a particular type of construction. To calculate this value the designer must know what an R value is and where to find it.

The U value represents an *amount of heat flow* through a cross section of construction that includes:

1. The inside air film.
2. A material or series of materials.
3. An air space(s).
4. The outside air film.

The R value represents *resistances to heat flow* of a particular (single) material, or an air space, or an air film. The sum of the individual resistance is R_{total} (R_T).

The U value is calculated by taking the reciprocal of the sum of the resistances of all materials, air films, and air spaces contained in the cross section of the construction.

$$U = \frac{1}{R_T}$$

As an example, the U value of the uninsulated frame wall shown in [16–6] is

$$U = \frac{1}{R_T} = \frac{1}{4.44} = 0.23$$

The U value of the same wall insulated with 3½-inch batts would be

$$U = \frac{1}{R_T} = \frac{1}{14.43} = 0.07$$

Remember that, if you want to stop heat flow, the *lower* the U value the better. Recently published codes and standards set maximum allowable average values for walls and roofs. These maximum values vary depending on the severity of the climate. The units for U are Btu* per hour-square foot-degree Fahrenheit.

16.5 Heat Losses

If we maintain a residential building enclosure at 72°F†, the space will continually lose heat to outdoor air that is at lower temperatures. Table 16–2 shows that winter outdoor design temperatures in all areas of the United States are less than the 72°F that we want to maintain in our residence. Heat will, therefore, flow from the inside to the outside of a building during the winter months anywhere we build in the United States. Because of this, the heat lost through the walls, the ceiling, and the floor of each room must be balanced by heat delivered to each room by the heating system.

A heating system should be designed by an engineer who specializes in this type of work. However, the drafter will prepare the heating plans and should be familiar with the design process. The first step is to calculate the heat loss. Heat escapes from a room in two ways:

1. Transmission through walls, ceiling, floor, windows, and doors.
2. Infiltration of cold air (and consequently exfiltration of warm air) through cracks around windows and doors.

Figure [16–7] is an approximate graphical explanation of the division of heat losses in a typical home.

An approximate division of the heat loss for conventional housing.

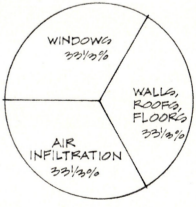

Figure 16–7

---

* Btu is the abbreviation for British thermal unit. It is a measurement of heat equal to that amount required to raise the temperature of one pound of water one degree Fahrenheit.
† Energy conserving guidelines recommend 68°F.

Design of Residential Climate Control Systems

277

16.6 Transmission Losses

Heat will be transmitted through construction materials, in a given period of time, in proportion to three factors:

1. The area of the surface of the material.
2. The difference in temperature between the inside air and the outside air.
3. The ability of the material to transmit heat. This is indicated by its coefficient of transmission, U.

The relationship between these factors is expressed in the formula

$$H = AU(t_i - t_o)$$

where H = heat loss each hour, Btu/hr
A = area of material, ft^2
U = coefficient of transmission, Btu/hr ft^2 °F
t_i = inside temperature, °F
t_o = outside design temperature, °F

U values for typical construction are given in Table 16–3. Outside design temperatures may be obtained from Table 16–2 or other published data, such as the *ASHRAE Handbook of Fundamentals*. Winter and summer outdoor design temperatures for the United States are shown graphically in [16–8 and 16–9]. The curved lines on these maps are called *isotherms*—lines of equal temperature.

Table 16–2. Outdoor Design Temperatures (°F)

City, State	Winter	Summer	Summer Mean Daily Range	City, State	Winter	Summer	Summer Mean Daily Range
Albany, NY	−6	88	23	Little Rock, AR	15	96	22
Albuquerque, NM	12	94	27	Los Angeles, CA	37	89	20
Amarillo, TX	6	95	26	Louisville, KY	5	93	23
Anchorage, AL	−23	68	15	Lubbock, TX	10	96	26
Atlanta, GA	17	92	19	Madison, WI	−11	88	22
Birmingham, AL	17	94	21	Medford, OR	19	94	35
Bismark, ND	−23	91	27	Memphis, TN	13	95	21
Boise, ID	3	94	31	Miami, FL	44	90	15
Boston, MA	6	88	16	Minneapolis, MN	−16	89	22
Brownsville, TX	35	93	18	Nashville, TN	9	94	22
Buffalo, NY	2	85	21	New Orleans, LA	29	92	16
Burlington, VT	−12	85	23	New York, NY	11	89	17
Charleston, SC	25	92	13	Norfolk, VA	20	91	18
Cheyenne, WY	−9	86	30	Oklahoma City, OK	9	97	23
Chicago, IL	−8	89	20	Omaha, NE	−8	91	22
Cincinnati, OH	1	90	21	Philadelphia, PA	10	90	21
Cleveland, OH	1	88	22	Phoenix, AZ	31	107	27
Columbia, MO	−1	94	22	Pittsburgh, PA	1	86	22
Denver, CO	−5	91	28	Portland, ME	−6	84	22
Des Moines, IA	−10	91	23	Portland, OR	17	85	23
Detroit, MI	3	88	20	Raleigh, NC	16	92	20
Dodge, KS	0	97	25	Richmond, VA	14	92	21
El Paso, TX	20	98	27	Sacramento, CA	30	98	36
Fort Worth, TX	17	99	22	St. Louis, MO	2	94	21
Fresno, CA	28	100	34	Salt Lake City, UT	3	95	32
Great Falls, MT	−21	88	28	San Antonio, TX	25	97	19
Honolulu, HI	62	86	12	San Diego, CA	42	80	12
Houston, TX	27	94	18	San Francisco, CA	35	77	20
Indianapolis, IN	−2	90	22	Seattle–Tacoma, WA	21	80	22
Jackson, MS	21	95	21	Tampa, FL	36	91	17
Jacksonville, FL	29	94	19	Tulsa, OK	8	98	22
Kansas City, MO	2	96	20	Washington, DC	14	91	18
Lake Charles, LA	27	93	17				

SOURCE: *ASHRAE Handbook of Fundamentals*, 1981.

Table 16–3. Coefficients of Transmission (U) Values for Building Components (BTU/hr-ft^2-°F)

Walls	
Wood siding, gypsum board interior, no insulation	0.21
Wood siding, gypsum board interior, R-11 (3½ in.) insulation	0.08
Wood siding, plastered interior, R-19 (6 in.) insulation	0.05
Brick veneer, plastered interior, no insulation	0.26
Brick veneer, plastered interior, R-11 (3½ in.) insulation	0.07
Brick veneer, plastered interior, R-19 (6 in.) insulation	0.05
8-in. solid brick, no interior finish	0.50
8-in. solid brick, furred and plastered interior	0.31
12-in. solid brick, no interior finish	0.36
12-in solid brick, furred and plastered interior	0.24
10-in cavity brick, no interior finish	0.34
10-in. cavity brick, furred and plastered interior	0.24

Partitions	
Wood frame, gypsum board, no insulation	0.29
4-in. solid brick, no finish	0.60
4-in. solid brick, plastered one side	0.51
4-in. solid brick, plastered both sides	0.44
6-in. solid brick, no finish	0.53
8-in. solid brick, no finish	0.48
Wood frame, gypsum board, R-11 insulation	0.08

Ceilings and Floors	
Frame, plastered ceiling, no flooring, no insulation	0.61
Frame, plastered ceiling, no flooring, R-19 (6 in.) insulation	0.05
Frame, plastered ceiling, no flooring, R-30 (9 in.) insulation	0.03
Frame, no ceiling, wood flooring, no insulation	0.34
Frame, no ceiling, wood flooring, R-19 (6 in.) insulation	0.05

Ceilings and Floors (continued)	
Frame, no ceiling, wood flooring, R-30 (9 in.) insulation	0.03
Frame, plastered ceiling, wood flooring, no insulation	0.22
Frame, plastered ceiling, wood flooring, R-19 (6 in.) insulation	0.04
Frame, plastered ceiling, wood flooring, R-30 (9 in.) insulation	0.03
3-in. bare concrete slab	0.68
3-in. concrete slab, parquet flooring	0.45
3-in. concrete slab, wood flooring on sleepers	0.25
2-in. lightweight concrete slab	0.30

Roofs	
Asphalt-shingled pitched roof, no ceiling, no insulation	0.52
Asphalt-shingled pitched roof, plastered ceiling, no insulation	0.31
Asphalt-shingled pitched roof, plastered ceiling, R-19 (6 in.) insulation	0.05
Asphalt-shingled pitched roof, plastered ceiling, R-30 (9-in.) insulation	0.03
Built-up flat roof, no ceiling, no insulation	0.49
Built-up flat roof, no ceiling, 2 in. board insulation	0.12
Built-up flat roof, plastered ceiling, no insulation	0.31
Built-up flat roof, plastered ceiling, 2 in. board insulation.	0.11

Windows and Doors	
Single-glazed windows	1.13
Double-glazed windows	0.45
Triple-glazed windows	0.28
1¾-in. solid wood doors	0.46
1¾-in. solid wood door with storm door	0.27

SOURCE: *ASHRAE Handbook of Fundamentals*, 1981.

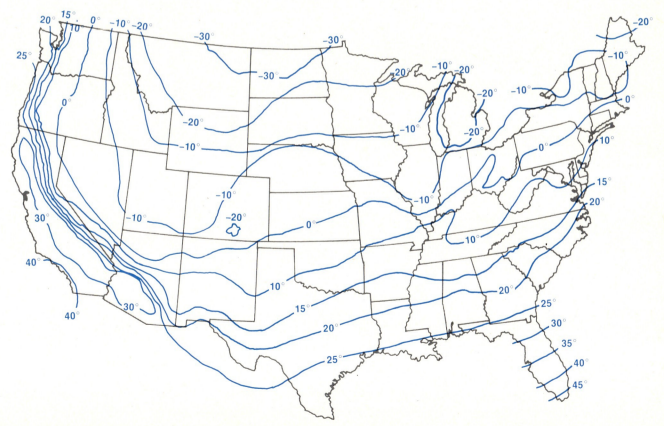

Figure 16–8 Isotherms for winter outdoor design temperatures.

Figure 16–9 Isotherms for summer outdoor design temperatures.

16.7 Heat Loss at Slab Perimeter

In calculating the heat loss of concrete slabs on grade, the only loss that is usually considered to take place is along and near the edges of the slab. Very little heat is dissipated into the ground below the slab. In most areas of the United States the edges of the slab should be insulated [16–10]. Table 16–4 gives the amount of heat loss (Btu/hr) for each linear foot of slab edge for either 2 inches (recommended) or 1 inch of rigid insulation.

A slab on grade should be insulated at the edges to reduce heat loss.

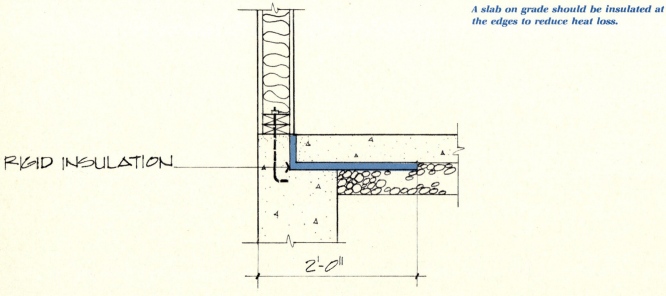

Figure 16–10

Table 16–4. Heat Loss of Concrete Floors at or near Grade Level per Foot of Exposed Edge (Btuh)[a]

Outdoor Design Temperature (°F)	Recommended 2-in. Edge Insulation	1-in. Edge Insulation	No Edge Insulation[b]
−20 to −30	50	55	75
−10 to −20	45	50	65
0 to −10	40	45	60

[a] Btuh is an accepted form of expressing Btu per hour.
[b] This construction not recommended; shown for comparison only.
SOURCE: *ASHRAE Handbook of Fundamentals*, 1981.

16.8 Air Infiltration Losses

Winter winds blow cold outdoor air into indoor spaces through cracks around windows and doors on the windward side of the house. This air is warmed by heating units near these locations. An equal amount of warmed air leaves through similar cracks on the leeward side. Losses due to infiltration must be considered as a part of the heat loss calculations. The basis for calculating hourly heat loss due to infiltration is the number of cubic feet per hour (cfh) of outdoor air that must be heated from outdoor design temperature to room temperature.

One method for estimating the amount of infiltration air is the *air change method*. This involves calculating the volume of air in each room and multiplying this by the number of air changes per hour under average conditions. Typical air change values resulting from infiltration are shown in Table 16–5.

Example 16–1

Using the air change method, find the rate of infiltration in cubic feet per hour of outdoor air entering a room that is 12 ft × 15 ft × 8 ft high, with openings on two sides.

Table 16–5 shows that, for rooms with windows on two sides, the predicted number of air changes per hour due to infiltration is 1.5. Therefore, the rate of infiltration for the room in this example is 12 × 15 × 8 × 1.5 = 2160 cfh.

After the rate of flow of outdoor air into the space is established, the calculation for the resulting hourly heat loss due to infiltration is found using the equation

$$H = 0.018 \text{ cfh} (t_i - t_o)$$

where H = heat loss each hour, Btuh
0.018 = factor accounting for the heat required to raise 1 cubic foot of air 1 degree Fahrenheit
cfh = infiltration rate, cubic feet per hour
t_i = inside design temperature, °F
t_o = outside design temperature, °F

Example 16–2

Using the infiltration rate found in Example 16–1, what would be the heat loss due to infiltration on a winter design day in Minneapolis, Minnesota?

From Table 16–2 we see that the winter outdoor design temperature is −16°F. Assuming that the indoor design temperature is 72°F, we can then calculate the heat loss due to infiltration as

$$H = 0.018 \times 2160 \times [72 - (-16)]$$
$$= 0.018 \times 2160 \times 88$$
$$= 3421 \text{ Btuh}$$

16.9 Heat Loss Calculations

In designing a heating system for a building, all of the heat losses discussed in the preceeding sections must be calculated and summarized. A suggested format for this is seen in Table 16–7 that uses as an example the home designed for Mr. and Mrs. Browne in Chapter 13. Typical heat loss calculations are shown for this residence assuming it to be located in the vicinity of Chicago, Illinois, rather than in the Southwest. Also, for Chicago, a stucco exterior wall surface has been used. The floor

Table 16–5. Air Changes Occurring Under Average Conditions in Residences, Exclusive of Air Provided for Ventilation[a]

Kind of Room	Number of Air Changes per Hour
Rooms with no windows or exterior doors	0.5
Rooms with windows or exterior doors on one side	1
Rooms with windows or exterior doors on two sides	1.5
Rooms with windows or exterior doors on three sides	2
Entrance halls	2

[a] For rooms with weather-stripped windows or with storm sash, use two-thirds these values.
SOURCE: *ASHRAE Handbook of Fundamentals*, 1981.

Design of Residential Climate Control Systems

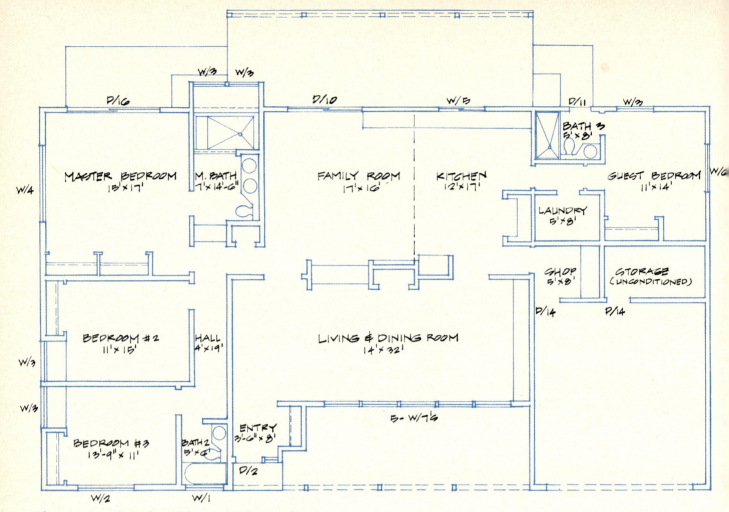

Figure 16–11 Floor plan of the Browne home (Chapter 13).

plan is shown in [16–11]. Assume that the home faces south in this location.

From Table 16–2 the winter outdoor design temperature in Chicago is −8°F. Indoor temperature can be assumed to be 72°F. The attic is unheated. Estimate infiltration by the air change method. Assume that the building is constructed as follows:

Walls: 2″ × 6″ stud walls with ½-inch stucco exterior; 5½-inch fiberglass batt insulation ($R = 19$); ½-inch gypsum board interior ($R_T = 22.4$, $U = 0.045$).
Ceiling: ½-inch gypsum board and 13½ inches of loose-fill fiber insulation having an $R = 30$ ($R_T = 31.8$, $U = 0.03$).
Windows: Single-glazed with weather stripping. See Table 16–6 for door and window sizes and U values.
Floor: Concrete slab on grade, 2-inch rigid insulation around edges.

The calculated Btuh values shown in Table 16–7 are the result of applying formulas for transmission loss, heat loss through the slab, and infiltration. The method of making the calculations for one of the rooms is shown in the following example.

Table 16–6. Doors and Windows for the Browne Home

Notation	Size	Area (ft²)	U
	Window Schedule		
W/1	2′-0″ × 4′-0″	8.0	1.13
W/2	3′-0″ × 6′-0″	18.0	1.13
W/3	3′-0″ × 4′-0″	12.0	1.13
W/4	2′-0″ × 8′-0″	16.0	1.13
W/5	3′-4″ × 5′-0″	16.6	1.13
W/6	3′-0″ × 5′-0″	15.0	1.13
W/7	2′-6″ × 3′-10″	9.6	1.13
	Exterior Doors		
D/2	6′-8″ × 3′-0″ × 1¾″	15.0 (without glass)	0.46
	2′-0″ × 2′-6″ door glass	5.0	1.13
	1′-6″ × 6′-8″ sidelight glass	10.0	1.13
D/10	6′-8″ × 8′-0″ glass	53.3	1.13
D/11	6′-8″ × 2′-8″ × 1¾″	17.8	0.46
D/14	6′-8″ × 2′-6″ × 1¾″	16.7	0.46
D/16	6′-8″ × 10′-0″ glass	66.7	1.13

Table 16-7. Heat Loss Calculation Table for the Browne Home [16-11]

Rooms	Building Elements Air Change Rate	Net Exterior Area Exposed Edge Length Room Volume	U Value Edge Loss Infiltration	Temperature Difference (°F)	Heat Loss (Btuh)	Total Heat Loss (Btuh)
Master bedroom	Glass	83 ft²	1.13	80	7503	
	Walls	173 ft²	0.045	80	623	
	Ceiling	255 ft²	0.03	80[a]	612	
	Floor	32 ft	40 Btu/ft		1280	
	1.0 change/hr	2040 ft³	2040 cfh	80	2938	12,956
Master bath	Glass	24.0 ft²	1.13	80	2170	
	Walls	64.0 ft²	0.045	80	230	
	Ceiling	101.5 ft²	0.03	80[a]	244	
	Floor	11 ft	40 Btu/ft		440	
	0.67 change/hr	812 ft³	544 cfh	80	783	3,867
Family room	Glass	53.3 ft²	1.13	80	4818	
	Wall	74.7 ft²	0.045	80	269	
	Ceiling	272.0 ft²	0.03	80[a]	653	
	Floor	16 ft	40 Btu/ft		640	
	1.5 changes/hr[b]	2176 ft³	3264 cfh	80	4700	11,080
Kitchen	Glass	16.6 ft²	1.13	80	1501	
	Wall (7 ft high)	67.4 ft²	0.045	80	243	
	Ceiling	204.0 ft²	0.03	80[a]	490	
	Floor	12 ft	40 Btu/ft		480	
	0.67 change/hr	1428 ft³	957 cfh	80	1378	4,092
Bath 3	Door	18.6 ft²	0.46	80	684	
	Wall	45.4 ft²	0.045	80	163	
	Ceiling	40.0 ft²	0.03	80[a]	96	
	Floor	8 ft	40 Btu/ft		320	
	0.67 change/hr	320 ft³	214 cfh	80	308	1,571
Guest bedroom	Glass	27 ft²	1.13	80	2441	
	Walls (exterior)	173 ft²	0.045	80	623	
	Wall (storage)[c]	88 ft²	0.08	40[d]	282	
	Ceiling	154 ft²	0.03	80[a]	370	
	Floor	25 ft	40 Btu/ft		1000	
	1.0 change/hr	1232 ft³	1232 cfh	80	1774	6,490
Shop	Door	16.7 ft²	0.46	40[d]	307	
	Walls (storage and garage)	87.3 ft²	0.08	40[d]	279	
	Ceiling	40 ft²	0.03	80[a]	96	
	Floor	8 ft	40 Btu/hr		320	
	2.0 changes/hr	320 ft³	640 cfh	40[d]	461	1,463

[a] A conservative approach would be to consider that the attic is ventilated to prevent moisture buildup and that the temperature in the attic is equal to that of the outside air.
[b] Exposed one side, but sliding doors are used frequently. Use conservative value of 1.5.
[c] Table 16-3. Wood frame partition with gypsum board surface and R-11 insulation.
[d] Temperature in garage and storage selected to be 32°F, midway between indoors and outdoors.

Table 16–7. (*continued*)

Rooms	Building Elements Air Change Rate	Net Exterior Area Exposed Edge Length Room Volume	U Value Edge Loss Infiltration	Temperature Difference (°F)	Heat Loss (Btuh)	Total Heat Loss (Btuh)
Living and dining room	Glass	48 ft²	1.13	80	4339	
	Walls (exterior)	144 ft²	0.045	80	518	
	Wall (garage)ᶜ	88 ft²	0.08	40ᵈ	282	
	Ceiling	448 ft²	0.03	80ᵃ	1075	
	Floor	35 ft	40 Btu/ft		1400	
	1.0 change/hrᵉ	3584 ft³	3584 cfh	80	5161	12,775
Laundry	Ceiling	40 ft²	0.03	80	96	96
Entry	Glass	15 ft²	1.13	80	1356	
	Walls	62 ft²	0.045	80	223	
	Door	15 ft²	0.46	80	552	
	Ceiling	28 ft²	0.03	80ᵃ	67	
	Floor	11.5 ft	40 Btu/ft		460	
	2.0 changes/hr	224 ft³	448 cfh	80	645	3,303
Bath 2	Glass	8 ft²	1.13	80	723	
	Wall	32 ft²	0.045	80	115	
	Ceiling	30 ft²	0.03	80ᵃ	72	
	Floor	5 ft	40 Btu/ft		200	
	0.67 change/hr	240 ft³	161 cfh	80	232	1,342
Bedroom 3	Glass	30 ft²	1.13	80	2712	
	Walls	168 ft²	0.045	80	605	
	Ceiling	151 ft²	0.03	80ᵃ	362	
	Floor	25 ft	40 Btu/ft		1000	
	1.0 change/hr	1210 ft³	1210 cfh	80	1742	6,421
Bedroom 2	Glass	12 ft²	1.13	80	1085	
	Wall	76 ft²	0.045	80	274	
	Ceiling	165 ft²	0.03	80ᵃ	396	
	Floor	11 ft	40 Btu/ft		440	
	0.67 change/hr	1320 ft³	884 cfh	80	1273	3,468
Hall	Ceiling	76 ft²	0.03	80	182	182
				Total		69,106

ᵉ Exposed on one side; weather-stripped windows offset by fireplace. Use 1.0.

Example 16–3

Compute the heat loss for the master bedroom.

First determine the areas of the various surfaces from the floor plan [16–11] and Table 16–6. Window W/4 on the west wall has 16 square feet of glass, while door D/16 on the north has 66.7 square feet of glass. Therefore, we list 83 square feet of glass in column 1 of Table 16–7. Now we can find the net area of exterior wall. Its gross area is 32 linear feet × 8 feet high = 256 square feet. Therefore, its net area is 256 square feet − 83 square feet glass are = 173 square feet. The ceiling area is the room width × length = 15 feet × 17 feet = 255 square feet. The U values for the walls and the ceiling are found in the construction specifications at the beginning of this section. The U value for the glass areas is found in Table 16–6. List these values in column 2 of Table 16–7. The temperature difference between indoors and outdoors is calculated by subtracting the outdoor design temperature ($-8°F$) from the indoor temperature ($72°F$). List the result ($80°F$) in column 3.

The heat loss for the walls is calculated by using the transmission loss equation:

$$H = AU(t_i - t_o) = 173 \times 0.045 \times 80 = 623 \text{ Btuh}$$

Similarly, the glass loss is $83 \times 1.13 \times 80 = 7503$ Btuh, and the ceiling loss is $255 \times 0.03 \times 80 = 612$ Btuh. These losses are listed in column 4.

To determine the floor losses, the exposed edge length of the floor is 15 feet + 17 feet = 32 feet (column 1). The heat loss for an outdoor design temperature of $-8°F$ is found in Table 16–4 to be 40 Btuh per foot of exposed edge when 2-inch edge insulation is used. This value is listed in column 2. The total floor loss is 40 Btuh/ft $\times$ 32 feet = 1280 Btuh (column 4).

The infiltration in the master bedroom is found using Table 16–5. This room falls under the classification of rooms with windows or exterior doors on two sides. The 1.5 air changes per hour shown must be multiplied by $\frac{2}{3}$ because the window is weather-stripped. This gives us 1.0 air change per hour. The volume of the room listed in column 1 is 15 feet $\times$ 17 feet $\times$ 8 feet high = 2040 cubic feet. Multiplying this by 1.0 air change per hour results in the infiltration value of 2040 cfh. This is listed in column 2. Using the infiltration loss equation:

$$H = 0.018 \text{ cfh } (t_i - t_o) = 0.018 \times 2040 \times 80 = 2938 \text{ Btuh}$$

This is shown in column 4.

16.10 Types of Heating Systems

Up until the mid-nineteenth century most residences had little more than a central fireplace or, if fortunate, several fireplaces located on opposing exterior walls. Heat was distributed by radiation from the fire. The Franklin stove made a major advancement in that its heat distribution took place by two methods: radiation from the hot metal stove sitting in the room, and also air convection of the room's air across the stove's surface. Even more significant was the eventual locating and enclosing of such a metal firebox in the basement and allowing the heated air to rise through ducts into the occupied space above. Thus the fuel was burned in a location remote from where the heat was being used. At the turn of the twentieth century, the development of electricity, fans, and pumps allowed warm fluids to be moved substantial distances from the combustion process. Today we can choose from a multitude of systems. Heating systems can be classified by the method used to move the heat to the occupied space:

1. Warm air.
2. Hot water.
3. Electric.
4. Passive solar.

16.11 Warm Air Systems

The *forced warm air system* has become the most popular heating method in new homes because of its economical first cost, its ability to provide heat quickly, and its compatibility with summer cooling systems. The system is comprised of three major components [16–12]:

1. The furnace.
2. The distribution system.
3. The control system.

In the furnace, the heating of the air that has been recirculated from the occupied space is provided by one of various sources. It could be from the burning of fuel such as oil or gas. It could be from electrical resistance or from a heat pump, or heat could be provided by hot water that has been heated by the sun.

The distribution system consists of supply and return ducts, a fan to move the air, grilles and registers, and filters. In the forced warm air system, the heated air is delivered to the various rooms at a temperature somewhere between 115 and 145°F. This warm air replaces the Btu loss due to transmission and infiltration.

If we have chosen 72°F as a suitable indoor temperature in winter, the room air should not drop below that temperature. Therefore to maintain 72°F, the room air will be drawn through a grille and returned to the furnace, where it will be reheated. It is best to provide a supply register and a return register for each room. However, in some smaller and less expensive installations, the return air travels through louvers cut in doors and down hallways to return to a single return air grille.

Because of moisture and odors, it is customary not to recirculate air from bathrooms or kitchens. Instead, it is exhausted to the outdoors. This is done with exhaust fans or weighted dampers that allow the air to escape but prevent wind from entering. An air intake on the suction side of the furnace brings in fresh "makeup" air to replace that which has been exhausted.

Design of Residential Climate Control Systems

The major components of a warm air system are the furnace, the distribution system, and the control system.

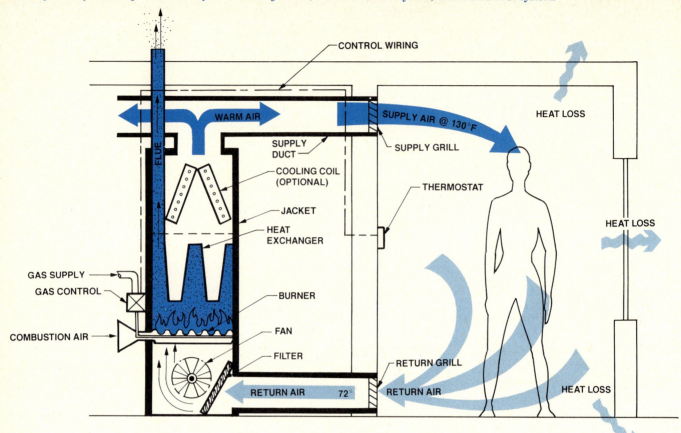

Figure 16–12

16.12 Types of Warm Air Furnaces

The forced warm air furnace can be designed to allow air to flow through it in a number of ways, thereby giving the designer freedom to place the furnace in a variety of locations. It can be placed in a basement, in a closet, or mounted horizontally in an attic or a crawl space [16–13 and 16–14]. The most common sources of heat used in forced warm air furnaces are oil, natural gas, and electricity. Heat by electricity can be produced by resistance elements or by a heat pump. The heat pump (see Section 16.21) is a refrigeration cycle in reverse. It is a convenient method of using electricity to produce heat in a mild climate.

Figure [16–15] shows a cutaway photograph of an actual up-flow, gas-fired, warm air furnace. This is the type of furnace that was shown in diagrammatic form in [16–12]. Return air enters at the bottom, passes through a filter, and enters the circular inlet (suction side) of a "squirrel cage" fan. Note that the electric drive motor is mounted in the inlet. The air is heated as it passes around the outside surface of the heat exchanger and is then exhausted upward to the distribution duct.

On the inside of the heat exchanger are the gas burners. The hot gases of combustion are carried up and out the flue pipe that is visible at the top of the furnace. This pipe extends through the roof of the house. On the side of the flue pipe is a box that houses a control device to save energy. Inside the box a small electric motor controls the position of a flue damper [16–16]. After the burner shuts off, the damper closes and prevents heat from leaving the heat exchanger and escaping up the flue. Table 16–8 shows typical specification data for a residential size warm air furnace.

Table 16–8. Typical Specifications for Up-Flow and Down-Flow Warm Air Furnaces[a]

	Model Number		
	G12Q3–82	G12Q3–110	G12Q3–137
Input (Btuh)	82,000	110,000	137,000
Output (Btuh)	63,000	84,000	105,000
Height (in.)	49	49	53
Width (in.)	16¼	21¼	26¼
Depth (in.)	26⅛	26⅛	26⅛

[a] Installation clearance requirements are: sides, rear, top, 1 in.; front, 6 in.

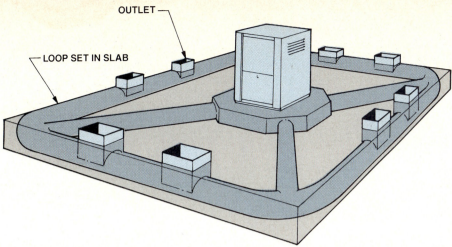

Air distribution may be through a perimeter system . . .

Figure 16–18

[16–19]. Smaller branch ducts carry the warm air to the different room registers. Flexible circular ducts are often used for the branch ducts. This type of system is most frequently used when air outlets direct air downward toward the exterior walls from registers located high on an interior wall or on a furred-down ceiling. The central main trunk system is frequently used in warmer climates for both heating and cooling where the proper distribution of cooling air is the primary consideration (see Section 16.29).

16.14 Warm Air Controls

Typically, there are three control devices that are used on most warm air systems—a room thermostat, a fan thermostat, and a high limit control. The last two devices are included in the furnace. The *room thermostat* turns the burner on automatically when the air temperature drops below a predetermined setting and turns the burner off when the desired temperature has been obtained. The room thermostat must be carefully located so that it will sense the average condition of the space(s).

Usually, location on an inside wall at 5'–0" height (where there is free air circulation) is best.

The purpose of the *fan thermostat* is to turn the fan motor on after the air in the furnace is heated enough to prevent the delivery of uncomfortably cool air. After the burner shuts off, the fan will continue to run until the temperature of the air passing the heat exchanger falls below a level preset on the thermostat. The warm air *high limit control* will shut off the burner if the air temperature in the furnace exceeds a predetermined setting.

16.15 Hot Water Systems

A *hot water heating system*, sometimes referred to as a *hydronic* system, circulates hot water to devices that release heat in the occupied space. The basic system consists of a boiler to heat the water, pipes and pumps to circulate the water, and radiators or convectors to distribute heat in the rooms.

In the past, very small systems (with the boiler located in a basement) allowed hot water to circulate by natural

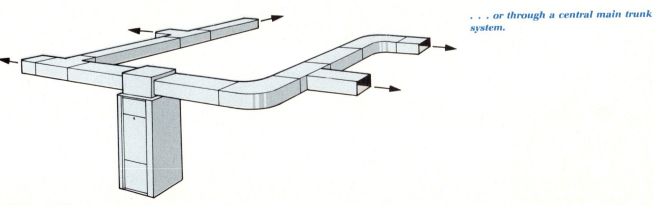

. . . or through a central main trunk system.

Figure 16–19

Design of Residential Climate Control Systems

convection. However, most contemporary systems use a small, electric pump to move the hot water. *Radiators*, as the name implies, distribute heat to the room by radiation. *Convectors*, on the other hand, are designed so that the cooler room air is heated by contact with a finned tube [16–20]. The hot water passing through the radiator or convector is cooled as it gives up its heat to the room. This cooler water (10 to 20°F cooler than that supplied) returns to the boiler to be reheated. Further details concerning convectors and sizing information are provided in Section 16.18.

16.16 The Boiler

In a hot water heating system the boiler heats the water but not necessarily to the boiling point. The heating within the boiler can be done in several ways. A *combustion boiler* burns some type of fuel and the released thermal energy heats a sealed metal jacket or tubing

Hot water systems distribute heat through radiators and convectors.

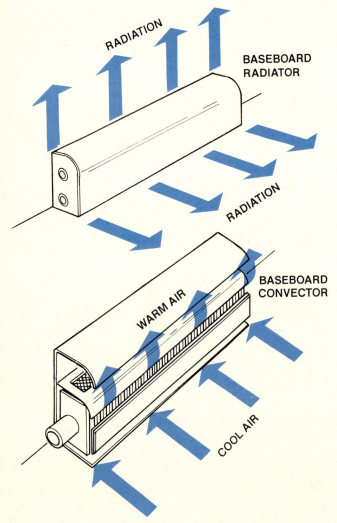

Figure 16–20

A residential hot water heating system boiler . . . the gas burner heats water circulating through tubing.

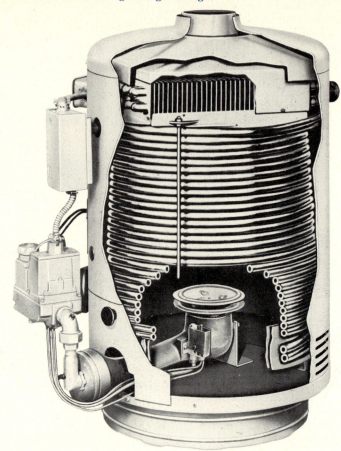

Figure 16–21

that encloses the water [16–21]. The water is heated by conduction of heat through the metal enclosure. The fuel burned is commonly oil or natural gas, depending on which is the most economical to use. A constant supply of combustion air must be available. The furnace is designed to mix the proper ratio of fuel and air for the most efficient burning in the combustion chamber. The hot gases, after releasing heat to the metal surfaces, travel up the flue pipe to the atmosphere.

Example 16–4
Select a natural gas-fired boiler to provide hot water heat for the Browne home (Chapter 13).

From the heat loss estimate, (Table 16–7), we see that 69,106 Btuh output capacity must be provided. The specification data in Table 16–9, line 2, "Max. heat loss load," shows that the Model HW-80P is not large enough. We will select Model HW-100P with a capacity of 72,000 Btuh.

In an *electric boiler* there is no burning of fuel and no exhaust gases that require a flue. A coil of high-resistance wire is inserted into the water tank. This coil is heated by electrical current passing through it, and water in contact with the coil is thereby heated.

Table 16–9. **Typical Boiler Specifications for Hot Water Heating Systems**

Model:	HW-80P	HW-100P	HW-120P	HW-160P	HW-200P
Gases:	Natural and Propane	Natural and Propane	Natural	Natural and Propane	Natural and Propane
Max. Btu input, American Gas Association rating	80,000	100,000	120,000	160,000	199,000
Max. heat loss load (Btu)	57,600	72,000	86,400	108,800	136,000
Height (in.)	26¾	26½	28⅛	29⅜	32⅜
Depth (in.)	34¾	37½	37½	40¾	40¾
Width (in.)	28¾	28	28	29¾	29½

Another method of heating water, in areas of plentiful sunshine, is by *solar collectors* [16–22]. Water (or an antifreeze solution) will reach temperatures of 180 to 190°F in the collector. The heated fluid passes through a heat exchanger in the storage tank. Here it heats a separate quantity of water, which is then circulated in a hot water heating system or used to heat air in a warm air system. A backup method of heating the water is usually provided for periods of extended cloudy weather.

Boiler controls in all of the systems typically regulate the temperature of the supply water to between 190 and 220°F. With further control devices, it is possible to save energy by automatically lowering this supply water temperature as the outside air temperature rises. When heat is called for by the room thermostat, an electric pump is activated to circulate the hot water to the radiators or convectors.

16.17 Hot Water Piping Systems

There are four piping arrangements that are generally used to circulate hot water to the heating elements that

A solar collector can be used to heat a fluid that circulates through a heat exchanger in a storage tank.

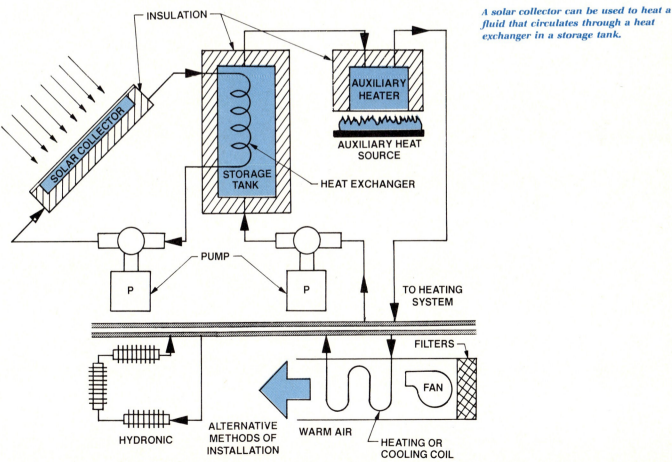

Figure 16–22

Design of Residential Climate Control Systems

Heated water may be distributed through a series loop system . . .

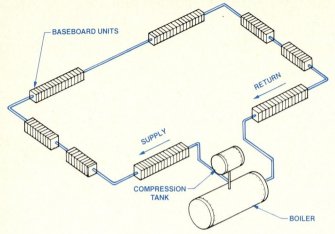

Figure 16–23

. . . or through a two-pipe reverse return system . . .

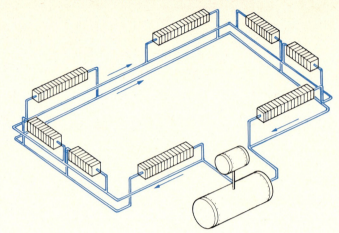

Figure 16–25

are located in the spaces to be heated. These are the series loop system, the one-pipe system, the two-pipe reverse return system, and the two-pipe direct return system.

A *series loop* system is usually run at the perimeter of the house [16–23]. The water flows through each baseboard convector (radiator) in series. The water flowing through the first convector may be 20°F higher than that flowing through the last convector in the circuit. A valve at each heating element is not possible in a series loop since any closed valve would shut off the entire loop. Control of heat output is by means of a damper at each baseboard convector that reduces the convection of air over the fins. This manual control would not be satisfactory to everyone. The series loop is used in small homes since it is inexpensive to install.

A *one-pipe* system is often chosen for residential systems [16–24]. It offers better control than the series loop system, since each convector can be shut off by closing its valve. Special fittings act to divert part of the flow into each convector, while water at the proper temperature flows past to heat the more distant convectors.

A *two-pipe reverse return* system is the best choice for larger buildings with long runs [16–25]. It requires more piping than either the series loop or the one-pipe systems, but it provides nearly the same hot water temperature to all convectors. The cooler water leaving each convector does not mix with the hot water supply but is collected in the return loop. Note that all water must travel the same distance before returning to the boiler. Thermostatic controls can be used in each room, if desired, to regulate the flow of water.

A *two-pipe direct return* system is mentioned here only so that it will be avoided [16–26]. Although it uses less return pipe than the reverse return system, it has inherent problems. The path of water through the first convector is much shorter than that through the others. More water will flow through the shorter path; thus the nearer convectors will transfer the most heat energy, and the more distant ones will transfer less.

. . . or distributed through a one-pipe system . . .

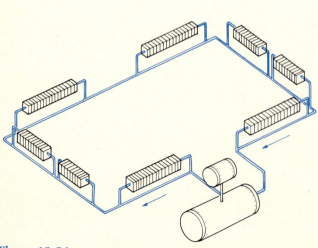

Figure 16–24

. . . or through a two-pipe direct return system.

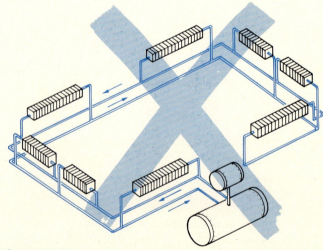

Figure 16–26

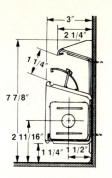
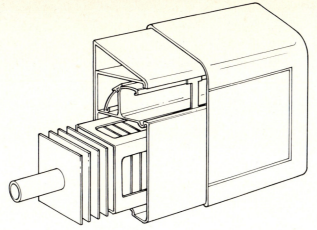

A typical baseboard type convector... with heat output ratings (Btuh/ft).

Type E-10	Flow rate[a]		Average Water Temperature(°F)																
	gal/min	ft/sec	240	235	230	225	220	215	210	205	200	195	190	185	180	175	170	165	160	155	150
	4	2.36	1070	1040	990	960	930	890	860	810	780	740	710	670	630	600	560	530	490	450	410
	1	0.59	1010	980	940	910	880	840	810	770	740	700	670	630	600	570	530	500	460	430	390

[a] Ratings at water flow rate of 4 gal/min (2000 lb/hr) should be used for E-10 Baseboard, Series-Connnected Systems, where the water flow rate through the baseboard unit is equal to or greater than 4 gal/min. For other piping arrangements resulting in lower water flow rate, or where the water flow rate is not known, the rating at the standard water flow rate of 1 gal/min (500 lb/hr) must be used.

Figure 16–27

16.18 Sizing Baseboard Convectors

Figures [16–27 and 16–28] show convector types and give manufacturer's data for determining the length of convector required. Selection is based on an assumed water flow rate and an average temperature of the water supplied.

Example 16–5

Determine the length of convectors required for each room of the Browne home.

The first step is to determine the location and type of convectors needed in each room. A heating system layout of the Browne home is shown in [16–29]. The designer should attempt to place the convectors below

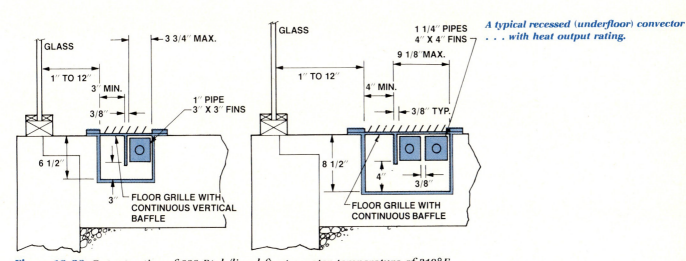

A typical recessed (underfloor) convector ... with heat output rating.

Figure 16–28 Output rating of 930 Btuh/lineal ft. at a water temperature of 210°F minimum. Rating is based on 0°F outdoor temperature and 70°F room temperature and only for glass walls (not conventional walls). Average temperature of down-draft, 47°F. Average air velocity, 60 ft/min; inside glass temperature, 25°F.

Design of Residential Climate Control Systems 293

Boiler location, convector layout, and piping schematic for the Browne home.

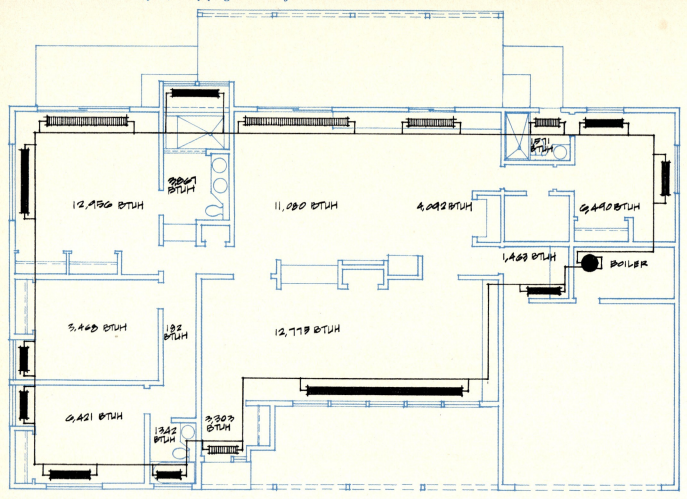

Figure 16-29

Table 16–10. Heat Losses and Convector Sizes for the Browne Home

Room	Heat Loss (Btuh)	Lineal Feet of Convector
Master bedroom	12,956	15[a]
Master bath	3,867	5
Family room	11,080	12[a]
Kitchen	4,092	5[a]
Bath 3	1,571	2[a]
Guest bedroom	6,490	8
Shop	1,463	2
Living and dining room	12,775	16
Laundry	96	b
Entry	3,303	4[a]
Bath 2	1,342	2
Bedroom 3	6,421	8
Bedroom 2	3,468	4
Hall	182	b

[a] Includes recessed convector.
[b] Minimal heat loss through ceiling. Heat will be gained from other rooms.

windows if at all possible. The warm air rising from the convector will counteract the cool air falling from the cold glass. For the master bedroom, we see that a baseboard convector would interfere with the sliding glass door. In this case we may use a recessed convector along the north wall. Under the west window we will use a standard baseboard convector.

To calculate the length of convector needed for each room we will assume a hot water flow rate of 500 lb/hr (1 gal/min) and an average water temperature of 210°F. Table 16–10 shows the heat loss for each room (from Table 16–7) and the length of convector required for each room. The length of convector for the master bedroom is found by using an output rating of 810 Btuh/ft for baseboard convectors [16–27] and an output rating of 930 Btuh/ft for recessed convectors [16–28]. Assume that equal lengths of baseboard and recessed convectors will be used. Then the average output value is

$$\frac{930 + 810}{2} = 870 \text{ Btuh/ft}.$$

The total length of convectors in the master bedroom is 12,956 Btuh heat loss ÷ 870 Btuh/ft convector output = 14.9 feet. Use 15 feet.

16.19 Hot Water Radiant Heating

The *hot water radiant heating system* utilizes copper tubing that has been embedded in a concrete floor or in a plastered ceiling [16–30 and 16–31]. Water flowing through the loops of tubing creates large warm surfaces. The sensation of chill in a cold room is caused by loss of body heat to surrounding surfaces, rather than by the temperature of the air. If the temperature of the surrounding surfaces is such that the body heat is not lost to the surface, the enclosed space will be perceived to be comfortable at a much lower air temperature. This will result in lower utility costs.

Heat in floor slabs eliminates the coldness of concrete. Usually, a slab temperature of 85°F will keep the occupants quite comfortable even with air temperatures slightly less than 60°F. Radiant ceilings can be kept at a higher temperature, say 100 to 120°F. Each room may have a separate piping loop and a thermostat that activates a separate pump for that room.

In areas of the country where quick heating is needed only in the morning and evening, radiant heating may be unsatisfactory. Concrete slabs can take up to 10 hours to come up to desired temperatures and 8 hours to cool down. It is possible to include controls that somewhat offset this "lag" problem. An outdoor air sensor can be provided that allows the system to anticipate a change in load before the need develops within the house.

16.20 Heat Pumps

The heat pump can be thought of as a refrigeration machine running in reverse. Instead of taking unwanted heat from the inside and rejecting it to the outdoors, the heat pump extracts heat from the outside air and pumps it inside to warm the indoor air [16–32]. There is recoverable heat in cold outdoor air even at low temperatures. In the summer, a simple switch of a valve position allows the unit to operate as a conventional cooling unit. The heat pump is powered by electricity and, like electric resistance heating (Section 16.21), is clean and requires no combustion air or flue pipe [16–33].

The heat pump has the ability to provide more heat than electric resistance heating per unit of electrical energy input. Its efficiency varies with the temperature of the outside air. For instance seasonal efficiency of a unit in Jacksonville, Florida, may be a 3 to 1 ratio of heat output to electrical energy input. In Chicago, Illinois, this ratio may be 2 to 1. The heat pump will operate and provide more heat than the equivalent electrical

Hot water radiant heating uses water circulating through tubing embedded in a concrete floor slab . . .

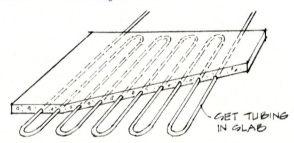

Figure 16–30

. . . or through tubing attached to ceiling joists and embedded in plaster.

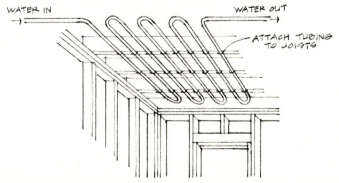

Figure 16–31

The heat pump's winter cycle . . . heat is removed from the outside air . . . in summer the coil's functions are reversed.

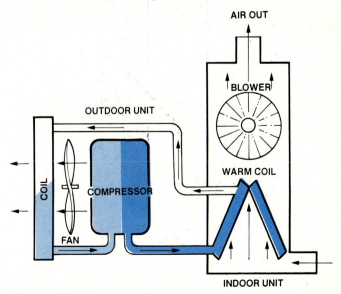

Figure 16–32

Design of Residential Climate Control Systems

A heat pump system . . . the compressor is mounted outside . . . heated (or cooled) refrigerant is piped to a blower unit inside the house.

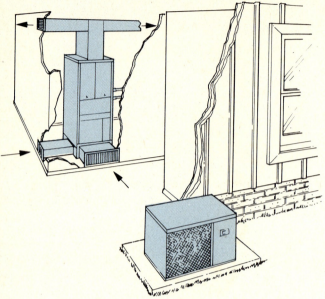

Figure 16–33

input down below 0°F outside temperature. However, at temperatures below 30°F, its capacity (based on accepted methods of sizing the equipment) must be supplemented with more expensive electrical resistance heating.

The heat pump, with its air circulation, cooling, filtering, humidifying, and dehumidifying ability can do a better job of climate control than electric resistance heating, where no air circulation is used. The final selection criteria for a complete climate control system usually gets down to the availability and costs of various fuels in the area. If the cost of natural gas is low enough, a conventional warm air furnace with an add-on cooling unit may be less expensive in the long run than the all-electric heat pump. For further explanation of the refrigeration cycle, see Section 16–26.

16.21 Electric Heating Systems

Electric heating systems convert electrical energy into heat energy by passing electric current through resistance wiring. This is probably the most convenient form of heating. It does not require outside combustion air, a flue pipe, or provision for storage and delivery of special fuels. The first cost for electric heating equipment is usually less expensive than gas, oil, or coal burning units. However, in most areas of the country, electricity is quite a bit more expensive than these other fuels per unit of heating output.

Electricity can be used to produce both radiant and convection type heat. Radiant systems use resistance wiring embedded in the ceiling or floor [16–34]. Electric resistance baseboard convection units are similar in appearance to hot water baseboard units and provide almost instantaneous heat. With a thermostat in each room, electric heating systems are very easy to control. The disadvantages of electric radiant and convective heating systems are that they have no provision for controlled air circulation, filtration, humidification, and cooling.

16.22 Cooling Systems

Mechanical cooling devices did not become common until the turn of the twentieth century after the development of the electric motor. Up until the 1920s, forced ventilation was the only common type of mechanical cooling. Methods of refrigerating air were developed for commercial buildings in the 1920s, but it wasn't until after World War II that residential and small commercial size refrigeration equipment was produced. Now, central refrigeration systems are standard for many homes and most business and industry establishments.

16.23 Evaporative Cooling

Using the evaporation of water is the oldest known method in man's attempt to produce cooling for comfort.

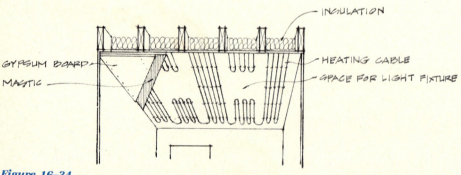

Electric radiant heating uses resistance wiring embedded in a ceiling (or floor).

Figure 16–34

296   **Building Systems**

To evaporate 1 pound of water, approximately 1000 Btu must be supplied from the surrounding material(s). When perspiration is evaporated from your skin, Btus are drawn from the skin, giving a cooling sensation. Warm and relatively dry air can be cooled this same way. If the air is passed through a fine mist of water, the heat required to evaporate the water is taken from the air and the temperature of the air drops. The wet-bulb temperature* of the air gives an indication of the air's "dryness." The lower the wet-bulb temperature, the more moisture that can be evaporated into a given quantity of air.

Hot, arid climates are well suited to cooling by evaporative coolers. By means of a fan, the evaporative cooler draws hot dry outside air over a wetted pad. The resulting cooler, more humid air is supplied to the building's interior. The supply air temperature approaches the wet-bulb temperature of the outdoor air. As an example, consider a possible condition in Phoenix, Arizona, in June when the outside air temperature is 100°F and the wet-bulb temperature is 63°F. Air supplied by an evaporative cooler would easily be cooled to 67°F and would provide very satisfactory conditions. The fan in the unit would be sized to provide a complete air change every 2 minutes in the occupied area. The cooled air can be supplied to the rooms through the same duct system as used for a warm air furnace. After the air passes through the occupied area, it is rejected to the outside.

When outside air temperatures and especially humidity become excessive, evaporative cooling may be unsatisfactory. In Phoenix during August, the air temperature may rise to 109°F and the wet-bulb temperature to 76°F. The air could be cooled to 81°F with a humidity of 80%, but this would not provide a comfortable condition for most people. During this period of high temperature and humidity, mechanical refrigeration would normally be used. The selection of an evaporative cooler for use in your area should only be made after a careful review of the annual climatic data.

16.24 Heat Gain

Like the heat loss estimate used to size our heating equipment (Section 16.9), we must calculate a *heat gain estimate* in order to establish the size of refrigeration cooling equipment. This is frequently referred to as the *cooling load estimate*. The total heat gain of a residence is made up of the following components:

1. Heat gain from opaque surfaces such as walls and roofs. These surfaces may be in the shade or in direct sunlight.

2. Heat gain through glass. This is a combination of solar heat gain *and* transmission due to the difference between the indoor and outdoor temperatures.
3. The internal heat gain from people and the heat gain from appliances.
4. Infiltration loss. This loss is not as significant in the summer as it is in the winter. (Infiltration has been neglected in our load estimating in the following pages.)

Heat gain estimates become more complicated than heat loss estimates due to the effect of the sun on walls and roofs, and the solar radiation passing through windows. Residential cooling load estimates have been simplified by some manufacturers. The method described in this chapter is known as the *24-hour method*.

Table 16-11 presents a convenient format for calculating cooling loads using the 24-hour method. This form makes use of simplified engineering factors and was specially devised for typical house construction. Its use is based on the assumption that the structure's mass absorbs heat energy and that the interior temperature can vary between 72 and 78°F. The load calculation estimate assumes an average indoor temperature of 75°F. This gradually changing variation of about 6 degrees is quite acceptable, and the resulting room conditions are well within the comfort zone as described by ASHRAE. This daily "swing" enables the air conditioning equipment to draw on the cooling effect stored in the structure to augment its capacity during peak load periods.

The 24-hour method has certain advantages:

1. Smaller equipment may be used for the residence, requiring smaller ductwork, smaller power sources, and reduced first costs.
2. This smaller equipment will operate for longer periods of time—up to 24 hours (continuous) on hot days.
3. Operating costs should be lower. For any house, in theory, a large unit and a small unit will remove the same amount of heat over 24 hours, but the larger unit will operate fewer hours. Since they both do the same work, the power consumption would theoretically be the same for both. But actually, the more frequent cycling of the larger unit is more wasteful of power.

The 24-hour method is generally applicable, but it does have limitations for more complex designs. It is used here *as an example* to present only the basic idea of cooling load estimating. A knowledgeable mechanical system designer should always be consulted before equipment is selected.

---

* The wet-bulb temperature is obtained by putting a wetted fabric wick over the bulb of a normal thermometer and passing air over it at a rapid rate.

Table 16–11. Residential Cooling Load Estimate for the Browne Home

Orientation	Overhang	Heat Gain Factors (from Tables)	Entire House Quantity	Entire House Btuh Heat Gain	Living and Dining Room Quantity	Living and Dining Room Btuh Heat Gain	Entry Quantity	Entry Btuh Heat Gain	Kitchen Quantity	Kitchen Btuh Heat Gain	Family Room Quantity	Family Room Btuh Heat Gain	Master Bedroom Quantity	Master Bedroom Btuh Heat Gain
	Windows		Heat gain = heat gain factor (Table 16–12) × quantity (area in square feet) = Btuh											
N/S	48 in.	24	273	6552	48	1152	15	360	17	408		1272	67	1608
NE/NW														
E/W	48 in.	43	55	2365									16	688
SE/SW														
	Walls		Heat gain = heat gain factor (Table 16–13) × quantity (linear feet of perimeter) = Btuh											
E/W	48 in.	11 × 0.75[a] × 0.66	61	332			3.5	19					17	93
S	48 in.	11 × 0.75[a] × 0.66	50	272	24	131	6[b]	33						
N	48 in.	15 × 0.5[c] × 0.75 × 0.66	87[d]	323	11.5	43			12	45	8[b]	30	5[b]	19
	Roof		Heat gain = heat gain factor (Table 16–14) × quantity (area in square feet) = Btuh											
		2 × 0.67[e]	2005	2687	448	600	28	38	204	273	272	364	255	342
	Floor		Heat gain = heat gain factor (Table 16–14) × quantity (area in square feet) = Btuh											
		0												
	Internal		Heat gain = 440 Btuh × 2 persons × number of bedrooms + 1800 Btuh for kitchen = Btuh											
				5320		3520				1800				
	Total heat gain													
				17851		5446[g]		452		2526		1666		2750
			Cooling load = total heat gain × summer climate factor (Table 16–15)[h] = Btuh											
				13924		4248[g]		353		1970		1299		2145
			Approximate cooling air quantity = cooling load ÷ 30 = cfm											
				464		142[g]		12		66		43		72

[a] Uncorrected factor from Table 16–13 = 11.
Correction for light-colored walls = 0.75
Correction for different U value $= \frac{0.045}{0.068} = 0.66$

[b] Length of perimeter reduced by width of full-length glass.

[c] Uncorrected factor from Table 16–13 = 15.q6
Correction for north wall = 0.5
Correction for light-colored walls = 0.75
Correction for different U value $= \frac{0.045}{0.068} = 0.66$

[d] Also includes walls other than north that are shaded.

[e] Uncorrected factor from Table 16–14 = 2.
Correction for different U value $= \frac{0.03}{0.045} = 0.67$

[f] Includes ½ of hallway ceiling area.

[g] These values are artificially high because all of the internal gain for the house (except the kitchen) has been listed under the living room and dining room for convenience since it is a central room.

[h] Summer climate factor for Chicago:
Summer outdoor design temperature = 89°F
Daily range = 20°
Interpolating from Table 16–15

$\frac{(1.00 - 0.82)}{5} = 0.036$

$0.82 - 0.036 = 0.784$

Use 0.78 as climate factor.

Table 16–11. (continued)

Bedroom 2		Bedroom 3		Master Bath		Bath 2		Bath 3		Guest Bedroom		Laundry		Shop	
Quantity	Btuh Heat Gain	Quantity	Btuh Heat Gain	Quantity	Btuh Heat Gain	Quantity	Btuh Heat Gain	Quantity	Btuh Heat Gain	Quantity	Btuh Heat Gain	Quantity	Btuh Heat Gain	Quantity	Btuh Heat Gain
		18	432	16	384	8	192	19	456	12	288				
12	516	12	516							15	645				
11	60	11	60	4	22					14	76				
		14	76			5	27								
				7	26			8[b]	30[b]	22	82			13	48
203[f]	272	189[f]	253	102	137	30	40	40	54	154	206	40	54	40	54
	848		1337		569		259		540		1297		54		102
	661		1043		444		202		421		1012		42		80
	22		35		15		7		14		34		1		3

16.25 Using the Cooling Load Estimate Form

The Residential Cooling Load Estimate Form (Table 16–11) provides a basis for calculating the heat gain through four main elements of the building structure—the windows, the walls, the roof, and the floor. It also makes provision for calculating the internal heat gain. The form has spaces for separating the windows and the walls into types based on orientation and overhang. The appropriate heat gain factors are then listed for each. These factors are obtained from Tables 16–12 and 16–13. The roof and floor heat gain factors found in Table 16–14 are also listed.

The heat gain in Btuh for the entire house and for each individual room is found by listing the quantity in square feet or linear feet for each structural element in the quantity columns and multiplying by the heat gain factors. The internal heat gain is calculated using a factor based on the number of bedrooms. After summing up the heat gain columns to determine the total heat gain, the cooling load is found by multiplying by the summer climate factor found in Table 16–16. Finally, the approximate cooling air quantities are found by dividing the cooling loads by a factor of 30.

Design of Residential Climate Control Systems

Table 16–12. Solar Heat Gain and Transmission through Windows or Glass Doors (Btuh/Ft² Sash Area)[a]

Windows Facing	Roof Overhang (in.)				
	0	12	24	36	48
N/S	30	27	24	24	24
NE/NW	43	41	39	36	34
E/W	57	56	51	47	43
SE/SW	51	48	42	36	33

[a] *Notes:*
1. Based on venetian blinds or roll shades full drawn. For omission of venetian blinds (no inside shading) use 1.17 times values in table.
2. For awnings use values for 48 in. overhang.
3. For double glazing use 0.80 times values in table.
4. Shading due to roof overhang applies to single story house. For two-story house, figure shading for second floor, none for the first floor.
5. Windows shaded all day by trees or buildings should be included as north windows.
6. Consider outside doors with glass as windows. For Kool shade, use 0.60 times value in table.

SOURCE: Carrier Corporation.

Table 16–14. Heat Gain through Sunlit Pitched and Flat Roofs and through Floors (Btuh/Ft²)[a]

Construction	U	Factor
Roof		
No insulation	0.32	14
2 in. insulation, $R = 7$	0.098	4
4 in. insulation, $R = 11$	0.071	3
6 in. insulation, $R = 19$	0.045	2
Floor		
Underside exposed		6
Over conditioned space		3
Slab, cool basement, closed crawl space		0

[a] *Notes:*
1. Pitched roof area is taken as the area projected on a horizontal plane, i.e. ceiling area.
2. No positive ventilation in attic. (With positive attic ventilation, use 0.75 times values in table.)
3. For white marble chip roof, use 0.75 times values in table.
4. Roof construction listed as ordinarily encountered in residences. The heat gain factor is directly proportional to the heat transmission coefficient (U).

SOURCE: Carrier Corporation.

The data and calculated values shown in Table 16–11 are for the Browne home assuming that it is built in the Chicago, Illinois area and that it faces south. Refer to Section 16.9 for building construction details. The following paragraphs describe the various facets of the cooling load form and its accompanying tables and describe in more detail how the values are obtained.

Table 16–12 gives window heat gain factors on the basis of Btuh per square foot of window area for various compass orientations and roof overhangs. The footnotes cover corrections to be applied to these factors for omission of inside shading, for awnings or other external shading, and for double glazing.

Table 16–13. Heat Gain through Sunlit and Shaded Walls (Btuh per Linear Foot of Length)[a]

Wall Construction	U	Roof Overhang (in.)				
		0	12	24	36	48
Frame or heavy masonry	0.27	61	55	49	44	42
Frame, 1 in. insul., $R = 4$	0.13	30	27	24	21	20
Frame, 2 in. insul., $R = 7$	0.098	21	19	17	15	15
Frame, 4 in. insul., $R = 11$	0.068	15	14	12	11	11
Light masonry	0.46	104	94	84	75	71

[a] *Notes:*
1. Based on 8 ft wall height.
2. For north or shaded walls, use 0.5 times factors for no overhang.
3. Wall adjoining attic space should be taken as roof.
4. Wall adjoining unconditioned space should be included as shaded wall.
5. Shading due to roof overhang applies to single-story house. For two-story house, figure shading for second floor, none for first floor.
6. Based on dark-colored walls. For light-colored walls use 0.75 times values in tables.
7. Wall construction listed as ordinarily encountered in residences. The heat gain factor is directly proportional to the heat transmission coefficient (U).

SOURCE: Carrier Corporation.

Table 16–13 gives wall heat gain factors on the basis of Btuh per linear foot of exposed perimeter for various wall constructions and roof overhangs. The footnotes cover corrections to be applied to these factors for different wall colors, exposures, and shading. Heat gain factors are shown in the table for only a few typical wall constructions and U values. The heat gain factors are directly proportional to U values. For wall constructions not listed, determine the correct U value from the data in Table 16–3 and arrive at the estimated heat gain factor by proportion.

Table 16–14 gives roof heat gain factors on the basis of Btuh per square foot projected area for various roof conditions. The footnotes cover corrections to be applied to these factors for conditions and constructions other than those upon which the table is based. Table 16–14 also gives heat gain factors for various types of floors.

Calculations for the entire house and the various rooms are made as follows:

1. *Entire house:* The cooling load estimate form can be used to establish the cooling load either for the entire house or for the house on a room-by-room basis. It is more accurate to make the room-by-room load calculation and to establish the air quantity for each room accordingly. The data for the entire house then become the total of the data for the individual rooms. These totals can be recorded on the proper lines in the entire house column.

   You may, however, want to determine only the load for the entire house to make a preliminary estimate or to establish the size of a cooling unit to be used in an existing home with a satisfactory air distribution system. In such cases, the total window area, the total wall perimeter, and so on, are placed in the entire house quantity column, and only the total cooling load and cooling cfm are calculated.

2. *Windows:* Select the glass heat gain factor from Table 16-12 for each window based on its orientation and roof overhang. For example, the factor for a south window with venetian blinds, double glazing, and a 24-inch overhang, is 24 × 0.8, or 19.2 Btuh per square foot of window area. Enter this value in the heat gain factors column. Enter the window area in square feet for each orientation in the quantity column. Determine the heat gain Btuh by multiplying the heat gain factor by the quantity value.

3. *Walls:* Select the wall heat gain factor from Table 16-13 for the proper roof overhang and wall construction or U value. For example, the factor for a light-colored frame wall with 2-inch insulation and 24-inch overhang is 17 × 0.75 or 12.75 Btuh per linear foot of exposed perimeter. Enter this value in the heat gain factor column. Enter the linear feet of outside wall perimeter for each orientation in the quantity column. Determine the heat gain Btuh by multiplying the heat gain factor by the quantity value.

   Solid doors (no glass), because of minor infiltration during summer cooling, are considered part of the wall. Any glass in doors should be included as window area. Walls, or those parts of walls that consist of glass from floor to ceiling (commonly called window walls), should be treated as glass only and omitted from the perimeter length when figuring the heat gain through the walls.

   The wall factors are based on an 8-foot wall height. For wall heights appreciably greater than 8 feet, the factors should be increased proportionately. A wall adjoining an attic space, such as might be encountered in the expansion attic type of construction, should be figured as roof. A wall adjoining a closed but non-conditioned space on a lower floor, such as a wall next to a garage, should be figured as a shaded wall.

4. *Roof:* Select the roof heat gain factor from Table 16-14 for the proper roof construction or U value. For example, the factor for a 4-inch insulated roof is 3.0 Btuh per square foot projected area—that is, the area projected on a horizontal plane or ceiling area. For roofs that are essentially flat, use the full area of the roof surface. Enter this value in the heat gain factor column. Enter the roof area in square feet in the quantity column. Use the basic room areas, but include with each room all adjacent areas (such as closets and halls) that do not require separate air supplies but whose heat gain must be included. Determine the heat gain Btuh by multiplying the heat gain factor by the quantity value.

5. *Floors:* Select the floor heat gain factor from Table 16-14 for the proper condition. For example, there is zero heat gain for a concrete slab on ground. Enter this value in the heat gain factor column. Enter the floor area in square feet in the quantity column. Use the basic room areas, but include with each room all adjacent areas (such as closets and halls) that do not require separate air supplies but whose heat gain must be included. Determine the heat gain Btuh by multiplying the heat gain factor by the quantity value.

6. *Internal heat gain:* People give off heat that must be removed from the inside space. Each person adds about 440 Btuh of heat gain. This includes the heat that must be removed to condense the moisture evaporated by the body (latent heat). The number of people in a home is usually assumed to be two times the number of bedrooms. For example, in an average three-bedroom house, the heat gain from people would be: 2 × 3 × 440 Btuh = 2640 Btuh.

   In addition to heat gain from people, there is internal heat gain from cooking and appliances in the kitchen. This is estimated to be an average of 1800 Btuh and is shown in the heat gain Btuh column for the kitchen.

7. *Total heat gain:* Find the sum of the figures in the heat gain Btuh columns. The heat gains, as calculated, are based on an outdoor design temperature of 95°F and a daily temperature range of 20°F. Table 16-2 lists the summer outdoor design temperatures for various locations in the United States. Also the summer mean daily temperature range is listed for each location.

8. *Cooling load:* To adjust the total heat gain for summer outside design conditions other than 95°F and 20°F range, it is necessary to multiply the total heat gain values by a summer climate factor. This value is obtained from Table 16-15. For example, the factor for an outdoor design temperature of 100°F and a daily range of 25°F is 1.11. Determine the cooling load by multiplying the total heat gain values by the summer climate factor.

9. *Cooling air quantity:* The approximate cooling air quantities for the various rooms and for the entire house are found by dividing the cooling load values by a factor of 30. This factor is based on an air temperature leaving the cooling coil approximately 20°F

Table 16–15. Summer Climate Factor

Daily Temperature Range (°F)	Outside Design Temperature (°F)			
	90	95	100	105
15	0.90	1.08	1.26	1.45
20	0.82	1.00	1.18	1.37
25	0.74	0.93	1.11	1.30
30	0.66	0.84	1.03	1.21

SOURCE: Carrier Corporation.

below room temperature, and includes an allowance for normal heat gain to the supply ductwork.

The cooling capacity required for the Browne home is 13,924 Btuh. This value will be used to select the size of the cooling equipment. It should be noted here that the cooling capacity required for the Browne home may not be as great as you might have expected. There are several reasons for this. First, the house is very well insulated. Second, the windows are all well shaded by a 48-inch overhang. Third, the 24-hour method of cooling and load calculation results in the selection of a smaller piece of cooling equipment than would be required if constant indoor temperatures are to be maintained. For those homeowners who prefer excess capacity in their cooling equipment and a smaller temperature swing, provision can be made when selecting actual equipment by using capacity multipliers.

16.26 The Compression Refrigeration Cycle

Refrigeration can be defined as removing heat from a space where it is not wanted and ejecting it in a place where it is not objectionable. The cooling of a typical residential or small commercial building is usually accomplished by a *compression refrigeration machine*. In compression refrigeration, a refrigerant is circulated through various components by a compressor. The refrigerant changes from a liquid to a gas then back to a liquid during its movement through the system.

Figure [16–35] shows a schematic diagram of a compression refrigeration machine. Cooling occurs when the liquid refrigerant passes through a valve and enters the *evaporator* coil. Because of the low pressure maintained in the evaporator by the suction of the compressor, the

Schematic diagram of a compression refrigeration machine.

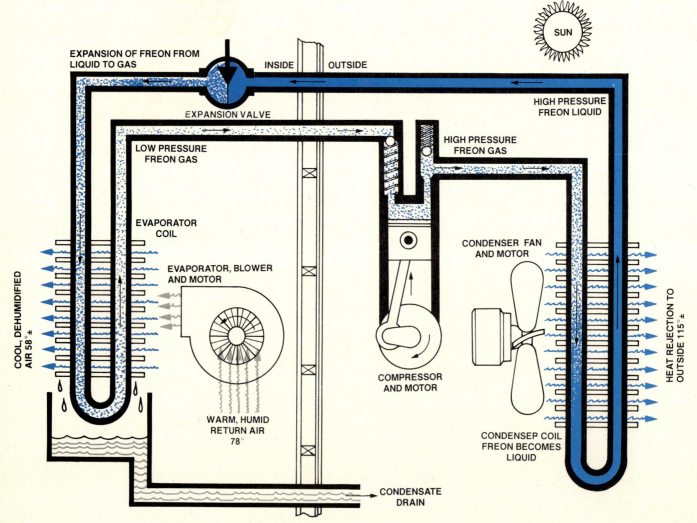

Figure 16–35

Air is cooled by passing over the finned surfaces of an evaporator coil.

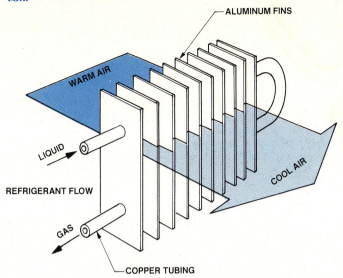

Figure 16–36

refrigerant boils. The heat required for the boiling comes from the evaporator tubing which becomes quite cold (for example, 45°F). This cold coil is used to cool air that is recirculated from the room.

After the refrigerant has boiled to a gas it must be recycled back to a liquid form. To do this the compressor draws the gas into its intake and its piston raises the pressure (and also the temperature) of the gas. This high-pressure and high-temperature gas then passes through a coil where the relatively cooler outside air is blown over it. As the high-pressure gas is cooled, it condenses back to a liquid. Thus this coil is called the *condenser*. The liquid refrigerant is now ready to begin another cycle by reentering the evaporator coil to create further cooling.

In summary, the evaporator absorbs heat from the inside air [16–36]. The condenser dissipates the heat absorbed by the evaporator to the outside. The condenser, therefore, must be placed where it can give off its heat without causing objectionable consequences.

16.27 Typical Air Conditioning Equipment

The major components of the compression refrigeration cycle are the expansion valve, the evaporator coil, the compressor, and the condenser coil [16–37]. A thermostat is also required to control the system. The expansion valve and the evaporator coil are usually located inside the building where a fan blows recirculated room air over it. Filtered return air from the room will have a temperature of approximately 78°F. This air will be cooled by about 20°F to a temperature of 58°F and will then be resupplied to the room through supply ducts.

The compressor and condenser coil, along with a fan to blow outside air over the condenser coil, are located outside the building. These components are usually placed in a single package called the *condensing unit*. The condensing unit can be located on the roof or on a concrete slab on the ground. It is preferable for this unit to be in as cool a place as possible and located where the noise will not be objectionable.

Schematic diagram of a typical residential compression refrigeration cooling system . . . air is blown over an evaporator mounted in a warm air furnace . . . the condensing unit is outside.

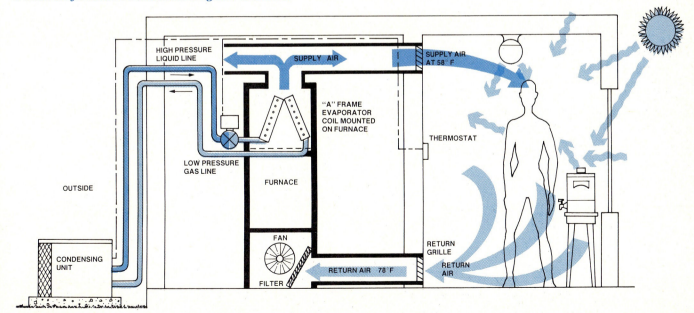

Figure 16–37

Design of Residential Climate Control Systems

A split type air conditioning system has the condensing unit mounted outside and the evaporator mounted inside.

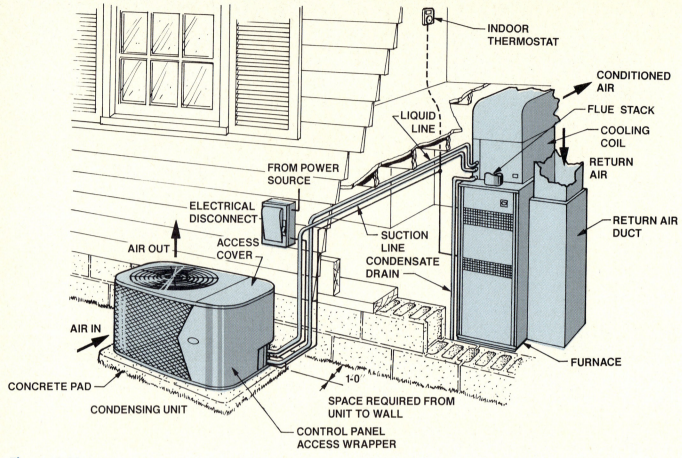

Figure 16–38

The condensing unit on the outside is connected to the evaporator coil on the inside by two refrigerant lines. When the equipment is operating, the larger tube (the low-pressure gas) will be cold, while the smaller tube (the high-pressure liquid) will be warm. The cold tube should be insulated. There will also be electric supply and control wiring to the condensing unit.

The system just described is called a *split system* [16–38]. The components are assembled in two prefabricated enclosures—one located outside and the other inside. It is also called an *add-on system*, because the evaporator coil is normally added to a forced warm air furnace. The furnace fan circulates air to the rooms through a conventional forced warm air distribution system.

A *single-package* air conditioner embraces all four basic components of the refrigeration cycle in a single package or housing. Primarily, it is designed to be located outdoors [16–39] where it may be mounted on a slab on grade or on the roof.

A single package central air conditioning unit contains all four basic components.

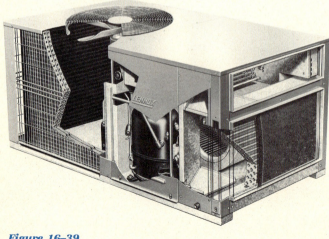

Figure 16–39

16.28 Sizing the Air Conditioning System

Once the cooling load estimate has been completed, we will know the number of Btu per hour (Btuh) that must

304 Building Systems

Table 16–16. Evaporator Coil Specifications

	Unit Model No.					
	018	024	030	036	042	048
Nominal capacity (Btuh)	18,000	24,000	30,000	36,000	42,000	48,000
Air quantity range (cfm)	450–750	600–1000	750–1250	900–1500	1050–1750	1200–2000
Height	1′–0¾″	1′–1½″	1′–5 5/16″	1′–6 5/16″	1′–8 5/16″	2′–0 3/16″
Width	1′–10″	1′–10″	1′–10″	1′–10″	1′–10″	1′–10″
Depth	1′–2 3/16″	1′–5½″	1′–5½″	1′–9″	1′–9″	2′–0″

SOURCE: Carrier Corporation.

Table 16–17. Condensing Unit Specifications

	Unit Model No.					
	001	002	003	004	045	005
Nominal capacity[a] (Btuh)	18,300	25,600	28,700	33,600	42,200	47,800
Width	1′–10″	1′–10″	1′–10″	1′–10″	1′–10″	1′–10″
Length	2′–10¼″	2′–10¼″	2′–10¼″	2′–10¼″	2′–10¼″	2′–10¼″
Height	1′–4″	1′–4″	1′–4″	2′–0″	2′–0″	2′–0″

[a] Actual capacity based on a number of variables, including temperature of outside air, the type of evaporator coil connected, length of refrigerant lines, and so on.

SOURCE: Carrier Corporation.

be removed by the cooling equipment. The cooling equipment is rated in Btuh or in tons of refrigeration. A ton of refrigeration is equivalent to 12,000 Btuh.* The tons of capacity can, therefore, be found by dividing the Btuh of cooling capacity required by 12,000. In the example of the Browne home, the tons of capacity required is 13,924 ÷ 12,000 = 1.16 tons.

A typical evaporator coil for an up-flow system.

Figure 16–40

* A ton of refrigeration is actually the amount of cooling produced by melting a ton of ice (32°F solid to 32°F liquid) in 24 hours. 2000 lb × 144 Btu/lb = 288,000 Btu/day or 12,000 Btuh.

If a cooling system is installed with or added to an existing forced warm air system, two components must be selected—an evaporator coil and a condensing unit. Figure [16–40] shows a typical evaporator coil for an up-flow system. Simplified specification data are listed in Tables 16–16 and 16–17.

Appropriate air conditioning units can be selected from the data of Tables 16–16 and 16–17. For the Browne home, we see that evaporator coil Model 018 (Table 16–16) will give 18,000 Btuh of cooling. Although we only need 13,924 Btuh, Model 018 is the smallest available size and is adequate. For the condensing unit (Table 16–17), we see that Model 001 will provide 18,300 Btuh.

16.29 Forced Air Distribution

The same room air outlets are usually used for both heating and cooling in forced air systems. The location of the outlets should be based on which season (heating or cooling) predominates for the geographic location. In cold locations it is advisable to place outlets in or near outside walls where the greatest amount of heat loss occurs. Cold down drafts below windows can be counteracted by blowing air up along the wall or window from floor or low, side wall outlets.

Figure [16–41] shows the air pattern produced by a low, exterior wall outlet in both the heating and cooling seasons. In warm climates, locating the supply outlets high on the side wall gives the best room distribution during the cooling season. Figure [16–42] shows the air patterns produced by a high, side wall outlet. The stagnant zones have relatively large variations of room temperature. Locating the return air intake in the stagnant

Air patterns from a low, exterior wall outlet.

Air patterns from a high, side wall outlet.

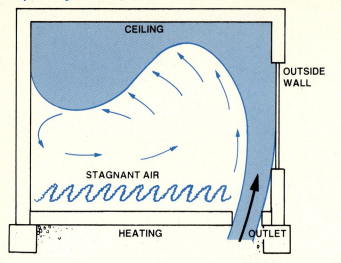
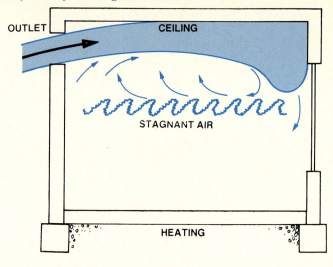
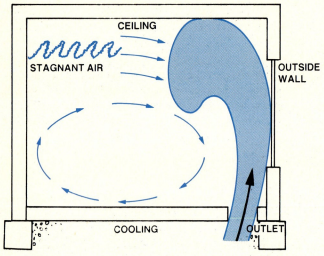

Figure 16-41

Figure 16-42

zone will return the warmest air during the cooling cycle and the coolest air during the heating cycle.

16.30 Air Duct Construction and Sizing

Air ducts are constructed of various materials, such as glass fiber board, galvanized steel, and aluminum. Underslab ducts can be made from circular galvanized steel or cement asbestos pipe. Smaller branch ceiling ducts are frequently made from flexible ducts consisting of an inner steel spiral that is interlocked with a fiberglass mesh. It is covered with 1-inch fiberglass insulation and a vinyl vapor barrier.

After the designer determines which season (heating or cooling) has the predominate influence on the system, it can be determined if the air should be supplied from underfloor ducts or from ducts in or near the ceiling. It is then possible to lay out the duct runs.

The quantity of air to be supplied to each space can be quickly estimated by using the formulas:

cooling cfm = heat gain for space $\div$ 30
heating cfm = heat loss for space $\div$ 70

The cooling cfm is based on an air temperature leaving the cooling coil approximately 20°F below room temperature and includes an allowance for normal heat gain to the supply ductwork. The heating cfm is based on an air temperature leaving the heating unit at 65°F above room temperature and allows for a 20% heat loss in the supply ducts. The results, therefore, are conservative. The largest cfm, either from heating or cooling, will be used to size the duct work.

Table 16–18. Recommended and Maximum Air Duct Velocities for Residences and Light Construction

System Components	Velocities (fpm)	
	Recommended	*Maximum*
Air intakes[a]	500	800
Filters[a]	250	300
Heating coils[a]	450	500
Cooling coils[a]	450	450
Fan outlets	100–1600	1700
Main ducts	700–900	800–1200
Branch ducts	600	700–1000

[a] Velocities for these components are for gross face area, not the net free area. Other velocities are for the net free area.
SOURCE: Carrier Corporation.

Example 16–6

The master bedroom of the Browne home has a heat loss of 12,956 Btuh and a heat gain of 2,145 Btuh. How many cfm must be supplied to the room by a warm air heating system? By a refrigerated cooling system?

Warm air: $12{,}956 \div 70 = 185$ cfm
Cool air: $2{,}145 \div 30 = 72$ cfm

Low air velocity in ducts is good because it results in a quieter system. However, the lower the velocity, the larger the ducts must be. When ducts are made too small in order to save on material and installation costs, the system can be too noisy. Small ducts offer more resistance to airflow and therefore require more fan energy to move the same quantity of air. This means higher operating cost. Table 16–18 gives recommended air velocities through various system components. These values are used to determine the size of the components.

The formula for determining the size of a duct is

$$A = \frac{Q}{V}$$

where A = cross-sectional area of the duct, ft^2
Q = quantity of air, cfm (ft^3/min)
V = velocity, fpm (ft/min)

Example 16–7

Determine the size of the branch duct supplying warm air to the master bedroom of the Browne home using the recommended velocity in Table 16–18.

From Table 16–18 we see that the recommended velocity for a branch duct is 600 fpm. The maximum required airflow from the calculations in Example 16–6 is 185 cfm. Therefore,

$$A = \frac{185 \text{ ft}^3/\text{min}}{600 \text{ ft/min}} = 0.31 \text{ ft}^2 = 44.64 \text{ in}^2$$

If we were to use a round branch duct, the diameter would be found by the following:

$$A = \frac{\pi d^2}{4}$$

$$d = \sqrt{\frac{4A}{\pi}}$$

$$= \sqrt{\frac{4 \times 44.64}{\pi}}$$

$$= \sqrt{56.8}$$

$$= 7.5 \text{ in.}$$

Use the next standard size = 8-in. duct.

16.31 Planning and Designing the Entire System

The steps in planning and designing a complete heating and cooling system for a residence can be seen in the following example. We will design a heating and cooling system for the Browne home using a gas-fired warm air furnace and an add-on cooling system. The heat loss and gain quantities determined in Tables 16–7 and 16–11 are summarized in Table 16–19. The airflow quantities are calculated using the formulas of Section 16–30.

A suggested approach is to:

1. Locate furnace and condensing unit.
2. Select register locations and types.
3. Make a duct layout.
4. Determine furnace specifications.
5. Determine cooling equipment specifications.
6. Size ducts.
7. Select diffusers.

1. *Locate furnace and condensing unit.* In looking for a central location, we find a closet shown on the south side of the master bath [16–43]. This is a satisfactory location for the furnace. The condensing unit should be placed outside, preferably in a shady spot, as close as possible to the furnace room. However, remember that there will be some noise and hot air associated with this unit, so we don't want it adjacent to the patio. A location on the northwest corner of the master bedroom might be the best that we can do. It should be shaded by plantings.

2. *Select register locations and types.* For the cold Chicago climate, heating is the primary climate control problem. It would be best to supply air at the perimeter, under the windows, to offset cold down-drafts. Small floor diffusers, which are suitable for this house, deliver roughly 100 cfm. The rooms will require one or two diffusers, depending on the calcu-

Table 16–19. Heating and Cooling Requirements for the Browne Home

Room	Winter heating		Summer Cooling	
	Heat Loss (Btuh)	Airflow for Heating (cfm)	Heat Gain (Btuh)	Airflow for Cooling (cfm)
Living/dining	12,775	183	4,248	142
Entry	3,303	47	353	12
Kitchen	4,092	58	1,970	66
Family room	11,080	158	1,299	43
Master bedroom	12,956	185	2,145	72
Bedroom 2	3,468	50	661	22
Bedroom 3	6,421	92	1,043	35
Guest bedroom	6,490	93	1,012	34
Master bath	3,867	55	444	15
Bath 2	1,342	19	202	7
Bath 3	1,571	22	421	14
Laundry	96	1	42	1
Shop	1,463	21	80	3
Hall	182	3	[b]	
	69,106	987[a]	13,920	466

[a] The cfm requirement for winter conditions is greater than that for summer. Therefore, use the winter cfm for designing the ductwork.

[b] Hall heat gain included in bedrooms 2 and 3.

lated airflow requirements and the room configurations. Since the heating airflow requirements are greater, they will be used to determine the number of diffusers and to size the ducts. Locate the diffusers on the heating and cooling system layout [16–43]. Then a total of 17 diffusers are required.

3. *Make a duct layout.* With perimeter floor outlets we will need ducts under the slab. We will select the perimeter-loop system shown in [16–18]. The air distribution duct layout for the Browne home is shown in [16–43]. Return air grilles will be placed in the ceiling of all rooms supplied except the bathrooms, family room, kitchen, laundry, and entry. This air will be ducted back, above the ceiling, to the furnace. In laying out the feeders the following guidelines have been used:
   a. The distance between points where feeders connect should not exceed 35 feet.
   b. The number of diffusers between adjacent feeder connections to the loop should not exceed three.
   c. Connect all feeders to the loop at 90° and not closer than 18 inches to any diffuser.
   d. The distance of any diffuser from any feeder should not exceed 15 feet.
   e. If the distance between two adjacent diffusers on the same run of loop exceeds 20 feet, provide another feeder between them.
   f. No diffuser should be located on a feeder duct.
4. *Determine furnace specifications.* The furnace must be of the down-flow type and must have at least 69,106 Btuh of output. From Table 16–8 we see that Model G12Q3–110 is the closest choice that exceeds our requirements.
5. *Determine cooling equipment specifications.* If we are to install an add-on cooling system on a down-flow furnace, we must install the evaporator coil under the furnace. We require a cooling capacity of 13,920 Btuh. From Table 16–16 we see that a Model 018 evaporator coil provides 18,000 Btuh and is sufficient. Table 16–17 shows that a Model 001 condensing unit with an 18,300 Btuh capacity will be satisfactory.
6–7. *Size ducts and select diffusers.* The following steps can be used as a guide to the design and sizing of the feeder and perimeter ducts:
   a. Identify diffusers by number and feeders by letter [16–43].
   b. Assign the heat to be delivered by each diffuser using the requirements summarized in Table 16–19.
   c. Using the duct layout [16–43], find the heat that must be supplied through each feeder, assuming that each diffuser is served by the nearest feeder (Table 16–20).
   d. Measure and list the length of each feeder along with its heat supply requirements (Table 16–21).
   e. With the feeder length and its Btuh requirements, use Table 16–22 to select its diameter (Table 16–21).
   f. The perimeter duct diameter will be the same as that of the largest feeder. In this example it is 9 inches.

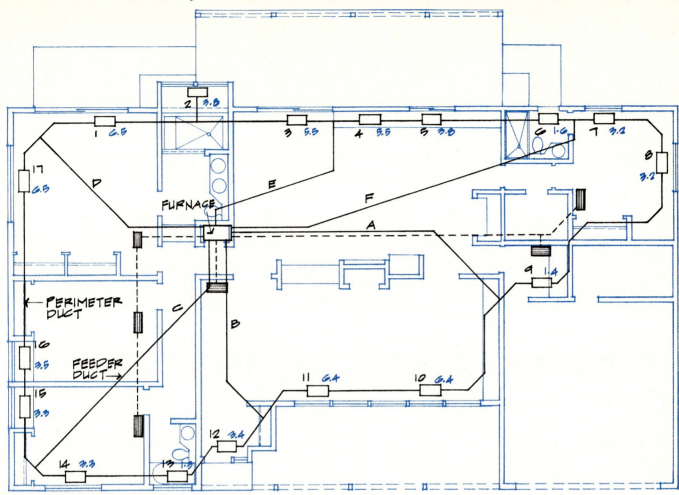

A perimeter loop air distribution duct system designed for the Browne home . . . feeder ducts are lettered for reference . . . diffusers are numbered and show heat delivery in 1000 Btuh.

 RETURN AIR GRILLE
---- RETURN AIR DUCT

Figure 16–43

Table 16–20. Heat to be Supplied by Feeder Ducts in Browne Home (1000 Btuh)

	Feeder A		Feeder B		Feeder C		Feeder D		Feeder E		Feeder F	
	Diffuser	Heat	Diffuser	Heat	Diffuser	Heat	Diffuser	Heat	Diffuser	Heat	Diffuser	Heat
	9	1.4	11	6.4	14	3.3	17	6.5	3	5.5	6	1.6
	10	6.4	12	3.4	15	3.3	1	6.5	4	5.5	7	3.2
			13	1.3	16	3.5	2	3.8	5	3.8	8	3.2
Total		7.8		11.1		10.1		16.8		14.8		8.0

Table 16–21. **Feeder Duct Sizes for Browne Home**

Feeder	Heat Delivery (1000 Btuh)	Feeder Length (ft)	Feeder Diameter[a] (in.)
A	7.8	33	7
B	11.1	21	8
C	10.1	32	7
D	16.8	24	9
E	14.8	18	8
F	8.0	40	7

[a] From Table 16–22.

Table 16–22. **Feeder Duct Diameters (in.) for Various Heat Delivery Capacities**

Heat Delivery (Btuh)	Length of Feeder (ft)			
	10–20	21–40	41–60	61–80
Up to 6,999	6	6	7	7
7,000 to 8,999	7	7	7	7
9,000 to 9,999	7	7	7	8
10,000 to 10,999	7	7	8	8
11,000 to 12,999	8	8	8	8
13,000 to 13,999	8	8	8	9
14,000 to 14,999	8	8	9	9
15,000 to 17,000	8	9	9	9

SOURCE: *ASHRAE 1973 Systems Handbook.*

EXERCISES

16–1. What is the winter outdoor design temperature for Omaha, Nebraska?

16–2. For effective air conditioning, what are the variables that must be controlled?

16–3. What is meant by a "split system"? Draw a diagram to accompany your explanation.

16–4. Given the wall section shown in [16–6] except that the studs are 2 x 6's instead of 2 x 4's, determine the total resistance if the air space is filled with 5½ inches of batt insulation. What is the overall U factor of this wall?

16–5. For Omaha, Nebraska, how much heat would be lost on a winter design day through 280 linear feet edge of a slab with 2 inches of edge insulation?

16–6. What is the U factor for an asphalt-shingled pitched roof with a plastered ceiling and R30 (9-in.) insulation?

16–7. The size of a corner bedroom is 12 ft. x 15 ft. x 8 ft. Compute the Btuh loss due to infiltration if the inside is to be maintained at 70°F and the outside temperature is 10°F. Windows are on both sides.

16–8. Select the model of a natural gas-fired warm air furnace for a house that has a calculated heat loss of 96,000 Btuh. Estimate the minimum size of room in which you would put the furnace. List the type of pipes, ducts, wires, and so on, that would enter and leave the furnace space.

16–9. Select the model of a natural gas-fired boiler for a house that has a calculated heat loss of 96,000 Btuh. Estimate the minimum size of room in which you would put the boiler. List the number and type of pipes, ducts, wires, and so on, that would enter and leave the boiler room.

16–10. What is the conventional unit of heat in the United States?

16–11. The conditions in a meeting room are 78°F and 60% relative humidity. Would most people be comfortable? Explain your answer.

16–12. Explain how a typical fireplace heats a room.

16–13. Name three common ways of heating water in a hydronic heating system.

16–14. In a central air conditioning system, where is the condensing unit usually located? Why?

16–15. In a heat pump installation, where is the heat obtained for warming a building?

16–16. List the three most common sources of energy for heating a building.

16–17. What are the two main portions of the heating load?

16–18. What main sources of heat are part of the cooling load?

16–19. If one knows the U value, how is the total resistance (R_T) determined?

16–20. Name the disadvantages of radiant heating.

17 Plumbing Systems

17.1 Plumbing

The plumbing system for a home or a light commercial building includes two major subsystems—water supply and waste disposal. Water supply consists of pipes, valves, fittings, and other accessories that distribute water from the city main (or another source) to fixtures such as sinks, toilets (also called *water closets*), bathtubs, and showers. Part of this water is sent through a water heater to provide hot water. The water and waste disposal subsystem consists of pipes and fittings that conduct the "used" water and other waste products to the municipal sewer or to a local disposal facility.

17.2 Water Supply

The water supply to a home or a small building is normally provided by a municipal system. The water is checked and treated, if necessary, to ensure that it meets minimum standards of cleanliness. It is piped through city mains at a pressure that is usually about 50 pounds per square inch (psi).

The owner of a proposed structure will request that the city provide service to the building site. The city will excavate the street to the property line and tap onto the streen main [17–1]. The tap will include a pipe from the street main to the property line. This will usually include two valves—one near the main called the *corporation cock*, and one near the property line called the *curb cock*. The vertical valve stem of the curb cock can be 4 to 5 feet long, depending on the depth of the piping. It is placed inside a pipe for protection. This allows the water to be shut off to the building without reexcavating.

The owner or contractor will connect to the curb cock and bring the water supply line through or under the foundation wall and into the house. Any piping outside the building must be located below the frost line to prevent freezing. The service cock allows the occupant to shut off the supply. Next, the meter is installed to measure the quantity of water used. Some cities require that the dial face of the meter be visible from outside the house. The meter might be mounted near grade close to a small window or a clear glass block in the foundation wall to allow the meter reader to see the meter dial. In mild weather locations, the meter may be located outside, just below grade and near the curb cock. A check valve prevents water from the house being pulled back into the city main in case of a break in the main.

If water is to be softened for household purposes, a supply line should first be installed to outside hose bibbs and other locations that do not require soft water. A softener, necessary in locations where water is "hard," removes calcium and other minerals from the water. It must be regenerated periodically and consequently, needs access to a drain. It must also be located near an electrical outlet. After the water is softened, it can be distributed to the desired fixtures having a cold water requirement and to the water heater.

A portion of the cold water supply is routed to the water heater. Usually, the heater is combined with a storage tank. Water is heated by electric, gas, or solar heaters. If a boiler is used in the house heating system, this is sometimes used to heat water for other applications as well. In this case the boiler would contain a separate coil to heat the domestic hot water.

Water heaters have a thermostat to permit adjusting the temperature to between 120 and 150°F. The lower the temperature setting, the less heat loss from the stored hot water. Storage tank capacities available are: 30 gallons (apartment size), 40, 50, 65, 75, and 100 gallons. A 40-gallon gas-fired tank is commonly specified for the average family. A larger tank may be required if an electric heater is used (due to the slower recovery rate). If solar collectors are used, the storage capacity must be increased to allow for nights and cloudy days. Some backup means of heating should also be provided.

17.3 Supply Pipes and Sizing

A variety of materials are used for water supply piping. Copper tubing is often preferred since it does not corrode easily. Black and galvanized steel pipe will rust and develop leaks after a number of years of service. Copper tubing is joined by soldering. Steel pipe is joined with screwed fittings. Plastic pipe has gained in popularity since many plumbing codes now allow its use for water supply as well as for waste disposal. The joints are fused together with a solvent or with heat.

The water supply system for a home starts at the city main—pipes should be installed with a slight slope to permit draining the system by a valve at the low end.

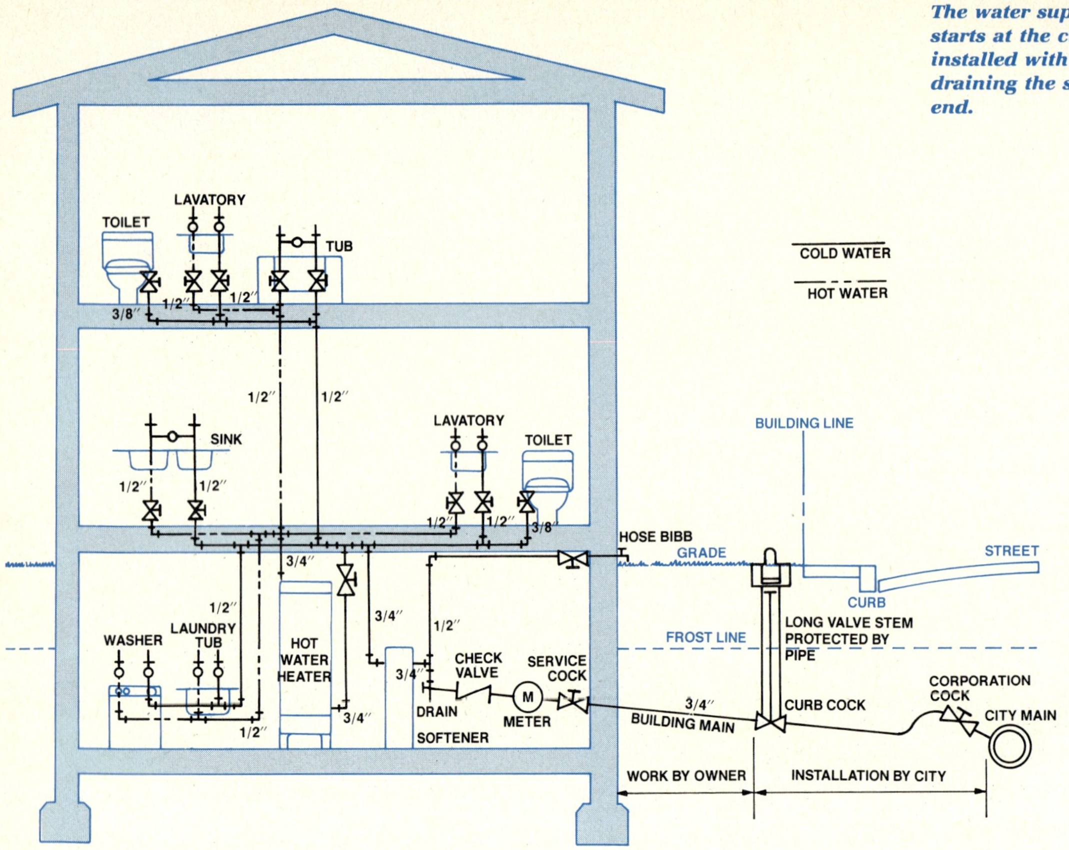

Figure 17–1

Three general categories of pipes are seen in [17–1]. The largest pipe is the main supply pipe. This leads to feeder risers that distribute water to the individual fixture risers. Those are the smallest pipes. Piping diagrams use standard symbols to show fittings that join the pipes and other common parts such as valves and meters [17–2].

Pipe sizing is based on a number of variables, such as the quantity of water required by the fixtures, the available water pressure, and the pressure loss resulting from friction in long runs of piping. Table 17–1 simplifies the sizing procedure by giving minimum sizes recommended by the Federal Housing Administration.

17.4 Water and Waste Disposal

The disposal system consists of pipes, traps, vents, and cleanouts. These items are all necessary to operate and maintain the system with a minimum of trouble [17–3]. Each fixture that must dispose of water and/or waste is connected to piping leading eventually to the municipal sewer or to a private treatment system.

A *fixture trap* is located in or near each fixture to prevent sewer gases in the piping from entering the occu-

Table 17–1. Minimum Water Supply Pipe Sizes

	Pipe Diameters (in.)	
Pipe Applications	*Hot Water*	*Cold Water*
Fixture risers		
Toilet, flush tank		⅜
Lavatory	⅜	⅜
Bathtub	½	½
Shower	½	½
Kitchen sink	½	½
Laundry sink	½	½
Feeder risers		
Bathroom group[a] (plus one or more	¾	¾
Three fixtures (other than bathroom group)	¾	¾
Bathroom group[a]	½	½
Two fixtures	½	½
Hose bibb		½
Supply lines[b]	¾	¾

[a] A bathroom group consists of a toilet, a lavatory, and a bathtub or shower stall.

[b] A 1-in. supply line should be provided to a house with more fixtures than is equivalent to three bathrooms, a kitchen, and laundry facilities.

SOURCE: Federal Housing Administration

Piping diagrams use standard symbols.

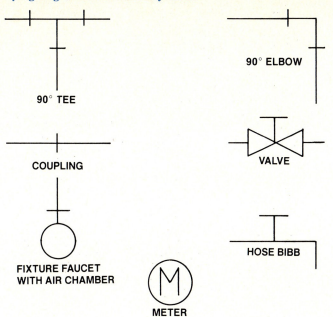

Figure 7-2

The water and waste disposal system includes drain pipes and vent pipes.

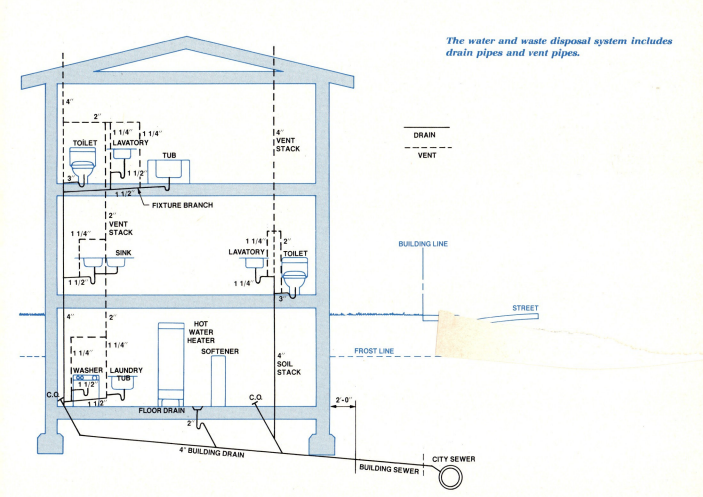

Figure 17-3

313

pied area. The trap catches and holds a portion of the wastewater from each discharge. This provides a water seal as shown in [17–4]. A *vent* must be installed on the outlet side of the fixture trap. This is needed to prevent suction from emptying the trap.

The piping following the trap leads to the *fixture branch*. The fixture branch is a nearly horizontal pipe that conducts the waste from one or more fixtures to either a *building drain* or to a *waste* or *soil stack* (vertical disposal system pipes open to the atmosphere are called *stacks*). A soil stack receives discharge from a toilet, whereas a waste stack does not. Soil stacks are often 4 inches in diameter, whereas waste stacks are usually 3 inches in diameter.

The waste or soil stack must be extended through the roof. It is called a *vent stack* above the highest branch. The size of the vent is given in Table 17–5. In some parts of the country where the vent stack might become clogged with snow and ice, its size must be at least 4 inches in diameter as it passes through the roof. In this case, if the vent stack is not required to be 4 inches in diameter for its entire length, it must be increased to 4 inches in diameter at least 1 foot before it passes through the roof.

The stack(s) empties into the building drain. This is usually a 4-inch-diameter extra-heavy cast iron pipe located under the basement floor. It runs out at a slope of ¼ inch per foot and extends 6 feet beyond the foundation wall. At this point it is connected to the *building sewer*. The building sewer may be made of 4-inch cast iron, 4-inch plastic, or 6-inch vitrified clay. It extends to the city sewer or to a private disposal system.

Clean outs are provided at strategic locations in the building drain. This allows a snakelike tool to be used to clean out stoppages that may occur between the fixtures and the city sewer. The cleanout operation can also be performed from the roof by extending a cleaning tool down the vent pipe and into the drainage system.

17.5 Disposal Pipe Sizing

The pipes, traps, and vents are sized based on the expected flow through the fixtures they serve. The flow is estimated in terms of drainage *fixture units*. The fixture unit values for various fixtures are given in Table 17–2. Trap sizes for various plumbing fixtures are shown in Table 17–3. The maximum number of drainage fixture units that may be connected to horizontal fixture branches and to stacks is shown in Table 17–4, while the size of vents is found in Table 17–5. Finally, the maximum number of fixture units that may be connected to building drains and sewers is given in Table 17–6.

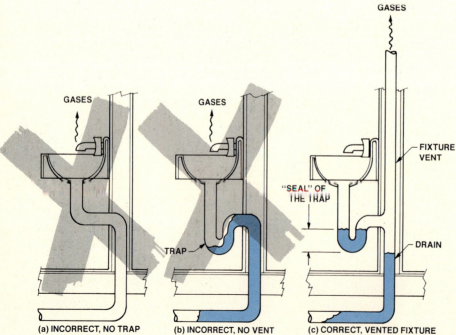

A properly designed fixture trap prevents sewer gases from entering the room.

Figure 17–4

Table 17–2. Drainage Fixture Unit Values for Various Plumbing Fixtures

Type of Fixture or Group of Fixtures	Drainage Fixture Unit Value (d.f.u.)
Automatic clothes washer (2-in. standpipe)	3
Bathroom group consisting of a water closet, lavatory, and bathtub or shower stall:	
Flushometer valve closet	8
Tank-type closet	6
Bathtub (with or without overhead shower)[a]	2
Bidet	1
Clinic sink	6
Combination sink-and-tray with food waste grinder	4
Combination sink-and-tray with one 1½-in. trap	2
Combination sink-and-tray with separate 1½-in. traps	3
Dental lavatory	1
Dental unit or cuspidor	1
Dishwasher, domestic	2
Drinking fountain	½
Floor drains with 2-in. waste	3
Kitchen sink, domestic, with dishwasher 1½-in. trap	3
Kitchen sink, domestic, with food waste grinder	2
Kitchen sink, domestic, with food waste grinder and dishwasher 2-in. trap	3
Kitchen sink, domestic, with one 1½-in. trap	2
Laundry tray (one or two compartments)	2
Lavatory with 1¼-in. waste	1
Shower stall, domestic	2
Showers (group) per head	2
Sinks:	
Flushing rim (with valve)	6
Service (P trap)	2
Service (trap standard)	3
Pot, scullery, etc.	4
Surgeon's	3
Urinal, pedestal, syphon jet blowout	6
Urinal, stall, washout	4
Urinal, wall lip	4
Urinal trough (each 6-ft section)	2
Wash sink (circular or multiple) each set of faucets	2
Water closet, tank-operated	4
Water closet, valve-operated	6
Fixtures not listed above:	
Trap size 1¼ in. or less	1
Trap size 1½ in.	2
Trap size 2 in.	3
Trap size 2½ in.	4
Trap size 3 in.	5
Trap size 4 in.	6

[a] A shower head over a bathtub does not increase the fixture unit value.
SOURCE: National Standard Plumbing Code.

Table 17–3. Sizes of Nonintegral Traps for Plumbing Fixtures

Plumbing Fixture	Trap Size (in.)
Bathtub (with or without overhead shower)	1½
Bidet	1¼
Combination kitchen sink, domestic, dishwasher, and food waste grinder	2
Combination sink and wash (laundry) tray	1½
Combination sink and wash (laundry) tray with food waste grinder unit	1½[a]
Dental lavatory	1¼
Dental unit or cuspidor	1¼
Dishwasher, commercial	2
Dishwasher, domestic (nonintegral trap)	1½
Drinking fountain	1¼
Floor drain	2
Food waste grinder—commercial use	2
Food waste grinder—domestic use	1½
Kitchen sink, domestic	1½
Kitchen sink, domestic, with dishwasher	1½
Kitchen sink, domestic, with food waste grinder unit	1½
Laundry tray (one or two compartments)	1½
Lavatory (barber shop, beauty parlor or surgeon's)	1½
Lavatory, common	1¼
Lavatory, multiple type (wash fountain or wash sink)	1½
Shower stall or drain	2
Sink (flushing rim type, flush valve supplied)	3
Sink (service type with floor outlet trap standard)	3
Sink (service trap with P trap)	2
Sink (surgeon's)	1½
Sink, commercial (pot, scullery, or similar type)	2
Sink, commercial (with food grinder unit)	2

[a] Separate trap required for wash tray and separate trap required for sink compartment with food waste grinder unit.
SOURCE: National Standard Plumbing Code.

Table 17-4. Sizes of Horizontal Fixture Branches and Stacks

	Maximum Number of Fixture Units That May Be Connected to:			
Diameter of Pipe (in.)	Any Horizontal Fixture Branch[a]	Stack Sizing for Three Stories in Height or Three Intervals	Stack Sizing for More Than Three Stories in Height	
			Total for Stack	Total at One Story or Branch Interval
1½	3	4	8	2
2	6	10	24	6
2½	12	20	42	9
3	20[b]	48[b]	72[b]	20[b]
4	160	240	500	90
5	360	540	1100	200
6	620	960	1900	350
8	1400	2200	3600	600
10	2500	3800	5600	1000
12	3900	6000	8400	1500
15	7000			

[a] Does not include branches of the building drain.

[b] Not more than two water closets or bathroom groups within each branch interval nor more than six water closets or bathroom groups on the stack.

Stacks shall be sized according to the total accumulated connected load at each story or branch interval and may be reduced in size as this load decreases to a minimum diameter of ½ of the largest size required.

SOURCE: National Standard Plumbing Code.

Table 17-5. Sizes of Vents

Size of Soil or Waste Stack (in.)	Fixture Units Connected	Maximum Length of Vent (ft) Diameter of Vent Required (in.)							
		1¼	1½	2	2½	3	4	5	6	8
1½	8	50	150							
1½	10	30	100							
2	12	30	75	200						
2	20	26	50	150						
2½	42		30	100	300					
3	10		30	100	100	600				
3	30			60	200	500				
3	60			50	80	400				
4	100			35	100	260	1000			
4	200			30	90	250	900			
4	500			20	70	180	700			
5	200				35	80	350	1000		
5	500				30	70	300	900		
5	1100				20	50	200	700		
6	350				25	50	200	400	1300	
6	620				15	30	125	300	1100	
6	960					24	100	250	1000	
6	1900					20	70	200	700	
8	600						50	150	500	1300
8	1400						40	100	400	1200
8	2200						30	80	350	1100
8	3600						25	60	250	800
10	1000							75	125	1000
10	2500							50	100	500
10	3800							30	80	350
10	5600							25	60	250

SOURCE: National Standard Plumbing Code.

Table 17-6. Sizes of Building Drains and Sewers[a]

Diameter of Pipe (in.)	Maximum Number of Fixture Units That May Be Connected to Any Portion of the Building Drain or the Building Sewer, Including Branches of the Building Drain			
	Fall per Foot			
	1/16 in.	1/8 in.	1/4 in.	1/2 in.
2			21	26
2½			24	31
3		36[b]	42[b]	50[b]
4		180	216	250
5		390	480	575
6		700	840	1,000
8	1,400	1,600	1,920	2,300
10	2,500	2,900	3,500	4,200
12	2,900	4,600	5,600	6,700
15	7,000	8,300	10,000	12,000

[a] On-site sewers that serve more than one building may be sized according to the current standards and specifications of the Administrative Authority for public sewers.

[b] Not over two water closets or two bathroom groups.

SOURCE: National Standard Plumbing Code.

Example 17–1

Size the fixture branches, traps, and vents for the bathroom shown in [17–5].

First list the fixtures, their fixture unit values from Table 17–2, and the trap sizes from Table 17–3.

	Fixture Units	Trap Size (in.)
Lavatory	1	1¼
Toilet (W.C.)	4	3 (built into toilet)
Shower	2	2

From Table 17–4 we see that a 1½-inch horizontal fixture branch is the smallest size used and will handle up to three fixture units. Since the lavatory has only one fixture unit, we will use a 1½-inch branch [17–6]. This line combines with the branch from the toilet (4 fixture units).

The branch from the toilet then must handle 4 + 1 fixture units. From Table 17–4 we would select a 2-inch branch; however, the branch cannot be smaller than the fixture trap (3 inches for a toilet), so we use a 3-inch branch. The branch from the shower (2 fixture units) must be at least 2 inches to match its trap size. When it joins the branch carrying the flow from the toilet and lavatory, a total of 7 fixture units (1 + 4 + 2) must be handled. Thus the continuing branch must be at least 2½ inches according to Table 17–4. Here again, however, we must consider that a 3-inch branch is connected, so we must continue with at least that size.

The sizing of vents is done in a similar manner using Table 17–5. The lavatory will have a 1¼-inch vent since this is the smallest size used and will handle up to 8 fixture units. The toilet vent size is based on its 3-inch branch. The table shows that a 1½-inch vent is needed if the vent pipe is less than 30 feet long. The 2-inch shower trap is connected to a 2-inch pipe leading to the 3-inch branch from the toilet. From Table 17–5 we can see that the shower vent from this 2-inch pipe can be 1¼ inches if it is less than 30 feet long.

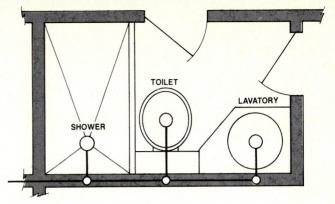

A typical bathroom plan ... showing drain connections.

Figure 17–5

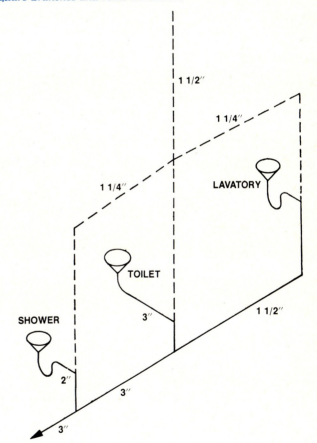

Drainage piping diagram for a bathroom ... sizes of horizontal fixture branches and vents are shown.

Figure 17–6

Plumbing Systems

Drainage system layout for the Browne home.

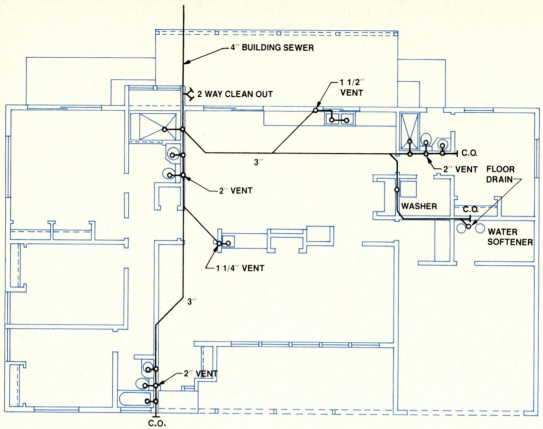

Figure 17-7

Isometric diagram of the Browne home drainage system.

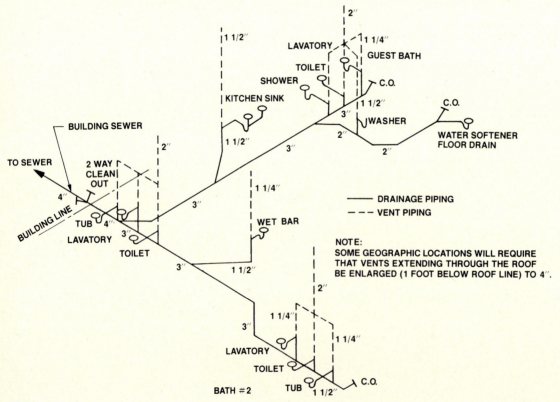

Figure 17-8

318

Water distribution system layout for the Browne home.

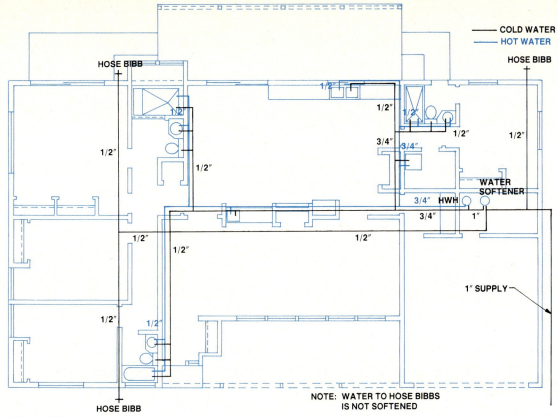

Figure 17-9

A further example of drainage system sizing can be seen in the layouts for the Browne home [17-7 and 17-8]. Figure [17-8] is an isometric diagram showing the schematic arrangement of the drainage piping. The water supply system layout for the Browne home is shown in [17-9].

EXERCISES

17-1. What is the proper size for the cold water supply pipe feeding a lavatory, a shower, and a laundry sink?

17-2. What determines the minimum depth that the building water supply is buried?

17-3. Investigate methods of preventing water hammer in a water supply system. Describe them.

17-4. Determine the number of fixture units connected to the building drain of the residence in which you live.

17-5. For your home, what is the minimum size building sewer required?

17-6. What is the required minimum depth of water seal in a trap?

17-7. Use one of your school's restrooms as an example and assume that all fixtures are connected to the same branch. Draw an isometric diagram of the piping. Determine the number of drainage fixture units connected to the branch. Determine the necessary trap sizes. Determine the necessary branch sizes. Show the sizes on the piping diagram.

17-8. Make a sketch of the plumbing system in your home as you believe it to be. Show the sizes of all pipes.

17-9. Draw a simple section view sketch showing a bathroom on the first floor of a house and another bathroom directly above on the second floor. On this sketch indicate the following:
1. Building sewer
2. Building drain
3. Soil and waste stacks
4. Vent stacks
5. Fixture branches
6. Traps

Plumbing Systems

18 Electrical Systems

In less than 100 years the use of electricity in the home has grown from the first single light bulb to a multitude of work-saving devices and other amenities that are now being operated by computer-controlled switching. By the mere closing of a switch, buildings are lighted, wheels are turned, food is cooked, ice is made, distant events are seen, and many other tasks are performed.

Electricity is a form of energy (a flow of electrons) that, unlike fuels or even heat, cannot be stored. (In a battery, small amounts of electrical energy can be stored as chemical energy.) It must be used during the same instant in which it is generated. It is clean, convenient, and easy to transmit in comparison to the burning of a fuel and the piping or ducting of a heated fluid. A disadvantage of electricity is its expense in terms of natural resources. To create it, nonrenewable fuel must be consumed (except for hydroelectric, wind, solar, or geothermal generation). Commercial electrical power is commonly produced by steam-driven turbines that drive generators. This fuel-to-heat-to-electricity conversion usually has an efficiency of less than 40%. When we compare this to a gas-fired furnace with an efficiency of 70 to 80%, we can conclude that the choice of using electricity or some other form of energy must be made carefully.

18.1 Basic Electrical Terminology

The following terms are basic to the understanding of electrical systems:

Current (I): The flow of electrons through a conductor is called current. The unit of measure of electron flow is the *ampere*. An ampere is the amount of electron flow caused by an electrical "pressure" (potential difference) of 1 volt in a circuit with a resistance of 1 ohm.

Voltage (V): The electrical "pressure" or potential difference produced by an electrical energy source is called *voltage* and is measured in *volts*. In a fully charged battery this voltage is essentially constant and thus has the ability to cause an unchanging current in the same direction. Therefore, the voltage produced by a battery is called *direct current* (d-c) voltage. This is different from the voltage normally produced by public utilities that varies in a cyclic fashion at 60 times each second. During this very short period the voltage rises and falls and passes from a positive to a negative value. This causes the current to flow in one direction during half the cycle, and in the opposite direction during the other half cycle. This is known as *alternating current* (a-c) and the voltage is called a-c voltage.

Resistance (R): The flow of current in an electric circuit is resisted due to the size and type of material through which the current passes. The unit of measurement of resistance is the *ohm*. Materials display different resistances to the flow of electric current. Most metals have lower resistance and therefore are called *conductors* because they conduct electricity easily. Copper and aluminum are the most frequently used conductor materials for electrical wiring. On the other hand, materials that tend to prevent or highly resist electrical flow are called *insulators*. Porcelain, glass, mica, rubber, and certain plastics are frequently used to insulate conductors.

Circuit: For electricity to flow and do useful work there must be a completed loop of wiring that contains: (1) a source of voltage, (2) an electrical device (or load), and (3) a device (switch) to start or stop the flow [18–1].

18.2 Electric–Hydraulic Analogy

The flow of electricity in an electrical circuit can be compared to the flow of water in a piping circuit. In the piping circuit of [18–2] the flow of water is proportional to the pressure and inversely proportional to the friction. In an electrical circuit the current is proportional to the voltage and inversely proportional to the resistance. The greater the voltage, the greater the current. The greater the resistance, the lower the current. This relationship between voltage, current, and resistance is expressed in an equation called *Ohm's Law*:

$$I = \frac{V}{R}$$

where I is expressed in amperes, V in volts, and R in ohms.

Electricity flows in a circuit containing a source of voltage, an electrical load, and a switch.

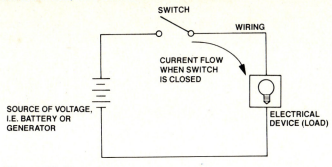

Figure 18–1

Electricity flows in a wiring circuit similar to water flowing in a piping circuit.

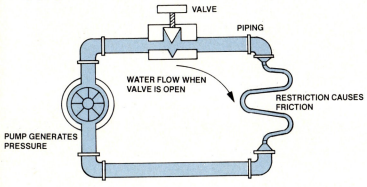

Figure 18–2

18.3 Electrical Power

Power is defined as the rate at which energy is used, or the amount of energy used per unit of time. In electrical terms power is measured in *watts*, which is the product of voltage times amperage. Electrical devices are marked with their power rating expressed in watts. For a device such as an incandescent light bulb, the wattage is determined by multiplying the voltage times the amount of amperage that the device draws to operate. A light bulb rated at 100 watts will use 100 watts of power while connected in a 120 volt circuit through which 0.833 amperes is flowing (120 volts × 0.833 ampere = 100 watts). A *kilowatt* is equal to 1000 watts.

Electrical energy use can be determined by multiplying the power rating of a device by the length of time that it is used:

Energy = Power × Time

For instance, if a 100-watt light bulb is burned for 10 hours, you would use 100 watts × 10 hours, or 1000 watt-hours. This is the same as 1 kilowatt-hour.

18.4 Series and Parallel Circuits

Electrical devices can be connected (wired) in a circuit in two different ways. Figure [18–3] shows a *series* circuit with a 120-volt source. You might think of this as an older-style string of Christmas tree bulbs. All bulbs must be lit or none will be lit, since the same current must flow through each bulb in sequence. If one bulb burns out, the circuit is broken (open) and no current can flow. If you imagine this as a water piping system, the flow of water would stop.

Figure [18–4] shows a *parallel* circuit—the type found in building wiring circuits. Each fixture has the same voltage applied to it. Also, each device can be operated independently of the others. The failure of one bulb, for example, does not affect the others.

18.5 Wire Sizes

Current flow through a wire produces heat. If the wire is too small for the amount of current, overheating will occur, causing power to be lost and the insulation to deteriorate. A *short circuit* may result. This is a very high flow of current from the "hot" wire to the neutral

Electrical devices can be connected in a circuit in series . . .

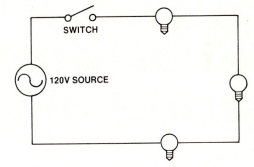

Figure 18–3

. . . or connected in parallel.

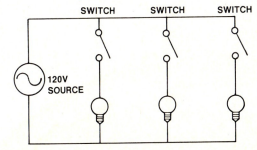

Figure 18–4

Electrical Systems

321

wire or to the ground. The high current causes a very high temperature, melting the metal conductor with explosive force. Sparks of molten metal and electrical arcing can ignite nearby combustible materials.

Wire sizes, then, are selected based on the current the wire will carry within certain temperature limits, and on the heat resistance capability of the insulation covering the wire [18–5]. Table 18–1 shows the safe current carrying capacity of wires with two different types of insulation: T, thermoplastic; and RHW, moisture- and heat-resistant rubber. Number 12 wire is generally recommended for branch lighting circuits in a home.

Conductors for building wiring are made in different sizes and types . . . sizes and number of strands shown are relative and not exact.

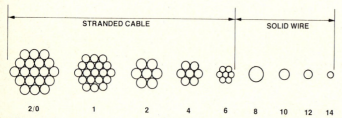

Figure 18–5

Table 18–1. Allowable Current-Carrying Capacity of Insulated Copper Conductors (amperes)

Wire Size	Type of Insulation	
	T	RHW
14	15	15
12	20	20
10	30	30
8	40	45
6	55	65
4	70	85
3	80	100
2	95	115
1	110	130
0(1/0)	125	150
00(2/0)	145	175
000(3/0)	165	200

SOURCE: Extracted from National Electrical Code.

18.6 Electrical Generation and Distribution

One source of commercially generated electrical energy is by means of steam-driven turbines turning electrical generators [18–6]. Alternating current (a-c) power is usually produced at a voltage of 13,800 volts. In order to transmit the energy "cross country" in relatively small wires, its voltage is increased by means of a transformer to as high as 500,000 volts. The higher the voltage, the less the current and thus the smaller the conductor required. This makes the system more economical. If the transmission distance is relatively short, the voltage may only be raised to 69,000 volts. These "high-tension" wires are supported on high towers.

When the power reaches the city or town where it is to be used, it will go through a transformer substation where its voltage will be reduced to possibly 12,500 or 4160 volts (other possible voltages are 2400, 7200, or 13,200 volts). From here the power may be distributed under ground or above ground on power poles to a transformer near the building that will use the power. This final transformer reduces the voltage to that required in the building. For residences and small commercial buildings this voltage would probably be 120/240-volt three-wire service.

18.7 Service Entrance

The *service entrance* is that part of the wiring system that brings power from the electric power company's distribution system at the property line to the building. Figures [18–7] and [18–8] show installations for above-ground and underground service entrances. Included in the service entrance is a meter to measure the amount of electricity used.

The size of the service entrance wiring is an important consideration because it sets the ultimate limit on the amount of power that may be used in the house. Factors used in selecting the wiring size are the number and types of electrical appliances and devices to be used plus an allowance for possible future additions and activities. The current capacity required of the service entrance may vary from a minimum of 60 amperes to 200 or more amperes.

The amperage of the service for a home can be determined by first estimating the total load of the electric equipment from Table 18–2. For example, let us suppose that the total wattage required for a home is 35,000 watts. The minimum service would be

$$\text{amperes} = \frac{\text{watts}}{\text{volts}}$$

$$= \frac{35{,}000}{240}$$

$$= 145.8$$

Since a 20% expansion factor is commonly added, the required service would be 145.8 × 1.2 = 175 amperes. Use 200 amperes, the next standard size.

A typical electrical energy system . . . commercial electric power is transmitted at high voltages and then distributed at lower voltage to meet customer requirements.

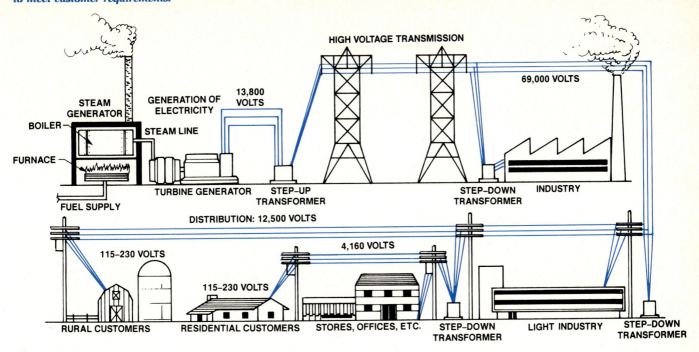

Figure 18–6

Electrical power service for a building may be above ground . . .   *. . . or the service may be underground.*

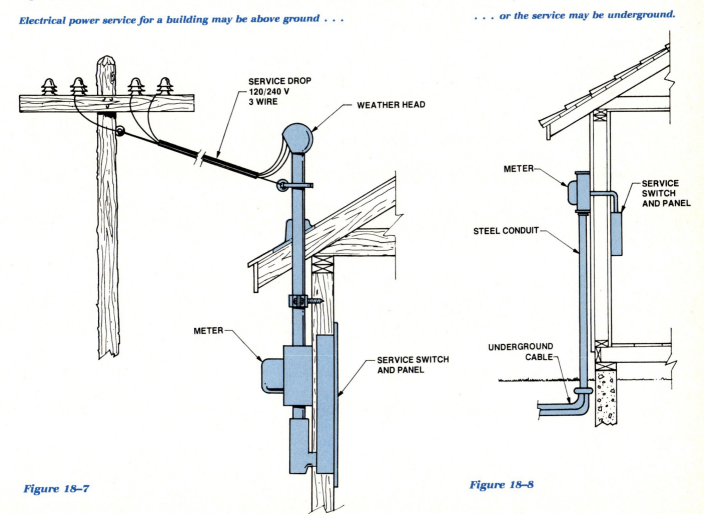

Figure 18–7   *Figure 18–8*

Table 18–2. Electrical Power Requirements for a Home

Electrical Equipment	Typical Load (watts)
Lighting fixtures	3 watts/ft^2
Central air conditioning or heat pump	1,600 watts/ton
Dishwasher	1,200
Automatic washer	700
Electric clothes dryer	5,000
Electric range/oven	12,000
Electric water heater	3,000
Exhaust fan (attic)	300
Iron	1,000
Microwave oven	1,450
Portable heater	1,300
Refrigerator	500
Refrigerator/freezer	800
Freezer	500
Room air conditioner	1,400
Swimming pool pump	1,500
Swimming pool sweep	1,000
Electric spa heater	12,000
Table saw	1,000
Television	300

18.8 Electrical Service

Once the electrical service enters the house it will pass through the *building service switch panel* [18–9]. This panel contains not only the main switch, but also, a *circuit breaker* or a *fuse* for each "hot" line [18–10 and 18–11]. Opening the main switch will interrupt the electrical current to the entire house. The two hot wires and the neutral wire then enter the *building load center*. This center distributes the electricity into a series of branch circuits serving different areas or functions within the building. Each branch circuit also has a circuit breaker or a fuse in the load center that will automatically open and break the circuit if there is an overload. A branch of the neutral wire is also continued on to a ground connection.

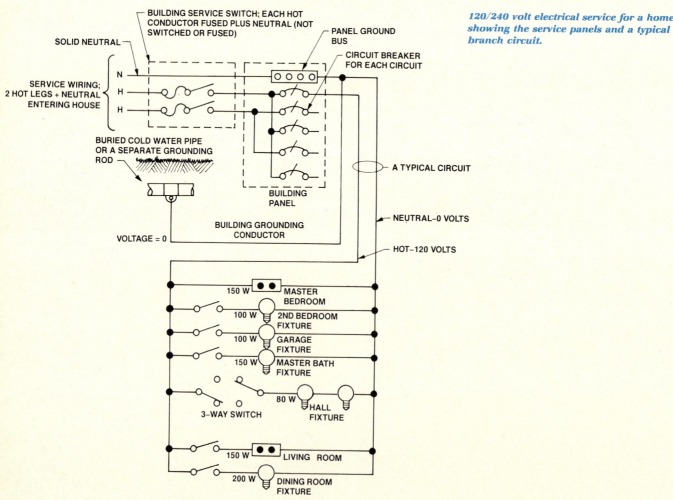

120/240 volt electrical service for a home, showing the service panels and a typical branch circuit.

Figure 18–9

This compact type of circuit breaker is capable of providing overcurrent protection for two different branch circuits.

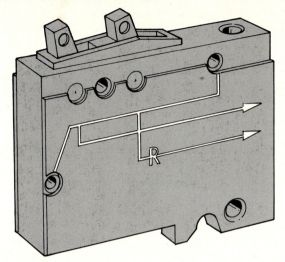

Figure 18–10

Common types of nonrenewable element fuses . . . (a) plug type and (b) cartridge type.

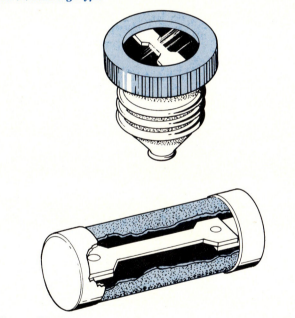

Figure 18–11

18.9 Safety

Two means are provided in electrical code requirements to protect people from shock and electrocution. The first is the use of *grounding receptacles,* and the second is the use of *ground-fault circuit interrupters.*

Figure [18–12] shows the typical three-wire circuit required for a grounding receptacle. The black (or red) hot wire has a voltage higher than that of the white neutral wire. The grounding system is the green wire (or a bare wire, or the metal conduit used to enclose the conductors). The neutral bus bar in the building panel is a copper strip to which the neutral and ground wires from all circuits are connected. This neutral bus is then securely connected to metal buried in the ground (either a rod driven into the ground or cold water pipes buried in the ground).

The power cord for the washer shown in [18–13] is connected to a branch circuit with a three-prong grounding plug. The center prong is connected to the metal cabinet of the appliance. If the black (hot) wire were to accidentally contact the cabinet, current would flow back through the green wire to ground and, consequently, open the circuit breaker. If the cabinet were not connected to ground, a person coming in contact with the cabinet and also touching ground would receive a shock and possibly be electrocuted. Large appliances and most power tools are required to have grounding cords and plugs. Many power hand tools are now double-insulated to eliminate the need for a grounding plug.

Some appliances are not provided with a three-prong plug. This can present a safety hazard that can be avoided by the use of a ground-fault circuit interrupter (GFCI) [18–14]. In a branch circuit that is working properly, the current is the same in the hot wire as in the neutral wire. The GFCI senses this condition. If the two currents are not of equal magnitude, meaning that current is flowing to ground through some improper path, the GFCI opens the circuit. The *National Electrical Code* (NEC) now requires ground-fault circuit interrupters in new

A three wire circuit is required for a grounding receptacle.

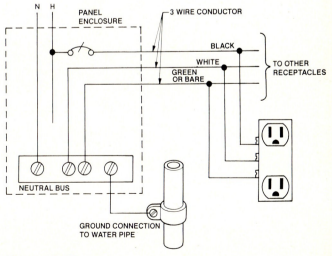

Figure 18–12

Electrical Systems

325

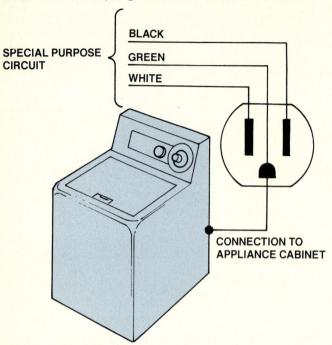

This washer is connected to a branch circuit with a three prong plug . . . the center prong is connected to the metal cabinet.

Figure 18-13

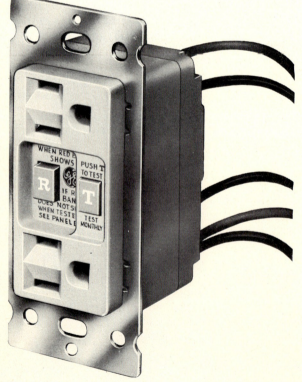

Ground-fault circuit interrupters can be installed in place of regular outlets . . . note indication, reset, and test features.

Figure 18-14

residential construction for bathroom, garage, and outdoor receptacles. They are also recommended for kitchen counter and laundry receptacles. Interrupters can be installed on individual outlets or can be incorporated in the branch circuit breaker, thus protecting all outlets on the circuit. Interrupters have a built-in self-test button and should be checked monthly for proper functioning.

18.10 Lighting Fixtures, Receptacles, and Switches

Whenever possible, buildings should be designed to take maximum advantage of natural lighting. It not only helps to create a pleasant environment but also saves energy. In any case, light from artificial sources must be provided at night and on overcast days. Artificial lighting is a key element in the design of an interesting and properly functioning building.

There are two basic methods of illumination—general and local. General lighting is a system designed to give uniform lighting throughout the area under consideration. Overhead fluorescent lights in an office provide general illumination of this type. Local lighting provides a small area of high-level lighting such as a lamp on a desk or a flood lamp over the kitchen sink.

Locating and selecting proper lighting fixtures requires careful study of the various visual tasks to be carried on in the space. These requirements must then be matched with the capabilities of the various lighting fixtures available. A blend of both built-in and portable fixtures is usually desirable. Fluorescent fixtures are more efficient than incandescent fixtures; however, their light quality is not always desirable. Figure [18–15] provides an idea of the basic classifications of lighting fixture types that are available.

Precise calculations are rarely necessary to design residential lighting. The lighting needs are so typical for homes that the architect can select sizes based on past experience. The main concern is to select fixtures that will give the appropriate atmosphere and appearance. A broad range of "moods" can be obtained by using different types of lighting. For example, direct fluorescent lighting is not flattering to the appearance of skin. For this reason it is too harsh for living room or bedroom use. It is best reserved for areas where a large quantity of light is more important than the quality of the lighting effect. Fluorescent lighting is usually used in the kitchen, basement, garage, and workshop. It is not recommended for the bathroom, if that is where facial make-up will be applied. Incandescent lighting (the typical light bulb) is a soft warm light appropriate for living spaces. Its effect can be altered somewhat by the type of fixture used.

A fixture that causes most of the light to shine up instead of down is called an *indirect light*. Indirect light-

Many types of lighting fixtures are available to serve a wide variety of needs.

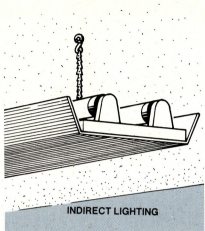

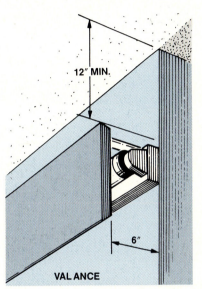
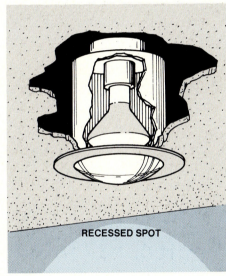

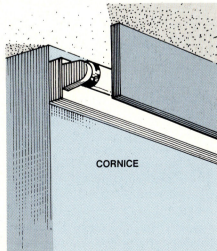
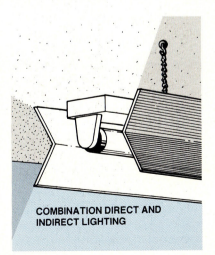

Figure 18–15

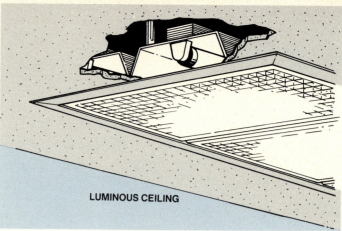
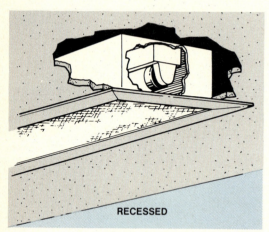

Figure 18–15 (continued)

ing is subtle and soft since it reaches the room by first being reflected off the ceiling [18–16]. Indirect fluorescent lighting is soft enough to use in living spaces. Indirect lighting may not be strong enough by itself to light certain activities such as reading, sewing, or recreational activities, so supplementary *direct lighting* is used. Direct lighting, where most of the light is directed downward toward the activity, can come in various forms. Fixtures may direct the light to a confined spot to accent a painting or a plant or they may spread it over the whole area. The architect or drafter must know how to select the proper lighting for different types of settings.

Placement of wall receptacles is less optional. The various building codes have minimum requirements for the location of these items. The codes are concerned with safety more than convenience although some of the regulations provide both. For example, no point along a wall can be more than six feet from a wall receptacle. This requirement reduces the need for extension cords since a cord from a lamp or TV is approximately 6 feet long.

Avoiding extension cords is a precaution against fire. You may wish to provide more outlets than required by code. In the kitchen of a modern home, there are usually more outlets than required by code because of the increased number of electrical appliances that have become available.

Switches must be located for convenience and economy. Light switches are usually located by the latch side of a door, inside the room. At times a room may be entered from two directions and may require the light to be operated from two places. This is common in kitchens, halls, and stairways. Switches that operate a light from two locations are called *three-way switches* [18–17]. Lights operated from two locations use three-way switches symbolized by "S_3". In this hall, the two light fixtures "A" can be turned on and off from either end of the hall. A *four-way switch* may be used with three-way switches in order to operate a light from three locations. This is expensive and should be avoided unless required by the design.

Indirect light is reflected light.

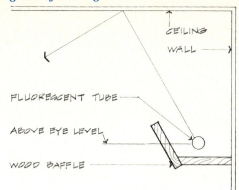

Figure 18–16

Three-way switches are used to operate a light from either of two locations.

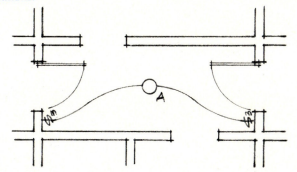

Figure 18–17

18.11 Electrical Layout

Electrical wiring in a building is rigidly controlled by building codes and should be installed by licensed electricians. However, the location of switches, fixtures, outlets, and controls must be determined by the designer. There are some basic rules that should be followed:

1. Outlets should be installed on an average of one for every 12 linear feet of wall.
2. Kitchen outlets should be installed on an average of one for every 4 linear feet of wall.
3. The main light source for each room should be controlled by a wall switch located at the room's entrance(s).
4. Not all lights and outlets in the room should be on the same circuit.
5. Walls between doors should always contain at least one outlet.
6. The height of all outlets should be listed on the plans. There are three switch variations that the designer may use:

1. *Single pole switch:* One switch controls a single fixture or multiple fixtures [18–18].

A single-pole switch controls lighting from one location.

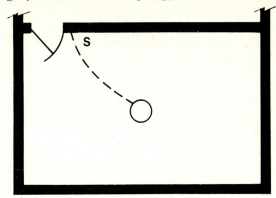

Figure 18–18

2. *Three-way switches:* Two three-way switches control one or more fixtures [18–19].

Three-way switches control lighting from two locations.

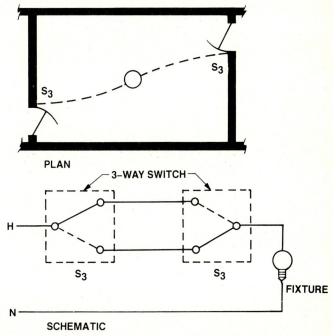

Figure 18–19

Electrical Systems

329

3. *Four-way switch:* A combination of three-way and four-way switches control one or more fixtures from three different locations in a room [18–20].

Three-way and four-way switches are used to control lighting from three locations.

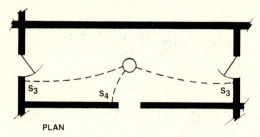

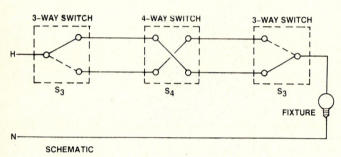

Figure 18–20

Some guidelines for the location of switches are as follows:

1. Indicate the height as well as the location of switches.
2. Lights for halls and stairways should be controlled from both ends.
3. Rooms that have only lamps should have an entry switch that controls an outlet into which at least one lamp is plugged.
4. The garage light should be controlled from one three-way switch in the garage and one three-way switch just inside the house.
5. Wall switches are preferred to pull strings in closets.
6. If the furniture arrangement in a bedroom is known, consider controlling room lighting from both the bedside as well as the room entrance.

18.12 Low-Voltage Switching

This method of switching control is becoming a very popular method of controlling electrical loads, and should be increasingly popular in view of the availability of computerized load management systems. With a low-voltage system, all lights in the house can be turned on or off from one point, for example, the bedroom. The switching system operates on 24 volts, so the control wiring size is small and inexpensive—like that used for the doorbell. A low-voltage control circuit diagram is shown in [18–21].

Switches are of the momentary contact type and as many as desired can be wired in parallel. This eliminates the complicated wiring for three-way and four-way switches. Also, switches can be added later with no complicated wiring changes. Since much of the heavier 12-gauge 120-volt wiring is eliminated, the overall cost of wiring is reduced.

18.13 Electrical Plans

Electrical plans should be as complete as possible so that the installation does not create surprises when the electrician has to make arbitrary decisions during construction. Using the floor plan, the designer should plan the exact location of all lighting fixtures, outlets, and appliances. The proper electrical symbols, as shown in [18–22], are then drawn on the floor plan.

A low voltage switching circuit . . . lights can be controlled from multiple, remote locations.

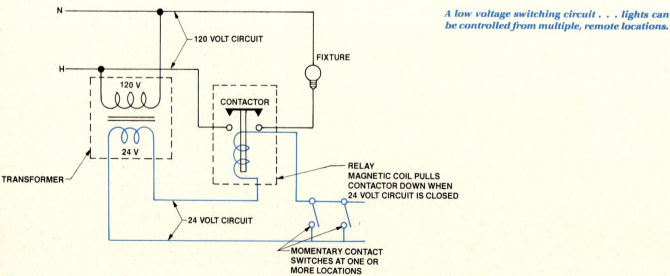

Figure 18–21

Electrical drawings use standard symbols.

Extracted from ANSI Y32.9–1972, American National Standard Graphic Symbols for Electrical Wiring and Layout Diagrams Used in Architecture and Building Construction, with the permission of the publisher, The Institute of Electrical and Electronic Engineers, 345 East 47th Street, New York, N.Y. 10017.

[a] Outlets requiring special identification may be indicated by the use of upper case letter abbreviations adjacent to the standard outlet symbol, for example: WP-Weatherproof, VT-Vaportight, WT-watertight, RT-Raintight, DT-Dusttight, EP-Explosionproof, R-Recessed, G-Grounded, UNG-Ungrounded.

[b] Use numeral or letter as a subscript alongside the symbol, keyed to explanation in the drawing list of symbols, to indicate type of receptacle or usage.

[c] Use subscript letters to indicate function (DW-Dishwasher, CD-Clothes Dryer, etc.).

Figure 18–22

Electrical plan for the Browne home.

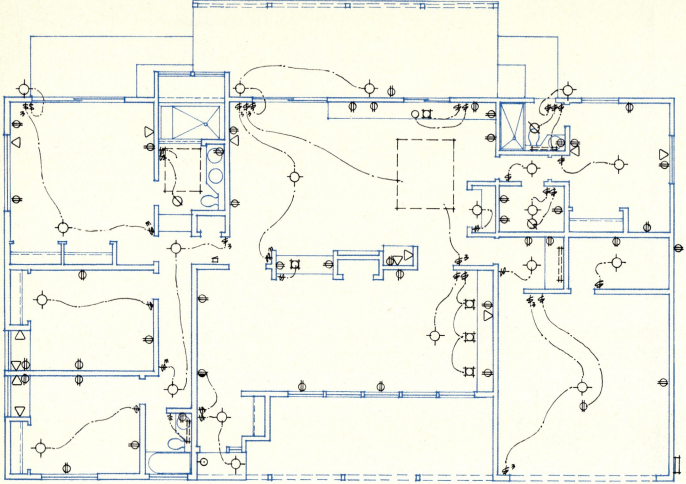

Figure 18–23

The exact position of each wire is not the responsibility of the designer, but rather of the electrician. However, the designer must show which switch controls which fixture or outlet. The designer should also locate the main panel and any subpanels, giving amperage information for each. Finally, an electrical fixture schedule with a symbol legend should be shown. Figure [18–23] shows the electrical plan for the Browne home.

EXERCISES

18–1. What is electricity? Define an ampere. Define a watt.

18–2. Check the electrical panel in your home. If the circuit breakers are not identified as to what they serve, determine this and place a diagram inside the panel door.

18–3. Make a sketch of your home's floor plan. Place proper symbols on the plan showing all electrical fixtures and devices.

18–4. Identify all special-purpose outlets in your home. Determine the power required by each outlet.

18–5. Lay out the outlets, lights, and switches for a home designated by your instructor. Show the symbols for each device. Show switching.

18–6. Draw a diagram showing how electric current is supplied to a ceiling light from the service entrance. Show wiring, switches, fuses, and circuit breakers.

18–7. Name three types of switches that might be used in a home. When would each be used?

18–8. What amperage capacity is necessary to serve a house with a 28,000-watt load (120/240 volts)?

18–9. The grounded neutral in a three-wire system is identified by what color of wire? What other wire colors are commonly used, and what do they signify?

18–10. It is desired to move the automatic toaster to a new location in a small restaurant. The nameplate on the toaster shows it to be rated at 2500 watts and it operates on 240-volt current. What is the amperage of the unit? Will No. 14 wire be adequate for this connection?

18–11. What is a circuit breaker?

18–12. Using prices in your locality make a comparison cost estimate of providing a low-voltage switching system for the Browne home instead of a conventional switching system.

IV

Construction Documentation

19 Construction Documents

Once the client is satisfied with the building design, the architect begins preparation of the technical documents from which the building will be constructed. These documents include the specifications, the working drawings, and the contract between the owner and the contractor. Working drawings show sizes, structural arrangement, shape, and location, while specifications indicate procedures and quality. The contract itself is often a standard form with minor changes made for each job. Variations of the contract will not be discussed in this book.

19.1 Architectural Specifications

Not all parts of a building can be clearly represented by drawings. For instance, it would be difficult to show texture or to "draw" a color of paint. Yet color and texture are important parts of a structure. Hardware, flooring, wall finishes, paneling, roofing, and lighting fixtures must be described in detail, and specific instructions for their application or installation must be given. Attempting to draw these instructions would be unwieldy. These tasks are much more easily performed by written instructions. This is where *specifications* of a project are most valuable. They are written instructions that are difficult to be shown graphically, but which are necessary for the completion of the work [19–1].

In the profession of architecture a standard format for the preparation of specifications has been adopted that makes their writing easier. In a like manner, standardization of the various chapters or "divisions" of the specifications makes comprehension easier. You should not concern yourself at this point with how to prepare the instructions that are required in each division of the specifications. This is a specialty in itself. It will, however, be of assistance to you to know that they are organized into 16 separate, standard divisions. These are:

Division	1	General Requirements
Division	2	Site Work
Division	3	Concrete
Division	4	Masonry
Division	5	Metals
Division	6	Wood and Plastics
Division	7	Thermal and Moisture Protection
Division	8	Doors and Windows
Division	9	Finishes
Division	10	Specialties
Division	11	Equipment
Division	12	Furnishings
Division	13	Special Construction
Division	14	Conveying Systems
Division	15	Mechanical
Division	16	Electrical

By use of these standardized divisions, you can describe what must be done and how it must be accomplished for those parts of a structure that are better de-

Specifications are an important part of the construction documents.

Figure 19–1

scribed in words than with a drawing. The specifications, along with the drawings, form two parts of the construction documents that help a builder to construct a building accurately and with minimum confusion. Accuracy in production of all parts of the documents is necessary to assure comprehension.

Figure [19–2] is an example of a specification for insulation. There may be several types of insulation in a building; if so, several more paragraphs would be needed. Insulation is, of course, only one item out of hundreds that would be described in a typical specification.

Notice that this specification describes the required U value for the wall or roof containing the insulation. The U value is a measure of the amount of heat a wall will transmit. Its use is discussed in more detail in Chapter 16. A certain thickness of insulation in the wall or roof is required to achieve this value. With this type of specification, calling out the thickness of the insulation in the drawings would be redundant and could cause confusion. The architect would have to calculate the thickness required and enter the correct thickness on the drawings. Any change in the insulation material or the wall material at a later date could cause the dimension on the drawing to be incorrect. Since the person making the changes may not be the person who drew the original drawings, it is possible that the dimension may not be adjusted properly. Thus any redundancy would create the possibility for an error. This is more apparent when you realize that hundreds of such relationships between specifications and drawings may exist.

A typical insulation specification.

Thermal and Moisture Protection
Division 7
Section 7A
Building Insulation

Part 1: General

1.1 Included herein is all wall and roof insulation required by drawings. Refer to drawings for location.

1.2 Following is a specification for type and general location of insulation. These locations are not all-inclusive. Insulation in miscellaneous areas as shown on the drawings and as required for a complete installation shall be furnished and installed.

1.3 Work not included consists of pipe, ducts, and equipment insulation, which is specified under Section 15.

Part 2: Materials

2.1 *Exterior Wall and Roof Insulation*
Batt or blanket insulation shall be mineral wool, Federal Specification HH–1–521E, 1984, width as required by framing; actual thickness shall provide a U value of 0.08 for the completed exterior wall construction and a U value of 0.04 for the completed roof construction as determined in accordance with recognized methods in agreement with the ASHRAE Handbook and Product Directory Fundamentals. Computations for establishing insulation thickness for the specified U value shall be submitted for approval.

2.2 *Marking*
Insulation shall bear identifying marks indicating grade of material and standards under which it is produced.

2.3 *Delivery and Storage*
Insulation shall be delivered to the site in undamaged condition and stored in fully covered, well-ventilated areas.

2.4 *Samples*
Two square feet of insulation together with the manufacturer's installation instructions shall be submitted to the architect for approval.

Part 3: Execution

3.1 *Installation*
Insulation shall be installed only when construction has advanced to the point that remaining construction operations will not damage the insulation.
Where electric outlets, ducts, pipes, vents, or other utility items occur, insulation shall be placed on the cold or weather side of the item. Installation, except as otherwise specified, shall be in accordance with the manufacturer's approved instructions.
Batt or blanket insulation shall be installed between framing members; and insulation facings shall be secured to the sides of the framing members to provide continuous seal and so that the entire weight of the insulation will be carried by the framing members.

Figure 19–2

Any references to insulation on the drawings that are covered by the specification should simply say "BATT INSULATION" or "BLANKET INSULATION," with no thickness mentioned. It would be appropriate to call out the thickness of the insulation (such as "4" BATT INSULATION") only if the specification made no reference from which a thickness could be derived.

19.2 Working Drawings

If it were possible to describe machinery, electrical circuits, or buildings verbally in enough detail to assure construction, there would be less need to make drawings. Just as primitive man found it easier to explain complex ideas by pictures, so the architect today can explain more clearly and exactly how a building is constructed by drawing much of the instructions, rather than attempting to use only words. Architectural drawings, therefore, are a form of communication.

As a form of language, drawings should be very clear to all who read them. By establishing rules for this "language," we can make the directions given by the drawings more easily understood. Many persons use the architectural drawings in their work. They are used by the builder and subcontractors, bankers, appraisers, building departments that issue permits, environmental control agencies, building inspectors, leasing agents, and the owner or tenant of the building. All must be able to understand the language used in drawing the plans. To accomplish this, the rules of preparing drawings must be carefully followed.

Working drawings include architectural and engineering information. On a large job this information will be on separate sheets and may be done by different offices. Architectural sheets describe the configuration of the site, the building, and the building elements. Engineering drawings describe the building site and the various systems of the building that require calculations in their design. These systems include structural, mechanical, plumbing, and electrical. The remainder of this chapter and the chapters that follow will discuss standard procedures for producing architectural and engineering working drawings.

19.3 Organization of Working Drawings

While a machine drafter may be able to show the top, front, and side views of a component part of a mechanical device on a single sheet of paper, the architectural drafter will likely require several larger sheets to display equivalent views of a building project. Moreover, architectural drawings are most commonly organized in their order of construction assembly. Therefore, *topographic maps* or *site plans* ("top" views of the land area) usually precede the *foundation drawings*. These are followed by *floor plans* ("top" views of each floor), and *elevations* (the front, side, and rear views of the structure). Following the elevations are the building *cross sections* (views cut through the building to show structural methods). In many cases the cross sections are followed by *wall sections*, indicating specific construction methods and finishes. Next come the *interior elevations*, which show finish materials, heights of fixtures, and cabinetry.

Finally, the architectural segment of the working drawings set will include the *construction details* of the building (such as windows, doors, cabinets, and so on) and the chartlike *schedules* that show paint colors, floor finishes, and wall and ceiling treatments that are more easily listed than drawn. The typical sequence of a set of architectural drawings for a home is shown in [19-3]. These are bound into a "set" of drawings for ease in handling by the contractors, subcontractors, and building inspectors [19-4].

Architectural drawings are arranged in a prescribed sequence.

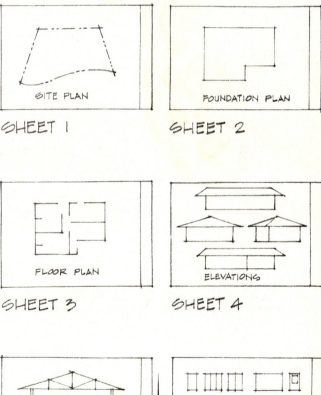

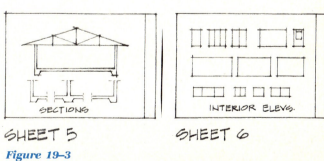

Figure 19-3

Construction Documents

337

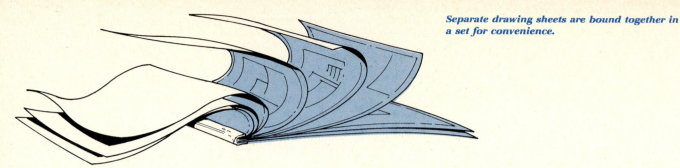

Separate drawing sheets are bound together in a set for convenience.

Figure 19–4

A home may not require formal engineering drawings. In this case, engineering information is included on the architectural sheets. Larger projects will use separate sheets after the architectural sheets to describe the structural, mechanical, plumbing, and electrical systems. Figure [19–5] shows a typical drawing sheet index from a light construction project. The order of drawings, especially in the engineering portion, may vary with the size and type of project. Each architectural office is also different and may establish individualized procedures to best suit its needs.

A typical drawing sheet index for a light construction project

A-1	Site Plan	M-1	Mechanical Room Plan
A-2	Floor Plan and Foundation Plan	M-2	HVAC Piping
		M-3	HVAC Air System
A-3	Elevations	M-4	HVAC Schedules
A-4	Building Section and Wall Sections	P-1	Plumbing Plan
		P-2	Plumbing Risers
A-5	Details and Schedules	E-1	Electrical Plan, Power
S-1	Framing Plan	E-2	Electrical Plan, Lighting
S-2	Structural Details		
MPE-1	Utility Site Plan		

Figure 19–5

19.4 Standards and Symbols

Architectural symbols and conventions are standardized to clarify the work and to provide consistency of interpretation. The more commonly used symbols are illustrated in [19–6] to [19–8]. Material symbols are not a substitute for notes. Each material must be "called out" (specified) even when its symbol is shown. The symbol shows the extent of the area to which the note applies. Symbols also help make a detail more readable by making a clearer distinction between materials.

Material symbols.

BRICK | FIREBRICK | CARPET

CLAY TILE | CONCRETE | CONCRETE BLOCK

EXISTING CONSTRUCTION TO BE REMOVED | GLASS: SHEET, PLATE, FLOAT | GRAVEL

CONCRETE: INSULATING | MARBLE | STEEL

PLASTIC | RESILIENT FLOORING | SAND OR FILL

FINISH WOOD, SECTION | PLYWOOD, SECTION | ROUGH WO SECTION, CONTINUOL FRAMING

Figure 19–6

338   Construction Documentation

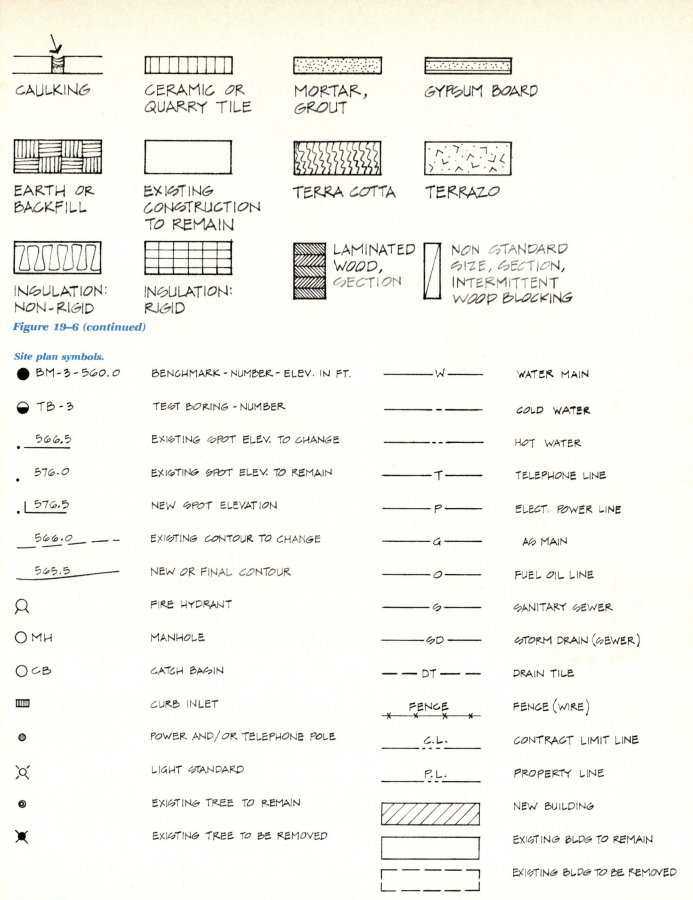

Figure 19-6 (continued)

Site plan symbols.

Figure 19-7

Reference symbols.

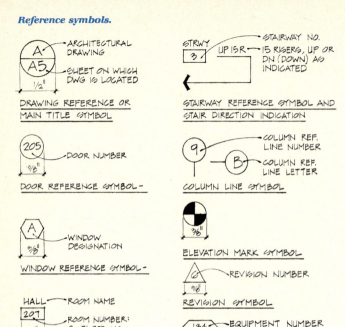

Figure 19–8

Stick-on title blocks may be used when preprinted sheets are unavailable.

Figure 19–9

19.5 Title Blocks

The size and location of the drawing sheet title block is usually standardized for each firm. It is commonly placed along the right-hand edge [25–1 to 25–7] or in the lower right-hand corner of the sheet. The right-edge location is usually preferred because it allows quick identification of each sheet as the set of drawings is unrolled. Also, this location allows ample space for the numerous data that should be included there.

Required information in the title block area includes the identity of the work; the name and address of the architect, and the name of the client; the names or initials of drafters, designers, and checkers of the work; revision blocks; and spaces for professional seals. In addition, each sheet must be numbered and dated. Precut drawing sheets usually have title blocks and borders preprinted on them. The name of the firm may also be included when preprinted title blocks are used. Stick-on title blocks may be obtained for use on sheets that are cut from roll stock [19–9]. These can be of a standard format or of a special design that includes the name of the firm.

EXERCISES

19–1. What type of information is found in the specifications in comparison to the type of information found in the drawings?

19–2. Under which standard division would the following items be found in the specifications?
   (a) Types of brick required.
   (b) Quality of lumber used.
   (c) Types of electrical insulation specified.

19–3. Give examples of items included in the following specification divisions.
   (a) Division 7: Thermal and Moisture Protection
   (b) Division 9: Finishes
   (c) Division 10: Specialties
   (d) Division 11: Equipment
   (e) Division 13: Special construction
   (Hint: Manufacturers' literature covering standard specification divisions may be found in *Sweet's Catalogs*. Every architectural firm and many libraries have a set of these catalogs.)

19–4. Using [19–5], on what working drawing sheets would you expect to find the following information?
   (a) Dimensions of paving.
   (b) Material used for siding.
   (c) Size of beams and joists.
   (d) Clearance between the furnace and surrounding walls.
   (e) Location of light fixtures and switches.

19–5. Where would you locate a roof plan in a set of working drawings? Why?

19–6. Where would you look to find the colors of the interior walls?

19–7. What kind of symbol would you use if you could not find a standard symbol for a material in your detail? (Hint: *Architectural Graphic Standards* by Ramsey & Sleeper, John Wiley, is a time-honored reference for commonly used architectural drawing symbols and details.)

19–8. Design a title block for the full length of the right edge of an 18- x 24-inch sheet. Include places for all the necessary information.

20 Developing Plans

20.1 Site Plans

Originally, we examined the site plan as part of the presentation drawings. The *working drawing site plan* has several differences. For example, no rendering is used. Usually, the outline of the building walls is shown instead of the outline of the roof. If the roof outline is shown, it is usually drawn with hidden (dashed) lines. The building must be dimensioned with respect to the property lines as many times as necessary in order to positively fix its location. A building that has two adjacent sides parallel to the property lines requires only two such dimensions to fix its location [20–1].

If no property lines are parallel to building walls, additional dimensions [20–2] or angles [20–3] are required. The dimensions of the building itself need not be shown on the site plan. These dimensions are shown at a larger scale on the floor plan. All other features to be built or installed on the site by the contractor should be dimensioned on the site plan.

A feature that is typical of most jobs is the paving. The paving configuration must be dimensioned as well as its position with respect to the property lines or the building [20–4]. Free-form driveways found at some homes should be based on arcs of circles for ease of dimensioning and constructing. If a truly free-form drive is desired, a series of points along its edge must be dimensioned. The contractor must be given specific instructions for laying out form work for the shape desired. A series of dimensions is the only way that this can be done.

Sidewalks and patios are other types of paving that must be dimensioned on the site plan unless they are dimensioned at a larger scale on the floor plan. Extensive landscaping may require a separate *landscape plan* where types and locations of plantings are shown. Existing trees to be preserved should be identified. Existing items to be removed, such as paving, foundations, or structures, should be noted on the site plan. Utility service lines may be shown on the architectural site plan for homes or on an engineering site plan for larger projects.

Only two dimensions are required to position this building.

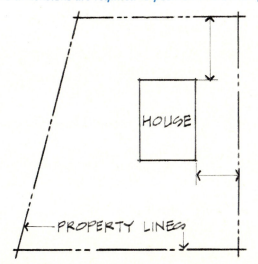

Figure 20–1

Four dimensions can be used to position this building . . . the dimensions are parallel or perpendicular to the same property line.

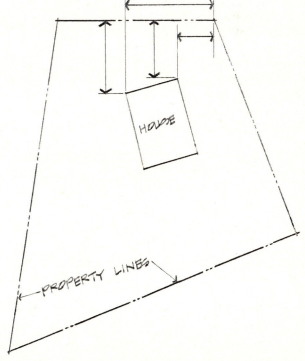

Figure 20–2

341

Two dimensions and two angles can be used to position this building . . . the dimensions are perpendicular to the sides of the building.

Land contours are shown on site plans with a series of equal elevation lines . . . each perspective view provides a three-dimensional interpretation of the corresponding plan view.

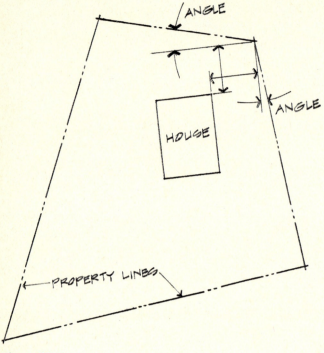

Figure 20–3

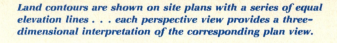

Paving must be dimensioned on the site plan.

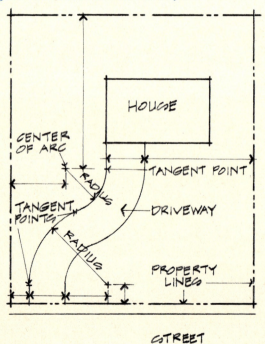

Figure 20–4

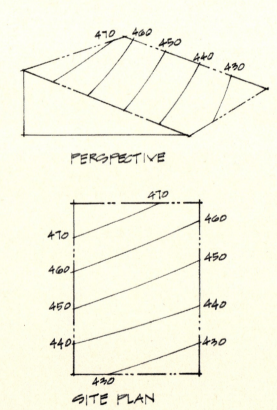

Figure 20–5

342

If the site is sloping, contours should be shown. *Contours* are lines connecting a series of points each of which is located at the same distance above sea level [20–5]. The elevation (distance in feet above sea level) is indicated by a number interrupting each contour line or marked near it. The vertical distance (*contour interval*) between all lines is the same on a site plan. Because of this, closely spaced lines represent steeper slopes than lines spaced farther apart. The contour interval may be different on different site plans.

If a building is built on sloping ground, the site plan will show different contour lines touching the building. The elevation of such a building must show the line of the sloping grade as it touches the building [20–6]. If part of a sloped site is leveled for a building, new contours are created on the site plan [20–7]. Final contours are often drawn as solid lines while the old contours are drawn dashed.

Although working drawing site plans are not rendered, simplified symbols are used for trees [20–8]. Single or double circles may be used to indicate trees, or a large dot representing the trunk of an existing tree may be

New contours are created when a sloped site is leveled . . . both new and old contour lines are drawn.

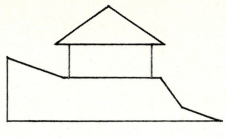

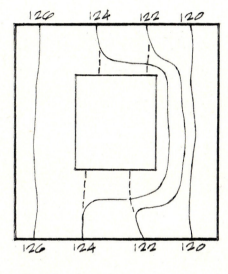

Figure 20–7

The elevation view of a building on sloping ground shows the sloping grade line.

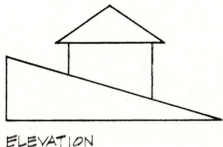

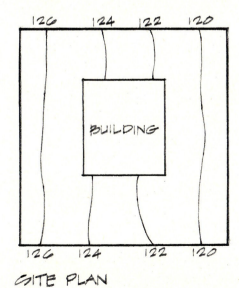

Figure 20–6

Working drawing site plans use simplified symbols to locate existing and new trees.

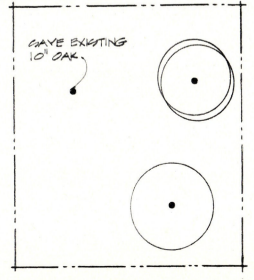

Figure 20–8

Developing Plans

used. The contractor must be informed which trees are to be removed, which are to be saved, and what new trees are to be planted.

20.2 Foundation Plans

The *foundation plan* shows the layout of the foundation walls, piers, and footings and locates them with dimensions [20–9]. If a building has a basement, the foundation plan is combined with the basement plan. Alterations to the foundation wall, such as vents, changes in elevation, and insertion of sleeves for mechanical purposes, are noted and dimensioned where necessary. If a concrete slab is used, the thickness of the slab and the size of its reinforcing is noted.

Although the convention varies, solid lines are usually used to represent the wall lines, while dashed lines show the edges of the footing. The footing is not dimensioned on the foundation plan. It is dimensioned, however, in a wall section.

20.3 Floor Plans

The *working drawing floor plan* is similar to the presentation floor plan in that they both view the same part of the building from the same orientation. They differ, however, in the information that is included. The working drawing floor plan is usually drawn with walls left undarkened, although wood grain [20–10] or light shading is sometimes used. Wood [20–11] or insulation symbols are sometimes drawn at the corners and around openings in the walls. Furniture and floor textures are omitted. There is no attempt to make the plan look three-dimensional or realistic. The contractors using the working drawings have seen many plans before and

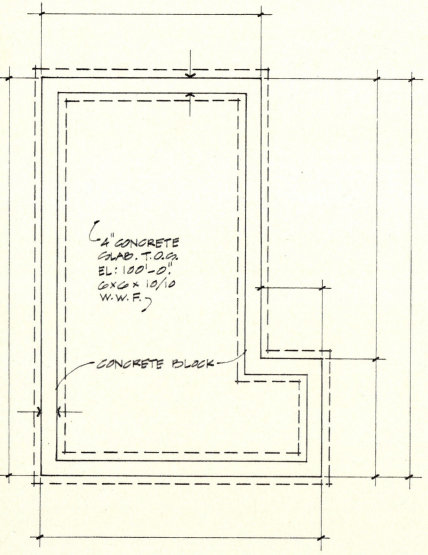

A foundation plan with dimension lines and slab notation . . . dashed lines show the edges of the footing.

Figure 20–9

Walls on working drawing floor plans are usually left undarkened, but a wood grain symbol may be used for a wood framed wall.

The wood grain symbol is sometimes drawn only at selected corners.

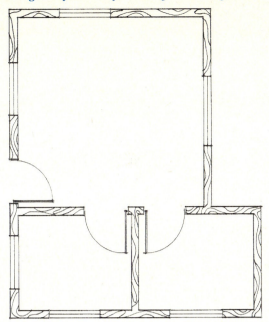

Figure 20-10

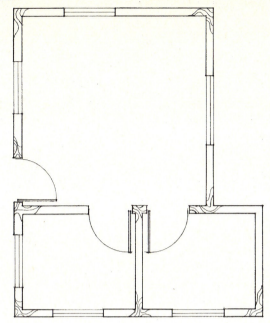

Figure 20-11

understand them without the embellishment necessary for lay persons.

The working drawing floor plan does include partition locations, built-in cabinetry, plumbing fixtures, and a variety of other information, such as electrical switch and fixture locations (residential only) and surface material references. The floor plan is drawn to scale, and it is dimensioned to precisely locate walls, door and window openings, and any special features. This drawing is the most used of the various architectural drawings. For this reason it usually contains cross-referenced data from the other drawings. By this means the builder is directed to other sheets within the set to find such things as exterior and interior elevations, structural cross sections, and specification information on doors and windows.

The positions and important features of all walls are located on the floor plan by dimensions [20-12 and 20-13]. The outside walls have two or three dimension lines, depending on the complexity of the plan shape. The line of dimensions closest to the building locates the wall openings (windows and doors). The middle dimension line locates changes in the building shape. The outermost dimension line gives the overall length. The overall length for each side must be shown on *all* sides of the plan. The dimension lines are parallel to the walls. It may seem repetitious to repeat the overall length on opposite sides of the building, but it provides an important reference for the person who is not intimately familiar with the building. For example, the contractor cannot assume that the building is rectangular until you verify it for him with dimensions.

For residential frame construction, windows and doors should be located (center to center) with center lines [20-12]. For masonry construction, these features should be located by dimensioning to the edges of openings [20-13]. Dimensions given to the edges of windows and doors in a stud wall stop at the window or door side of the stud adjacent to the opening. The dimension across the opening, then, is the *rough opening* (R.O.) dimension. Dimensions given to the edges of openings in a masonry wall are to the window or door side of the masonry bordering the opening. The dimension across the opening, then, is the measurement of the *masonry opening* (M.O.).

Usually interior features are dimensioned within the interior of the plan, while dimensions relating to exterior features lie outside the plan. Interior walls are located with a sequence of dimensions (a "string") running from outside to outside of the exterior walls. The dimension lines should run continuously through the plan. Do not skip back and forth with short dimension lines. Dimensions are more easily read when aligned into a single line. Residential wood frame walls may be dimensioned to their center line if they are on the interior. They may also be dimensioned to one or both faces of the studs. Masonry walls are dimensioned to one or both faces.

All rooms should have names. In complicated homes and commercial construction, each room is assigned a number. These numbers are usually marked in a square or rectangle positioned under or adjacent to the room name [20-14]. Windows are identified with letters in hexagons; doors are identified with numbers in circles. The geometric shapes around the letters and numbers may

Developing Plans

345

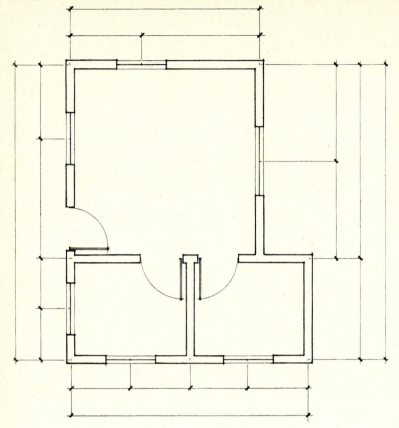

Residential frame construction . . . windows and doors are located with center to center dimensions.

Figure 20–12

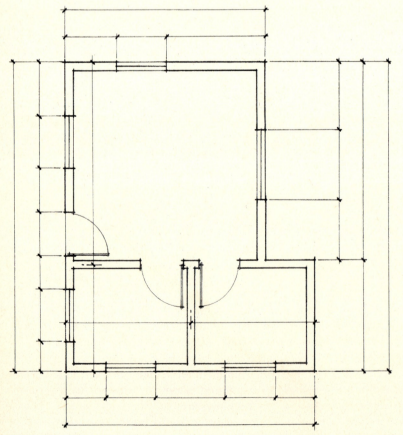

Masonry construction . . . windows and doors are located by dimensions to the edge of openings.

Figure 20–13

Rooms are named and assigned numbers . . . windows and doors are identified with letters and numbers shown in geometric symbols.

Reference symbols on a floor plan identify locations where details and sections have been made.

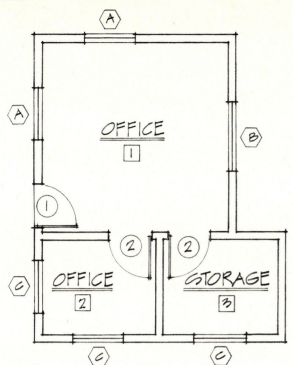

Figure 20–14

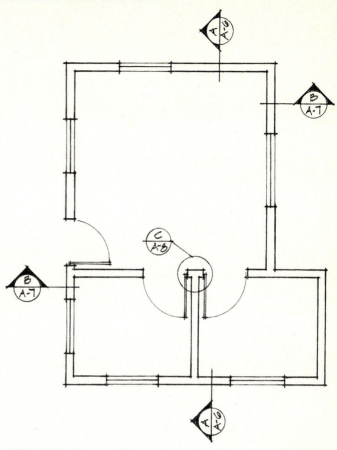

Figure 20–15

vary from office to office. The letters and numbers refer to schedules elsewhere in the drawings that list information that is too lengthy to show on the plan.

The floor plan also shows reference symbols to identify locations where details originate and where wall and building sections have been cut [20–15]. Typically, these are two part symbols. The upper number identifies the individual detail or section number; the lower number identifies the drawing sheet on which this detail or section is shown. The locations where detail drawings have been made are circled and marked with an adjacent reference symbol. Building section reference symbols have two section arrows that are aligned on opposite sides of the plan and point in the same direction. The wall section reference symbol has a similar-appearing arrow but is not used in pairs. Single wall section arrows are located on walls as necessary to identify differences in individual wall configurations. Note that all lettering on a drawing is positioned to read from the bottom or right side of the sheet.

20.4 Roof Plans

The *roof plan* is an optional drawing that is omitted from many projects. It is useful to clarify slopes for drainage on flat roofs [20–16] and to show the configuration of a sloped roof [20–17] when it is not clear from the

The floor plan for a flat roof helps clarify drainage slopes.

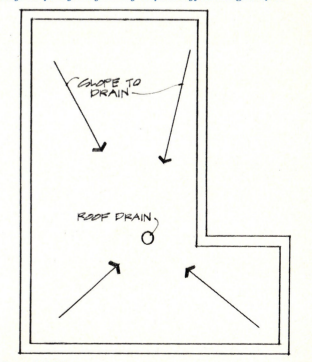

Figure 20–16

Developing Plans

347

A roof plan may be used to show a roof configuration that is not clear on the elevations.

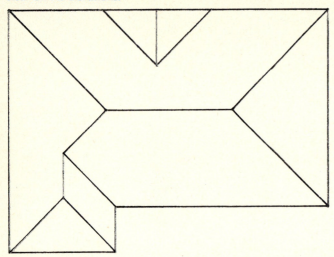

Figure 20–17

elevations. It may be combined with the site plan if the scale is large enough to show the needed detail.

20.5 Schedules

A *schedule* is a detailed list of building components. The materials and finishes on the interior surfaces of a building are identified in a *finish schedule* that is keyed to the room numbers on the floor plan [20–18]. Window information is provided in a *window schedule* that is keyed to the letters marked on the floor plan [20–19]. Door sizes, materials, and other information may be found in a *door schedule* that is keyed to the numbers marked on the floor plan [20–20].

The finish schedule shows materials and finishes on the interior surfaces of the various rooms in a building.

FINISH SCHEDULE										
NO.	ROOM	CEILING	N. WALL	E. WALL	S. WALL	W. WALL	WAINSCOT	BASE	FLOOR	REMARKS
1	FOYER	GYP. BD.	BRICK	GYP. BD.	GLASS	GYP. BD.	—	VINYL	BRICK	
2	RECEPTION	ACOUS. BD.	↓	↓	—	↓	—	↓	BRICK	GRAPHICS E. WALL
3	WAITING	↓	↓	↓	GYP. BD.	↓	—	↓	CARPET	
4	SEC. OFFICE	↓	GYP. BD.	↓	↓	↓	—	↓	V.T.	
5	SEC. OFFICE	↓	↓	↓	↓	↓	—	↓	V.T.	
6	GEN. MGR.	GYP. BD.	↓	BRICK	↓	↓	—	↓	CARPET	
7	ASST. MGR.	↓	↓	GYP. BD.	↓	BRICK	—	↓	↓	
8	OFFICE	ACOUS. BD.	↓	↓	↓	GYP. BD.	—	↓	V.T.	
9	OFFICE	↓	↓	↓	↓	↓	—	↓	V.T.	
10	OFFICE	↓	↓	↓	↓	↓	—	↓	V.T.	
11	OFFICE	↓	↓	↓	↓	↓	—	↓	V.T.	
12	TOILET	↓	CER. TILE	CER. TILE	CER. TILE	CER. TILE	—	↓	CER. TILE	
13	TOILET	↓	↓	↓	↓	↓	—	↓	↓	
14	JANITOR	↓	GYP. BD.	GYP. BD.	GYP. BD.	GYP. BD.	—	↓	V.T.	
15	HALL	↓	↓	↓	↓	↓	VINYL C'V'R	↓	V.T.	

Figure 20–18

WINDOW SCHEDULE						
Mark	Description	Size	Material	Glass	Detail	Remarks
A	CASEMENT	2'–0" × 6'–0"	Aluminum	½" insulated	Sheet A9	
B	CASEMENT	3'–0" × 6'–0"	Aluminum	½" insulated	Sheet A9	
C	DOUBLEHUNG	2'–6" × 4'–6"	Aluminum	½" insulated	Sheet A9	
D	DOUBLEHUNG	3'–0" × 5'–0"	Aluminum	½" insulated	Sheet A9	
E	AWNING	4'–0" × 2'–0"	Aluminum	½" insulated	Sheet A9	
F	FIXED	3'–0" × 8'–0"	Aluminum	½" insulated	Sheet A9	

The window schedule shows detailed information on the windows of a building . . . windows are identified by letters marked on the floor plan.

Figure 20–19

MARK	SIZE	TYPE	QTY.	MAT'L	HEAD	JAMB	SILL	REMARKS
				DOOR SCHEDULE				
1	3'×7'×1¾"	A	1	ALUM & GLASS	H-1	J-1	S-1	DK. BRONZE ALUM. FRAMES & BRONZE TEMP. GLASS
2	3'×6'⁸×1¾"	C	1	SOLID WOOD	DETAIL 9/9	DETAIL 6/9	–	
3	3'×6'⁸×1¾"	D	1	H.C. WOOD	H-2	J-2	–	
4	3'×6'⁸×1¾"	D	1	H.C. WOOD	H-2	J-2	–	
5	3'×6'⁸×1¾"	D	1	H.C. WOOD	H-2	J-2	–	
6	3'×6'⁸×1¾"	D	1	H.C. WOOD	H-2	J-2	–	

The door schedule shows detailed information on the doors of a building . . . doors are identified by numbers marked on the floor plan.

Figure 20–20

EXERCISES

20–1. What are the differences between a working drawing site plan and a presentation site plan?

20–2. List the notes and dimensions that are needed on a site plan.

20–3. Draw the site plan in [20–21] at a convenient scale. Apply all necessary dimensions. Assume that the building is 30'–0" × 60'–0". Make minor adjustments to the drive so that you can use radii to dimension its shape and position. Assume that the drive is 15'–0" wide.

20–4. Draw a cross section through the site shown in [20–22] at the location shown by the arrows. Assume that the site is 1000 feet wide. Use a convenient scale.

20–5. Is the land formation in the center of the site shown in [20–23] a ridge or a depression? How do you know?

20–6. Draw a foundation plan for the house in [7–19] at a scale of ¼" = 1'–0". Dimension the plan.

20–7. Draw the floor plan for the house in [7–20] at a scale of ¼" = 1'–0". Dimension the plan. Assign numbers to the rooms. Identify the windows and doors with appropriate letters and numbers.

20–8. Draw the roof plan for the house in [7–17] at a scale of ¼" = 1'–0".

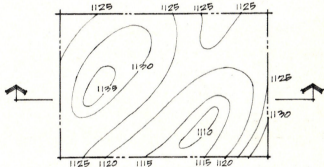

Figure 20–22

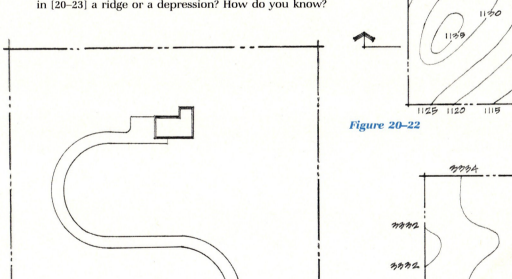

Figure 20–21

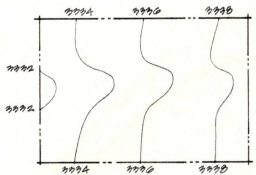

Figure 20–23

Developing Plans

21 Developing Elevations and Building Sections

21.1 Elevations

The *working drawing elevations* are similar in configuration to the presentation elevations but are not rendered. In addition, they show the footing and foundation as a dashed line. Working drawing elevations include the minimum amount of information necessary to construct the building. Resist the temptation to "show every shingle" or "draw every brick" in the building. Such work is time consuming and expensive. What is required by the builder is a minimal but clear indication of the materials that are to be used. Too much detail drawing on an elevation can confuse rather than enlighten the builder. In addition, changes and alterations are more easily made if the drawing is kept simple and readable.

Material symbols resemble those in the presentation drawings but much less of the symbol is drawn. The symbol is usually shown only at each edge of the material, leaving the central part open for notes [21–1]. The edges of material symbols may stop at 60° or 70° or in an irregular pattern. The edge of the material symbol used on each side of the elevation drawing should slant in the same direction on every elevation.

Typically, elevations have very few dimensions. Vertical dimensions that do not appear in detail drawings are shown on the elevations. The heights of windows and other major features are usually shown in section views, thus eliminating the need for them on the elevations. One set of major dimensions that may be repeated on the elevations is the height of the footing and of the roof structure with respect to the floor structure [21–2]. These heights (also called *elevations*) are seen in other details but may be helpful if shown on the elevation drawing as well. Note the shape of the symbol denoting elevation. These dimensions are especially needed for commercial buildings or complicated residences that have many floor and roof levels.

The height of the roof ridge may be omitted because the roof slope symbol establishes the height of the roof [21–3]. The ridge location is fixed once the starting point of the roof is dimensioned. The slope symbol is an upside-down right triangle. The altitude of the triangle is the number of units that the roof rises for the number of units shown measured horizontally.

Elements usually noted in the vertical dimension string are: the bottom of the footing, the top of the floors (called "top of finished floor"), and a location on some easily

Material symbols on working drawing elevations are shown only at the edge of the material . . . the symbol edge should slant in the same direction on every elevation.

The height of the footing and the roof structure with respect to the floor is often shown on elevations . . . describe the level on each extension line.

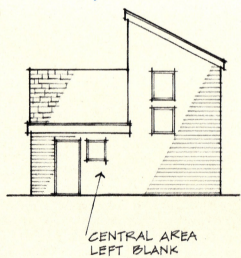

Figure 21–1

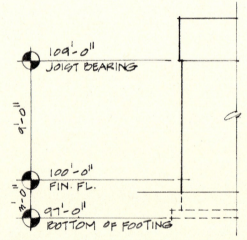

Figure 21–2

Elevation dimensions for important features are shown for more complex structures . . . the roof slope symbol establishes the overall height of the roof.

An expanded elevation provides an undistorted view of the angled face.

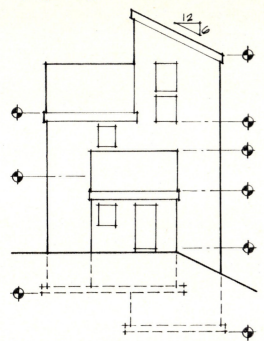

Figure 21–3

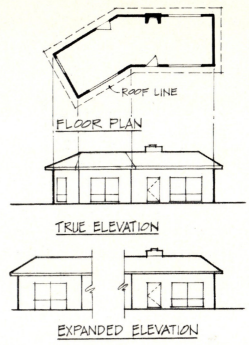

Figure 21–4

identifiable structural member at the roof such as the bearing of the horizontal roof joists (flat roofs) or the top of the double plate in the wall, (both of which are at the same height). Commercial buildings with steel structures can use the top of the structural steel or the bearing of open web steel joists. Since there is some flexibility as to what levels are "called out," always describe the level on the extension lines [21–2].

Call out all materials that appear in the elevation. Materials repeated throughout the elevations need not be noted in every view if their symbols are similar in appearance and the views are on the same sheet.

Both interior and exterior elevations will be drawn. Elevations are always drawn of all exterior walls. However, elevations are not drawn of all interior walls. Rather, views are drawn of only those partitions that require particular instructions and information for the builder, such as bathroom walls, kitchen walls with cabinetry, fireplace walls, and other walls against which cabinets or fixtures are installed [25–6].

In some situations a *true* multiview projection of an elevation from a plan view could present a confusing and distorted view. This is particularly true if some walls of the building are not at right angles to others. An example of such a building is shown in [21–4]. Note how a true elevation of the plan might tend to confuse the building contractor. In this case an *expanded elevation* is used to provide an undistorted view of the angled face. This helps to clarify the nature of the construction requirements. It also relieves you of the need to produce the more time consuming distorted view.

21.2 Cross Sections

Cross sections are views drawn primarily to describe structural framing procedures for the builder. Wall composition and framing at selected locations are exposed to view as in the presentation building section. It should be understood that these drawings are used to clarify the structural systems that are employed. *They should not be confused with interior elevations.*

A common mistake is to attempt to show an elevation view of the wall beyond the place where the section was cut [21–5]. This complicates the picture and can be confusing to the builder. Regardless of whether the section is for an entire building or for a component (such as a wall or fireplace), show only the relevant information *existing at the line of the cut*.

Avoid the temptation to combine cross-sectional information with other data. Information to help clarify the building section and to orient the viewer may be included. Room names and numbers and elevations (vertical dimensions) of major elements are sometimes shown. Detail reference symbols may be used to note portions that are drawn at a larger scale elsewhere in the set [21–6].

An overdrawn section . . . the line work and lettering is professional and the information is accurate, but the usefulness is reduced by including too much information and showing a wall elevation beyond the cut line.

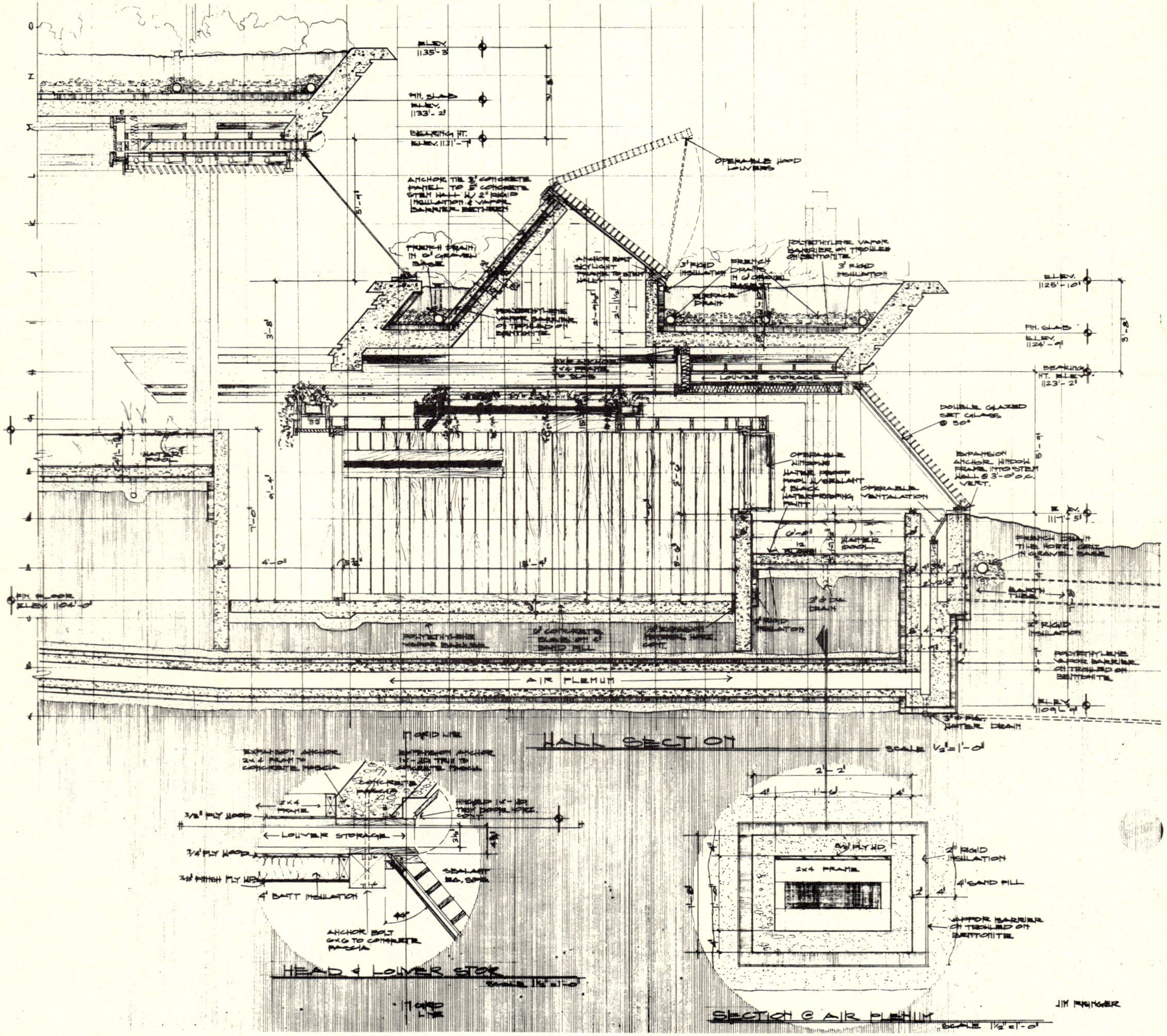

Figure 21-5

Detail reference symbols may be used on a section to note portions drawn at a larger scale elsewhere.

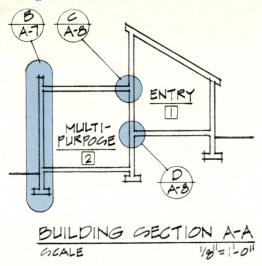

Figure 21–6

EXERCISES

21-1. What is the difference between working drawing elevations and presentation elevations?

21-2. Draw a working drawing elevation of the front of the house in [7–19]. Make assumptions for any information not known. Use a ¼" = 1'–0" scale.

21-3. What is the difference between working drawing building sections and presentation building sections?

21-4. Draw a building section across the short dimension of the house in [7–20]. Select the exact postion yourself. Use a ¼" = 1'–0" scale.

Developing Elevations and Building Sections

353

22 Developing Details

22.1 Detail Drawings

These drawings are the most difficult and challenging part of architectural drawing. They are commonly referred to as *details*. They show at large scale those elements of a building that are not practical to describe on small-scale drawings, such as elevations and plans. Because the items that require detailing must fit precisely into the total structure, it is important to be careful in their drawing. Windows, doors, and custom cabinetry are examples of items that are often drawn in large detail. Weatherproofing and surface treatments are also most commonly shown on detail drawings. The accurate assembly of framing parts is dependent on carefully drawn detail drawings.

22.2 Wall Sections

Many detail drawings are drawn as section views. The largest detailed sections are the *wall sections* that usually precede all others in a set of working drawings. The wall section shows the extent of a wall from footing to roof [22–1]. The scale for a wall section is usually $\frac{3}{4}'' = 1'-0''$ or $1'' = 1'-0''$ and must be stated on the drawing.

Material symbols are shown for all materials. If an area contains only one material, it is not entirely filled with the symbol. This is done to save time, to reduce the amount of graphite on the sheet, and to provide a clear space for other symbols and for leader arrows from notes. The material symbol is shown at the edge of the material, or at opposite ends if the space is long and narrow, such as a wall.

Vertical dimensions are shown on wall sections. All materials and elements are identified. Notes have their left edges aligned vertically and are placed as close as possible to the referenced item so the leaders can be short and direct. Reference symbols are shown if part of a wall section is to be enlarged in another detail.

Several wall sections are usually needed. Sections that show the connection of the roof and ceiling to the wall (where the members are perpendicular and parallel to the wall) are usually held to only the minimum number required. Wall sections are titled using letters corresponding to the section reference symbols marked on the floor plan.

22.3 Door and Window Details

Details are required showing how the doors and windows fit into the walls [22–2 to 22–5] in commercial construction and custom residential work. They are usually omitted for standard residential construction. Many types of windows are available [22–6]. Although door and window units have different sectional views, the

This wall section is a detail drawing of the wall from the footing to the roof.

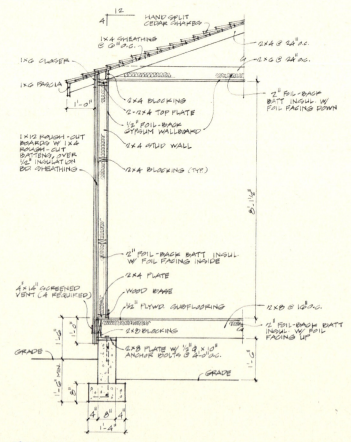

Figure 22–1

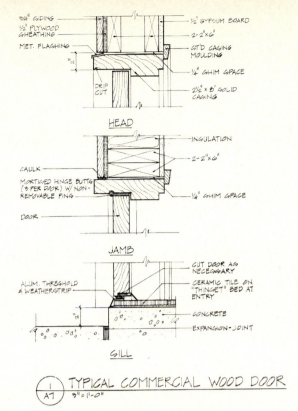

Figure 22–2 Typical commercial wood door.

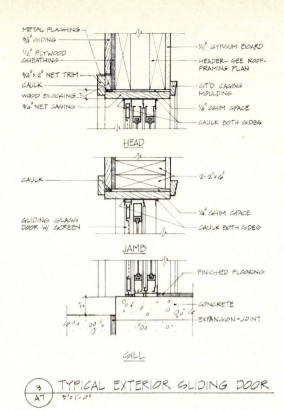

Figure 22–4 Typical exterior sliding door.

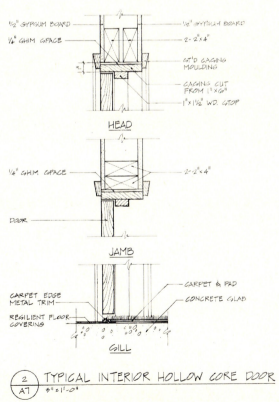

Figure 22–3 Typical interior hollow core door.

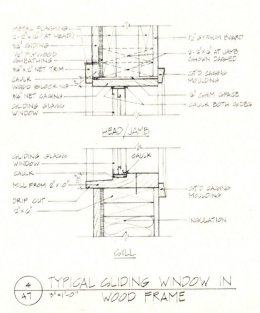

Figure 22–5 Typical sliding window in a wood frame.

Many types of windows are available.

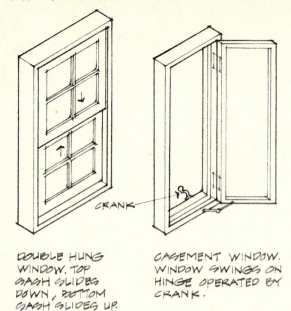

DOUBLE HUNG WINDOW. TOP SASH SLIDES DOWN, BOTTOM SASH SLIDES UP.

CASEMENT WINDOW. WINDOW SWINGS ON HINGE OPERATED BY CRANK.

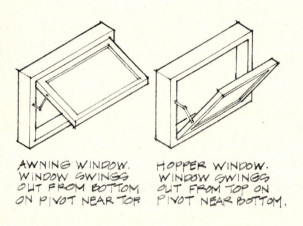

AWNING WINDOW. WINDOW SWINGS OUT FROM BOTTOM ON PIVOT NEAR TOP

HOPPER WINDOW. WINDOW SWINGS OUT FROM TOP ON PIVOT NEAR BOTTOM.

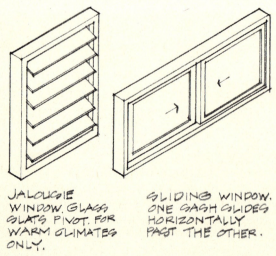

JALOUSIE WINDOW. GLASS SLATS PIVOT. FOR WARM CLIMATES ONLY.

SLIDING WINDOW. ONE SASH SLIDES HORIZONTALLY PAST THE OTHER.

Figure 22-6

basic requirements for detailing them are similar. The details are usually in three parts consisting of head, jamb, and sill sections. The *head* is the top of the opening, the *jamb* is the side, and the *sill* is the bottom of the opening. The head and jamb are usually drawn the same except for the framing adjacent to the unit and the flashing above the head. The head must support the wall above the door or window. Consequently, it must act as a beam. The structural member over an opening is called the *lintel*.

The lintel is made of two wood members (2 × 4's through 2 × 12's) or single wood members (4 × 6's through 4 × 12's) that are also called *headers*. The wood members are set on edge and increase in size as the opening gets wider. Minimum sizes for these members should be designed by engineering methods. For drawing purposes in home design you can usually assume that two 2 × 4's will span openings up to 2'–0", two 2 × 6's up to 3'–0", two 2 × 8's up to 4'–0", two 2 × 10's up to 5'–0", and two 2 × 12's up to 6'–0". Greater spans may be achieved with high-quality lumber.

The jamb does not have headers. The studs are doubled on the sides of the window or door unit, but are not turned on edge. They remain in the same relative orientation as other studs in the wall. A small space (about ¼ inch) is shown between the unit and the framing. This is the shim space and is the clearance required to slide a unit into the wall after the framing is in place.

All material symbols are shown in a door or window detail. All materials are called out at least once in the three views. A material, such as a wall covering, that is in the same relative position in all views and whose symbol is the same in all views need not be called out in all views. This is to save time and to reduce clutter in the detail. If you omit its identification, the type of material must be obvious to one who has never seen the drawing before.

The door unit may be fabricated in a factory or on the job by a carpenter. In either case it has a simple profile and is easily drawn. The window unit is prefabricated and is often complicated in profile. This is especially true of metal windows. Since the carpenter will only install the window, not fabricate it, the exact configuration of the window need not be drawn. The parts of the window profile that touch the wall must be drawn accurately, but the internal workings of hollow windows, for example, are not of interest to us. Those mechanisms and components of a window that are prefabricated and do not affect the fitting of the window into the wall may be simplified in drawing [22–7]. The criteria for simplifying the actual configuration is that it must be recognized as a window unit by the person(s) who will use the drawing.

The dimensions of the rough opening (the space between the rough framing members) are shown. The distance from the rough head to the floor is also shown

Window details can be simplified on working drawings.   **Partial sections are used to show special construction details.**

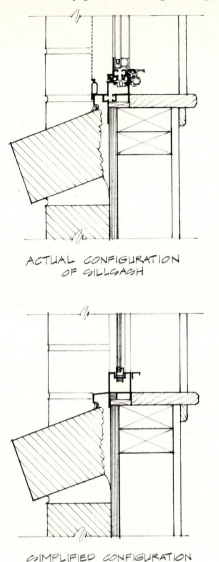

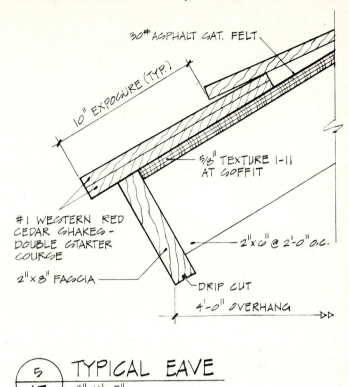

Figure 22–8

Figure 22–7

to set the height of the opening. Door and window details are usually drawn at a scale of $3'' = 1'-0''$. Manufacturer's details of several types of doors and windows are shown in Appendix D.

22.4 Miscellaneous Details

Any construction configuration that must be assembled by the contractor must have its own detail if it is not clear from other drawings. Every corner and connection in the building need not be drawn, however, since many items are built in accordance with standard construction practice. Miscellaneous details are drawn at various scales. Scales of $1\frac{1}{2}'' = 1'-0''$ and $3'' = 1'-0''$ are common.

If walls differ only in certain places, the other parts of the walls need not be duplicated. Supplementary details that are actually partial wall sections may be shown to explain variations without redrawing the entire wall [22–8 and 22–9].

22.5 Detail Drawing Sequence

A well-planned, sequential procedure, such as the six-step process shown in [22–10], is recommended when drawing details to obtain clean, neat results and to avoid smudging. Although detail drawing is meticulous work, it is also among the most enjoyable. This results because you will be called upon often to use innovative ideas in solving construction puzzles. You must be careful, however, to avoid the common tendency to "over-detail" a drawing.

Details should not be unnecessarily complex. They should not show items that could easily be shown elsewhere or items that are so common a part of construction practice that they do not need to be drawn at all. As an example, the manufacturers of many building components (for example, kitchen cabinets and dishwashers) fabricate their products away from the job site. In these

Developing Details

Partial sections may be sufficient to explain variations without redrawing an entire area.

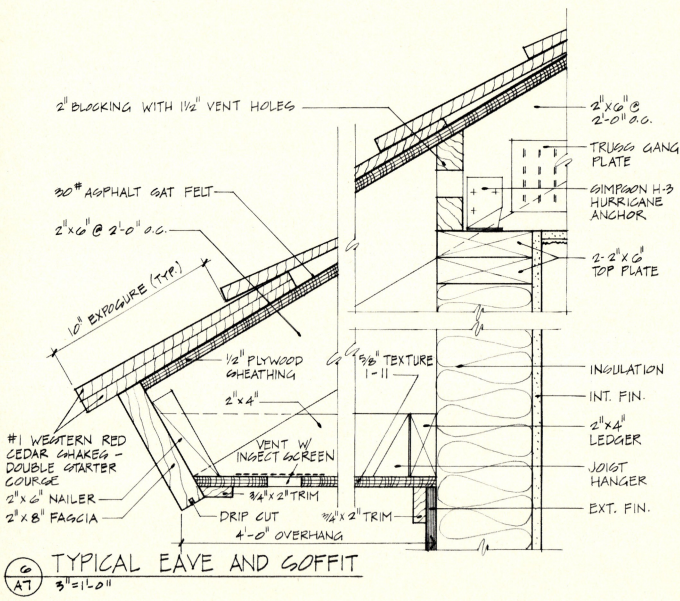

Figure 22–9

Sequential steps in drawing a detail.

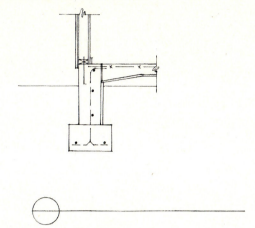

Figure 22–10A Lightly layout work

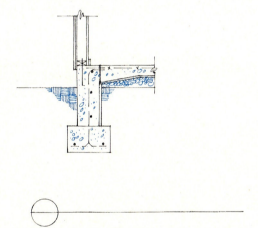

Figure 22–10B Add material symbols

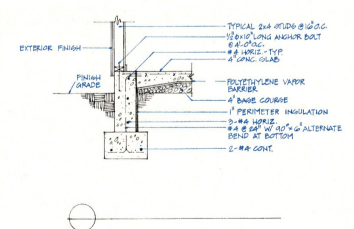

Figure 22–10C Add notes

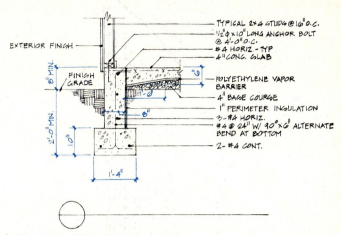

Figure 22–10D Add dimensions

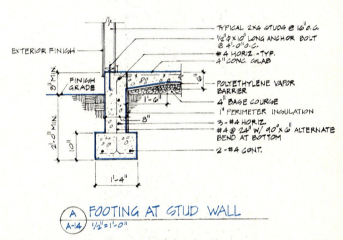

Figure 22–10E Darken outlines and add titles

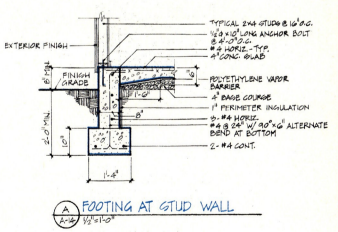

Figure 22–10F The finished work

instances you will only need to indicate their location (usually on an elevation) and to specify the item by manufacturer and catalog number. This restricts the contractor in selecting alternative units at a lower price, however, so you must make it clear if substitutes of equal quality are allowed. This is usually done in the specifications.

22.6 Clarity in Communications

It is important that architectural drawings be explicit, clear, and concise. Repetition should be avoided to reduce confusion. Redundancies in drawings (for example, showing a particular dimension in several places on the drawing) have the same effect as stammering in verbal communications. Both will confuse the reader or listener. A good drafter will adhere to the principle of "Say it once and say it right." Also, the more places that a dimension is repeated on the drawings, the more chance for error if a correction is overlooked during a design change.

Those who enjoy drafting must resist the tendency to draw too much. Repetitive dimensions and over-rendered details take extra time to draw and add little to the work. In fact, overdrawn work often confuses those attempting to read the prints. Excessive crosshatching, unnecessary notes, and extra dimensions do not clarify the drawing. Instead, they tend to obscure the clear picture that you are attempting to present.

Note in [22-11] how a simple detail of a concrete retaining wall can become confusing to a person reading the drawing. This drawing is overdrawn. It has repetitious notes, redundant dimensions, errors, and excessive material designations. Some dimensions are contradictory and confusing. The drawing in [22-12] is more properly drawn. It has a minimum but adequate number of notes and details. The material indications and dimensions are just sufficient to clarify the work and to permit construction. The drawing is easier to read and easier to use in construction.

22.7 The Drawing Check

As you proceed through the drawings for a set of plans, one of your most important tasks will be to "troubleshoot" the drawings in progress. This involves careful study of the drawings to discover and correct any errors that may have been made. For this work, proficiency increases with experience. It is usually a lot easier to discover someone else's errors than your own.

The check is more effective if done in an orderly manner. Prior to beginning the check, make a set of prints of your work. Mark all errors and changes in red pencil on the prints. Complete all markings prior to beginning

A crowded and unnecessarily detailed drawing is difficult to understand.

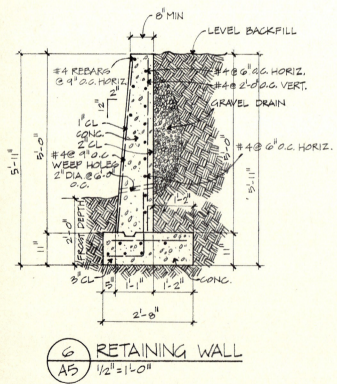

Figure 22–11

Simplify the drawing as much as possible.

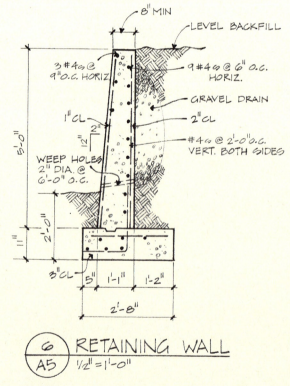

Figure 22–12

the corrections on the original drawings. As you make corrections, mark through the red notes on the print with a yellow pencil. When you have completed the corrections, you should review your marked-up set to see that all red marks now have matching yellow marks. Those that don't should be reviewed to see that corrections have been made. After your own check, your supervisor may want to make his own "red-line" set of new prints of your work. You may also be given the task of "red-lining" prints of other drafters to ensure that all errors are caught before construction begins.

EXERCISES

22–1. Name three typical types of detail drawings found in a set of working drawings. What scales are used for these details?

22–2. List 10 details that would be considered to be miscellaneous details. These are details that do not fit into any of the major categories of details. You will not be able to find all these in the text. Examine a set of working drawings and participate in group discussion to complete the list.

22–3. What elements, notes, and dimensions are included in a wall section? A door detail? A window detail?

22–4. The details in [22–13 to 22–17] include omissions and errors. Practice "red-lining" drawings by checking these details. Compare your conclusions with the corrected details shown in [22–18 to 22–22].

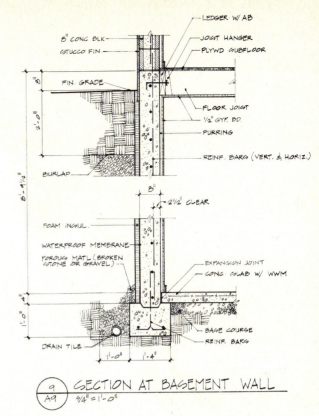

Figure 22–14

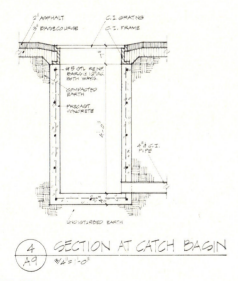

Figure 22–13

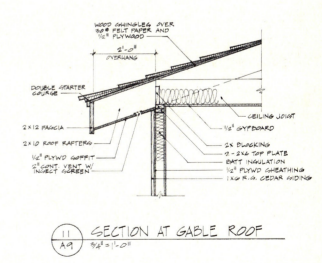

Figure 22–15

Developing Details

361

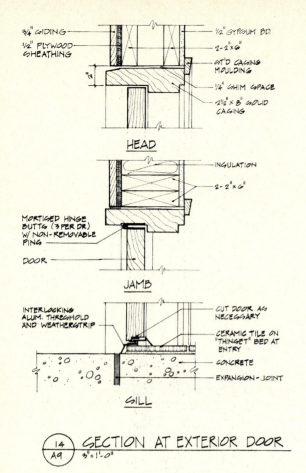

Figure 22–16

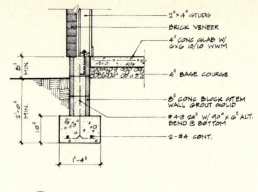

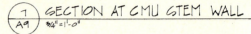

Figure 22–17

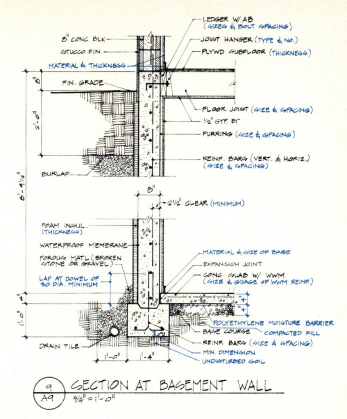

Figure 22-19

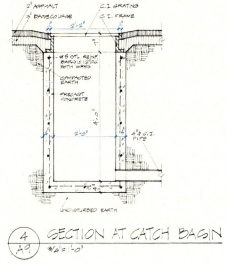

Figure 22-18

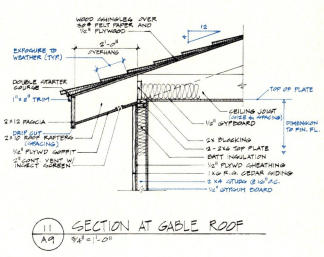

Figure 22-20

363

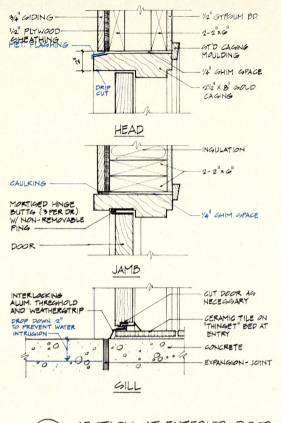
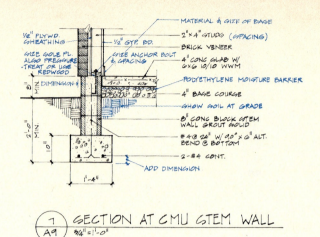

Figure 22–21

Figure 22–22

23 Developing Stair and Fireplace Details

Stairs in the past have ranged from the very steep and narrow in frontier homes to very grand in historic mansions [23–1 and 23–2]. Most stairs built today tend to fall somewhere between the extremes in an attempt to achieve a balance of economy, attractiveness, and utility [23–3].

23.1 Stair Details

Stairs are designed for comfort and safety. If a stair is too steep, it will be tiring to climb. If it does not have uniform and correct proportions, it may cause one to trip and fall. Residential stairs may be steeper than commercial stairs. This is because the occupants of a house use the same stairs daily and are used to them. Also, the frequency of use for residential stairs is less than for commercial stairs.

The horizontal part of a stair is called the *tread*. The vertical element is the *riser*. All of the effective individual tread lengths added together equal a distance called the *run*. All the risers added together equal a distance called the *rise* [23–4]. When designing interior stairs for multiple-story buildings the total rise for the stairs is more than the floor-to-ceiling height. The space accommodating the structure between the ceiling and the next floor must also be included.

Figure 23–1 Staircase in the Ruggles House, Columbia Falls, Maine.

Figure 23–2 Hanging staircase at Shirley Plantation Charles City County, Virginia.

A contemporary staircase . . . the visual limits of the surrounding spaces are extended through this stair due to its openness.

Figure 23–3

Specific terms are used to describe stairway elements.

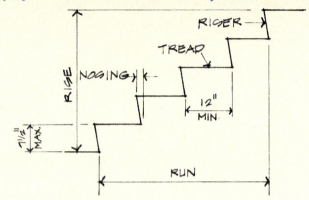

Figure 23–4

The maximum riser height for a residential stair is 8 inches. The minimum residential tread width is 9 inches. The maximum riser height for a commercial stair is 7½ inches. The minimum commercial tread width is 10 inches. The tread should overhang the riser by 1 inch. This overhang is called the *nosing*. It helps reduce the problem of people kicking the riser as they climb the stair. The nosing may be created by an overhang or by slanting the riser.

Exterior stairs should have slightly shorter risers and slightly wider treads to make them safer. This also makes them easier to use in bad weather. A 6-inch riser and a 12-inch tread is a common exterior step size.

Minimum stairway requirements . . .

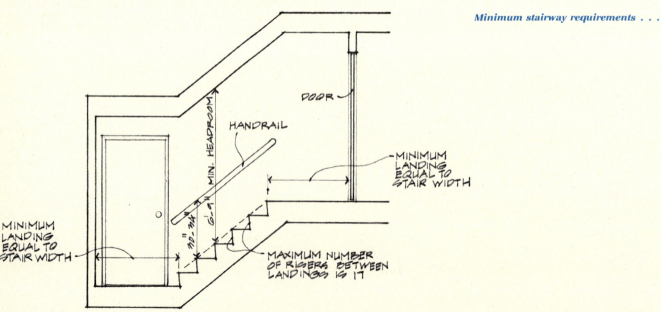

Figure 23–5

Construction Documentation

Stairs may be arranged in an L shape . . .

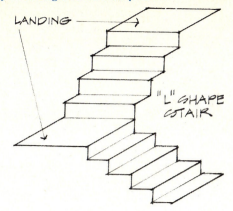

Figure 23–6

. . . or arranged in a U shape.

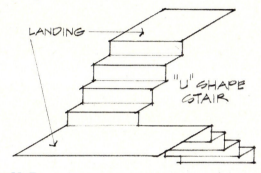

Figure 23–7

To design an interior stairway that meets acceptable proportions, use the following guidelines:

Riser Height × Tread Width = a number whose magnitude is 72 to 75

(2 × Riser Height) + Tread Width = a number whose magnitude is 24 to 25.

All stairs should have handrails [23–5]. The top of the handrail should be 30 to 34 inches above the tip of the nosing. The ceiling and any other obstructions above the stairway should be a minimum of 6'–9" above the tip of the nosing. Stairs are limited to a maximum of 17 risers between landings. This limitation helps prevent accidents due to fatigue.

If a stairway requires more than 17 risers, it must be interrupted with a landing at least equal in length to the stair width. A *landing* is a section of floor at the top, bottom, and sometimes in between groups of steps. Stairs may be straight run, L-shaped [23–6], or U-shaped [23–7]. The "winder" stair [23–8] changes direction with wedge-shaped steps and is prohibited in nonresidential buildings. It is not recommended for homes either, due to the danger it presents for tripping and falling.

A "winder" stair shape . . . not recommended.

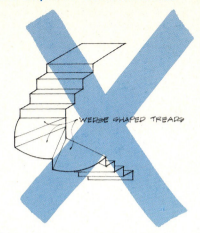

Figure 23–8

The width of a residential stair should be a minimum of 3'–0". If the center-to-center spacing of studs on either side of a stair opening is 3'–6", the clear space remaining for the stair will be about 3'–0". The width of commercial stairs varies with the number of people using it. Refer to the appropriate governing code to select the minimum dimension.

Residential and light commercial stairs are usually wood while commercial stairs may be steel or concrete. Wood stairs are supported by two or three stringers [23–9]. Stairs over 3 feet wide should have three stringers. Stringers are cut from 2 × 12's. Stair treads should be ¾ to 1¼ inches thick. Risers may be thinner or omitted for an open rise stair. The stringers are fastened to double headers at the top. They may be notched and set on a 2 × 4 *ledger* [23–9]. They should be prevented from sliding off the ledger by securing the bottom to the floor with a 2 × 4 *kick plate*. The opening in the floor around the stair is framed with double floor joists called *headers*

Construction details for wood stairs.

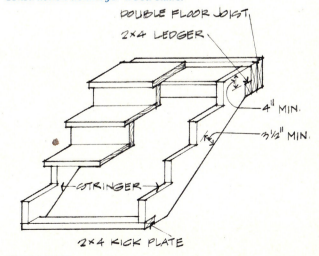

Figure 23–9

Developing Stair and Fireplace Details

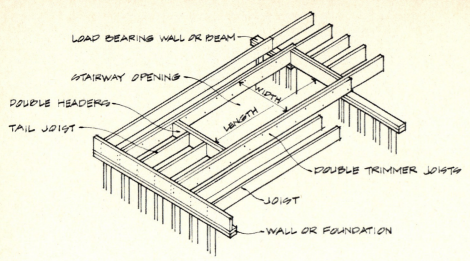

Floor opening framing for stairs . . . length of opening parallel to joists.

Figure 23–10

and *trimmers* [23–10 and 23–11]. In contemporary homes, the stairs are usually carpeted.

To design a stair, you must first determine the floor-to-floor distance that the stair spans. The sum of the floor joist size, thickness of floor materials, and the ceiling height is the floor-to-floor height [23–12].

Example 23–1

8′–0″	ceiling height
0½″	ceiling material
7¼″	joist depth
0¾″	floor material
8′–8½″	floor-to-floor height

Now divide the floor-to-floor height by 7¼ inches (a typical riser size) to find the number of risers required.

$$\frac{8'-8\frac{1}{2}''}{7\frac{1}{4}''} = \frac{104.5''}{7.25''} = 14.4 \text{ risers}$$

Since all risers must be equal height, this figure must be rounded to either 14 or 15 risers. Selection of 14 risers will cause the riser height to be greater than 7¼ inches. Selection of 15 risers will result in a riser height of less than 7¼ inches. Divide the floor to floor height by 14 risers to see if the resulting riser height is acceptable.

$$\frac{104.5''}{14} = 7.46'' \text{ riser height}$$

7.46 inches is the design height if 14 risers are used. This is an acceptable riser size.

Now select a suitable tread width. Ten inches will be examined to see if it is compatible with a 7.46-inch riser height.

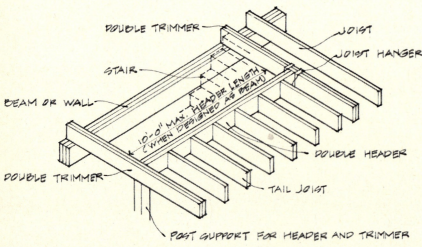

Floor opening framing for stairs . . . length of opening perpendicular to joists.

Figure 23–11

368   Construction Documentation

Computing floor-to-floor height for stairs.

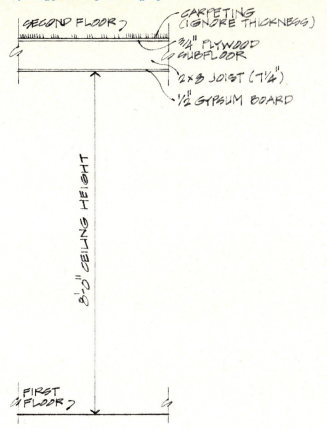

Figure 23-12

Riser Height × Tread Width = 72 to 75
7.46 × 10 = 74.6, which is between the limits 72 and 75

(2 × Riser Height) + Tread Width = 24 to 25
(2 × 7.46) + 10 = 24.92, which is between the limits 24 and 25

A 10-inch tread width is, therefore, compatible with a 7.46-inch riser height.

Finally, determine the space required for the stairway. A stair with 14 risers has 13 treads. The total stair run is 13 treads × 10 inches per tread.

13 × 10 inches = 130 inches, or 10′–10″

Therefore, space for a stairway with a length of 10′–10″ plus landings must be provided in the floor plan.

23.2 Nonresidential Stairs

In nonresidential construction, stairs are usually concrete or metal.* The choice of putting metal or concrete

---
* This section is adapted from American Stair Corporation literature.

interior stairs in a building depends principally on the building design, aesthetics, past cost experience, and personal preference.

Reinforced concrete buildings often have concrete stairs because carpenters and concrete laborers are readily available. However, it is not unusual for concrete buildings to have metal stairs. This is because metal stairs are frequently less expensive. Also, metal stairs are often put in concrete buildings when the stairs are to be heavily used because experience has shown that metal stairs typically have more uniform treads and risers than wood-formed concrete stairs.

Once the basic stair type has been chosen, the architect needs to consider the best method of construction. Metal stairs are available in two basic configurations—custom metal stairs and prefabricated stair systems. The custom metal stair is built on a job-by-job basis by metal fabricating shops to meet specific architectural design specifications. Each stair is designed anew for each job. The stairs are normally end-wall-supported since they are built to fit the designed stairwells. Field adjustments to compensate for construction irregularities may be difficult and certainly costly to correct. Therefore, each floor must be measured during the construction phase and prior to fabrication to ensure a proper fit. If concrete treads are used, they are normally poured on the site.

Prefabricated metal stair systems are built in a standard factory assembly line process with stringers, risers, and treads to meet specifications. These metal stair systems are side-wall-supported, allowing adjustment for stairwell construction irregularities.

Prefabricated steel stairs may be obtained several stories high [23–13]. Details of this type of stair are shown in [23–14]. These stairs are shop-fabricated and shop-erected into towers. The towers are then transported to the project for placement. Each tower contains the complete stairs for up to four floors or 40-foot heights. The towers can be stacked one upon the other, like building blocks, until the height of the building is attained.

A prepoured concrete tread that is field installed with the stair is immediately usable. It eliminates construction difficulties while concrete is drying. These stair systems are particularly economical in buildings that require many runs of standard stairs. Systems are also available in open riser design, with special treads, or with metal pans for field-poured treads.

A hybrid metal stair system is a stacked stair that consists of two or three floors of preassembled stairs trucked to the jobsite preconnected. They are limited in use since the building must be built around them, and the job must be within economical shipping distance of the stair suppliers. Generally, these stairs are not used in buildings over four stories high.

Concrete stairs may be made with metal forms. These pre-engineered factory built forms assure that poured concrete stairs are uniform, stair after stair, floor after

Prefabricated steel stairs may be obtained several stories high.

Figure 23–13

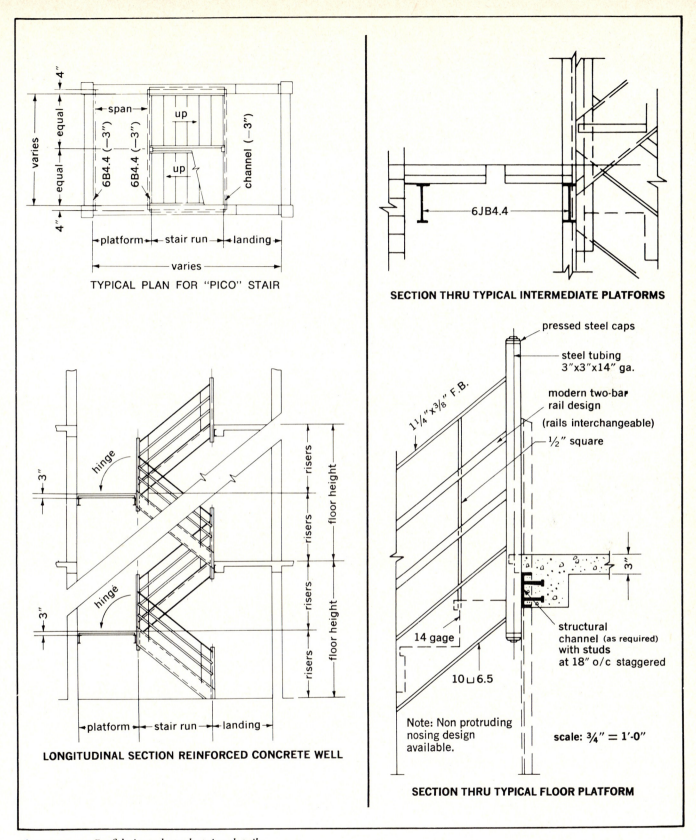

Figure 23-14 Prefabricated steel stairs details.

floor, regardless of the contractor used or the geographical area. [23–15] Patching to repair broken nosings, tilted risers, and crooked treads are reduced. The form becomes an aesthetic, integral part of the finished stair.

Concrete stairs can also be made with wood forms built in the field. The wood forms can become vulnerable to worker traffic, sometimes resulting in damaged risers or treads. Therefore, wood forming of stairs may require workers to use ladders and hoists for travel between floors. This delays easy access from floor to floor for a period of time.

Railings for interior stairs must serve two purposes—aesthetics and safety. Railing systems for both metal pan and concrete stairs are available. Designs are available using both square tubing and round tubing. It is recommended that railings be specified to be compatible with the products of the selected stair suppliers.

Spiral stairs are sometimes popular for supplementary

Prefabricated metal forms for building reinforced concrete stairs . . . these systems complete with metal riser fronts, reinforcing, and metal stringers, are welded into a rigid one-piece unit that remains in place after the concrete is poured.

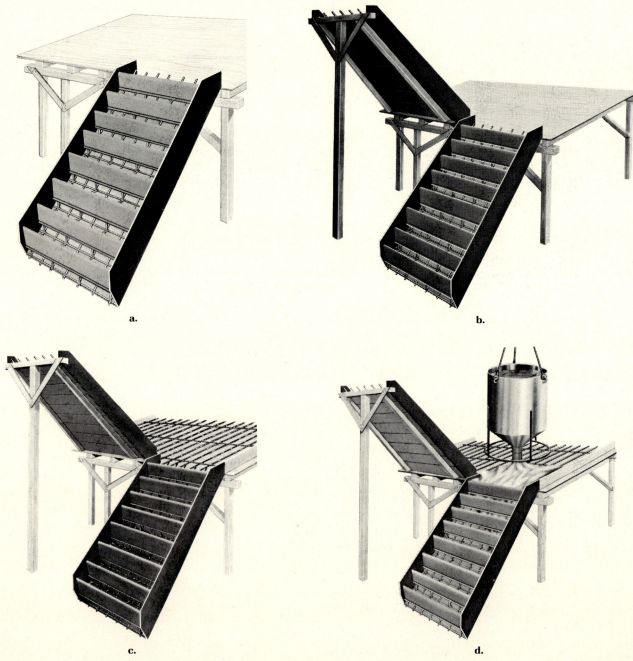

a.

b.

c.

d.

Figure 23–15

Spiral stairs are generally large and eye catching.

Figure 23–16

A traditional-style fireplace, open on one side.

Figure 23–17

entrance or exit and may also be used as visual features. They are not as easy to use as straight stairs and cannot be used to carry large pieces of furniture up or down. In nonresidential applications they are generally large and eye-catching [23–16]. Since codes require exit stairs for nonresidential buildings to be enclosed in fire-resistant construction, open spiral stairways are always supplementary to the required minimum number of "fire stairs."

EXERCISES

23–1. What conditions affect the tread size of the stair?
23–2. When is a landing required? What is the minimum size for a landing?
23–3. What is a nosing? Why is it needed? What size is a nosing?
23–4. The second floor of a two-story house is made up of 2×10's with a ⅝-inch subfloor. A ⅜-inch underlayment covers the subfloor. The ceiling of the first floor is ½-inch gypsum board. The ceiling height of the first floor is 7′–11″. Design a stair from the first floor to the second floor. How many risers are there? How many treads? What is the tread and riser size? How long is the total run?

23.2 Fireplaces

At one time wood-burning fireplaces were a necessity for heating. Their charm and the cozy atmosphere they create have kept them popular long after they were no longer essential for practical heating purposes. With the increasing interest in energy conservation, however, the wood-burning fireplace is again becoming useful as a supplementary or alternative heat source. The fireplaces of today, whether masonry or prefabricated steel, are much more efficient than the older versions.

Fireplaces may be open on one, two, or three sides [23–17]. Due to the lightweight steel flues that are now available, prefabricated fireplaces may be installed that are open on all sides [23–18]. The *flue* is hung from the ceiling or supported by thin steel members rising from the base. Free-standing metal fireplaces are available in many shapes and colors [23–19]. In this example, the flue exposed in the two-story space is an important visual feature.

Although the trend in fireplace styles is toward contemporary, traditional designs are still used. Facing materials for fireplaces may be stone, brick, or wood, or a combination of these materials [23–17] and [23–20] to [23–22].

Glass doors may be used to keep fire brands from popping out of the firebox [23–23]. They can also be used to keep the fireplace from using room air for combustion if the unit has a separate source of air from the outside. Drawing in room air increases infiltration of cold air into the room to replace the air that has been lost to the fireplace.

Fireplaces can be open on all sides

Figure 23-18

A free-standing prefabricated metal fireplace.

A fireplace in a wood covered wall.

Figure 23-19

Figure 23-20

Wood facing may be used on a fireplace.

Figure 23–21

A fireplace with brick and wood paneling.

Figure 23–22

Glass doors make a fireplace safer and more efficient if an outside source is available for combustion air.

Figure 23–23

A fireplace should not be placed where traffic must pass in front of it [23–24 and 23–25]. If the fireplace is the hub around which a conversational furniture grouping is centered, traffic is best routed so that the view of the fireplace is not interrupted.

Figure [23–26] shows typical details of a masonry fireplace. A masonry fireplace requires a masonry or con-

This fireplace is located at the "dead end" of the room so that through traffic does not pass in front of it.

Figure 23–24

Developing Stair and Fireplace Details

375

Better traffic pattern . . . fireplace is at the "dead end" of the room . . . the view of the fireplace is not interrupted.

Not recommended . . . traffic must pass in front of the fireplace.

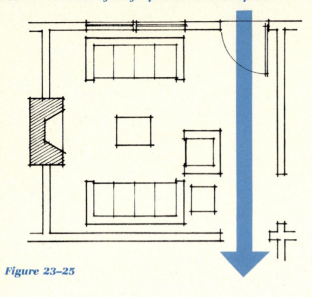
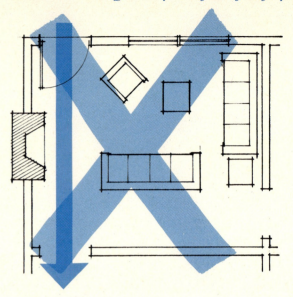

Figure 23–25

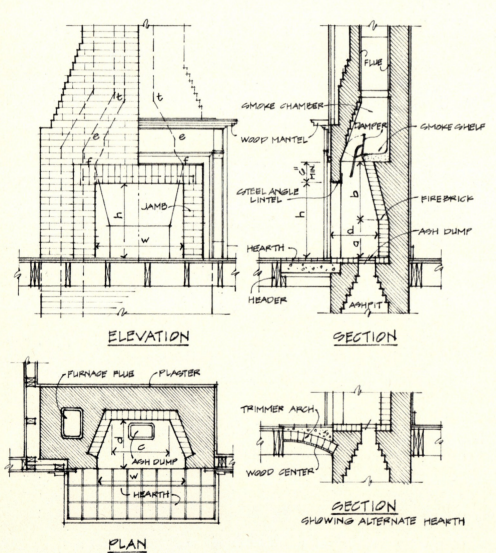

Figure 23–26 *Typical details of a masonry fireplace.*

Table 23–1. Recommended Dimensions for Fireplaces and Sizes of Flue Lining Required[a] (in.)

Size of Fireplace Opening		Depth d	Minimum Width of Back Wall c	Height of Vertical Back Wall a	Height of Inclined Back Wall b	Size of Flue Lining Required	
Width w	Height h					Standard Rectangular (Outside Dimensions)	Standard Round (Inside Diameter)
24	24	16–18	14	14	16	8½ × 13	10
28	24	16–18	14	14	16	8½ × 13	10
30	28–30	16–18	16	14	18	8½ × 13	10
36	28–30	16–18	22	14	18	8½ × 13	12
42	28–32	16–18	28	14	18	13 × 13	12
48	32	18–20	32	14	24	13 × 13	15
54	36	18–20	36	14	28	13 × 18	15
60	36	18–20	44	14	28	13 × 18	15
54	40	20–22	36	17	29	13 × 18	15
60	40	20–22	42	17	30	18 × 18	18
66	40	20–22	44	17	30	18 × 18	18
72	40	22–28	51	17	30	18 × 18	18

[a] Letters at the top of each column refer to [23–26].

crete foundation. As in the rest of the house, this foundation must distribute the weight of the fireplace and the chimney over a wide enough area so that the masonry will not sink into the ground. The minimum footing should extend at least 6 inches beyond the foundation on all sides and should be 8 inches thick for one-story houses and 12 inches thick for two-story houses. All footings that are in ground that is subject to freezing must be located below the frost line.

The *hearth* should be made of a noncombustible material, such as brick or clay tile. It should extend at least 20 inches out from the fireplace opening and 12 inches on either side of the opening. The hearth protects the floor from sparks and burning logs that may fall out of the fireplace. The depth of a fireplace should be about two-thirds the height of the opening. Recommended fireplace dimensions are shown in Table 23–1.

The fireplace chimney should extend at least 3 feet above flat roofs and at least 2 feet above a roof peak that is within 10 feet of the chimney [23–27]. No wood should be in contact with a chimney. A 2-inch space should be provided between any wood framing and a masonry chimney [23–28]. The 2-inch space should be filled with nonmetallic, noncombustible, loose material. Mortar is not appropriate since it would become a part of the chimney and eliminate the 2-inch space between the chimney and wood.

Care must be taken to keep water from entering the house at the point where the chimney passes through the roof. Metal *flashing* is built into the chimney and lapped with the roof shingles [23–29]. If the chimney pierces the roof below the peak, a *cricket* must be built on the upper side to keep water from pooling between the sloped roof and the chimney.

With the generation of heat becoming more important than just beauty, the prefabricated metal fireplace unit has become popular. These manufactured units that are designed for maximum heat yield to the home are far more effective than the traditional, custom masonry fireplace [23–30]. Metal units can be as attractive as masonry fireplaces since the only metal that shows is in the firebox. The metal unit is normally surrounded with wood framing [23–31]. The framing is then covered with any material that the owner desires. These fireplaces may be obtained with vents and fans that send additional heat into the fireplace room or into other rooms of the

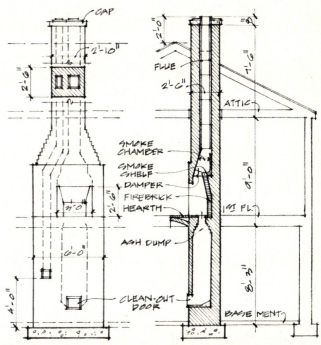

Figure 23–27 Elevation and section of a masonry fireplace from foundation to top of flue.

Developing Stair and Fireplace Details

A 2" space must be provided between wood framing and the chimney.

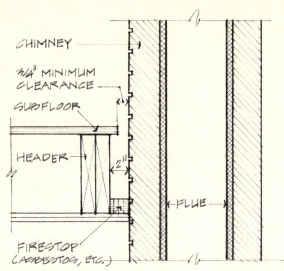

Figure 23-28

Prefabricated fireplace units are designed for maximum heat yield to the home.

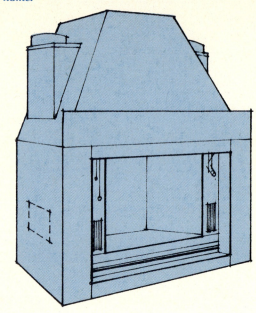

Figure 23-30

Care must be taken to prevent water leaks between the chimney and the roof.

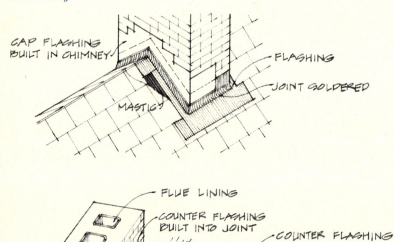

Figure 23-29

Metal fireplace units may be concealed behind wood framing . . . the framing can be covered with any materials the owner desires.

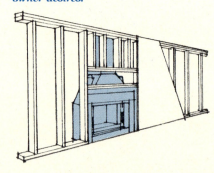

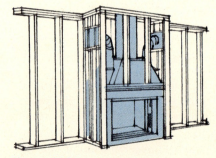

Figure 23-31

Fireplace units may have fans and vents to circulate heat.

A Heatilator prefabricated metal fireplace unit . . . arrows show cool air being drawn into the fireplace and warm air being returned to the room.

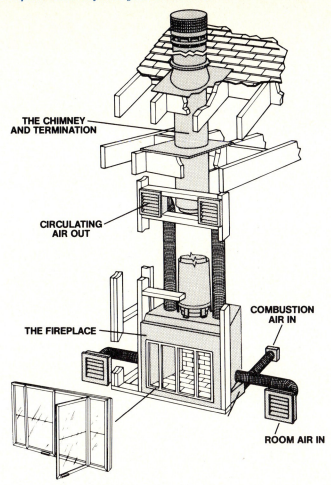

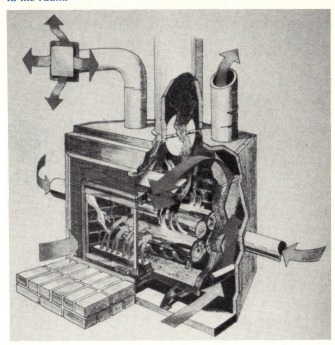

Figure 23–32

Figure 23–33

Installation of a metal fireplace unit . . . the flue is erected on the basic unit . . .

house [23–32]. Figures [23–33] to [23–38] show steps in the installation of a prefabricated metal fireplace unit.

Fireplace units may be positioned in many different orientations on a floor plan [23–39]. A variety of unit sizes are available. Figures [23–40] and [23–41] show a few of the sizes offered by one manufacturer.

The flues for prefabricated fireplace units are usually metal [23–42 and 23–43]. A double metal tube with insulation in between carries the smoke through the framing and out the roof. Metal tubes may be installed in different positions. Flue sections are available with angles in them so that a variety of turns can be made between the fireplace and the roof [23–44].

The part of the flue exposed to the outside may be painted or surrounded by wood framing [23–45]. The framing may be covered with siding or shingles or other light material. All chimneys must extend above the roof high enough to cause a draft in the flue. Chimneys that are too low will not draw the smoke up due to obstruction of the air currents by the roof. "Rules of thumb"

Figure 23–34

Developing Stair and Fireplace Details

. . . *ductwork is attached for circulating air,*

Figure 23-35

. . . *brick veneer is applied,*

Figure 23-37

. . . *detailing is added to the framing,*

Figure 23-36

. . . *and the fireplace is finished.*

Figure 23-38

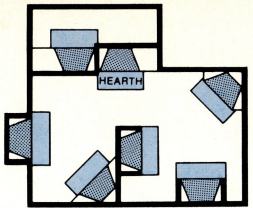

Fireplace units may be positioned in a variety of orientations.

HEARTH

Figure 23–39

5 15/16″
25 1/8″
37 3/4″
21 1/4″
28 3/4″
37″
5 5/8″
1 7/8″
1228 WITH GLASS DOORS
21 1/4″*
38 1/4″*
1238 WITH GLASS DOORS
21 1/4″*
43″*
1243 WITH GLASS DOORS
*Add 3/4″ to dimensions for "SHC" glass doors.
A
D
E
F
B
C
CORNER INSTALLATION

B1200 FRAMING DIMENSIONS

INSTALLATION	1228	1238	1243
A	49 1/2″	56 1/4″	59 5/8″
B	21″	30 1/2″	35 1/4″
C	70″	79 1/2″	84 1/4″
D	10 1/2″	15 1/4″	17 5/8″
E	35″	39 3/4″	42 1/8″
F	24 1/2″	24 1/2″	24 1/2″
G WITHOUT	2 1/2″	2 1/2″	2 1/2″
G WITH*	8″	8″	8″
G WITH**	11″	11″	11″
H	37″	46 1/2″	54 1/4″
J	5″	5″	5″

*COMBUSTION AIR KIT CAK-4
**COMBUSTION AIR KIT CAK-6

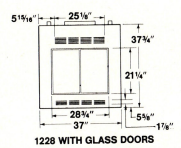

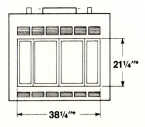

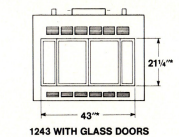

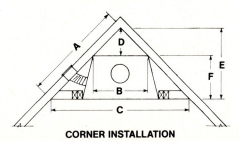

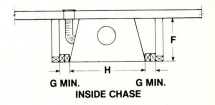

F
H
G MIN.
G MIN.
INSIDE CHASE
B
F
J
H
OUTSIDE CHASE

NOTE: DIAGRAMS & ILLUSTRATIONS NOT TO SCALE

Figure 23–40 *Typical fireplace unit sizes.*

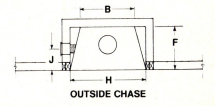

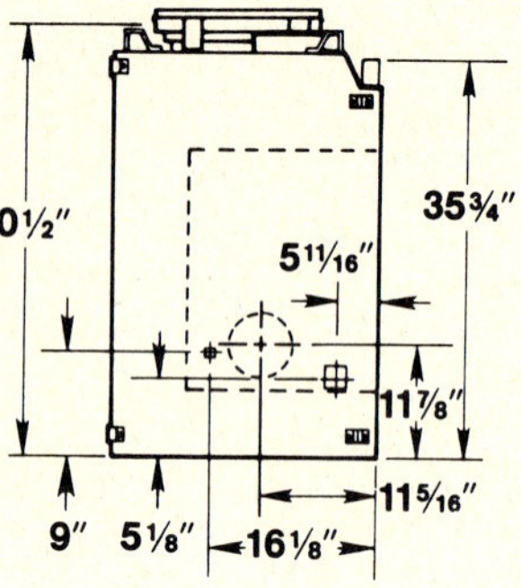

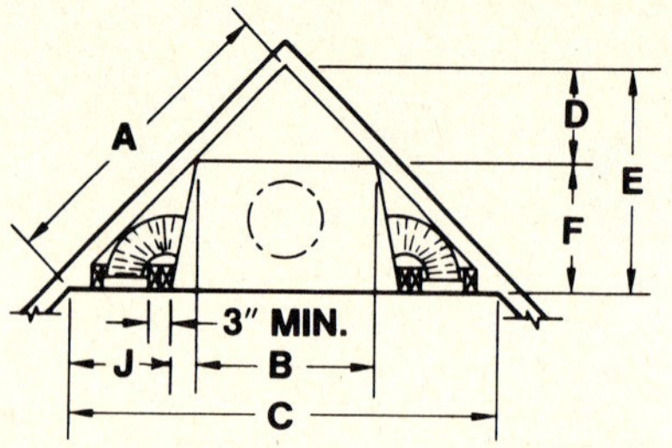

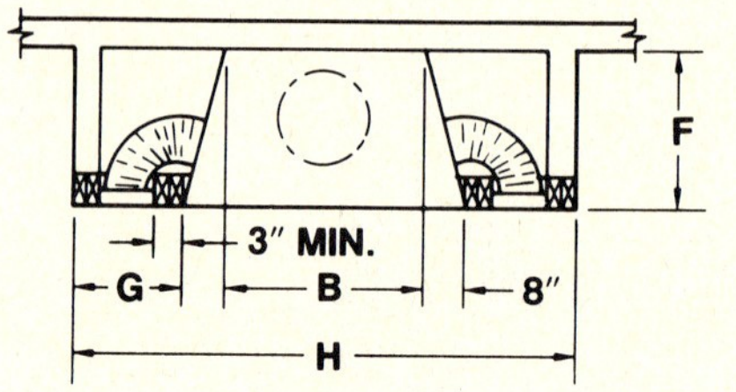

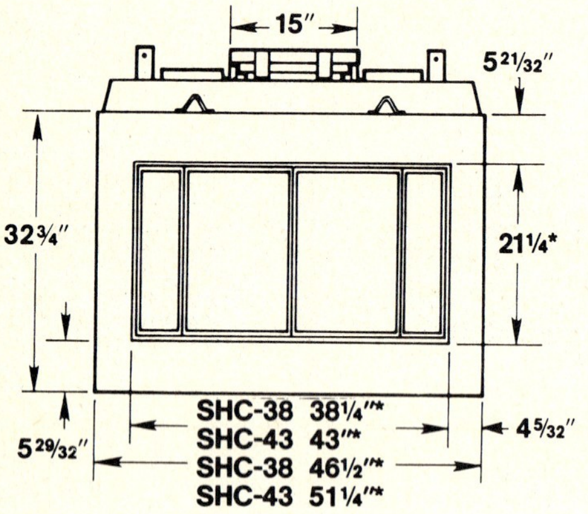

WITH GLASS DOORS

*Add ¾″ to dimensions for "SHC" glass doors.

ENERGIZER FRAMING DIMENSIONS

INSTALLATION		SHC-38	SHC-43
A_1	—	56¼	59⅝
B_1	B_2	30½	35¼
C_1	—	79½	84¼
D_1	—	15¼	17⅝
E_1	—	39¾	42⅛
F_1	F_2	24½	24½
G_1	—	14¼	14¼
H_1	—	75	79¾
J_1	—	16½	16½
—	A_2	68½	71¾
—	C_2	96¾	101½
—	D_2	23⅞	26¼
—	E_2	48⅜	50¾
—	G_2	16⅝	16⅝
—	H_2	79¾	84½
—	J_2	25⅛	25⅛

[1]Standard fireplace installed with natural convection (gravity) system or 180-FAK-3 Forced Air Kit.
[2]Fireplace installed with HD6-250-B Forced Air Kit.

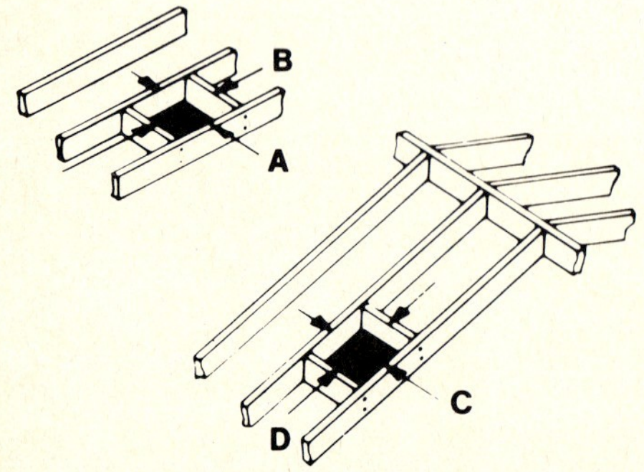

FRAMING DIMENSIONS FOR CHIMNEY ROUTE

Minimum allowable (includes clearance)

Type Flue	Ceiling Opening "A"	Ceiling Opening "B"	Roof Openings Pitch	Roof Openings "C"	Roof Openings "D"
AK10, Vertical	17″	17″	0/12	17″	17″
AK10, Offset 30°	17″*	26″*	6/12	17″	19″
(offset applies only to			12/12	17″	24″
ceiling openings)			60°	17″	34″
AS8/TF8, Vertical	14½″	14½″	0/12	14½″	14½″
AS8/TF8, Offset 30°	14½″*	25″*	6/12	14½″	17″
(offset applies only to			12/12	14½″	21½″
ceiling openings)			60°	14½″	30″

*Note:
Align chimney opening in same direction as offset flue pipe.

Figure 23–41 *Typical fireplace unit sizes (continued).*

Metal fireplace flues are double tubes with insulation in between.

Figure 23–42

Metal flues may be installed in different positions.

NOTE: Non-combustible Chase top must be used within 3 feet of underside of termination.

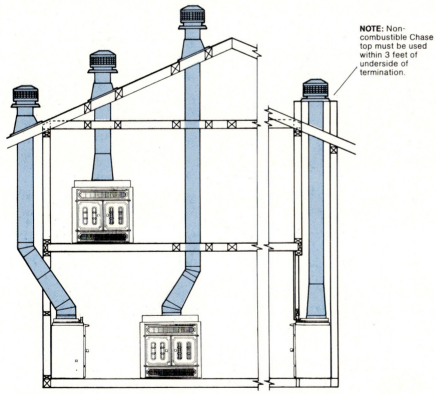

Figure 23–43

Metal flue sections are made with angles so that a variety of turns can be made.

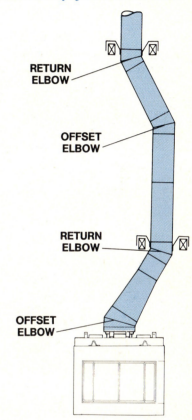

RETURN ELBOW

OFFSET ELBOW

RETURN ELBOW

OFFSET ELBOW

A minimum of one 12" length of flue or starter section must be installed between the offset and return

Figure 23–44

383

A metal flue may be covered with wood framing and siding.

Figure 23–45

for height above the roof are the same for metal flues as for masonry chimneys [23–46].

Traditional all-masonry fireplaces are more expensive than the metal units and have additional foundation requirements. The light metal units require only a strengthened floor structure below them.

EXERCISES

23–5. List the different types of fireplaces.

23–6. Name the main elements of a fireplace.

23–7. What are the advantages of a masonry fireplace over a prefabricated metal fireplace unit? What are the advantages of a prefabricated metal fireplace unit over a masonry fireplace?

23–8. A fireplace has an opening 28 inches wide by 24 inches high. How deep should the firebox be?

23–9. A chimney sets 12′–0″ away from the ridge on a roof that slopes 6 in 12. How high above the point of contact with the roof must the chimney rise?

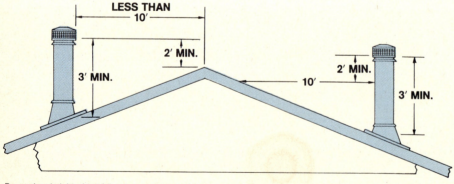

Flues and chimneys have specific height requirements.

Remember, height of total fireplace system must be not less than 12′0″ nor greater than 80′0″.

Figure 23–46

384   Construction Documentation

24 Engineering Drawings

24.1 Types of Engineering Drawings

The working drawings related to the construction of the sheltering and social aspects of a building (such as the walls, roof, doors, and windows) are called *architectural drawings.* Typically they do not require numerical calculations but are based on judgements in regard to appearance, function, and code requirements. Those drawings for which numerical calculations are required are called *engineering drawings.* They fall into two categories: structural and environmental control.

Commercial construction projects require separate sheets for the engineering drawings. The numbers for these drawing sheets have a prefix indicating the type of drawing on that sheet. The letter "S" represents structural, an "M" represents mechanical work, "E" is for electrical, and "P" stands for plumbing. A site plan showing mechanical, electrical, and plumbing information might be called "MPE." Sometimes the plumbing is included in the mechanical section under the prefix "M."

The order of the engineering drawing sheets is usually the structural followed by the mechanical, electrical, and plumbing. The different types of engineering drawing sheets may be drawn by the same or different engineering offices. If the engineering drawings are done in the same office as the architectural sheets, they usually are not drawn by the same person. It is also common practice for the engineering drawings to be prepared at the same time that the architectural sheets are drawn. Because of these circumstances, it is easier to start the numbering system over with each type of drawing sheet. The first structural sheet will be S-1 and not a continuation of the numbers on the architectural sheets. The first mechanical sheet will be M-1, and so on. The engineering site plans precede the other sheets in each group. All engineering drawings follow the architectural sheets [19–5].

The types and formats of engineering drawings required are similar for each commercial project. This helps to compensate for the dissimilar and complex nature of the engineering systems of each job. For residences where the engineering systems are not particularly large or complex, an explanation of their construction details may be done using notes and specifications rather than formal engineering drawings.

24.2 Structural Working Drawings

Residential structural drawings may consist of only a *roof framing plan* for a slab-on-grade one-story house. This framing plan may be included as one of the architectural sheets. It may also be combined with another drawing, such as the site plan [25–1] or the floor plan. If the first floor is wood structure, its framing plan may be shown on the foundation plan. These framing plans, when combined with the floor or foundation plan, are only partially drawn, usually with dashed lines. The architectural plans have too much other information on them to allow a complete framing plan to be superimposed. A simple roof truss system may be partially described in dashed lines on the elevation.

Nonresidential structural drawings typically are separate from other drawings. The *foundation plan* [24–1] will show dimensions for the foundation walls and openings in the wall; changes in footing, foundation wall, and slab elevations; joints in the slab and other information about the slab; references for details [24–2]; and other information necessary to build the foundation. All plans should have a north arrow. If a project has columns, it is possible that a schedule will be used to describe the size and reinforcing in the footings and the reinforcing in the columns if they are concrete [24–3].

A *framing plan* is provided for all floors and the roof of a non-residential building [24–4]. The framing plan shows the position of the framing members, that is, wood or steel joists and beams. The sizes of members are called out and elevations should be noted. Reference symbols are shown for details [24–5].

24.3 Mechanical Working Drawings

Commercial building projects require one or more sheets describing the heating, ventilating, and air conditioning (*HVAC*) systems of the building. A *mechanical*

Partial foundation plan for a nonresidential building.

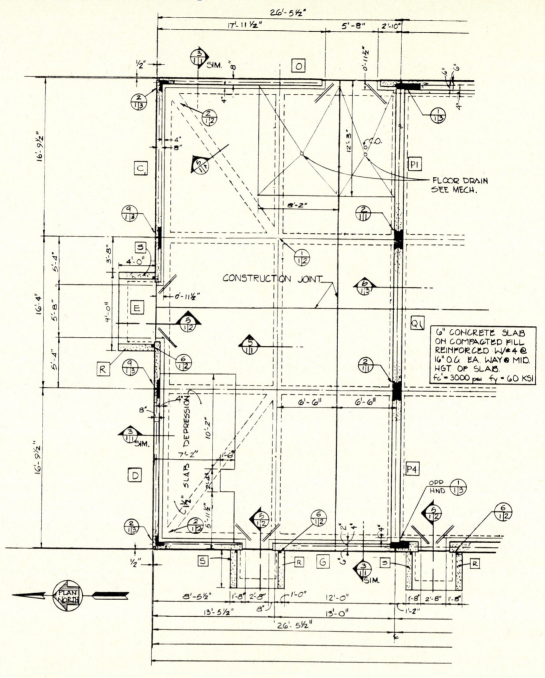

Figure 24–1

A foundation detail that has been referenced in the foundation plan of [24–1].

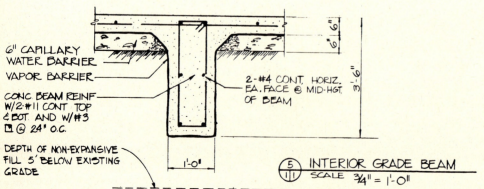

Figure 24–2

A typical column and footing schedule.

Column and Footing Schedule

Column	Footing	Footing Reinforcing	Column Reinforcing
A-1	3'-0" × 3'-0" × 1'-0"	4 #4 E.W.	4 #8
A-2	4'-0" × 4'-0" × 1'-0"	5 #4 E.W.	4 #10
A-3	4'-6" × 4'-6" × 1'-0"	5 #4 E.W.	4 #10

Figure 24-3

A roof framing plan for a nonresidential building.

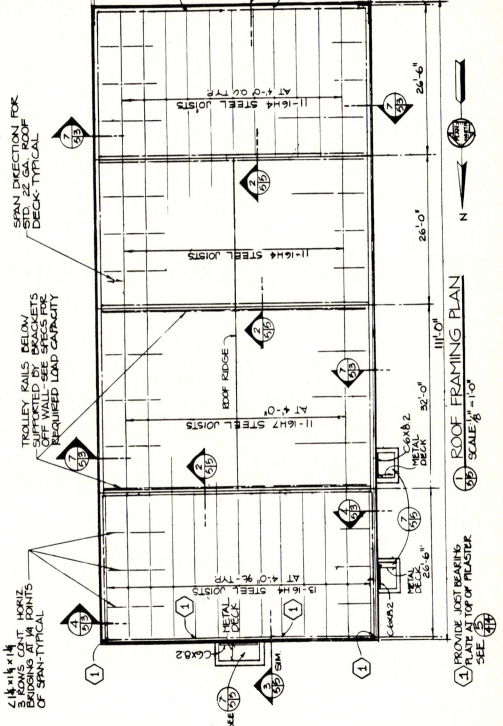

Figure 24-4

A detail referenced on the left of the roof framing plan of [24-4].

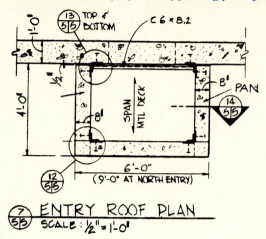

Figure 24-5

A typical mechanical symbols legend.

MECHANICAL LEGEND	
SYMBOL	DESCRIPTION
—HWS—	HEATING WATER SUPPLY
--HWR--	HEATING WATER RETURN
—⋈—	GATE VALVE
—⋈—	GLOBE VALVE
—AAV	AUTOMATIC AIR VENT
—⊢—	GAGE COCK
—⋈—	BALANCING COCK
—⊙	RISER DOWN (ELBOW)
—○	RISER UP (ELBOW)
—⊙—	RISER OR DROP
—▶—	DIRECTION OF FLOW
—‖—	FLOW INDICATOR
Ⓣ	THERMOSTAT
▫D.G.	DOOR GRILLE
O.A.	OUTSIDE AIR
S.A.	SUPPLY AIR
R.A.	RETURN AIR
M.D.	MOTORIZED DAMPER
MBD	MANUAL BALANCING DAMPER
F.D.	FIRE DAMPER
⬡	NOTE BY SYMBOL IDENTIFICATION
—LR—	LIQUID REFRIGERANT LINE
—SR—	SUCTION REFRIGERANT LINE
	SOLENOID VALVE
	PLUG VALVE W/ MEMORY STOP
A.C.U.	AIR CONDITIONING UNIT
	3-WAY CONTROL VALVE
—‖—	UNION
	THERMOMETER WELL
	CHECK VALVE
	STRAINER
A.F.F.	ABOVE FINISHED FLOOR
EXH.	EXHAUST
REG.	REGISTER
C.D.	CEILING DIFFUSER
EXR	EXHAUST REGISTER
RG	RETURN AIR GRILLE
UH	UNIT HEATER

Figure 24-6

site plan is required to show existing utility lines in the street and the new lines connecting them to the building. Symbols are used to describe the various parts of the mechanical system. Although it would be desirable to use a common set of symbols that are standard in every office, an entirely standard system has not been devised.* Every office's symbols differ slightly. Therefore, always supply a *mechanical symbols legend* showing all the symbols that you have used. Figure [24-6] is a brief legend showing a few of the more common symbols.

A *mechanical floor plan* showing duct locations and sizes, grille locations and sizes, direction of airflow through registers, amount of air moved, and other mechanical information is required [24-7]. The HVAC information is superimposed on a simplified floor plan, called a *shell*. It is drawn to the same scale as the architectural floor plan. The shell is drawn with light lines and shows walls, windows, doors, room numbers, and room names. There are no material symbols or detailed architectural information on this sheet. *Mechanical detail drawings* [24-8] and other supplementary drawings are referenced on the mechanical floor plan.

Often the shell is simply a reproducible print of the architectural floor plan that has been made before detailed information is added. The mechanical information is drawn very dark and is easily distinguished from the wall lines. The shell should be oriented with north in the same direction on the sheet as it is on the architectural floor plan.

The mechanical plan requires the use of many *notes*. Often they are lengthy and too cumbersome to fit onto the plan. Therefore, a numbering system is frequently used on the plan or other drawings [24-8]. These numbers refer to a list of notes that are located elsewhere on the sheet. The number representing the note on the plan is enclosed in a circle, a triangle, or a hexagon to make it more easily identified. The notes include information that cannot be easily conveyed in symbol form. The mounting height of grilles or the identification of certain types of dampers are items that typically require notes.

* *ASHRAE Handbook of Fundamentals,* 1981.

A partial mechanical plan for a nonresidential building.

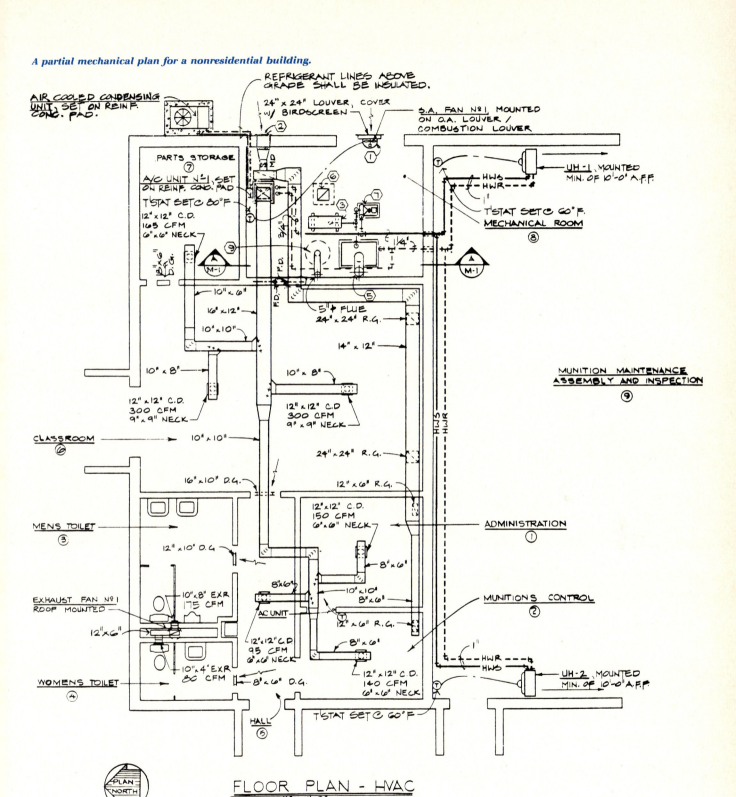

Figure 24-7

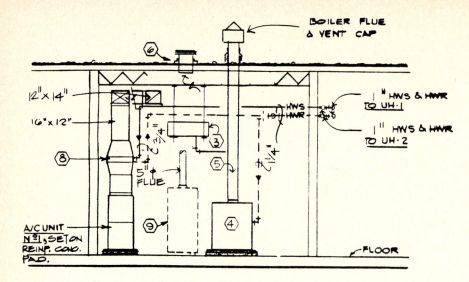

A section showing mechanical information ... the reference is found on drawing [24–7]. This detail makes use of numbered and listed notes that are too lengthy to fit onto the drawing.

NOTES BY SYMBOL "⬡"

1. MOUNT S.A. FAN N°1 W/ OUTSIDE AIR/COMBUSTION AIR LOUVER ABOVE MECH. ROOM DOOR.
2. 12"x8" OUTSIDE LOUVER, COVER W/ BIRDSCREEN.
3. EXPANSION TANK, SUSPEND FROM STRUCTURE ABOVE.
4. GAS FIRED H.W. BOILER, SET ON REINF. CONC. PAD.
5. 10"⌀ BOILER FLUE UP THRU ROOF.
6. ROOF MOUNTED RELIEF AIR UNIT, 12"x12" OPENING.
7. H.W. PUMP, SET ON REINF. CONC. PAD.
8. DUCT MOUNTED HOT WATER COIL (HWC-1).
9. DOMESTIC WATER HEATER, SEE PLBG PLANS.

Figure 24–8

It is usually easier to locate and understand note type information if it is arranged in the form of a *schedule*. Typical schedules are the "Mechanical Equipment Schedule" [24–9], the "Exhaust Fan Schedule" [24–10], and the "Grille and Diffuser Schedule" [24–11]. Each schedule identifies the items that fit into the mechanical details [24–12]. Other examples of mechanical details would be "Gas Pipe Support Detail," "Typical Boiler Flue Thru Roof Detail" [24–13], "Underfloor Duct Detail," "Toilet Room Exhaust Discharge Detail," "Typical Branch Take-off [24–14]," "Rooftop Unit," and "Mounting Curb Flashing Detail."

As in structural drawing requirements, *residential* mechanical drawing requirements are less formal than for commercial work. Depending on how complicated the mechanical system is, the drawings may range from a complete set (as described for commercial work) to none. Usually some form between these extremes is used. One

A typical mechanical equipment schedule.

Mechanical Equipment Schedule								
				Air Quantity				Heat Capacity (kW)
Mark	Manufacturer	Model	Description	CFM	ESP (in.)	HP	Volts	
Unit 1	Lennox	CHA8–953	Single-zone Rooftop HTG/CLG Unit	3500	4	3	208/3	31.8
Unit 2	Lennox	CHA8–413	Single-zone Rooftop HTG/CLG Unit	1275	4	3	208/3	114.0
Unit 3	Hastings	EHV-9-G	Rooftop Heating/vent Unit	9000	5	½	208/3	18.6

Figure 24–9

A typical exhaust fan schedule.

Exhaust Fan Schedule								
			Air Quantity					
Mark	Manufacturer	Model	CFM	ESP (in.)	HP	RPM	Volts	Remarks
EF 1	Penn	WXT-82	225	⅛	$\frac{1}{12}$	1140	120/1	Kitchen Hood Exhaust
EF 2	Duo-Aire	I-71	Extt. 3600 Sup 3168	⅝	E-½ S-(2)⅓		208/3	
EF 3	Nutone	8832	70	$\frac{1}{10}$	100 W		120/1	Ceiling Exhaust

Figure 24–10

A typical grille and diffuser schedule.

Grille and Diffuser Schedule				
Mark	Manufacturer	Model	Finish	Remarks
D-5	Titus	272-RLF	Off-white	Wall S.A. Diffuser w/A6–275 Volume Extractor
D-6	Titus	TXR-3	Prime coat	24″ × 25″ Perforated R.A. Diffuser Drop-in Invert T-Bar
G-8	Titus	33 GL	Anodized Aluminum	Heavy-duty R.A. Grille w/30° Blades

Figure 24–11

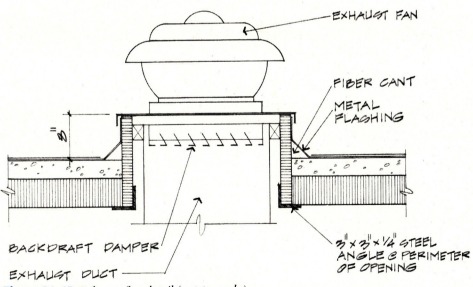

Figure 24–12 *Exhaust fan detail (not to scale).*

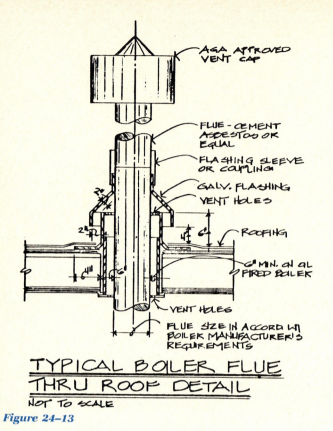

Figure 24–13

method is to provide the mechanical contractor with the general mechanical requirements. This would include sizes of the spaces to be conditioned, number of windows, type of insulation, and location of the furnace and air conditioning equipment. A floor plan and elevations could also include this information.

The engineering office of the mechanical contractor's equipment supplier might design the mechanical system and provide *shop drawings* describing the equipment and method of installation. Shop drawings usually are drawn by the shop that is to supply and install the various manufactured or fabricated items that are specified for a building. They may be prepared using the architect's drawing as a guide as to how the equipment should be installed, or they may be drawn without reference to the architectural drawings. The architect would review the supplier's shop drawing of the HVAC system to see if the proposed design is satisfactory. If approved, the mechanical system is installed directly from the shop drawings. In this case they do not become part of the architectural set but are filed in the architect's office for future reference.

If the architect wishes to have control over the mechanical equipment installation earlier in the process than at the time the shop drawings are being reviewed, it may be desirable to include a schematic drawing in the architectural set. This schematic would show the location of diffusers, equipment, and duct runs but would not include the sizes of these items. Schedules, legends, and details may be omitted due to the simplicity of residential systems. Since there is usually only one furnace in a house, a table or schedule need not be prepared.

The mechanical information described in drawings for commercial buildings must also be conveyed between parties involved in residential construction, but the simplicity of the residential work allows it to be transmitted by less formal means than detailed engineering drawings. The drafter in charge of the working drawings will have to decide how much must be drawn and how much can be handled in other ways.

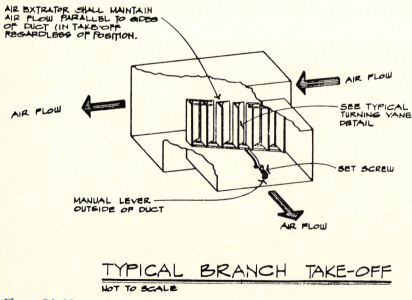

Figure 24–14

24.4 Electrical Working Drawings

Residential electrical drawing requirements differ from mechanical drawing requirements in two ways. First, much of the electrical work is visible to the building occupants and is actively used each day. This causes some parts of the electrical system, such as the lighting and wall receptacles, to require extra attention from the architect. The lighting fixtures must be selected in accord with appearance and a determination of the amount of light needed. The wall receptacles should be placed according to code and functional requirements. The lighting system is never left to the supplier to design, and the wall receptacle layout should not be the responsibility of the contractor.

On the other hand, the technical aspects of the electrical system—the wiring, fuses, connections, and so on—do not affect the function of the house. The wires are more easily hidden than ductwork, and their locations receive almost no attention from the drafter. Architects rarely supply circuit drawings for the electrical lines for a house or ask to approve a supplier's drawings. Normally the only drawings associated with the wiring of a house are the electrician's sketches for his own use. Usually, they are not instrument drawn, nor reproducible, and are discarded after the work is complete. Since residences are smaller than commercial buildings, separate electrical sheets need not be drawn to show the lighting switches, and receptacles. Their locations are usually shown on the architectural floor plan (see Section 18.13).

As in mechanical work, *commercial* projects require separate electrical sheets and a formal presentation of the electrical requirements. Electrical *wiring drawings* are required and are separate from the *lighting drawings*. The lighting drawing is sometimes called the *reflected ceiling plan* [24–15]. It is a ceiling plan drawn as if it were seen in a mirror on the floor of the building. Everything on the ceiling should be shown so that light fixtures are not in conflict with mechanical grilles. Symbols are used for incandescent lighting, while rectangular fluorescent lighting is shown with its actual shape drawn to scale.

In an office building most lighting is provided by recessed fluorescent fixtures set in a 2- × 4-foot grid of acoustical ceiling board. Each light has a letter near it that refers to a *lighting fixture schedule* [24–16]. This schedule describes in detail the various types of lights used.

The path of the wiring is shown on drawings for commercial projects. It is drawn on the *electrical power plan* [24–17], and it is sometimes shown on the reflected ceiling plan or lighting plan. The various items using electricity are connected with lines representing the number of wires required. Each circuit is assigned to a panelboard, where the fuses or circuit breakers are located. The panel, switch, and outlet locations are shown.

A common electrical schedule is the *panel board* or *circuit schedule* [24–18]. It is this schedule that describes the function of each circuit, the wattage of the circuit, the amperage rating of each fuse or breaker, and in some cases the conduit and wire size. Notes, details, and an *electrical legend* always accompany the electrical drawing [24–19]. The legend contains both lighting symbols and wiring symbols.

The total amount of power assigned to each circuit is controlled by code requirements. The wiring design is prepared to meet the code regulations and, for economy, to run the wires the shortest distances possible. A typical detail accompanying the electrical plans might be a "Service Transformer Pad Detail" or a "Smoke Detector Fixture Mounting Detail" [24–20].

The *electrical site plan* precedes the other electrical drawings [24–21]. It is similar to the mechanical site plan in function and may be combined with it.

If you are preparing residential drawings, you may select the simplified approach to electrical drawing instead of the more detailed commercial approach if the required information can be conveyed clearly.

A partial electrical power plan for a nonresidential building.

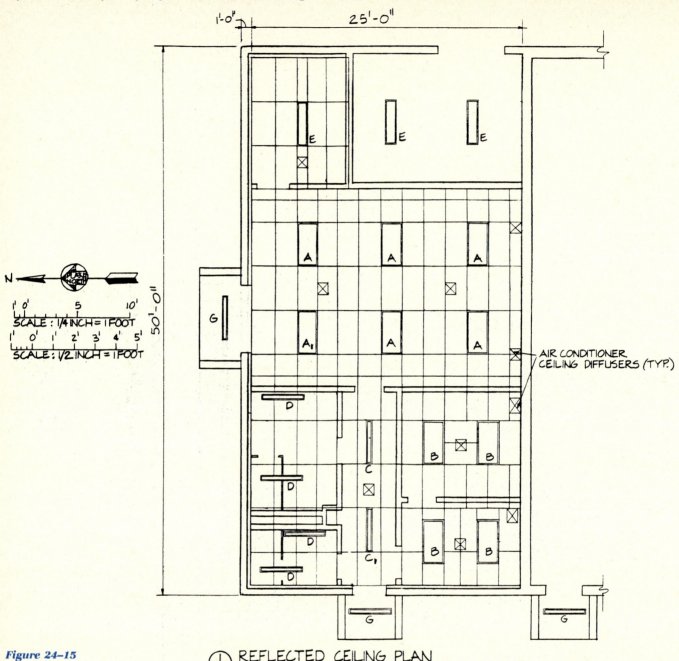

Figure 24–15

A typical lighting fixture schedule.

Lighting Fixture Schedule					
Type	Description	No. and Type of Lamps	Lens	Mounting	Manufacturer and Number
A	2' × 4' Fluorescent Grid Traffer—Flush Aluminum Door	2-F40 CW	Prismatic Acrylic	Recessed	Williams #5222-KA
B	Downlight	1-150 W A-21	Drop Opal	Recessed	Marco #52-T200
C	Wall Cylinder	1-75 W R-30	—	Surface Wall	Solo #9344

Figure 24–16

A partial reflected ceiling plan for a non-residential building.

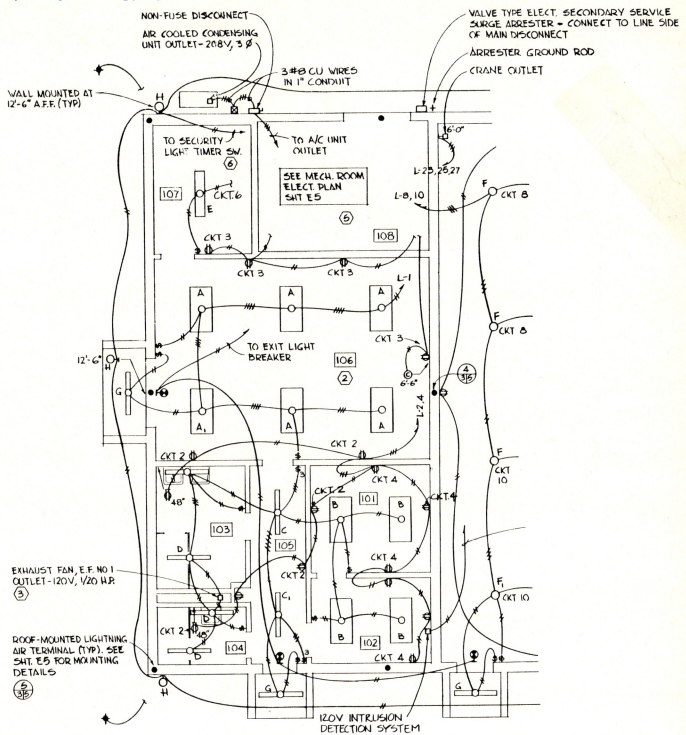

Figure 24–17

A typical electrical circuit schedule for a nonresidential building.

Circuit Schedule

Main Distribution Panel L, 120/208V, 3 Phase, S.N. 125 amp Main Breaker

Circuit	No. of Poles	Breaker Size	Load	Connected Watts
1	1	20	Lighting-Room 106	1152
2	1	20	Recept.-Room 101, 103, 104, 105, 106	1260
3	1	20	Recept.-Room 106, 107, 108	1080
4	1	20	Recept.-Room 101, 102	1080
5	1	20	Recept.-Room 109, 110	720
6	1	20	Lighting-Room 101, 102, 103, 104, 105, 107, 108, E.F. no. 1	1304
7	1	20	Recept.-Room 111	720
8	1	20	Lighting-Room 109	1080
9	1	20	Recept.-Room 109, 110	720
10	1	20	Lighting-Room 109	1080
11	1	20	Lighting-Room 110	1152
12	1	20	H.W. Pump no. 1, 120V, 1∅, ¼ HP	667
13	1	20	Lighting-Room 111	1152
14	1	20	Unit Heaters (2) 120V, ⅛ HP; S.A. Fan No. 1, 1/30 HP	1020
15	1	20	Boiler Control	600
16	1	20	Security Lighting	1040
17, 19, 21	3	50	Air Cooled Condensing Unit; A/C Unit No. 1, 208V, 3∅	7992
18, 20, 22	3	20	Air Compressor, 208V, 3∅, 3 HP	3816
23, 25, 27	3	15	Crane, 208V, 3∅, 1 HP	1440
24			Spare	
26				
28				
42				

Figure 24–18

A typical electrical symbols legend.

Figure 24-19

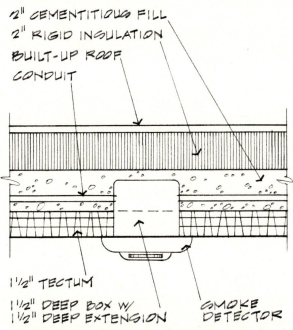

Figure 24-20 *Smoke detector fixture mounting detail.*

A partial electrical site plan for a nonresidential building.

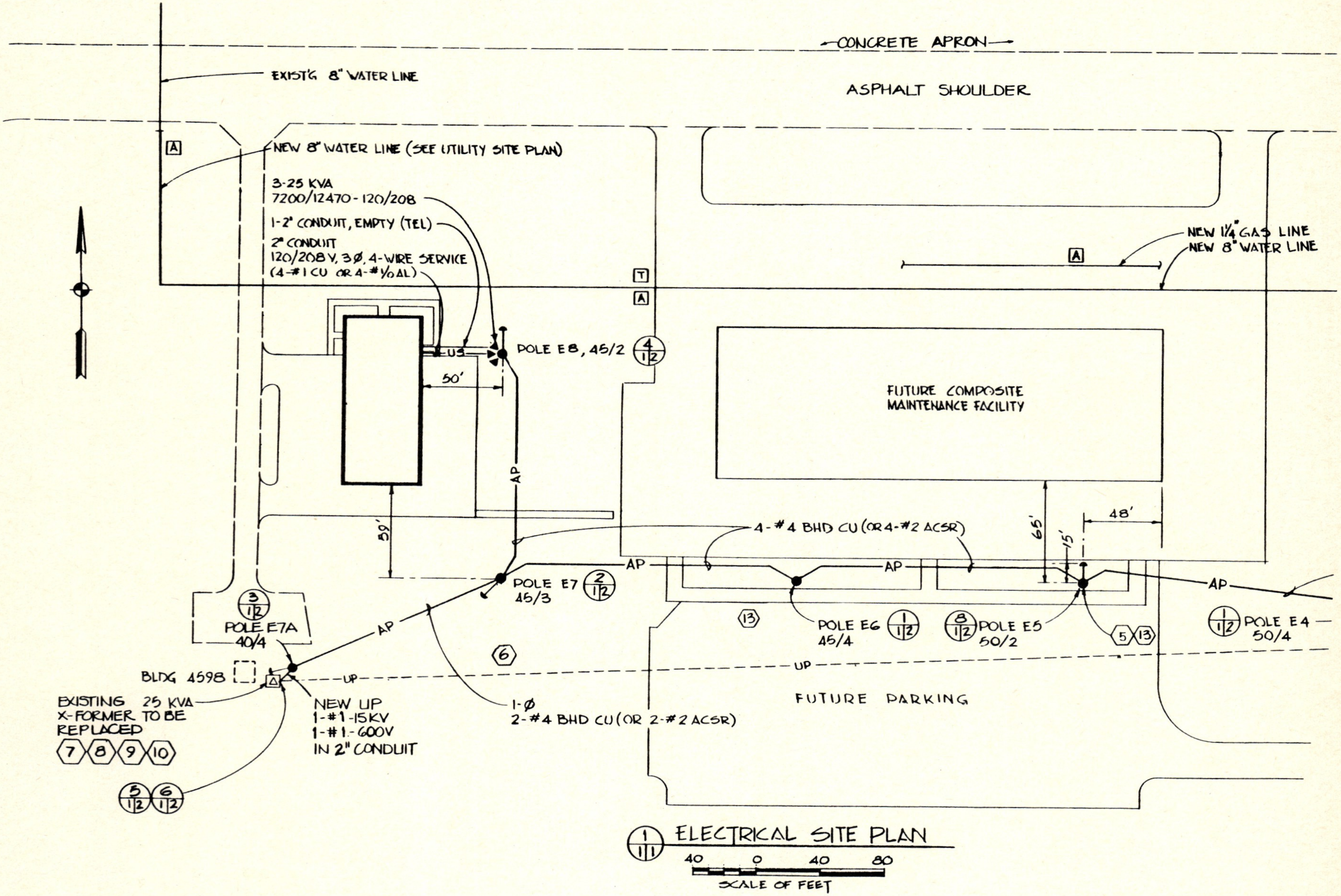

Figure 24-21

24.5 Plumbing Working Drawings

The method used to draw *residential* plumbing drawings is similar to that used for electrical work. You as an architectural designer are concerned only with those parts of the plumbing system that are seen and used daily. You are also relatively unconcerned with the supply and drain piping as long as they do not affect the architectural aspects of the house, are installed competently and according to code (some walls require 2 × 6 studs rather than 2 × 4 studs), and function properly. You may determine where the piping crosses the site from the utility service mains to the point where it enters the building, and you must determine where the fixtures are located in the house. The contractor will normally lay the piping between these points. The contractor will usually work from his own schematic sketches. These are usually drawn without instruments and on nonreproducible paper. No other plumbing drawings are usually required for a house.

In addition to selecting the location, the architect must select the style, size, and color of the kitchen, bath, and other plumbing fixtures. In small homes, the selection emphasizes economy. In more expensive homes, even the selection of the type of faucets and handles become an important decision. The location of the fixtures is shown on the architectural floor plan (see Chapter 17). Information about type, color, and size are included in the specifications. Usually, this information is not included on the drawing.

As in the other engineering drawings, *commercial* projects require considerably more plumbing drawings than do residential projects. As in mechanical and electrical working drawings, the *plumbing floor plan* uses a shell outline [24–23]. The plumbing lines are drawn darker than the wall lines on the shell to reduce confusion between the two. The location and size of the plumbing lines are shown. Various valves, cleanouts, and other accessories are located. Notes, schedules, and details are required. A typical *plumbing schedule* is the "Fixture Piping Schedule" [24–22]. This schedule shows the sizes of the piping connected to each fixture. *Water closet* (W.C.) is an architectural term meaning toilet. *Lavatory* is commonly used instead of "sink" or "washbasin" when referring to the type of sink used in a bathroom. Typical plumbing details would be "Water Heater Connection Detail," "Water Service Entrance Detail" [24–24], "Sump Pump Detail," and "Roof Drain Detail."

A typical plumbing fixture piping schedule.

Fixture Piping Schedule					
Symbol	Fixture	Hot Water HW	Cold Water CW	Waste	Vent
A	Water Closet (Flush Valve)	—	1"	4"	2"
B	Lavatory	½"	½"	1¼"	1¼"
C	Shower	¾"	¾"	2"	1½"

Figure 24–22

Engineering Drawings

A partial plumbing plan for a nonresidential building.

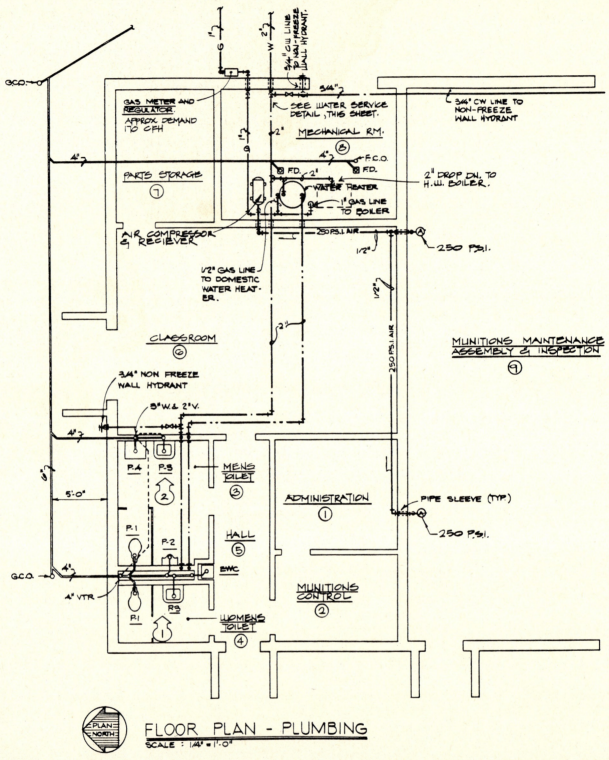

Figure 24–23

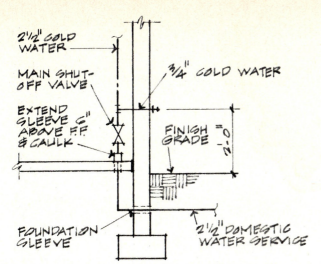

Figure 24-24 Water service entrance detail.

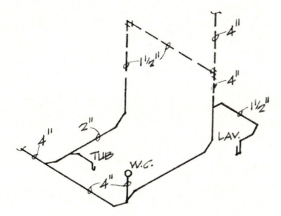

Figure 24-25 Waste riser isometric.

Another type of drawing required for commercial plumbing work is the *plumbing isometric* [24-25]. This is a schematic drawing showing how the drain system is vented. The water supply system and the drain system venting may also be shown in an elevation schematic drawing. A *plumbing symbols legend* is also required [24-26]. If the building is not too complex, the *plumbing site plan* may be combined with the mechanical and electrical site plan.

Although the environmental control (HVAC) drawings appear at the end of a set of working drawings and are sometimes abbreviated, they are very important. Not only do they represent a large percentage of the cost of a job, but they directly affect the comfort of the building occupants. This work should be planned along with the architectural aspects so that all systems will be compatible with the appearance and function of the building and with each other.

A typical plumbing symbols legend.

PLUMBING SYMBOLS		
SECTION I — LINE SYMBOLS		
SYMBOL	DESCRIPTION	
———	SANITARY DRAIN	
—V—	SANITARY VENT	
—SD—	STORM WATER DRAIN	
—·—	COLD WATER	
—··—	HOT WATER	
—···—	HOT WATER RETURN	
—G—	NATURAL GAS, LOW PRESSURE	
—*G—	MEDIUM OR HIGH PRESSURE GAS	
—A—	COMPRESSED AIR	
—V—	VACUUM	
→	DIRECTION OF FLOW	
⌐	DIRECTION OF PITCH DOWN	
-----	DASHED PIPING INDICATES EXISTING	
≠≠≠≠	DASHED CROSS HATCHED PIPING INDICATES EXISTING TO BE REMOVED OR ABANDONED AS NOTED	
⇧	PLUMBING RISER	
⬡	NOTES BY SYMBOL	
P-4	PLUMBING EQUIPMENT NUMBER	
FD ▣	FLOOR DRAIN	
⊙	ROOF DRAIN	
●	HUB DRAIN	
SD ▣	SHOWER DRAIN	
SECTION II — VALVES, FITTINGS, ETC.		
⋈	GATE VALVE	
⋈	GLOBE VALVE	
⋈	ANGLE VALVE	
⋈	BUTTERFLY VALVE	
⋈	CHECK VALVE	
●	BACKWATER VALVE	
▭	BACKFLOW PREVENTER	
⋈	GAS COCK	
⋈	BALANCE VALVE	
⋈	AIR OPERATED VALVE	
⋈	MOTOR OPERATED VALVE	
⋈	GAS PRESSURE REGULATOR	
⋈	PRESSURE REDUCING VALVE	
⋈	PRESSURE OR TEMP. RELIEF VALVE	
⋈	FLOW SWITCH	
⊳⊲	CONCENTRIC REDUCER	
⊳⊲	ECCENTRIC REDUCER	
‖	UNION	
⊸	CLEANOUT (TYPE AS INDICATED)	
⊢	WALL C.O.	
⊸	AIR DROP	
⊸	VALVE IN VERTICAL (TYPE AS NOTED OR SPEC'D)	
▨	FLEXIBLE CONNECTION	
⊸	STRAINER	
⊸	WATER HAMMER ARRESTOR	
⇧ AAV	AUTOMATIC AIR VENT	
⊸	HOSE BIBB OR WALL HYDRANT (AS NOTED)	
⊡ YH	YARD HYDRANT	
⊙	VACUUM BREAKER	

Figure 24-26

Engineering Drawings

401

EXERCISES

24-1. Note that the upper surface of the concrete floor slab [24-1] is not at the same level throughout. Locate the parts of the slab that change level. Describe the changes in level in terms of location, square footage affected, and the number of inches that the level changes. Since the change in level at the floor drains is not specified, describe how this will be determined.

24-2. List the sizes of steel joists shown in [24-4]. How far apart are they spaced?

24-3. Locate the thermostats in [24-7]. The thermostat symbol may be found in [24-6]. Find the fire dampers in [24-7]. What do you think is the purpose of a fire damper?

24-4. How many light fixtures are used in the reflected ceiling plan [24-15]? How many different types of light fixtures are used?

24-5. Refer to [24-17]. Which room has lights that can be turned on from two different locations? Which rooms have electrical outlets that are positioned approximately 4 feet above the floor?

24-6. Refer to [24-21]. What size is the conduit that carries the electrical lines into the building? What size is the conduit for the telephone lines that go into the building?

24-7. Locate the floor drains in [24-22]. Floor drain symbols may be seen in [24-26]. What size is the water supply line that enters the building? What size is the gas supply line that enters the building? What sizes are the sewer lines that leave the building?

25 A Working Drawing Case Study

As in previous chapters, we wish to bring you closer to architectural drawing in the "real world" by presenting an actual project. The example that follows is a continuation of the design of the home for Mr. & Mrs. Browne that was described in Chapter 13. After acceptance of his design by the Brownes, architect Smith turned the work over to one of the drafters in his office. With his guidance and assistance, the drafter developed the working drawings shown in [25–1] to [25–7].

Note the logical progression of the work prepared by the drafter. The drawings are arranged in the most usual order of construction. The *site plan* indicating the placement of the home on the lot is shown on the first sheet [25–1]. Also included on this sheet is a diagram of the roof framing plan. Although not a standard practice, Smith found that in this instance combining the roof framing plan with the site plan cut down on drafting time. Next in sequence is the *foundation plan* that also shows the foundation details [25–2].

The *floor plan* of the home follows next [25–3]. General notes added to the drawing replace many instructions that would otherwise either have to be drawn or specified separately in writing. The floor plan shows the Browne's home as it would appear from the air with the roof and upper 4 ft of wall removed. Careful dimensioning assures the correct location of walls. Partitions to be installed are indicated by special designations described in the notes located on the sheet. Window and door types are indicated by number. The location of the light fixtures and receptacles are also indicated. You should not attempt to indicate plumbing pipes, electric wiring, or air conditioning details on the architectural floor plan.

Next in order are the *elevations* [25–4]. With elevation drawings, the drafter is communicating information to the builder that will enable him to construct the exterior of the structure. After the elevations, Smith's drafter prepared the *cross sections* [25–5]. These views show portions of the skeleton frame of the home. They show the supporting structural framework and the sizes of component members. In this instance, cross-sectional views have been shown at two different locations to clarify the structural aspects of the building. Building sections are usually drawn at the same scale as the elevations and floor plan. Note that these cross sections are drawn twice as large. By using a scale of ½" = 1'–0", the drafter was able to show the walls with enough detail to avoid drawing separate wall sections. This is a timesaving procedure, and it makes the building sections more clear and useful. It is not, however, standard practice.

Interior elevations [25–6] were included to show the kitchen and bath cabinetry, the fireplace, the beverage bar, and the storage wall at the north end of the dining area. Note that several details of construction have been cross-referenced to detail drawings on the next sheet. The window and door schedules, located on the interior elevations sheet, show the types of doors and windows and the framing sizes. Auxiliary items such as glass and hardware style would be difficult to describe on drawings. Therefore, these items are covered in separate written specifications (not shown) prepared as a supplement to the working drawings. Finally, the *details sheet* [25–7] shows in larger scale special items such as the door and window heads, jambs, and sills, structural attachments, and complicated details such as the pass-through window from the kitchen to the patio, and the plant shelf in the master bath.

Steps in *actual* construction of the home for the Browne family are shown in the photographic sequence [25–8] to [25–23].

EXERCISES

A first step to learning to draw working drawings is understanding how to "read" working drawings. Complete the following exercises to familiarize yourself with the drawings in [25–1] to [25–7].

25–1. For what purpose are 2 × 6's used in the roof framing?
25–2. What is the roof slope?
25–3. What is the thickness and type of roof sheathing material?
25–4. How many square feet are in the house?
25–5. What is the spacing of the exterior wall studs? What is the interior wall stud spacing?
25–6. What is the siding material?
25–7. How large are the overhangs?

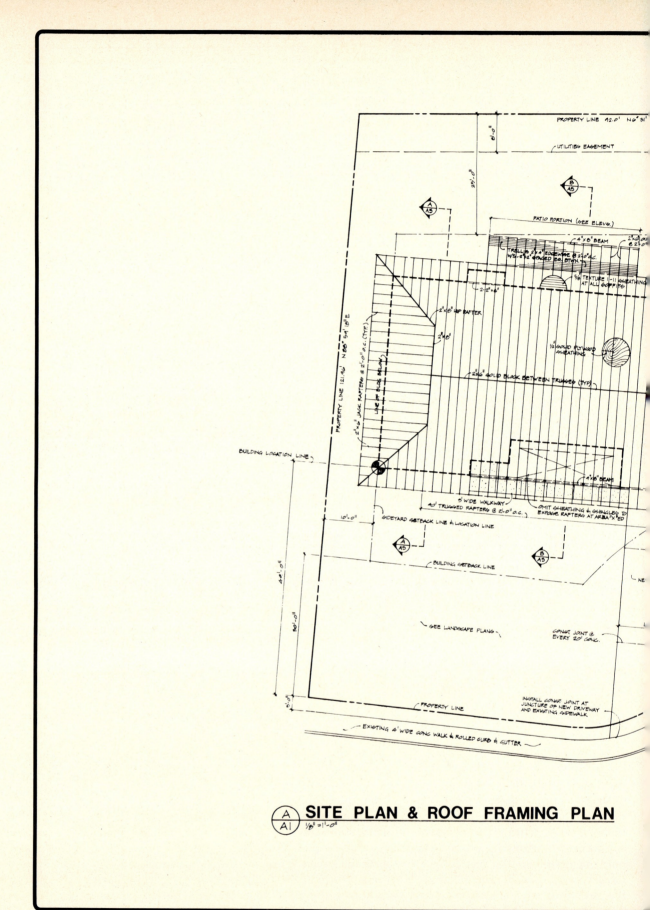

Figure 25-1 The site plan.

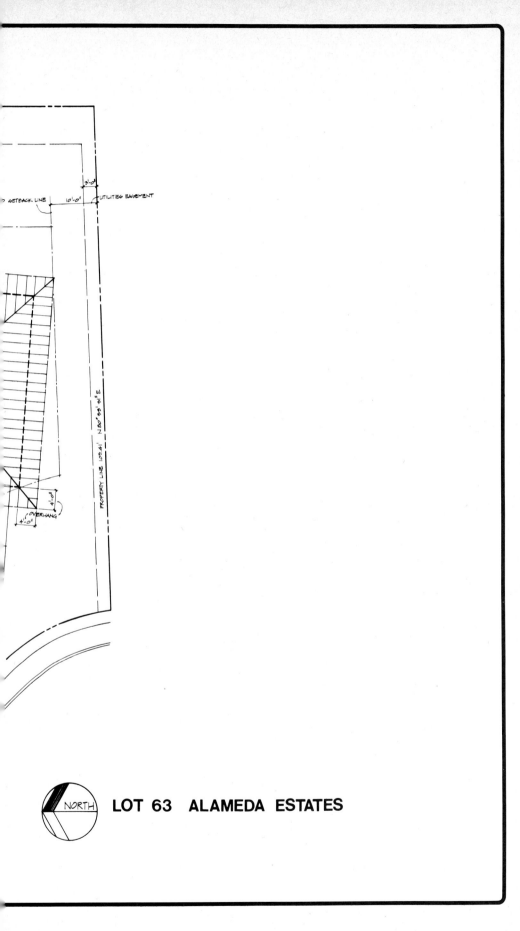

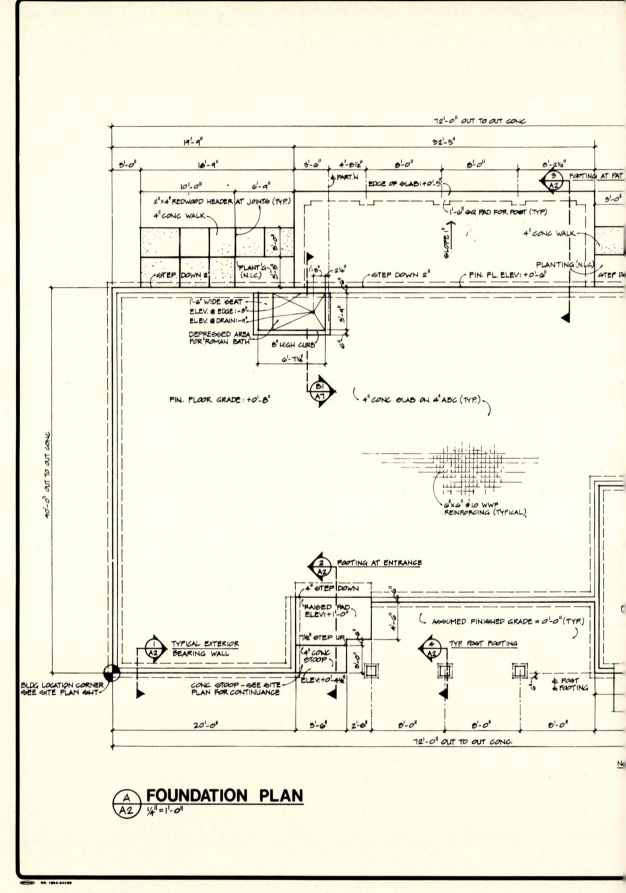

Figure 25–2 The foundation plan.

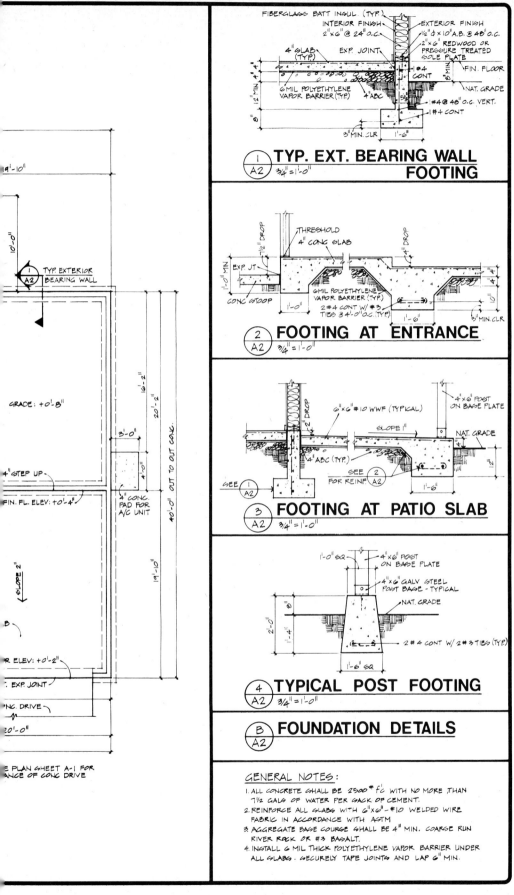

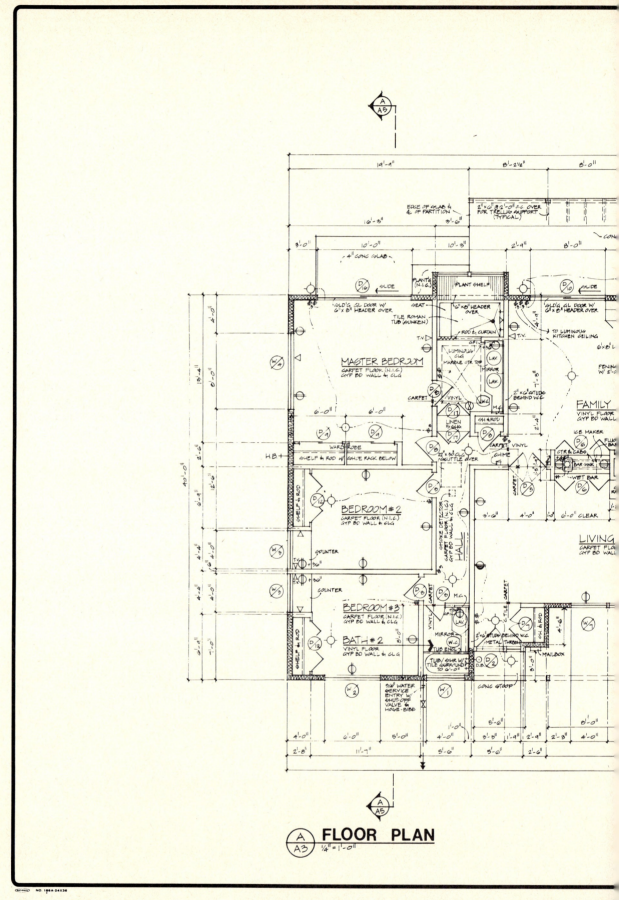

Figure 25-3 The floor plan.

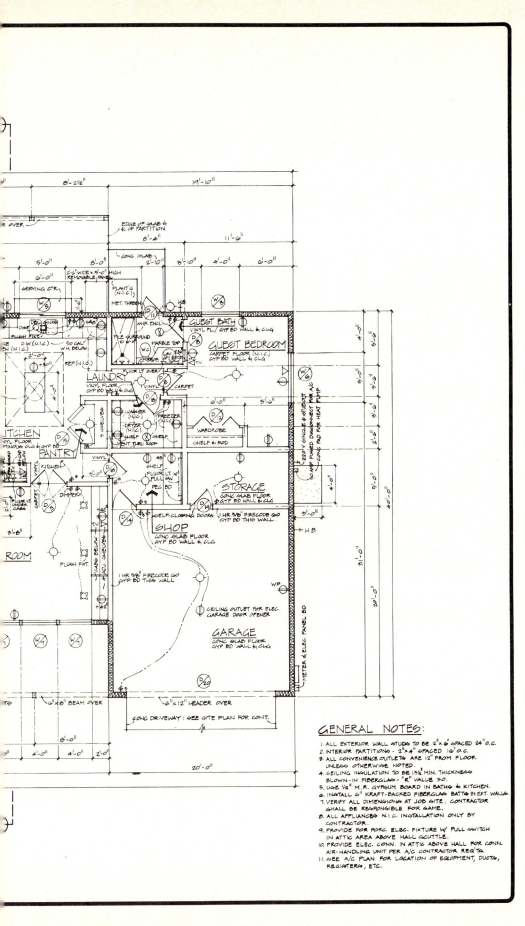

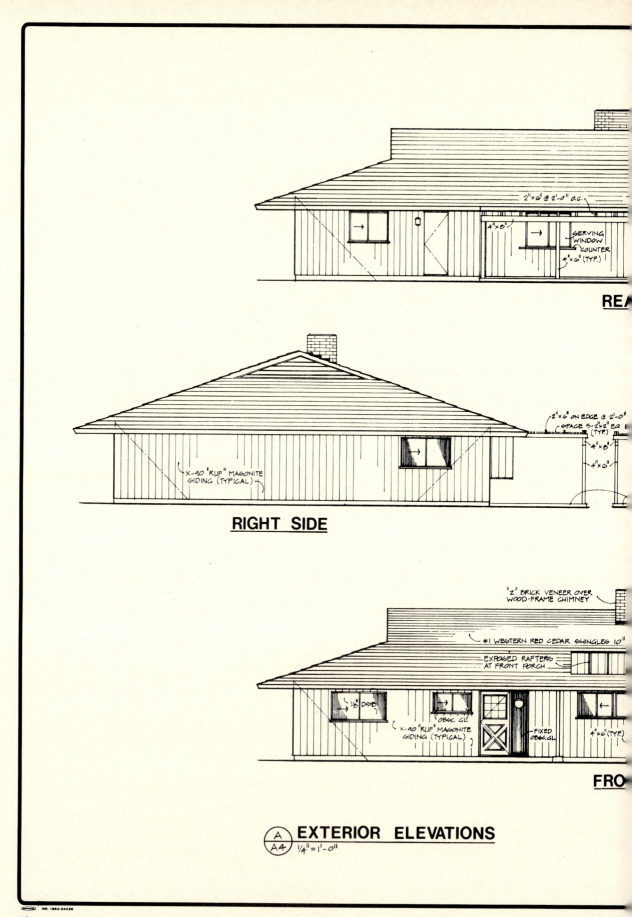

Figure 25-4 The elevations.

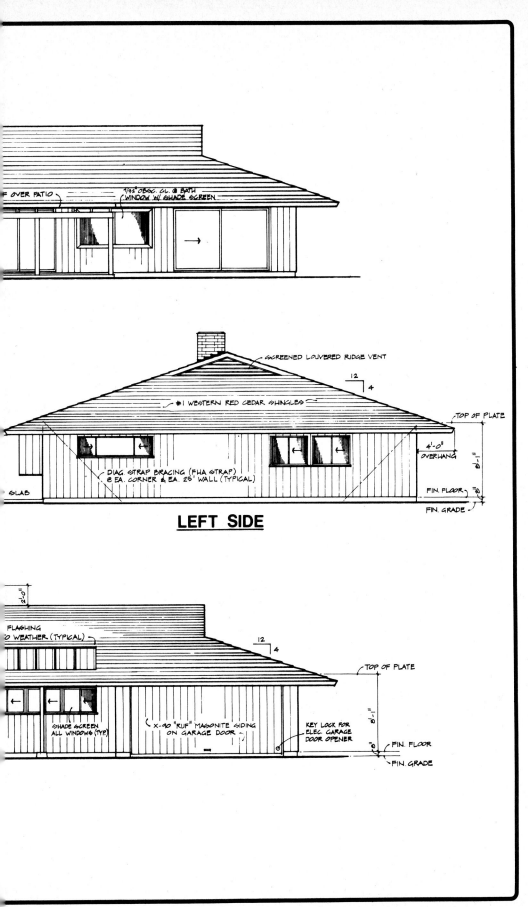

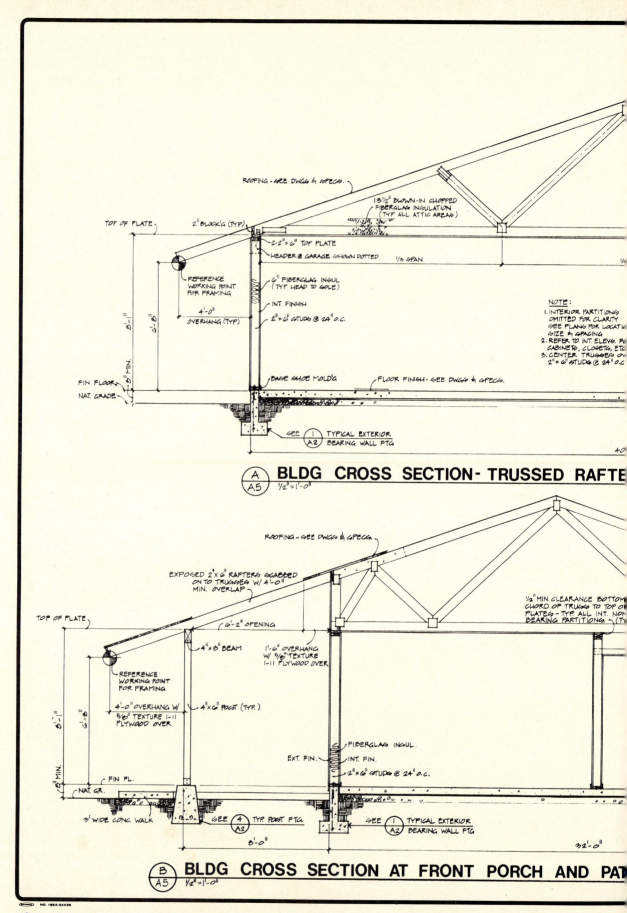

Figure 25-5 *The cross sections.*

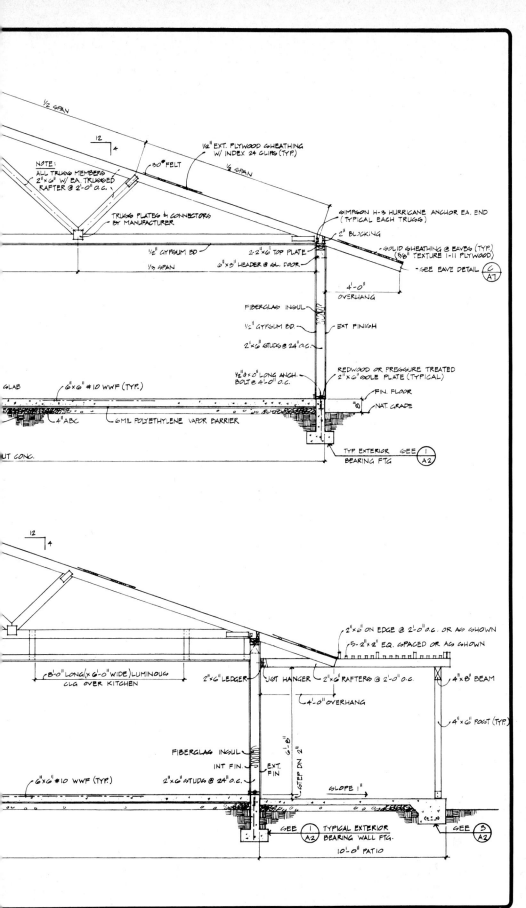

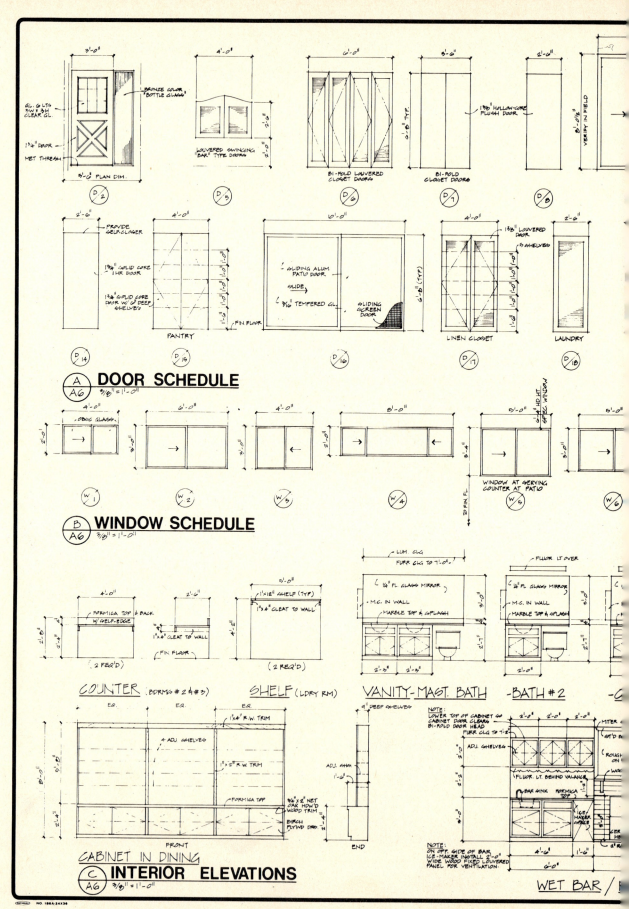

Figure 25-6 The interior elevations.

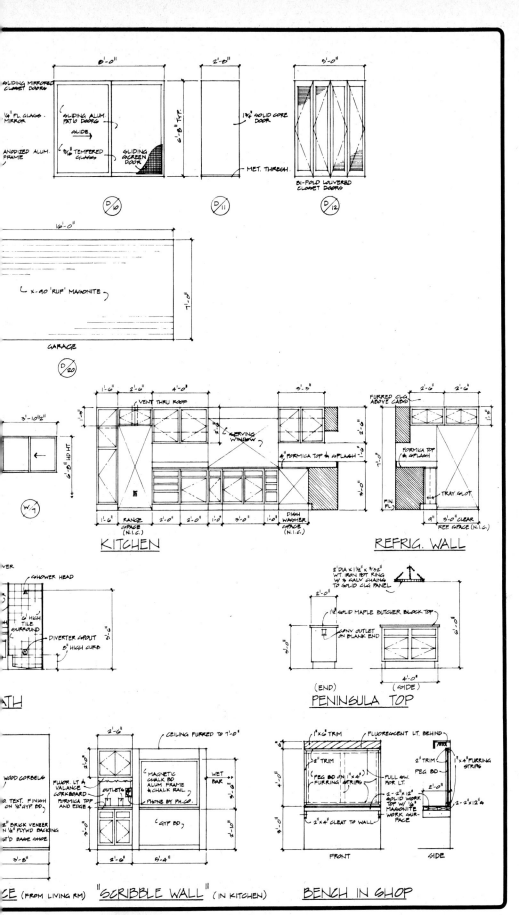

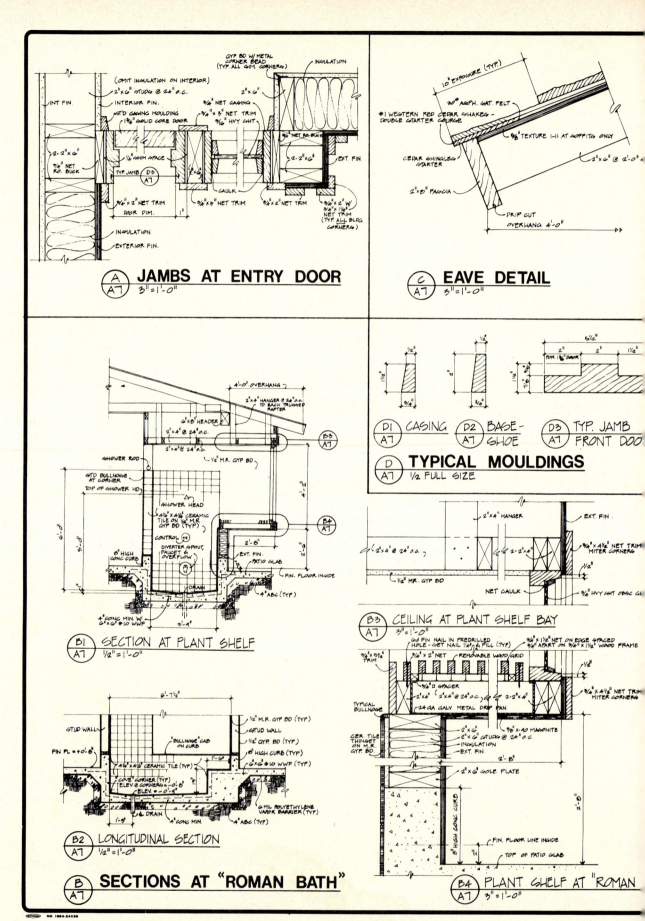

Figure 25-7 The details.

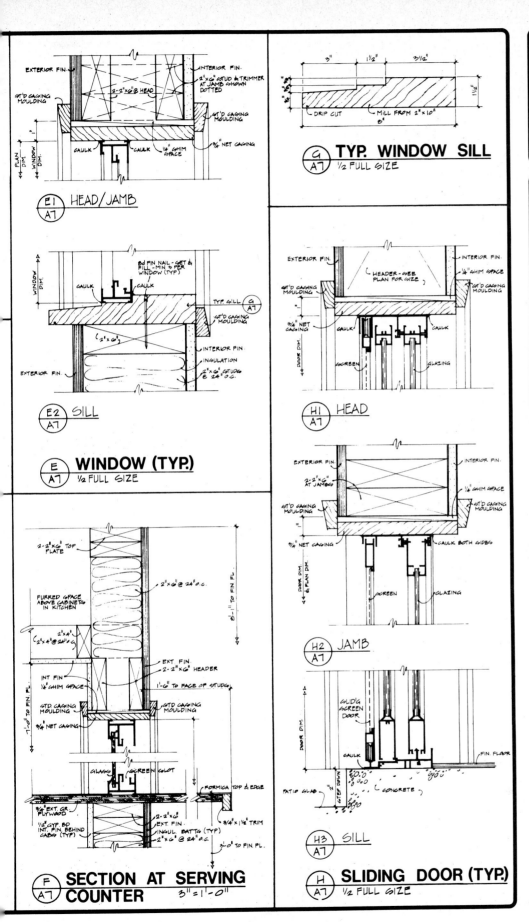

The undeveloped building site.

Figure 25–8

Trenches dug for foundations. . . . reinforcing bar for concrete set in place.

Figure 25–9

Concrete foundations poured.

Figure 25–10

Plumbing set in place.

Figure 25–11

Floor slab poured.

Figure 25–12

Wall studs nailed to sill plates.

Figure 25–13

Wall framing completed.

Figure 25–14

Exterior wall sheathing added. . . . roof trusses started.

Figure 25–15

Roof trusses completed.

Figure 25–17

A view of the roof trusses and vent.

Figure 25–16

Roof sheathing nailed to trusses.

Figure 25–18

Interior framing . . . prefabricated fireplace set in place.

Figure 25–19

Siding applied over wall sheathing . . . rear view of house.

Figure 25–20

Installation of roof shingles.

Figure 25–21

Gypsum board nailed to interior wall studs.

Figure 25–22

The completed Browne home with landscaping.

Figure 25-23

25-8. What types of windows are used?
25-9. How many square feet of mirrors are used in the bathrooms?
25-10. What is the size and material of the fascia?
25-11. What is the size of a typical bearing wall footing?
25-12. What size steel mesh is used in the patio slab?
25-13. What size are the members of the trusses?
25-14. What is the size and type of ceiling material?
25-15. What material is specified for the vanity tops in the bathrooms?
25-16. What is the thickness and material of the vapor barrier under the floor slab?
25-17. What is the thickness and material of the soffits?
25-18. What is the roofing material?
25-19. Identify the lights controlled by the three-way switches.
25-20. How many 2'-6"-wide doors are used?

Looking at each drawing sheet and at the set of drawings as a whole, discuss the following questions.

25-21. Are there any standard drawing practices described in this book that have not been followed? Why do you suppose this was done?
25-22. Are there any omissions in describing certain features of the home?
25-23. Are there any other drawings that should have been provided?
25-24. Would you have arranged the drawings differently on the sheets?
25-25. How do these drawings differ from the climate control, plumbing, and electrical system drawing examples in the book that used the Browne home floorplan?
25-26. What design features of this home would you change to better suit the climate of the area in which you live?
25-27. How well would the general style of this home satisfy the demands of the average homebuyer in your area?
25-28. Would this home meet the zoning ordinances and building code requirements in your area?
25-29. If you have access to a copy machine that has enlarging capabilities, make enlarged copies of the house plans for the Browne home. Using these sheets as "checkprints" mark any errors or omissions with a red pencil.
25-30. Draw the plans for a home of your own design.

V

Computers
in
Architectural
Drawing
and
Design

26 Computer Equipment

26.1 Introduction

Although computers have been available for a number of years, architectural offices have only recently begun to use them extensively. Since architectural offices are relatively small compared with industrial and commercial corporations, the initial cost of computing systems has been difficult to justify. In recent years, however, as the cost and size of computers have decreased, the types of services available have increased. Many architectural firms can now afford and find ample applications for computers. The mathematical capabilities of computers are readily adaptable to engineering design, such as for structures and environmental control systems. Architectural offices that perform a significant amount of engineering work may be able to justify their own computer to help with this function alone. With the advent of desk-top computers many offices that could not previously justify larger units have been able to buy machines that can also assist with bookkeeping, payroll, specification writing, data filing, general typing, and other non-mathematical functions.

Before examining the computer functions that are most useful to an architectural office, we need to understand the components of a computer system. A computer system consists of two groups of components. The physical components that perform computations and transfer information are referred to as *hardware*. The various sets of instructions that are used to direct the function of the hardware are called computer programs or *software*. Hardware falls into three categories: the solid-state electronic computing equipment, the documentation equipment, and the equipment that is used to communicate with the computer. This communication may require several devices that collectively are called the *workstation*.

26.2 The Workstation

The most familiar device used to send information into the computer is a *keyboard* [26-1]. Computer keyboards are similar to typewriter keyboards except that they usually contain more keys. In addition to the alphabet, num-

A computer keyboard is similar to a typewriter keyboard.

Figure 26-1

bers, and symbols, computer keyboards usually have other special keys that are used to send brief or lengthy special instructions to the computer. Such instructions might include directing the computer to perform several calculations, to arrange spaces in a floor plan, to plot a perspective view of a building, or to perform a multitude of other functions.

Another device that may be used to send messages to the computer is a *digitizer*. A digitizer is a smooth-surfaced board ranging in size from several inches [26-2] to several feet on a side [26-3]. The surface may be completely blank, but more commonly it has a blank area surrounded by printed symbols and commands [26-4]. The underside has a grid of hundreds of electronically sensitive points.

A digitizer is more graphically oriented than a keyboard. A signal is sent to the computer when a pencil-like stylus or a *puck* (sometimes referred to as a cursor) is brought close to the electronically sensitive surface of the digitizer [26-5 and 26-6]. The signal may be a specific command to the computer or it may be a record of the position of the puck on the board. Commands to record graphic symbols or to perform certain drafting

A workstation with a small digitizer.

This large digitizer resembles a drawing board.

Figure 26–2

Figure 26–3

The surface of a digitizer board commonly has a blank area surrounded by printed symbols and commands.

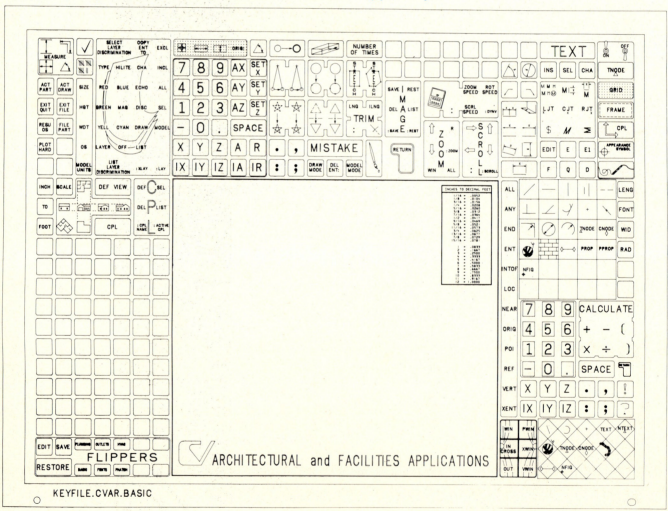

Figure 26–4

426

A puck may be used to send a command to the computer by positioning it over a symbol on the digitizer.

Figure 26–5

functions may be sent by positioning the puck over the appropriate symbol that is printed on the surface of the digitizer. In the line-drawing mode the computer records the movement of the puck over the blank area as lines matching the configuration of the puck's path. By mixing linework and symbol signals, information necessary to produce a drawing may be entered into the computer memory [26–7].

Before discussing a third input device, it is useful at this point to describe how the information going into the computer may be reviewed visually. It is important to see what information is going into the computer to ensure accuracy and to have a base on which to add more information. A video display *monitor* is used with the keyboard, digitizer, and other input devices to provide a "picture" of the written, numerical, and graphic information being exchanged between the user and the computer. The monitor is a *cathode ray tube* (CRT) similar to a television screen [26–8]. The resolution of the screen varies widely between computer systems. An ordinary TV set may be used as a monitor with many small personal or home computers but the resolution is very limited. The monitors used in large specialized computer graphics systems have much higher resolution. Other types of visual displays, including *liquid-crystal displays* (LCD), such as are found in hand calculators and watches, are being developed.

The puck may also be used to record specific locations on the digitizer board.

Figure 26–6

Computer Equipment

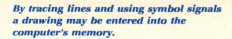
By tracing lines and using symbol signals a drawing may be entered into the computer's memory.

Figure 26-7

The monitor provides a visual record of the written, numerical, and graphic input.

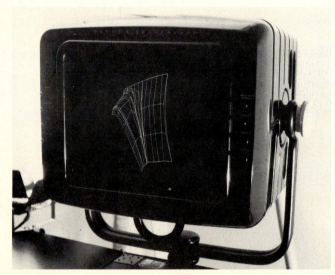

Figure 26-8

Linework, symbols, letters, and numbers appear on the monitor screen when they are entered by using an input device. After such information is seen to be correct, the computer may be instructed to perform calculations or other functions using the data. The results of the computation will appear on the screen and more information and instructions may be added. In the larger computer-aided design systems, two monitors are commonly used—one for primarily written and numerical information and the other for graphical information. In current practice the graphic monitor is frequently a full-color display.

An electronic *light pen* may be used to add or alter information directly on the monitor screen [26-9]. This process is similar to the use of a puck on a digitizer

A light pen may be used directly on the monitor screen to create and modify drawings and to enter commands.

Figure 26-9

428

Computers in Architectural Drawing and Design

board. The monitor screen may have a group of symbols that, when touched with the pen, will send instructional signals to the computer. The screen also has a blank area on which pen movement will be recorded as lines in the computer.

The workstation is usually located in an ordinary office environment, but the treatment of lighting may need modification. Just as you may see reflections of windows or lamps on your TV screen at home, the images on a computer monitor may be obscured by similar reflections. Outdoor light should not be allowed to fall on the monitor screen. Artificial light must also be controlled in the area where a monitor is located so as to prevent reflections on the viewing screen. Temperature, relative humidity, and sound control need not be different from those normally found in a modern office.

26.3 The Computing Equipment

The heart of the computer system is the computing unit, whose principal function is to perform many thousands of calculations in a very short period of time. Its essential components are an aritimetic-processing unit, a memory, and a control unit to manage the interactions of these devices and the input and output equipment. In very small computers all of these items may be packaged together along with an input keyboard and possibly even some form of output device. These computers are known as *microcomputers* [26–10]. They are also sometimes referred to as personal or home computers.

Very large computers are known as central or *mainframe* computers [26–11]. Due to their size and special environmental requirements, mainframe computers are usually housed in a special room accompanied by large auxiliary memory units and large high-speed printers.

Very small computers—known as microcomputers or personal computers—have their essential components combined in one package.

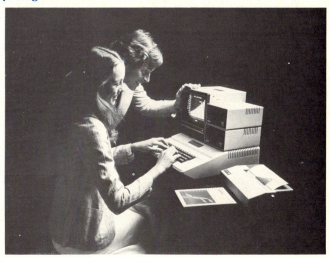

Figure 26–10

Figure 26–11

Very large computers—known as central or mainframe computers—are usually housed in a special room.

Computer Equipment

429

Medium-size computers are called minicomputers.

Figure 26–12

Between these extremes there are medium-size units called *minicomputers* [26–12]. These units are often installed in the same room as the workstation. Due to the great advances in solid-state electronics in recent years, the calculating power of minicomputers is now very close to that of the mainframes of just a few years ago.

Architectural offices are most likely to use the larger models of the microcomputers if very extensive graphic applications are desired. In large offices several microcomputers at individual workstations may be interfaced with a single minicomputer. Routine calculations and graphic manipulations, expecially in regard to input and output, are processed by each microcomputer. More lengthy calculations and expanded memory requirements are shifted to the minicomputer.

The *memory* unit is a very important part of the computing equipment. It is used to store the data to be processed, the final and intermediate results of any calculations, and the software instructions that dictate how the calculations are to be made and displayed or printed. The memory unit also serves as a library in which drawings, specifications, letters, and accounting information can be stored. Commands entered at the workstation will cause the computer to perform a series of tasks previously entered into memory. The tasks might include listing material "takeoffs," drawing perspective views, arranging floor plans, writing specifications, and a multitude of other mathematical and nonmathematical procedures.

In order to create a drawing on a computer, there are two basic types of data that must be stored in memory. First is the drafting program or instructions that tell the computer how to make the drawing. Although large, the size of this data *is not* related to the number of drawings in the system. The second type of data is that developed by the program to define the subject material on each drawing. The size of the data in this case *is* related to the number of drawings in the system as well as to the size and complexity of each drawing.

It takes about 25,000 words to store the instructions necessary to create (draw) an average architectural or engineering drawing. A set of thirty drawing sheets would require the computer to store at least 750,000 words, which is too many for the built-in memory of a typical microcomputer. Therefore an auxiliary storage system is needed. Minicomputers and mainframes also use auxiliary memory units to increase their capacity as needed. *Magnetic tape, hard discs*, and *floppy discs* are common auxiliary memory devices. Punched cards and paper tape have also been used with some of the older systems.

To store completed projects and other information not regularly used, "off-line" storage devices must be provided. This is to allow new projects to be entered into the system because on-line memory has a finite capacity. Floppy discs are used with microcomputers and magnetic tape is used with larger computers for off-line storage.

Auxiliary memory storage systems give the computer a much greater computing capability than it would have if it could only store programs and data within its central processing unit.

The computing equipment's output (results of computations and other performed tasks) is displayed on a monitor at the workstation throughout the exchange between the user and the computer. To obtain a printed copy of the output, documentation equipment is required.

26.4 The Documentation Equipment

The display of the conclusion of the computing process (charts, graphs, perspectives, floor plans, lists, structural designs, and so on) has limited use if it is merely shown as a picture on a CRT screen. The output of most computer work must be printed on paper to be a useful tool in any architectural office. Computer systems therefore also include machines that can print and plot written and graphic results. Small desk-top computer systems usually have their printing equipment located adjacent to the workstation. Larger computers and their associated high-speed printing equipment often make enough noise to be bothersome. They are therefore best located in a room separate from the general work area. It should have sound-deadening properties.

Computer printing equipment is usually referred to as printers or plotters, depending on their primary use. *Printers* are designed primarily for alphanumeric (letter and number) output similar to that of a standard typewriter. Some types of printers can produce graphical output as well. In this case, rather than having individual alphabet and number elements (like a typewriter), the letters and numbers are formed by using a series of tiny dots. The dots can then also be used to form lines and graphic symbols. *Plotters* are designed primarily to print graphical output. They can produce alphanumeric output as well but are not designed for high-speed printing of large quantities of small, standard print. Lines drawn by plotters are usually continuous rather than being formed by a series of dots.

Electromechanical *pen plotters* employ several types of pens and two types of plotting surfaces. Pencils, ball point pens, and ink pens may be used as the marking devices. The quality of the drawing increases from the first to the last of these. The mechanism that holds the paper may be flat (*flat-bed plotters* [26–13]) or cylindrical (*drum plotters* [26–14]). Flat-bed plotters are available in a variety of sizes corresponding to standard drawing sizes. The pen travels left and right on a horizontal bar that moves up and down on a flat drawing surface. Drum plotters print on paper in contact with a cylindrical drum. If the paper is fed from a roll, the drawing can be quite long. The width of the drum may vary from the width of standard typing paper to that of large drawing sheets. The drum holding the paper rotates in both directions so that a pen mounted on a fixed bridge can draw lines in the direction of rotation of the drum. The pen also moves back and forth on the bridge to draw lines parallel to the axis of the drum. The combination of these two movements enables lines to be drawn at any angle or curvature.

Computer-drawn linework is not always drawn in the sequence that a drafter would follow to complete a sheet. Since the computer memory contains all the data necessary to produce a drawing, the lines, notes, symbols,

A flat-bed plotter holds the paper on a flat surface . . . it may also have digitizing capabilities.

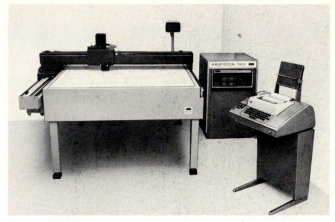

Figure 26–13

A drum plotter holds the paper on a rotating drum.

Figure 26–14

and numbers may be applied to the drawing sheet in a more efficient sequence. A drum plotter, for example, may plot along one end of a sheet and as the drum rotates back and forth it will gradually roll the sheet past the pen bridge so that the drawing is completed from one end to the other. In contrast, the drafter usually applies object lines first and then finishes with notes and dimensions. It is no advantage for the computer to print notes forward (the first word first and the last word last). The computer output program may be

A variety of plotter linework styles may be selected.

Figure 26–15

A variety of lettering styles may also be selected.

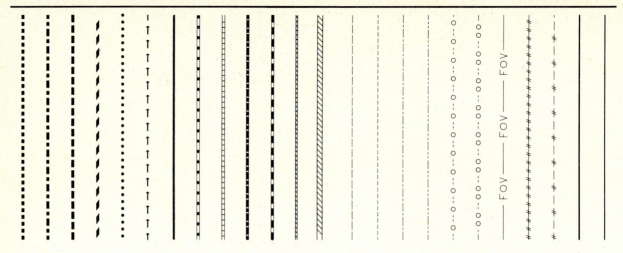

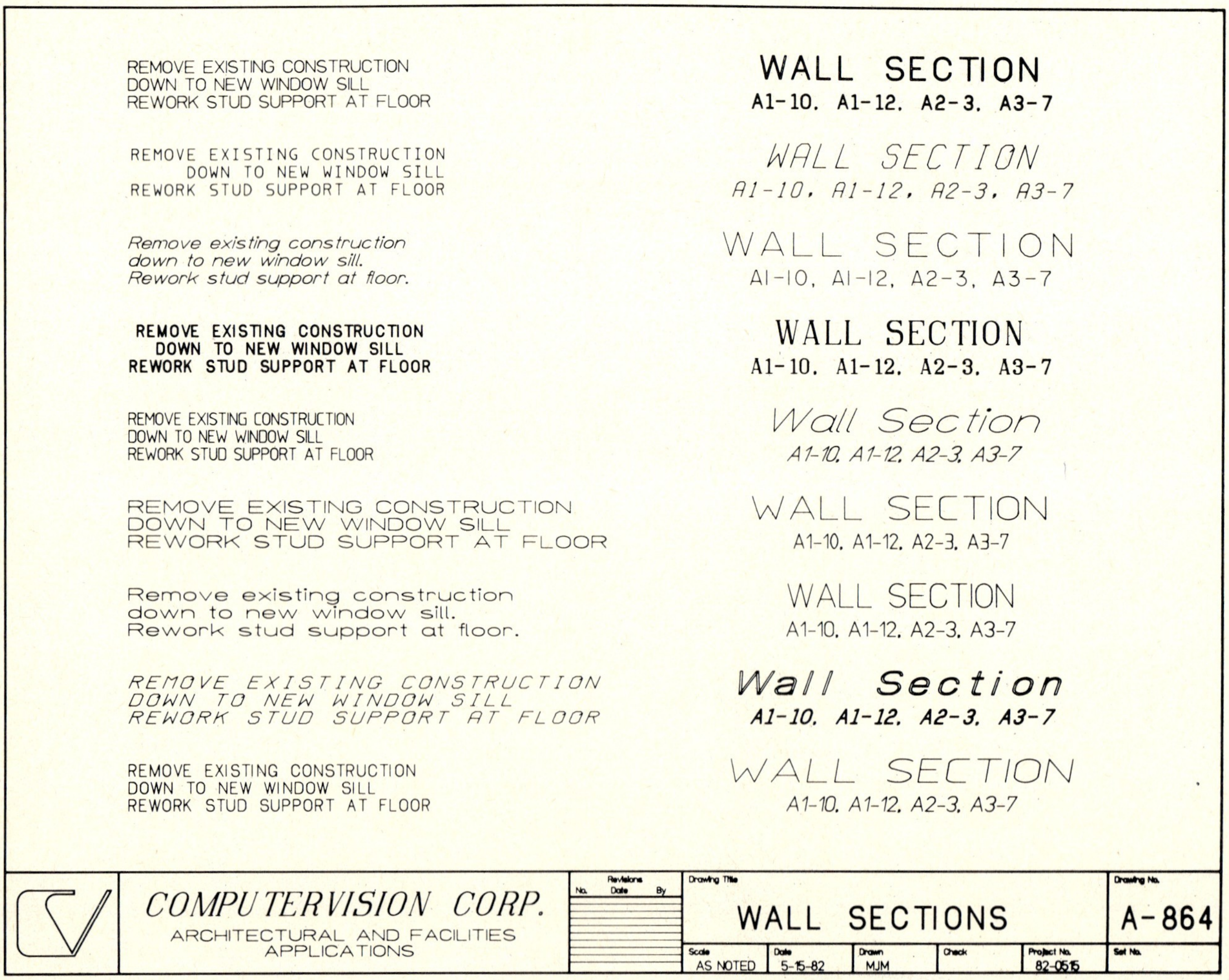

Figure 26–16

designed to print all data based on the position of the pen at a particular moment. This may result in notes, dimensions, and linework being plotted both from left to right and right to left.

A variety of plotter linework styles may be readily selected [26–15]. Colored lines may also be drawn by plotters that hold several pen points. A variety of lettering styles is also available [26–16]. Many symbols can be printed without a drafter forming them individually on a digitizer. The symbol picture on the digitizer need merely be touched with the cursor for the image to be printed on the drawing sheet [26–17]. The size of the symbol library and the ease which new symbols may be drawn and stored for future use varies greatly between the many graphic software and computer systems.

A faster printing device that does not use pens is the *electrostatic plotter*. The quality of printing with this type of plotter has greatly improved in recent years. Modern high speed units can very quickly print drawings to any scale with accuracy and line quality rivaling pen plotters. Large electrostatic plotters usually print the drawing in a progressive fashion starting at one end and gradually proceeding to the other as the paper moves steadily through the machine. The image appearing on the computer screen or stored in memory is recreated in the form of an electrostatic charge on paper or reproducible vellum or film. This charge attracts a black powder to form a visible image that is made permanent by passing through a fixer.

Computers and printing equipment work best in an environment of controlled temperature and humidity. Temperatures in the 60 to 75 °F range and relative humidity from 35 to 70 percent will limit expansion and contraction of component parts and drawing paper. Maintaining these conditions contributes to smooth functioning and accuracy in drawing. Rapid temperature changes should also be avoided. Since the equipment generates heat, this problem must be considered when designing the air conditioning for the space.

26.5 Equipment Selection

The various components of a computer system may be purchased separately or as a package. When purchasing separate items, it is very important to make a careful analysis of their compatibility with each other. This is especially true of a system having graphic capabilities. Some manufacturers supply graphic computer systems only as a complete package of hardware and software. These "turnkey" systems are closely integrated to perform a specific design function and are kept updated as new developments arise.

Another point to keep in mind in equipment selection is that there are major differences between systems in their ability to "multitask." Some systems can only perform one function at a time, such as plotting a drawing, creating a drawing on a monitor, or digitizing a drawing. Others can do more than a single task at one time. The ability to do this has a major impact on productivity and scheduling in an architectural or engineering office.

EXERCISES

26–1. Explain the function of a digitizer.
26–2. Visit a local architectural office and list the types of computer equipment used. What is the function of each? Is the plotter a flatbed or a drum type?
26–3. What is a light pen?
26–4. For personal use would you purchase a microcomputer? Why?
26–5. Describe the operation of the memory unit of a digitial computer.
26–6. What is a floppy disk?

Symbols may be printed on a drawing by touching the desired symbol picture on the digitizer.

Figure 26–17

27 Computer Applications

27.1 Computer Software

Before any computer system can be put to practical application, the necessary sets of instructions or *programs* must be written or purchased to direct the computing and associated equipment. The computer manufacturer usually supplies only the most elementary programs with the purchase of the computer. Other specialty programs must be carefully selected and purchased to suit your specific needs.

The specialized programs sold by each computer manufacturer are usually designed to operate only on their equipment. It is therefore very important when selecting a computer system to look carefully at both the hardware and software capabilities of each manufacturer's products. Some special purpose computer programs have also been written by educational institutions and by companies that are not directly associated with any one hardware manufacturer. Programs of this type are usually designed to run successfully on the most popular models of computers from several major manufacturers with only minor modifications.

No matter how well a computer program is written, a certain amount of time must be allocated for training operators before productive use can be expected. Software (as well as hardware) that is easier to learn to use is said to be "user friendly." Training courses are often provided by manufacturers or software suppliers at their headquarters or at your office when a large purchase is made. Additional information and modifications to widely used programs are available by joining "users' groups" that share practical application techniques.

In the following sections we will briefly look at the general application areas of computer systems in architectural drawing and design offices. These areas are: design calculations, word processing, computer-aided drafting, and computer-aided design. Many programs are commercially available in each of these areas.

27.2 Design Calculations

An architectural office that does not do its own engineering analysis and design may have limited use for a computer's ability to perform rapid structural and HVAC calculations. On the other hand, those offices that regularly do this type of work may wonder how they ever operated at a profit before the advent of the computer. The computer's ability to calculate structural and equipment size requirements is extremely useful. However, it offers an even greater service in being able to optimize the selections. Structural and mechanical engineering calculations involve the juggling of a great number of variables. The design process requires weighing these variables against each other for maximum performance, economy, and safety.

The engineer has to make assumptions about materials, systems, and sizes that are interrelated. It is impossible for the human mind to comprehend the interrelated consequences of all decisions, especially in terms of cost. Due to the great speed of the computer, a large number of options can be explored rapidly and optimum solutions can be found. The ramifications of changes in structural and HVAC systems can quickly be explored, giving both the engineer and the architect data on which to base design decisions.

27.3 Word Processing

The previously tedious and inefficient task of cutting up old specifications and pasting them together with newly written segments is now made relatively simple by the computer. Computer programs are available with complete specifications on them. The specification writer may delete or add segments to the computer program without handling paperwork. This procedure not only makes the preparation of specifications faster but also makes the document more accurate. There is less chance of omitting critical data or including extraneous or dated information. Once the specifications are complete, the computer prints them, thus saving hours of typing.

Bookkeeping, a function necessary in all offices, can also be computerized. Billing and payroll data can be stored on the computer. Such information can be called up on the monitor, updated, and returned to the computer memory by pushing a few buttons on the keyboard at the workstation. Meeting notes, correspondence, and other general information formerly kept in a file cabinet can be stored on the computer instead. Also, the routine task of typing letters can be done on the computer. Correction of typographical errors and general editing can be done on the monitor before the computer proceeds to type the text on paper. Changing typed material after the text is printed simply means that the original text is retrieved from the computer's memory, displayed on the monitor, edited electronically, and then a fresh copy is printed. The obsolete copy itself is not corrected. It is usually discarded.

27.4 Computer-Aided Drafting

The long process of constructing a perspective drawing requires that several decisions be made prior to the first pencil mark. The distance of the viewer from the building, the height of the viewer, the angle of the view, and even the sides of the building to be viewed all affect the form of the perspective drawing. Although an experienced drafter can readily make such decisions, considerable work is invested before one can tell from the drawing in progress just what will be seen in the final rendering. Often, when working by hand, only one or two perspectives may be drawn because of the labor required. This limits the designer's and the client's ability to judge what the constructed building will look like from all directions. The graphic capability of computers has drastically changed this limitation.

After plan and elevation data for a proposed building have been entered into a computer, schematic perspectives can be shown in a few seconds on the monitor from any viewer position [27–1]. You can seem to "walk"

Plan and elevation data entered in a computer can quickly produce perspective views from various directions.

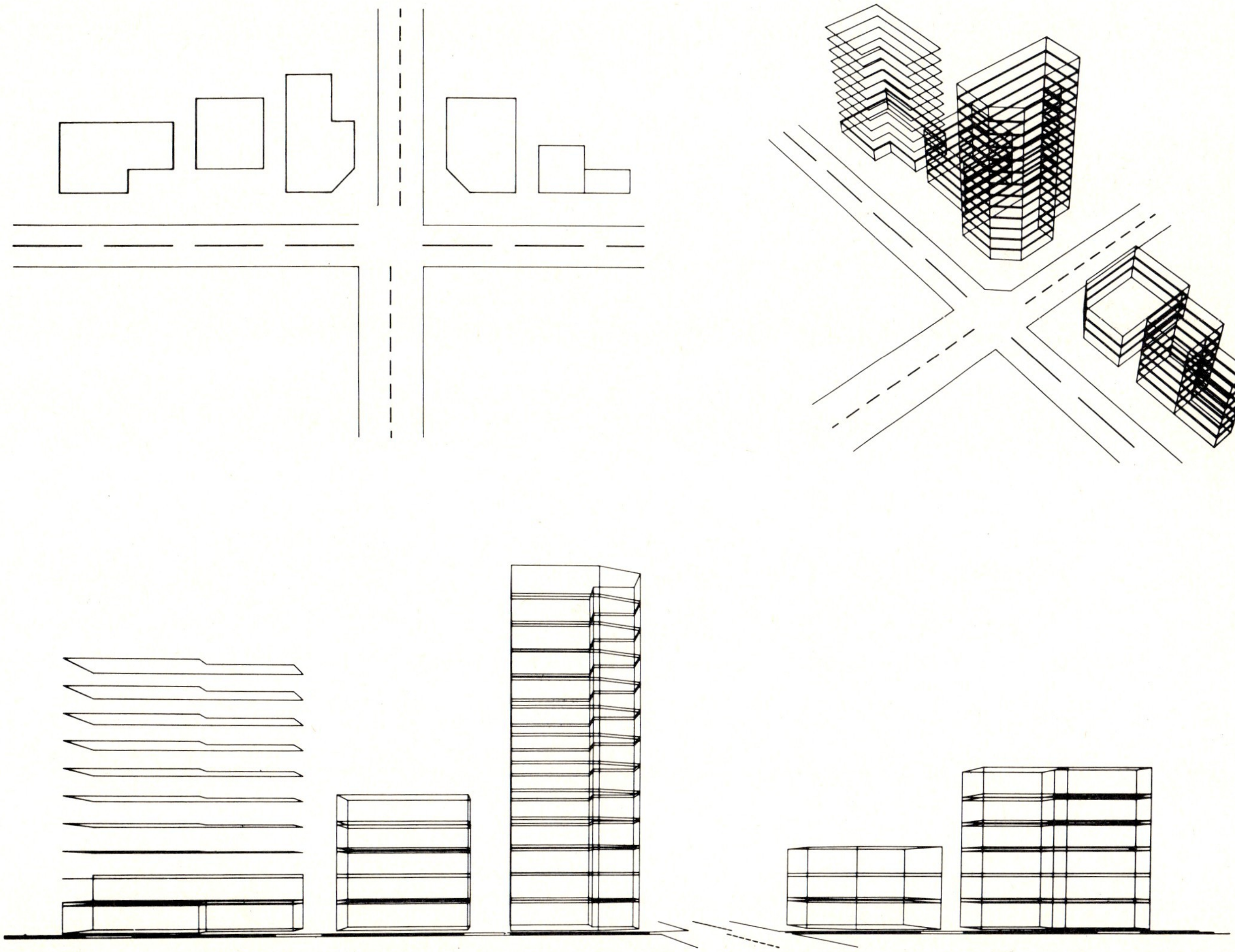

Figure 27–1

Computer Applications

around the building as the computer turns the schematic picture around on the screen while you watch. Such a walk around the building is a useful experience for both yourself and your client. Any of several views can be selected for printing. The printed schematic can be overlaid with tracing paper and a final rendering developed.

Three-dimensional examination is also very useful for site configurations and building interiors [27–2]. Building

Computer-drawn floor plans and perspectives are also useful for evaluating interior arrangements.

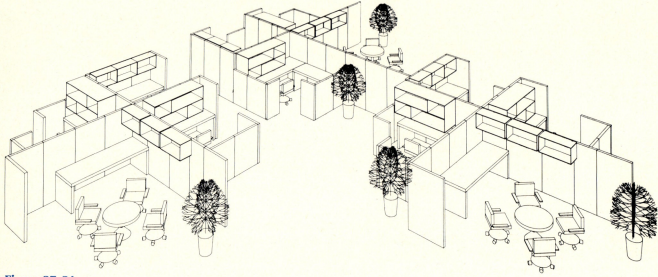

Figure 27–2A

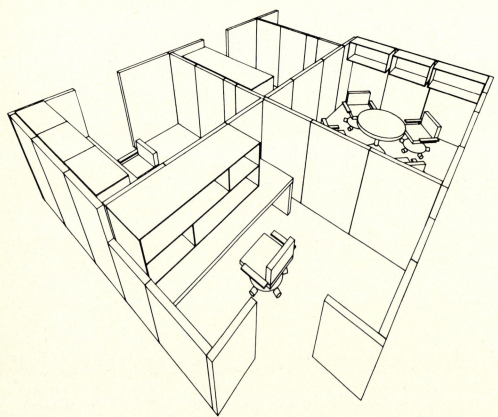

Figure 27–2B

436 Computers in Architectural Drawing and Design

Figure 27-2C

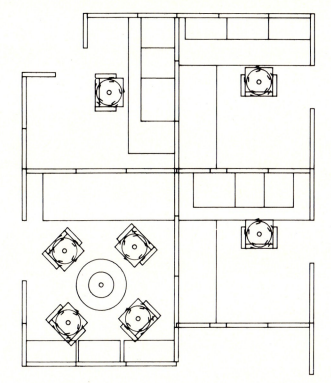

Figure 27-2D

exteriors can also be modeled for clarification and marketing purposes [27-3]. In addition to perspective, other types of pictorial views may be drawn, such as isometric and other types of paraline drawings. Details and working drawings can also be plotted by the computer at a great saving of time [27-4 thru 27-7]. Word processing and linework are easily mixed, such as in the various building schedules [27-8].

27.5 Computer-Aided Design

Thus far the computer uses described have been essentially those replacing manual activities. The design capability of a computer may seem to emulate the thinking process of a designer. However, it operates the same for design decisions as it does for other activities. In designing, the architect can type into the computer the criteria for a floor plan arrangement. The computer can then determine an optimum arrangement of spaces and report on the monitor the preferred solution. The

Building exteriors may be modeled on the computer for clarification and marketing.

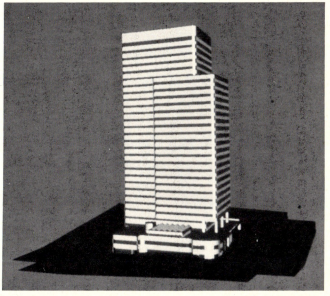

Figure 27-3

process is one of trial and error, wherein the computer proposes to itself different options and then evaluates them mathematically on the basis of the priorities set by the designer.

The great speed of the machine in making such evaluations makes it seem as if the machine is designing, but it is merely reporting an optimum mathematical relationship. This space-manipulating ability can save the designer time in developing plans for buildings with complicated functions, but certainly it is not the complete design process. The computer tool is valuable in that it can save the designer time in certain of the routine sequences of operations and decisions previously studied in this book that are necessary to produce buildings.

When using the design capabilities of the computer, it is always necessary to recognize the importance of selecting the most appropriate computer software that will perform the analysis required. It is also very important to understand the assumptions on which the software selected is based. Being able to evaluate, interpret, modify, and write computer programs will be important design functions for the architectural designers and drafters of the future.

A computer-drawn floor plan.

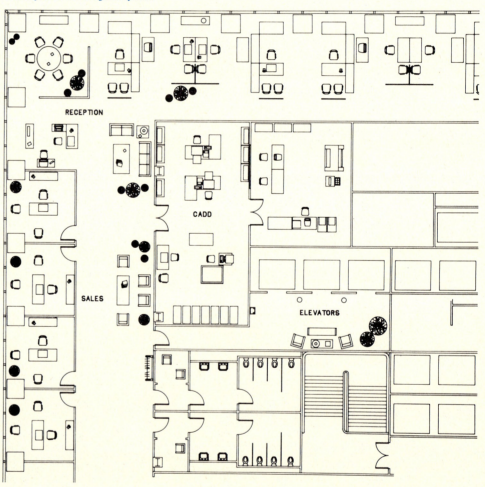

Figure 27-4

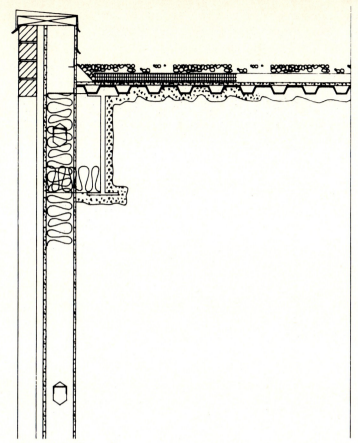

A computer-drawn wall section.

Figure 27-5

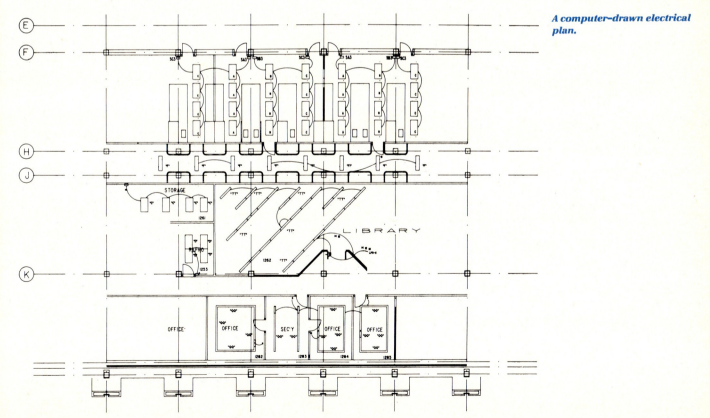

A computer-drawn electrical plan.

Figure 27-6

HVAC drawings may be prepared on a computer.

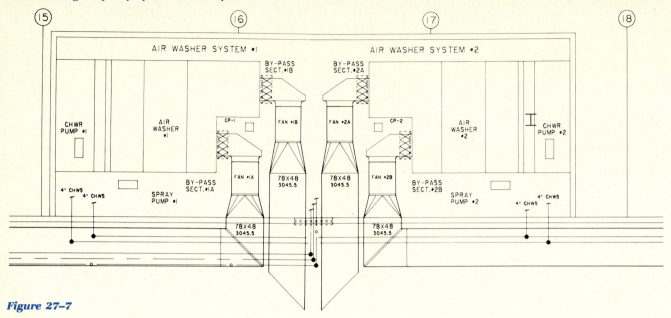

Figure 27-7

Word processing and linework may be combined on computer prepared building schedules.

Figure 27-8

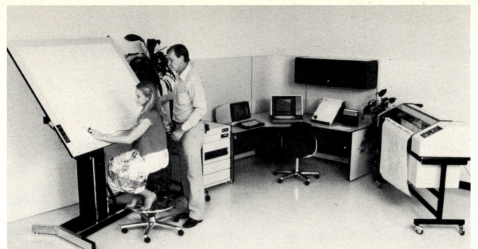

A drafting room of the future for some . . . the drafting room of the present for others.

Figure 27–9

27.6 Conclusions

The continuing drop in computer cost and the increase in capability will surely change the process for producing work in architectural and other drafting-oriented offices. Professionals and drafters will have to continue to understand the issues and concepts of architectural design and drafting but may perform somewhat different physical tasks. More pushing of pens on screens and less pushing of pencils on paper is no doubt in the future of the building-oriented professions. Before a machine can assist in making "aesthetic" decisions, however, more work will have to be done to reduce aesthetics to a mathematical basis. Since aesthetic quality is difficult to describe verbally, not to mention in numerical form, aesthetic judgment will most likely remain the prerogative of the human mind for some time [27–9].

EXERCISES

27–1. Visit a local architectural office that uses computer aided drafting equipment. What software is used?

27–2. What are the advantages and disadvantages of word processing?

27–3. What are the advantages and disadvantages of computer aided drafting?

27–4. How has the computer improved the design proficiency *potential* of the average architect?

VI

Appendixes

Architectural and Construction Abbreviations

The purpose of using abbreviations is to save time and space while still communicating a precise message. Part of the ability to "read blueprints" is the ability to translate certain standard abbreviations into their full meaning. However, due to several types of specialized work being combined in some projects, the same abbreviation may convey a confusing variety of meanings. Thus "SS" might mean "single strength" to the glass manufacturer, "stainless steel" to the metal worker, "select structural" to the carpenter, "structural steel" to the iron trades, and "slop sink" to the plumber.

To avoid overlapping and to ensure clarity of drawings, the following are the preferred abbreviations to use on architectural drawings, unless a special abbreviation legend accompanies the drawing or unless standard drafting procedures are superseded by instructions from the client, or by other standards (such as Corps of Engineers standards, and so on).

Standard Abbreviations List

Above finished counter	AFC
Above finished floor	AFF
Above finished grade	AFG
Acoustic	AC
Acoustic plaster	AC PL
Acoustic tile	AC T
Actual	ACT
Additional	ADD
Adhesive	ADH
Adjustable	ADJ
Aggregate	AGGR
Air conditioning	AIR COND
Air conditioning unit	ACU
Alternating current	AC
Aluminum	AL or ALUM
American Institute of Architects	AIA
American Institute of Steel Construction	AISC
American Institute of Timber Construction	AITC
American National Standards Institute	ANSI
American Plywood Association	APA
American Society of Heating, Refrigerating, and Air Conditioning Engineers	ASHRAE

Standard Abbreviations List

American Society for Testing and Materials	ASTM
American wire gauge	AWG
American Wood Preservers Institute	AWPI
Amount	AMT
Ampere	AMP
Anchor bolt	AB
Angle (in degrees)	∢
Angle (structural)	∟
Approximate	APPROX
Architectural	ARCH
Architectural Woodwork Institute	AWI
Area	A
Area drain	AD
Asbestos	ASB
Asphalt	ASPH
Asphaltic concrete	ASPH CONC
Assembly	ASSEM
Associated General Contractors of America	AGC
At	@
Automatic	AUTO
Avenue	AVE
Average	AVG
Balcony	BALC
Basement	BSMT
Baseplate	BP
Bathroom	B
Bathtub with shower	BTS
Batten	BATT
Beam	BM
Bearing	BRG
Bearing plate	B PL
Bedroom	BR
Bench mark	BM
Between	BET
Beveled	BEV
Bidet	BDT
Block	BLK
Blocking	BLKG
Blower	BLO
Board	BD
Board feet	BD FT
Both sides	BS
Both ways	BW
Bottom	BOT
Boulevard	BLVD
Bracket	BRKT

Standard Abbreviations List

Brass	BR
Brick	BRK
Brick Institute of America	BIA
British thermal unit	BTU
Broom closet	BC
Building	BLDG
Building line	BL
Built-in	BLT-IN
Built-up	BU
Bulletin board	BB
Button	BUT
Buzzer	BUZ
By (used as 2 × 4)	×
Cabinet	CAB
Candela	cd
Candlepower	CP
Carpet	CPT
Cast iron	CI
Cast in place	CIP
Catalog	CAT
Catch basin	CB
Caulking	CLKG
Ceiling	CLG
Ceiling diffuser	CD
Celsius	C
Cement	CEM
Cement plaster	CEM PLAS
Center	CTR
Center to center	C to C
Center line	₵ or CL
Centimeter	cm
Ceramic	CER
Ceramic tile	CT
Chalkboard	CHKBD
Chamfer	CHAM
Channel (structural)	C
Check	CHK
Cinder block	CIN BL
Circle	CIR
Circuit	CKT
Circuit breaker	CIR BKR
Class	CL
Classroom	CLRM
Cleanout	CO
Clear	CLR
Closet	CLO or CL
Clothes dryer	CL D
Cold water	CW
Column	COL
Combination	COMB
Common	COM
Concrete	CONC
Concrete block	CONC B
Concrete masonry unit (concrete block)	CMU
Concrete Reinforcing Steel Institute	CRSI
Construction	CONST
Construction Specifications Institute	CSI
Continuous	CONT
Contractor	CONTR
Contractor furnished	CF
Control joint	CJ
Copper	COP or CU
Corridor	CORR
Counter	CTR
Countersink	CSK
Courses	C
Cover	COV
Cross section	X-SECT
Cubic	CU
Cubic feet	CU FT
Cubic feet per minute	CFM
Cubic yard	CU YD
Damper	DMPR
Decibel	db
Deep, depth	DP
Degree	° or DEG
Department	DEPT
Detail	DET
Diagonal	DIAG
Diagram	DIAG
Diameter	DIA
Diffuser	DIFF
Dimension	DIM
Dining room	DIN RM
Direct current	DC
Dishwasher	DW
Disposal	DISPL
Distance	DIST
Ditto	" or DO
Divided or division	DIV
Door	DR
Double	DBL
Double-hung	DH
Double-strength (glass)	DS
Douglas Fir	DF
Dowel	DWL
Down	DN
Downspout	DS
Drain	D or DR
Drawing	DWG
Drinking fountain	DF
Dry bulb	DB
Dryer	D
Drywall	DW
Duplicate	DUP
Each	EA
Each face	EF
Each way	EW
East	E
Elbow	ELL
Electric(al)	ELECT
Electric panel board	EPB
Elevation	EL or ELEV
Elevator	ELEV
Enclosure	ENCL
Engineer	ENGR
Entrance	ENT
Equal	EQ
Equipment	EQUIP
Estimate	EST
Excavate	EXC
Exhaust	EXH
Existing	EXIST'G
Expansion bolt	EB
Expansion joint	EXP JT

Standard Abbreviations List

Exposed	EXPO
Extension	EXT
Exterior	EXT
Exterior grade	EXT GR
Fabricate	FAB
Face brick	FB
Face of studs	FOS
Fahrenheit	F
Family room	FAM R
Federal Housing Administration	FHA
Feet	' or FT
Feet per minute	FPM
Fiberglass-reinforced plastic	FRP
Figure	FIG
Finish(ed)	FIN
Finished all over	FAO
Finished floor	FIN FL
Finished floor elevation	FFE
Finished grade	FIN GR
Finished opening	FO
Firebrick	FBRK
Fire extinguisher	F EXT
Fire extinguisher cabinet	FEC
Fire hose cabinet	FHC
Fire hydrant	FH
Fireproof	FP
Fitting	FTG
Fixture	FIX
Flammable	FLAM
Flange	FLG
Flashing	FL
Flexible	FLEX
Floor	FLR
Floor drain	FD
Floor sink	FS
Flooring	FLG
Flourescent	FLUOR
Folding	FLDG
Foot	' or FT
Footing	FTG
Forward	FWD
Foundation	FND
Four-way	4-W
Frame	FR
Front	FR
Full size	FS
Furnace	FURN
Future	FUT
Gallon	GAL
Galvanized	GALV
Galvanized iron (galvanized steel)	GI
Gauge	GA
General Services Administration	GSA
Glass	GL
Glass block	GL BL
Glazed structural unit	GSU
Glue-laminated	GLUELAM
Government	GOVT
Grade	GR
Grade beam	GB

Standard Abbreviations List

Grating	GRTG
Gravel	GVL
Grille	GR
Ground	GRND
Grout	GT
Gymnasium	GYM
Gypsum	GYP
Hall	H
Hardboard	HBD
Hardware	HDW
Hardwood	HDWD
Head	HD
Header	HDR
Heater	HTR
Heating	HTG
Heating/ventilating/air conditioning	HVAC
Heavy duty	HD
Height	HT
Hexagonal	HEX
Highway	HWY
Hollow core	HC
Hollow metal	HM
Horizontal	HORIZ
Horsepower	HP
Hose bibb	HB
Hospital	HOSP
Hot water	HW
Hot water heater	HWH
Hour	HR
House	HSE
Hundred	C
I-beam (structural)	S
Illuminate	ILLUM
Incandescent	INCAND
Inch	" or IN.
Inflammable	INFL
Information	INFO
Inside diameter	ID
Inside face	IF
Inspect(ion)	INSP
Install	INST
Insulate(d)(ion)	INS
Interior	INT
Interior grade	INT GR
International Conference of Building Officials	ICBO
Invert	INV
Jamb	JMB
Janitor's sink	JS
Janitor's closet	JC
Joint	JT
Joist	JST
Joist and plank	J & P
Junction	JCT
Junction box	J-BOX
Kelvin	K
Kiln dried	KD
Kilogram	kg
Kilovolt	KV
Kilowatt	KW
Kitchen	KIT
Kitchen cabinet	KCAB
Kitchen sink	KSK

Architectural and Construction Abbreviations

Standard Abbreviations List

Knockout	KO
Label	LBL
Laboratory	LAB
Laminate(d)	LAM
Landing	LDG
Latitude	LAT
Laundry	LAU
Lavatory	LAV
Leader	LDR
Left	L
Length	LGTH
Level	LEV
Library	LIB
Light (pane of glass)	LT
Linear feet	LIN FT
Linen closet	L CL
Linoleum	LINO
Live load	LL
Living room	LR
Location	LOC
Long	LG
Longitude	LNG
Lumber	LBR
Machine bolt	MB
Manhole	MH
Manufacture(r)	MFR
Marble	MRB
Mark	MK
Masonry	MAS
Masonry opening	MO
Material	MAT
Maximum	MAX
Mechanical	MECH
Medicine cabinet	MC
Medium	MED
Membrane	MEMB
Metal	MET
Metal lath and plaster	MLP
Meter	m
Mile	MI
Millimeter	mm
Minimum	MIN
Mirror	MIRR
Miscellaneous	MISC
Modular	MOD
Molding	MLDG
Mullion	MULL
National Association of Home Builders of the U.S.	NAHB
National Association of Women in Construction	NAWIC
National Bureau of Standards	NBS
National Lumber Manufacturer's Association	NLMA
Natural grade	NAT GR
Noise reduction coefficient	NRC
Nominal	NOM
North	N
Not applicable	NA
Not in contract	NIC
Not to scale	NTS
Number	NO. or #
Oak	O
Office	OFF

Standard Abbreviations List

On center	OC
One-way	1-W
Open web	OW
Opening	OPG
Opposite	OPP
Opposite hand	OPH
Ounce	OZ
Outside diameter	OD
Outside face of concrete	OFC
Outside face of studs	OFS
Overhead	OH
Painted	PTD
Pair	PR
Panel	PNL
Parallel	PAR or $\parallel$
Partition	PTN
Passage	PASS
Pavement	PVMT
Penny (nail size)	d
Per	/
Percent	%
Perforate	PERF
Perimeter	PERIM
Perpendicular	PERP or $\perp$
Piece	PC
Plan	PLN
Plaster	PLS
Plasterboard	PL BD
Plastic	PLAS
Plastic tile	PLAS T
Plate	PL or $\mathcal{L}$
Plate glass	PL GL
Platform	PLAT
Plumbing	PLMB
Plywood	PLY
Polished	POL
Polyethelyne	POLY or PE
Polystyrene	PS
Polyvinyl chloride	PVC
Position	POS
Pound	LB or #
Pounds per square foot	PFS
Pounds per square inch	PSI
Precast	PRCST
Prefabricated	PREFAB
Preliminary	PRELIM
Premolded	PRMLD
Property	PROP
Public address system	PA
Pull chain	PC
Pushbutton	PB
Quantity	QTY
Quarry tile	QT
Quart	QT
Radiator	RAD
Radius	RAD
Random length and width	RL&W
Range	R
Receptacle	RECP
Recessed	REC
Redwood	RDWD
Reference	REF
Refrigeration	REF
Refrigerator	REFRIG

Standard Abbreviations List

Register	REG
Reinforce, reinforcing	REINF
Reinforcing bar	REBAR
Required	REQ
Resilient	RES
Resistance	RES
Return	RET
Revision	REV
Revolutions per minute	RPM
Right	R
Right hand	RH
Riser	R
Road	RD
Roof	RF
Roof drain	RD
Roofing	RFG
Room	RM
Rough	RGH
Rough opening	RO
Round	RD or ϕ
Rubber base	RB
Rubber tile	RBT
Schedule	SCH
Screw	SCR
Second	s or SEC
Section	SECT
Select	SEL
Select structural	SS
Self-closing	SC
Service	SERV
Sewer	SEW
Sheathing	SHTHG
Sheet	SHT
Sheet metal	SM
Shower	SH
Siding	SDG
Sill cock	SC
Similar	SIM
Single-hung	SH
Single-strength (glass)	SS
Sink	SK
Slop sink	SS
Society of American Registered Architects	ARA
Socket	SOC
Soil pipe	SP
Solid block	SLD BLK
Solid core	SC
South	S
Southern Building Code Congress International	SBCC
Southern Forest Products Association	SFPA
Southern Pine Inspection Bureau	SPIB
Specifications	SPEC
Square	□ or SQ
Square feet	SF or ϕ
Square inches	SQ IN or ⊞
Stainless steel	SST
Stairs	ST
Stand pipe	ST P
Standard	STD
Station point	SP

Standard Abbreviations List

Steel	STL
Stirrup	STIR
Stock	STK
Storage	STO
Storm drain	SD
Street	ST
Structural	STR
Structural clay tile	SCT
Substitute	SUB
Supply	SUP
Surface	SUR
Surface four sides	S4S
Surface two edges	S2E
Suspended ceiling	SUSP CLG
Switch	S or SW
Symbol	SYM
Symmetrical	SYM
Synthetic	SYN
System	SYS
Tack board	TK BD
Tangent	TAN
Tar and gravel	T & G
Technical	TECH
Tee	T
Telephone	TEL
Television	TV
Temperature	TEMP
Temporary	TEMP
Terra-cotta	TC
Terrazzo	TZ
Thermostat	THERMO
Thickness	THK
Thousand	M
Thousand board feet	MBM
Three-way	3-W
Threshold	THR
Tissue paper	TP
Toilet	TOL
Tongue and groove	T & G
Top of wall	TW
Tread	TR
Two-way	2-W
Typical	TYP
Undercut door	UCD
Underwriters' Laboratory, Inc.	U.L.
Unfinished	UNFIN
U.S. Bureau of Land Management	BLM
U.S. Department of Housing and Urban Development	HUD
U.S. Standard Gauge	USG
Urinal	UR
Utility	UTIL
V-joint	VJ
Vanishing point	VP
Vanity	VAN
Vapor barrier	VB
Vent through roof	VTR
Vent stack	VS
Ventilation	VENT
Ventilator	V
Vertical	VERT

Architectural and Construction Abbreviations

Standard Abbreviations List

Vertical grain	VG
Vestibule	VEST
Vinyl	VIN
Vinyl asbestos tile	VAT
Vinyl base	VB
Vinyl tile	VT
Vinyl wall covering	VWC
Vitreous clay tile	VCT
Volt	V
Volume	VOL
Wainscot	WSCT
Wall cabinet	WCAB
Wall vent	WV
Waste stack	WS
Water	W
Water closet (toilet)	WC
Water Heater	WH
Waterproof	WP
Watt	W

Standard Abbreviations List

Weatherproof	WP
Weephole	WH
Weight	WT
Welded wire fabric	WWF
West	W
Wet bulb	WB
White pine	WP
Wide flange (structural)	W
Window	WDW
With	w/
Without	WO
Wood	WD
Working point	WPT
Wrought iron	WI
Yard	YD
Year	YR
Yellow pine	YP
Zinc	ZN

B Glossary of Architectural and Construction Terms

Acoustics—The science of sound and sound control.

Acrylic—A noncrystalline thermoplastic with good weather resistance, shatter resistance, and optical clarity; sometimes used for glazing. (Common trade names are Plexiglas and Acrylite.)

Adhesive—A natural or synthetic material, usually in liquid or paste form, used to cement materials together.

Admixture—A prepared substance added to concrete to alter it or to achieve certain characteristics.

Adobe—An unburned brick dried in the sun; found primarily in the southwestern region of the United States.

Aggregate—The inert ingredients of concrete; normally sand and crushed rock.

Air-Dried Lumber—Lumber that has been stored in yards or sheds for a length of time after cutting. (For the United States as a whole the minimum moisture content of thoroughly air-dried lumber is 12 to 15%. The average is somewhat higher.)

Air-Entrained Concrete—Concrete containing millions of tiny air bubbles that increase workability, resist deterioration due to the freeze–thaw cycle, and reduce water requirement.

Alcove—A recessed space or portion of a larger room.

Alligatoring—Coarse checking pattern on paint caused by weathering.

Alloy—The combination of a metal with other metals or elements to achieve desirable characteristics.

Anchor Bolts—Bolts used to secure a wood sill plate or steel column base to a concrete or masonry floor or wall [B–1].

Apron—The inside trim board placed immediately under the window sill; also a paved area, such as the juncture of a driveway with the street or with a garage entrance.

Arcade—A series of arches supported by columns or piers. [B–2].

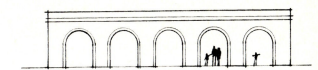

Figure B–2 Arcade

Arch—A curved structural member designed to support its weight and the weight above it [B–3].

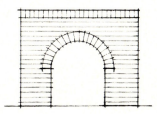

Figure B–3 Arch

Areaway—A recessed area below grade affording access, air, and light to a cellar or basement [B–4].

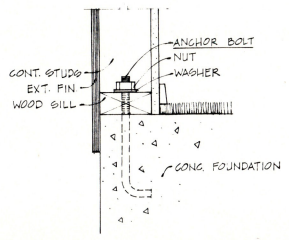

Figure B–1

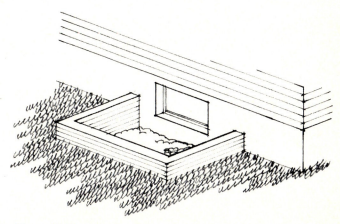

Figure B–4 Areaway

Arris—The sharp edge formed by the meeting of two planes or surfaces, especially found on edges of moldings and doors.

Asbestos Cement—A material formed from a mixture of Portland cement and asbestos fibers.

Ash Pit—The ash depository usually located beneath the fireplace hearth.

Asphalt—A residue from evaporated petroleum. Not soluble in water but soluble by other petroleum products. Melts when heated. Used widely for making flooring tile, waterproofing roofs and exterior walls, panels, and so on.

Asphaltic Concrete—A mixture of asphalt and aggregate. Spread and rolled while hot. Used for paving roads and driveways.

Astragal—A molding attached to one of a pair of swinging doors, against which the other door strikes.

Atrium—An open court or central hall within a building.

Attic—The space between the ceiling and the roof.

Awning Window—An outswinging window that is hinged along the top edge.

Backfill—Replacement of excavated earth or gravel into the space around a building wall after foundations are in place.

Balcony—A platform projecting outward from the wall of a building, above ground level.

Balloon Framing—Distinguished by two-story-high studs, to the faces of which are nailed supporting members for the second floor [14–41].

Baluster (Banister)—An upright support of a railing, such as alongside a stairway [B–5].

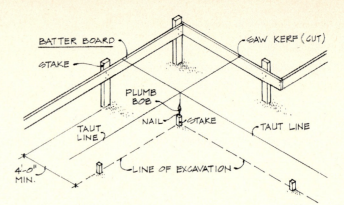

Figure B–6

Bay Window—A window projecting out from the walls of a building, either square or polygonal in shape.

Beam—A horizontal structural member that is designed to carry loads perpendicular to its span [B–7].

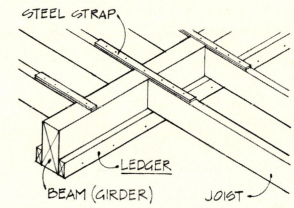

Figure B–7

Beam Ceiling—A ceiling where the ceiling beams are exposed to view.

Bearing Partition—A partition (wall) that supports a vertical load (floor or roof) in addition to its own weight.

Bearing Plate—A metal plate used to distribute a load over a larger area.

Bed Joint—Horizontal joints in masonry work [B–8].

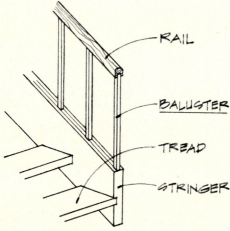

Figure B–5

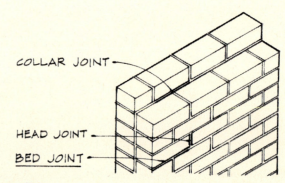

Figure B–8

Bar Chair or Chair—A device used to support reinforcing bars during concrete placement.

Baseboard—The finish board covering the intersection of the interior wall and floor [14–55].

Batt—A piece of insulation designed to be installed between two framing members.

Batten—Narrow strips of wood or metal used to cover joints in walls or as decorative vertical members over plywood, wide boards, metal siding, or roofing [14–60].

Batter Boards—Reference boards erected at a given offset distance from the building and set prior to excavation. Used to establish line of excavation [B–6].

Bench Mark—A surveyor's reference mark placed on some permanent object that is fixed to the ground and from which land measurements and grades are established.

Blind Nailing—Driving nails in such a way that the holes are concealed. Usually driven at an angle in the tongue of tongue-and-groove flooring [14–60].

Blocking—Small wood members placed between joists to prevent twisting. Also miscellaneous sizes of wood used as spacers and filler pieces [B–9].

Bow Window—A window projecting out from the walls of a building, either curved or semicircular in shape.

Box Beam—A hollow, built-up structural member.

Brick Veneer—A facing of brick laid against and fastened through sheathing to the studs of a frame wall, or a facing of brick laid against a concrete or masonry wall [14–55].

Bridging—Crossed braces used between joists to stiffen and prevent twisting [B–10].

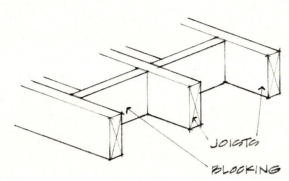

Figure B–9

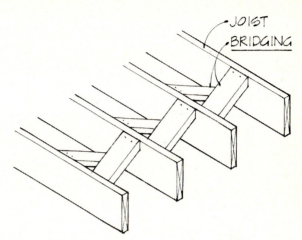

Figure B–10

Board Foot—A unit of measure for lumber. (Equals volume of a board with nominal dimensions of 1 inch thick × 12 inches × 12 inches)

Bond—The pattern in which the masonry units are arranged in a wall; also the mortar joint between two adjacent masonry units [14–32].

Bond Beam—A reinforced concrete beam used to strengthen masonry walls.

Buck—Rough framing members around doors and windows.

Built-Up Roof—Roofing composed of three to five layers of asphalt-saturated felt laminated with coal tar pitch, asphalt, or other bonding agent. The top is generally finished with crushed slag or gravel. Used on flat or low-pitched roofs [B–11].

Figure B–11

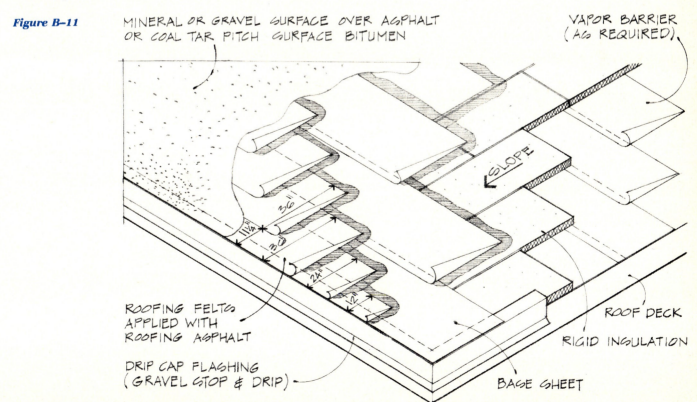

Glossary of Architectural and Construction Terms

Bullnose—Rounded edge trim units.
Butt Joint—The juncture where ends of the two timbers or other members meet in a square-cut joint, end to end, or edge to edge.
Butts—Hinges applied to the edge of a door [B–12].

AT EXPANSION JOINT OR AROUND WINDOW AND DOOR OPENINGS
Figure B–14

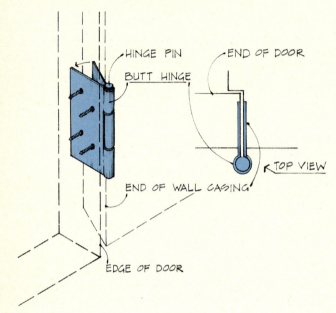

Figure B–12

Call Out—An instructional note on a drawing with a leader to the feature.
Camber—A slight upward bend in a structural member [B–13].

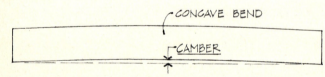

Figure B–13

Cant Strip—A beveled strip used to avoid a sharp bend in roofing material.
Cantilever—A beam or girder that is free at one end and fixed at the other.
Cap—A covering for a post or wall.
Capillary Action—Tendency of water to move into small spaces regardless of gravity.
Carport—A garage that is not fully enclosed.
Casement—A window whose frame is hinged along the vertical side.
Casing—Molding of various widths and thicknesses used to trim the edges of door and window openings.
Caulking—The waterproof compound or the application of these compounds to seal points of contact between two materials or surfaces. Used for weatherproofing [B–14].

Cavity Wall—A hollow wall formed by firmly linked masonry walls, providing an insulating air space between [14–33].
Cement—A substance used to unite two materials; also a material used with sand, gravel, and water to make concrete.
Chamfer—A beveled edge formed by removing the sharp corner of a piece of material.
Chase—A recessed space or passage through a structural element to accommodate ducts, pipes, or conduits.
Chord—The horizontal members of a truss.
Clapboard—A long, thin board, thicker on one edge, overlapped and nailed on to serve as exterior siding.
Cleat—A small board fastened to another member and serving as a supporting brace.
Collar Beam—A horizontal tie beam connecting two opposite rafters at a level above the wall plate to add rigidity [B–15].

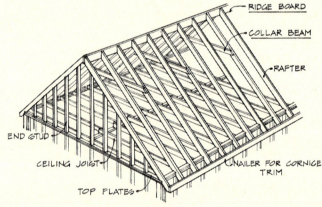

Figure B–15

Concrete—Ordinarily, a combination of Portland cement, sand, coarse aggregate, and water.
Control Joint—A groove in concrete construction to regulate the location of cracks.
Coping—A protective masonry or metal cap or top course to prevent water penetration.
Corbel—A shelf or ledge formed by building successive courses of masonry out from the wall.
Core—The inner layer or layers of plywood.
Corner Brace—A diagonal member at the corner of a wood-frame wall to stiffen and strengthen the wall [14–41].
Cornice—Overhang of a pitched roof at the eave line. Usually

consists of a fascia board, a soffit for a closed cornice, and appropriate moldings [B–34].

Counter Flashing—A flashing used under the regular flashing.

Course—A horizontal row of bricks, stone, tile, blocks, or other building material.

Cove—Molded concave-shaped trim usually used on inside corners.

Crawl Space—The shallow, unfinished space usually surrounded by the foundation wall that is between the floor joists and the ground, when there is no basement.

Cricket—A flashing saddle used between a sloping roof and a chimney [B–18].

Cripple—A structural member that is cut less than full length, such as a stud above a door or window opening [14–43].

Cross Bracing—Boards fastened diagonally across structural members, such as studs, to provide rigidity [14–41].

Crown Molding—Decorative molding used above eye level at the top of cabinets, at ceiling corners, or under a roof overhang.

Cul-De-Sac—A street or court with no outlets that provides a circular turn around for automobiles.

Cupola—A small decorative structure built on a roof.

Curtain Wall—An exterior wall that provides no structural support.

Dado Joint—A groove on the face of a board that has been properly cut to receive the perpendicular end of another board to form a joint. Often used in cabinet construction.

Dead Load—A constant weight or pressure causing a load on a structural member.

Decibel—A unit for measuring the relative intensity of sound.

Dew Point—Temperature at which water vapor in the atmosphere begins to condense as a liquid.

Dome—A hemispherical structure.

Dormer—A minor gable in a pitched roof, usually having a window(s) on the front face [B–16].

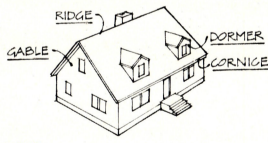

Figure B–16

Double-Glazing—An insulating window pane formed of two pieces of glass with a sealed air space between them.

Double-Hung Windows—Windows having top and bottom sashes each capable of vertical movement in its own grooves.

Downspout—A vertical drain pipe to carry rainwater from the roof to the ground.

Drain—A pipe to carry wastewater.

Dressed Size—The actual size of lumber after surfacing the rough wood to a finished size.

Drip—A projection or groove designed to cause rainwater to drip beyond its normal position of fall.

Dry Pack—To fill by packing tightly with a damp concrete mixture.

Dry Rot—Decay in seasoned timber caused by fungus.

Dry Well—A pit or shallow well located on porous ground used for the disposal of rainwater.

Drywall—A wall finished with gypsum wallboard or other material, rather than with plaster [14–65].

Duct—A conduit, usually of sheet metal, used for air distribution throughout a building [16–39].

Duplex Outlet—Electrical wall outlet having two plug receptacles.

Easement—A right or privilege for some specific use of a piece of property held by someone other than the owner. Usually used for placement of public utility lines.

Eave—The lower part of a roof projecting over a wall [B–34].

Efflorescence—Whitish powder of crystals caused by water-soluble salts that come to the surface when water evaporates from brick or other masonry construction.

Elbow—An L-shaped pipe fitting.

Ell—An addition to a building that lies at a right angle to the main section.

Enamel—A pigmented paint with a hard, shiny surface finish.

Epoxy—A synthetic resin with excellent adhesion properties.

Excavation—A cavity or hole formed by cutting, digging, or scooping.

Expansion Joint—A bituminous fiber or synthetic strip used to separate blocks or slabs of concrete [B–14]. Discourages cracking due to expansion or contraction resulting from temperature change.

Facade—The face or front of a building.

Face Brick—Better-quality brick used on the exposed surface of a wall.

Facia (or Fascia)—A flat board, band, or face used sometimes by itself, but usually in combination with molding. Often used at the outer face of a cornice or at the end of rafters [B–34].

Fill—Sand, gravel, or loose earth used to bring a subgrade up to a desired level.

Firebrick—Brick having a great resistance to cracking or other deterioration from the effects of heat [23–27].

Firecut—The angular cut at the end of a joist designed to rest on a masonry wall [B–17].

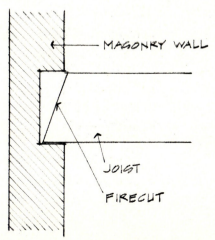

Figure B–17

Glossary of Architectural and Construction Terms

Firestops—Horizontal blocks placed between studs to impede the spread of fire [14–41 and 23–28].

Firewall—A fire-resistant wall used to subdivide a building and prevent the spreading of a fire from one area to another.

Flagstone—Thin, flat stones used for walks, floors, walls, and steps.

Flashing—The material or the application of this material to seal and protect joints formed between different surfaces or materials; usually made of metal [B–18].

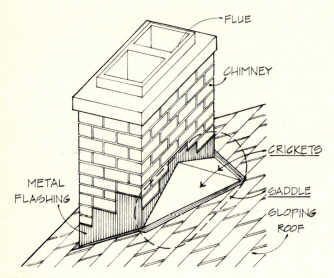

Figure B–18

Flue—The space or passage in a chimney through which smoke, gas, or other fumes ascend. Each passage is called a *flue*. One or more flues and the surrounding masonry make up the chimney [B–18].

Flue Lining—Terra-cotta pipe used as the inner lining for chimneys [B–18].

Footings—A secure element, usually made of concrete, used to support a particular portion of a structure [14–4].

Foundation—The entire supporting arrangement of a structure [14–4].

Framing—The rough structural lumber used to construct a building—the studs, joists, rafters, beams, and so on.

Frieze—The horizontal trim member connecting the soffit of the cornice with the wall [B–34].

Frost Line—The depth of frost penetration in soil [14–5 and 14–6].

Furring—Strips of wood or metal applied to a wall or other surface to level it, create an insulating air space, and/or serve as a fastening base for a finish material.

Gable—Vertical triangular end of a building having a double sloping roof [B–16]. Also a specific roof shape [6–21].

Galvanic Action—The deteriorating electrolytic reaction between two different metals or alloys when they are in contact with one another with moisture present.

Galvanizing—The process of applying a coating of zinc to steel for protection against corrosion.

Gambrel Roof—A gable roof with two pitches, the lower steeper than the upper [6–21].

Garrett—The part of the attic just under the roof.

Geodesic Dome—A dome-shaped structure formed of triangular panels [6–41].

Girder—A large or principal horizontal beam used to support concentrated loads at isolated points along its length [B–7].

Glazing—A term describing glass in a frame or the work of installing glass in a frame.

Grade—The level of the ground around a building.

Grade Line—The point at which the ground rests against the foundation wall.

Gradient—The inclination of the ground, a road, or piping. Expressed in percent.

Gravel Stop—The strip of metal with a vertical lip used to retain the gravel around the edge of a built-up roof.

Grounds—Guides used around openings and at the floor line to provide a finish line for plaster.

Grout—A fluid mixture of cement, sand, and water used to fill joints and cavities in masonry or tile.

Grubbing—The removal of unwanted roots, stumps, and so on, from a site.

Gunite—A trade name for pneumatically placed concrete.

Gusset—A flat piece of wood, plywood, or metal used to provide a connection at the intersection of wood members [B–19].

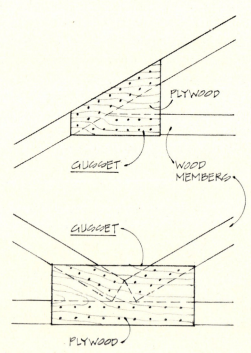

Figure B–19

Gutter—A trough at the edge of a roof used to carry off rainwater.

Gypsum—Hydrated sulfate of calcium used to make plaster and plasterboard.

Hanger—A metal strap used to support piping or the ends of joists [B–20].

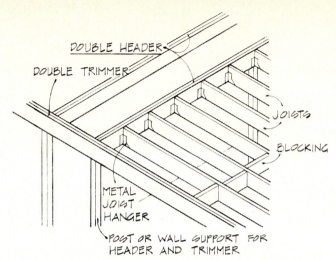

Figure B–20

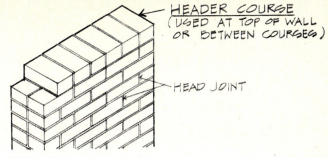

Figure B–22

Hardwood—Wood from trees having broad leaves, in contrast to needles.
Heat Joint—The vertical joint between masonry units [B–22].
Header—(a) A beam placed perpendicular to joists and to which joists are fastened in framing [B–20]; (b) a wood lintel [B–21].

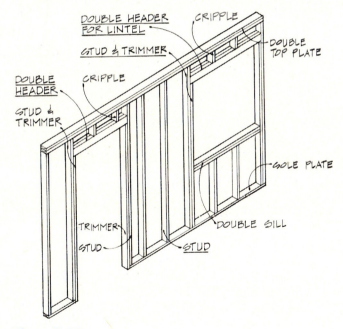

Figure B–21

Header Course—A masonry course in which the smallest surface of the units are exposed and the largest surface is horizontal [B–22].

Headroom—The vertical clearance in a room or on a stairway.
Hearth—The inner or outer floor of a fireplace, usually made of concrete, stone, or brick [23–26].
Heartwood—Wood extending from the center of the tree to the sapwood.
Hinge—Device on which doors, windows, cabinets, and so on, may turn or swing to open or close [B–12].
Hip—The exterior edge formed by the meeting of two sloping roof surfaces which have their wall plates running in different directions [B–23]. Also a specific roof shape [6–21].

Figure B–23

Honeycomb—Concrete that is poorly mixed, placed, or vibrated, resulting in air pockets.
Hose Bibb—A water faucet with its outlet threaded for the attachment of a hose.
Humidifier—A device usually attached to a furnace for the purpose of increasing the relative humidity in a building.
I-Beam—A metal beam with a cross section resembling the letter I.
Insulation—Construction materials used for protection from sound, heat, cold, or fire. *Acoustic* insulation affords protection from sound. *Thermal* insulation is used for protection from heat or cold.
Jack Rafter—A short rafter that spans the distance from a

Glossary of Architectural and Construction Terms 457

wall top plate to a hip rafter, or from a valley rafter to a ridge [B–24].

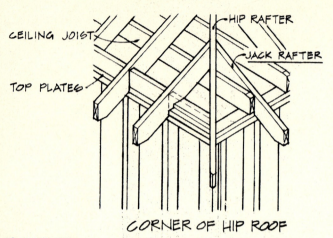

Figure B–24

Jalousie—A type of window consisting of several long, thin, horizontal pivoted glass panels [B–25].

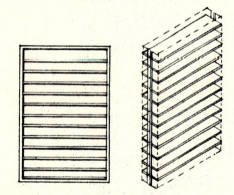

Figure B–25

Jamb—The side and head lining of a door, window, or other opening [B–26].

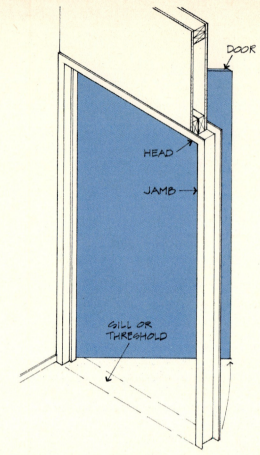

Figure B–26

Jetting—Drilling with high-pressure water or air jets.
Joist—One of a series of parallel beams used to support floor and ceiling loads that are supported in turn by larger beams, girders, or bearing walls [B–15].
Kiln-Dried Lumber—Lumber that has been dried in a kiln or oven.
King Post—The center upright support in a roof truss.
Laitance—Mortar or grout scum on the surface of concrete.
Lally Column—A metal column filled with concrete.
Laminated Material—Material made under pressure using superimposed layers of materials impregnated with glue.

Landing—A platform between flights of stairs or at the termination of a flight of stairs [B–27].

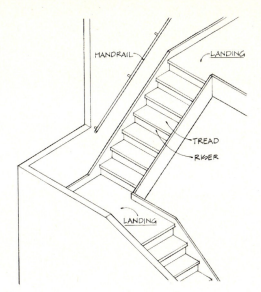

Figure B–27

Lath—A building material of wood, metal, gypsum, or insulating board that is fastened to the frame of a building to act as a plaster base.

Latitude—Perpendicular distance on a map in a north or south direction from the equator expressed in degrees, minutes, and seconds [B–28].

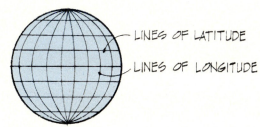

Figure B–28

Lattice—A framework made of crossed or interlaced wood or metal strips.

Lavatory—A washbasin or a room equipped with a washbasin.

Leader—A vertical downpipe that carries rainwater from the gutter to the ground.

Ledger—Horizontal member supporting joists above. Also called ribbon, girt, purlin, or stringer [B–7].

Light—Space in a window for a single pane of glass. Also a single pane of glass [B–30].

Lintel—A horizontal member that supports the wall and roof load over an opening, such as a door or window [13–21].

Live Load—The moving or movable external load on a structural member, including weight of furniture, people, and so on.

Longitude—Perpendicular distance on a map in an east or west direction from a standard north-south line, expressed in degrees, minutes, and seconds [B–28].

Lookout—A short framing timber used to support an overhanging portion of a roof, extending from the wall to the underside surfacing of the overhang.

Lot Line—The line formed by the legal boundary of a piece of land.

Louver—An opening with a series of slats so arranged as to permit ventilation, but to exclude rain, light, or vision.

Mansard—A specific type of roof shape [6–21].

Mantel—The shelf above a fireplace. Also the decorative trim around a fireplace [23–26].

Masonry—Building materials such as block, stone, or brick which are set in place by a mason and bonded together by mortar.

Mastic—A permanently plastic waterproof adhesive material used in sealing joints [23–29].

Millwork—Building materials made of finished wood and manufactured in millwork plants or planing mills. Includes such items as inside and outside doors, window and door frames, mantels, panelwork, stairway banisters, moldings, and interior trim. Does not normally include flooring, ceiling, or siding.

Miter Joint—Joining of two pieces of wood at an angle that bisects the joining angle. Example: the miter joint between the side and head casing of a door is made at a 45° angle.

Modular Construction—Construction using building components whose sizes are based on a standardized unit of measurement.

Moisture Barrier—Sheet material that has the quality to retard the penetration of vapor or moisture into walls, ceilings, floors, and so on.

Mortar—A bonding agent for stone and brick made of cement or lime, sand, and water.

Mortise—A slot cut into a board, plank, or timber, usually edgewise, to receive a tenon of another piece of timber to form a joint [B–29].

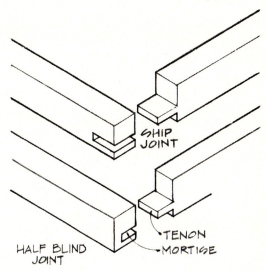

Figure B–29

Mullion—The vertical bar or divider in the frame between windows, doors, or other openings [B–30].

Glossary of Architectural and Construction Terms

Muntin—Any short thin bar within a window frame, either vertical or horizontal, separating the lights [B–30].

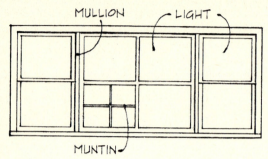

Figure B–30

Neat—Cement or plaster that has been mixed with water only, with no aggregate.

Newel—A post to which the end of a stair railing is fastened.

Nominal Size—The nearest larger round numbers to the actual dimensions of masonry and lumber.

Nonbearing Wall—A wall supporting no load other than its own weight.

Nosing—The rounded edge of a stair tread [23–4].

On Center (O.C.)—The measurement of spacing for studs, rafters, joists, partitions, and so on in a building. Measured from the center line of one member to the center line of the next.

Outlet—Any type of electrical connection allowing electrical current to be drawn from the system for appliances or lighting.

Outrigger—An extension of a rafter beyond the wall line by attaching a smaller member to the larger to form an overhang. (Also known as an "outlooker.")

Overhang—The horizontal distance that a roof projects beyond a wall.

Pallet—A strong wood skid used to help move stacks of block or brick.

Panel—A thin, flat surface framed by a thicker material.

Parapet—That portion of a wall that extends above a roof (or edge of a roof).

Pargeting—The application of a thin coat of cement mortar to a masonry wall.

Parquet Flooring—Flooring, usually wood blocks, laid in an alternating or inlaid pattern to form pleasing designs.

Partition—An interior wall of a building.

Penny—A measure of length of nails. The term originally indicated price per hundred (see Appendix F).

Periphery—The boundary of a piece of land or of a building.

Pier—A masonry pillar usually used to support the floor framing.

Pigment—White or colored matter, usually in the form of an insoluble powder, mixed with oil, water, and so on to make paint.

Pilaster—A rectangular pier attached to a wall to strengthen it.

Pile—A vertical member driven into the ground to help bear the load of an overhead structure [14–11].

Pitch—The inclined slope of a roof. Also, the ratio of total rise (vertical) to total run (horizontal). Example: a roof that has an 8-foot rise in a 24-foot run has a ⅓ pitch. Also used to describe coal tar used in roofing.

Plate—Horizontal member to which other members are fastened. Example: the sole plate is the horizontal bottom member of a frame wall. The top plate is the top horizontal member supporting ceiling joists, rafters, and so on. [B–31].

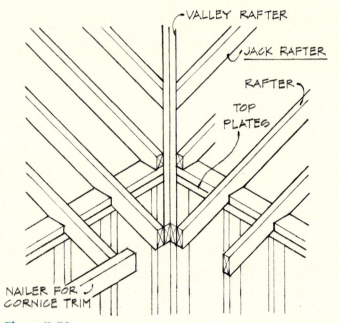

Figure B–31

Plumb—Describes something that is exactly aligned vertically (perpendicular to the horizontal).

Ply—The number of layers of roofing material, plywood, veneer in plywood, or layers of built-up materials in any finished piece.

Plywood—A piece of wood composed of three or more plies (layers) of wood bonded together with glue. Usually laid with the grain of adjoining plies at right angles to one another. Almost always composed of an odd number of plies to provide balanced construction rigidity.

Portland Cement—Calcined hydrated ground limestone used as the binding agent in making concrete.

Post-and-Beam Construction—A type of building construction in which roof and floor loads are carried by beams that are supported by columns. [14–47].

Precast—A concrete building unit that has been formed at a location other than its final position in the building or structure.

Primer—The first coat of paint applied to the material. Serves as a base for subsequent layers of paint.

Purlins—Horizontal roof framing members laid over trusses or other framing to support the roof deck.

Putty Coat—Final smooth coat of interior plaster.

Quoins—Large stones set in the corners of masonry buildings for aesthetic effect.

Rabbet—A rectangular groove cut on the edge of a board to form a corner joint [B–32].

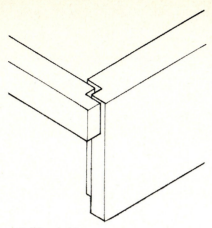

Figure B–32 Rabbet joint.

Rafter—One of a series of structural members running from the eave to the ridge of a roof designed to support roof loads. Flat roof rafters are sometimes called *roof joists* [B–15].
Rail (of a door)—A horizontal piece of framework or paneling in a door.
Rake Joint—A recessed mortar joint made by tooling.
Register—The outlet of a heating or cooling air duct. Usually equipped with an adjustable grille to regulate the airflow.
Reinforced Concrete—Concrete with 0.2% or more of reinforcing bars or wire mesh to improve its strength.
Relative Humidity—The amount of water vapor in the atmosphere expressed as a percentage of the maximum quantity that could be present at a given temperature and pressure.
Retaining Wall—A wall designed to hold back an earthen embankment.
Reveal—The side of an opening for a door or window, between the frame and the outer surface of the wall.
Reverberation—The lingering of sound within a space (after the source is terminated) due to multiple reflections of the sound.
Ridge Board—Horizontal line at the junction of the upper edges of two sloping surfaces [B–16].
Ridge Pole—The highest horizontal timber in a gable roof. It is supported by and attached to the upper ends of the ridge rafters [B–15].
Riprap—Stones placed randomly to prevent soil erosion.
Rise—In stairs, the vertical height of a step or a flight of stairs [23–4].
Riser—Each of the vertical boards closing the spaces between the treads of a stairway [B–27]. Also, a vertical duct or pipe.
Rocklathe—Flat gypsum sheets used as a plaster base.
Roof Sheathing—Boards or sheets of plywood that are attached to the top edges of rafters or trusses to tie the roof together and support the roofing material [B–34].
Rough Opening—A framed, unfinished opening constructed to receive finished units such as doors, windows, and cabinets.
Rowlock—A masonry course in which the units are laid on their narrow, long face with the small end of the units exposed.

Run—In stairs, the width of a step or the horizontal distance covered by a flight of stairs [23–4].
Saddle—Two small sloping triangular surfaces meeting in a horizontal ridge. Used at the back side of a chimney or other vertical surface as it penetrates a sloping roof [B–18].
Sapwood—The outer zone of wood next to the bark of a tree.
Sash—A single frame constructed to securely hold one or more panes of glass.
Scab—A short, flat piece of lumber which is bolted, nailed, or screwed to two butting pieces to splice them together [B–33].

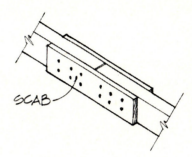

Figure B–33

Screed—A strip of material placed at intervals along a wall to be plastered to gauge the thickness of the plaster. Similarly, a screed is used to pour concrete level to a predetermined thickness.
Sealant—Material used to fill and seal the surface of a joint, especially an expansion joint.
Septic Tank—A buried concrete or steel settling tank that uses bacterial action to process sewage.
Shake—A thick, split wood shingle; it yields a thicker more irregular butt edge than a shingle [B–34].
Sheathing—Structural covering, usually wood boards or plywood, used over studs or rafters of a structure [B–34].
Shed Roof—A single plane roof that slopes in only one direction [6–21].
Sheeting—Vertical construction used to temporarily hold back the walls of an excavation during construction. (Do not confuse with sheathing.)
Shellac—Transparent coating made by dissolving lac, a resinous secretion of the lac bug, in alcohol. (Lac bugs are insects that thrive in tropical climates.)
Shim—A thin member, usually of wood, that is used to level and steady a member while it is being secured.

Shingle—A roofing unit of wood, slate, tile, asbestos, or asphalt material used as a covering and applied in an overlapping fashion [B–34].

Slump Test—A test for mixed concrete to determine consistency.

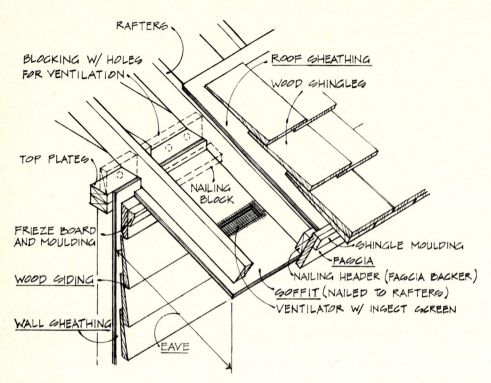

Figure B–34

Shiplap—Boards with overlapping rabbeted edges [14–60].
Siding—The finish covering of an outside wall of a frame building [B–34].
Sill—The horizontal member across the bottom of a door or window opening [B–21]. Also a horizontal member supported by a foundation wall or piers that in turn supports the upright members of a frame [B–1].
Sleeper—Horizontal member used to support a structure above. Especially the wood strips between a concrete slab and a finished wood floor [B–35].

Smoke Chamber—The portion of a chimney flue that is located directly above the fireplace.
Soffit—The visible underside of an overhang [B–34].
Soil Stack—A vertical plumbing sewage discharge pipe [17–3].
Soldier Course—A row of masonry in a wall that is laid vertically with the narrow side exposed.
Soleplate—The horizontal member between the floor and the wall studs and to which the studs are nailed [B–21].
Span—The horizontal distance between structural supports such as joists, beams, and trusses.
Square—Trade nomenclature for an area of 100 square feet. Most commonly used to specify quantities of roofing material.
Stile—The upright or vertical member of a door, panel, or screen.
Stirrup—A U-shaped metal strap used to support framing members.
Stool—The interior horizontal ledge across the bottom of a window.
Stretcher Course—A row of masonry in a wall laid horizontally with the long narrow face exposed.
Stringer—The inclined structural supporting member cut to receive the stair treads and risers [23–9].
Stucco—Mixture of sand, Portland cement, and water. May be tinted and applied as plaster.
Stud—One of a series of slender wood or metal vertical mem-

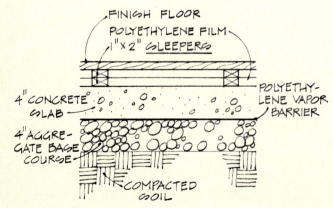

Figure B–35

bers placed as supporting elements in a wall or partition. Plural: studs or studding [B-21].

Subfloor—Rough boards or plywood laid over joists upon which finish flooring will be laid [23-12 and 23-28].

Swale—A wide, shallow depression in the ground to form a channel for storm water drainage.

Termite Shield—Sheet metal used to block the passage of termites.

Terrazzo—Flooring material made from small chips of marble set in cement and ground down and polished.

Threshold—The beveled tread member of an entrance [B-26].

Tie—A wood member that binds a pair of principal rafters at the bottom.

Toenail—To drive nails into wood at an angle.

Tongue-and-Groove—A carpentry joint in which the jutting edge of one board fits into the grooved edge of a mating board.

Translucent—Having the capability to transmit light but diffusing it so that objects beyond cannot be clearly distinguished.

Transom—A small hinged window over a door.

Transparent—Having the capability of transmitting light so that objects beyond can be seen clearly.

Trap—A U-shaped pipe below plumbing fixtures that provides a water seal to prevent passage of gases and sewer odors [17-4].

Tread—Horizontal part of a step [B-27].

Trimmer—A rafter or joist around an opening in a floor or roof.

Truss—A braced framework of structural members, usually arranged in triangular units, capable of supporting loads over a long span [14-78].

Valley—Internal angle formed by the juncture of two roofs with sloping sides.

Valley Rafter—The diagonal rafter at the juncture of two intersecting sloping roofs [B-31].

Vapor Barrier—Material such as paper, metal, or paint used to prevent vapor from passing into and through walls [B-35].

Varnish—A transparent, glossy, hard surface-coating material.

Vehicle—The liquid portion of paint that holds the pigments or solids in suspension.

Veneer—A thin sheet or wall of non-load-bearing facing material.

Vent Stack—A vertical pipe placed in the plumbing system for ventilation and pressure equalization [17-3].

Vermiculite—An aggregate used in lightweight concrete. Made from expanded mica.

Vestibule—A small lobby or entrance room.

Wainscot—Decorative or protective covering on the lower part of an interior wall that differs in finish from the remainder of the wall.

Wall Tie—A metal piece that connects wythes of masonry to each other or to other material, such as a wall [14-36 and 14-55].

Warp—Twisting of a board from its original shape.

Water/Cement Ratio—Ratio of water to cement in a concrete mix. Governs the strength of the resulting mix.

Water Stop—Material used to provide a weatherproof connection between a wall and a floor below grade.

Waterproof—Impervious to water or water vapor, even under constant pressure.

Weather Stripping—A strip of metal, fabric, or plastic, employed to make exterior openings weathertight.

Weepholes—Small openings left in retaining walls, foundations, window casings, and so on to permit water to escape [14-55].

Wythe—Refers to a single thickness of masonry wall [14-33].

C Program Development Case Study

This appendix describes a study done by an architectural firm leading to a building design program for a Rural Electric Cooperative. As part of the research, an analysis of the existing facility was done. A schematic floor plan illustrating the requirements of the program and a proposed final floor plan are included. Following is a list of the contents of this appendix.

I. Purpose of Study
   Employee Work-Flow Questionnaire
   Department Work-Flow Questionnaire
II. Method of Study
III. Forecasting
IV. Findings
V. Recommendations
   Organizational Chart
   Activity Matrix
   Space Program
   Proportional Space Needs Chart
   Optimum Work-Flow Diagram
   Floor Plan
   Blank Space Program Form

I. PURPOSE OF STUDY
   This study was made to accomplish the following:
   A. Evaluate the efficiency of office work flow through the use of graphic techniques such as activity matrix and work-flow diagrams to identify existing or potential problem areas in personnel work flow and arrangement.
   B. Increase management contact and control to minimize unnecessary staff expansion and overhead.
   C. Provide a pleasant working environment for present and future staff while achieving the first two objectives.
   D. Minimize capital improvements to the highest cost-effective priorities within an overall 10-year expansion plan.

EMPLOYEE WORK-FLOW QUESTIONNAIRE

NAME _____ POSITION _____ NO. _____ LOCATION NO. _____

1. Job duties (brief description) _____
   _____
   _____

2. Check and describe items used at your work station.

   FURNITURE
   - ____ desk (30 in. x 60 in.)
   - ____ desk (36 in. x 72 in.)
   - ____ chair
   - ____ visitor chair (number) _____
   - ____ other (describe) _____

   STORAGE
   - ____ files (no. drawers) _____
   - ____ dead storage _____
   - ____ confidential files (no. drawers) _____
   - ____ shelves _____
   - ____ clothes _____
   - ____ display (literature, etc.) _____
   - ____ other _____

   EQUIPMENT
   - ____ typewriter
   - ____ telephone
   - ____ calculator
   - ____ other (describe) _____

3. With whom do you communicate? (Describe incoming or outgoing communications with telephone, intercom, or paper.) Use a "C" to indicate where confidentiality is needed.

Position No.	Times/Month	Purpose
_____	_____	_____
_____	_____	_____
_____	_____	_____
_____	_____	_____
_____	_____	_____
_____	_____	_____
_____	_____	_____

4. Where do you go when you leave your work station?

Location No.	Times/Month	Position No.	Purpose
_____	_____	_____	_____
_____	_____	_____	_____
_____	_____	_____	_____
_____	_____	_____	_____
_____	_____	_____	_____
_____	_____	_____	_____
_____	_____	_____	_____
_____	_____	_____	_____
_____	_____	_____	_____

5. Who comes to your work station?
   Position No.   *Times/Month*   *Purpose*
   _____   _____   _____
   _____   _____   _____
   _____   _____   _____

6. To whom do you report problems?
   Position No.   *Times/Month*   *Position No.*   *Times/Month*
   _____   _____   _____   _____
   _____   _____   _____   _____

7. Who reports problems to you?
   Position No.   *Times/Month*   *Position No.*   *Times/Month*
   _____   _____   _____   _____
   _____   _____   _____   _____
   _____   _____   _____   _____

8. Check and describe your work schedule.
   _____ Flexible schedule _____
   _____ Fixed schedule _____
   _____ Other _____

9. How many times per day do you enter the building? _____
10. Do you have a key to the building? _____
11. Describe problems you have with the following in your work:
    a. Location _____
    b. Noise _____
    c. Lighting _____
    d. Heating/cooling _____
    e. Storage _____
    f. Equipment _____
    g. Furniture _____
    h. Distractions _____
    i. Available space _____
    j. Parking _____
    k. Other (toilets, conference area, kitchen, etc.) _____
    _____
    _____
    _____
    _____

DEPARTMENT WORK-FLOW QUESTIONNAIRE

DEPARTMENT _____   Name _____   Position _____

1. Department duties (brief description) _____

2. With whom does your department communicate? (Describe incoming or outgoing communications which involve telephone, intercom, or paper.)

Who	Times/Month	Purpose

3. With which departments does your department work most frequently?

Department	Times/month	Purpose

4. What additional equipment do you anticipate in your department?

Purchased Recently	Not Yet Purchased	Delivery Date

5. What is the nature of the contact your department has with the outside public? _____

6. What records does your department store?

Type	Yearly Increase (no. file drawers)

7. What is your policy on record retirement? _____

8. What is your policy for destroying records? _____

9. Does your department require a conference room? How many people would use it at one time? How often would your department use the room? _____

10. Does your department require a work room? What type of equipment would you need in it? _____

11. Do you have any special needs for waiting, storage, or other purposes? _____

12. Indicate on the attached organization chart the names and classifications of each employee in your department.
13. Check the type of space required by each person in your department:

Position No.	Private	Semi-Private	Office Pool	Other (Describe)
_____	_____	_____	_____	_____
_____	_____	_____	_____	_____
_____	_____	_____	_____	_____
_____	_____	_____	_____	_____
_____	_____	_____	_____	_____
_____	_____	_____	_____	_____
_____	_____	_____	_____	_____
_____	_____	_____	_____	_____
_____	_____	_____	_____	_____
_____	_____	_____	_____	_____
_____	_____	_____	_____	_____
_____	_____	_____	_____	_____
_____	_____	_____	_____	_____
_____	_____	_____	_____	_____

II. METHOD OF STUDY

A work-flow study was developed (1) to evaluate the present working conditions of the Coop offices in terms of physical arrangement and space requirements, and (2) to conceptually design alternative solutions to space usage. The study was organized into the following activities:

A. *Office Employee Survey:* To establish a data base and identify work-flow problems, every office employee was asked to complete an Employee Work-Flow Questionnaire (p. 466). This questionnaire identified the furnishings and equipment needed at each work station, the number of communications made, the physical contact between employees, and the reasons these contacts were made. Finally, it requested the employee to record complaints about their work environment, if any.

The department heads were then asked to review these questionnaires and comment on the validity of the information. Comments were minimal, so an Activity Matrix was developed. Also, each department head completed an Employee Work-Flow Questionnaire along with a Department Work-Flow Questionnaire (p. 468).

B. *Activity Matrix:* To consolidate the data, an Activity Matrix (p. 473) was developed showing all interrelated physical contacts between employees. This matrix provided a crosscheck of the work-flow questionnaires against each other to be sure that all employee contacts were considered.

Because the physical work contacts were only estimates, the matrix was categorically divided into a range of contacts. Fewer than 20 contacts per month totally between two employees were not considered to be important enough to merit adjacent work stations. More than 80 per month (approximately 4 per day) were considered a level at which adjacency of work stations was considered to be important.

A preliminary draft of this matrix was reviewed with each department head and their comments requested. Several changes were then noted as the overall work-flow picture began to develop.

C. *Architectural Analysis:* Concurrently with the work-flow survey and the activity matrix, a room-by-room evaluation was made of the existing building. Interior and exterior problems with the structure were noted along with mechanical, plumbing, lighting, finishes, and circulation problems.

D. *Work-Flow Diagram:* To graphically illustrate and quantify the work relationship, an existing conditions work-flow diagram was developed for those situations where there were more than 80 total contacts per month between locations. This diagram was similar to the Optimum Work-Flow Diagram (p. 480). A location may include several work stations and much trip activity.

The objective of the work-flow diagram was to minimize the trip/distance between locations where possible. It was determined that some trips indicated were temporary and should not be included in this analysis, although they were indicated on the questionnaires.

Each department head reviewed a preliminary work-flow diagram along with the activity matrix and was requested to make comments.

E. *Assumptions:* At this point it was necessary to eliminate some unknowns by stating their presupposed condition. For example, it was assumed that consumer member growth for the next few years would be proportional to the last 10 years. The development of these assumptions are important reference points to which future actual conditions may be related to determine change in expected needs or requirements.

F. *Projections:* It was necessary to project factors of change such as consumer membership. This particular factor affects the organization, size, employees, and operational context of the Cooperative.

G. *Space Program:* Based on standards of office use, each existing office position, work space, and unoccupied area was studied to qualify their net present and future space needs. This net area was factored by 40% to allow for gross square-footage items such as elevations, toilets, corridors, walls, and so on (pp. 474–478). The total of present and future gross space needs were then compared to the actual gross area of the existing building to determine the space available for expansion and/or the space shortage overall.

H. *Conceptual Design Considerations:* Consolidating the above information and findings, several design concepts were sketched to eliminate or minimize distorted space use and excessive trip/distance between locations and to qualify the need for the use of space. In this step nonproductive spaces such as corridors and walls were evaluated against their original intent and need. Also, unnecessary trips that could be converted to electronic communication were identified and evaluated. Management consideration for department controls (i.e., department head located physically adjacent to that department) were incorporated.

The shape and size of existing spaces were evaluated for the constraints on proper use of the space by work stations. Flexibility of space usage appeared to be a key design consideration.

I. *Alternative Identification:* Because there were several potential solutions, it was necessary to identify the most feasible solution within the limits of cost and benefit to overall working conditions. From the alternatives one scheme was selected for the Cooperative. Growth of consumer membership, expansion of computer usage, and increased in-house engineering services were the primary determining factors. Government policy and additional services or duties to the membership were considered secondary because of the limitation in forecasting these factors.

III. FORECASTING

A. *Assumptions*
1. The major influence on number of clerical and office personnel of the Cooperative is the number of consumer memberships. Changes in membership will affect each department proportionally as in the past 10 years.
2. The basic organizational structure, job duties, and services offered by the Cooperative will not change in the next 10 years. Specifically, the department organization will remain, with engineering design remaining an in-house function. The duties of additional personnel will fall into the same categories.
3. The population change in membership will continue the trend established between 1971 and 1981.
4. The basic requirement for net space of each work station will remain the same.
5. Contacts made between work stations will continue to be valid as identified on the work-flow questionnaires.
6. Hard-copy file documents and records will be stored in dead files with some form of microfilm or computer access developed for working files.

B. *Projections*
1. Based on the 10-year trend between 1971 and 1981, the total consumer membership is expected to be 30,208 by 1992, growing at 4.2% annual average compounded.
2. The number of office-related personnel in the Cooperative by 1992 will be 66 as compared to 42 in 1982. This is divided in departments as follows:

	1971	1982	1992
General offices	2	2	3
Administrative	4	10	14
Business	9	16	22
Public relations	1	2	4
Engineering	1	9	19
Field services	3	3	4
Total	20	42	66

The impact of consumer growth will primarily affect clerical or technical areas directly related to consumer service. Based on Assumption 2 the management, staff, and nonoccupied support spaces were considered individually for expansion of space.

3. From the projections listed, it follows that the net square foot requirement will increase from 9690 square feet in 1982 to 12,370 square feet in 1992. Based on 35% for space such as walls, corridor, mechanical, toilets, and so on, the total gross square footage required in 1992 will be 16,700 square feet.

IV. FINDINGS

A. *Problem Analysis:* From data collected in the work-flow questionnaires along with interviews with management, the Activity Matrix was developed to illustrate contacts between individual positions. Additional information was collected to establish the present Organizational Chart (p. 472). This chart illustrates department organization and lines of responsibility. The work contacts over 80 per month were separated from the Activity Matrix to identify the most serious work-flow problems.

To spatially define the needs for each position, a Space Program (pp. 474–478) was developed assigning net work area to each employee and support area. This space program was combined into present and future net space requirements by department. The future space requirements were based on a 10-year projection of employees per department. To graphically illustrate the results of this study, the Proportional Space Needs Chart (p. 479) was developed. To identify how the distance between locations could best be provided, an Optimum Work-Flow Diagram (p. 480) was developed.

B. *Problem Identification:* From the study it was determined that there are a number of major restrictions to work flow and overall flexibility in the existing building. These are:
1. Although the present gross building area (25,110 square feet excluding the warehouse) is sufficient to accommodate the projected future gross footage needs (16,700 square feet), the excessive corridor space (1980 square feet) and the limited-use basement (7890 square feet) reduce the functionally available square footage to 15,240 square feet.
2. The elongated building shape (excluding the community room) is roughly 190 feet long by 60 feet wide and further restricts efficient use of the space for efficient work flow.
3. The building is segmented into a large number of small office spaces along the corridors. From the Space Program it was determined that approximately 3400 square feet is presently needed for large open offices compared to the existing 2200 square feet. Since the larger area provides more flexibility and better management control, it is estimated that the 10-year projected needs for open offices will reach 5600 square feet (3400 more than existing), or 33.5% of the future gross square footage needs.
4. Because of the rapid growth in certain areas of the Cooperative and the above conditions, the departments have in the past been divided throughout the building, hindering efficient management contact and control by department heads. In comparing the existing work-flow conditions to an optimum work-flow pattern, it was determined that by simply reducing the physical trip distance between locations, time spent moving from position to position (for contacts exceeding 80 per month) could be reduced by 39.7%. Assuming under these conditions that movement to and from locations takes 5% of the total man-hours, approximately 820 man-hours could be saved per month if the optimum work-flow pattern was developed.
5. The extensive use of bearing wall construction throughout the building restricts the development of open office areas or elimination of some corridors. Additionally, only two exterior walls of the building are designed for physical expansion.
6. The double set of main entry doors were to provide separate access for the community room, but, in fact, create confusion to the entering public.
7. The location of the receptionist is not visually accessible to either entry, creating additional confusion and causing unnecessary interruption to the cashier counter nearby.

V. RECOMMENDATIONS

Based on findings developed from this study it has been determined that a new Floor Plan (p. 481) will provide the maximum utilization of space for the least cost in meeting the objectives of this study. Since some capital improvements will generate a more rapid amortization by reducing overhead and management costs, the following priorities in this 10-year plan are recommended.
A. Locate the billing operation and the computer near the consumer records to reduce travel and excessive personnel requirements.
B. Consolidate business office personnel in a large, flexible office space with adjacent manager's office to provide control and permit future expansion.
C. Locate the receptionist for better visibility to the public and to control traffic.
D. Consolidate consumer relation offices near the waiting area to afford convenient public access.
E. Consolidate public relations and administrative assistant offices to provide staff contact and possibly reduce personnel.
F. Provide cashier station space for one person.
G. Arrange field superintendents' offices to allow space for equipment and control of traffic by the dispatcher.
H. Utilize a less accessible space for an employee-break area and mailroom.
I. Provide space in the engineering department for drafting, computer equipment, and future employees.
J. Zone the mechanical system for efficient controls with minimum accessibility for nonauthorized personnel.
K. Develop an exterior graphics system to avoid public confusion at the main entrance.
L. Minimize access to the main computer room by utilization of remote terminals.

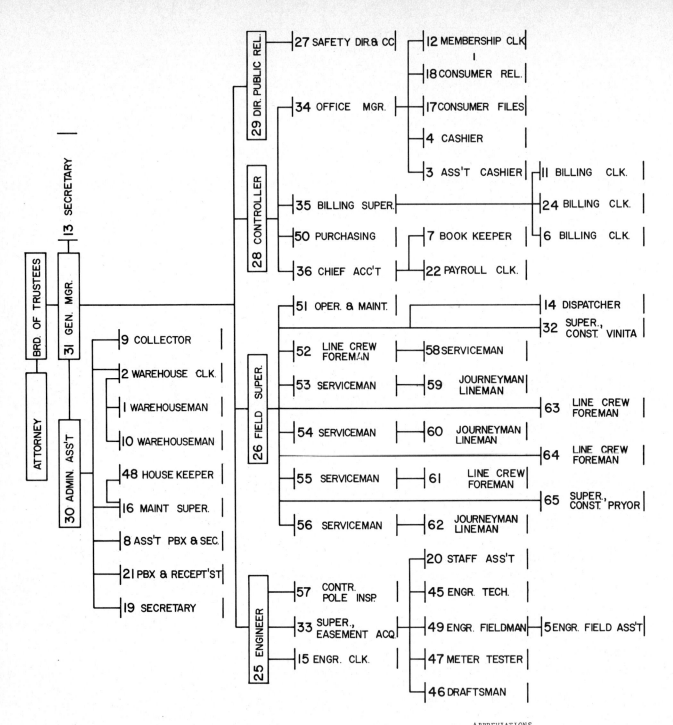

NORTHEAST OKLAHOMA REC
ACTIVITY MATRIX

DATE: SEPTEMBER 20, 1982
SOURCE: EMPLOYEE WORK FLOW QUESTIONAIRES

james j adams, p.c.
architecture — planning
p.o. box 526 — nevada mo
(417) 667-3568   64772

LEGEND OF SYMBOLS
- ○ <= 20 CONTACTS PER MONTH
- ● 21- 50 CONTACTS PER MONTH
- ■ 51-100 CONTACTS PER MONTH
- ◢ 101-200 CONTACTS PER MONTH
- ◼ > 200 CONTACTS PER MONTH

SPACE PROGRAM FOR: Rural Electric Cooperative   PROJECT NO. P78-13   DATE 2-2-83   PAGE 1 OF 9

Description of Area-Subareas	Area No.	Space Requirements Present	Space Requirements Future	Adjacent Area Nos.	Fixture & Equipment	Remarks
SUMMARY (Net sf)		9,690	12,370			
General Offices	G	940	1,060			
Admin. Dept.	A	880	1,010			
Field Dept.	F	360	480			
Engr. Dept.	E	970	2,140			
Business Dept.	B	2,920	3,440			
Pub. Rel. Dept.	P	370	590			
General	-	3,250	3,650			
35%		3,390	4,330			
Net		9,690	12,370			
Estimated Gross Demand		13,080	16,700			Exist. sf. (gross) 17,220 1st floor; 7,890 Basement; 25,110 Act.Gross

NOTES:

james j adams
architecture / planning   s main st   nevada mo 64772   417·667·3568

SPACE PROGRAM FOR: Rural Electric Cooperative   PROJECT NO. P78-13   DATE 2-2-83   PAGE 2 OF 9

Description of Area-Subareas	Area No.	Space Requirements Present	Space Requirements Future	Adjacent Area Nos.	Fixture & Equipment	Remarks
GENERAL OFFICES	G	940	1,060			1,270 GSF
General Mgr.	20	180			Desk (Conf. 6 chairs)	
G.M. Secretary	19	120			Desk 3x6 - 4 chairs	
Board Room	21	500			16 chairs & table	existing
Storage	-					
Kitchen	22	80			existing	existing
Toilets	23	60				existing

NOTES:

james j adams
architecture / planning   s main st   nevada mo 64772   417·667·3568

SPACE PROGRAM FOR: Rural Electric Cooperative   PROJECT NO. P78-13   DATE 2-2-83   PAGE 3 OF 9

Description of Area-Subareas	Area No.	Space Requirements Present	Future	Adjacent Area Nos.	Fixture & Equipment	Remarks
ADMINISTRATION DEPT.	A	880	1,010			
30. Admin. Ass't.	17	120			Desk w/4 chairs	existing
19. Admin. Ass't Secy	16	140			Desk w/3 chairs 7 files	existing
9. Collector	16	60				ex. shar
21. PBX Operator & Receptionist	48	60			Desk & console	bad location
8. Ass't PBX & Secy	15	80	128		Desk	
2. Warehouse Clerk	26	60			Engineer files	
10. Warehouseman	30	30				share w/1.
1. Warehouseman	30	30			Desk chair & counter	share w/10.
48. Housekeeper	45				No desk	share w/16. area in gen. stor.
16. Maintenance Super.	45					
Gen. Storage & Supply	45	300				

NOTES:

james j adams
architecture / planning   s main st   nevada mo 64772   417·667·3568

SPACE PROGRAM FOR: Rural Electric Cooperative   PROJECT NO. P78-13   DATE 2-2-83   PAGE 4 OF 9

Description of Area-Subareas	Area No.	Space Requirements Present	Future	Adjacent Area Nos.	Fixture & Equipment	Remarks
FIELD DEPT.	F	360	480			
26. Field Super.	34	120			Desk w/3 chairs	existing
32. Area Super. (Vinita)	35	120			Desk w/3 chairs	existing
14. Dispatcher		120			Desk w/1 chair & files	needs ass't. during day

NOTES:

james j adams
architecture / planning   s main st   nevada mo 64772   417·667·3568

SPACE PROGRAM FOR: Rural Electric Cooperative   PROJECT NO. P78-13   DATE 2-2-83   PAGE 5 OF 9

Description of Area-Subareas	Area No.	Space Requirements Present	Future	Adjacent Area Nos.	Fixture & Equipment	Remarks
ENGINEERS DEPARTMENT	E	970	2,140			
25. Engineer	59	120			Desk w/3 chairs 2 files	existing
15. Engr. Clerk	61	80			Desk & Chair & CRT	existing
33. Super.Easement Acy	61	90			Desk & 2 chairs	share map table
49. Engr. Fieldman	61	90			Desk & 2 chairs	share map table
45. Engr. Tech.	61	90	720		Desk & 2 chairs	share map table
20. Staff Ass't	61	60			Desk & Chair	
47. Meter Tester	27	60			Desk & Chair	Test equip. in van & meters in WH 30.
46. Draftsman	60	120			Draft table, printer, flat files	Several flat files to be added Dept. expanding
5. Engr. Field Ass't	61	60				part-time
General Stor		200	300			
Test Lab			150			new

NOTES:

james j adams
architecture / planning   s main st   nevada mo 64772   417·667·3568

SPACE PROGRAM FOR: Rural Electric Cooperative   PROJECT NO. P78-13   DATE 2-2-83   PAGE 6 OF 9

Description of Area-Subareas	Area No.	Space Requirements Present	Future	Adjacent Area Nos.	Fixture & Equipment	Remarks
BUSINESS DEPARTMENT	B	2,920	3,440			
28. Controller	18	120			Desk w/3 chairs & cred.	existing
34. Office Mgr	49	120			Desk w/3 chairs & cred.	existing
12. Member. Clerk	43	90			Desk w/chair and 2-4 d. file	existing
17. Cons. Record Clerk	43	470	520		Elec.file (3) Desk & chair	mail in other area
18. Cons. Relation Clerk	46	120			Desk w/3 chairs 1 file & disp.	
4. Cashier	53	80			Desk & chair with/counter	ex. night dep.
3. Ass't Cashier	53	80			Desk & Chair with/CRT	ex. night dep.
35. Billing Super	55	110			Desk w/2 chairs 3 - file cab.	existing
11. Billing Clerk	55	80			CRT w/desk & chair 4 files	
6. Billing Clerk	55	80			CRT w/desk & chair 4 files	
24. Billing Clerk	55	80			CRT w/desk & chair 4 files	

NOTES:

james j adams
architecture / planning   s main st   nevada mo 64772   417·667·3568

SPACE PROGRAM FOR: Rural Electric Cooperative   PROJECT NO. P78-13   DATE 2-2-83   PAGE 7 OF 9

Description of Area-Subareas	Area No.	Space Requirements Present	Future	Adjacent Area Nos.	Fixture & Equipment	Remarks
(CONTINUED) BUSINESS						
23. Purchaser	26	120			Desk w/2 chairs Catalog bookcase 3 files	Being phased combine space
50. Ass't Purchaser	26					
36. Chief Acc't	56	120			Desk w/3 chairs 2 files	
22. Payroll Clerk	57	90			Desk & chair 2 files	
7. Bookkeeper	57	100			Desk w/CRT chair 2 files	
Business Storage		610				
Computer		450			Some storage	Need adequate vent & heat

NOTES:

james j adams architecture / planning s main st nevada mo 64772 417-667-3568

SPACE PROGRAM FOR: Rural Electric Cooperative   PROJECT NO. P78-13   DATE 2-2-83   PAGE 8 OF 9

Description of Area-Subareas	Area No.	Space Requirements Present	Future	Adjacent Area Nos.	Fixture & Equipment	Remarks
PUBLIC RELATIONS	P	370	590			
29. P.R. Director	14	150			Desk w/4 chairs large amt files	existing
27. Safety Director	29	120			Desk w/2 chairs 2 files	
Dead storage		100				Expect growth possible 2-3 men

NOTES:

james j adams architecture / planning s main st nevada mo 64772 417-667-3568

SPACE PROGRAM FOR: Rural Electric Cooperative   PROJECT NO. P78-13   DATE 2-2-83   PAGE 9 OF 9

Description of Area-Subareas	Area No.	Space Requirements Present	Future	Adjacent Area Nos.	Fixture & Equipment	Remarks
GENERAL AREA		3,250	3,650			
Lobby	2	250			6 chairs	now (11) combine for community room lobby
Mail Room	25	300				Work top not right
Copier	24	100			Machine & paper storage	
Dead Storage	lower	800				Ample for REC size
Dark Room	lower	300				existing
Meeting Room	lower	1,500			50 people	

NOTES:

james j adams
architecture / planning   s main st   nevada mo 64772   417·667·3568

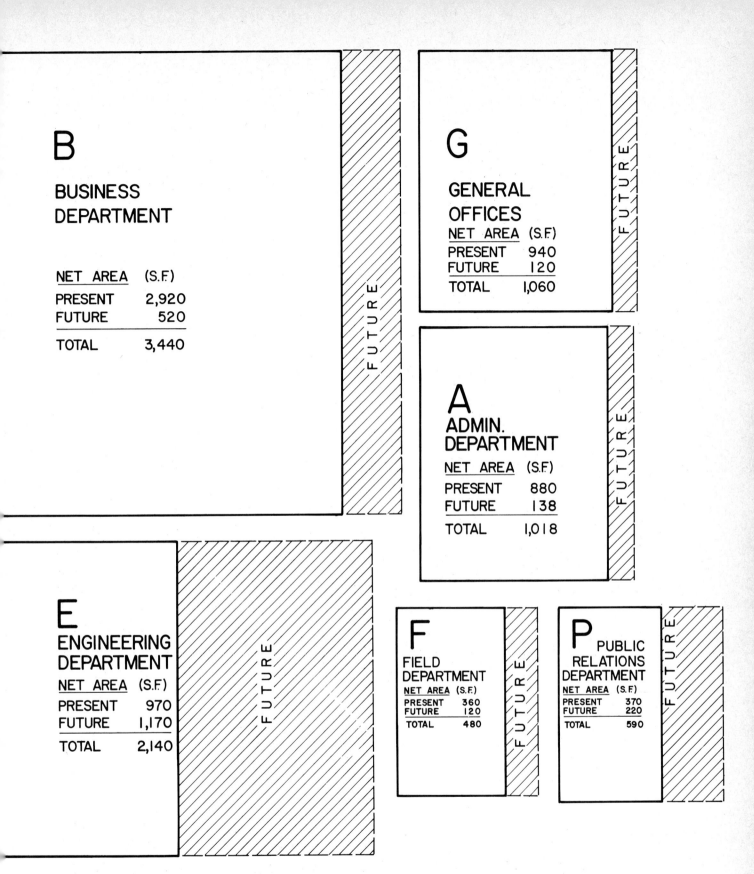

PROPORTIONAL SPACE NEEDS
NORTHEAST OKLAHOMA REC (PRESENT & FUTURE)

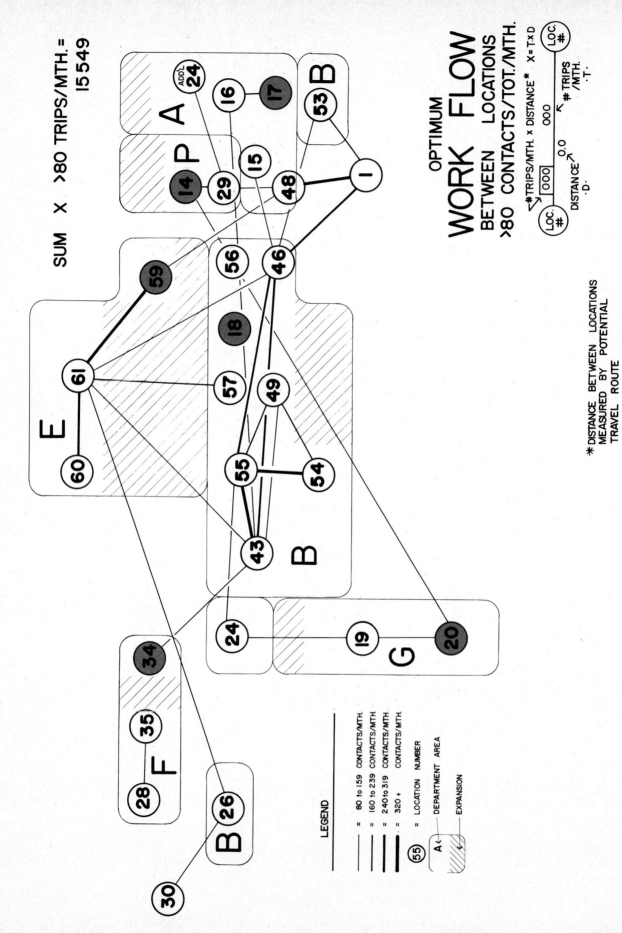

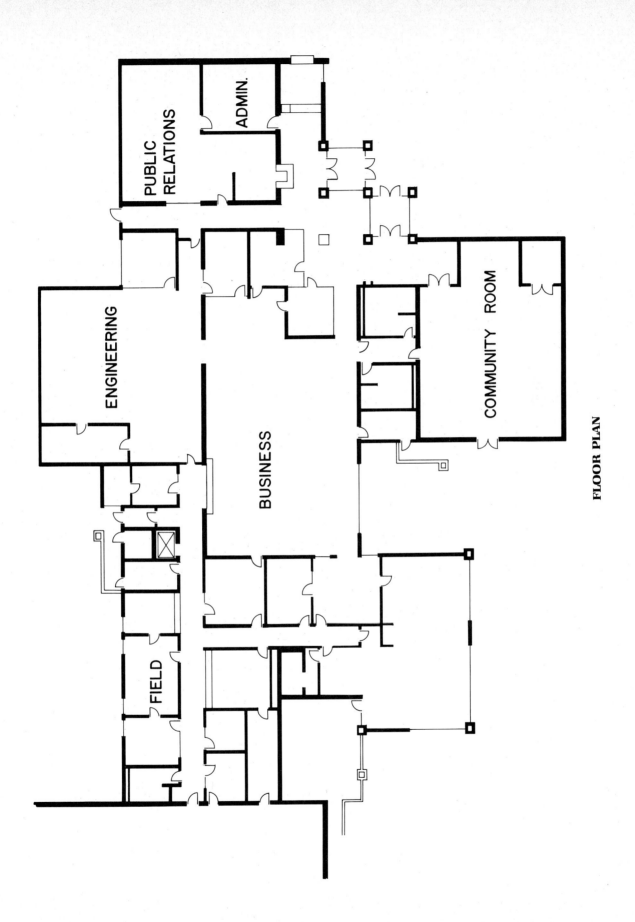

FLOOR PLAN

D Doors and Windows

Wood Double Hung Windows*

Figure D–1

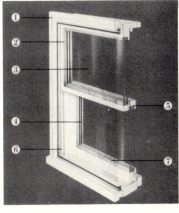

Figure D–2

Specifications:

1. *Frame:* Shall be kiln-dried Western pine treated with a water-repellant, preservative and insect toxicant. All exposed exterior surfaces shall be factory-primed. Basic jamb width shall be 4 9/16" (14 mm). Side jambs shall have screw-type adjusters to allow frame alignment. Frame shall include brick mold and sill nosing with weather stripping, hardware and all inside stops applied.

2. *Sash:* Shall be 1 5/8" at check rail made with kiln-dried Western pine, treated with a water repellant, preservative and insect toxicant. Sash shall be assembled with mortise and tenon corner joints, then secured with screws. Compressible jamb shall allow both sash to be removed without tools. Finger-lift groove shall be continuous across bottom sash. Exposed exterior surfaces shall be factory-primed. Sash shall allow convenient disassembly for field replacement of glass and parts.

3. *Finish:* All exposed surfaces shall be factory primed. Interior wood surfaces shall be unfinished to allow painting or staining.

4. *Glass:* Shall be 7/16" (11 mm) hermetically-sealed insulating glass with lites of 3/32" (2.3 mm) clear select-quality glass separated by 1/4" (6.3 mm) air space. Exception: all picture window units shall be 3/4" (19 mm) hermetically-sealed insulating glass with lites of 3/16" (5 mm) and 3/8" (10 mm air space).

5. *Glazing Gasket.* Insulating glass shall be glazed in sash with flexible extruded vinyl gasket, heat welded at the corners. Replacement of glass shall be possible without requiring putty or other glazing compound.

6. *Weatherstripping.* Shall be stainless steel jamb liner weatherstrip combined with flexible vinyl bulb system at head, sill and check rail, plus additional metal leaf weatherstrip at the head.

7. *Hardware.* Shall provide two coil-spring balances, encased in vinyl cylinders, per sash. Spring balances shall be specially treated for quiet operation. Positive lock shall insure firm sash closure.

8. *Screen.* Shall be "silent" charcoal fiberglass screen cloth (18 × 16 mesh). White aluminum frame shall be held in place with spring-loaded plungers at the sides and by brick mold routing at the head.

9. *Removable Divided Lite Grilles:* Shall be extruded white vinyl to achieve the effect of a divided lite sash. Grilles shall be easily removable without removing glass panels.

---

*Descriptive, tabular, photographic, and diagramatic materials for wood windows and doors have been supplied for this appendix through the courtesy of the Caradco Corporation, Rantoul, Illinois. These materials have been extracted from Caradco catalogs to provide realistic examples of door and window sizes and specifications as they are typically provided by the various architectural and construction related industries. It is not the intent of the authors to recommend this particular product in preference to others. However, the authors are most appreciative of the privilege afforded them to present this product information for student use.

Wood Double Hung Windows

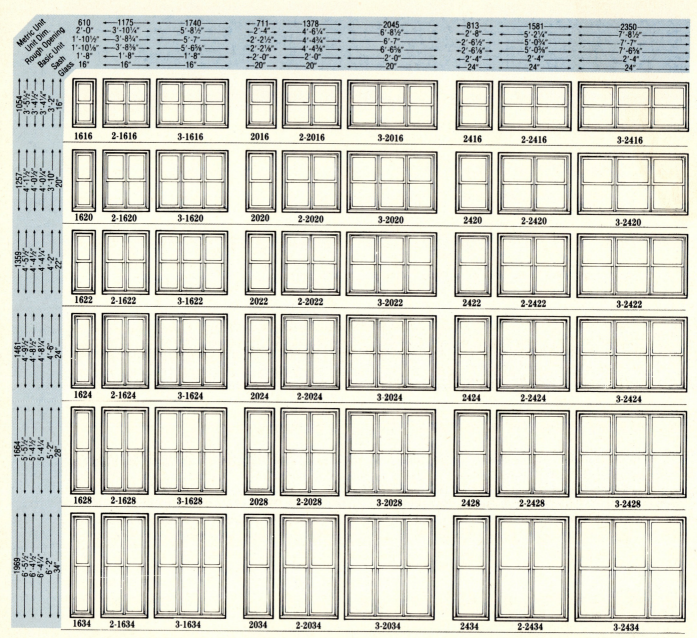

Dimension Explanation:

Metric Unit: Unit dimension in metric (mm soft conversion).

Unit Dim.: Overall unit size including trim.

Rough Opening: Inside dimension from stud to stud.

Basic Unit: Dimension from outside of jamb to outside of jamb. Does not include brick mold or subsill.

Figure D–3

Glass: Actual size of glass per sash. (Does not apply to picture units where nominal glass sizes are used.)

Coding System: Primed double-hung unit numbers are actual glass size. This does not apply to picture units where actual glass size are used.

Wood Double Hung Window Details

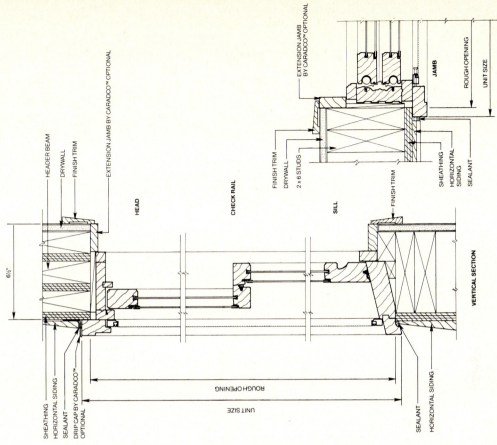

Figure D-5

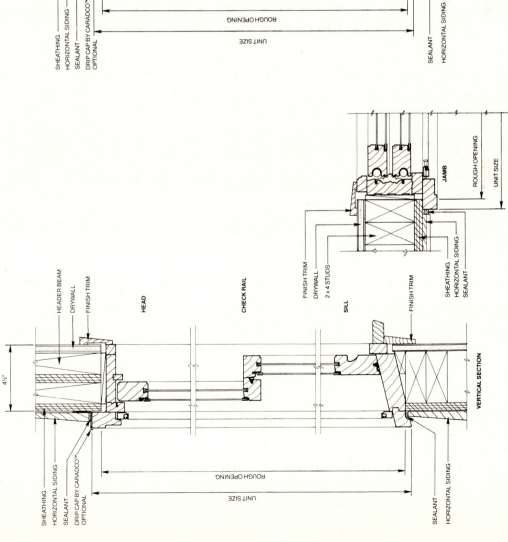

Figure D-4

Wood Double Hung Window Details

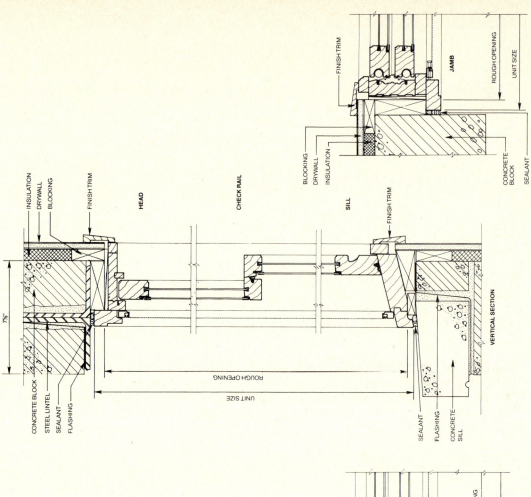

Figure D-7

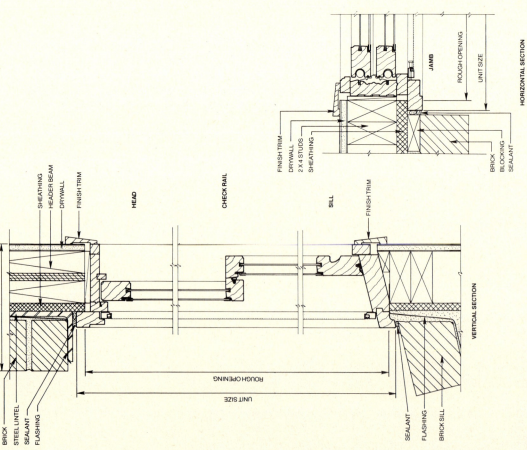

Figure D-6

Wood Casement Windows

Figure D–8

Specifications:

1. *Frame:* Shall be kiln-dried Western pine treated with a water-repellant, preservative and insect toxicant. All exposed exterior surfaces shall be factory-primed. Basic jamb width shall be 4 9/16" (14 mm). Assembled frame shall include brick mold and sub-sill, weatherstripping and hardware.
2. *Sash:* Shall be 1 3/4" (44 mm) thick kiln-dried Western pine, treated with a water-repellant, preservative and insect toxicant. Sash corner joints shall be mortise and tenon, then secured with screws. All exposed exterior surfaces shall be factor-primed. Sash shall allow convenient disassembly for field replacement.
3. *Finish:* All exposed surfaces shall be factory primed. Interior wood surfaces shall be unfinished to allow painting or staining.
4. *Glass:* Shall be 7/16" (11 mm) hermetically-sealed insulating glass with lites of 3/32" (2.3 mm) clear select-quality glass separated by 1/4" (6.3 mm) air space. Exception: all picture window units shall be 3/4" (19 mm) hermetically-sealed insulating glass with lites of 3/16" (5 mm) and 3/8" (10 mm) air space.
5. *Glazing Gasket.* Insulating glass shall be glazed in sash with flexible extruded vinyl gasket, heat welded at the corners. Replacement of glass shall be possible without requiring putty or other glazing compound.
6. *Weatherstripping.* Shall combine a stainless steel leaf applied to the sash with a complete second system of flexible vinyl bulb applied to the frame.
7. *Hardware.* Sash shall be hinged with a sliding nylon shoe reinforced with steel in a stainless steel track. All hinges shall be concealed from exterior view and protected from weather. Roto-operator shall be worm-gear type with die-cast case finished in Chestnut Bronze. Positive closure shall be insured by a die-cast cam action lock in matching Chestnut Bronze. All units 51" and taller shall have two sash locks. Operator arm shall have nylon roller that allows easy disconnect from sash track without tools, allowing casement to open 90° for inside washing.
8. *Screen.* Shall be "silent" charcoal fiber-glass screen cloth (18 × 16 mesh) set in Chestnut Bronze aluminum frame. Frame shall be held in place with two spring plungers and retaining pins. Nylon grommets in frame shall be factory installed.
9. *Triple Glazing.* Shall be select-quality glass set in a rigid white vinyl frame with flexible tubular vinyl weatherstrip fused in place. Panel secures to outside of the sash with nylon fasteners.
10. *Removable Divided Lite Grilles:* Shall be extruded white vinyl to achieve the effect of a divided lite sash.

Wood Casement Windows

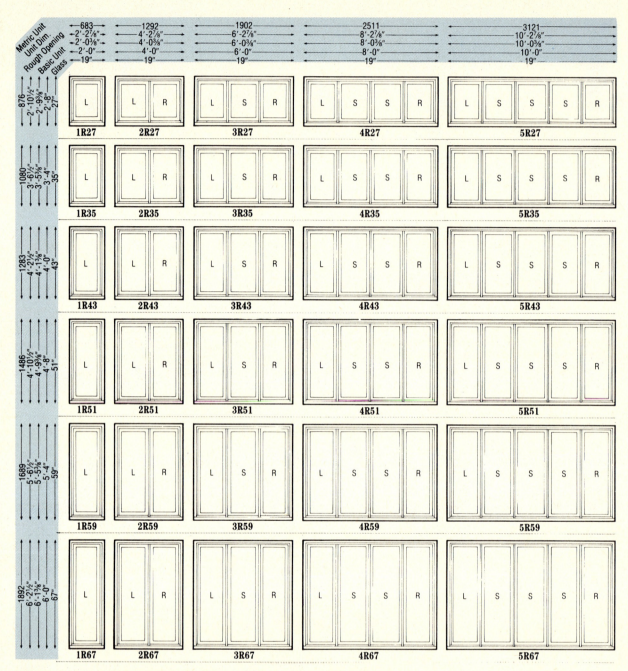

Formula for Rough Opening Size of Multiple Units
Width: Add ⅜″ to Basic Unit
Height: Add ⅜″ to Basic Unit

Formula For Masonry Opening
Width: Add ½″ to Unit Dim.
Height: Add ¼″ to Unit Dim.

Figure D–9

Wood Casement Window Details

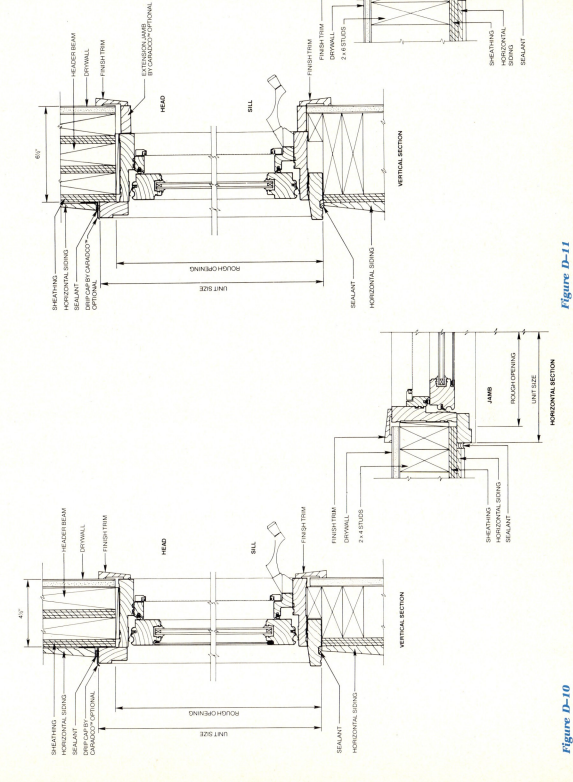

Figure D-11

Figure D-10

Wood Casement Window Details

2 x 4 FRAME WALL BRICK VENEER
SCALE: 3" = 1'-0"

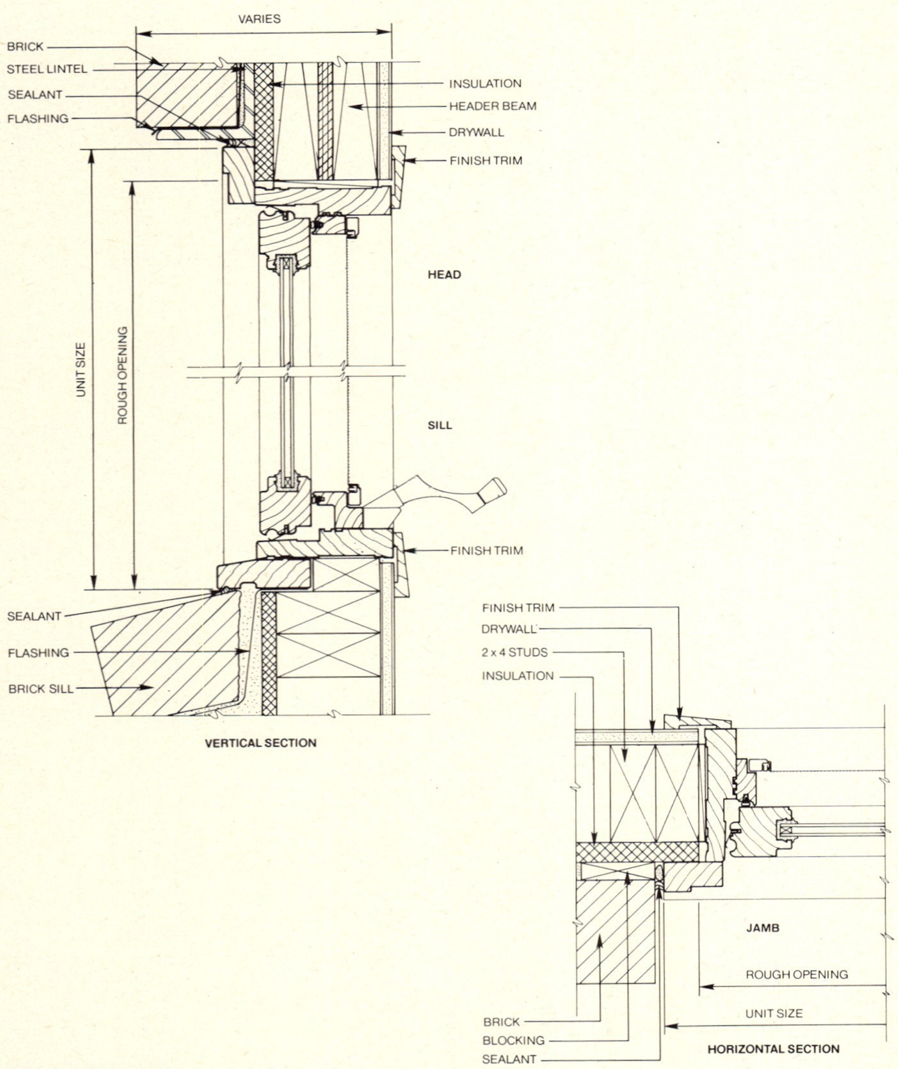

8" MASONRY WALL
SCALE: 3" = 1'-0"

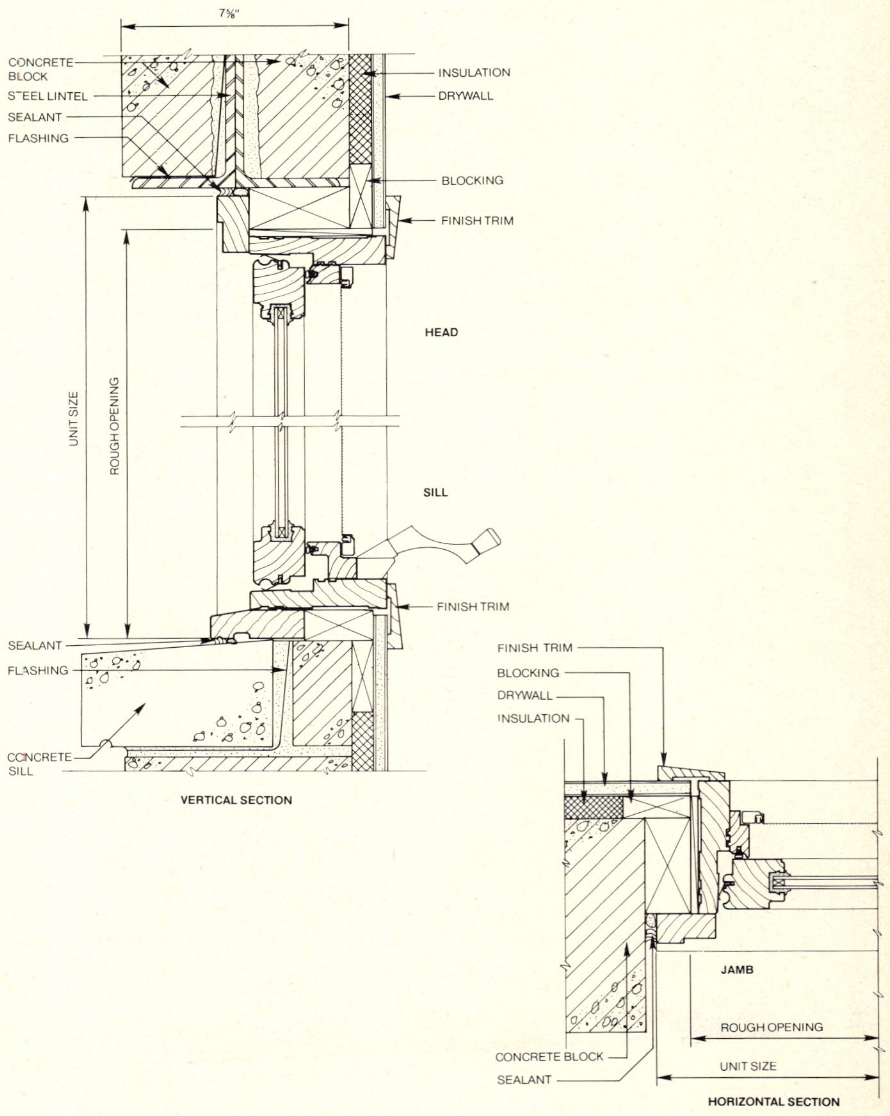

Figure D-12

Figure D-13

490

Wood Horizontal Slider Windows

Figure D–14

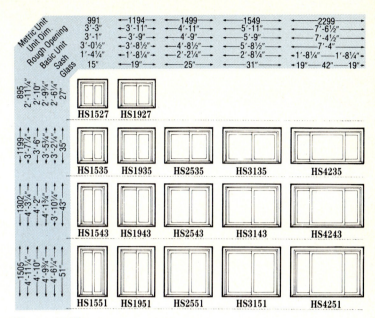

Figure D–15

Specifications:

1. *Frame:* Shall be kiln-dried Western pine, treated with a water repellant, preservative and insect toxicant. All exposed exterior surfaces shall be factory-primed. Basic jamb width shall be 4 9/16" (116 mm). Assembled frame shall include brick mold with weather-stripping and hardware applied.
2. *Sash:* Shall be kiln-dried Western pine, treated with a water-repellant, preservative and insect toxicant. Sash corner joints shall be mortise and tenon, then secured with screws. All exposed exterior surfaces shall be factory-primed. Sash shall allow convenient disassembly for field replacement of glass and parts.
3. *Finish:* All exposed surfaces shall be factory primed. Interior wood surfaces shall be unfinished to allow painting or staining.
4. *Glass:* Shall be 7/16" (11 mm) hermetically-sealed insulating glass with lites of 3/32" (2.3 mm) clear select-quality glass separated by 1/4" (6.3 mm) air space. Exception: all picture window units shall be 3/4" (19 mm) hermetically-sealed insulating glass with lites of 3/16" (5 mm) and 3/8" (10 mm) air space).
5. *Glazing Gasket.* Insulating glass shall be glazed in sash with flexible extruded vinyl gasket, heat welded at the corners. Replacement of glass shall be possible without requiring putty or other glazing compound.
6. *Weatherstripping.* Shall combine a dual-durometer vinyl weatherstrip installed at the lock jamb, a vinyl interlock and two vinyl bulbs on the meeting stiles, a compression vinyl weatherstripping system at the head and a precision fit between operating sash and vinyl-capped track at the sill.
7. *Hardware.* The slider operating sash shall glide across a high-rise aluminum track capped with vinyl. A vinyl liner within the bottom rail of the sash and a vinyl cap on the top rail shall provide a smooth vinyl-to-vinyl contact on both sliding surfaces. A convenient finger pull shall be installed on the lead stile of the sash and a matching luggage-type sash lock shall provide positive closure at the meeting stiles.
8. *Screen.* All screens shall be "silent" charcoal fiberglass screen cloth (18 × 16 mesh). A white aluminum frame shall be held in place by spring tension, without clips or fasteners.

Wood Sliding Window Details

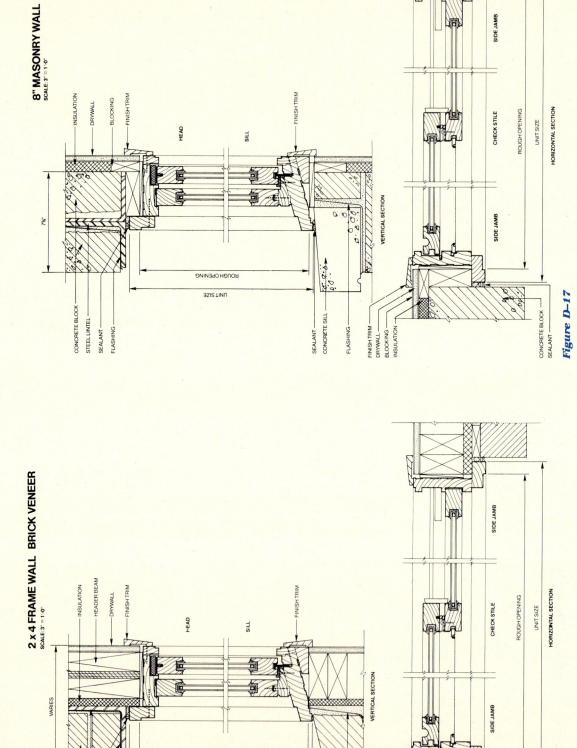

Figure D-17

Figure D-16

Wood Sliding Window Details

2 x 6 FRAME WALL WOOD SIDING

SCALE: 3" = 1'-0"

Figure D–18

2 x 4 FRAME WALL WOOD SIDING

SCALE: 3" = 1'-0"

Figure D–19

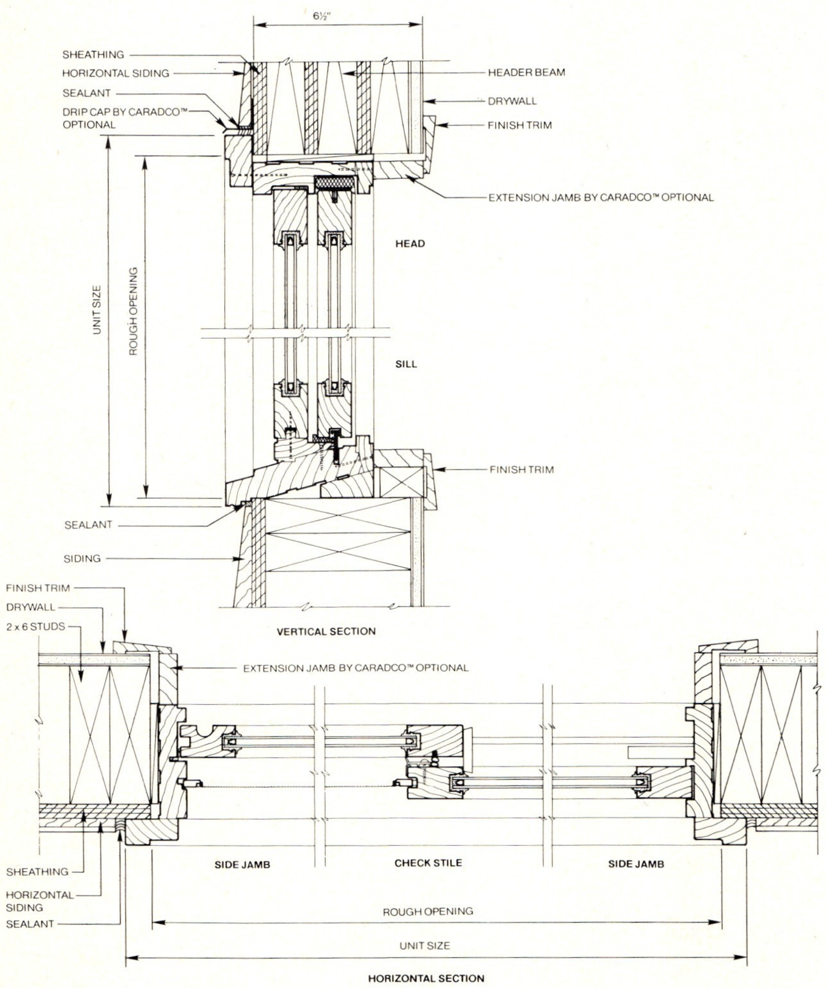

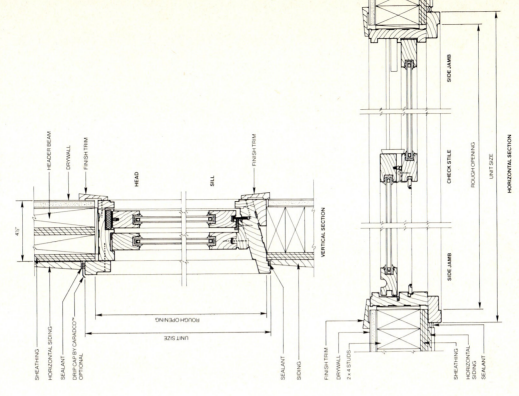

Wood Awning Windows

Figure D–20

Figure D–21

Specifications:

1. *Frame:* Shall be kiln-dried Western pine, treated with a water-repellant, preservative and insect toxicant. All exposed exterior surfaces shall be factory-primed. Basic jamb width shall be $4\frac{9}{16}''$ (14 mm). Assembled frame shall include brick mold and sub-sill, with weather-stripping and hardware applied.
2. *Sash:* Shall be $1\frac{3}{4}''$ (44 mm) thick kiln-dried Western pine, treated with a water-repellant, preservative and insect toxicant. Sash corner joints shall be mortise and tenon, then secured with screws. All exposed exterior surfaces shall be factory-primed. Sash shall allow convenient disassembly for field replacement of glass and parts.
3. *Finish:* All exposed surfaces shall be factory primed. Interior wood surfaces shall be unfinished to allow painting or staining.
4. *Glass:* Shall be $\frac{7}{16}''$ (11 mm) hermetically-sealed insulating glass with lites of $\frac{3}{32}''$ (2.3 mm) clear select-quality glass separated by $\frac{1}{4}''$ (6.3 mm) air space. Exception: all picture window units shall be $\frac{3}{4}''$ (19 mm) hermetically-sealed insulating glass with lites of $\frac{3}{16}''$ (5 mm) and $\frac{3}{8}''$ (10 mm air space).
5. *Glazing Gasket.* Insulating glass shall be glazed in sash with flexible extruded vinyl gasket, heat welded at the corners. Replacement of glass shall be possible without requiring putty or other glazing compound.
6. *Weatherstripping.* Shall combine a stainless steel leaf applied to the sash with a complete second system of flexible vinyl bulb applied to the frame.
7. *Hardware.* Sash shall be hinged with a sliding nylon shoe reinforced with steel in a zinc dichromate plated steel track. All hinges shall be concealed from exterior view and protected from weather. Roto-opertor shall be worm-gear type with die-cast finished in Chestnut Bronze. Scissor-type operator arm shall allow for easy disconnect from sash to permit awning to open past 90° for washing from the inside. Push bar operators also shall be available.
8. *Screen.* Shall be "silent" charcoal fiber-glass screen cloth (18 × 16 mesh) set in Chestnut Bronze aluminum frame. Frame shall be held in place with two spring plungers and and retaining pins. Nylon grommets in frame shall be factory installed to accept screen.
9. *Triple Glazing.* Shall be select-quality glass set in a rigid white vinyl frame with flexible tubular vinyl weatherstrip fused in place. Panel secures to outside of the sash with nylon fasteners.
10. *Removable Divided Lite Grilles:* Shall be extruded white vinyl to achieve the effect of a divided lite sash. Grilles shall be easily removable without removing glass panels.

Wood Awning Windows

N Series (Narrow): 15″ Glass Height
R Series (Regular): 19″ Glass Height
W Series (Wide): 23″ Glass Height
XW Series (Extra Wide): 31″ Glass Height

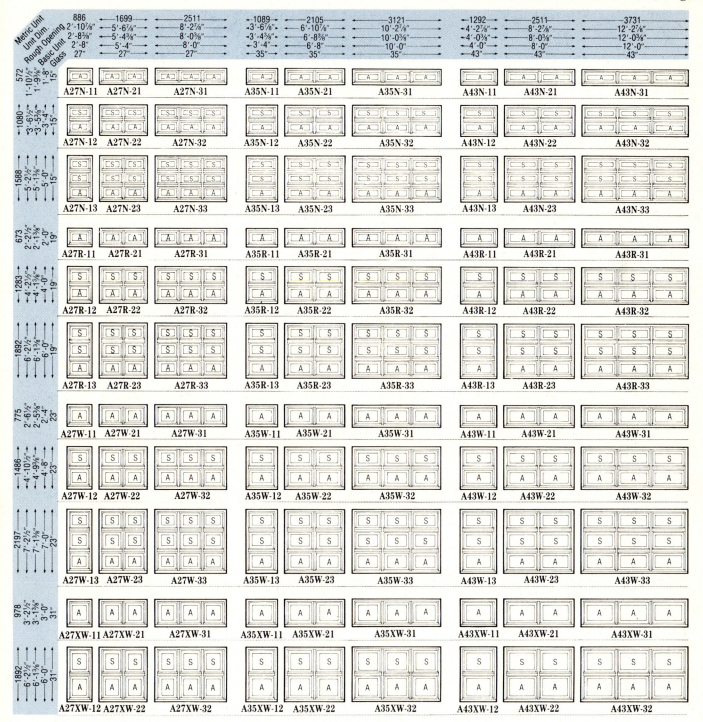

Coding System: The unit codes for primed awning above are based on glass size. Example: an assembled twin primed awning would be coded as A35N-12. The first letter indicates an awning unit. The number 35 indicates glass width in inches. The letter N indicates (narrow) 15″ glass height. The -12 indicates 1 unit in width and 2 units in height.

Figure D–22

Wood Awning Window Details

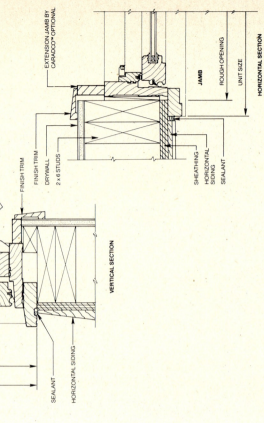

2 x 6 FRAME WALL WOOD SIDING
SCALE: 3" = 1'-0"

Figure D-24

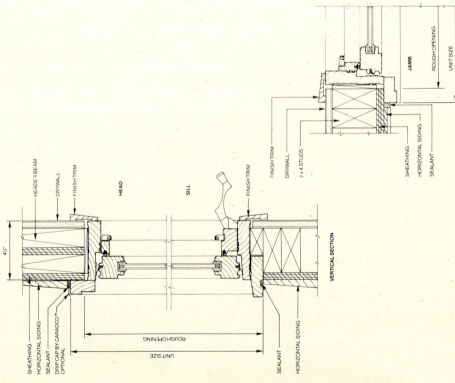

2 x 4 FRAME WALL WOOD SIDING
SCALE: 3" = 1'-0"

Figure D-23

Wood Awning Window Details

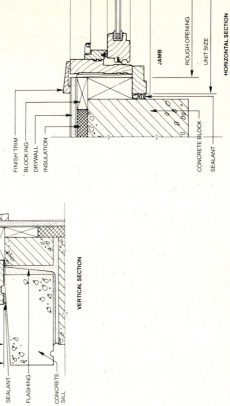

Figure D-26

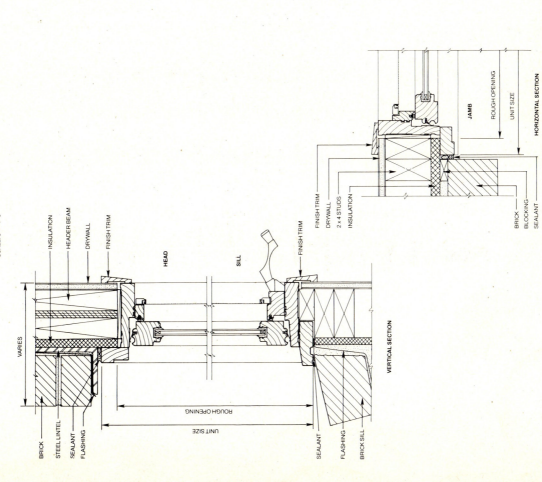

Figure D-25

Wood Sliding Glass Doors

Figure D–27

31" Glass – Sidelight, 2 Door and 3 Door Units

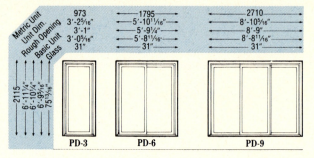

43" Glass – Sidelight, 2 Door and 3 Door Units

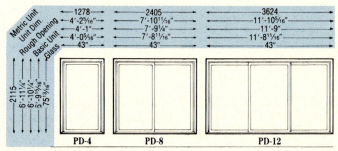

Note: New size patio doors scheduled for 1983 introduction will have rough openings of: 3′1½″ x 6′8″, 4′1½″ x 6′8″, 6′0″

Figure D–28

Specifications:
1. *Frame.* The wood frame shall be kiln-dried Western pine, precision-milled and fitted, and treated with water repellant, preservative and insect toxicant. All exposed exterior surfaces shall be factory-primed. Assembled frame shall include brick mold with weatherstripping and hardware applied. A heavy wood insert shall separate the two-piece aluminum sill to provide a positive thermal break. Threshold shall be hardwood. Basic jamb width shall be 4 9/16″ (116 mm).
2. *Door Panels.* Shall be kiln-dried Western pine treated with a water-repellant, preservative and insect toxicant. Wood door panels shall be assembled with mortise and tenon corner joints, secured with screws for structural strength. Exposed exterior surfaces shall be factory-primed. Two-panel doors shall be field reversible.
3. *Glass.* Insulating glass shall be 5/8″ (16 mm) overall, composed of two sheets of 3/16″ (4.8 mm) clear tempered glass with ¼″ (6 mm) air space.
4. *Glazing Gasket.* Caradco insulating glass shall be glazed in flexible extruded vinyl, heat welded at the corners.
5. *Weatherstripping.* Shall be vinyl bulb gasket weatherstrip installed at the lock jamb, a vinyl interlock and a vinyl bulb on the stationary panel meeting stile, a center-fin pile weatherstrip at the head and the sill.
6. *Hardware.* Shall be two sets of adjustable tandem steel ball-bearing rollers to allow fingertip operation of the movable panel. Inside/outside handle set shall incorporate a positive locking mechanism and an additional security deadbolt shall be standard. Two acetal plastic rollers on the top rail of the movable panel shall be provided to insure smooth operation and positive weatherstrip contact.
7. *Screen.* All screens shall be "silent" charcoal fiberglass screen cloth (18 × 16 mesh). Two adjustable rollers at top and bottom shall be provided to assure smooth screen operation. Screen shall be factory prefinished.

Options:
8. *Wood Grilles:* Wood grilles in a colonial divided lite design shall be available as an option. (Diamond design grilles are available on special order.) Grille bars shall be 5/8″ (16 mm) × ½″ (13 mm) thick with full surround. Steel pins in wood surround shall attach grille to door panel. Wood grilles shall be unfinished Western pine to allow for painting or staining.
9. *Key Lock:* Key lock shall be available as an option to allow locking and unlocking from the exterior.

Wood Sliding Glass Door Details

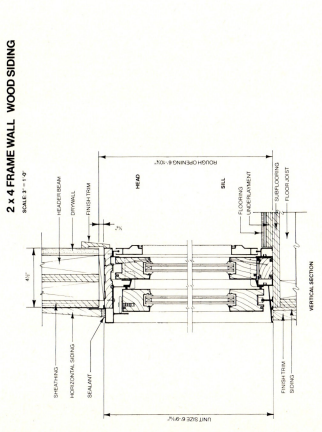

Figure D-29

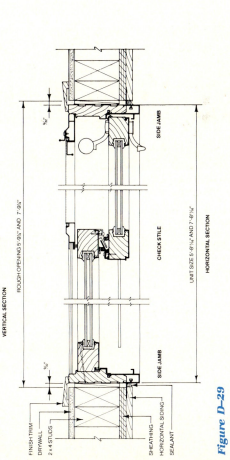

Figure D-30

Wood Sliding Glass Door Details

2 x 4 FRAME WALL BRICK VENEER

SCALE: 3" = 1'-0"

Figure D–31

8" MASONRY WALL

SCALE: 3" = 1'-0"

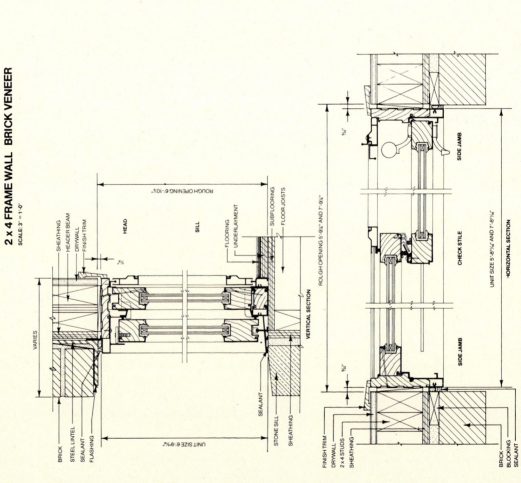

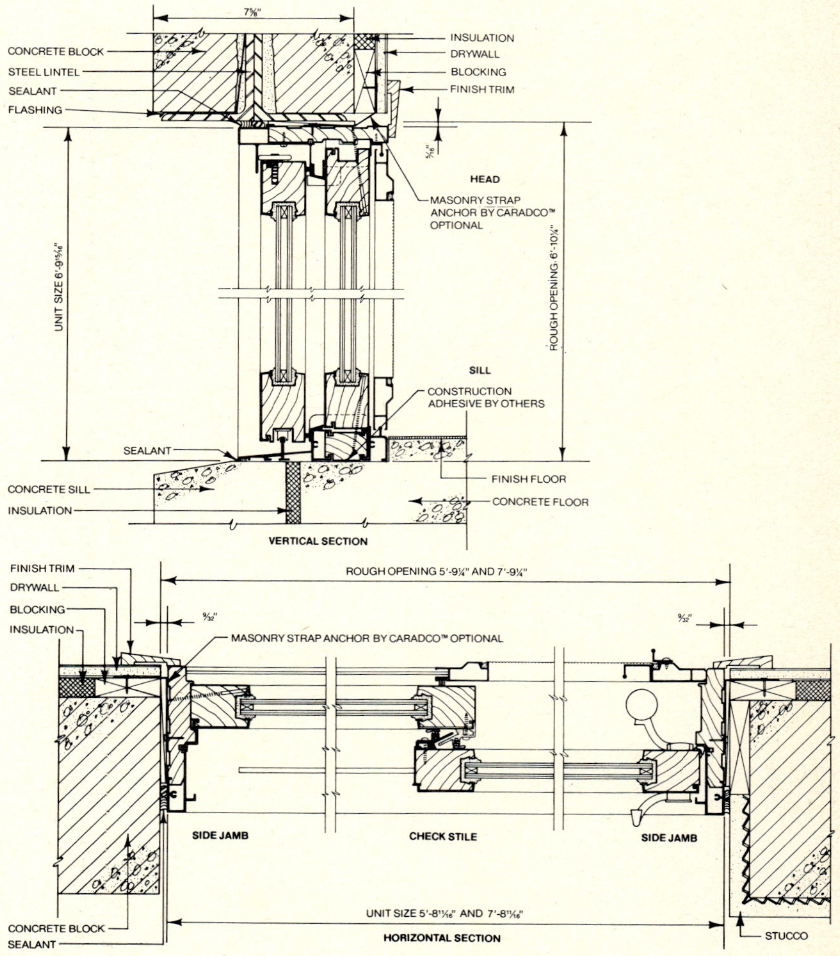

Figure D–32

E Structural Tables

Table E–1. Floor or Ceiling Live Loads

Location	Live Load (psf)
Dwelling rooms (other than sleeping quarters)	40
Dwelling rooms (sleeping quarters and attic floors)	30
Ceiling joist-attics (served by permanent or disappearing stair)	30
Ceiling joist-attics (limited storage roof slope over 3 in 12)	20
Ceiling joists-attics (without storage roof slope 3 in 12 or less)	10
Stairs	60
Public stairs and corridors (two-family dwellings)	60
Garages and carports (passenger cars)	75
Balconies and porches	60
Sidewalks and driveways	250

SOURCE: HUD Minimum Property Standards, 1973 ed.

Table E–2. Roof Loads

Roof Slopes	Live Load[a] (psf)
Slope 3 in 12 or less:	
Minimum load	20
Roof used as deck	40
Slope over 3 in 12:	
Minimum load	15

[a] Psf on horizontal projection of roof area.
SOURCE: HUD Minimum Property Standards, 1973 ed.

Table E–3. Properties of Southern Pine Lumber

	2–4 in. Thick, 5 in. and Wider			2–4 in. Thick, 2–4 in. Wide	
	Extreme Fiber in Bending[a]		Modulus of Elasticity,	Extreme Fiber in Bending[a]	
Grade[b]	F_b (psi)	$1.15F_b$ (psi)	E (psi)	F_b (psi)	$1.15F_b$ (psi)
Dense Sel Str KD	2200	2550	1,900,000	2500	2900
Dense Sel Str	2050	2350	1,800,000	2350	2700
Sel Str KD	1850	2150	1,800,000	2150	2450
Sel Str	1750	2000	1,700,000	2000	2300
No. 1 Dense KD	1850	2150	1,900,000	2150	2450
No. 1 Dense	1700	1950	1,800,000	2000	2300
No. 1 KD	1600	1850	1,800,000	1850	2150
No. 1	1450	1650	1,700,000	1700	1950
No. 2 Dense KD	1550	1800	1,700,000	1800	2050
No. 2 Dense	1400	1600	1,600,000	1650	1900
No. 2 KD	1300	1500	1,600,000	1550	1800
No. 2	1200	1400	1,600,000	1400	1600
No. 3 Dense KD	875	1000	1,500,000	1000	1150
No. 3 Dense	825	950	1,500,000	925	1075
No. 3 KD	750	850	1,500,000	850	975
No. 3	700	800	1,400,000	775	900
Construction KD			1,500,000	1100	1150
Construction			1,400,000	1000	1050
Standard KD			1,500,000	625	725
Standard			1,400,000	575	650
Utility KD			1,500,000	275	325
Utility			1,400,000	275	325
Stud KD	800[c]	925	1,500,000	850	975
Stud	725[c]	900	1,400,000	775	900

[a] When designing members that include at least three together (floor joists), use the column "$1.15\ F_b$." When designing members that are not at least three together (a single beam), use the column "F_b."

[b] Sel. Str., select structural; KD, kiln dried to a moisture content of 15% or less; where KD is not shown, the material is dried to a moisture content of 19% or less.

[c] Applies to 5- and 6-in. widths only.

SOURCE: Southern Pine Use Guide, Southern Forest Products Association.

Table E-4. Recommended Spans (ft-in.) for Southern Pine Floor Joists: 30-psf Live Load[a]

Size and Spacing in.	in. O.C.	Dense Sel Str KD and No. 1 Dense KD	Dense Sel Str, Sel Str KD, No. 1 Dense and No. 1 KD	Sel Str, No. 1 and No. 2 Dense KD	No. 2 Dense, No. 2 KD and No. 2	No. 3 Dense KD	No. 3 Dense	No. 3 KD	No. 3
2 × 5	12.0	10–3	10–0	9–10	9–8	9–3	8–11	8–6	8–3
	13.7	9–9	9–7	9–5	9–3	8–7	8–4	8–0	7–9
	16.0	9–3	9–1	8–11	8–9	8–0	7–9	7–5	7–2
	19.2	8–9	8–7	8–5	8–3	7–3	7–1	6–9	6–6
	24.0	8–1	8–0	7–10	7–8	6–6	6–4	6–0	5–10
2 × 6	12.0	12–6	12–3	12–0	11–10	11–3	10–11	10–5	10–1
	13.7	11–11	11–9	11–6	11–3	10–6	10–3	9–9	9–5
	16.0	11–4	11–2	10–11	10–9	9–9	9–6	9–0	8–9
	19.2	10–8	10–6	10–4	10–1	8–11	8–8	8–3	8–0
	24.0	9–11	9–9	9–7	9–4	8–0	7–9	7–4	7–1
2 × 8	12.0	16–6	16–2	15–10	15–7	14–10	14–5	13–9	13–3
	13.7	15–9	15–6	15–2	14–11	13–11	13–6	12–10	12–5
	16.0	15–0	14–8	14–5	14–2	12–10	12–6	11–11	11–6
	19.2	14–1	13–10	13–7	13–4	11–9	11–5	10–10	10–6
	24.0	13–1	12–10	12–7	12–4	10–6	10–2	9–9	9–5
2 × 10	12.0	21–0	20–8	20–3	19–10	18–11	18–5	17–6	16–11
	13.7	20–1	19–9	19–4	19–0	17–9	17–2	16–5	15–10
	16.0	19–1	18–9	18–5	18–0	16–5	15–11	15–2	14–8
	19.2	18–0	17–8	17–4	17–0	15–0	14–6	13–10	13–5
	24.0	16–8	16–5	16–1	15–9[c]	13–5	13–0	12–5	12–0
2 × 12	12.0	25–7	25–1	24–8	24–2	23–0	22–4	21–4	20–7
	13.7	24–5	24–0	23–7	23–1	21–7	20–11	19–11	19–3
	16.0	23–3	22–10	22–5	21–11	19–11	19–4	18–6	17–10
	19.2	21–10	21–6	21–1	20–8	18–3	17–8	16–10	16–3
	24.0	20–3	19–11	19–7	19–2[c]	16–3	15–10	15–1	14–7

[a] *Floor Joists—30-psf live load.* Sleeping rooms and attic floors. (Spans shown in lightface type are based on a deflection limitation of L/360. Spans shown in color, boldface type are limited by the recommended extreme fiber stress in bending value of the grade and includes a 10-psf dead load.)

[b] Abbreviations are explained in Table E–3.

[c] The span for No. 2 grade, 24 in. O.C. spacing is: 2 × 10, **15–8**; 2 × 12, **19–1.**

SOURCE: Southern Pine Use Guide, Southern Forest Products Association.

Table E-5. Recommended Spans (ft-in.) for Southern Pine Floor Joists: 40-psf Live Load[a]

Size and Spacing		Grade[b]							
in.	in. O.C.	Dense Sel Str KD and No. 1 Dense KD	Dense Sel Str, Sel Str KD, No. 1 Dense and No. 1 KD	Sel Str, No. 1 and No. 2 Dense KD	No. 2 Dense, No. 2 KD and No. 2	No. 3 Dense KD	No. 3 Dense	No. 3 KD	No. 3
2 × 5	12.0	9–3	9–1	8–11	8–9	8–3	8–0	7–8	7–4
	13.7	8–11	8–9	8–7	8–5	7–9	7–6	7–2	6–11
	16.0	8–5	8–3	8–2	8–0	7–2	6–11	6–7	6–5
	19.2	7–11	7–10	7–8	7–6	6–6	6–4	6–0	5–10
	24.0	7–4	7–3	7–1	7–0[c]	5–10	5–8	5–5	5–3
2 × 6	12.0	11–4	11–2	10–11	10–9	10–1	9–9	9–4	9–0
	13.7	10–10	10–8	10–6	10–3	9–5	9–2	8–9	8–5
	16.0	10–4	10–2	9–11	9–9	8–9	8–6	8–1	7–10
	19.2	9–8	9–6	9–4	9–2	8–0	7–9	7–4	7–1
	24.0	9–0	8–10	8–8	8–6[c]	7–1	6–11	6–7	6–4
2 × 8	12.0	15–0	14–8	14–5	14–2	13–3	12–11	12–4	11–11
	13.7	14–4	14–1	13–10	13–6	12–5	12–1	11–6	11–1
	16.0	13–7	13–4	13–1	12–10	11–6	11–2	10–8	10–3
	19.2	12–10	12–7	12–4	12–1	10–6	10–2	9–9	9–5
	24.0	11–11	11–8	11–5	11–3[c]	9–5	9–1	8–8	8–5
2 × 10	12.0	19–1	18–9	18–5	18–0	16–11	16–5	15–8	15–2
	13.7	18–3	17–11	17–7	17–3	15–10	15–5	14–8	14–2
	16.0	17–4	17–0	16–9	16–5	14–8	14–3	13–7	13–1
	19.2	16–4	16–0	15–9	15–5	13–5	13–0	12–5	12–0
	24.0	15–2	14–11	14–7	14–4[c]	12–0	11–8	11–1	10–9
2 × 12	12.0	23–3	22–10	22–5	21–11	20–7	20–0	19–1	18–5
	13.7	22–3	21–10	21–5	21–0	19–3	18–9	17–10	17–3
	16.0	21–1	20–9	20–4	19–11	17–10	17–4	16–6	16–0
	19.2	19–10	19–6	19–2	18–9	16–3	15–10	15–1	14–7
	24.0	18–5	18–1	17–9	17–5[c]	14–7	14–2	13–6	13–0

[a] *Floor Joists—40-psf live load.* All rooms except sleeping rooms and attic floors. (Spans shown in lightface type are based on a deflection limitation of L/360. Spans shown in color, boldface type are limited by the recommended extreme fiber stress in bending value of the grade and includes a 10-psf dead load.)

[b] Abbreviations are explained in Table E-3.

[c] The span for No. 2 grade, 24 in. O.C. spacing is: 2 × 5, **6–10**; 2 × 6, **8–4**; 2 × 8, **11–0**; 2 × 10, **14–0**; 2 × 12, **17–1.**

SOURCE: Southern Pine Use Guide, Southern Forest Products Association.

Table E-6. Recommended Spans (ft-in.) for Southern Pine Ceiling Joists: 10-psf Live Load[a]

Size and Spacing		Grade[b]									
in.	in. O.C.	Dense Sel Str KD and No. 1 Dense KD	Dense Sel Str, Sel Str KD, No. 1 Dense and No. 1 KD	Sel Str, No. 1 and Dense No. 2 KD	No. 2 Dense, No. 2 KD and No. 2	No. 3 Dense KD	No. 3 Dense	No. 3 KD	No. 3	Construction KD	Construction	Standard KD	Standard
2 × 4	12.0	13–2	12–11	12–8	12–5	12–2	12–0	11–6	11–0	12–2	11–10	9–11	9–6
	13.7	12–7	12–4	12–1	11–10	11–7	11–3	10–9	10–4	11–7	11–4	9–3	8–11
	16.0	11–11	11–9	11–6	11–3	10–10	10–5	10–0	9–6	11–0	10–9	8–7	8–3
	19.2	11–3	11–0	10–10	10–7	9–11	9–6	9–1	8–8	10–4	9–11	7–10	7–6
	24.0	10–5	10–3	10–0	9–10	8–10	8–6	8–2	7–9	9–3	8–10	7–0	6–9
2 × 5	12.0	16–11	16–7	16–3	15–11	15–1	14–7	13–11	13–5				
	13.7	16–2	15–10	15–7	15–3	14–1	13–8	13–0	12–7				
	16.0	15–4	15–1	14–9	14–6	13–0	12–8	12–1	11–8				
	19.2	14–5	14–2	13–11	13–8	11–11	11–7	11–0	10–8				
	24.0	13–5	13–2	12–11	12–8[c]	10–8	10–4	9–10	9–6				
2 × 6	12.0	20–8	20–3	19–11	19–6	18–5	17–10	17–0	16–5				
	13.7	19–9	19–5	19–0	18–8	17–2	16–8	15–11	15–5				
	16.0	18–9	18–5	18–1	17–8	15–11	15–6	14–9	14–3				
	19.2	17–8	17–4	17–0	16–8	14–6	14–1	13–6	13–0				
	24.0	16–4	16–1	15–9	15–6[c]	13–0	12–8	12–0	11–8				
2 × 8	12.0	27–2	26–9	26–2	25–8	24–3	23–6	22–5	21–8				
	13.7	26–0	25–7	25–1	24–7	22–8	22–0	21–0	20–3				
	16.0	24–8	24–3	23–10	23–4	21–0	20–5	19–5	18–9				
	19.2	23–3	22–10	22–5	21–11	19–2	18–7	17–9	17–2				
	24.0	21–7	21–2	20–10	20–5[c]	17–2	16–8	15–10	15–4				
2 × 10	12.0	34–8	34–1	33–5	32–9	30–11	30–0	28–8	27–8				
	13.7	33–2	32–7	32–0	31–4	28–11	28–1	26–9	25–11				
	16.0	31–6	31–0	30–5	29–9	26–9	26–0	24–10	23–11				
	19.2	29–8	29–2	28–7	28–0	24–5	23–9	22–8	21–10				
	24.0	27–6	27–1	26–6	26–0[c]	21–10	21–3	20–3	19–7				

[a] *Ceiling Joists—Drywall Ceiling—10-psf live load.* No future sleeping rooms and no attic storage, roof slopes 3 in 12 or less. (Spans shown in lightface type are based on a deflection limitation of L/240. Spans shown in color, boldface type are limited by the recommended extreme fiber stress in bending value of the grade and includes a 5-psf dead load.)

[b] Abbreviations are explained in Table E-3.

[c] The span for No. 2 grade, 24 in. O.C. spacing is: 2 × 5, 12–6; 2 × 6, 15–3; 2 × 8, 20–1; 2 × 10, 25–7.

SOURCE: Southern Pine Use Guide, Southern Forest Products Association.

Table E-7. Recommended Spans (ft-in.) for Southern Pine Ceiling Joists: 20-psf Live Load[a]

Size and Spacing		Grade[b]										
in.	in. O.C.	Dense Sel Str and No. 1 Dense KD	Dense Sel Str, Sel Str KD, No. 1 Dense and No. 1 KD	Sel Str, No. 1 and Dense No. 2 KD	No. 2 Dense	No. 2 KD	No. 2	No. 3 Dense KD	No. 3 Dense	No. 3 KD	No. 3	Construction KD	Construction	Standard KD	Standard
2 × 4	12.0	10-5	10-3	10-0	9-10	9-10	9-10	8-10	8-6	8-2	7-9	9-3	8-10	7-0	6-9
	13.7	10-0	9-9	9-7	9-5	9-5	9-5	8-3	8-0	7-8	7-3	8-8	8-3	6-7	6-3
	16.0	9-6	9-4	9-1	8-11	8-11	8-11	7-8	7-4	7-1	6-9	8-0	7-8	6-1	5-10
	19.2	8-11	8-9	8-7	8-5	8-5	8-3	7-0	6-9	6-5	6-2	7-4	7-0	5-6	5-4
	24.0	8-3	8-1	8-0	7-10	7-9	7-5	6-3	6-0	5-9	5-6	6-7	6-3	4-11	4-9
2 × 5	12.0	13-5	13-2	12-11	12-8	12-8	12-6	10-8	10-4	9-10	9-6				
	13.7	12-10	12-7	12-4	12-1	12-1	11-8	9-11	9-8	9-3	8-11				
	16.0	12-2	11-11	11-9	11-6	11-3	10-9	9-3	8-11	8-6	8-3				
	19.2	11-5	11-3	11-0[c]	10-8	10-3	9-10	8-5	8-2	7-9	7-6				
	24.0	10-8	10-5[d]	10-3[c,e]	9-6[d]	9-2	8-10	7-6	7-4	7-0	6-9				
2 × 6	12.0	16-4	16-1	15-9	15-6	15-6	15-3	13-0	12-8	12-0	11-8				
	13.7	15-8	15-5	15-1	14-9	14-9	14-3	12-2	11-10	11-3	10-11				
	16.0	14-11	14-7	14-4	14-1	13-9	13-2	11-3	10-11	10-5	10-1				
	19.2	14-0	13-9	13-6[c]	13-0	12-6	12-0	10-3	10-0	9-6	9-2				
	24.0	13-0	12-9[d]	12-6[c,e]	11-8	11-2	10-9	9-2	8-11	8-6	8-3				
2 × 8	12.0	21-7	21-2	20-10	20-5	20-5	20-1	17-2	16-8	15-10	15-4				
	13.7	20-8	20-3	19-11	19-6	19-6	18-9	16-0	15-7	14-10	14-4				
	16.0	19-7	19-3	18-11	18-6	18-1	17-5	14-10	14-5	13-9	13-3				
	19.2	18-5	18-2	17-9[c]	17-2	16-6	15-10	13-7	13-2	12-7	12-1				
	24.0	17-2	16-10[d]	16-6[c,e]	15-4	14-9	14-2	12-1	11-9	11-3	10-10				
2 × 10	12.0	27-6	27-1	26-6	26-0	26-0	25-7	21-10	21-3	20-3	19-7				
	13.7	26-4	25-10	25-5	24-11	24-11	24-0	20-6	19-10	18-11	18-4				
	16.0	25-0	24-7	24-1	23-8	23-1	22-2	18-11	18-5	17-6	16-11				
	19.2	23-7	23-2	22-8[c]	21-10	21-1	20-3	17-3	16-9	16-0	15-6				
	24.0	21-10	21-6[d]	21-1[c,e]	19-7	18-10	18-1	15-6	15-0	14-4	13-10				

[a] *Ceiling Joists—Drywall Ceiling—20-psf live load.* No future sleeping rooms but limited storage available. (Spans shown in light face type are based on a deflection limitation of L/240. Spans shown in color, boldface type are limited by the recommended extreme fiber stress in bending value of the grade and includes a 10-psf dead load.)
[b] Abbreviations are explained in Table E-3.
[c] The span for No. 1 grade is: 2 × 5, 19.2 O.C., 10-10; 24 O.C., 9-8; 2 × 6, 19.2 O.C., 13-3; 24 O.C. 11-10; 2 × 8, 19.2 O.C., 17-5; 24 O.C., 15-7; 2 × 10, 19.2 O.C., 22-3; 24 O.C., 19-11.
[d] The span for No. 1 KD grade, 24 in. O.C. is: 2 × 5, 10-2; 2 × 6, 12-5; 2 × 8, 16-5; 2 × 10, 20-11.
[e] The span for No. 2 Dense KD grade, 24 in. O.C. is: 2 × 5, 10-0; 2 × 6, 12-3; 2 × 8, 16-2; 2 × 10, 20-7.

SOURCE: Southern Pine Use Guide, Southern Forest Products Association.

Table E-8. Recommended Spans (ft-in.) for Southern Pine Rafters—Low Slope: 20-psf Live Load[a]

Size and Spacing in.	in. O.C.	Dense Sel Str and No. 1 Dense KD	Dense Sel Str, Sel Str KD, No. 1 Dense and No. 1 KD	Sel Str, No. 2 Dense KD	No. 1	No. 2 Dense	No. 2 Dense KD	No. 2	No. 3 Dense KD	No. 3 Dense	No. 3 KD	No. 3
2 × 5	12.0	13-5	13-2	12-11	12-11	12-8	12-8	12-6	10-8	10-4	9-10	9-6
	13.7	12-10	12-7	12-4	12-4	12-1	12-1	11-8	9-11	9-8	9-3	8-11
	16.0	12-2	11-11	11-9	11-9	11-6	11-3	10-9	9-3	8-11	8-6	8-3
	19.2	11-5	11-3	11-0	10-10	10-8	10-3	9-10	8-5	8-2	7-9	7-6
	24.0	10-8	10-5[c]	10-3[d]	9-8	9-6	9-2	8-10	7-6	7-4	7-0	6-9
2 × 6	12.0	16-4	16-1	15-9	15-9	15-6	15-6	15-3	13-0	12-8	12-0	11-8
	13.7	15-8	15-5	15-1	15-1	14-9	14-9	14-3	12-2	11-10	11-3	10-11
	16.0	14-11	14-7	14-4	14-4	14-1	13-9	13-2	11-3	10-11	10-5	10-1
	19.2	14-0	13-9	13-6	13-3	13-0	12-6	12-0	10-3	10-0	9-6	9-2
	24.0	13-0	12-9[c]	12-6[d]	11-10	11-8	11-2	10-9	9-2	8-11	8-6	8-3
2 × 8	12.0	21-7	21-2	20-10	20-10	20-5	20-5	20-1	17-2	16-8	15-10	15-4
	13.7	20-8	20-3	19-11	19-11	19-6	19-6	18-9	16-0	15-7	14-10	14-4
	16.0	19-7	19-3	18-11	18-11	18-6	18-1	17-5	14-10	14-5	13-9	13-3
	19.2	18-5	18-2	17-9	17-5	17-2	16-6	15-10	13-7	13-2	12-7	12-1
	24.0	17-2	16-10[c]	16-6[d]	15-7	15-4	14-9	14-2	12-1	11-9	11-3	10-10
2 × 10	12.0	27-6	27-1	26-6	26-6	26-0	26-0	25-7	21-10	21-3	20-3	19-7
	13.7	26-4	25-10	25-5	25-5	24-11	24-11	24-0	20-6	19-10	18-11	18-4
	16.0	25-0	24-7	24-1	24-1	23-8	23-1	22-2	18-11	18-5	17-6	16-11
	19.2	23-7	23-2	22-8	22-3	21-10	21-1	20-3	17-3	16-9	16-0	15-6
	24.0	21-10	21-6[c]	21-1[d]	19-11	19-7	18-10	18-1	15-6	15-0	14-4	13-10
2 × 12	12.0	33-6	32-11	32-3	32-3	31-8	31-8	31-2	26-7	25-10	24-8	23-9
	13.7	32-0	31-6	30-10	30-10	30-3	30-3	29-2	24-11	24-2	23-0	22-3
	16.0	30-5	29-11	29-4	29-4	28-9	28-1	27-0	23-0	22-4	21-4	20-7
	19.2	28-8	28-2	27-7	27-1	26-7	25-8	24-8	21-0	20-5	19-6	18-10
	24.0	26-7	26-1[c]	25-7[d]	24-3	23-9	22-11	22-0	18-10	18-3	17-5	16-10

[a] *Rafters—Low Slope (3 in 12 or less)—With No Finished Ceiling—20-psf live load.* (Spans shown in lightface type are based on a deflection limitation of L/240. Spans shown in color, boldface type are limited by the recommended extreme fiber stress in bending value of the grade and includes a 10-psf dead load.)
[b] Abbreviations are explained in Table E-3.
[c] The span for No. 1 KD 24 in. O.C. is: 2 × 5, 10-2; 2 × 6, 12-5; 2 × 8, 16-5; 2 × 10, 20-11; 2 × 12, 25-5.
[d] The span for No. 2 Dense KD, 24 in. O.C. is: 2 × 5, 10-0; 2 × 6, 12-3; 2 × 8, 16-2; 2 × 10, 20-7; 2 × 12, 25-0.

SOURCE: Southern Pine Use Guide, Southern Forest Products Association.

Table E-9. Recommended Spans (ft-in.) for Southern Pine Rafters—High Slope: 20-psf Live Load[a]

Size and Spacing		Grade[b]													
in.	in. O.C.	Dense Sel Str KD	Dense Sel Str	No. 1 Dense KD and Sel Str KD	Sel Str	No. 1 Dense	No. 1 Dense KD	No. 1	No. 1 KD	No. 2 Dense	No. 2 Dense KD	No. 2	No. 2 KD	No. 3 Dense	No. 3 Dense KD	No. 3	No. 3 KD	Construction	Construction KD	Standard	Standard KD

Size	O.C.	Dense Sel Str KD	Dense Sel Str	No.1 Dense KD & Sel Str KD	Sel Str	No.1 Dense	No.1 Dense KD	No.1	No.1 KD	No.2 Dense	No.2 Dense KD	No.2	No.2 KD	No.3 Dense	No.3 Dense KD	No.3	No.3 KD	Constr	Constr KD	Stand	Stand KD
2×4	12.0	11-6	11-3	11-6[c]	11-1	11-3	11-2	11-0	10-8	10-6	10-2	9-8	8-2	7-11	7-7	7-3	8-7	8-2	6-6	6-3
	13.7	11-0	10-9	11-0[c]	10-7	10-9	10-5	10-3	10-0	9-10	9-6	9-1	7-8	7-4	7-1	6-9	8-0	7-8	6-1	5-10
	16.0	10-5	10-3	10-5[c]	10-0	10-0	9-8	9-6	9-3	9-1	8-10	8-5	7-1	6-10	6-6	6-3	7-5	7-1	5-7	5-5
	19.2	9-10	9-8	9-6	9-2	9-2	8-10	8-8	8-5	8-4	8-1	7-8	6-6	6-3	6-0	5-8	6-9	6-6	5-1	5-5
	24.0	9-1	8-11	8-6	8-2	8-2	7-11	7-9	7-7	7-5	7-3	6-10	5-9	5-7	5-4	5-1	6-1	5-9	4-7	4-5
2×5	12.0	14-9	14-6	14-4	13-11	13-9	13-4	13-1	12-8	12-6	12-0	11-6	9-10	9-7	9-1	8-10				
	13.7	14-1	13-10	13-5	13-3	13-3	12-6	12-3	11-10	11-8	11-3	10-10	9-3	8-11	8-6	8-3				
	16.0	13-5	13-1	12-5	12-1	11-11	11-6	11-4	11-0	10-9	10-5	10-0	8-6	8-3	7-11	7-8				
	19.2	12-4	11-11	11-4	11-0	10-10	10-6	10-4	10-0	9-10	9-6	9-1	7-9	7-7	7-3	7-0				
	24.0	11-1	10-8	10-2	9-10	9-9	9-5	9-3	9-0	8-10	8-6	8-2	7-0	6-9	6-5	6-3				
2×6	12.0	18-0	17-8	17-6	17-0	16-9	16-3	16-0	15-6	15-3	14-8	14-1	12-0	11-8	11-2	10-9				
	13.7	17-3	16-11	16-5	15-11	15-8	15-3	15-0	14-6	14-3	13-9	13-2	11-3	10-11	10-5	10-1				
	16.0	16-4	16-0	15-2	14-9	14-6	14-1	13-11	13-5	13-2	12-9	12-3	10-5	10-1	9-8	9-4				
	19.2	15-1	14-7	13-10	13-6	13-3	12-10	12-8	12-3	12-0	11-7	11-2	9-6	9-3	8-10	8-6				
	24.0	13-6	13-0	12-5	12-0	11-10	11-6	11-4	11-0	10-9	10-5	10-0	8-6	8-3	7-11	7-7				
2×8	12.0	23-9	23-4	23-1	22-5	22-1	21-6	21-1	20-5	20-1	19-4	18-7	15-10	15-5	14-8	14-2				
	13.7	22-9	22-4	21-7	21-0	20-8	20-1	19-9	19-1	18-9	18-1	17-5	14-10	14-5	13-9	13-3				
	16.0	21-7	21-0	20-0	19-5	19-2	18-7	18-4	17-8	17-5	16-9	16-1	13-9	13-4	12-9	12-4				
	19.2	19-11	19-2	18-3	17-9	17-6	17-0	16-8	16-2	15-10	15-4	14-8	12-7	12-2	11-7	11-3				
	24.0	17-10	17-2	16-4	15-10	15-8	15-2	14-11	14-5	14-2	13-8	13-2	11-3	10-11	10-5	10-0				
2×10	12.0	30-4	29-9	29-5	28-8	28-3	27-5	26-11	26-1	25-7	24-8	23-8	20-3	19-8	18-9	18-1				
	13.7	29-0	28-6	27-7	26-9	26-3	25-7	25-3	24-5	24-0	23-1	22-2	18-11	18-5	17-6	16-11				
	16.0	27-6	26-10	25-6	24-10	24-5	23-9	23-4	22-7	22-2	21-4	20-6	17-6	17-0	16-3	15-8				
	19.2	25-5	24-6	23-3	22-8	22-4	21-8	21-4	20-7	20-3	19-6	18-9	16-0	15-7	14-10	14-4				
	24.0	22-8	21-11	20-10	20-3	19-11	19-4	19-1	18-5	18-1	17-5	16-9	14-4	13-11	13-3	12-10				

[a] *Rafters—High Slope* (over 3 in 12)—*With No Finished Ceiling*—20-psf live load + 15-psf dead load—*heavy roofing*. (Spans shown in lightface type are based on a deflection limitation of L/180. Spans shown in color, boldface type are limited by the recommended extreme fiber stress in bending value of the grade and includes a 15-psf dead load.)
[b] Abbreviations are explained in Table E-3.
[c] The span for Select Structural KD, 2 × 4, 12 in. O.C. is 11-3; 13.7 in. O.C., 10-9; and 16 in. O.C., 10-3.

SOURCE: Southern Pine Use Guide, Southern Forest Products Association.

Table E-10. Recommended Spans (ft-in.) for Southern Pine Rafters—High Slope: 40-psf Live Load[a]

Size and Spacing		Dense Sel Str KD	Sel Str Dense	No. 1 Dense KD and Sel Str KD	No. 1 Dense	No. 1 KD	No. 2 Dense KD	No. 2 Dense	No. 2 KD	No. 2	No. 3 Dense KD	No. 3 Dense	No. 3 KD	No. 3	Construction KD	Construction	Standard KD	Standard
in.	in. O.C.																	
2 × 4	12.0	9-1	8-11	9-1[c]	8-11	8-11	8-9	8-5	8-2	7-9	6-6	6-3	6-0	5-9	6-10	6-6	5-2	4-11
	13.7	8-8	8-7	8-8[c]	8-7	8-4	8-2	7-10	7-7	7-3	6-1	5-11	5-8	5-5	6-5	6-1	4-10	4-8
	16.0	8-3	8-1	8-3[c]	8-0	7-8	7-7	7-3	7-1	6-8	5-8	5-5	5-3	5-0	5-11	5-8	4-6	4-3
	19.2	7-9	7-8	7-7	7-4	7-0	6-11	6-8	6-5	6-1	5-2	5-0	4-9	4-7	5-5	5-2	4-1	3-11
	24.0	7-3	7-1	6-9	6-6	6-3	6-2	5-11	5-9	5-6	4-7	4-5	4-3	4-1	4-10	4-7	3-8	3-6
2 × 5	12.0	11-8	11-6	11-5	10-11	10-8	10-6	10-1	9-11	9-7	7-10	7-8	7-3	7-0				
	13.7	11-2	11-0	10-8	10-3	9-11	9-9	9-6	9-4	8-7	7-4	7-2	6-10	6-7				
	16.0	10-8	10-5	9-11	9-6	9-2	9-1	8-9	8-7	8-0	6-10	6-7	6-4	6-1				
	19.2	9-10	9-6	9-0	8-8	8-5	8-3	8-0	7-10	7-3	6-3	6-0	5-9	5-7				
	24.0	8-10	8-6	8-1	7-10	7-6	7-5	7-2	7-0	6-6	5-7	5-5	5-2	5-0				
2 × 6	12.0	14-4	14-1	14-0	13-5	13-0	12-9	12-4	12-2	11-3	9-7	9-4	8-11	8-7				
	13.7	13-8	13-5	13-1	12-6	12-2	12-0	11-7	11-4	10-6	9-0	8-9	8-4	8-0				
	16.0	13-0	12-9	12-1	11-7	11-3	11-1	10-8	10-6	9-9	8-4	8-1	7-8	7-5				
	19.2	12-0	11-7	11-0	10-7	10-3	10-1	9-9	9-7	8-11	7-7	7-4	7-0	6-9				
	24.0	10-9	10-5	9-10	9-6	9-2	9-0	8-9	8-7	7-11	6-9	6-7	6-3	6-1				
2 × 8	12.0	18-10	18-6	18-5	17-8	17-1	16-10	16-4	16-0	15-5	12-8	12-4	11-9	11-4				
	13.7	18-0	17-9	17-3	16-6	16-0	15-9	15-3	14-5	13-10	11-10	11-6	11-0	10-7				
	16.0	17-2	16-9	15-11	15-3	14-10	14-7	14-1	13-4	12-6	11-0	10-8	10-2	9-10				
	19.2	15-10	15-4	14-7	14-2	13-11	13-4	12-9	12-2	11-9	10-0	9-9	9-3	8-11				
	24.0	14-2	13-8	13-0	12-6	12-1	11-11	11-4	10-11	10-6	8-11	8-8	8-3	8-0				
2 × 10	12.0	24-1	23-8	23-6	22-10	22-6	21-10	21-6	20-10	20-5	16-2	15-8	14-11	14-5				
	13.7	23-0	22-7	22-0	21-1	20-5	20-1	19-5	19-1	18-5	15-1	14-8	14-0	13-6				
	16.0	21-10	21-5	20-4	19-6	18-11	18-7	17-8	17-1	16-5	14-0	13-7	12-11	12-6				
	19.2	20-3	19-7	18-7	17-10	17-3	17-0	16-2	15-7	14-11	12-9	12-5	11-10	11-5				
	24.0	18-1	17-6	16-7	15-11	15-5	15-2	14-5	13-11	13-5	11-5	11-1	10-7	10-3				

[a] Rafters—High Slope (over 3 in 12)—With No Finished Ceiling—40-psf live load + 15-psf dead load—heavy roofing. (Spans shown in light face type are based on a deflection limitation of L/180. Spans shown in color, bold face type are limited by the recommended extreme fiber stress in bending value of the grade and includes a 15-psf dead load.)

[b] Abbreviations are explained in Table E-3.

[c] The span for Select Structural KD, 2 × 4, 12 in. O.C. is 8-11; 13.7 in. O.C., 8-7; and 16 in. O.C., 8-1.

SOURCE: Southern Pine Use Guide, Southern Forest Products Association.

Table E–11. Structural Glued Laminated Timber Spans[a,b]

Span ft	Spacing ft	Roof Beams: Total Load-Carrying Capacity							Floor Beams Total Load
		20 psf	*25 psf*	*30 psf*	*35 psf*	*40 psf*	*45 psf*	*50 psf*	*55 psf*	*50 psf*
8	4	—	—	*3⅛ × 4½	*3⅛ × 4½	*3⅛ × 4½	*3⅛ × 4½	*3⅛ × 4½	*3⅛ × 6	*3⅛ × 6
	6	—	—	*3⅛ × 4½	*3⅛ × 6	*3⅛ × 6	*3⅛ × 6	*3⅛ × 6	*3⅛ × 6	*3⅛ × 6
	8	—	—	*3⅛ × 6	*3⅛ × 6	*3⅛ × 6	*3⅛ × 6	*3⅛ × 6	*3⅛ × 6	*3⅛ × 7½
10	4	—	—	*3⅛ × 6	*3⅛ × 6	*3⅛ × 6	*3⅛ × 6	*3⅛ × 6	*3⅛ × 6	*3⅛ × 7½
	6	—	—	*3⅛ × 6	*3⅛ × 6	*3⅛ × 6	*3⅛ × 7½	*3⅛ × 7½	*3⅛ × 7½	*3⅛ × 7½
	8	—	—	*3⅛ × 6	*3⅛ × 7½	*3⅛ × 7½	*3⅛ × 7½	*3⅛ × 7½	*3⅛ × 7½	*3⅛ × 9
	10	—	—	*3⅛ × 7½	*3⅛ × 7½	*3⅛ × 7½	*3⅛ × 9	*3⅛ × 9	*3⅛ × 9	*3⅛ × 9
12	6	—	—	*3⅛ × 7½	*3⅛ × 7½	*3⅛ × 7½	*3⅛ × 7½	*3⅛ × 9	*3⅛ × 9	*3⅛ × 9
	8	—	—	*3⅛ × 7½	*3⅛ × 7½	*3⅛ × 9	*3⅛ × 9	*3⅛ × 9	*3⅛ × 9	*3⅛ × 10½
	10	—	—	*3⅛ × 9	*3⅛ × 9	*3⅛ × 9	*3⅛ × 10½	*3⅛ × 10½	*3⅛ × 10½	*3⅛ × 12
	12	—	—	*3⅛ × 9	*3⅛ × 9	*3⅛ × 10½	*3⅛ × 10½	*3⅛ × 10½	*3⅛ × 12	*3⅛ × 12
14	8	—	—	*3⅛ × 9	*3⅛ × 9	*3⅛ × 10½	*3⅛ × 10½	*3⅛ × 10½	*3⅛ × 10½	*3⅛ × 12
	10	—	—	*3⅛ × 9	*3⅛ × 10½	*3⅛ × 10½	*3⅛ × 12	*3⅛ × 12	*3⅛ × 12	*3⅛ × 13½
	12	—	—	*3⅛ × 10½	*3⅛ × 10½	*3⅛ × 12	*3⅛ × 12	*3⅛ × 13½	*3⅛ × 13½	*3⅛ × 13½
	14	—	—	*3⅛ × 10½	*3⅛ × 12	*3⅛ × 12	*3⅛ × 13½	*3⅛ × 13½	*3⅛ × 15	*3⅛ × 15
16	8	—	—	*3⅛ × 10½	*3⅛ × 10½	*3⅛ × 10½	*3⅛ × 12	*3⅛ × 12	*3⅛ × 12	*3⅛ × 13½
	12	—	—	*3⅛ × 12	*3⅛ × 12	*3⅛ × 13½	*3⅛ × 13½	*3⅛ × 15	*3⅛ × 15	*3⅛ × 16½
	14	—	*3⅛ × 12	*3⅛ × 12	*3⅛ × 13½	*3⅛ × 13½	*3⅛ × 15	*3⅛ × 16½	*3⅛ × 16½	*3⅛ × 16½
	16	—	*3⅛ × 12	*3⅛ × 13½	*3⅛ × 13½	*3⅛ × 15	*3⅛ × 16½	*3⅛ × 16½	3⅛ × 16½	*5⅛ × 15
18	8	—	—	*3⅛ × 12	*3⅛ × 12	*3⅛ × 12	*3⅛ × 13½	*3⅛ × 13½	*3⅛ × 13½	*3⅛ × 15
	12	—	*3⅛ × 12	*3⅛ × 13½	*3⅛ × 13½	*3⅛ × 15	*3⅛ × 15	*3⅛ × 16½	3⅛ × 16½	3⅛ × 16½
	16	—	*3⅛ × 13½	*3⅛ × 15	*3⅛ × 16½	*3⅛ × 16½	3⅛ × 16½	*5⅛ × 15	*5⅛ × 16½	*5⅛ × 16½
	20	—	*3⅛ × 15	*3⅛ × 16½	3⅛ × 16½	3⅛ × 18	3⅛ × 18	*5⅛ × 16½	5⅛ × 16½	5⅛ × 16½
20	8	—	—	*3⅛ × 12	*3⅛ × 13½	*3⅛ × 13½	*3⅛ × 15	*3⅛ × 15	*3⅛ × 15	3⅛ × 16½
	12	—	*3⅛ × 13½	*3⅛ × 15	*3⅛ × 15	*3⅛ × 16½	3⅛ × 16½	3⅛ × 16½	*5⅛ × 15	*5⅛ × 16½
	16	—	*3⅛ × 15	*3⅛ × 16½	3⅛ × 16½	3⅛ × 18	3⅛ × 18	*5⅛ × 16½	5⅛ × 16½	5⅛ × 18
	20	—	*3⅛ × 16½	3⅛ × 16½	3⅛ × 18	*5⅛ × 16½	5⅛ × 16½	5⅛ × 16½	5⅛ × 18	5⅛ × 19½
24	8	—	—	*3⅛ × 15	*3⅛ × 15	*3⅛ × 16½	3⅛ × 16½	3⅛ × 16½	3⅛ × 18	5⅛ × 16½
	12	—	*3⅛ × 16½	3⅛ × 16½	3⅛ × 16½	3⅛ × 18	*5⅛ × 16½	5⅛ × 16½	5⅛ × 16½	5⅛ × 19½
	16	—	3⅛ × 16½	3⅛ × 18	5⅛ × 16½	5⅛ × 16½	5⅛ × 18	5⅛ × 18	5⅛ × 19½	5⅛ × 21
	20	—	3⅛ × 18	5⅛ × 16½	5⅛ × 18	5⅛ × 18	5⅛ × 19½	5⅛ × 19½	5⅛ × 21	5⅛ × 22½
28	8	—	*3⅛ × 16½	3⅛ × 16½	3⅛ × 18	3⅛ × 18	5⅛ × 16½	5⅛ × 16½	5⅛ × 16½	5⅛ × 19½
	12	—	3⅛ × 18	5⅛ × 16½	5⅛ × 16½	5⅛ × 18	5⅛ × 18	5⅛ × 19½	5⅛ × 19½	5⅛ × 22½
	16	—	5⅛ × 16½	5⅛ × 18	5⅛ × 18	5⅛ × 19½	5⅛ × 19½	5⅛ × 21	5⅛ × 22½	5⅛ × 24
	20	—	5⅛ × 18	5⅛ × 19½	5⅛ × 19½	5⅛ × 21	5⅛ × 22½	5⅛ × 24	5⅛ × 25½	5⅛ × 25½
32	8	—	3⅛ × 18	5⅛ × 16½	5⅛ × 16½	5⅛ × 18	5⅛ × 18	5⅛ × 19½	5⅛ × 19½	5⅛ × 22½
	12	—	5⅛ × 18	5⅛ × 18	5⅛ × 19½	5⅛ × 19½	5⅛ × 21	5⅛ × 21	5⅛ × 22½	5⅛ × 25½
	16	—	5⅛ × 19½	5⅛ × 19½	5⅛ × 21	5⅛ × 22½	5⅛ × 22½	5⅛ × 24	5⅛ × 25½	5⅛ × 27
	20	5⅛ × 19½	5⅛ × 21	5⅛ × 21	5⅛ × 22½	5⅛ × 24	5⅛ × 25½	5⅛ × 27	5⅛ × 28½	6¾ × 27

Span ft	Spacing ft	Roof Beams: Total Load-Carrying Capacity 20 psf	25 psf	30 psf	35 psf	40 psf	45 psf	50 psf	55 psf	Floor Beams Total Load 50 psf
36	12	—	5⅛ × 19½	5⅛ × 21	5⅛ × 21	5⅛ × 22½	5⅛ × 24	5⅛ × 24	5⅛ × 25½	6¾ × 25½
	16	—	5⅛ × 21	5⅛ × 22½	5⅛ × 24	5⅛ × 25½	5⅛ × 25½	5⅛ × 27	5⅛ × 28½	6¾ × 28½
	20	5⅛ × 21	5⅛ × 22½	5⅛ × 24	5⅛ × 25½	5⅛ × 27	5⅛ × 30	6¾ × 27	6¾ × 28½	6¾ × 30
	24	5⅛ × 22½	5⅛ × 24	5⅛ × 25½	5⅛ × 28½	5⅛ × 30	6¾ × 27	6¾ × 28½	6¾ × 30	6¾ × 33
40	12	5⅛ × 19½	5⅛ × 21	5⅛ × 22½	5⅛ × 24	5⅛ × 25½	5⅛ × 25½	5⅛ × 27	6¾ × 25½	6¾ × 28½
	16	5⅛ × 22½	5⅛ × 24	5⅛ × 25½	5⅛ × 27	5⅛ × 27	5⅛ × 28½	6¾ × 27	6¾ × 28½	6¾ × 31½
	20	5⅛ × 24	5⅛ × 25½	5⅛ × 27	5⅛ × 28½	6¾ × 27	6¾ × 28½	6¾ × 30	6¾ × 31½	6¾ × 34½
	24	5⅛ × 25½	5⅛ × 27	5⅛ × 28½	6¾ × 27	6¾ × 28½	6¾ × 31½	6¾ × 33	6¾ × 34½	6¾ × 36
44	12	5⅛ × 22½	5⅛ × 24	5⅛ × 25½	5⅛ × 27	5⅛ × 27	5⅛ × 28½	6¾ × 27	6¾ × 28½	6¾ × 31½
	16	5⅛ × 24	5⅛ × 25½	5⅛ × 27	5⅛ × 28½	5⅛ × 30	6¾ × 28½	6¾ × 30	6¾ × 31½	6¾ × 34½
	20	5⅛ × 25½	5⅛ × 28½	5⅛ × 30	6¾ × 28½	6¾ × 30	6¾ × 31½	6¾ × 33	6¾ × 34½	6¾ × 37½
	24	5⅛ × 27	5⅛ × 30	6¾ × 28½	6¾ × 30	6¾ × 31½	6¾ × 34½	6¾ × 36	6¾ × 37½	6¾ × 39
48	12	5⅛ × 24	5⅛ × 25½	5⅛ × 27	5⅛ × 28½	5⅛ × 30	6¾ × 28½	6¾ × 30	6¾ × 30	6¾ × 34½
	16	5⅛ × 25½	5⅛ × 28½	5⅛ × 30	6¾ × 28½	6¾ × 30	6¾ × 31½	6¾ × 31½	6¾ × 34½	6¾ × 37½
	20	5⅛ × 28½	5⅛ × 30	6¾ × 30	6¾ × 31½	6¾ × 31½	6¾ × 34½	6¾ × 36	6¾ × 37½	8¾ × 37½
	24	5⅛ × 30	6¾ × 30	6¾ × 31½	6¾ × 33	6¾ × 34½	6¾ × 37½	6¾ × 39	8¾ × 36	8¾ × 39
52	12	5⅛ × 25½	5⅛ × 27	5⅛ × 30	5⅛ × 31½	6¾ × 30	6¾ × 30	6¾ × 31½	6¾ × 33	6¾ × 37½
	16	5⅛ × 28½	5⅛ × 30	6¾ × 30	6¾ × 31½	6¾ × 33	6¾ × 33	6¾ × 34½	6¾ × 37½	8¾ × 37½
	20	5⅛ × 30	6¾ × 30	6¾ × 31½	6¾ × 33	6¾ × 34½	6¾ × 37½	6¾ × 39	8¾ × 36	8¾ × 40½
	24	6¾ × 30	6¾ × 31½	6¾ × 33	6¾ × 36	6¾ × 37½	6¾ × 40½	8¾ × 37½	8¾ × 39	8¾ × 42
56	12	5⅛ × 27	5⅛ × 30	6¾ × 28½	6¾ × 30	6¾ × 31½	6¾ × 33	6¾ × 34½	6¾ × 34½	8¾ × 36
	16	5⅛ × 30	6¾ × 30	6¾ × 31½	6¾ × 33	6¾ × 34½	6¾ × 36	6¾ × 37½	8¾ × 36	8¾ × 40½
	20	6¾ × 30	6¾ × 31½	6¾ × 34½	6¾ × 36	6¾ × 37½	8¾ × 36	8¾ × 37½	8¾ × 39	8¾ × 43½
	24	6¾ × 31½	6¾ × 34½	6¾ × 36	6¾ × 39	8¾ × 36	8¾ × 39	8¾ × 40½	8¾ × 42	8¾ × 46½
60	12	5⅛ × 30	6¾ × 28½	6¾ × 31½	6¾ × 33	6¾ × 34½	6¾ × 36	6¾ × 36	6¾ × 37½	8¾ × 39
	16	6¾ × 30	6¾ × 31½	6¾ × 34½	6¾ × 36	6¾ × 37½	6¾ × 39	8¾ × 37½	8¾ × 37½	8¾ × 43½
	20	6¾ × 31½	6¾ × 34½	6¾ × 36	6¾ × 39	8¾ × 37½	8¾ × 39	8¾ × 40½	8¾ × 42	8¾ × 46½
	24	6¾ × 34½	6¾ × 36	6¾ × 39	8¾ × 37½	8¾ × 39	8¾ × 42	8¾ × 43½	8¾ × 45	8¾ × 49½
64	12	6¾ × 28½	6¾ × 31½	6¾ × 33	6¾ × 34½	6¾ × 36	6¾ × 37½	6¾ × 39	6¾ × 40½	8¾ × 42
	16	6¾ × 31½	6¾ × 34½	6¾ × 36	6¾ × 37½	6¾ × 39	8¾ × 37½	8¾ × 39	8¾ × 40½	8¾ × 46½
	20	6¾ × 34½	6¾ × 36	6¾ × 39	6¾ × 40½	8¾ × 39	8¾ × 40½	8¾ × 42	8¾ × 45	8¾ × 49½
	24	6¾ × 36	6¾ × 39	8¾ × 37½	8¾ × 40½	8¾ × 42	8¾ × 43½	8¾ × 46½	8¾ × 49½	8¾ × 52½
68	12	6¾ × 30	6¾ × 33	6¾ × 34½	6¾ × 36	6¾ × 39	6¾ × 40½	8¾ × 37½	8¾ × 39	8¾ × 43½
	16	6¾ × 33	6¾ × 36	6¾ × 39	6¾ × 40½	8¾ × 39	8¾ × 40½	8¾ × 42	8¾ × 43½	8¾ × 48
	20	6¾ × 36	6¾ × 39	8¾ × 37½	8¾ × 40½	8¾ × 42	8¾ × 43½	8¾ × 45	8¾ × 48	8¾ × 52½
	24	6¾ × 39	8¾ × 37½	8¾ × 40½	8¾ × 42	8¾ × 45	8¾ × 46½	8¾ × 49½	8¾ × 52½	10¾ × 52½
72	12	6¾ × 33	6¾ × 34½	6¾ × 37½	6¾ × 39	6¾ × 40½	8¾ × 39	8¾ × 40½	8¾ × 42	8¾ × 46½
	16	6¾ × 36	6¾ × 37½	6¾ × 40½	8¾ × 39	8¾ × 40½	8¾ × 42	8¾ × 43½	8¾ × 45	8¾ × 51
	20	6¾ × 37½	8¾ × 37½	8¾ × 40½	8¾ × 42	8¾ × 43½	8¾ × 46½	8¾ × 48	8¾ × 51	10¾ × 51
	24	6¾ × 40½	8¾ × 40½	8¾ × 42	8¾ × 45	8¾ × 46½	8¾ × 49½	8¾ × 52½	10¾ × 49½	10¾ × 55½
76	12	6¾ × 34½	6¾ × 36	6¾ × 39	6¾ × 40½	8¾ × 39	8¾ × 40½	8¾ × 42	8¾ × 43½	8¾ × 49½
	16	6¾ × 37½	6¾ × 40½	8¾ × 39	8¾ × 42	8¾ × 43½	8¾ × 45	8¾ × 46½	8¾ × 48	10¾ × 51
	20	6¾ × 40½	8¾ × 40½	8¾ × 42	8¾ × 45	8¾ × 46½	8¾ × 48	8¾ × 51	10¾ × 48	10¾ × 54
	24	8¾ × 39	8¾ × 42	8¾ × 45	8¾ × 46½	8¾ × 49½	8¾ × 52½	10¾ × 49½	10¾ × 52½	10¾ × 58½

80	12	6¾ × 36	6¾ × 39	6¾ × 40½	8¾ × 39	8¾ × 39	8¾ × 42	8¾ × 43½	8¾ × 45	8¾ × 46½	8¾ × 52½
	16	6¾ × 39	8¾ × 39	6¾ × 42	8¾ × 42	8¾ × 43½	8¾ × 45	8¾ × 46½	8¾ × 49½	8¾ × 51	10¾ × 54
	20	8¾ × 39	8¾ × 42	8¾ × 45	8¾ × 45	8¾ × 46½	8¾ × 49½	8¾ × 51	8¾ × 49½	10¾ × 51	10¾ × 57
	24	8¾ × 42	8¾ × 45	8¾ × 46½	8¾ × 46½	8¾ × 49½	8¾ × 52½	10¾ × 51	10¾ × 52½	10¾ × 55½	10¾ × 61½
84	12	6¾ × 37½	6¾ × 40½	6¾ × 39	8¾ × 39	8¾ × 42	8¾ × 43½	8¾ × 45	8¾ × 46½	8¾ × 48	10¾ × 51
	16	8¾ × 37½	8¾ × 40½	8¾ × 39	8¾ × 43½	8¾ × 45	8¾ × 48	8¾ × 49½	8¾ × 51	8¾ × 52½	10¾ × 55½
	20	8¾ × 40½	8¾ × 43½	8¾ × 43½	8¾ × 46½	8¾ × 48	10¾ × 49½	10¾ × 49½	10¾ × 51	10¾ × 54	10¾ × 60
	24	8¾ × 43½	8¾ × 46½	8¾ × 46½	8¾ × 49½	10¾ × 51	10¾ × 51	10¾ × 52½	10¾ × 55½	10¾ × 58½	10¾ × 64½
88	12	6¾ × 39	8¾ × 39	8¾ × 42	8¾ × 42	8¾ × 43½	8¾ × 45	8¾ × 46½	8¾ × 49½	8¾ × 51	10¾ × 54
	16	8¾ × 40½	8¾ × 43½	8¾ × 43½	8¾ × 48	8¾ × 48	8¾ × 49½	8¾ × 52½	10¾ × 49½	10¾ × 52½	10¾ × 58½
	20	8¾ × 43½	8¾ × 46½	8¾ × 46½	8¾ × 51	10¾ × 49½	10¾ × 51	10¾ × 52½	10¾ × 54	10¾ × 55½	—
	24	8¾ × 45	8¾ × 49½	8¾ × 52½	10¾ × 51	10¾ × 54	10¾ × 51	10¾ × 55½	10¾ × 58½	10¾ × 61½	—
92	12	6¾ × 40½	8¾ × 40½	8¾ × 43½	8¾ × 43½	8¾ × 45	8¾ × 48	8¾ × 49½	8¾ × 51	8¾ × 52½	10¾ × 55½
	16	8¾ × 42	8¾ × 45	8¾ × 48	8¾ × 48	8¾ × 49½	8¾ × 52½	10¾ × 51	10¾ × 52½	10¾ × 54	10¾ × 61½
	20	8¾ × 45	8¾ × 48	8¾ × 51	8¾ × 51	10¾ × 49½	10¾ × 52½	10¾ × 54	10¾ × 57	10¾ × 58½	—
	24	8¾ × 48	8¾ × 51	10¾ × 51	10¾ × 54	10¾ × 54	10¾ × 55½	10¾ × 58½	10¾ × 61½	10¾ × 64½	—
96	12	8¾ × 39	8¾ × 42	8¾ × 45	8¾ × 48	8¾ × 48	8¾ × 49½	8¾ × 51	8¾ × 52½	10¾ × 51	10¾ × 58½
	16	8¾ × 43½	8¾ × 46½	8¾ × 49½	8¾ × 52½	10¾ × 51	10¾ × 52½	10¾ × 54	10¾ × 54	10¾ × 57	10¾ × 64½
	20	8¾ × 46½	8¾ × 49½	8¾ × 52½	10¾ × 52½	10¾ × 54	10¾ × 57	10¾ × 57	10¾ × 58½	10¾ × 61½	—
	24	8¾ × 49½	8¾ × 52½	10¾ × 52½	10¾ × 55½	10¾ × 58½	10¾ × 60	10¾ × 60	10¾ × 64½	—	—
100	12	8¾ × 40½	8¾ × 43½	8¾ × 46½	8¾ × 49½	8¾ × 49½	8¾ × 51	10¾ × 49½	10¾ × 52½	10¾ × 54	10¾ × 60
	16	8¾ × 45	8¾ × 48	8¾ × 51	10¾ × 51	10¾ × 51	10¾ × 52½	10¾ × 55½	10¾ × 57	10¾ × 58½	—
	20	8¾ × 48	8¾ × 52½	10¾ × 52½	10¾ × 54	10¾ × 54	10¾ × 57	10¾ × 58½	10¾ × 61½	10¾ × 64½	—
	24	8¾ × 51	10¾ × 52½	10¾ × 55½	10¾ × 58½	10¾ × 58½	10¾ × 60	10¾ × 63	—	—	—

[a] **Table specifications:**
This beam design table applies for straight, simply-supported, laminated timber beams. Other beam support systems may be employed to meet varying design conditions.
Roofs should have a minimum slope of ¼ inch per foot to eliminate water ponding.
Total load carrying capacity includes beam weight. Floor beams are designed for uniform loads of 40 psf live load and 10 psf dead load.
Allowable stresses:
Bending stress F_b = 2400 psi (reduced by size factor C_F) except those marked * in which cases F_b = 2000 psi (reduced by size factor C_F).
Shear stress, F_v = 165 psi.
Modulus of elasticity, E = 1,700,000 psi except those marked * in which cases E = 1,500,000 psi.
For roof beams, F_b and F_v were increased 15% for short duration of loading.
Deflection limits:
Roof beams—L/180 span for total load.
Floor beams—L/360 span for 40 psf live load only.
Values for preliminary design purposes only. For more complete design information, see the AITC *Timber Construction Manual*.

[b] **Cantilevered and Continuous Span Systems.**
Cantilever beam systems may be comprised of any of the various types and combinations of beam illustrated below. Cantilever systems permit longer spans or larger loads for a given size member than do simple span systems, provided member size is not controlled by compression perpendicular to grain at the supports or by horizontal shear. Substantial design economies can be effected by decreasing the depths of the members in the suspended portions of a cantilever system.

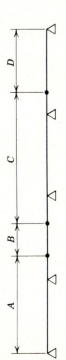

Cantilevered Beam Systems. *A* is single cantilever, *B* is a suspended beam, *C* has a double cantilever, and *D* is a beam with one end suspended.
For economy, the negative bending moment at the supports of a cantilevered beam should be equal in magnitude to the positive moment.
Consideration must be given to deflection and camber in cantilevered multiple spans. When possible, roofs should be sloped the equivalent of ¼ inch per foot of horizontal distance between the level of the drain and the high point of the roof to eliminate water pockets, or provisions should be made to ensure that accumulation of water does not produce greater deflection and live loads than anticipated. Unbalanced loading conditions should be investigated for maximum bending moment, deflection, and stability.
Continuous span beams are commonly used in both building and bridge construction to reduce maximum moments, thus reducing the section size required.
Design aids for cantilever and continuous span beam systems may be found in the AITC "Timber Construction Manual."
Glued laminated timber beams are often tapered or curved to meet architectural requirements, to provide pitched roofs, or to provide a minimum depth of beam at the point of bearing.

SOURCE: American Institute of Timber Construction.

Table E-12. Wood Decking Spans (ft-in.) 2-Inch Decking Spans[a,b]

	Douglas Fir-Larch		Douglas Fir South		Hem-Fir		Mountain Hemlock		Mountain Hemlock-Hem-Fir		Western Hemlock		Engelmann Spruce-Alpine Fir (Engelmann Spruce-Lodgepole Pine)		Lodgepole Pine		Ponderosa Pine-Sugar Pine (Ponderosa Pine-Lodgepole Pine)		Idaho White Pine		Western Cedars		White Woods (Western Woods)	
	Select	Comm.	Select	Comm.	Select	Comm.	Select	Comm.	Select	Comm.	Select	Comm.	Select	Comm.	Select	Comm.	Select	Comm.	Select	Comm.	Select	Comm.	Select	Comm.
Floor Decking: 10-psf Dead Load/40-psf Live Load/L/480 Deflection Limit																								
Simple	5-6	5-5	5-0	4-11	5-0	4-11	4-11	4-8	4-11	4-8	5-0	5-3	4-11	4-8	5-0	4-8	5-0	4-11	4-8	4-11	4-8	4-6	4-8	4-6
Controlled random	6-0	5-11	5-6	5-4	5-6	5-4	5-4	5-1	5-4	5-1	5-6	5-9	5-4	5-1	5-6	5-1	5-6	5-4	5-1	5-1	5-1	4-11	5-1	4-11
Roof Decking: 10-psf Dead Load/20-psf Live Load/L/240 Deflection Limit																								
Simple	8-9	8-7	8-1	7-10	8-1	7-10	7-10	7-5	7-10	7-5	8-1	8-5	7-10	7-5	7-10	7-5	8-1	7-10	7-5	7-5	7-5	7-3	7-5	7-3
Controlled random	9-7	9-5	8-10	8-7	9-0	8-7	8-7	8-1	8-7	8-1	8-10	9-2	8-7	8-1	8-7	8-1	8-4	8-7	8-10	8-7	8-1	7-10	8-1	7-10
Roof Decking: 10-psf Dead Load/30-psf Live Load/L/240 Deflection Limit																								
Simple	7-8	7-6	7-1	6-10	7-3	6-10	6-10	6-6	6-10	6-6	7-1	7-4	6-10	6-6	6-10	6-8	6-8	6-10	7-1	6-10	6-6	6-4	6-6	6-4
Controlled random	8-4	8-2	7-8	7-6	7-10	7-6	7-6	7-1	7-6	7-1	7-8	8-0	7-6	7-1	7-6	7-4	7-4	7-6	7-8	7-6	7-1	6-10	7-1	6-10
Roof Decking: 10-psf Dead Load/40-psf Live Load/L/240 Deflection Limit																								
Simple	7-0	6-10	6-5	6-3	6-7	6-3	6-3	5-11	6-3	5-11	6-5	6-8	6-3	5-11	6-3	6-1	6-1	6-3	6-5	6-3	5-11	5-9	5-11	5-9
Controlled random	7-7	7-5	7-0	6-10	7-2	6-10	6-10	6-5	6-10	6-5	7-0	7-4	6-10	6-5	6-10	6-8	6-8	6-10	7-0	6-10	6-5	6-3	6-5	6-3

[a] Spans are for 4- to 12-in.-wide lumber manufactured and used at a maximum moisture content of 19%. Spans are given in feet-inches for normal load duration.
[b] Joist and Plank grades run to pattern may be used as follows:
No. 1—Use Select spans for all species.
No. 2—Use Commercial spans for all species.
No. 3—Douglas Fir-Larch use Douglas Fir South Select spans.
No. 3—Douglas Fir, South and Western Hemlock use Mountain Hemlock Commercial spans.
No. 3—Hem-Fir and Mountain Hemlock use Western Cedar Commercial spans.
SOURCE: Western Wood Products Association, *Product Use Manual* 6.1 d/we, Yeon Building, Portland, OR 97204.

Table E-13. Wood Decking Spans (ft-in.) 3-Inch Decking Spans[a,b]

	Douglas Fir-Larch		Douglas Fir South		Hem-Fir		Mountain Hemlock		Mountain Hemlock Hem-Fir		Western Hemlock		Engelmann Spruce Alpine Fir (Engelmann Spruce-Lodgepole Pine)		Lodgepole Pine		Ponderosa Pine-Sugar Pine (Ponderosa Pine-Lodgepole Pine)		Idaho White Pine		Western Cedars		White Woods (Western Woods)	
	Se-lect	Comm. lect	Se-lect	Comm. lect	Se-lect	Comm. lect	Se-lect	Comm. lect	Se-lect	Comm. lect	Se-lect	Comm. lect	Se-lect	Comm. lect	Se-lect	Comm. lect	Se-lect	Comm. lect	Se-lect	Comm. lect	Se-lect	Comm. lect	Se-lect	Comm.
Floor Decking: 10-psf Dead Load/40-psf Live Load/L/480 Deflection Limit																								
Simple	9-2	9-0	8-5	8-3	8-8	8-5	8-3	7-9	8-3	7-9	8-5	7-9	8-3	7-9	8-0	8-0	8-0	7-9	8-5	8-3	7-9	7-6	7-9	7-6
Controlled random	10-6	10-4	9-8	9-5	9-11	9-8	9-5	8-11	9-5	8-11	9-8	8-11	9-5	8-11	9-2	9-2	9-2	8-11	9-8	9-5	8-11	8-8	8-11	8-8
Roof Decking: 10-psf Dead Load/20-psf Live Load/L/240 Deflection Limit																								
Simple	14-7	14-4	13-5	13-1	13-9	13-5	13-1	12-5	13-1	12-5	13-5	12-5	13-1	12-9	12-9	12-9	12-5	13-5	13-1	12-5	12-0			
Controlled random	16-9	16-5	15-5	15-1	15-9	15-1	15-1	14-3	15-1	14-3	16-1	14-3	15-1	14-8	14-8	14-8	14-3	15-5	15-1	14-3	13-9	14-3	13-9
Roof Decking: 10-psf Dead Load/30-psf Live Load/L/240 Deflection Limit																								
Simple	12-9	12-6	11-9	11-6	12-0	11-9	11-6	10-10	11-6	10-10	12-3	10-10	11-6	11-2	11-2	11-2	10-10	11-9	11-6	10-10	10-6	10-10	
Controlled random	14-8	14-4	13-6	13-2	13-9	13-6	13-2	12-5	13-2	12-5	14-1	12-5	13-2	12-10	12-10	12-10	12-5	13-6	13-2	12-5	12-0	12-5	12-0
Roof Decking: 10-psf Dead Load/40-psf Live Load/L/240 Deflection Limit																								
Simple	11-7	11-5	10-8	10-5	10-11	10-8	10-5	9-10	10-5	9-10	10-8	9-10	10-5	10-2	10-2	10-2	9-10	10-8	10-5	9-10	9-6	9-10	
Controlled random	13-4	13-1	12-3	11-11	12-6	12-3	11-11	11-3	11-11	11-3	12-3	11-3	11-11	11-7	11-7	11-7	11-3	12-3	11-11	11-3	10-11	11-3	10-11

[a] Spans are for 4- to 12-in.-wide lumber manufactured and used at a maximum moisture content of 19%. Spans are given in feet-inches for normal load duration.
[b] Joist and Plank grades run to pattern may be used as follows:
No. 1—Use Select spans for all species.
No. 2—Use Commercial spans for all species.
No. 3—Douglas Fir-Larch use Mountain Hemlock Commercial spans.
No. 3—Douglas Fir South use Western Cedar Commercial spans.

SOURCE: Western Wood Products Association, *Product Use Manual* 6.1d/we, Yeon Building, Portland, OR 97204.

Table E-14. Wood Roof Truss Spans (ft)[a]

Load	55 psf with 15% Duration Factor For 40-psf Snow Load and Shingle Roof or 30-psf Snow Load and Heavy Roof, Such as Tile				55 psf with 33% Duration Factor or 47 psf with 15% Duration Factor For 30-psf Wind Load with Tile Roof or 30-psf Snow Load with Shingle Roof				47 psf with 33% Duration Factor or 40 psf with 15% Duration Factor For 30-psf Wind Load of 20-psf Snow Load and Shingle Roof. Meets FHA-Minimum Property Standards				40 psf with 25% Duration Factor For 20-psf Live Load (Construction for Rain, Not Snow) and Shingle Roof			
	Chord Size				Chord Size				Chord Size				Chord Size			
Pitch	2×4 Top 2×4 Bot.	2×6 Top 2×4 Bot.	2×4 Top 2×6 Bot.	2×6 Top 2×6 Bot.	2×4 Top 2×4 Bot.	2×6 Top 2×4 Bot.	2×4 Top 2×6 Bot.	2×6 Top 2×6 Bot.	2×4 Top 2×4 Bot.	2×6 Top 2×4 Bot.	2×4 Top 2×6 Bot.	2×6 Top 2×6 Bot.	2×4 Top 2×4 Bot.	2×6 Top 2×4 Bot.	2×4 Top 2×6 Bot.	2×6 Top 2×6 Bot.
2/12	23	23	26	38	25	26	28	29	29	30	31	45
2.5/12	26	27	31	43	28	31	31	35	35	33	37	50
3/12	29	31	35	47	31	35	34	39	39	37	42	55
3.5/12	32	35	39	51	34	39	37	44	44	40	47	60
4/12	34	39	43	55	36	43	40	47	47	42	51	63
5/12	37	45	49	60	40	49	43	54	54	46	57	69[b]
6/12	39	50	54[b]	62[b]	41	54[b]	45	59[b]	59[b]	47	62[b]	71[b]
7/12	39	54[b]	58[b]	63[b]	42	58[b]	45	63[b]	63[b]	48[b]	66[b]	72[b]
2/12	22	23	25	37	24	25	27	29	29	40	29	31	43
2.5/12	26	27	31	42	28	31	30	35	35	46	32	37	49
3/12	28	31	35	46	31	35	34	39	39	51	36	42	54
3.5/12	31	35	39	50[b]	33	39	37	44	44	55[b]	39	47[b]	59[b]
4/12	33	38	43[b]	54[b]	36	43[b]	39	47[b]	47[b]	59[b]	42[b]	51[b]	63[b]
5/12	37[b]	45[b]	49[b]	59[b]	39[b]	49[b]	43[b]	54[b]	54[b]	64[b]	46[b]	57[b]	69[b]
6/2[c]	32	38	48	52	35	42	38	47	57[b]	40	50	60[b]
6/2.5	30	34	45	48	32	39	35	43	53	37	46	56[b]
6/3	27	30	41	44	29	34	32	39	48	34	41	51
6/3.5	23	23	35	38	25	27	28	30	42	30	33	44
6/4	21	19	31	34	22	22	25	25	37	26	27	39

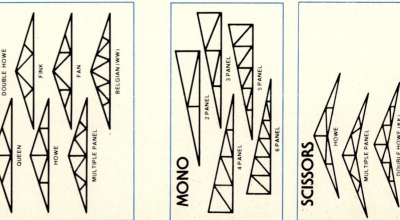

COMMON: SIMPLE KINGPOST, QUEEN, HOWE, DOUBLE HOWE, FINK, FAN, MULTIPLE PANEL, BELGIAN (WW)

MONO: 2 PANEL, 3 PANEL, 4 PANEL, 5 PANEL, 6 PANEL

SCISSORS: HOWE, MULTIPLE PANEL, DOUBLE HOWE (KK)

FLAT

Depth									
16"	—	22	—	—	—	25	—	—	27
18"	24	23	—	26	25	27	27	28	29
20"	25	24	29	27	26	29	28	30	31
24"	28	27	33	30	29	32	32	33	34
28"	30	30	37	33	32	35	34	37	37
30"	31	31	39	34	33	36	36	42	38
32"	33	32	40	35	34	38	37	43	39
36"	35	34	43	37	37	40	40	45	42
42"	37	37	46	40	40	43	43	49	45
48"	39	40	50	42	43	45	46	54	48
60"	42	44	56	45	47	48	51	58	53
72"	44	48	60	47	51	50	55	64	57

Note: Positive drainage must be provided to prevent any possibility of ponding.

[a] These overall spans are based upon 4" nominal bearing each end, 24" o.c. spacing, a live load deflection limited to $L/360$ maximum and use of lumber properties as follows: Lumber: 1KD SP. 2×4 f_b = 1850 psi; f_t = 1050 psi; f_c = 1450 psi; E = 1.8 × 10^6; 2×6 f_b = 1600 psi; f_t = 1050 psi; f_c = 1450 psi; E = 1.8 × 10^6. Allowable spans for 2 × 4 top chord trusses using sheathing other than plywood (e.g., spaced sheathing or 1× boards) may be reduced slightly.

[b] Trusses exceeding 14 ft height at peak can be shipped in two pieces.

[c] 6/12 = Top chord pitch, 2/12 = Bottom chord pitch.

SOURCE: Copyright 1979 Alpine Engineered Products, Inc.

Flat roof truss depths are O/A

2 PANEL, 3 PANEL, 4 PANEL, 5 PANEL, 6 PANEL, 7 PANEL, 8 PANEL

Table E–15. Wood Floor Truss Spans: Spacing 2′-0″ O.C.[a]

	55 psf	Overall	60 psf
Joist 12 in. Deep			
No. 2 K.D. M.G. S.P.	18′-0″		17′-4″
No. 2 Dense K.D. S.P.	19′-2″		18′-6″
No. 1 K.D. S.P.	19′-8″		18′-10″
No. 1 Dense K.D. S.P.	21′-0″		20′-4″
No. 1 D.F. 19%	19′-2″		18′-6″
S.S.D.F. 19%	20′-4″		19′-8″
Joist 14 in. Deep			
No. 2 K.D. M.G. S.P.	19′-8″		18′-10″
No. 2 Dense K.D. S.P.	20′-10″		20′-0″
No. 1 K.D. S.P.	21′-4″		20′-6″
No. 1 Dense K.D. S.P.	23′-0″		22′-2″
No. 1 D.F. 19%	20′-10″		20′-0″
S.S.D.F. 19%	22′-0″		21′-2″
Joist 16 in. Deep			
No. 2 K.D. M.G. S.P.	21′-0″		20′-2″
No. 2 Dense K.D. S.P.	22′-2″		21′-6″
No. 1 K.D. S.P.	22′-10″		22′-0″
No. 1 Dense K.D. S.P.	24′-10″		23′-10″
No. 1 D.F. 19%	22′-2″		21′-6″
S.S.D.F. 19%	23′-10″		22′-10″
Joist 18 in. Deep			
No. 2 K.D. M.G. S.P.	22′-6″		21′-6″
No. 2 Dense K.D. S.P.	23′-8″		22′-10″
No. 1 K.D. S.P.	24′-4″		23′-4″
No. 1 Dense K.D. S.P.	26′-6″		25′-4″
No. 1 D.F. 19%	23′-8″		22′-10″
S.S.D.F. 19%	25′-4″		24′-4″
Joist 20 in. Deep			
No. 2 K.D. M.G. S.P.	23′-8″		22′-8″
No. 2 Dense K.D. S.P.	25′-0″		24′-2″
No. 1 K.D. S.P.	25′-10″		24′-8″
No. 1 Dense K.D. S.P.	28′-0″		26′-10″
No. 1 D.F. 19%	25′-0″		24′-2″
S.S.D.F. 19%	26′-8″		25′-8″
Joist 22 in. Deep			
No. 2 K.D. M.G. S.P.	24′-10″		23′-10″
No. 2 Dense K.D. S.P.	26′-4″		25′-10″
No. 1 K.D. S.P.	27′-0″		26′-0″
No. 1 Dense K.D. S.P.	29′-4″		28′-2″
No. 1 D.F. 19%	26′-4″		25′-10″
S.S.D.F. 19%	28′-2″		27′-2″

[a] *Notes:*
1. Typical spans and depths based on visual graded lumber. Spans may be increased in certain depths with the use of machine stress rated lumber in lieu of visual graded.
2. All spans figured with no allowable unit stress increase.
3. All spans figured at a maximum spacing of 24 in. O.C.
4. Spans include 4-in. bearings.
5. S.P., Southern Pine; D.F., Douglas Fir; S.S.D.F., Select Structural Douglas Fir.

SOURCE: TrusWal Systems, Inc.

Table E-16. Steel Solid Web Joist Spans: Maximum Allowable Clear Spans (ft-in.)[a]

USG Joist Style[b]	Joists Spacing (in.)	Floor Loading (psf)										
		10 Dead 30 Live		10 Dead 40 Live		10 Dead 50 Live						
		1-Span	2-Span	1-Span	2-Span	1-Span	2-Span					
115SJ20*	12	30-0	33-9	27-4	30-9	25-4	28-6					
	16	27-4	30-8	24-10	28-0	23-0f	25-11					
	24	23-0f	26-10	20-7f	24-5	18-10f	22-8					
115SJ16*	12	25-1f	31-6	22-6f	28-8	20-6f	25-11f					
	16	21-10f	27-9f	19-7f	24-5f	17-10f	21-11f					
	24	17-10f	21-10f	15-11f	19-1f	14-6f	17-10f					
95SJ20	12	25-7	28-9	23-2	26-2	21-7	24-4					
	16	23-2	26-2	21-1	23-10	19-7	22-1					
	24	19-11f	22-10	17-10f	20-10	16-4f	19-4					
95SJ16*	12	23-10	26-10	21-7	24-5	20-1	22-8					
	16	21-7	24-5	19-8	22-3	17-11f	20-7					
	24	17-11f	21-3	16-0f	19-5	14-7f	18-0f					
925SJ20	12	25-0	28-2	22-8	25-8	21-1	23-9					
	16	22-8	25-7	20-8	23-4	19-2	21-7					
	24	19-6f	22-4	17-6f	20-4	15-11f	18-10					
925SJ16*	12	23-4	26-3	21-2	23-11	19-7	22-2					
	16	21-2	23-10	19-4	21-9	17-7f	20-2					
	24	17-7f	20-10	15-8f	19-0	14-4f	17-7					
75SJ20	12	21-0	23-8	19-1	21-7	17-8	20-0					
	16	19-1	21-6	17-5	19-7	16-1	18-2					
	24	16-8f	18-9	15-0f	17-1	13-7f	15-10					
75SJ16	12	19-7	22-1	17-10	20-1	16-6	18-8					
	16	17-10	20-1	16-2	18-3	15-1f	17-0					
	24	15-1f	17-6	13-6f	15-11	12-4f	14-10					
75SJ13*	12	17-10	20-1	16-2	18-3	14-11f	17-0					
	16	15-11f	18-3	14-2f	16-8	12-11f	15-5					
	24	12-11f	15-6f	11-7f	13-5f	10-6f	11-11f					
725SJ20	12	20-5	23-0	18-7	21-0	17-2	19-5					
	16	18-7	20-11	16-11	19-1	15-8	17-8					
	24	16-2f	18-3	14-7f	16-8	13-4f	16-8					
725SJ16	12	19-1	21-6	17-4	19-7	16-1	18-2					
	16	17-4	19-6	15-10	17-9	14-7	16-6					
	24	14-8f	17-0	13-1f	15-6	12-0f	14-5					

USG Joist Style[b]	Joists Spacing (in.)	Floor Loading (psf)					
		10 Dead 30 Live		10 Dead 40 Live		10 Dead 50 Live	
		1-Span	2-Span	1-Span	2-Span	1-Span	2-Span
725SJ13*	12	17-4	19-6	15-10	17-10	14-7	16-6
	16	15-8f	17-9	14-0f	16-2	12-10f	15-0
	24	12-10f	15-6f	11-5f	13-5f	10-5f	11-11f
60SJ20	12	17-6	19-8	15-11	18-0	14-10	16-8
	16	15-11	17-11	14-6	16-4	13-6	15-2
	24	13-11	15-8	12-7	14-4	11-7f	13-2
60SJ16	12	16-4	18-5	14-10	16-10	13-10	15-7
	16	14-10	16-8	13-6	15-4	12-7	14-2
	24	12-10f	14-7	11-6f	13-4	10-6f	12-5
60SJ13	12	14-11	16-10	13-6	15-4	12-6	14-2
	16	13-6	15-4	12-4	13-11	11-2f	12-11
	24	11-2f	13-4	10-0	12-1	9-1f	11-4
55SJ20	12	16-4	18-5	14-10	16-9	13-10	15-6
	16	14-10	16-9	13-6	15-3	12-6	14-2
	24	12-11	14-7	11-10	13-4	10-11f	12-4
55SJ16	12	15-2	17-2	13-10	15-8	12-10	14-6
	16	13-10	15-7	12-7	14-3	11-8	13-3
	24	12-1f	13-7	10-10f	12-5	9-10f	11-6
55SJ13	12	13-11	15-8	12-7	14-3	11-8	13-3
	16	12-7	14-3	11-6	13-0	10-6f	12-0
	24	10-6f	12-5	9-5f	11-4	8-7f	10-6
55SJ10*	12	12-8	14-5	11-6f	13-1	10-6f	12-2
	16	11-2f	13-1	10-0f	11-10f	9-1f	10-6f
	24	9-1f	10-6f	8-1f	9-0f	7-5f	7-11f

[a] Based upon allowable design stress (values followed by "f"), or (all others) upon live-load deflection limitation of L/360, whichever is less.
[b] For joists designated with an asterisk, h/t ratio exceeds 150, requiring web stiffeners at all reactions and concentrated loads: *all joists must be checked for web crippling.*
[c] Joist reinforcing required for a minimum distance of 0.1 span to each side—total of 0.2 of a span—from center support.
SOURCE: United States Gypsum.

Table E-17. Open Web Steel Joist Spans: H Series Shortspan Joists Standard Load Table[a-d,g]

(a) For Joist Depths 8 to 16 In. Inclusive

Joist Designation	8H3	10H3	10H4	12H3	12H4	12H5	12H6	14H3	14H4	14H5	14H6	14H7	16H4	16H5	16H6	16H7	16H8
Nominal Depth[e] (in.)	8	10	10	12	12	12	12	14	14	14	14	14	16	16	16	16	16
Resist. Moment (in.-kips)	91	116	148	140	180	222	260	165	212	259	307	369	221	289	344	413	478
Max. End React. (lb)	2400	2500	2800	2800	3200	3600	3900	3200	3500	3800	4200	4600	3800	4300	4600	4900	5200
Approx. Wt.[f] (lb/ft)	5.0	5.0	6.1	5.2	6.2	7.1	8.2	5.5	6.5	7.4	8.6	10.0	6.6	7.8	8.6	10.3	11.4
Span in Feet:																	
8	600																
9	533																
10	480 460	500	560														
11	436 345	455	509														
12	400 266	417	467	467	533	600	650										
13	359 209	385 337	431 417	431	492	554	600										
14	310 167	357 270	400 334	400 393	457	514	557	457	500	543	600	657					
15	270 136	333 219	373 271	373 320	427 418	480	520	427	467	507	560	613					
16	232 112	302 181	350 223	350 264	400 345	450 404	488 480	400 366	438	475	525	575	475	538	575	613	650
17		268 151	329 186	323 220	376 287	424 337	459 400	376 305	412 398	447	494	541	447	506	541	576	612
18		239 127	305 157	288 185	356 242	400 284	433 337	340 257	389 336	422 393	467	511	422 413	478	511	544	578
19		214 108	273 133	259 157	332 206	379 241	411 286	305 218	368 285	400 334	442 399	484 470	400 351	453 432	484	516	547

518

Span	193	247	233	300	360	390	275	350	380	420	460	368	430	460	490	520
20	193 / 92	247 / 114	233 / 135	300 / 177	360 / 207	390 / 246	275 / 187	350 / 245	380 / 287	420 / 342	460 / 403	368 / 301	430 / 370	460 / 437	490	520
21			212 / 117	272 / 152	336 / 179	371 / 212	249 / 162	320 / 212	362 / 248	400 / 295	438 / 348	334 / 260	410 / 320	438 / 377	467 / 454	495
22			193 / 101	248 / 133	306 / 155	355 / 185	227 / 141	292 / 184	345 / 215	382 / 257	418 / 302	304 / 226	391 / 278	418 / 328	445 / 395	473 / 454
23			176 / 89	227 / 116	280 / 136	328 / 162	208 / 123	267 / 161	326 / 189	365 / 225	400 / 265	279 / 198	364 / 243	400 / 287	426 / 346	452 / 398
24			162 / 78	208 / 102	257 / 120	301 / 142	191 / 108	245 / 142	300 / 166	350 / 198	383 / 233	256 / 174	334 / 214	383 / 253	408 / 304	433 / 350
25							176 / 96	226 / 125	276 / 147	327 / 175	368 / 206	236 / 154	308 / 190	367 / 224	392 / 269	416 / 310
26							163 / 85	209 / 111	255 / 131	303 / 156	354 / 183	218 / 137	285 / 169	339 / 199	377 / 239	400 / 275
27							151 / 76	194 / 99	237 / 117	281 / 139	337 / 164	202 / 122	264 / 151	315 / 177	363 / 214	385 / 246
28							140 / 68	180 / 89	220 / 104	261 / 125	314 / 147	188 / 110	246 / 135	293 / 159	350 / 192	371 / 220
29												175 / 99	229 / 121	273 / 143	327 / 172	359 / 198
30												164 / 89	214 / 110	255 / 129	306 / 156	347 / 179
31												153 / 81	200 / 99	239 / 117	287 / 141	332 / 162
32												144 / 74	188 / 90	224 / 107	269 / 128	311 / 148

[a] Based on Allowable Stress of 30,000 psi.

[b] Allowable total safe load in pounds per linear foot.

[c] The black figures in the table give the total safe uniformly distributed load-carrying capacities, in pounds per linear foot, of H-Series High Strength Steel Joists. The weight of dead loads, including the joists, must in all cases be deducted to determine the live load-carrying capacities of the joists. The load table may be used for parallel chord joists installed to a maximum slope of ½-inch per foot.

The blue figures in this load table are the live loads per linear foot of joist which will produce an approximate deflection of 1/360 of the span. Live loads which will produce a deflection of 1/240 of the span may be obtained by multiplying the blue figures by 1.5. In no case shall the total load capacity of the joist be exceeded. Section 5.9 of the "Specifications for Open Web Steel Joists J- & H-Series" limits the design live load deflection as follows: Floors—1/360 of span where a plaster ceiling is attached or suspended; 1/240 of span for all other cases.

[d] Loads above heavy lines are governed by shear.

[e] Tests on steel joists designed in accordance with the Standard Specifications have demonstrated that the Standard Load Tables are applicable for concentrated top chord loadings (such as are developed in bulb-tee roof construction) when the sum of the equal concentrated top chord loadings does not exceed the allowable uniform loading for the joist type and span and the loads are placed at spacings not exceeding 33" along the top chord.

SOURCE: Standard Load Tables copyright by Steel Joist Institute. Reprinted by permission.

Table E-17. Open Web Steel Joist Spans: H Series (continued)

(b) For Joist Depths 18 to 22 In. Inclusive

Joist Designation	18H5	18H6	18H7	18H8	18H9	18H10	18H11	20H5	20H6	20H7	20H8	20H9	20H10	20H11	22H6	22H7	22H8	22H9	22H10	22H11
Nominal Depth[e] (in.)	18	18	18	18	18	18	18	20	20	20	20	20	20	20	22	22	22	22	22	22
Resist. Moment (in.-kips)	325	383	466	540	627	705	814	365	406	499	602	701	789	912	422	526	653	776	873	1,009
Max. End React. (lb)	4500	4800	5200	5400	5900	6600	7600	4800	5100	5400	5600	6400	7000	7900	5400	5600	5800	6700	7200	8100
Approx. Wt.[f] (lb/ft)	8.0	9.2	10.4	11.6	12.6	14.0	15.8	8.4	9.6	10.7	12.2	13.2	14.6	16.4	9.7	10.7	12.0	13.8	15.2	16.9
Span in Feet:																				
18	500	533	578	600																
19	474	505	547	568	621															
20	450	480	520	540	590				510	540	560	640								
21	429 409	457	495	514	562	629		457	486	514	533	610								
22	409 356	436 420	473	491	536	600		436	464	491	509	582	636		491	509	527	609		
23	391 312	417 368	452 441	470	513	574	633 619	417 380	443 434	470	487	557	609		470	487	504	583	626	
24	375 274	400 324	433 388	450 444	492 484	550 546	608 548	400 335	425 382	450	467	533	583		450 446	467	483	558	600	648
25	347 243	384 286	416 343	432 393	472 428	528 483	585 487	384 296	408 338	432 411	448	512	560	632	432 395	448	464	536	576	623
26	321 216	369 255	400 305	415 349	454 380	508 429	563 435	360 263	392 300	415 365	431	492 476	538	608	415 351	431 426	446	515	554	600
27	297 193	350 227	385 272	400 312	437 340	489 383	543	334 235	371 268	400 326	415 392	474 425	519 480	585 545	386 313	415 380	430	496	533	579
28	276 173	326 204	371 244	386 280	421 305	471 344	543 390	310 211	345 240	386 292	400 352	457 381	500 431	564 488	359 281	400 341	414	479 468	514	579

520

559 539	540 487	523 441	506 401	491 366	476 335	463 307	450 282	438 260	426 240	415 222	405 205	395 191	381 177	364 165	347 154			
497 473	480 428	465 387	450 352	436 321	424 294	411 269	400 247	389 228	379 210	369 195	360 180	346 167	330 156	315 145	301 136			
462 421	447 381	432 345	419 314	406 286	394 261	383 240	372 220	362 203	353 187	340 173	323 161	308 149	293 139	280 129	267 121			
400 379	387 343	374 311	363 282	352 257	341 235	331 216	322 198	314 183	301 169	286 156	272 145	259 134	247 125	235 116	225 109			
386 307	373 277	361 251	342 228	322 208	303 190	286 175	271 160	256 148	243 136	231 126	219 117	209 109	199 101	190 94	181 88			
335 253	313 228	293 207	275 188	258 172	243 157	230 144	217 132	206 122	195 112	185 104	176 96	167 89	159 83	152 78	145 72			
545 440	527 397	510 360	494 327	479 298	465 273	451 250	439 230	427 212	416 195	400 181	380 168							
483 388	467 350	452 317	438 288	424 263	412 240	400 220	389 203	378 187	364 172	346 159	329 148							
441 343	427 310	413 281	400 255	388 233	376 213	366 195	356 179	341 165	324 153	307 141	292 131							
386 317	373 286	361 259	350 236	339 215	329 196	320 180	310 166	293 152	278 141	264 130	251 121							
372 263	360 238	346 215	325 196	305 178	288 163	272 150	257 137	243 127	230 117	219 108	208 100							
322 216	301 195	282 177	264 161	249 147	234 134	221 123	209 113	198 104	187 96	178 89	169 82							
289 190	270 171	253 155	238 141	223 129	210 118	199 108	188 99	178 91	169 84	160 78	152 72							
524 351	507 317	490 287	475 261	461 238	447 218	434 200	419 183											
455 309	440 280	426 253	413 230	400 210	388 192	377 176	363 162											
407 274	393 248	381 224	369 204	358 186	347 170	337 156	323 143											
372 252	360 227	348 206	338 187	327 171	311 156	294 143	278 132											
359 220	345 199	323 180	303 164	285 149	269 136	254 125	240 115											
304 184	284 166	266 150	249 137	234 125	221 114	208 104	197 96											
258 155	241 140	225 127	212 116	199 106	187 96	177 88	167 81											
29	30	31	32	33	34	35	36	37	38	39	40	41	42	43	44			

521

Table E-17. (Continued)

(c) For Joist Depths 24 to 32 In. Inclusive

Joist Designation	24H6	24H7	24H8	24H9	24H10	24H11	26H8	26H9	26H10	26H11	28H8	28H9	28H10	28H11	30H8	30H9	30H10	30H11	32DH9	32DH10	32DH11
Nominal Depth[e] (in.)	24	24	24	24	24	24	26	26	26	26	28	28	28	28	30	30	30	30	32	32	32
Resist. Moment (in.-Kips)	462	576	716	851	957	1,106	784	925	1,040	1,203	846	1,000	1,124	1,300	909	1,075	1,207	1,397	1,149	1,291	1,494
Max. End React. (lb)	5600	5800	6000	7000	7500	8200	6700	7200	7600	8300	6700	7200	7700	8400	6800	7500	8100	8700	8600	9200	10300
Approx. Wt.[f] (lb/ft)	10.3	11.5	12.7	14.0	15.5	17.5	12.8	14.8	16.2	17.9	13.5	15.2	16.8	18.3	14.2	15.4	17.3	18.8	17	18	20
Span in Feet:																					
24	467	483	500	583	625																
25	448	464	480	560	600																
26	431	446	462	538	577	631															
27	415 375	430	444	519	556	607															
28	393 336	414 406	429	500	536	586	515	554	585	638											
29	366 303	400 365	414	483	517	566	496	533	563	615											
30	342 273	387 330	400	467 457	500	547	479	514	543	593	479	514	550	600	453	500	540	580			
31	320 248	374 299	387 373	452 414	484 465	529	462	497	524	572	462	497	531	579	439	484	523	561			
32	301 225	363 272	375 339	438 376	469 423	513 482	447	480	507	553	447	480	513	560	425	469	506	544	538	575	644
33	283 205	352 248	364 309	424 343	455 386	497 440	432 418	465	490	535	432	465	497	542	412	455	491	527	521	558	624
34	266 188	332 227	353 283	412 314	441 353	482 402	419 380	450 445	475	519	419	450	481	525	400	441	476	512	506	541	606
35	251 172	313 208	343 259	400 288	429 323	469 369	406 346	436 405	461 456	503	406 404	436	467	509	389	429	463	497	491	526	589

36	37	38	39	40	41	42	43	44	45	46	47	48	49	50	51	52	53
572	557	542 / 528	528 / 488	515 / 452	502 / 420	490 / 391	479 / 364	468 / 340	458 / 318	448 / 297	438 / 279	429 / 262	415 / 246	398 / 232	383 / 218	368 / 206	355 / 194
511	497	484 / 460	472 / 426	460 / 395	449 / 366	438 / 341	428 / 318	418 / 296	409 / 277	400 / 259	390 / 243	374 / 228	358 / 215	344 / 202	331 / 190	318 / 180	306 / 170
478	465 / 443	453 / 409	441 / 378	430 / 350	420 / 325	410 / 303	400 / 282	391 / 263	378 / 246	362 / 230	347 / 216	332 / 203	319 / 191	306 / 179	295 / 169	283 / 159	273 / 151
483	470	458 / 426	446 / 395	435 / 367	424 / 341	414 / 318	405 / 297	395 / 278	387 / 260	378 / 244	370 / 229	363 / 215	355 / 202	348 / 191	341 / 180	335 / 170	328
450	438 / 436	426 / 402	415 / 372	405 / 345	395 / 320	386 / 298	377 / 278	368 / 259	360 / 242	352 / 227	345 / 213	338 / 200	331 / 188	322 / 177	309 / 166	298 / 157	286 / 148
417	405 / 387	395 / 357	385 / 331	375 / 306	366 / 285	357 / 265	349 / 247	341 / 230	333 / 215	326 / 202	319 / 189	311 / 177	298 / 167	287 / 157	276 / 148	265 / 139	255 / 132
378 / 359	368 / 330	358 / 305	349 / 282	340 / 262	332 / 243	324 / 226	316 / 211	309 / 196	299 / 184	286 / 172	274 / 161	263 / 151	252 / 142	242 / 134	233 / 126	224 / 119	216 / 112
467	454 / 432	442 / 399	431 / 369	420 / 342	410 / 318	400 / 295	391 / 275	382 / 257	373 / 240	365 / 225	357 / 211	350 / 198	343 / 186	336 / 175	329 / 165	321 / 156	309 / 147
428 / 410	416 / 378	405 / 349	395 / 322	385 / 299	376 / 278	367 / 258	358 / 241	350 / 225	342 / 210	335 / 197	328 / 184	321 / 173	312 / 163	300 / 153	288 / 144	277 / 136	267 / 128
400 / 364	389 / 336	379 / 310	369 / 287	360 / 266	351 / 247	343 / 229	335 / 214	327 / 200	320 / 187	313 / 175	302 / 164	289 / 154	278 / 144	267 / 136	256 / 128	247 / 121	237 / 114
372 / 311	362 / 287	353 / 265	344 / 245	335 / 227	327 / 211	319 / 196	305 / 183	291 / 171	279 / 159	267 / 149	255 / 140	245 / 131	235 / 124	226 / 116	217 / 110	209 / 103	201 / 98
461 / 401	449 / 370	437 / 341	426 / 316	415 / 292	405 / 272	395 / 253	386 / 235	377 / 220	369 / 205	361 / 192	353 / 180	346 / 169	334 / 159	321 / 150	308 / 141	297 / 133	
422 / 352	411 / 324	400 / 299	390 / 276	380 / 256	371 / 238	362 / 221	353 / 206	345 / 193	338 / 180	328 / 168	314 / 158	301 / 148	289 / 139	277 / 131	267 / 124	256 / 117	
400 / 312	389 / 288	379 / 266	369 / 246	360 / 228	351 / 211	343 / 197	334 / 183	319 / 171	305 / 160	291 / 150	279 / 140	268 / 132	257 / 124	247 / 117	237 / 110	228 / 104	
372 / 267	362 / 246	353 / 227	344 / 210	327 / 194	311 / 181	296 / 168	283 / 156	270 / 146	258 / 137	247 / 128	237 / 120	227 / 112	218 / 106	209 / 100	201 / 94	193 / 88	
456 / 339	443 / 312	432 / 288	421 / 266	410 / 247	400 / 229	390 / 213	381 / 199	373 / 186	364 / 173	348 / 162	334 / 152	320 / 143					
417 / 297	405 / 274	395 / 253	385 / 234	375 / 217	366 / 201	357 / 187	345 / 174	330 / 163	315 / 152	302 / 142	289 / 133	277 / 125					
389 / 264	378 / 243	368 / 225	359 / 208	350 / 193	337 / 179	322 / 166	307 / 155	293 / 145	280 / 135	268 / 127	257 / 119	246 / 111					
333 / 238	324 / 219	316 / 202	308 / 187	298 / 174	284 / 161	271 / 150	258 / 140	247 / 130	236 / 122	226 / 114	216 / 107	207 / 100					
296 / 191	280 / 176	266 / 162	252 / 150	240 / 139	228 / 129	218 / 120	208 / 112	198 / 105	190 / 98	181 / 92	174 / 86	167 / 81					
238 / 158	225 / 146	213 / 135	202 / 124	193 / 115	183 / 107	175 / 100	167 / 93	159 / 87	152 / 81	146 / 76	139 / 71	134 / 67					

Table E-17. (Continued)

(c) For Joist Depths 24 to 32 In. Inclusive

Joist Designation	24H6	24H7	24H8	24H9	24H10	24H11	26H8	26H9	26H10	26H11	28H8	28H9	28H10	28H11	30H8	30H9	30H10	30H11	32DH9	32DH10	32DH11
54											193	229	257	297	208	246	276	319	263	295	342
											92	108	121	139	106	125	140	161	142	160	184
55											186	220	248	287	200	237	266	308	253	285	329
											87	102	115	132	101	118	133	152	135	152	174
56											180	213	239	276	193	229	257	297	244	274	318
											83	97	109	125	95	112	126	144	128	144	165
57															187	221	248	287	236	265	307
															90	106	119	137	121	136	156
58															180	213	239	277	228	256	296
															86	101	113	130	115	129	148
59															174	206	231	268	220	247	286
															81	95	108	123	109	123	141
60															168	199	224	259	213	239	277
															77	91	102	117	104	117	134
61																			206	231	268
																			99	111	128
62																			199	224	259
																			94	106	121
63																			193	217	251
																			90	101	116
64																			187	210	243
																			86	96	110

[a] Based on Allowable Stress of 30,000 psi.
[b] Allowable total safe load in pounds per linear foot.
[c] The black figures in the table give the total safe uniformly distributed load-carrying capacities, in pounds per linear foot, of H-Series High Strength Steel Joists. The weight of dead loads, including the joists, must in all cases be deducted to determine the live load-carrying capacities of the joists. The load table may be used for parallel chord joists installed to a maximum slope of ½-inch per foot.
   The blue figures in this load table are the live loads per linear foot of joist which will produce an approximate deflection of 1/360 of the span. Live loads which will produce a deflection of 1/240 of the span may be obtained by multiplying the blue figures by 1.5. In no case shall the total load capacity of the joist be exceeded. Section 5.9 of the "Specifications for Open Web Steel Joists J- & H-Series" limits the design live load deflection as follows: Floors—1/360 of span. Roofs—1/360 of span where a plaster ceiling is attached or suspended: 1/240 of span for all other cases.
[d] Loads above heavy lines are governed by shear.
[e] Indicates Nominal Depth of Steel Joists only.
[f] The weights per foot as shown in these tables are approximate only. Such weights are shown only for the convenience of the designer. They cannot be used in figuring prices or determining shipping weights.
[g] Tests on steel joists designed in accordance with the Standard Specifications have demonstrated that the Standard Load Tables are applicable for concentrated top chord loadings (such as are developed in bulb-tee roof construction) when the sum of the equal concentrated top chord loadings does not exceed the allowable uniform loading for the joist type and span and the loads are placed at spacings not exceeding 33" along the top chord.

SOURCE: Standard Load Tables copyright by Steel Joist Institute. Reprinted by permission.

Table E-18. Steel Roof Deck Loads[a]

Narrow Rib Deck Type NR

Deck Type	Span Condition	Design Thickness	Uniform Total (Dead & Live) Load in Pounds Per Sq. Ft. Span Length—c. to c. Joists or Purlins									
			4-0	4-6	5-0	5-6	6-0	6-6	7-0	7-6	8-0	8-6	9-0
NR 22	Simple	0.0295	74	58	47								
NR 20	Simple	0.0358	90	72	58	48	40						
NR 18	Simple	0.0474	121	95	77	64	54	46					
NR 22	2	0.0295	80	64	51	42							
NR 20	2	0.0358	96	76	62	51	43						
NR 18	2	0.0474	124	98	79	66	55	47	40				
NR 22	3 or more	0.0295	100	79	64	53	45						
NR 20	3 or more	0.0358	120	95	77	64	53	46					
NR 18	3 or more	0.0474	155	122	99	82	69	59	51	44			

Intermediate Rib Deck Type IR

Deck Type	Span Condition	Design Thickness	4-0	4-6	5-0	5-6	6-0	6-6	7-0	7-6	8-0	8-6	9-0
IR 22	Simple	0.0295	86	68	55	45							
IR 20	Simple	0.0358	106	83	68	56	47	40					
IR 18	Simple	0.0474	141	112	90	75	63	54	46	40			
IR 22	2	0.0295	93	74	60	49	41						
IR 20	2	0.0358	112	88	72	59	50	42					
IR 18	2	0.0474	145	114	93	76	64	55	47	41			
IR 22	3 or more	0.0295	116	92	74	62	52	44					
IR 20	3 or more	0.0358	140	110	89	74	62	53	46	40			
IR 18	3 or more	0.0474	181	143	116	96	80	68	59	51	45	40	

Wide Rib Deck Type WR

Deck Type	Span Condition	Design Thickness	5-0	5-6	6-0	6-6	7-0	7-6	8-0	8-6	9-0	9-6	10-0
WR 22	Simple	0.0295	89	70	56	46							
WR 20	Simple	0.0358	112	87	69	56	47	40					
WR 18	Simple	0.0474	154	118	94	76	63	53	45				
WR 22	2	0.0295	98	81	68	58	50	43					
WR 20	2	0.0358	125	103	87	74	64	56	49	43			
WR 18	2	0.0474	165	136	115	98	84	73	64	57	51	45	40
WR 22	3 or more	0.0295	122	101	85	70	58	49	42				
WR 20	3 or more	0.0358	156	129	108	87	72	60	52	45			
WR 18	3 or more	0.0474	207	171	143	120	98	81	69	59	51	45	40

[a] Steel decks complying with SDI Basic Design Specifications are available from member companies in 1½-, 2-, 3-, 4½-, 6-, and 7½-in. depths; 6-, 8-, 9-, and 12-in. centers; with and without stiffening elements.

Notes:
1. Load tables are calculated using Section Properties.
2. Loads shown in tables are uniformly distributed total (dead plus live) loads in psf. Loads in white areas are governed by live load deflection not in excess of L/240 × span. The dead load included is 10 psf. All other loads are governed by the allowable flexural stress limit of 20,000 psi for a 33,000 psi minimum yield. Where heavy construction loads or other unusual concentrated loads are anticipated during the lifetime of the deck, the specified live load must be increased to offset the effects of the abnormal concentrated loading.
3. The rib width limitations shown are taken at the theoretical intersection points of the flange and web projections.
4. Span length assumes center-to-center spacing of supports. Tabulated loads shall not be increased by assuming clear span dimensions.
5. Bending Moment formulae used for flexural stress limitation are:

Simple & Two Span $\quad M = \frac{wl^2}{8}$

Three Span or more $\quad M = \frac{wl^2}{10}$

6. Deflection formulae for deflection limitation are:

Simple Span $\quad \Delta = \frac{5\,wl^4}{384\,EI}$

Two & Three Span $\quad \Delta = \frac{3\,wl^4}{384\,EI}$

7. Normal installations covered by these tables do not require midspan fasteners for spans of 5 ft. or less.

SOURCE: Steel Deck Institute.

Fasteners and Fastening Systems

Wood, most commonly used in residential construction, is usually nailed together. *Nails* used to fasten pieces of wood together and to other construction materials are designated by their size and shape or purpose [F-1]. The term *"penny"* is used to indicate the length of a wire nail. The "penny" designation is adapted from an old English system that was used to designate the price per hundred nails. Since the British abbreviation for penny is the letter "d," nails used in construction such as "16 penny" and "10 penny" are abbreviated on drawings and in specifications as "16d" and "10d." Figure [F-2] shows the relative proportions of common nails of various lengths. The accompanying table shows the actual lengths of nails corresponding to their "penny" sizes.

Size	Length (in.)
2d	1
3d	1¼
4d	1½
5d	1¾
6d	2
7d	2¼
8d	2½
9d	2¾
10d	3
12d	3¼
16d	3½
20d	4
30d	4½
40d	5
50d	5½
60d	6

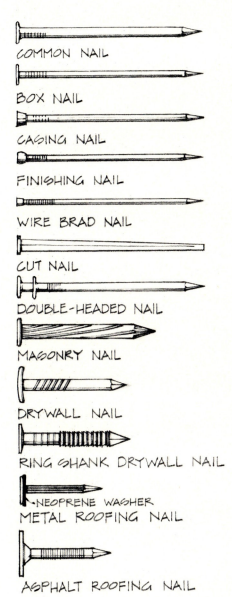

Figure F-1 *Nail types.*

Common wire nails are most often used. Box nails are employed for fine work to avoid splitting the wood. Finish nails have a smaller head to allow them to be "set" below the finished surface of the wood for fine work. The small hole resulting from setting can be filled with putty or wood paste, then painted or stained to produce a nearly invisible fastening technique. Several special-type nails, such as drywall nails and masonry nails, are used for selected applications, as their name implies. Cut nails are used for concrete and masonry. Double-headed nails are used in formwork or other

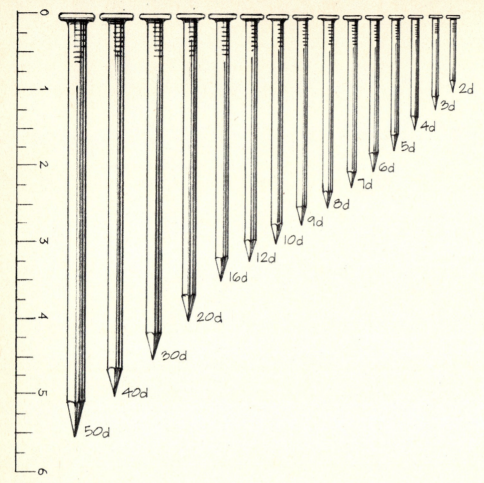

Figure F–2 Nail sizes.

applications where it is desirable to remove the nail after it has been driven. Staples and machine-driven nails are gradually replacing the conventional fastening systems employing a hand-held hammer.

Bolts, nuts, and washers are also used to fasten construction materials. The commonly used standard types are shown in [F-3]. Bolts are usually used to fasten heavier wood pieces together and to secure wood to other structural components. Carriage bolts are often used to fasten two pieces of wood together. The square neck under the head end of the bolt serves to prevent it from turning in the wood as the nut is tightened. Washers are seldom used under carriage bolt heads.

Machine bolts are used in heavier work to connect pieces of wood, or to fasten wood to other structural members. These are most often used with flat washers to avoid marring the wood. They are sometimes used in combination with special glues to produce a particularly rigid joint. Bolts with a short 90° bend at the unthreaded end are often used to secure wood to masonry or concrete. In this case they are known as *"anchor bolts,"* and are set into the masonry or concrete while it is being placed [B-1].

Another fastener commonly used in wood construction is the *screw*. This fastener can be plated with cadmium or galvanized with zinc to resist rust and corrosion. Screws come in many different sizes, shapes, and head types. Some of the more commonly used types are shown in [F-4]. The head styles for each of the three types of screws are generally available for all three types except for sheet metal screws, which are not made with flat or oval heads. Regular slotted drives are standard for all of the screw types shown. Phillips and one-way drives are available for machine screws and wood screws. The Allen (socket) drive is normally used only on machine screws.

Sheet metal screws have a special thread designed to thread into plain holes in thin sheet metal. Machine screws are used to thread into mating threaded holes or to pass through plain holes and have a nut on the end. Wood screws are designed to thread into wood.

Small brass wood screws are often used in light cabinet work or elsewhere if the tensile or shear strength of the fastener is not critical. Flat head screws can be set flush with the surface of the material in countersunk holes. When used to join two pieces of wood, the holes may be drilled deeper and filled with glue-in wood dowels to produce an almost invisible joint [F-5].

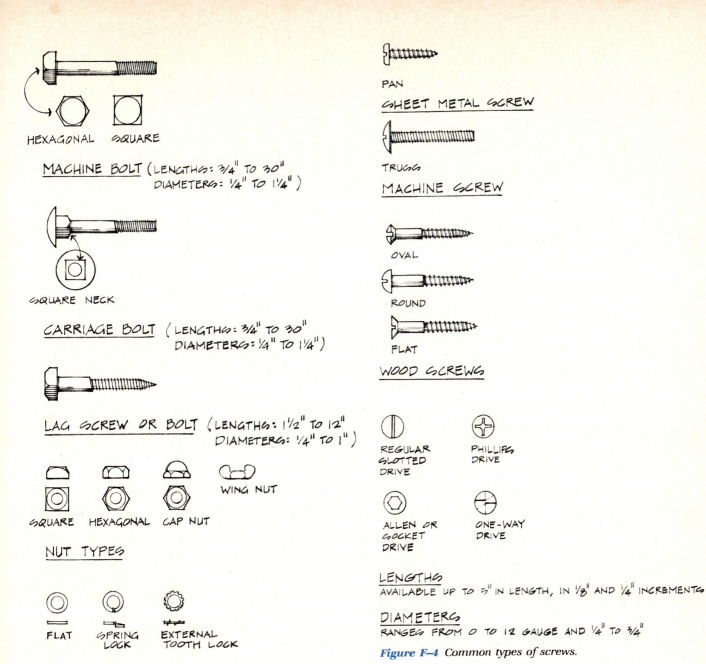

Figure F–3 Standard types of bolts, nuts, and washers.

Figure F–4 Common types of screws.

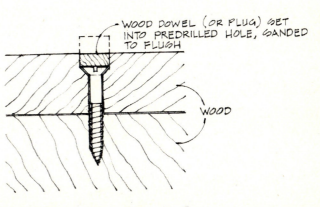

Figure F–5 Countersunk screw.

Some special-purpose fasteners are shown in [F-6]. They are especially useful for fastening applications where the material to which the fastener is being attached is relatively soft or weak and/or there is no access to the back surface of the material to apply a standard washer and nut.

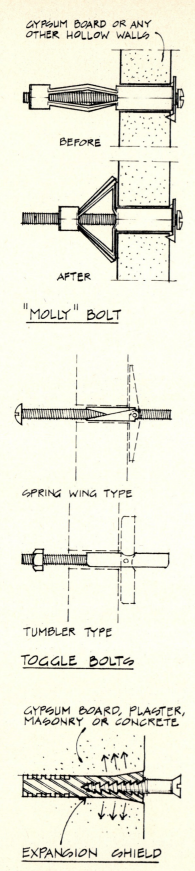

Figure F–6 Special-purpose fasteners.

Index

A

Abbey, 4
Abbreviations, 445
Acoustical privacy, 126
Active solar energy system, 148
Adams, James J., 180
Add-on system, 304
Adjustable triangle, 49
Aerial perspective, 84
Aerial positioning, 20
Aesthetic considerations, 111
Aggregate, 233
Air change method, 281
Air infiltration, 281
Alignment pins, 104
Alternating current, 320
Altitude, solar, 156
Anatolia, 3
Anchor, 241
Angle, profile, 156
Angle of incidence, 156
Applique, 105
Architect, 219
Architect's scale, 55
Architectural drawings, 385
As-built drawing, 7
Atmospheric effects, 21
Automobiles, 189
Axis
  major, 34, 35
  minor, 35
Axle, 34
Axonometric, 76
Axonometric drawing, 77
Azimuth, solar, 156

B

Babylon, 264
Balance, 120
Balloon, 182
Balloon framing, 242
Bank, branch, 170
Bar joist, 237

Barrier, vapor, 233
Basement wall, 237
Bathtub, 144
Bay window, 145
Beam compass, 51
Beams
  exposed, 245
  laminated wood, 246
Bedroom, 140
Bending failure, 264
Bergmann, Richard, 6
Bevel siding, 248
Bird's eye view, 31
Bite, 47
Block
  concrete, 193, 231
  title, 340
Blueline print, 61
Board
  gypsum, 251
  panel, 393
Board-and-batten, 249
Body language, 11
Boiler, 290
  combustion, 290
  electric, 290
Branch, fixture, 314
Branch bank, 170
Break line, 65
Breaker, circuit, 234
Brick, 187, 193
Brick veneer, 247
Browne, Henry, 219
Brush, drafting, 59
Bubble, 182
Bubble diagram, 181
Budget, 170
Building code, 171
Building drain, 314
Building load center, 234
Building model, 209
Building orientation, 151
Building paper, 255
Building section, 197

Building sewer, 314
Building systems costs, 170
Built-up roofing, 254

C

Cabin, log, 227
Cabinet oblique, 80
Callicrates, 4
Carpentry costs, 173
Carpeting, 186
Carport, 146
Case study, 465
Cast shadows, 194
Castello D'Acqua, 7
Catal Huhuk, 3
Cathedral, Gothic, 113
Cathode ray tube, 427
Cavalier oblique, 80
Cavity wall, 238
Ceiling framing, 251
Center, building load, 234
Center line, 65
Central main trunk, 288
Centre Le Corbusier, 122
Chipboard, 209
Circle template, 51
Circuit, 320
    parallel, 321
    short, 321
Circuit breaker, 234
Circuit schedule, 393
Closed flat collector, 150
Closet
    linen, 123, 145
    water, 311, 399
Cock
    corporation, 311
    curb, 311
Code
    building, 171
    energy, 177
    National Building, 171
    National Electrical, 171
    One and Two Family Dwelling, 171
    Standard Building, 171
    Uniform Building, 171
Codes, 171
Coefficient of transmission, 277
Coil, evaporator, 305
Collector
    closed flat, 150
    open flat, 150
    parabolic, 150
    solar, 291
Colonial, 111
Colonial Revival, 111

Combustion boiler, 290
Comfort, 273
Commercial, 8
Compass, 51
    beam, 51
Competition drawing, 6
Computer, main-frame, 429
Concrete, 187
Concrete block, 193, 231
Condensing unit, 303
Conduction, 274
Conservation, energy, 146
Conservatory, 163
Considerations, aesthetic, 111
Construction
    geometric, 65
    light, 8
    post-and-beam, 242
    prefabricated, 260
    roof, 253
Construction lines, 18
Continuous spread footing, 230
Contour exercise, 17
Contour interval, 343
Contours, 343
Contrast, value, 40
Control
    infiltration, 151
    residential climate, 273
Convection, 274
Convector, 290
Cooling, evaporative, 296
Cooling load estimate, 297
Cooling systems, 296
Core, shadow, 42
Corporation cock, 311
Costs
    building systems, 170
    carpentry, 173
    formwork, 172
    material, 171
Counter top, kitchen, 141
Cricket, 377
Cross section, 351, 403
CRT, 427
C-shaped joists, 242
Curb cock, 311
Current, 320
    alternating, 320
    direct, 320
Curtain wall, 243
Curve drawing, 51
Curves
    French, 54
    irregular, 54

Cutting plane, 71
Cutting-plane line, 65
Cycle, refrigeration, 302

D

Damper, flue, 288
Da Vinci, Leonardo, 5
Dead load, 265
Deciduous tree, 162
Decking, 270
Deflection, 268
Deflection failure, 264
Delineation, 199
Depth, 18
   frost, 228
Depth illusion, 21
Design process, 179
Design sketches, 4
Detail, 354
Details, 72
Details sheet, 403
Developer, 61
Devices, shading, 156
Diagram, bubble, 181
Diazo printing, 61
Diazo process, 60
Diffuser, 308
Digitizer, 425
Dimension line, 65, 99
Dimensioning, 99
Dimetric, 77
Dining room, 135
Direct current, 320
Direct gain heating, 153
Direct lighting, 328
Disc
   floppy, 430
   hard, 430
Display, liquid-crystal, 427
Display model, 211
Dividers, 57
Dome, 118
   geodesic, 118
Door schedule, 348
Dormer window, 146
Drafting brush, 59
Drafting film, 60
Drafting machine, 49
Drain, building, 314
Drawing
   as-built, 7
   axonometric, 77
   competition, 6
   curve, 51
   freehand, 11
   line, 48
   oblique, 79
   orthographic, 67
   paraline, 76
   perspective, 75, 82
   pictorial, 75
   presentation, 5
   shop, 392
Drawing tools, 45
Drawings
   architectural, 385
   engineering, 385
   presentation, 183
   schematic, 183
   shop, 8, 393
   structural, 385
   working, 6
Driveway, 128
Drum plotter, 431
Duct, 307
Dulseal, 105
Dutch hip, 118

E

Earth-shelter, 151
Effects, atmospheric, 21
Egyptian, 3
Electric boiler, 290
Electrical legend, 393
Electrical site plan, 393
Electrostatic plotter, 433
Elevation, 69, 350, 403
   expanded, 351
   interior, 69, 403
   schematic, 182
Elevations, 403
Ellipse template, 52
Energy code, 177
Energy conservation, 146
Energy systems, 146
Engineering drawings, 385
Engineer's scale, 55
Engraving, 8
Entrance, service, 322
Entry foyer, 128
Envelope, 273
Equinox, 162
Eraser, 59
Erasing shield, 59
Estimate
   cooling load, 297
   heat gain, 297
Evaporative cooling, 296
Evaporator coil, 305
Exercise, contour, 17

Expanded elevation, 351
Exposed beams, 245
Extension line, 65, 99
Eye judgment, 30

F

Facade, 69
Failure
  bending, 264
  deflection, 264
  shear, 264
Fallingwater House, 121
Family room, 135
Fasteners, 527
Federal, 111
File, floor, 186
Film, drafting, 60
Finish schedule, 348
Fireplaces, 373
Fixative, 101
Fixture branch, 314
Fixture trap, 312
Fixture units, 314
Flagstone, 187
Flashing, 377
Flat-bed plotter, 431
Flat roof, 115
Flat scale, 55
Flat slab, 235
Floor plan, 74, 403
  plumbing, 399
Floor tile, 186
Floors, 233
Floppy disc, 430
Flue, 373
Flue damper, 288
Folded plate roof, 118
Footing
  continuous spread, 230
  pad, 231
  spread, 228
  stepped, 231
Forced warm air system, 285
Foreshortening, 22
Formwork costs, 172
Foundation plan, 344, 385, 403
Foundations, 227
Four-way switches, 328, 329
Foyer, entry, 128
Framing
  balloon, 242
  ceiling, 251
  platform, 241, 242
  steel, 237, 242
  wall, 246

Framing plan, 385
Framing window, 242
Freehand drawing, 11
Freehand sketching, 11
French curves, 54
Frost depth, 228
Furnace, warm air, 286
Furniture, 135, 186, 199

G

Gable, 115
Gambrel roof, 115
Garage, 146
Geodesic dome, 118
Geometric construction, 65
Glass, 194
Glossary, 451
Gothic, 112
Gothic cathedral, 113
Grade, 231
Grass, 187
Gravel, 187
Greek Revival, 112
Greek temple, 4
Ground line, 85
Guggenheim Museum, 121
Guide, lettering, 59
Gypsum board, 251

H

Hallway, 123
Hammurabi, 264
Handrails, 367
Hard disc, 430
Hardware, 425
Harold Brooks Home, 113
Head, 356
Header, 235, 242, 356
Hearth, 377
Heat gain estimate, 297
Heat losses, 277
Heat pump, 295
Heat transfer, 274
Heating
  direct gain, 153
  radiant, 295
Herb Greene House, 120
Hip roof, 115, 117
Holder, lead, 45
Home, precut, 260
Horizon line, 22, 85, 90
Huggles House, 112
Hydronic system, 289
Hyperbolic paraboloid roof, 119

I

Ictinus, 4
Illusion, 12
   depth, 21
   space, 43
Incidence, angle of, 156
Indirect gain passive system, 153
Indirect light, 326
Infiltration, air, 281
Infiltration control, 151
Ink, 4
Insulation, 151, 239
Insulator, 275, 320
Interior elevation, 69, 403
Interval, contour, 343
Irregular curves, 54
Isolated gain passive system, 154
Isometric, 77
   plumbing, 399
Isotherm, 278

J

Jamb, 242, 356
Joist, 233, 234
   bar, 237
   steel, 236
Joists
   C-shaped, 242
   open web steel, 242
Jones, E. Fay, 9
Judgment, eye, 30

K

Kahn, Louis, 119
Keyboard, 425
Kick plate, 367
Kimball Museum, 119
Kitchen, 135
Kitchen counter top, 141
Kitchen layout, 140
Kitchen storage, 141

L

Laminated wood beams, 246
Landing, 367
Language, body, 11
Laundry, 123
Laundry room, 145
Lavatory, 399
Layout, kitchen, 140
LCD, 427
Lead
   pencil, 60
   ultrathin, 46
Lead holder, 45
Lead pointer, 45
Leader, 65
Leaf shapes, 200
Leaves, 196
Le Corbusier, 11, 12, 122
Ledger, 367
Legend
   electrical, 393
   mechanical symbols, 388
Le Modulor, 122
Leroy, 106
Letter spacing, 97
Lettering, 95
   template, 106
   transfer, 105
Lettering guide, 59
Light, 40
   direct, 328
   indirect, 326
Light construction, 8
Light pen, 428
Lighting fixture schedule, 393
Line
   break, 65
   center, 65
   cutting-plane, 65
   dimension, 65, 99
   extension, 65, 99
   ground, 85
   horizon, 22, 85, 90
   material symbol, 65
   object, 65
   picture plane, 90
   true length, 90
Line drawing, 48
Line rendering, 197
Linen closet, 123, 145
Lines, construction, 18
Linework, 62
Lintel, 356
Liquid-crystal display, 427
Live load, 265
Living room, 129
Load
   dead, 265
   live, 265
Load-bearing, 237
Loads, roof, 501
Log cabin, 227
Loop, series, 292
Losses
   heat, 277
   transmission, 278
Low-voltage switching, 330
Lumber sizes, 235

M

Mactac, 105
Machine
   drafting, 49
   refrigeration, 302
Magnetic tape, 430
Main-frame computer, 429
Major axis, 34, 35
Mansard roof, 117, 118
Map, zoning, 172
Marker, 14
Masonry opening, 345
Matboard, 209
Material costs, 171
Material symbol line, 65
Measurement, shadow, 190
Mechanical pencil, 45
Mechanical site plan, 385
Mechanical symbols legend, 388
Memory unit, 430
Metal siding, 250
Metal stair, 369
Method, air change, 281
Methods, timesaving, 102
Meyer, Doug, 7
Microcomputer, 429
Minicomputer, 430
Minimum standards, 220
Minor axis, 35
M.O., 345
Model, display, 211
Model building, 209
Modular units, 262
Modulus, section, 265
Monitor, 427, 429

N

National Building Code, 171
National Electrical Code, 171
Noise, 125
Nominal size, 233, 234
Nonresidential, 8
Normal, 156
Nosing, 366
Notes, 388

O

Object line, 65
Oblique, 76, 80
   cabinet, 80
   cavalier, 80
   plan, 81
Oblique drawing, 79
One and Two Family Dwelling Code, 171
One-pipe system, 292
One-point perspective, 28, 83
Open divided scale, 56
Open flat collector, 150
Open web, 237
Open web steel joists, 242
Opening
   masonry, 345
   rough, 345
Ordinance, zoning, 172
Orientation, building, 151
Orthographic drawing, 67
Orthographic projection, 67
Overhang, 157

P

Pad footing, 231
Panel board, 393
Paneling, 252
Paneling, wood, 193
Paper
   building, 255
   sepia print, 61
   sketching, 60
Parabolic collector, 150
Paraline drawing, 76
Parallel circuit, 321
Parallel rule, 49
Parthenon, 4
Passive energy control system, 151
Pattern, traffic, 124
Paving, stone, 187
Payne, John Howard, 111
Pearce-McAllister House, 111
People, 195
Pen, 14
   light, 428
   plotter, 431
Pencil, mechanical, 45
Pencil lead, 60
Pendant, 138
Pens, technical, 47
Perimeter, slab, 280
Perimeter distribution system, 288
Perspective, 21
   aerial, 84
   bird's-eye, 84
   one-point, 28, 83
   three-point, 94
   two-point, 27, 89
   worm's-eye, 84
Perspective drawing, 75, 82
Perspective sketch, 24
Photocompositor, 106
Photoreproduction, 102
Pictorial drawing, 75
Picture plane, 85

Picture plane line, 90
Pier, 232
Piling, 232
Pin registration, 103
Pins, alignment, 104
Plan
    electrical site, 393
    floor, 74, 403
    foundation, 344, 385, 403
    framing, 385
    mechanical site, 385
    plot, 70
    reflected ceiling, 393
    roof, 70, 347
    roof framing, 385
    schematic, 182
    screened, 103
    site, 70, 388, 403
Plan oblique, 81
Plane
    cutting, 71
    picture, 85
    viewing, 27
Plans
    presentation, 185
    site, 337
Plants, 200
Plate
    kick, 367
    sill, 235, 242
    sole, 242
    top, 242
Plot plan, 70
Plotter, 431
    drum, 431
    electrostatic, 433
    flat-bed, 431
    pen, 431
Plumb, 242
Plumbing, 311
Plumbing floor plan, 399
Plumbing isometric, 399
Plumbing schedule, 399
Plywood sheathing, 247
Pocket scale, 55
Point
    station, 85, 90
    vanishing, 22, 23, 85
    wedge, 51
Pointer, lead, 45
Polystyrene, 210
Pond, roof, 153
Position, sketching, 16
Positioning, aerial, 20
Post-and-beam construction, 242
Precut home, 260

Prefabricated construction, 260
Presentation drawing, 5
Presentation drawings, 183
Presentation plans, 185
Print, 60
    blueline, 61
Printer, 431
Printing, diazo, 61
Privacy, acoustical, 126
Process
    design, 179
    diazo, 60
Processing, word, 434
Profile angle, 156
Projection, orthographic, 67
Proportion, 121
Protractor, 58
Puck, 425
Pump, heat, 295
Pyramid, 3
Pyramid roof, 118

Q

Queen Anne, 112
Queen Anne-style, 114

R

R values, 275
Radiant heating, 295
Radiation, 274
Ranch style, 114
Rapidograph, 106
Reflected ceiling plan, 393
Refrigeration cycle, 302
Refrigeration machine, 302
Registration, 103
    pin, 103
Regulations, 171
Relative size, 19
Rendering, 185, 199
    line, 197
    wash, 198
Residential, 8
Residential climate control, 273
Resistance, 275, 320
    thermal, 276
Rhombus, 53
Rhythm, 120
Ribbed slab, 235
Rise, 365
Riser, 365
R.O., 345
Robie House, 115
Rockbed, 167
Roof construction, 253
Roof framing plan, 385

Roof loads, 501
Roof plan, 70, 347
Roof pond, 153
Roofing, built-up, 254
Roofs, 253
   flat, 115
   folded plate, 118
   gambrel, 115
   hip, 115, 117
   hyperbolic paraboloid, 119
   mansard, 117, 118
   pyramid, 118
   storage, 153
Room
   dining, 135
   family, 135
   laundry, 145
   living, 129
Room size, 146
Rough opening, 345
Rubber stamps, 106
Rules, 6
   parallel, 49
Run, 365

S

St. Paul's Cathedral, 7
Saltbox, 111
Sand, 187
Scale, 55
   architect's, 55
   engineer's, 55
   flat, 55
   open divided, 56
   pocket, 55
   value, 40
Schedule, 348
   circuit, 393
   door, 348
   finish, 348
   lighting fixture, 393
   plumbing, 399
   window, 348
Schematic drawings, 183
Schematic elevation, 182
Schematic plan, 182
Screened plan, 103
Scriber, 106
Section, cross, 351, 403
Section modulus, 265
Sections, 71
   building, 197
Sepia print paper, 61
Series loop, 292
Service entrance, 322
Sewer, building, 314

Shade, 40, 202
Shading, 151, 155
Shading devices, 156
Shadow core, 42
Shadow measurement, 190
Shadows, 189
Shakes, wood, 192
Shear failure, 264
Sheathing, 243, 254
   plywood, 247
   wall, 235
Sheet, details, 403
Shell, 388
Shield, erasing, 59
Shingles, 193
Shop drawings, 8, 392, 393
Short circuit, 321
Shower stall, 144
Siding
   bevel, 248
   metal, 250
   wood, 192, 193
Sill, 242, 356
Sill plate, 235, 242
Site plan, 70, 337, 388, 403
Sizes
   lumber, 235
   nominal, 233, 234
   relative, 19
   room, 146
Sketchboard, 11
Sketches, 11
   design, 4
   perspective, 24
Sketching, 11
   freehand, 11
Sketching paper, 60
Sketching position, 16
Slab
   flat, 235
   ribbed, 235
Slab perimeter, 280
Socrates, 148
Software, 425
Solar altitude, 156
Solar azimuth, 156
Solar collector, 291
Sole plate, 242
Soleri, Paolo, 5
Space illusion, 43
Spacing, lettering, 97
Specifications, 335
Split system, 304
Spread footing, 228
Stack, 314
Stair, metal, 369

Stall, shower, 144
Stamps, rubber, 106
Standard Building Code, 171
Standards, minimum, 220
Station point, 85, 90
Steel framing, 237, 242
Steel joist, 236
Steel stud, 242
Stepped footing, 231
Stikybac, 105
Stone paving, 187
Storage, kitchen, 141
Storage roof, 153
Storage wall, 153
Structural drawings, 385
Structural tables, 501
Stud, 241
    steel, 242
Subflooring, 235, 236
Sun, 146
Sun position, 195
Sun's rays, 189
Sunspace, 154
Switches
    four-way, 328, 329
    three-way, 328, 329
Switching, low-voltage, 330
Symbols, 338
Symbols legend, 388
Systems
    active solar energy, 148
    add-on, 304
    cooling, 296
    energy, 146
    forced warm air, 285
    hydronic, 289
    indirect gain passive, 153
    isolated gain passive, 154
    one-pipe, 292
    passive energy control, 151
    perimeter distribution, 288
    split, 304
    warm air, 285

T

Tables, structural, 501
Tape, magnetic, 430
Technical pens, 47
Template, 51
    circle, 51
    ellipse, 52
Template lettering, 106
Temple, Greek, 4
Thermal resistance, 276
Thermosiphon, 155

Thermostat, 289
Three-point perspective, 94
Three-way switches, 328, 329
Tile, 145
Timesaving methods, 102
Title block, 340
Tools, drawing, 45
Tooth, 47
Top plate, 242
Traffic pattern, 124
Transfer, heat, 274
Transfer lettering, 105
Transmission, coefficient of, 277
Transmission losses, 278
Trap, fixture, 312
Tread, 365
Tree, 162
Triangles, 49
    adjustable, 49
    work, 140
Trimetric, 77
Trimmers, 368
True length line, 90
Trunk, central main, 288
Trusses, 254, 257
Tube, cathode ray, 427
Tudor, 114
Two-point perspective, 27, 89

U

Ultrathin lead, 46
Underlayment, 235, 236
Uniform Building Code, 171
Units
    condensing, 303
    fixture, 314
    memory, 430
    modular, 262
Unity, 120

V

Value, 37–40
Value contrast, 40
Value scale, 40
Values, R, 275
Vanishing point, 22, 23, 85
Vapor barrier, 233
Vault, 118
Vellum, 47, 60
Veneer, brick, 247
Vent, 314
Victorian, 112
View, bird's eye, 31
Viewing plane, 27
Voltage, 320

W

Wade House, 113
Wall
  basement, 237
  cavity, 238
  curtain, 243
  storage, 153
Wall framing, 246
Wall sheathing, 235
Warm air furnace, 286
Warm air systems, 285
Wash rendering, 198
Water, 187
Water closet, 311, 399
W.C., 399
Web, open, 237
Wedge point, 51
Window
  bay, 145
  dormer, 146
  framing, 242
  schedule, 348

Wood paneling, 193
Wood shakes, 192
Wood siding, 192, 193
Word processing, 434
Work triangle, 140
Working drawings, 6
Workstation, 425
Worm's-eye perspective, 84
Wren, Christopher, 7
Wrico, 106
Wright, Frank Lloyd, 114, 121
Wythe, 238

X

Xerography, 105

Z

Zip-a-tone, 105
Zones, 127
Zoning map, 172
Zoning ordinance, 172